D0079158

PALAEOECONOMY

BRITISH ACADEMY MAJOR RESEARCH PROJECT

The Early History of Agriculture

Management Committee:
    Professor J. G. D. Clark, Sc.D., F.B.A.
    Professor Sir Joseph Hutchinson, C.M.G., Sc.D., F.R.S.
    Dr. G. H. S. Bushnell, Ph.D., F.S.A.
    Dr. R. G. West, Ph.D., F.R.S.
    E. S. Higgs, M.A., B.Comm. (Director)

Assistant Director, British Academy Fellow:
    M. R. Jarman, M.A.

Documentary Secretary:
    H. N. Jarman, B.A.

Associates:
    C. Vita-Finzi, Ph.D., University College, London
    D. Webley, B.Sc., D.I.C., M.A., Agricultural Development and Advisory Service, Cardiff

Research Associates:
    A. J. Legge, B.A., Churchill College
    R. W. Dennell, B.A., Pembroke College
    D. A. Sturdy, Ph.D., Trinity College
    P. F. Wilkinson, Ph.D., Gonville and Caius College (Department of Anthropology, Otago, Dunedin, New Zealand)
    G. W. W. Barker, Ph.D., St John's College (Department of Ancient History, Sheffield)

The help of the following bodies and institutions is acknowledged: The Institute of Animal Physiology, Babraham; The Plant Breeding Institute, Cambridge; The National Institute of Agricultural Botany, Cambridge; and The Department of Quaternary Research, Cambridge University.

PALAEOECONOMY

being the second volume of Papers in Economic Prehistory
by members and associates of the British Academy Major
Research Project in the Early History of Agriculture

London (Founded 1901)

edited by

E. S. HIGGS

Faculty of Archaeology and Anthropology, University of Cambridge

CAMBRIDGE UNIVERSITY PRESS

Published by the Syndics of the Cambridge University Press
Bentley House, 200 Euston Road, London NW1 2DB
American Branch: 32 East 57th Street, New York, N.Y. 10022

© Cambridge University Press 1975

Library of Congress Catalogue Card Number: 74–76576

ISBN: 0 521 20449 6

First published 1975

Text set in 11/12 pt. Photon Times, printed by photolithography,
and bound in Great Britain at The Pitman Press, Bath

CONTENTS

S
421
B74
v.2

I am well aware that scarcely a single point is discussed in this volume on which facts cannot be adduced, often apparently leading to conclusions directly opposed to those at which I have arrived.

Charles Darwin, *The Origin of Species*

INTRODUCTION

The first decision facing this British Academy Major Research Project was the direction in which the Project should go, the way in which to approach its assignment, the study of 'prehistoric agriculture in Europe'. In considering the currently accepted hypotheses relating to this subject it was found that in spite of the massive literature the conclusions reached are unsatisfactory and leave unexplored alternative explanations at least as likely as those customarily preferred. It was evident that to isolate European agriculture from similar phenomena elsewhere could only lead to a biased Eurocentric view of a matter of world-wide significance to studies of prehistoric man. Similarly, prehistoric agriculture could not properly be understood unless it was placed within the context of prehistoric economies in general.

The task was a formidable one for, with the isolated exception of Grahame Clark's *Prehistoric Europe: the Economic Basis*, published some twenty years earlier, little or nothing had been done to further research into prehistoric economies as a coherent study, such work as there has been on the subject consisting largely of the compilation of data in innumerable appendices. Furthermore, this data had been compiled largely for other purposes than those of archaeology, or more usually as a formal exercise with no particular purposes in mind. As a result the data were usually of limited use except to support – as and when required – existing and sometimes conflicting hypotheses.

It was decided that the Project would confine its attention to aspects of the study which seemed on a rational, but necessarily subjective basis to be both worthwhile and attainable with archaeological data. A first priority was the formation of a theoretical framework within which to work to this end. It was felt that current archaeology offered little in the way of such worthwhile objectives, nor did it have the necessary theoretical scope.

It was then necessary to form concepts, methods, and techniques additional to those in current use to meet the requirements of the selected objectives. Inevitably the choice had to be made between the pursuit of these newly formulated objectives with less than satisfactory techniques, or the pursuit of only such objectives, however trivial they may seem, as lay within the range of well accepted and tried methods. It was decided to adopt the former course with the help of such techniques as we were able to devise.

It was also decided that practice should be used to test theory before publication, so that we could avoid the danger of publishing theoretical approaches which might eventually prove to be impracticable, a fate which seems to await many current hypotheses.

This volume continues to follow this policy. It provides a number of instances where conclusions have been arrived at by the application of the hypotheses and methods proposed previously, and a body of information for future use.

Wilkinson, in his study of the musk ox uses data derived from ethology, anthropology, and archaeology. He stresses the importance of ethology to prehistory. By the study of the behaviour of animals it is possible to predict much of the behaviour of the human groups exploiting them, for, as he points out, where human beings are dependent to any extent upon a particular animal, the way of life followed by each of the species concerned must be and remain at least tolerable to the other. Where such relationships have continued for long periods of archaeological time it can be inferred that a close economic and ethological relationship was established, by whatever technology it may have been executed. He suggests that the study of palaeoeconomy provides a firm basis upon which to estimate the reliability for archaeological puposes of ethnographic parallels.

From Wilkinson's conclusions it is difficult not to draw the inference that human culture is a part, but certainly not the pre-eminent part, of the behaviour of the species. It is a factor which can best be studied in relation to other variables as one of many factors subject to natural selection.

Sturdy uses territorial analysis, ethology, anthropology, and archaeology in his study of prehistoric reindeer economies. He suggests that the way of life of the reindeer was so narrowly restricted that human groups dependent upon it had no option but to adjust their way of life and hence their institutions to it. He finds that ethological considerations have a predictive value in interpreting archaeological data.

The implication that the Palaeolithic reindeer cave sites of, for instance, the Dordogne, were no more than temporary camp sites in a seasonal round must have a profound effect upon the inferences drawn from the data, and upon typological considerations which commonly lead to a sterile cultural catalogue.

Dennell and Webley, by territorial analyses and pedological studies of the long-occupied tell sites of Bulgaria, demonstrate how the apparently homeostatic period of the Neolithic-Bronze Age was brought to an end by unforeseen geomorphological changes resulting from over-population and consequent over-exploitation of a brittle environment. Whether or not the necessary adjustment to these new conditions was brought about by indigenous adaptations or by invasions is of little consequence, but certainly such a disturbed economic situation would have increased the opportunity for an invasion by less unfortunate peoples from more stable regions. It is a reminder that over-population is a recurrent event in prehistory at least as far back as Neolithic times and is in fact inherent in the human situation and that a viable economic niche will in the long term be occupied and human behaviour will adapt to it. The last point is basic to the understanding of palaeoeconomic studies.

Barker employs territorial techniques for the consideration of the settlement of central Italy and shows that from Middle Palaeolithic times onwards economic adaptation can be seen broadly as rational responses to the opportunities offered by technology and resources. The process of settlement intensification in historic times for example is seen as the culmination of a long-term trend of great antiquity rather than a response to the occasion of particular political events.

Jarman and Webley consider in similar time perspective the settlement of an area of southern Italy. It is seen that even in an area which from a traditional archaeological viewpoint appears to have undergone recurring and dramatic change there are factors which continue unchanged as critical behavioural constants for long periods. Consideration of historical data from the archaeological perspective can in addition be seen to deepen our understanding of processes involved in short-term change.

December 1973

E.S.H.
M.R.J.

Glossary

The following terms are used in this volume.

Site catchment: The total area from which the contents of a site have been derived. It may be greater than the site territory (*Proc. prehist. Soc.* 1970, **36**).

Site territory: The territory surrounding a site which is exploited habitually by the inhabitants of the site. Its defence is not implied (*ibid.*).

Site territory (hunters and gatherers): The area which lies within two hours' walking distance from the site (*Proc. prehist. Soc.* 1967, **33**).

Site territory (farmers): The area which lies within one hour's walking distance from the site (*Proc. prehist. Soc.* 1970, **36**).

Annual territory: The total area exploited by a human group throughout the year. It may contain one or more site territories (*ibid.*).

Preferred site: A site occupied for a long period or repeatedly occupied (*Papers in Economic Prehistory*, 1972).

Transit site: A site fleetingly occupied (*Proc. prehist. Soc.* 1967, **33**).

Complementary resources: Resources with mutually exclusive distributions which, if exploited by a single human group with a mobile economy, will allow a higher population than could otherwise be maintained (*Papers in Economic Prehistory*, 1972).

Casual resources: Resources occasionally used such as medicines, relishes, and the like (*Proc. prehist. Soc.* 1970, **36**).

Mobile economies: Includes those practised by pastoralists and hunter-gatherers. Essentially mobile moving from place to place (*Proc. prehist. Soc.* 1967, **33**).

Mobile-cum-sedentary economies: Economies which comprise both mobile and sedentary elements (*ibid.*).

Land quality and classifications: *Papers in Economic Prehistory*, 1972.

Brittle environment: one which is precariously balanced.

Economic niches: Resources are utilised by means of mobile, mobile-cum-sedentary and sedentary economies. They are the principal components of the total economic exploitation.

Resources, the maximum range of distribution of which is from sea, through lowlands to mountain top (Figure 1a), are integrated at the primary level of technology by short distance (Figure 1a, 1.2.3) or, where complementary resources are far apart, long distance (Figure 1a, 4) transhumant economies. At this level the rare sedentary economies are ignored unless there is strong positive evidence to the contrary. In the long term with which we are concerned the inevitable population pressure makes them the least likely explanation on offer.

With technological development which increases the extractive capacity or enlarges the catchment area, sedentary economies increase, particularly in the lowlands where the potential is greater and the distance factor less restrictive. They disturb the pattern of exploitation of the mobile economies and up to the present day have continued to decrease their numbers and importance.

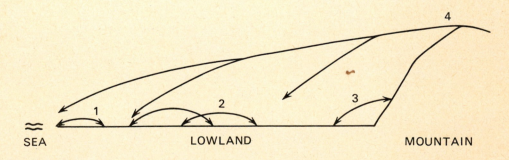

Palaeoeconomy

E. S. HIGGS AND M. R. JARMAN

Recent advances in its technical armoury, particularly the advent of the computer, have given to archaeology the appearance of a rapidly if unevenly developing subject. Many archaeologists have felt constrained to review and adapt the methods they employ in data retrieval, analysis, and exposition in the light of these developments. Of more moment, however, has been the increasing attention given to archaeological theory and the concern with the formulation of specific conceptual models. Many of the new methods and approaches put forward, however, have been borrowed directly and unaltered from other disciplines for which they were designed, and there has been little coherent attempt to formulate models with specifically archaeological objectives and data in mind. Whatever the various merits of these approaches may be they are an expression of a dissatisfaction with current archaeological theory and objectives and of a belief that more may be achieved by an extension of archaeological theory than by the elaboration of analytical methods.

In the nineteenth century a primary concern of archaeology was the need to establish a chronology. This interest has been largely taken over by scientific methods, and many of the traditional archaeological procedures have thus become redundant.

Another primary concern was the need to explain the artefacts recovered in excavations. The explanation was at first usually expressed within a geological framework, and an evolutionary stadial model was employed. The focus of attention shifted under the influence of late nineteenth-century nationalism (see Childe, 1956), particularly in Germany, and the 'culture-people hypothesis' became the main paradigm in the light of which archaeological data were considered. This hypothesis, most explicitly developed by Childe, proposed that archaeological 'cultures', defined in terms of artefactual groupings, be considered as representing prehistoric peoples. As Childe put it, the purpose was to rig up a culture with the trappings of personality, and the literature is in consequence full of 'the Magdalenians', 'the Natufians', and 'the Beaker Folk'.

A third factor was the Marxist influence which developed with the conflict between rival social and political systems. Childe accepted Durkheim's view that 'We can choose the form of our houses no more than the cut of our clothes; the one is imposed on us to the same degree as the other by social usage.' However, in selecting the social system as his deterministic priority he consigned other and more powerful directives, which he called 'instinctive' behaviour, to another discipline, thus depriving archaeology of a crucial key to the study of the mechanisms of prehistoric development.

Furthermore, the nineteenth century had always to take the supernatural into account in its considerations of man, endowed as he was with the gift of free will.

There seems no reason now why we should continue to be guided exclusively by nineteenth-century traditions and priorities, born as they were of the then contemporary needs, social conflicts, and climate of thought. We can surely pursue different priorities more in line with current needs, and one may wonder if this is best achieved by the elaboration of traditional archaeological models or whether there is not a better case for the reconsideration of basic objectives in the light of today's situation and intellectual climate.

AN ALTERNATIVE APPROACH

There is now no reason why, like the physical and behavioural sciences, we should not exclude the supernatural from our considerations. Throughout his history man has, in Ruth Benedict's phase, 'defended his uniqueness like a point of honour', and archaeologists have not been lacking in this respect. Whatever the merits of self-reassurance may be, there seems little justification for continuing in archaeology the search for criteria to demonstrate the critical differences between man and animals. Self-consciousness and reason, symbolism and language, can at best only be inferred by the most tenuous extrapolations from the available prehistoric data, and the soul leaves no skeleton. Not only are such criteria beyond the range of archaeological data, but it seems unnecessary and unhelpful to continue the obsession with human uniqueness. Everything above the molecular level is unique and the quality of uniqueness is the rule rather than the exception.

At the most optimistic assessment it must be said that the

human uniqueness standpoint offers only one of the possible views of human behaviour, a view which may actively obscure some of its important aspects. In highlighting human uniqueness and, in accordance with another major archaeological preoccupation, searching for the idiosyncratic and the individual within archaeological data, certain behavioural facets can never be adequately studied or evaluated. This can only be justified by the belief that these facets are less interesting, important, or worthy of study than those of traditional archaeological concern; a view which should perhaps be treated with reserve as it becomes increasingly obvious how little we understand of the motives for human actions, and how critical for the continued success of the species it may be to acquire this comprehension.

As studies in the behavioural sciences proceed it is becoming evident that crucially important aspects of human behaviour have more in common with the behaviour of other animals than we commonly allow. This view draws support from many fields, and is implicit in work in such diverse subjects as urban planning and criminal law (see Sachar, 1963; Tomlinson *et al.,* 1973). Clearly the principles of animal ethology and ecology must come into our consideration of human behaviour if we are to take this relationship into account, and there is every reason to include man in considerations of natural phenomena. If we do not know the nature and extent of biological influences or what over-riding biological principles exist, how can we hope to perceive to what extent man is subject to or independent of them, or to understand, in any wider sense than the purely descriptive or typological, archaeological 'cultural' variability?

Further, the pursuit of the social system as a primary controlling factor in human behaviour, even if it were practicable using archaeological data, is not wholly satisfactory in the climate of thought of today. The term 'social system' can be viewed as a clustering for the sake of convenience of a diversity of behavioural strands springing from a diversity of roots, each of which it may be more informative to follow individually. While many are willing, if pressed, to accept the proposition that ultimately all human culture and society is based upon and is only made possible by biological and economic viability, the tendency is to neglect the biological basis and concentrate upon the multitude of material and conceptual developments which has been erected on it.

There should be a branch of archaeology which digs more deeply and has as its primary interest basic aspects of human behaviour which underlie and form the fundamentals and directives of social systems. One may indeed suspect that the substantial convergence of different social systems in modern times must lead us to the conclusion that in the long periods of archaeological time (often of a thousand or more years in duration) the relatively simple prehistoric social systems, under biological evolutionary pressures, were probably so similar in their form and consequences that their dissimilarities would have had little significance in human prehistory. Furthermore, there are indications that the social system varies only within the permissible limits set by biological requirements; if these change, radical social change may be expected to follow swiftly, as is being experienced, often uncomfortably, in many areas undergoing rapid industrialisation.

A criticism sometimes levelled at attempts to view human behaviour in the context of biological principles is that they 'miss the point' – 'the point' presumably being that of human uniqueness. We may cling if we wish to the understandable belief that 'the most important thing about man is his humanity'. Even if this is accepted, however, it does not follow that the best way of understanding man is through his peculiarities. These 'anachronistically deterministic models', as biologically oriented approaches to archaeology have been called, are an attempt to eliminate the supernatural from our considerations of man. If a science of human behaviour is to be possible a search for over-riding principles or natural laws is of prime importance; and however unfashionable the term and ideas behind determinism may be, the very existence of natural laws presupposes a degree of determinism. With this objective in mind we can begin to establish archaeology as an intellectual discipline rather than the descriptive and technical exercise it is. The unidirectional trend of many aspects of human development indicates that there are indeed predictable laws of human behaviour; it may be profitable to concentrate on these, which are significant in the long archaeological record, but which may not appear, or may be swamped by the noise of innumerable short-term trivia, in the historic or anthropological record. Even in subjects concentrating on modern situations, such as sociology and psychology, where much data are available which can never be accessible to archaeology, and where the problems of sample control are greatly mitigated, the froth of short-term variables has impeded the formulation of accepted principles for some of the most crucial areas of study. This is evident in the endless, and perhaps never-to-be-ended, confusion as to the relative importance of environment and genotype in the formation of human personality.

Despite these developments in the climate of thought much of modern archaeology is cast in a traditional mould. At present one can perceive five main approaches to archaeology, although as with most classifications the edges are blurred and aspects of one approach are frequently to be found combined with another.

Artefactual explanation

This is in many ways the most primitive of archaeological approaches, as it has no declared purpose other than the collection, description, and classification of archaeological objects. The lack of an overall objective for these studies prevents anything more than the industrious accumulation of increasing amounts of information of uncertain value.

Palaeoethnography

The concern of ethnography is the characterisation of the races of man, including their habits, possessions, and distinguishing features. It has thus always been a descriptive and classificatory discipline rather than an analytic one, concerned with the collection and ordering of data rather than with processes and causality. Much of the main stream of archaeology over the past century has betrayed the same preoccupations, and even the apparently revolutionary 'New Archaeology' consists more often than not in the employment of new techniques rather than a reorientation of objectives. The definition of 'cultures' and the tracing of 'cultural influences' by the analysis of artefact and assemblage affinities remains the primary concern of many archaeologists, even though they may employ sophisticated concepts and equipment to this end.

Today it is popular to elaborate the framework within which such analyses are pursued, and one frequently encounters introductory affirmations of belief in the importance of other aspects, including evidence concerning the nature of the environment and economy. Consideration of these 'ancillary data' is rarely integrated into the work as a whole, however, and has little impact on the central concerns of the research.

The delimitation of peoples and tribes in prehistory does not in itself seem a worthwhile objective for the core of the discipline, especially as it has been demonstrated that one human group may practise two different stylistically based 'cultural' entities however they may be defined.

The systems approach

The 'systems' approach to archaeology, employing the principles and language of cybernetics, offers apparent theoretical advances, but has yet to yield much in the way of concrete results. In fact, perceptive archaeologists have for decades accepted that human communities are but one part of greatly more complex organisations, and while the concepts may not have been expressed in terms of 'homeostasis' and 'feedback', the complex interrelationship of different factors in the human environment has been implicit in much traditional archaeology. A severe limitation is placed on the efficacy of a systems ap-proach by the necessity of tailoring the method so rigidly to the eccentricities of archaeological data. It is one thing to propose that human communities are best studied in terms of the forces and relationships between social, demographic, economic, ecological, technological, and moral systems; the proposition loses something of its appeal when it is realised that in archaeology one can deal ineffectively or not at all with many of these aspects of human behaviour. These deficiencies result in an archaeology necessarily traditional in its basic concerns, although often expressed in misleadingly unfamiliar language.

A further disadvantage of this approach, in so far as it has yielded results to date, is that in emphasising the complexity of natural systems it concentrates attention on the apparent disadvantages of isolating simple over-riding mechanisms. This appears justified as long as the focus of study remains short-term and parochial; but a primary advantage of archaeological evidence is its capacity for use as a long-term record thus allowing the separation of logically explicable trends from random noise. Of course it is also true to say that little or nothing observable in human behaviour is truly random; it is related in some way to other factors in the system; but it must be treated as noise if its significance cannot effectively be pursued in terms of archaeological explanation.

The undoubted existence of myriad influences on human 'systems' has led some to reject the search for simple overriding factors. A conceptual circle or sphere is sometimes erected with innumerable interconnections but no beginning or direction. It is absurd, however, to consider that complex and multifactorial systems necessarily have no simple guiding principles, or that each definable aspect of such a system should necessarily be thought of as of equal significance.

Human palaeoecology

The last decade has seen a rise in interest concerning man's place in the ecosystem. This is related to a number of factors, in particular the growing public interest in ecology and environmental conservation. A reasonable term for the study of man's rôles in the prehistoric ecosystems of which he was a member is human palaeoecology.

Despite its many apparent attractions there is a number of grave difficulties in the pursuit of this approach to archaeology. The first of these is that the ecosystem, while a necessary philosophical concept in the light of which to consider the data of biological organisation, is inherently beyond empirical study in itself. 'The ecosystem is so all-embracing and so subtle that it seems to defy analysis' (Andrewartha & Birch, 1954). In order to study the subject it must be broken up into manageable units; aspects of, and relationships within, ecosystems can be studied and then related to the overall concept, but methods of data retrieval and analysis cannot now or in the foreseeable future begin to deal with the complexity of whole ecosystems even if these could be satisfactorily defined. If ecosystems themselves cannot be studied at the present day, how much more unrealistic it is to attempt to reconstruct and analyse prehistoric ecosystems, the vast preponderance of the evidence for which has irretrievably vanished, and which must thus be inferred from the few remaining traces.

A second primary drawback of an ecosystem model for archaeology is that it focuses attention on subsidiary aspects of the main objective. Archaeology is, or should be, a discipline concerned first and foremost with man, and while we necessarily accept the existence and relevance to our studies of ecosystems, this need not lead us to make them the central principle around which we arrange our hypotheses and data. It is clear that many features of human (and indeed other animal) behaviour transcend and cross-cut a number of ecosystems in which the populations participate. This is not to say that these behavioural features cannot be considered within the framework of an ecosystem model; but this is not necessarily the most appropriate model available. Many important human behaviour patterns are specifically designed to extract and integrate resources from a variety of ecosystems. As far as can be judged from the prehistoric record, the local ecology is not a directly determining factor for many human groups, although individual elements within it may have a strongly determining influence. This is witnessed by the common occurrence of very similar economies and tool-kits in widely differing ecological circumstances but where certain crucial economic resources remain unchanged. It is an expression of some of these difficulties inherent in the 'ecosystem approach' that many publications which are claimed to be concerned with the fashionable palaeoecology are in fact dealing either with the traditional environmental description or with aspects of palaeoeconomy.

Palaeoeconomy

Palaeoeconomic studies may be used to clothe with economic flesh the ethnic entities assumed from stylistic clusterings, and test their validity but its objectives are not confined to the augmentation of palaeoethnographic studies; it raises different problems and asks different questions. There is no reason to confine the questions asked to those of interest to palaeoethnographers. Its concern is with population technology and resources.

Palaeoeconomy is first about man and his behaviour; or, since 'behaviour' like 'the ecosystem' is too complex to study in itself, about those aspects of human behaviour which appear in the archaeological time perspective to have been of long-term significance. There are two major reasons for this focus of interest. In the first place, as many others have pointed out, the long time scale is a unique advantage of archaeology among the studies of man; it is therefore more profitable to exploit this quality of archaeological data in the search for long-term principles and directives than to strive to extend the historical narrative backwards in time to produce a pallid or romantic history. More important still is that archaeology, if it is to mature, must begin a search for natural laws governing human behaviour. If man is not to be considered supernatural – and, if he is so considered, a scientific study of man is impossible – then he is presumably subject to certain laws or principles, the study of which ought to be worth pursuing.

The primary human adaptation to the environment is the economy, man's management of his household. Artefactual explanation has not proved particularly informative in such matters, and thus does not have a prior place. Palaeoeconomic studies lay their main stress on a basic aspect of human behaviour which can be shown to conform to predictable laws over long time periods. Because no supernatural barrier, intellectual or otherwise, is assumed to exist between man and other organisms, animal studies are considered as relevant to our approach as anthropology or history. Indeed it is revealing to observe how similar many of the concerns, concepts, and even the language of much of animal ecology and ethology is to that of simple economics. The ethological concepts of territory and home range can usefully be applied to man. Nor should we be concerned myopically only with studies of primate behaviour. Animal (including human) behaviour is conditioned by the way the animals get their living, and in this respect primate behaviour is more removed from human behaviour than that of many other animals. In many ways the large carnivores offer more relevant comparative data than the primates. A further reason for the consideration of animal behaviour is that only thus can we hope to ascertain which behaviour patterns may be considered specifically and characteristically human. At present precisely similar patterns of behaviour tend to be considered very differently depending on whether they are undertaken by man or other animals. For example, migration and transhumance, which serve the same purpose of overcoming population limiting factors and seasonal imbalance of resources both for man and other animals, are described as 'cultural' behaviour in the first instance and as 'instinctive' behaviour in the second.

The commitment of palaeoeconomy to the search for trends of long-term significance directs its attention to the major factors which direct and determine human behaviour and development. Daryll Forde's attempt to pursue this goal in anthropology (1934) was doomed to failure by the lack of a sufficient time perspective. While anthropology can help by providing a known range of behavioural variables, it cannot select out the few which will be of importance in the long term. Our interest is in the constraints, rather than in the noise of choice which tends in any case to operate upon the short-term trivia, on the economic fat rather than on the basic necessities.

A major determining factor in the animal world is the relationship between populations and resources, and we may assume that the same factor is of similar importance in human behaviour. This crucial relationship has had an important long-term influence upon human decisions, whether this has been as the result of conscious responses to a situation or of subconscious responses due to biological feedback mechanisms. Such processes can be seen in the reaction of human populations to situations where the resource ceiling has been lifted by technological or environmental change, and no less where a corrective is necessary to unsuccessful efforts to overcome resource limitations. The extension of exploitation to inferior or marginal land in times of population pressure, and the effect of technology on the relationship between population and resources are two processes susceptible to study by archaeological means. However, relevant over-riding hypotheses are necessary in order to be able to consider past human behaviour coherently in relation to these and other factors.

RESOURCES

The extractive capacity of an animal species does not generally change on an archaeological time scale, and the study of the human exploitation of resources with a fixed technology can best begin with ethologically oriented territorial studies. The concept of territory in archaeology and the definitions of site exploitation territories and annual territories have been published elsewhere (Higgs *et al.*, 1967; Vita-Finzi & Higgs, 1970). Man, however, can lift the resource ceiling more quickly than the other animals by

(1) technological development which increases his extractive capacity within the available territory; and

(2) technological development which increases the available territory by reducing the degree to which the time–distance factor is limiting.

As resources in nature are unevenly distributed, the maintenance of the maximum population possible with the total available resources encounters the resistance of the time–distance factor, which is a major limiting constraint upon populations. Many basic aspects of past, as of modern, human behaviour are geared to the overcoming of

this constraint, and an important factor in human development has been the increasing capability to integrate effectively a diversity of widespread resources. We have in our earlier publications pointed out the importance of the time–distance factor and how the overcoming of its limitations has been a continuing process from dispersed hunter-gathering communities to urban agglomerations.

The data available to archaeology have in the past largely consisted of on-site data, both artefactual and biological. There has hitherto been little attempt to relate the two types of information, as they have usually been studied by different disciplines with different concepts and interests. In palaeoeconomy it is the relationship between them which is the principal interest, and it is vital for all the disciplines concerned that the importance of this relationship is recognised, for only thus can archaeological data be used to achieve its primary purpose: the creation of a scientific study of man. Furthermore, it has emerged that off-site data must be considered as of equal importance to on-site data. The consideration of the relationship between these two categories of information is of the first importance, but has so far been confined to broad environmental studies relevant perhaps to climatology and vegetation history, but contributing little more than some background scene-setting to the study of human behaviour. This has been of minimal value, and it is clear that the perceptible differences of climate and vegetation commonly have had little effect upon human behaviour. A further result of much of this work has been the great emphasis placed on the detection and analysis of change, often trivial in human terms, rather than continuity. This preoccupation can now be seen as misleading, at least in so far as it is indulged to the exclusion of concern with long-term constants. Territorial studies enable the relationship of on-site data to off-site data to be studied more precisely, in greater detail, and illuminate aspects of the relationship which are not perceptible by any other technique in current usage. In addition, as can be seen from some of the following papers, these studies tend to provide a necessary corrective to the view that human prehistory has been overwhelmingly dominated by change.

POPULATION

Chronological units such as those implied by the term Neolithic are thousands of years in duration, and isotopic dating commonly only gives an estimate of age to within several centuries. Few archaeological events, therefore, can be regarded as precisely contemporaneous but only as 'archaeologically contemporaneous', that is within a considerable range of time. There is little point, therefore, in erecting unworkable demographic models based on historical or ethnological data, whose primary concern is with phenomena of less than a few centuries in duration. While recognising the existence of short-term phenomena, a useful model for archaeological purposes will of necessity avoid the need for their consideration. Short-term models are in any case commonly based on data which are not available to archaeology and there is little point in putting forward untestable hypotheses and explanations. A basic demographic model for archaeological purposes must be concerned with long-term phenomena and trends of more than a few centuries duration, and must be based on archaeologically available data. Relevant subsidiary models can be created to deal with particular short-term situations, if the data are available, but these should not be allowed to swamp or distract us from the basic over-riding trend.

As in the rest of the animal world, human populations have the potential for a geometric rate of increase. As Sauvy (1969) puts it 'even the least prolific of uniparous animals can easily double their numbers in twenty years and through geometrical progressions this leads in a relatively short time to very high figures ... A primitive human population ... is more or less in the same position as an animal species: it multiplies until it reaches the maximum level allowed by its surroundings and the use it can make of these surroundings'. With developing technology the long-term trend is for the population level to rise, and despite the short-term oscillations of centuries the long-term curve continues upwards. With the data available to archaeology and its coarse chronology this is a trend we should be able to perceive and analyse in prehistory. Man through his technology has repeatedly succeeded in raising the restricting ceiling of the resources available to him − overcoming the 'resistance of the environment' in Sauvy's terms. The upward curve of human populations and their utilisation of resources will therefore not be smooth but will proceed in a series of steps, of upward jumps separated by plateaux of varying durations (Figure 1). These plateaux represent

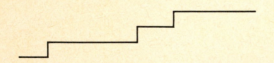

Figure 1. Schematic representation of population increase under the influence of developing technology.

periods wherein little understood and frequently unrecognised physiological and behavioural mechanisms, responding to the close proximity of the population to the acceptable ceiling, check population growth and produce a homeostatic, relatively stable situation (see Wynne-Edwards, 1962). How far such episodes can be perceived

by means of archaeological data has yet to be demonstrated; subsidiary and more detailed short-term models for brief archaeological periods may be employed for this purpose. For general archaeological as distinct from anthropological considerations, however, it is more profitable to treat the upward curve as the long-term norm and the plateaux as temporary and inevitably superseded exceptions.

Stress has been postulated as a principal cause of behavioural change. This argument has been elaborated by some authors with specific reference to the origins of agricultural economies, support being sought for the hypothesis that an exceptional stress situation gave rise to the first experiments in domestication. Stress, however, arising from the relationship between population and resources, occurs repeatedly in the long term and is inherent in the human situation. It has been argued that the various epideictic and physiological responses discussed by Wynne-Edwards and others would tend to maintain populations at levels below which stress might occur. On the contrary, however, the very existence of these mechanisms so widely among men and animals shows that such stress is ever-present in nature, and that while for a given population it may from time to time be relaxed, in the long term it must be viewed as a constantly recurrent factor. There is thus no need to resort to special cases to explain the presence or consequences of stress.

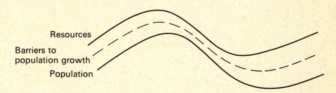

Figure 2. Schematic representation of the changing relationship between population and resources where both these factors are fluctuating.

Even in the short term, the homeostatic plateaux situations, resources will rarely if ever be constant, there being minor fluctuations due to factors beyond human control. If these changes in the available resources are sufficiently prolonged to cause population changes, the two factors will be changing at different rates. Demographic changes possess an internal dynamism which can only respond to feedback mechanisms from the environment much more slowly than the rate at which natural resources are likely to fluctuate. Figure 2 illustrates a situation in which a rise in population ultimately dependent upon an increase in available resources continues after the resources have begun to decrease. In this case increased pressure is brought to bear on the physiological and behavioural barriers to over-population and thus to over-exploitation of resources. Similarly, the reverse situation can occur, with the population continuing to decline for a period after the resources have begun to recover. Thus even over the short period – archaeologically speaking – of a few centuries periodic stress situations will recur.

Much has been made by the current archaeological generation of the importance of the use of scientific techniques and 'an interdisciplinary approach' in archaeology. It is hoped that this paper will encourage the view that while archaeology needs scientific aids, it is not enough for either participant that science should have the subsidiary rôle of providing only the technological devices with which to answer archaeological questions. It is only by bridging the gap at a theoretical level that a worthwhile discipline centred on man can be built, or that the sciences can make a major contribution to it. This demands the acceptance by archaeologists of the relevance of science theory to archaeological problems, and the acceptance by scientists that archaeology can contribute worthwhile objectives in which they can participate more fully than by the refinement of existing techniques.

BIBLIOGRAPHY

Andrewartha, H. G. & Birch, L. C. (1954) *The Distribution and Abundance of Animals*. Chicago: University of Chicago Press.

Childe, V. G. (1956) *Piecing Together the Past*. London: Routledge and Kegan Paul.

Forde, Daryll C. (1934) *Habitat, Economy and Society*. London: Methuen.

Higgs, E. S. (ed.) (1972) *Papers in Economic Prehistory*. Cambridge: Cambridge University Press.

Higgs, E. S., Vita-Finzi, C., Harris, D. R., & Fagg, A. E. (1967) The climate, environment and industries of Stone Age Greece: part III. *Proc. prehist. Soc.* **33**, 1–29.

Jarman, M. R. (1972) A territorial model for archaeology. In *Models in Archaeology*, ed. D. L. Clarke, pp. 705–35. London: Methuen.

Sachar, E. J. (1968) Behavioral science and criminal law. *Scientific American* **480**, 39–45.

Sauvy, A. (1969) *General Theory of Population*. London: Weidenfeld and Nicolson.

Slicher van Bath, B. H. (1963) *The Agrarian History of Western Europe A.D. 500–1850*. London: Edward Arnold.

Tomlinson, J., Bullock, N., Dickens, P., Steadman, P., & Taylor, E. (1973) A model of students' daily activity patterns. *Environment and Planning* **5**, 231–66.

Vita-Finzi, C. & Higgs, E. S. (1970) Prehistoric economy in the Mount Carmel area: site catchment analysis. *Proc. prehist. Soc.* **36**, 1–37.

Wynne-Edwards, V. C. (1962) *Animal Dispersion in Relation to Social Behaviour*. London: Oliver and Boyd.

2. THE RELEVANCE OF MUSK OX EXPLOITATION TO THE STUDY OF PREHISTORIC ANIMAL ECONOMIES

P. F. WILKINSON

In a survey of the relevance for prehistoric studies of contemporary experiments in the controlled exploitation of animal populations (Wilkinson, 1972a), the author concluded that, 'given a knowledge of the physiological and behavioural attributes of animals in prehistory, and of the technological competence of past human populations, it is possible to predict with a sufficient degree of accuracy optimal patterns of exploiting these resources, and to forecast the types of traces which these would leave in the archaeological record'. This paper attempts to illustrate the feasibility of this approach with reference to the exploitation of musk oxen (*Ovibos moschatus*).

The first section describes briefly some of the biological and behavioural attributes of modern musk oxen, which are influential in defining efficient patterns of exploiting musk oxen. Efficiency in this sense has been defined (Wilkinson, 1972b, p. 26) as exploitive relationships between human populations and populations of other animal species, which are consonant with existing technologies and are designed to optimise the yields obtained from the available resources without endangering the survival of these resources or exceeding their regenerative capacity. The attributes discussed can be interpreted plausibly as adaptations to the conditions of life in arctic or peri-glacial habitats, and there is no reason to assume that they have changed in important respects since the Pleistocene. The biology and behaviour of musk oxen limit efficient patterns of exploitation to two forms: they may be hunted for meat and robes as what I call a critical resource (see p. 23 for a definition); or they may be exploited for a combination of meat, milk, and underwool through some form of husbandry.

The second section reviews the ethnographic evidence for musk ox exploitation in North America and Greenland. Where musk oxen were exploited, they were hunted as a critical resource, when other resources failed unpredictably, or when it was necessary to visit areas lacking alternative resources. In conclusion, I discuss the value to prehistory of ethnographic data and conclude that many of the difficulties encountered by students of past cultural processes and phenomena do not apply to economic prehistorians.

The third section describes the types of archaeological traces which each hypothesised pattern of exploitation would leave and compares archaeological evidence for musk ox exploitation in North America and Eurasia with them. The archaeological evidence from North America suggests a direct continuity with ethnographically recorded patterns of exploitation, and musk oxen in prehistory seem to have played the role of a critical resource. In Eurasia there is no evidence that musk oxen were exploited prior to a late stage of the Upper Palaeolithic. The available evidence is highly inadequate, and the possibility that some form of husbandry was practised cannot be excluded beyond doubt. On the other hand, the evidence is more consistent with the view that musk oxen were exploited as a critical resource. It is suggested that the stimulus to musk ox exploitation was a decline in the diversity and abundance of many important game species after *c.* 25 000 B.P.

A concluding section evaluates the success of the methodology employed and discusses briefly its possible extension to other animals in prehistory.

THE BIOLOGICAL BASIS OF MAN–MUSK OX RELATIONSHIPS

If human populations are to thrive for long periods, they must not deplete or destroy the resources upon which they depend. The long survival of some past economies demonstrated archaeologically (e.g. Higgs *et al.*, 1967, for economies based upon red deer in Greece; Sturdy, 1972, for reindeer-based economies in the Upper Palaeolithic of northern Europe) indicates that the nature and intensity of prehistoric man's exploitation of animal populations often did not exceed tolerable levels. While it is self-evident that, particularly in the short term, technological ability and socio-cultural factors influence the ways in which animal populations are exploited, the biology and behaviour of the animals themselves play an important rôle. If it can be demonstrated with reasonable certainty that contemporary animals do not differ significantly in their biology and behaviour from prehistoric members of the same species, prehistorians can use zoological and ethological data to predict the manner in which they could have been exploited in the past, against which to test data from excavations.

In the following pages I outline briefly those biological and behavioural attributes of musk oxen which are, in my view, most influential in limiting the ways in which musk oxen can be exploited. I have pointed out elsewhere (Wilkinson, 1972c) that, because of their special interests, prehistorians may sometimes use non-archaeological techniques and theories differently from the way in which they are employed in the disciplines in which they were developed. For example, I interpreted the results of a metrical analysis of musk ox skulls in relation to contemporary zoological techniques for investigating prehistoric animal domestication (*ibid.* Chapter 12) rather than in terms of taxonomy (Tener, 1965). Provided that the techniques and theories so used are not misapplied and that interpretations of the results are not extended to unjustifiable limits, such an approach is legitimate and is justified by the special interests of prehistorians.

Distribution

Three aspects of the distribution of animals are relevant to prehistorians: changes through time in the distribution of a species; variations in the regional abundance of the animals at any given time; and the localised distribution of individual population units on a scale relevant to their exploitation by human populations.

Map 1 depicts the present world distribution of musk oxen. Harington (1961) and Wilkinson (1972c) discussed extensively long-term changes in the distribution of musk oxen. One major change occurred at the end of the Final Glacial. Prior to this, musk oxen occupied parts of Europe and Asia adjacent to the major ice masses and north of 50°. Finds securely dated to postglacial contexts are rare, but those from Hohensaaten (Dietrich, 1942), Norway (Hoel, 1933), Sweden (R. Skoglund, *in litt.*), the New Siberian Archipelago (Perry, 1883), and the Ural Mountains (Bader, 1965), for example, lie north of the former limits of musk oxen or within formerly glaciated areas and indicate a

northward movement of musk oxen as the Pleistocene glaciers retreated. Throughout most of Europe and Asia, musk oxen became extinct in the Early Postglacial, although they may have persisted for several millennia in parts of Siberia and Mongolia (Ehik, 1932; Vereschagin, 1967).

The distribution of musk oxen in the Late Pleistocene of Eurasia appears to have been markedly discontinuous. In Europe, finds of musk oxen are concentrated in the following areas: Switzerland and the upper Rhine Valley; the Austro-Yugoslavian foothills and the Moravian karst; the lower Rhine Valley, with a dubious extension into Belgium; and the southern and western portions of the North European Plain. A small, apparently isolated, population of musk oxen probably occupied the Dordogne *c.* 20 000 years ago. In the Soviet Union at this time the only firm evidence for musk oxen comes from the Desna Valley near Kiev (Klein, 1969), and later from the Ural Mountains (Bader, 1965; Rogachev, 1964). These finds are discussed more fully elsewhere (Wilkinson, 1972c, Appendix A).

Although it is tempting to ascribe this apparent discontinuity to differing intensities of investigation or to chance, the distribution of musk oxen today and during the past three centuries (the only period for which there is reasonably reliable evidence) has been similarly discontinuous. Maps 2–3 illustrate the distribution of musk oxen in the early

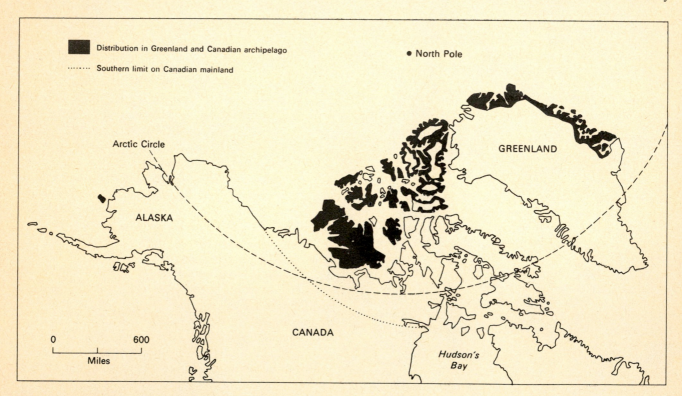

Map 1. Present distribution of free-living musk oxen.

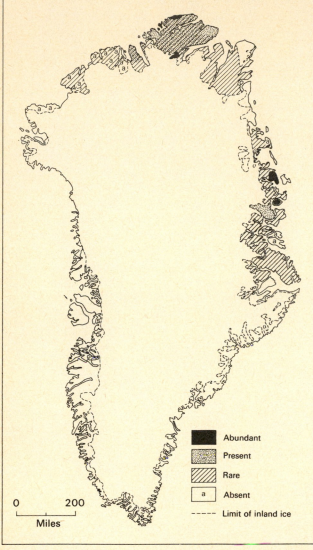

Map 2. Distribution and abundance of musk oxen in Greenland, 1901–25.

Legend:
- ■ Abundant
- ▦ Present
- ▨ Rare
- a Absent
- ----- Limit of inland ice

Scale: 0 — 200 Miles

and the resources accessible to them, and an understanding of highly localised patterns of animal distribution is relevant to this interest. Relevant data are rare, but Tener's (1963) survey of the distribution of musk oxen in the Queen Elizabeth Islands suggested that the localised distribution of individual population units was markedly discontinuous. Map 4 illustrates the distribution of population units north of Great Bear Lake, Canadian Northwest Territories, after 1953 (Kelsall *et al.*, 1971) and supports Tener's observations. Thus the localised distribution of musk oxen resembles their regional distribution, and individual population units are separated by areas with few or no musk oxen. This pattern of distribution is related to the effects of topography, geomorphology, and hydrography upon the types and abundance of important food species (Laverdière, 1954) and probably also to the depth and compactness of snow and ice cover in winter.

Movements

The frequency, regularity, and extent of movements by animals profoundly influence the manner in which they can be exploited. Whilst it has proved useful for zoologists to classify entire species as migratory or sedentary, for example, it has become increasingly clear that different populations of the same species and even different segments of single populations may often behave in very different fashions, depending on the nature and intensity of the stimuli to move. Since economic prehistorians are concerned with the relationship between individual human populations and the animal populations available to them, they cannot be satisfied with broad, zoological classifications, but must attempt to evaluate the possible impact of interpopulation differences in patterns of movements upon human exploitive strategies.

I have divided musk ox movements into three categories: seasonal movements, which are normally undertaken by entire population units; exploratory movements, usually by young adult bulls; and localised movements within seasonal feeding areas. I have also subdivided the study area into four regions: the Canadian archipelago; the Canadian mainland; Greenland; and Nunivak Island, which lies at *c*. 60° N off the Alaskan coast.

Canadian archipelago

The apparent infertility of the Canadian islands led some early explorers (e.g. Franklin, 1823; Sabine, 1823) to conclude that the musk oxen observed there in summer migrated to the mainland in winter, but later experience (Greely, 1886; Bernier, 1910) did not support this.

Seasonal and local movements on the islands are small

twentieth century. These maps indicate marked regional differences in the abundance of musk oxen, and core areas of relatively high densities are separated by large areas with few or no musk oxen. Lake Hazen, Ellesmere Island, is the best documented core area, but the region near Bathurst Inlet, the modern Thelon Game Sanctuary, Melville Island, and several parts of East Greenland have played a similar rôle. Evidence cited below suggests that the principal factor limiting the abundance and density of musk oxen is the quantity and accessibility of food in winter, and core areas probably depend on winter feeding conditions.

Economic prehistorians are concerned with the exploitive relationships between past human populations and are probably related to requirements of forage and shelter. Sheltered valleys are often occupied during storms (Sverdrup, 1904; Bernier, in Allen, 1913), but feeding activities are concentrated in exposed, windswept areas where the snow cover is lightest. Stefansson's (1924) belief that musk ox populations rarely moved more than a few miles per month in winter has been widely confirmed (MacMillan, in Hone, 1934; Harington, 1964; Bliss, 1971), but movements within summer feeding areas are probably greater.

Movements between islands have been reported (Manning & Macpherson, 1958, 1961; Harington, 1964; Freeman, 1971), but they are rare and usually involve only a few animals, often young adult bulls. A possible exception to this may have occurred recently on Banks Island. Musk oxen became extinct on Banks Island in the late nineteenth century. A few animals were seen there in the 1950s, which may have been immigrants from adjacent islands or possibly survivors of the indigenous population (Manning & Macpherson, 1958). Recent reports in the Canadian

press that there are 1500–2000 musk oxen on Banks Island are inconsistent with knowledge of rates of herd growth and may imply a large-scale immigration of musk oxen.

Canadian mainland

Critchell-Bullock (1930) appreciated the importance of food in regulating the movements of musk oxen, observing that movements were most frequent in areas poor in food. His belief that sexually active bulls were the most mobile, and senile bulls the least active, was confirmed by Hanbury (1904). Musk ox populations on the mainland are generally highly sedentary. Stefansson (1924) quoted the belief of Indian hunters that if they saw musk oxen in a given locality in one year and did not disturb them, they could be reasonably confident of finding them nearby the following year. None of the herds studied by Tener (1965) moved more than two miles per day on average in summer, although daily movements of up to twenty miles have occasionally been reported (Clarke, 1940). Two general patterns of short

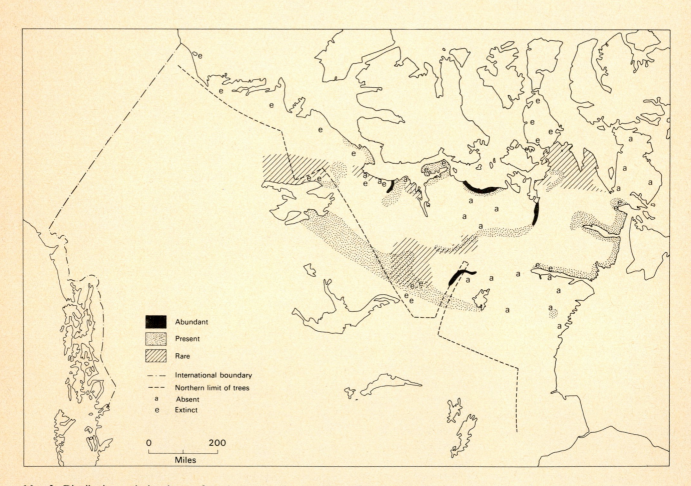

Map 3. Distribution and abundance of musk oxen on the Canadian mainland, 1901–25.

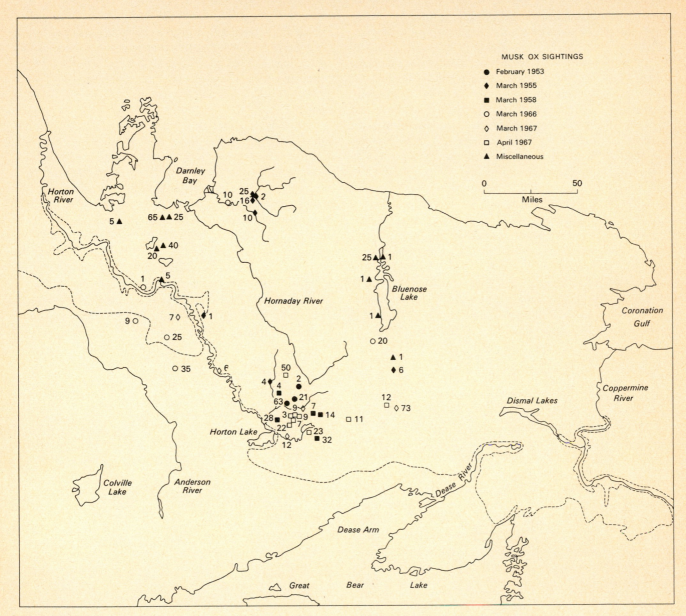

Map 4. Distribution of musk oxen north of Great Bear Lake after 1953. Broken line indicates northward limit of trees (redrawn after Kelsall *et al.*, 1971).

movements between seasonal feeding areas have been reported from the mainland. In the interior herds tend to spend the winter on windswept upland areas, where food is most easily accessible, and to move down to lakes and rivers in spring or summer to take advantage of the early flush of browse and grasses (Richardson, 1851; Banfield, 1951). In coastal areas musk ox populations tend to winter slightly inland on the windswept uplands and to descend to the coast in spring and summer (R. M. Anderson, in Hone, 1934). Longer seasonal movements are rare and probably

occur only near the Mackenzie River, where the tree-line curves north to *c.* 69° and where the forest–tundra ecotone offers abundant, unexploited food in winter (Richardson, 1836; MacFarlane, 1905). Exploratory movements undoubtedly occur on the mainland but have not been studied.

Greenland

Greenland has been relatively intensively studied and illustrates well inter-regional differences in patterns of move-

13

ment, although Rasmussen (1915) pointed out that behaviour in any given area fluctuated from year to year according to the depth of snow and the abundance of forage. In some areas such as Cape Morris Jesup (MacMillan, in Allen, 1913) and parts of East Greenland (Lynge, 1930), musk ox populations may not undertake seasonal movements in some years. In other parts of East and Northeast Greenland many groups spend the spring and summer near the coast and move inland and uphill in winter (Jennov, 1933; Hone, 1934; Pedersen, 1936, 1942). Pedersen (1936) observed a correlation between group size and movements; in his opinion large groups usually moved to winter feeding grounds earlier than small groups, but small groups moved more often than large. Local movements within seasonal feeding areas are small and follow the pattern observed in other areas (Pedersen, 1926–7; Johnsen, 1953; Hall, 1964). Long-distance movements of entire groups may occur infrequently (Pedersen, 1942), probably when ice-crusts render fodder inaccessible, but such movements are rare (Jennov, 1933) and usually involve very few animals (Johnsen, 1953).

Nunivak Island

Seasonal movements on Nunivak Island are short and are influenced by forage and snow cover. Most musk oxen there spend the winter in the coastal dunes, feeding on windswept stands of beach rye grass (Bos, 1967; Spencer & Lensink, 1970). Some populations remain near the coast in summer, but others move further inland, although there is little apparent regularity in these movements. Some animals occasionally move to small offshore islands in winter (J. J. Teal, *pers. comm.*), and reports of drowned animals (Buckley, Spencer, & Adams, 1954) imply that longer movements may be attempted, but the Etolin Strait separating Nunivak Island from the mainland never closes in winter. Local movements within seasonal feeding areas on Nunivak Island are very limited. Lent (1971) plotted the movements of two herds near Nash Harbour in summer. Map 5 reproduces Lent's results, which confirm the observations of Tener (1965) and Stefansson (1924).

Group size and composition

Many writers (e.g. Whitney, 1896; MacMillan, 1928; Tener, 1965; Freeman, 1971) have referred to seasonal changes in the size and composition of musk ox herds, but no thorough investigations have been conducted. Data are available only from two sources: Johnsen's (1953) survey of Northeast Greenland; and the work of Bos (1967) and the United States Bureau of Sport Fisheries and Wildlife in Alaska (U.S.B.S.F.W.). Both studies have serious limitations.

Johnsen was unable to age or sex many of the animals seen, and his study was limited to areas suitable for sledge travel. On Nunivak Island most observations were made in late winter/spring or late summer, and there is some uncertainty about the ageing and sexing of younger animals (Wilkinson, 1972c). Tables 1–2 summarise the results of the two surveys.

On Nunivak Island most bulls join mixed-sex groups in winter, when group size is greatest. In late winter the bulls begin to leave these groups, and the number of lone bulls and of all-male groups increases sharply and reaches a peak during the rutting season in late summer. The proportion of herds comprising only females and young is greatest in early summer, although a few bulls usually remain with or near these groups. The number of females in breeding harems averages 2.5, one-half of the number of adult cows (i.e. four years or greater) in mixed-sex groups in late winter, which supports the belief discussed below that musk ox cows breed only in alternate years. Non-breeding cows and bulls excluded from breeding activities form mixed-sex herds in the rutting season.

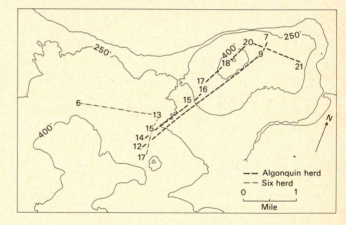

Map 5. Herd movements near Nash Harbour, Nunivak Island, in August 1969 (redrawn after Lent, 1971).

The figures from Northeast Greenland are less complete and show less regularity, but they are comparable to those from Nunivak Island. Mean herd size is greatest in early and late winter but may decline in mid-winter, perhaps because of the scarcity or inaccessibility of forage. The number of lone males and all-male herds is higher in summer than in winter, although the difference is less marked than on Nunivak Island, and February was the only month in which no such groups were observed. Herds of cows and young without bulls (6 per cent) were recorded only in August. The size of breeding harems was the same as on Nunivak Island, but group size at other seasons in Northeast Greenland was much smaller, which probably

THE RELEVANCE OF MUSK OX EXPLOITATION

Table 1. Herd size and composition, Nunivak Island
(Data from U.S.B.S.F.W. files, Bethel, and Bos, 1967)

Key. N = number of herds (including single males) seen; x = average number of musk oxen per herd; s = without; u = unknown.

Month	N	x	Per cent all-male herds	Per cent herds s bulls	x bulls in mixed herds	x cows in mixed herds
April	36	8.0	22.0	u	u	u
April	39	14.3	8.0	u	u	u
April	44	11.3	7.0	u	u	u
April	63	11.3	35.0	6.5	3.4	4.0
June–July	36	5.0	55.0	36.0	1.5	3.5
June–July	19	4.5	63.0	35.0	2.3	7.0
July	36	5.0	48.0	14.0	1.65	4.9
July	15	8.0	0.0	15.0	1.0	2.6
July	42	5.5	35.0	11.5	1.7	3.3
August	11	7.0	0.0	9.0	1.0	2.5
August	102	4.0	54.0	4.0	1.0	2.75
September	174	3.1	62.0	0.0	1.1	u
March	64	7.5	22.0	1.8	4.5	6.0
March	66	9.0	29.0	12.5	3.1	5.4

Table 2. Herd size and composition, Northeast Greenland
(Data from Johnsen, 1953)

Key. N = number of herds (including single males) seen; x = average number of musk oxen per head; s = without; u = unknown.

Month	N	x	Per cent all-male herds	Per cent herds s bulls	x bulls in mixed herds	x cows in mixed herds
April	16	5.0	44.0	u	u	u
April	23	4.5	40.0	u	u	u
May	42	4.2	45.0	u	u	u
May	11	2.4	64.0	u	u	u
June	13	1.6	78.5	u	u	u
June	9	1.8	30.0	u	u	u
July	3	4.3	7.5	0.0	u	u
July	6	2.5	40.0	u	u	u
August	10	2.9	80.0	0.0	1.0	2.0
August	17	3.5	41.0	6.0	1.5	2.5
August	7	1.9	53.0	u	u	u
August	5	3.4	60.0	u	u	u
September	13	2.1	61.0	0.0	1.0	1.0
September	7	8.5	14.0	u	u	u
October	24	3.8	58.0	0.0	1.6	1.5
October	13	2.5	58.0	u	u	u
November	2	1.5	100.0	0.0	u	u
December	1	1.0	100.0	0.0	u	u
February	6	2.0	66.0	0.0	1.0	1.0
February	2	7.0	0.0	u	u	u
March	20	4.95	40.0	u	u	u
March	15	8.6	14.0	u	u	u

reflects the relative sparseness of food in Northeast Greenland.

Herds of up to one hundred animals have been reported from the Canadian mainland (Hearne, 1795; Pike, 1892), the Canadian archipelago (McDougall, 1857), and Greenland (Koch, 1930; Pedersen, 1936), but these are unusual.

Despite Ogilvie's (1893) claim, there is no evidence that musk ox cows form single-sex herds or move to special areas for calving. Captive cows rarely stray far from the main herd when calving, and to do so would render free-living cows extremely vulnerable to predators.

Herd growth

Nunivak Island is the only area where rates of population increase have been studied for a long period. Tables 3–4 summarise the results of annual censuses since 1948. Despite the widespread belief that musk ox cows calve only in alternate years, Table 4 suggests that the number of calves observed is equivalent on average to 66 per cent and occasionally up to 90 per cent of the number of mature cows (usually assumed to be four years of age or older). This situation could arise if some cows were conceiving annually or if cows were sexually mature before four years of age. Data quoted above suggested that only one-half of the females over four years of age belonged to breeding harems, and it seems likely that younger females are breeding. Musk ox cows calve in alternate years because they suckle their young for one year or more after birth. It is difficult to envisage a mechanism by which calves might voluntarily wean themselves at four months to permit their mothers to breed annually, for although lactation in musk oxen is not a physiological barrier to conception, lactating cows rarely come into heat and breed. Jennings and Burris (1971) observed one cow on Nunivak Island which they believed had conceived as a yearling. The figures from Nunivak Island cannot be considered typical for musk oxen in their natural habitat, for this is a transplanted population, and Nunivak Island lacks predators and has very abundant forage, particularly in summer.

Freeman (1971) studied population dynamics in musk oxen near Jones Sound. He estimated that the average calf crop was 12.5 per cent of herd size, excluding solitary males. In two years on Ellesmere Island, however, no calves were observed, and the maximum calf crop there was 15.0 per cent. Freeman suggested elsewhere (Freeman, 1970) that a calf crop of 10.3 per cent was required to balance natural mortality, and he estimated that the probability that this would be achieved in his study area in any given year was only 0.47 per cent.

On theoretical grounds Leslie (1965) estimated that the

Table 3. Rate of population growth, Nunivak Island, 1948–68 (after Spencer and Lensink, 1970)

Year	Population size	Size of calf crop	Observed mortality		Increase[1]
1948–9	57	8	0[2]	0[3]	
1949–50	54	7	11	4	0.95
1950–1	60	16	1	3	1.11
1951–2	68	9	8	4	1.13
1952–3	75	15	2	4	1.10
1953–4	79	21	11	4	1.05
1954–5	97	19	3	9	1.23
1955–6	100	26	16	2	1.04
1956–7	118	25	8	2	1.18
1957–8	149	32	6	1	1.26
1958–9	167	39	14	6	1.12
1959–60	199	57	7	2	1.19
1960–1	224	69	32	2	1.13
1961–2	275	78	18	6	1.23
1962–3	333	73	20	3	1.22
1963–4	365	102	41	5	1.09
1964–5	406	108	61	15	1.09
1965–6	459	110	14	15	1.10
1966–7	531	120	30	11	1.15
1967–8	614	100	40	9	1.15
x			17.1	5.35	1.13

Notes

[1] $= \dfrac{\text{Herd size year } N}{\text{Herd size year } N-1}$.

[2] Inferred from total animals observed, but may include animals living but not seen.

[3] Includes remains found, some of which may have died prior to the year in which they were observed.

maximum rate of increase attainable by a free-living musk ox population was unlikely to exceed 1.16 per annum (i.e. herd size year $N + 1$/herd size year N). Leslie's predictions agree with observations from Nunivak Island but are much higher than Freeman's figures.

Musk ox cows usually produce only a single calf, and the harsh environment of the Arctic and the long suckling period of musk ox calves discourage twinning. Verifying occurrences of twinning in the wild is difficult. When herds are disturbed, calves may flee to the nearest adult, and observations of captive musk oxen have shown that a single cow may guard several calves while their mothers feed, although this has not been reported for free-living musk oxen. Mere sightings of cows with two or more calves do not constitute reliable proof of twinning. Twins have been reported from

Greenland (Manniche, 1912; Pedersen, 1936; Hall, 1964), the Canadian mainland (MacFarlane, 1905), the Canadian archipelago (Tener, 1965), and possibly from Nunivak Island (Spencer & Lensink, 1970). One pair of twins has also been born in captivity (Wilkinson, 1971b). Nonetheless, twinning in musk oxen is extremely unusual.

Table 4. Population increase,
Nunivak Island, 1948–66

Year	Mature females[1]	Calves[2]	Per cent calves[3]
1948–9	19	8	42.0
1949–50	18	7	38.8
1950–1	20	16	80.0
1951–2	22	9	40.0
1952–3	25	15	60.0
1953–4	27	21	78.5
1954–5	32	19	59.0
1955–6	33	26	78.0
1956–7	40	25	62.5
1957–8	50	32	64.0
1958–9	56	39	70.0
1959–60	66	57	86.5
1960–1	74	69	90.0
1961–2	90	78	87.0
1962–3	110	73	66.0
1963–4	120	102	85.0
1964–5	136	108	79.0
1965–6[4]	152	110	71.0

Notes
[1] Sex ratio of population assumed to be approximately equal; two-thirds of the females assumed to be mature sexually.
[2] Census in late summer; some mortality must have occurred.
[3] Per cent of adult females; in view of the mortality assumed, this under-estimates the proportion of calves actually born.
[4] Sex ratio of adults after this date biased in favour of males to an unknown degree.

Musk ox cows normally calve only in alternate years: females with yearlings are never accompanied by calves; the proportion of calves in herds rarely exceeds one-half the number of mature cows; and calves continue suckling for some twelve months after birth. Annual conception may occur occasionally (Stefansson, 1924; Pedersen, 1936), but high rates of herd growth probably indicate a lowering of the age of sexual maturity rather than annual conception.

Abundance

Partly as a result of severe over-exploitation, the numbers of musk oxen in the early twentieth century (when the first sur-veys of their abundance were conducted) were extremely low. Hone (1934) estimated the world population in the early 1920s at only c. 11 000. Anderson (1930), however, put the population of the Canadian archipelago at c. 12 000, and that of the Canadian mainland at c. 500. Hoare (1930) believed that there were only c. 9000 musk oxen in the Canadian islands. Thirty years later Tener (1963) counted only 8400 in the Queen Elizabeth Islands, and he put the mainland population at only 1500 (Tener, 1965). The present world population of musk oxen is probably between 17 000 and 22 000 (Tener, 1965; Vibe, 1958).

Estimates of the aboriginal population of North America and Greenland are necessarily speculative. Seton's (1929) estimate that there might have been almost one million musk oxen in North America in A.D. 1800 merits little confidence. Table 5 shows present densities of musk oxen in Canada and Greenland, but the very low densities undoubtedly reflect in part many years of intensive over-exploitation. Musk oxen in much of Greenland were less severely affected than in Canada. If the densities for Greenland are applied to the other areas, the potential population of the Canadian archipelago might be c. 70 000 and that of the mainland c. 45 000. These figures are not inconsistent with estimates of the numbers of musk oxen killed in post-contact times (Wilkinson, 1972c). Even if these estimates are seriously in error, musk oxen can never have been numerous compared with such species as caribou or bison. Estimates of former musk ox populations in Eurasia are hazardous, but there is no evidence that they were ever common there.

Table 5. Density of musk oxen per square mile

Area[1]	Number	Area[2]	Density[3]
Canadian archipelago	8 400	550 000	65
Canadian mainland	1 500	350 000	233
Greenland	10 000	80 000	8

Notes
[1] This is the surface area of each region; the area of potential musk ox range is undoubtedly much less.
[2] Square miles.
[3] Square miles per musk ox.

The food resources of musk oxen are abundant in most parts of the Arctic in summer, and there is no doubt that they could support large populations. The lack of moisture and the low winter temperatures are also conducive to excellent preservation of standing forage (foggage) in winter without serious loss of nutritive value. The chief factor limiting the size of populations is apparently the accessibility of winter fodder through the snow and ice cover. Few detailed studies of the relationship between snow and ice cover and population size have been conducted, but Pedersen (1936) pointed to Kaiser Franz-Joseph Fjord, where summer forage is abundant, but where its inaccessibility in winter results in a relatively low population density. Vibe (1967) described high mortality rates in East Greenland when deep snow and layers of ice rendered vegetation inaccessible, and he suggested that these conditions might occur cyclically.

Food

The types, diversity, and abundance of the staple food species of herbivores influence their potential for particular forms of exploitation. Table 6 summarises available data on the food preferences of free-living musk oxen in four areas and attempts to estimate their relative seasonal importance. These data come from the following sources: Hartz & Kruuse, 1911; Manniche, 1912; Lynge, 1930; Tener, 1965; Bos, 1967; and Spencer & Lensink, 1970.

Four important points emerge:

The diversity of foods consumed by free-living musk oxen is striking. Of the eighty-four species listed, seventy-three are chosen regularly. The only area in which many plant species are avoided is Nunivak Island, which is outside the natural range of free-living musk oxen.

Studies of the food preferences of reindeer/caribou (Kelsall, 1968), the only other large herbivore sharing the tundra habitat of the musk ox, indicate little or no competition for food between the two species. Musk oxen and reindeer have co-existed on Nunivak Island for forty years,

Table 6.   Food plants of free-living musk oxen

Key. Su = summer; St = staple; W = winter; Se = secondary; Ig = ignored; Au = autumn; Sp = spring.

Species	Thelon Game Sanctuary Season	Importance	Nunivak Island Season	Importance	Ellesmere Island Season	Importance	East Greenland Season	Importance
Alopecurus alpinus			Su	St	Su	St		
Festuca sp.			Su	St	Su	St		
Salix arctica			Su	St	Su	St	Su	St
Eriophorum sp.					W	St	Su	St
Eriophorum Scheuchzeri					Su	St		
E. angustifolium			Su/W	St/Se				
E. polystachum							Su	St
Alopecurus sp.					W/Su	St/St		
Oxyria digyna					Su	St		
Carex nardina					Su	St		
Carex sp.			Su	St	Su	St		
C. bigelowii			Su/W	St/St				
C. glareosa			Su	Ig				
C. aquatilis			Su/W	St/St				
Poa glauca					Su	St		
Potentilla pulchella					Su	Se		
Epilobium latifolium					Su	Se		
Melandrium triflorum					Su	St		
Erigeron compositus					Su	Se		
Polygonum viviparum					Su	St		
Cassiope tetragona					Su/Au	Ig		
Elymus arenarius			W	St				
E. mollis			Su/W	St/St				
Elymus sp.			Su	St				
Ledum palustre			W	St				
Arctostaphylos sp.			W	St				
A. alpinus			Su	St			Su	St
Salix pulchra			Su	St				
S. reticulata			Su/W	Se/St				
Calamagrostis canadensis			Su/Au/W	St/St/Se				
Rubus sp.			Su	St				
Rubus chamaemorus			W	Se				

Species	Thelon Game Sanctuary Season	Importance	Nunivak Island Season	Importance	Ellesmere Island Season	Importance	East Greenland Season	Importance
Angelica lucida			Su	St				
Arctagrostis latifolia			Au/W	St/Se				
Hierechloe alpina			Su	St				
Arenaria peploides			Su	St				
Lathyrus maritimus			Su	St				
Festuca rubra			Su	St				
Luzula sp.			Su/W	Ig/Se			Su	St
L. nivalis			W	Ig				
Sedum roseum			Su	Ig				
Ligusticum hulteni			Su	Se				
L. multelinoides			W	Ig				
Hylocomium sp.			W	Se				
Sphagnum sp.			W	Se				
Petasites frigidus			W	Se				
Trisetum sibiricus			W	St				
Loiseuleuria procumbens			W	St				
Cornus europea			W	Ig				
Cnidium ajanense			W	Ig				
Andromeda tetragona							Su	St
Rumex sp.			Su	St				
Ledum decumbens	Sp	St						
Empetrum nigrum	Sp	St	W/Su	St/St			Su	St
Betula nana			Su	St			Su	St
Vaccinium Vitis-Idaea	Sp	St						
V. uliginosum	Sp	St					Su	St
Betula glandulosa	Sp	St						
Cetraria nivalis	Sp	Se						
Alectoria ochroleuca	Sp	Se						
Rhytidium rugosum	Sp	Se						
Agropyron sp.	Sp	Ig						
Salix sp.	Sp/W/Au	St/Se/Se	W	Se	W	St		
S. alaxensis	Su	St	Su	Se				
S. Richardsonii	Su	Se						
S. arbusculoides	Su	Se						
Betula sp.	Su	Se						
Carex stans	Su	St			Su/W	St/St		
C. capitata	Su	St						
Juncus castaneus	Su	St						
Juncus sp.							Su	St
Poa alpina	Su	St			Su	St		
Poa sp.			Au/Su/W	St/St/Se	Su	St		
Equisetum arvense	Su	St	Su	St				
Puccinellia angustata					Su	St	Su	St
Festuca brachyphylla					Su/Su	St/Ig[1]		
Dryas integrifolia					Su	Se		
Dryas octopetala			W	St			Su	St
Saxifraga sp.					Su	Se		
S. oppositifolia							Su	St
Agropyron latiglume					Su	Ig		
Dupontia fisheri					Su	St		
Deschampsia brevifolia					Su	St		
Glyceria angustata							Su	St

Note. [1]There are two conflicting reports.

19

but there are no reports of serious competition, and the two species occupy largely distinct ranges. Musk oxen and arctic hares may occasionally compete for food, but not on an important scale.

There is no evidence that musk oxen are involved in complex grazing successions such as those recorded for many herbivores in African grasslands today (Bell, 1971), where the high biomass and diversity of herbivores can be maintained only by complex interactions in choice of foods, feeding behaviour, and patterns of movement.

In contrast to the lichens upon which reindeer/caribou depend, which may require up to thirty years to regenerate after heavy grazing or trampling (Klein, 1970), most of the species consumed by musk oxen renew themselves annually, which permits musk oxen to remain in restricted areas for long periods without seriously depleting staple foods.

The feeding behaviour of musk oxen is not understood in detail, but Tener (1965, p. 47) commented that 'as a rule musk oxen do not feed intensively in one spot in summer even in abundant vegetation . . . never remaining in one spot until all food is fully used'. Information on local patterns of movement cited above supports Tener's observations. Winter feeding habits may differ, since musk oxen are believed to be much less mobile in winter than in summer. Spencer and Lensink (1970), for example, believed that some groups severely overgraze certain parts of Nunivak Island in winter, although this claim demands confirmation (Wilkinson, 1973a).

Behaviour

Some aspects of musk ox behaviour, particularly in relation to domestication, have been discussed elsewhere (Wilkinson, 1972c, 1973b). The following is a selective account of those aspects of musk ox behaviour directly relevant to their exploitation by man.

When threatened by predators, musk oxen usually adopt a loose, semi-circular or linear formation facing the predators (Plate I). The mature bulls occupy the most vulnerable positions at the front and sides. Calves are protected between the flanks or beneath the bellies of their mothers. The phalanx is maintained until the danger has passed, except for occasional threatening sallies by in-

Plate I. Musk oxen in defensive group formation.

dividuals, which are often disciplined by the dominant bull. If predators approach within range, the musk oxen may attempt to gore them with a forward and upcurving sweep of the horns, but the horns are secondary in defence to the group-formation. Herds sometimes run uphill before adopting the defensive phalanx (Johnsen, 1953), which presumably minimises the risk of attacks from behind.

Musk oxen occasionally run greater distances from predators. Tener (1965), for example, reported that a group of thirty-eight fled from him in April. Stefansson (1921) believed that, when they fled, musk oxen ran further and were more difficult to catch than caribou. The rôle of experience is uncertain, but unconfirmed verbal reports from Nunivak Island, where musk oxen and men come into relatively frequent contact, suggest that the musk oxen there may be learning to flee from humans more often than formerly.

It is usually easy and safe for men to approach close to defensive groups, although the reactions of the animals vary according to the season, the composition of the group, and experience. Bernier (1910) reported that musk oxen on Melville Island were easy to approach, and Pedersen (1936) said that those near Scoresby Sound, East Greenland, paid little attention to humans although they were severely hunted in the early twentieth century. U. Møhl-Hansen (quoted by Anderson & Poulsen, 1958) stated that musk oxen in Peary Land, Northeast Greenland, were unafraid of men. Tyrell (1902) believed that herds with females and young were easily startled, but that adult bulls were virtually fearless. Stefansson (1924) found that even herds accustomed to being hunted were relatively easy to stalk from cover.

Wolves are the only regular predators of musk oxen, and the defensive formation offers excellent protection against wolves. The static phalanx is, however, particularly vulnerable to human hunters, even with primitive weapons. Humans can approach to within a few yards of defensive groups with little danger of being attacked. Although it is easy to slaughter musk oxen, recovering carcasses is difficult, since the defensive formation is usually maintained even after some of its members have been killed, although there are occasional exceptions to this rule (Madsen, 1901; Manniche, 1912). Although it is possible in theory for hunters to slaughter chosen animals and to go away and wait for the group to disband before retrieving their carcasses, this is an unattractive and often impossible proposition, particularly in winter, and entire social units have traditionally been slaughtered, even if not all their meat was required.

The defensive behaviour of single animals (usually bulls) is poorly understood, but they often occupy rocky rather than open areas, where they are less vulnerable to predators (B. Hubert, *pers. comm.*). Single animals show a greater tendency to flee than animals in groups; if pursued, however, they often take refuge with their hindquarters against a rock or cliff (J. J. Teal, *pers. comm.*), where they are relatively easy to kill.

Reactions to man

The preceding discussion suggests that defence against wolves depends upon group solidarity and that selective pressures have discouraged the exercise of aggressive tactics by individual animals. A similar passivity characterises the reactions of musk oxen to humans.

Parry (1821) and Greely (1888) believed that musk oxen never attacked men, but other authors have reported attacks by groups (Nathorst, 1901; Sverdrup, 1904) or, more commonly, by rutting bulls (Koldewey, 1874; Jennov, 1933; Johnsen, 1953). Experience with captive musk oxen suggests that the so-called attacks by groups were probably investigative rather than aggressive. The attacks by rutting bulls were probably attempts to frighten rather than to injure, and none of them resulted in injuries. There is only one reliable report of a man being killed by a musk ox, which occurred only when the animal was extremely provoked and frightened (J. J. Teal, *pers. comm.*).

Where they have been little hunted, musk oxen show no fear of man. Hanbury (1904) visited a remote area of the Canadian Barrens and reported that: 'Here the animals remain in their primeval state, exhibiting no fear, only curiosity. I approached several herds within thirty yards, photographed them at my leisure, moving round them as I wished and then retired, leaving them stupidly staring at me as if in wonder.' Even in areas where hunting was common, calves showed little fear of man. Manniche (1912) reported that a calf which survived the slaughter of its parental group attached itself to the hunters and showed no fear even of their dogs. On the basis of testimony from competent observers, a Canadian Royal Commission (Rutherford, McClean, & Harkin, 1922) concluded that 'when cows having young calves are killed, the calves show no fear of man and are easily led away, or will often follow without being led'. These comments suggest that taming, often an important element in domestication, may sometimes be unnecessary and that it does not require a sophisticated technology. The relevance to studies of prehistoric animal domestication of these observations has been discussed elsewhere (Wilkinson, 1972b and 1972c).

Social development

The social development of free-living musk oxen has not been studied, but reports about the distribution of particular age- and sex-classes permit useful inferences.

Calves suckle for some twelve months after birth. During this time they remain close to their mothers and probably form few social bonds except with other calves. Yearlings are rarely seen away from mixed-sex groups. Whether they remain with their mothers or even with the groups into which they were born is unknown. They have certainly ceased to suckle at this time, and their bond is probably to the group rather than to any individual animal. Data on two- and three-year-olds are sparse, since few observers have felt confident of distinguishing these classes, but have grouped them as subadults. Two-year-olds probably remain close to mixed-sex herds as protection against predators. The age at which females join breeding groups and at which males begin to compete for harems doubtless varies according to the quality, quantity, and availability of forage. On Nunivak Island most animals are sexually mature by three years of age, but Pedersen's (1936) estimate of four years probably applies in most other areas.

Once they are sexually mature, bulls are compelled to leave the protection of the main herds in early summer and cannot rejoin them until after the rutting season, in September or October. Most of the animals thus excluded form single-sex groups, since they would otherwise be very vulnerable to predation, and non-breeding females also form groups at this time. This suggests that musk oxen remain open to initiating new social contacts even as adults. A similar receptivity characterises musk oxen of all ages, and herds in the sense of permanent or semi-permanent aggregates of animals do not exist, but groups mix, fragment, and exchange members as they happen to meet (Teal, 1958).

The selective advantage of such behaviour is clear. Among sub-dominant bulls and non-breeding cows, protection from predators demands that they unite when they are excluded from breeding harems. The sparsity of food resources in most of the Arctic precludes high population densities and large herds. Musk ox bulls are polygynous, and a single bull may dominate breeding in a given area for several years. If herds were strictly closed, a high and possibly dangerous degree of inbreeding might develop.

Although musk oxen occupy restricted areas for long periods, there is no evidence that these areas are defended or that they are avoided by other groups or individuals. Like other non-territorial bovids (Ewer, 1968), musk ox bulls defend their harems during the rutting season.

Products

The products obtainable from animals influence the form and intensity of their exploitation by man. The principal products of musk oxen are meat, horn, hides, and underwool (*qiviut*).

Meat yields are high and are discussed in detail elsewhere (Wilkinson, 1972c, Chapter 6). Free-living adult bulls weigh 300–410 kg, and females 200–300 kg, and winter weight losses in most areas probably average *c*. 40 kg. The dressed weight of both sexes attains 55–60 per cent of live weight in late summer and proportionately less in winter.

Both sexes provide horn, although the horns of bulls are much larger and more useful than those of cows. Although useful, ethnographic data suggest that horn was rarely essential to any native arctic economies.

Musk ox hides are of excellent quality and, unlike caribou hides, they show little seasonal variation; nor are musk oxen particularly susceptible to the larvae of warble flies. On the other hand, the hides of bulls may weight up to 25 kg before cleaning, which is disadvantageous to mobile groups, and their long outer hairs easily collect dirt, which severely reduces their insulating properties.

The most valuable product of musk oxen is their *qiviut*, which grows beneath the outer hairs and is shed annually in spring. It rivals the finest textile fibres of the world. Yields from bulls reach *c*. 3000 g and those from mature cows probably do not exceed 2000 g. Fibre diameter averages *c*. 12.5 microns, compared with *c*. 13.0 microns for vicuña and *c*. 15.0 microns for cashmere. Fibre length ranges from 1.25–15.0 cm compared with a range of 1.25–6.5 cm for vicuña and 2.5–9.0 cm for cashmere (Wilkinson, 1972c).

If it can be assumed confidently that the attributes discussed have been constant through time and space and are not a product of recent, relatively unique circumstances, they can be used to predict past patterns of exploiting musk oxen. Knowledge of evolutionary rates makes it unlikely that important biological changes have occurred at least since the onset of the Final Glaciation, since musk oxen have occupied similar arctic or peri-glacial habitats throughout this period and the selective pressures upon them must have been relatively constant. The behavioural attributes discussed also seem explicable with reference to defence against predators, the necessity of avoiding excessive inbreeding, the scarcity of food in arctic and peri-glacial habitats, and other pressures which must have been relatively constant in recent millennia. Finally, the fact that musk oxen in different areas are biologically and behaviourally identical supports the belief that the attributes discussed represent widespread adaptations of long standing and are not a product of recent circumstances.

EFFICIENCY

It is axiomatic in economic prehistory that, in the long run, prehistoric human populations will have tended to exploit animals in what I have called an efficient manner. This does not necessarily impute a high degree of logic to the human groups in question; nor does it imply that there will never have been any exceptions to this generalisation. If, however, animals are exploited inefficiently, their numbers will decline or they may even become extinct, and the economies dependent upon them will disappear or be replaced by less destructive systems of exploitation. There may have been situations in the past in which the pressure of human populations upon space and the available resources was so low that inefficient forms of exploitation did not seriously harm the animal populations and in which the human groups could easily move to new areas if they did seriously deplete resources. In the time periods with which the economic prehistorian is usually concerned, however, demographic pressures will inevitably create situations in which the future growth or survival of human populations depends upon developing and maintaining efficient patterns of exploitation.

Human exploitation of animals at every level of technological and social development is necessarily selective with respect to the age and sex of the animals slaughtered; indeed non-human predators tend also to exploit their prey selectively (Jarman & Wilkinson, 1972, pp. 92–5). If animal populations are to be exploited for meat on a sustained basis without endangering their survival, exploitation must concentrate on those animals which are most easily replaced and which are least necessary for group defence and reproduction. In polygynous, gregarious species many males are superfluous to requirements of defence and propagation, and it is often a profitable strategy to slaughter these animals when they approach sexual maturity and maximum weight. Alternatively, males may be killed shortly after birth, since this creates a favourable balance between the number of females and young and the available forage. Old animals are easily replaced, and they are often less important for defence and reproduction than animals in their prime. Thus, the objective of most patterns of exploiting animal populations (whether the animals are free-living or domesticated) is to maintain a thriving nucleus of young and prime females with sufficient males to meet requirements of defence and propagation, and to concentrate exploitation upon young males and older animals of both sexes.

The preceding discussion of musk ox behaviour demonstrated that free-living musk oxen cannot be exploited in such a fashion because their defensive behaviour demands that entire social units be killed. In winter, social units normally contain males and females of all ages, but in summer they comprise predominantly females and young — the least expendable segment of the population. In theory, it is possible that lone bulls or younger bulls in single-sex groups might be exploited selectively, but these animals are often more difficult to locate and harder to hunt than females and young, and in practice there is no evidence that males were ever hunted selectively. Although the defensive formation of musk oxen would permit selective slaughter of chosen animals, the difficulties of retrieving carcasses are such that this is impracticable, particularly in winter.

The low density of musk oxen precludes their being exploited as a staple resource, by which I mean a resource which is regularly (perhaps seasonally) and intensively exploited and which forms an important part of the subsistence requirements of a human group. If musk oxen were exploited as a staple resource, their numbers would rapidly decline. Even if efforts were made to exploit them selectively with respect to age and sex, Freeman's studies (1970, 1971) revealed that the surplus segment of musk ox populations is often too small to support even small human populations. The discontinuous distribution of individual population units is a further disadvantage from a human point of view, since population units are often so scattered that it is impracticable to exploit sufficient population units to provide economically valuable quantities of meat.

Meat resources are usually abundant in the Arctic, and indigenous economies there have concentrated on varying combinations of exploiting seasonal abundances of fish, marine mammals, migratory birds, and caribou. Under normal circumstances, therefore, there is little pressure to make a special effort to exploit musk oxen, since other more abundant and more easily accessible meat sources are usually at hand. Opportunities for hunting musk oxen are often precluded by the demands of other more important subsistence activities. In winter, human settlements tend to be concentrated on the coast to exploit fish or marine mammals, whereas musk oxen tend to be inland in areas with shallower snow cover. In summer, when the musk oxen move down to the coast, many human groups move inland to fishing and hunting camps near lakes and rivers, and those groups which remain on the coast usually have abundant alternative resources. Human groups in the interior frequently move into the barren grounds in summer to exploit fish and caribou near lakes and rivers, where they might encounter musk oxen, but the availability of other resources usually discourages extensive reliance upon musk oxen. In winter musk oxen remain on the barrens when most caribou migrate south, and human groups also leave the barrens, so that they have no opportunity to exploit musk oxen.

A feature of traditional life in the Arctic has been the unpredictable failure of usually reliable or abundant resources. One efficient manner of exploiting musk oxen is as what I term a critical resource. A critical resource is one which is not exploited on a regular or seasonal basis and which is not exploited intensively, but without which survival in certain areas or periods is difficult or impossible. Such a strategy for exploiting musk oxen is clearly congruent with their biology and behaviour described above. There are two major situations in which musk oxen might be exploited in this fashion: when other resources fail unexpectedly; or on journeys through areas such as the Canadian Barrens in winter which lack alternative resources. The distinction between critical and staple resources (see p. 23 for a definition of the latter) is obvious. Two other classes of resources are widely recognised, emergency and casual resources, but both differ in important respects from a critical resource. Although a critical resource is sometimes used in emergencies, it may also be used purposefully on journeys through areas without alternative resources, but in which an emergency situation cannot justifiably be said to exist. Casual resources have been defined (Vita-Finzi & Higgs, 1970, p. 2) as those which 'serve as relishes, delicacies, medicines, and the like', and they differ very clearly from critical resources in the sense of my definition.

The scattered distribution of musk ox groups offers good protection against the total extermination of all the groups within a given area, and the infrequency of such hunts allows adequate time for the populations to recover. The relative immobility of musk ox groups and their static defensive behaviour are also advantageous. In times of crisis and on journeys in winter it is important to expend a minimum of time and energy in search of food. I have shown that musk oxen are relatively sedentary, and that this was appreciated by some Canadian Indians. In situations of stress and on journeys a high assurance of hunting success is important. The static defensive behaviour of musk oxen usually guarantees easy kills and large meat yields.

There is a second way in which musk oxen can be exploited efficiently; namely by domestication. I have suggested that there is usually little incentive to exploit musk oxen for meat in the Arctic because of the abundance of other meat sources. *Qiviut*, on the other hand, is a unique product there, and its high quality ensures its value in subsistence or cash economies. Because it is quickly degraded by sun and rain and spread by the wind after it has been shed, economically valuable quantities can be obtained only by plucking. This means that man must control the distribution of the musk oxen to make them available when plucking takes place. This control also facilitates the selective slaughter of age and sex classes, so that domesticated musk oxen can be exploited for meat as well as for *qiviut*. Some of the behavioural attributes discussed, such as gregariousness, slow social development, and catholicity of food preferences, are relevant to the potential of musk oxen for domestication, and these have been discussed at length elsewhere (Wilkinson, 1972c, 1973b).

The concept of efficient man-animal relationships can be extended profitably to animals in prehistory, since it derives from the biological and behavioural attributes of the animals involved, and it is often possible to establish with confidence the likelihood that these have changed through time. The probability that a particular strategy of exploitation was practised in the past depends not only upon the attributes of the individual species available, but also upon the nature and range of the other economic activities practised. In the modern Arctic, for example, there are only two large herbivores, reindeer/caribou and musk oxen, and human choice is sharply prescribed. Table 7 shows that in the past musk oxen have co-existed with many other large herbivores, and there was probably a lower risk of a serious failure of all other staple resources. More alternative animals were available on journeys and in times of crisis, reducing the probability that musk oxen would be exploited as a critical resource.

One important underestimated factor influencing patterns of exploiting animal populations is the exploitation of 'non-food' resources. Musk oxen became extinct on Banks Island in the late nineteenth century. Stefansson (1924) believed that they had been exterminated by the local Eskimos, and that the stimulus to this had been the wreck of McClure's *Investigator* at Mercy Bay, on the north coast, in 1853. The abundance of raw materials in the wreck induced many Eskimos to make unaccustomed journeys there, often in winter, when travelling was easiest, during which they had to rely upon musk oxen for food. Such intensive exploitation was inefficient in the sense of my definition, and musk oxen soon became extinct. A useful point for economic prehistorians to consider is that the nature of individual man-animal relationships is not simply a product of the biological and behavioural attributes of the animals themselves or of cultural factors, but may also depend upon the demands upon time and labour of other economic activities with different priorities in the total (often annual) subsistence cycle.

Prehistorians attempting to construct predictive models of past economic systems or of the individual relationships comprising these systems cannot treat each resource represented on archaeological sites as an independent variable. They must reconcile the hypothesised pattern of exploitation of each resource with the presence and abundance of all the other resources represented at the same site and at other sites believed to have been occupied by the same human group. This is the integrated approach to the study of prehistoric economies.

[Hence the importance of catchment as distinct from territorial analysis. *Editor*.]

The value of the concept of efficient man-animal relationships is that it permits predictions of the types of traces which particular patterns of exploitation would have

Table 7. The faunal associations of musk oxen

	1	2	3	4	5	6	7+	8	9	10	11+	12	13	14	15	16	17	18	19	20	21	22	23	24+	25+	26+	27+	28+	29+	30+	31	32+	33+	34+
Elephas primigenius		×		×	×	×			×	×	×	×	×	×		×	×	×		×		×		×	×	×	×	×	×			×		
Elephas trogontherii	×																																	
Elephas antiquus	×																																	
Allohippus süssenbornensis	×																																	
Equus fossilis			×																											×				
Equus caballus			×	×	×		×		×	×				×		×	×				×	×		×	×	×	×		×			×		
Equus aff. germanicus	×																				×													
Equus cf. hemionus	×																																	
Equus hydruntinus												×																						
Equus sp.		×												×										×	×	×	×							
Dicerorhinus etruscus	×																																	
Rhinoceros merckii						×	×																											
Rhinoceros tichorhinus					×	×	×			×				×			×	×	×				×		×		×	×	×					
Rhinoceros antiquitatis					×									×			×									×				×				
Sus cf. scrofa	×										×	×					×	×	×															
Hippopotamus major																				×														
Camelus sp.							×																											
Cervus elaphus				×		×			×	×	×	×	×	×		×	×		×			×		×	×		×	×	×					
Cervus acoronatus	×																																	
Megaloceros giganteus											×																							
Megaceros sp.							×																			×								
Pseudaxis sp.																		×																
Capreolus sp.		×							×			×	×	×			×							×	×		×	×	×					
Alces latifrons	×																																	
Alces alces	×					×	×		×				×			×	×	×				×		×	×	×	×	×	×	×	×	×	×	×
Rangifer tarandus	×																							×										
Euryceros pachyosteus							×																											
Bison sp.			×						×			×		×		×	×		×	×	×			×										
Bison priscus	×																																	
Bubalus teilhardi							×																											
Bos primigenius									×	×		×		×		×		×								×								

Note. + Archaeological sites.
Key to sites.

1 – Süssenborn
2 – Schlangenbühl
3 – Maidenhead
4 – Crayford
5 – Viry-Noureuil
6 – Précy
7 – Choukoutien
8 – Merseburg
9 – Barnwood
10 – Hamlin
11 – Pörgörlhegyer
12 – Ightham
13 – Freshford
14 – Fisherton
15 – Cosgrove
16 – Green Street Green
17 – Unkelstein
18 – Zbranki
19 – Neersen
20 – Dömitz
21 – Plumstead
22 – Langenbrunn
23 – Balver Höhle
24 – Gorge d'Enfer
25 – Kostenki 1-1
26 – Mezin
27 – Diuktai Cave
28 – Medvezh'ia
29 – Predmost
30 – Schaflochhöhle
31 – Escholtz Bay
32 – Thayngen
33 – Engigstciak
34 – Pelly Farm

25

left, against which to test and interpret data recovered by excavation. Further, it can guide archaeological fieldwork by suggesting the location of undiscovered sites and allows confident estimates of the size-range of human populations which could have been supported by particular exploitive strategies. Before applying this approach directly to the exploitation of musk oxen in prehistory, I shall test the hypothesis of efficient exploitation against the ethnographic data.

AN ETHNOGRAPHIC SURVEY OF MUSK OX EXPLOITATION

Although accounts of man–musk ox relationships cover only three centuries, sufficient data are available to test the hypothesis that primitive societies tend in general to exploit animals efficiently and that there are only two efficient ways in which musk oxen can be exploited. For convenience I have divided the data geographically into four areas: modern Alaska (including the Yukon Territory); the Canadian mainland; the Canadian archipelago; and Greenland. These areas are not all geographically distinct, but each has to some degree its own history of exploration, and they form convenient units for study.

Alaska (Map 6)

There is little evidence that musk oxen were ever exploited intensively in Alaska. Native informants reported that their 'grandfathers' hunted musk oxen on the North Slope (Russell, 1898; Brower, in Hornaday, 1911), and Stefansson (in Allen, 1913) stated that: 'during the winter 1899–1900 there died at Cape Smythe (or near there) the Eskimo man called Mangi by the whalers (probably Mangilanna). He was the last to die of Cape Smythe (Point Barrow) natives who had seen musk oxen in that vicinity. He was probably born between 1845 and 1850, as he was able to remember Maguire's visit to Point Barrow. [In the *Plover* in 1853.] A few years after Maguire's time – perhaps therefore about 1858 – there was a scarcity of food in winter at Cape Smythe. Mangi's father then went inland looking for caribou, and some distance up the Kunk River, which flows into Wainwright Inlet, they fell in with a band of thirteen musk oxen and killed them all. Since then, no-one near Point Barrow is known to have seen musk oxen or killed them.'

Gubser (1965) was told by Nunamiut Eskimo informants that musk oxen in Alaska began to decline in the early 1800s, but that they had traditionally been hunted in three main locations: on the lower Anaktuvuk River, above Umiat, and along the Colville River. He reported that musk oxen were hunted frequently, and Ingstad (1951) was informed by Nunamiut Eskimos that formerly 'the people lived mainly on musk oxen'. Surprisingly, Gubser was told that musk oxen were difficult to hunt without rifles, but rifles were extremely rare in Nunamiut territory until after the 1850s (Foote, 1965), well after the reported onset of the decline of musk oxen there. Gubser learned that musk oxen were valued for clothing, bedding, and shelter, but food was not mentioned. There is no evidence to support the claims of these modern informants, which I am inclined to doubt. For example, musk ox bones are absent from recent archaeological sites in Nunamiut territory (J. Cook, *pers. comm.*).

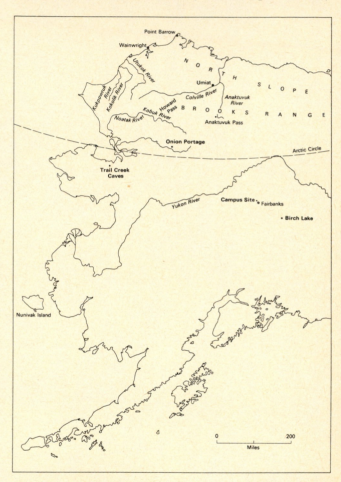

Map 6. Alaska: principal places mentioned in the text. Archaeological site names are in bold.

Musk oxen certainly did occupy Nunamiut territory at some period, and they were probably exploited occasionally, but there is no evidence that they were ever common there, that they were important in traditional economies, or that the Eskimos were responsible for their extinction, which probably occurred *c.* A.D. 1900 (Wilkinson, 1972c, Chapter 2). The only other account of musk ox exploitation in Alaska comes from the Chandalar Kutchin (McKennan,

1965), among whom musk oxen were hunted when they hapened to be encountered, sometimes by being driven over cliffs.

Foote's (1965) survey of traditional economies in Northwest Alaska before A.D. 1855 does not mention musk ox hunting. In fact, there is no evidence that musk oxen were ever common in Alaska in recent times. None of the Russian explorers in Alaska refers to musk oxen (Chévigny, 1965; Foote, 1965), although few of them visited the more northerly parts of the state. None of the later explorers to the north mentioned musk oxen either (Hooper, 1881; Wells, 1890; Bruce, 1895; Petrof, 1900; Ray, 1900). Only Turner (1886) believed that a few might survive north of the Romanzof Mountains, and the last two herds of musk oxen were killed in this general area near the turn of the century (McKennan, 1965). Earlier, Beechey (1831) and Richardson (1829) claimed that musk oxen existed in Alaska, although neither of them saw any.

In the present state of knowledge, the rarity and eventual disappearance of musk oxen in Alaska cannot be explained satisfactorily, but man can be excluded as an important agent of their extinction. With the dubious exception of some groups of Nunamiut, Alaskan Eskimos did not hunt musk oxen intensively. Where there is reliable evidence for their exploitation, as at Cape Smythe and among the Chandalar Kutchin, they were exploited as a critical resource, when other resources failed or when they were encountered by chance.

Canadian mainland (Map 7)

Ethnographic data from the Canadian mainland are relatively abundant. Since such reports by definition refer to the post-contact period, the probable degree of European influence must be estimated. For example, Franklin's (1823) report that Indians used to bring musk ox meat to Hudson's Bay Company forts does not necessarily indicate that they were traditionally hunted. Indrenius (1756), on the other hand, quoted data collected by Kalm on the west coast of Hudson's Bay from 1748–50 that the guard hairs of musk oxen were used to make face-nets as protection against mosquitoes. Barrow (1818) recorded that in a dispute near the mouth of the Coppermine River in 1770 some Indians 'threw all the tents and tent-poles into the river, destroyed a vast quantity of dried salmon, musk oxen flesh, and other provisions'. Dried musk ox meat was also used by the Sinimiut of the Pelly Bay area (Rae, 1850), and both of these reports undoubtedly reflect indigenous patterns of exploitation.

Musk oxen were not a staple resource. MacKenzie (1801), for instance, wrote of the Chipewyan Indians occupying the area from 60°–65°N and 100°–110°W that 'to the westward of them the musk ox may be found, but they

have no dependence upon it as an article of sustenance'. Parry (1828, vol. 4, p. 84) described feeding a group of Eskimos at Igloolik in 1882: 'at our meals I found every person much pleased with biscuit, which was supposed to be the dried flesh of the musk ox by those who had never seen the animal'. Elsewhere, however, musk oxen were undoubtedly exploited as a multi-purpose animal.

Products

Barrow's (1818) report from the Coppermine River does not indicate the economic importance of musk ox meat. Several observers of the Netsilik Eskimos (J. Ross, 1835; Rae, 1850; Balikci, 1964) agreed that the importance of musk ox meat fluctuated but that it was never very important. Rasmussen (1931), on the other hand, believed that in some periods musk ox meat attained at least seasonal importance among the Netsilik. Most groups of Iglulik Eskimos hunted musk oxen for meat occasionally (Damas, 1969), but it was important only to those near Wager Inlet. The Sauniktumiut southwest of Chesterfield Inlet relied heavily on musk ox meat as well as upon caribou (Steensby, 1917), and this may have been true of some groups of Netsilik who spent the winter in the interior, but Damas (1969, p. 118) wrote that 'although musk oxen inhabited this area, they were not an important factor in the Netsilik economy'. It is striking that, when Steensby (1917) described a group of Ukusiksillik Eskimos on the Hayes River in 1897 subsisting largely on musk ox meat, he emphasised that they were almost starving. Some Eskimos along the lower Back River occasionally hunted musk oxen for meat (Hanbury, 1904), but their staples were caribou and seals. Musk ox meat was relatively important among the Copper Eskimos near Bathurst Inlet (Jenness, 1922), which I earlier described as one of the core areas for musk oxen, but it was not particularly important to most other Copper Eskimo groups, although they certainly hunted musk oxen when they encountered them (Damas, 1969).

The use of musk ox horn was sporadic; although it was used when available, it was not highly valued on the mainland, perhaps because bone, antler, and wood served most of the same purposes. Among the Eskimos near the west coast of Hudson's Bay musk ox horn was used for ladles, gambling games, and riveted bows (Boas, 1901), as well as for barbs for fish-spears and attachments for manhole covers on kayaks (Boas, 1907) (Figure 1). Parry (1828, p. 208) noted that on the Melville Peninsula the bosses of horns, especially those of bulls, were used to make bowls and cups, adding that: 'of the smaller part of the horn they also form a convenient drinking-cup, sometimes turning it up artificially about one third from the point, so as to be almost parallel to the other part, and cutting it full of notches as a convenience in grasping it'. Spoons and bowls of musk ox horn were also made near Lyon Inlet, southeast Melville Peninsula (Parry, 1828).

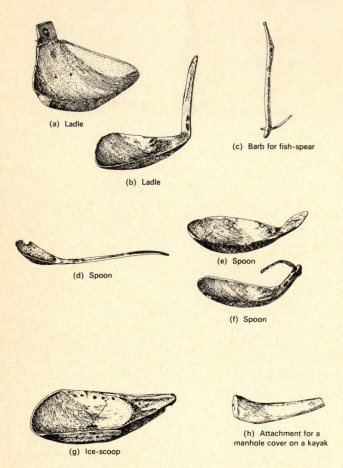

(a) Ladle

(b) Ladle

(c) Barb for fish-spear

(d) Spoon

(e) Spoon

(f) Spoon

(g) Ice-scoop

(h) Attachment for a manhole cover on a kayak

Figure 1. Artefacts of musk ox horn and bone from the west coast of Hudson's Bay (redrawn after Boas, 1901, 1907).

The Netsilik Eskimos made bows of musk ox horn, as well as fish leisters, blubber-pounders, and ladles (Nourse, 1879; Schwatka, 1885; Boas, 1907; Balikci, 1964) (Figure 2). The Caribou Eskimos made ladles and scoops for clearing ice from fishing holes out of musk ox horn (Birket-Smith, 1929), and those of the Boothia Peninsula straightened the horns by soaking them and used them as tent poles (Rasmussen, 1932). The use of musk ox horn was probably most extensive among the Copper Eskimos, and old kills and natural mortalities were also exploited for horn. The artefacts made included: blubber-pounders, tips of probes for seal holes, fish-spears, ulu handles, skin stretchers, knife blades, and snow-sounders (Stefansson, 1914a; Jenness, 1946) (Figures 3–5).

Ethnographic data confirm the belief (Comer, in Allen, 1913) that musk ox skins were unimportant in traditional arctic economies. Stefansson (1914a, p. 163) was told by Roxy, a Mackenzie Eskimo, that 'before Fort MacPherson was established musk ox skins were always thrown away' because they were too heavy to carry. Steensby (1910) and Birket-Smith (1929) said that they were not used for clothing because they attracted dirt.

When used, musk ox robes were employed as sleeping robes, although caribou and bear skins were preferred (J. Ross, 1835; Jenness, 1922). The Kinipetu, a small group living between Chesterfield Inlet and the Back River in the 1850s, used both musk ox and caribou robes (Steensby, 1917), but this was unusual. Anderson (1856) described the use of musk ox robes for tent coverings by the Ukusiksillik in the summer of 1855. The skins of calves were occasionally used for boots (Hearne, 1795; Schwatka, 1885), and Stefansson (1914a) saw sledges made of musk ox skins at Coronation Gulf and Repulse Bay, as did Schwatka (1885) on the Hayes River.

Some Copper Eskimos made toy bows from the ribs of musk oxen and caribou, and they preferred the longer ribs of musk oxen for making the bows of bow-drills (Stefansson, 1914a). Jenness (1946) listed the following which were made from the bones of caribou or, less often, musk ox: skin stretchers, needle cases, and harpoon sheaths from leg bones; skin stretchers from scapulae; handles, toggles, pins, and bows for drills from ribs, mouthpieces for drills from astragali. The stems of bow-drills were also made from musk ox or caribou bones. Birket-Smith (1929,

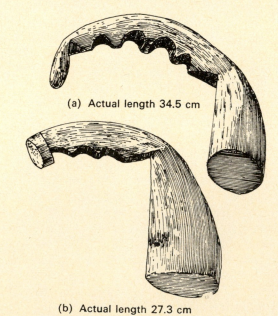

(a) Actual length 34.5 cm

(b) Actual length 27.3 cm

Figure 2. Musk ox horn blubber-pounders of the Netsilik Eskimos (redrawn after Boas, 1907).

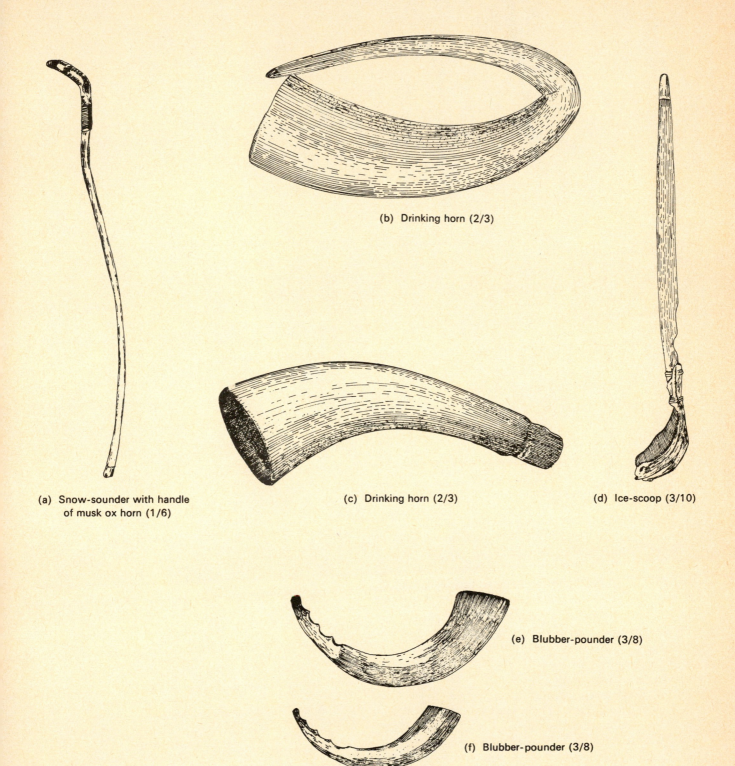

(b) Drinking horn (2/3)

(a) Snow-sounder with handle
of musk ox horn (1/6)

(c) Drinking horn (2/3)

(d) Ice-scoop (3/10)

(e) Blubber-pounder (3/8)

(f) Blubber-pounder (3/8)

Figure 3. Artefacts of musk ox horn from the Copper Eskimos (redrawn after Jenness, 1946).

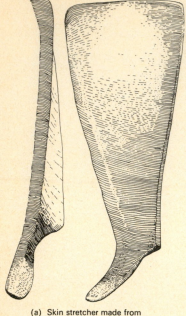

(a) Skin stretcher made from a scapula (1/2)

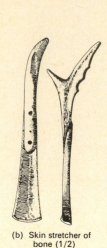

(b) Skin stretcher of bone (1/2)

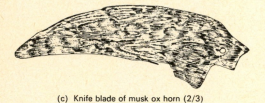

(c) Knife blade of musk ox horn (2/3)

Figure 4. Artefacts of musk ox bone and horn from the Copper Eskimos (redrawn after Jenness, 1946).

soup. J. C. Ross (1835) stated that 'musk oxen are said by the natives to be very numerous between the Isthmus of Boothia and Repulse Bay ... Their dung, when fresh, is considered a delicacy for the natives'.

Steensby (1910) suggested that musk ox fat might be used in lamps, but he did not indicate if this was done traditionally. Bladders, sections of the rectum, and the stomach were occasionally used as containers (Schell, 1972). The gristle of the ear of the musk ox was considered a delicacy by the Aivilik and Kinipetu Eskimos (Boas, 1907).

Hunting methods

The selective hunting of chosen age- and sex-groups of many animals by recent Eskimos is well documented (Stefansson, 1946; Gubser, 1965), but there is no ethnographic evidence to suggest that musk oxen were selectively slaughtered. Ethnographic accounts record several methods of hunting musk oxen and demonstrate that they were susceptible to primitive weapons. J. Ross (1835), for example, thought that bows and arrows were in-effectual against musk oxen, but Parry (1828) and Stefansson (1914a) recorded their use, although the latter

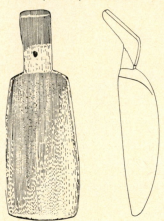

(a) Ladle with jointed handle (1/1)

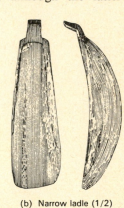

(b) Narrow ladle (1/2)

p. 145, fig. 44e) illustrated a marrow-extractor of musk ox bone, but caribou bones were used more frequently, and he also referred to a special type of fat-scraper made from a long bone with the epiphysis attached; although he appears not to have seen such a scraper, he was told that the long bones of bears or musk oxen and the bacula of walruses were preferred materials for these artefacts. Some Caribou Eskimos made scrapers from the mandibles of musk oxen.

Indrenius (1756) and Ellis (1748) described face-nets of musk ox hair used by the Eskimos near Hudson's Bay as protection against mosquitoes. Schell (1972) described an Eskimo mask in the Danish National Museum decorated with musk ox underwool. Otherwise neither the guard hairs nor the underwool of the musk ox were used by native groups in the Arctic.

Human consumption of the rumen contents of caribou was widespread, but only Richardson (1829) recorded that those of musk oxen were eaten. Eidlitz (1969) described the consumption of caribou faeces, either fresh or in blood

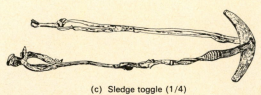

(c) Sledge toggle (1/4)

Figure 5. Ladles and sledge toggle of musk ox horn from the Copper Eskimos (redrawn after Jenness, 1946).

probably never saw them used. Stefansson (*ibid*. p. 96) described the efficiency of Copper Eskimo bows: 'At thirty or fifty yards members of our party have repeatedly seen an arrow pass through the thorax or abdomen of an adult caribou and fly several yards beyond.' Approaching within bow- or lance-range of defensive formations was easy and safe. Dogs were often employed (J. Ross, 1835; Birket-Smith, 1929), and their use reduced the probability that the animals will flee, although running humans could achieve the same effect.

The use of lances to hunt musk oxen was first reported by Jeremie (1926). Some Eskimos enraged musk oxen with arrows until they charged and then killed them with lances (Boas, 1888; Steensby, 1917; Birket-Smith, 1929). Driving musk oxen over cliffs is precluded by the topography of much of the Canadian arctic mainland and was described only among a few Central Eskimo groups (J. Ross, 1835). Musk ox drives were rare and were recorded only on the Back River (Pike, 1892), and among some Copper Eskimos, who commented that musk oxen could sometimes be driven right to camp sites before being killed, because, unlike caribou, musk oxen did not automatically flee from men (Jenness, 1922).

Unlike most marine and terrestrial mammals in the Arctic, musk oxen were not usually exploited on a strictly seasonal basis. Musk ox hunting was a secondary activity for some Copper Eskimos from June until mid-October and among the Iglulik Eskimos from mid-June until late December (Damas, 1969). On the other hand, winter hunts were the rule among some Netsilik groups (Balikci, 1964). Parry (1824) believed the Eskimos hunted musk oxen in summer and winter, but that the Indians hunted them only in summer, since the Indians left the barrens in winter. Winter hunts were most common along the coast of Hudson's Bay (Boas, 1901; Jeremie, 1926) as well as west-southwest of Coronation Gulf (Jenness, 1922). Amundsen (quoted by Steensby, 1917) and Birket-Smith (1929) believed that there was no definite season for musk ox hunts. Birket-Smith (1929, p. 112, emphasis added) agreed that there was no definite season for hunting musk oxen, but commented that 'it is to be supposed that the end of winter, *when caribou meat was scarce*, was especially the time for this hunting', which supports my belief that musk oxen were hunted as a critical resource. Some of the apparent discrepancies between reliable observers noted above may also reflect the fact that musk oxen were not exploited on a strictly seasonal basis.

As in Alaska, the Canadian mainland had a few areas famous for musk ox hunting, which reflects the discontinuous distribution of musk oxen referred to earlier. Balikci (1964) listed the following for the Netsilik Eskimos (Map 7): Kalusarvit (90°50′W, 60°30′N); along the Belcher River; the Hayes River near Chantrey Inlet; the Uqpik Hills (89°50′W, 68°30′N); and the Tinguqjuaq Hills (92°20′W, 68°20′N).

Written accounts show that bows, arrows, lances, and even knives were used for hunting musk oxen, and dogs, dog-sledges, and snow shoes were important (and probably essential) for winter hunts. There is no evidence, however, of specialised artefacts uniquely associated with musk ox hunting or with the utilisation of the carcasses and by-products of musk oxen.

The data, then, from the Canadian mainland support the hypothesis that musk oxen were exploited efficiently. In some areas musk oxen were apparently ignored, but throughout most of the Canadian mainland they were exploited as what I have called a critical resource.

Canadian archipelago (Map 8)

Data from the Canadian archipelago, although rare, suggest that in most areas musk oxen were not exploited intensively. Musk ox hunts were rare on eastern Ellesmere Island (Steensby, 1910), and Markham (1875, p. 171) reported the same about Banks Island, although he attributed this only to the inadequacy of the available technology. Musk oxen existed east and north of Minto Inlet, northwest Victoria Island, but the Eskimos of Dolphin and Union Straits rarely hunted them (Stefansson, 1914b). The Eskimos of western Victoria Island were believed to know of the existence of musk oxen on Banks Island but not to hunt them (Stefansson, 1921). In contrast musk oxen were hunted on the islands near the Melville Peninsula in the early nineteenth century (Damas, 1969).

Birket-Smith (1959) provided a striking illustration of the use of musk oxen as a critical resource. Early in the present century Polar Eskimos from northwestern Greenland started travelling in winter to Ellesmere and Axel-Heiberg Island to hunt musk oxen and polar bears for sleeping robes. Steensby (1910) believed that the stimulus to these journeys was a series of bad winters in northwestern Greenland which decimated the caribou populations there and caused the polar bears to move away, so that musk ox robes were needed as sleeping robes. Similar long journeys in search of musk oxen were undertaken by the Eskimos from Pond Inlet, Baffin Island, who went as far as Devon Island (Steensby, 1910), but the motivation of these hunts has never been clarified.

Musk oxen may occasionally have attained local importance in the Canadian archipelago, perhaps because alternative resources were less varied and abundant there than on the mainland. Some groups of Eskimos valued musk ox skins highly as sleeping robes (Freuchen, 1915), and horn spoons and ladles were important trade items among the

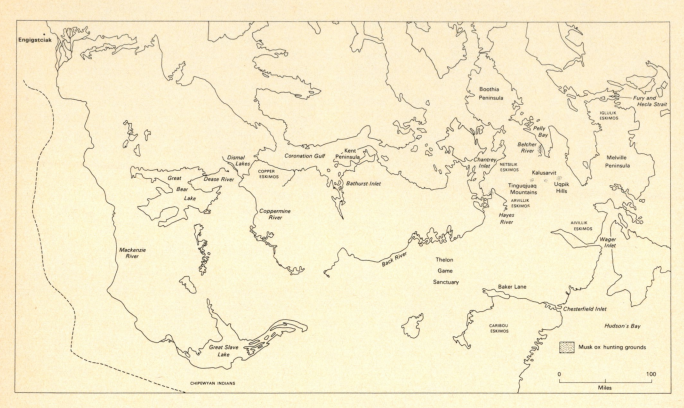

Map 7. Canadian mainland: principal places mentioned in the text. Archaeological site names are in bold.

Eskimos of Dolphin and Union Strait (Stefansson, 1914b). Tents of musk ox skins were seen near Prince Albert Sound, Victoria Island (Jenness, 1922), and Stefansson (1914b) described horn spoons and ladles from western Banks Island.

Greenland

Ethnographic data on musk ox exploitation in Greenland are lacking. On the east coast, Eskimos disappeared some time after 1823, when Clavering saw the last recorded group, a family of twelve on Clavering Island (Larsen, 1934). Musk oxen probably became extinct in Northwest Greenland by the mid-nineteenth century (Kane, 1856). There is little evidence to support Rasmussen's belief that they had been important in local economies there.

The only description of butchering practices comes from Greenland. McClintock (1859) was told that the Eskimos of Smith Sound removed the mandible with the skin but discarded the skull; since unfleshed skulls may weigh up to 25 kg, this is hardly surprising.

Summary

The preceding data demonstrate that traditional patterns of exploiting musk oxen fall into the category which I have called critical hunting. Musk oxen were usually hunted only when other resources failed, when they happened to be encountered, or in areas lacking alternative resources. Musk oxen were not a staple resource among any native arctic groups for which records are available.

The principal factors governing this relationship were the low density of musk oxen and their distribution in areas without sufficient resources, particularly in winter, to support permanent human populations. The rarity of musk oxen is not a new phenomenon, since Nicolas Jeremie, one of the earliest European observers of musk oxen commented (Jeremie, 1926, p. 20) in the late seventeenth century that: 'if they [musk oxen] were numerous enough to be worth hunting, they would soon have been destroyed by the natives.' Steensby (1910) noted that some parts of Greenland in which musk oxen were present were uninhabited by Eskimos because they did not possess sufficient resources to support viable economies.

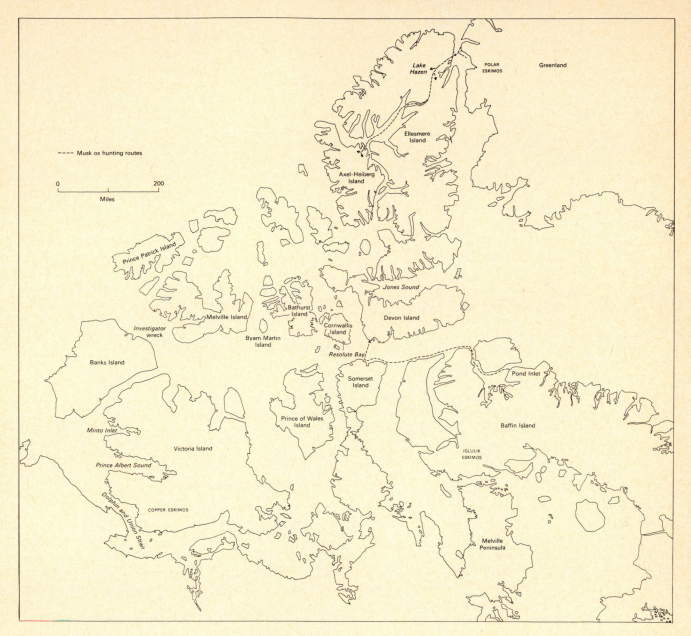

Map 8. Canadian archipelago: principal places mentioned in the text.

The observed relationship between Eskimos and musk oxen was an efficient one in my sense of the term, and I can find no evidence that the Eskimos were responsible for the widespread extermination of musk oxen prior to the arrival in the Arctic of Europeans and cash economies. I cannot accept the view (Allen, 1913; Stefansson, 1924; Hone, 1934) that Eskimos and musk oxen were traditionally incompatible, although they certainly became so after the development of the European fur trade (Wilkinson, 1972c).

Finally, the ethnographic evidence suggests that it might be profitable to apply a predictive model of efficient man–animal relationships to the study of man–musk ox relationships in prehistory. Binford (1968, p. 13) enumerated some of the difficulties of employing ethnographic parallels in archaeology: 'We can infinitely expand our knowledge of the lifeways of living peoples, yet we cannot construct the lifeways of past peoples unless we employ a more sophisticated methodology ... Fitting archaeological remains into ethnographically known patterns of life ... denies to archaeology the possibility of dealing with forms of cultural adaptation outside the range of variations known ethnographically.' Willey and Philips (1958, p. 2) made a similar implication: that 'archaeology ... concerns itself necessarily with the nature and position of unique events in space and time ...' I have argued elsewhere (Wilkinson, 1972d) that these limitations do not apply to economic prehistorians, since archaeological data represent traces of prehistoric man's participation in trophic-dynamic systems, the flow of energy through which was limited by the laws of thermodynamics, with their economic and behavioural consequences for human populations. Thus, unlike students of cultural processes, the economic prehistorian has a firm basis upon which to estimate the reliability of ethnographic parallels.

MUSK OXEN IN PREHISTORY

If musk oxen were exploited in either of the two efficient ways described earlier, the types of archaeological traces which each would leave are predictable.

If musk oxen were hunted as a critical resource, their bones would be rare in archaeological excavations, especially if they were hunted by travellers or at task-specific sites, since neither would often leave recognisable cultural deposits. When musk oxen were consumed at base camps, it is unlikely that entire skeletons would have been brought back. Butchering practices in Greenland suggest that mandibles might occur, and phalanges and possibly metapodials would be relatively numerous if the robes were kept. Horn would rarely survive. Vertebrae and pelves might be rare, but ribs and limb bones would probably be more common. Because selective hunting of musk oxen is usually impracticable, faunal samples should include a cross-section of age- and sex-classes. Samples from winter hunts would normally contain more mature bulls than samples from other seasons. The age of immature animals (which would occur in most samples) should permit reliable estimates of the hunting season on the basis of known sequences of dental eruption and attrition and epiphyseal fusion. In the case of winter hunts, evidence for dog-sledges and snow shoes might be expected.

Exploiting musk oxen for wool demands, at a minimum, taming the animals and controlling their location in spring to collect *qiviut* and to deliver and tame the calves. Since it is often easier for man to go to the animals than to bring them to his habitations (unless the two happen to coincide), these activities might have occurred away from easily recognised base-camps. If, as seems probable, such activities were seldom conducted more than a few times in precisely the

same location, they might rarely have left recognisable accumulations of debris for future archaeological excavation. Exploiting domesticated musk oxen for wool would almost certainly be associated with limited exploitation for meat. Since the animals would be tame and under human control, selective slaughter would be practicable, and the faunal samples left from such activities would be demonstrably different from those left by critical hunting. The most likely slaughter pattern would probably involve the following: slaughter of some males at three or four months of age in order that their dams might be bred annually; castration of most other males and slaughter at two or three years of age, giving an optimum yield of meat relative to maintenance-input; slaughter of adult bulls at ten years of age, after their optimal breeding period; and slaughter of females at twelve or fifteen years of age. Since domesticated animals could be slaughtered in chosen locations, complete skeletons would be more likely to occur than if the animals were hunted. The textile industry might involve some distinctive artefacts for knitting, weaving, felting, knotting, or spinning, but these would often be of organic materials and might rarely be preserved.

The following section compares archaeological evidence for musk ox exploitation against the predictive model developed in section one above. For convenience I have divided the data into Pleistocene and Post-Pleistocene finds and have employed the geographical subdivisions defined in the preceding section.

Alaska and the Yukon (Map 6)

Much of northern Alaska was not glaciated during the Wisconsin Glacial, and, with the Bering Land Bridge, is believed to have been rich in game. Laughlin's (1967, p. 421) claim that: 'the human adaptation to this region must surely have been that of big game hunters, living by means of scavenging dead mammoths and such bovids as caribou, bison and musk-ox, and by intentionally hunting live animals', awaits archaeological confirmation. Penetration of interior Alaska occurred at least by 17 300 ± 800 B.P. (Shell 6713A) at Driftwood Creek, on the Utukok River in the western Brooks Range, where the fauna probably included mammoth (Humphrey, 1966). Most sites in interior Alaska are undated, but occupation there was widespread and probably continuous after this time. Micro-blade sites in the interior, such as the Campus Site at College (Nelson, 1937) (Figure 6) and Birch Lake, sixty miles southeast of Fairbanks (Skarland & Giddings, 1948), may be related to the Epigravettian tradition of Asia. Further north, on the Kobuk River, Giddings (1960) and Anderson (1970) excavated a multi-level site at Onion Portage with a micro-blade tradition at the base, the Akmak complex. On the

North Slope, Solecki (1950) identified Epigravettian sites in the Kokolik and Kukpowruk River valleys, and my own fieldwork in 1970 confirmed his results for the former. Further east in the Brooks Range, in the Howard Pass area, a large habitation site with a micro-blade industry at Lake Itivlik and a probable winter camp at Kupiuak were located (Irving, 1962); other sites of this Arctic Small Tool Tradition were excavated at Ahlasurak and Kinyiksuvik. North of Anaktuvuk Pass, Solecki and Hackman (1951) excavated a site at Lake Natvakruak, and Campbell (1959, 1961a, 1961b) identified three complexes of finds, known as Tuktu, Kayuk, and Kogruk respectively.

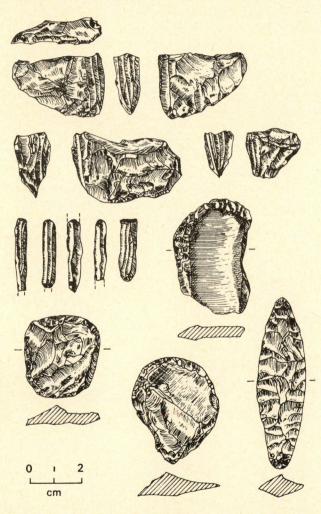

0 1 2
cm

Figure 6. Artefacts from the Campus site at College (redrawn after Bandi, 1969).

Faunal remains are rare at all inland Alaskan sites. At Trail Creek Cave (Larsen, 1968) and at some levels of Onion Portage, for example, musk oxen are absent. Most inland sites were located on routes of caribou migrations, or near lakes and rivers for fishing and perhaps fowling. Although this does not necessarily exclude musk ox hunting, it is unlikely to have been an important focus of subsistence activities. The emphasis of early Alaskan economies was marine, probably with seasonal exploitation of the hinterland (Larsen & Rainey, 1948), and musk oxen are also absent from all early coastal sites.

The only archaeological evidence of musk ox exploitation comes from Birnirk Period sites near Point Barrow (Ford, 1959). At Kugusugaruk, ten miles southwest of Barrow, corpses dressed in parkas of bird or animal skins lay in rows on brown bear, polar bear, or musk ox skins. The burials were undated, but were probably only between 200 and 300 years old. Burials at the village of Nunavak, possibly dating from A.D. 800 to 1250, were wrapped in musk ox or polar bear skins. At Kugok, an early Birnirk site post-dating A.D. 500, fragments of musk ox robes were found near Burials 2 and 5 in Mound A, but were not recorded from Mound B. At the type-site of Birnirk itself two fragments of musk ox horn were recovered from the floor of House A, the age of which is uncertain. Fragments of musk ox horn were recovered also from Structure B, which was probably recent. The site of Nunagiak, near Wainwright, yielded two spoons of musk ox horn, and the apparently recent finds from Utkiavik, which Ford purchased from Eskimo excavators, included a musk ox horn ladle.

In the Yukon, musk ox remains have been reported only from the Pelly Farm Site (MacNeish, 1964). Radiocarbon dates were indecisive, suggesting an age of 6000–3000 B.C.

The reasons for the absence of musk oxen from pre-Birnirk sites remain unclear, and the rarity of all faunal remains complicates the matter. Musk oxen may have been exploited, but the location of sites suggests that economies in the interior were based on caribou, as were recent native economies in the interior. In coastal sites, faunal remains are more common and indicate heavy reliance on fish and marine mammals and secondarily on caribou and birds. Musk oxen may not have existed in Alaska, although it seems probable that they did, and they are known from late Wisconsin gravels, near Fairbanks, but they may have been ignored. It is significant that the first appearance of musk oxen in native Alaskan economies coincides with the earliest evidence for dog-sledges. The use of musk ox robes may imply that the animals were killed in winter, when the robes are at their best and when it is easiest to transport heavy robes overland, and when dog-sledges would be indispensable to hunters. Whatever the situation, musk oxen were exploited at the most sporadically in Alaska, and claims that Eskimos were responsible for their extermination find no support.

Canadian mainland (Map 7)

Archaeological evidence for musk ox exploitation on the Canadian mainland falls into two classes: sites reported by early explorers, most of which are probably relatively recent; and those located by archaeologists.

Simpson (1843, p. 292) at Franklin Point found 'several old Esquimaux camping places, and human skulls and bones were seen in various situations. One skeleton lay alongside that of a musk-bull, in such manner as rendered it extremely probable that the dying beast had gored the hapless hunter'. Artefacts of musk ox horn on the Melville Peninsula, near Lyon Inlet, and on the coast of Fury and Hecla Strait (Bartlett, in Hone, 1934) are interesting, since there are no historical records of musk oxen from there, although Parry (1828, vol. 2) recorded that local Eskimos in that area decorated their clothing with musk ox teeth. Richardson (1829) did not mention musk oxen in that area. Harington (1961) speculated if this indicated that prehistoric man had exterminated musk oxen, but the evidence is inconclusive.

Archaeological investigations have linked musk ox exploitation to three technological complexes. The oldest site with musk oxen is Engigstciak, 25 km inland south of Herschel Island (MacNeish, 1956). MacNeish recognised nine complexes of artefacts, which he ordered chronologically, although they were not clearly stratified. The New Mountain Complex, the third-oldest, included a micro-blade and a macrolithic element, with lanceolate points and several types of burin. There were no traces of habitations, and the location of the site suggests that it was probably used in summer; complementary winter sites may exist on the coast. The fauna was predominantly caribou, but included bison, moose, musk oxen, and mountain goats larger than modern forms. MacNeish suggested an age of 4000–5000 years for the New Mountain Complex.

Finds made by Harp (1961) near Baker Lake and along the Thelon River may be related typologically to the New Mountain Complex. Geomorphological evidence suggests that they are less than 5000 years old. Two badly weathered musk ox skulls were dubiously associated with site SL-5, at Schultz Lake, the location of which on a game trail approaching a lake suggested that it was principally a caribou-hunting camp. One of the skulls bore cut marks, probably made by a steel blade, and both may post-date the original occupation of the site. Harp (1961) believed that a badly deteriorated ladle of musk ox horn from site BvL-3, at Beverley Lake, originated from a recent Caribou Eskimo occupation. Musk oxen were absent from all other sites in this area.

Musk ox exploitation was a secondary activity at some Dorset culture sites on the coast and in the interior.

Rousselière (1964) excavated an early Dorset site at Kugarjuk 4, southeast Pelly Bay, probably post-dating 700 B.C. The site lay 4 km from the mouth of the Pelly River, where the steep banks and a small lake facilitated hunting. No traces of dwellings were found. The artefacts included one doubtful scraper, a few retouched flakes, three microblades, burin spalls, and a slate plaque with one polished edge. A single bone was tentatively identified as musk ox. I noted earlier that southeast Pelly Bay was traditionally a favoured area for musk ox hunting.

Harp (1958, p. 245) surveyed the Dismal Lakes area, between the Coppermine and Dease Rivers, concluding that: 'judging from the finds I made, perhaps it may also be assumed that musk ox was formerly an important game animal in this area', but his claim demands corroboration. Sites with Dorset affinities occur in Newfoundland, and Harp (1969–70) found a small, flat amulet at Port-aux-Choix, on the northwest coast, which has been taken to resemble a seal, a bear, or a musk ox. Musk oxen are believed never to have occupied this area, and the resemblance is tenuous.

About A.D. 1000 Dorset artefacts were replaced in most of the Canadian Arctic by the Thule culture. Like the Dorset, the Thule economy was heavily marine-orientated. The artefacts included several types of harpoon head, bows and arrows, bird-arrows, bolas stones, leisters, fish-hooks, bow-drills, hand-drills, ground-slate ulus, adzes, picks, and hammerstones. Evidence of dog-sledges appears for the first time, although recent finds of Dorset-type artefacts in the Canadian archipelago suggest that they may have been present earlier.

The Thule site of Naujan, on the Melville Peninsula, yielded a spoon of musk ox horn from House 6, and a scraper-blade made on a musk ox radius also occurred (Mathiassen, 1927). Whale, walrus, and seal dominated the fauna; caribou were reasonably common and a few musk ox bones also occurred. Mathiassen (*ibid.*) investigated a second Thule site, at Igluligardjuk, on the southern coast of Chesterfield Inlet. Faunal remains were predominantly caribou, bearded seal, and other seals, but a few teeth and complete bones of musk oxen occurred. Both of these sites were probably occupied in autumn or winter, and a small winter camp at Aivilik also yielded a single bone of musk ox (*ibid.*).

Due west of Chesterfield Inlet Harp (1959) distinguished several sites along the Thelon River with a Thule element, probably the summer camps of groups which wintered on the coast. Faunal remains were rare, but the location of the sites suggested that caribou were the chief game.

MacNeish (1951) surveyed interior sites in the Northwest Territories. He located forty sites, which he divided tentatively into four artefactual complexes: the

Tahlateili, Artillery Lake, Lockhart, and Whitefish, in decreasing order of antiquity. No faunal remains were found, but the lacustrine and riverine distribution of the sites implied an economy based on caribou, fish, and perhaps water fowl.

These data suggest that musk oxen were never intensively exploited on the Canadian mainland. At coastal sites, the presence of musk oxen correlates with the presence of dog-sledges, but this is not observed at inland sites. The difference can probably be explained with reference to the seasonal movements of musk oxen. Inland sites were probably visited in summer and coastal sites in winter (and perhaps also at other seasons). I noted earlier that in winter many musk oxen move slightly inland, and that in summer musk oxen in the interior often descend to stands of willow near lakes and rivers. Thus musk oxen were probably inaccessible to hunters on the coast in winter unless they had sledges; in summer, however, groups moving inland to fish and hunt caribou near lakes and rivers would have stood a greater chance of encountering musk oxen.

Canadian archipelago (Map 8)

Parry (1828) found the remains of six houses on Byam Martin Island associated with bones of caribou, polar bear, and musk ox. Three more houses at Beverley Inlet produced a fauna of seal and musk ox, and two other musk ox skulls were found associated with an unidentified group of stones nearby. Markham (1875) also described musk ox bones from Byam Martin Island. The antiquity of these sites is unknown. Feilden (in Nares, 1878, vol. 1) reported numerous musk ox bones near old houses on the Bache Peninsula, eastern Ellesmere Island. On Banks Island, McClure (1856) said that old camp sites were numerous in the southeast and that musk ox bones occurred at most. During their biological survey of Prince of Wales Island, Manning and Macpherson (1961) observed several old camps, but reported that musk ox bones were rare. On Banks Island, on the other hand, they counted more than 200 musk ox skulls near a hill-top site close to the junction of the Muskox and Thomsen Rivers (Manning, 1956; Manning & Macpherson, 1958).

For practical reasons, archaeological excavations have been rare in the Canadian archipelago. Mathiassen (1931) recorded a single musk ox skull, probably associated with cultural debris, on the south coast of Southampton Island, and Eskimo informants told him that musk ox teeth occurred at the settlement of Kuk, on the west side of York Bay, but independent evidence for the former existence of musk oxen on this island is lacking, and these finds may be imports.

Collins (1950, 1951) excavated a site with Thule affinities near Resolute Bay, on the south coast of Cornwallis Island. Seal was the principal faunal element, followed by bowhead whale and walrus; caribou and musk oxen were rare, but bones of dogs and foxes were common.

Musk ox and caribou bones were minor elements at a site in McCormick Inlet, on the west coast of Hecla and Griper Bay, Melville Island (Henoch, 1964). Two dates bracket the occupation of this site: 1740 ± 190 B.P. (I-840) and 1150 ± 160 B.P. (GSC-148). The five artefacts found there included a large point with a straight base and two lateral notches close to the base (Taylor, 1964).

A site with generalised Dorset/Thule affinities at Cape Sparbo, Devon Island, produced bones of caribou and musk oxen (Lowther, 1962, & *pers. comm.*); the musk ox bones included several metacarpals.

In contrast, musk ox exploitation on Banks Island, Ellesmere Island, and Axel-Heiberg Island may sometimes have been comparatively intensive. A site at Shoran Lake, north-central Banks Island, produced 115 fragments of musk ox bone, 52 of caribou, and 6 bird bones (Taylor, 1967). Large bifacial quartzite points were the most common tools. Similar points have been dated 2910 ± 105 B.P. (I-2053) and 2990 ± 125 B.P. (I-2054) in the pre-Dorset levels of the Buchanan Site, southern Victoria Island.

East of a small creek at the southern end of Shoran Lake, Taylor (1967) excavated the Umingmak (Musk Ox) Site. This site, formerly next to the lake, covered an extensive area, but Taylor divided the finds into twelve zones and three complexes, each including early pre-Dorset material. The artefacts of each complex were similar, but differed markedly from other pre-Dorset sites, such as the Menez Site and NiNg-7. For example, burins with grinding facets were frequent at the latter but rare at the Umingmak Site. Micro-blades, which occurred in small numbers at the Umingmak Site, were absent from the other sites, but these had chert blades unknown from the Umingmak Site. Large, ovate, bifacial points occurred at all the sites but were rarer than in pre-Dorset sites on Victoria Island. A total of 1245 bone fragments were identified, comprising 85 per cent musk ox, 6.3 per cent caribou, 6.3 per cent bird, and some fox and hare. Taylor (1967, p. 227) commented that 'this whole-hearted devotion to musk ox [was] probably a seasonal stress'. The location of this site and the apparent absence of houses suggest that it was a summer camp, and the large area may imply that it was visited over a long period, so that the numerous musk ox bones may reflect prolonged rather than intensive exploitation. The skeletal elements represented are unreported, but skulls did occur.

Maxwell (1960) surveyed northern Ellesmere Island near Lake Hazen. The Lonesome Site (Tj-Aq-1) in Conybeare Bay was probably occupied sporadically in winter and summer, since both houses and tent rings occurred. Feature

2, a tent ring with a windbreak, two caches, and three fox traps, yielded bones of caribou, musk ox, hare, and seal, in decreasing order of abundance. Artefacts included an antler knife-handle with traces of an iron blade and a fragment of a sledge shoe. The presence of iron need not indicate a recent date; Ross (1819) reported that the Polar Eskimos of Northwest Greenland used meteoric iron. Feature 20, an isolated tent ring, lacked artefacts, but produced rare bones of caribou, musk ox, and seal. Feature 31, a tent ring with several caches and fox traps, which Maxwell interpreted to indicate a temporary occupation rather than a transient visit, produced a cylindrical bone harpoon on a wooden shaft, an antler harpoon head, the tip of a tanged arrow, and worked and unworked pieces of amber. Caribou bones dominated the fauna. Hare bones were next numerous, followed by musk ox, fox, and seal. Feature 35 was probably a similar semi-permanent tent ring and included two hearths. Hare bones dominated the fauna, followed by caribou, geese and other fowl, seal, musk ox, and fox in decreasing abundance. Three houses classified as winter dwellings produced faunal remains, but only one (Feature 21) included musk ox, associated with caribou, seal, hare, and polar bear. An adjacent midden included 500 fox mandibles.

The Stone Lamp Site produced no traces of dwellings, and the only artefact found was a soapstone lamp; the associated fauna included rare seal bones and one musk ox metapodial.

A single site in Archer Fjord, the Haematite Site (Tj-Ao-1), comprised two tent rings, two fox traps or caches, and four large caches, and was probably a summer camp. An antler prong for a fish-spear was the only artefact found, but the fauna included musk ox and caribou bones.

The Basil Norris Site (Tk-Ap-1) in Discovery Harbour comprised fifteen tent rings and one probable house. Faunal remains were numerous, including musk ox, seal, caribou, hare, and fox in decreasing order of importance.

The inland area near Lake Hazen is today unsuitable for winter occupation, and only three possible winter camps were found there. The Dryas Valley Site (Ua-Av-6), in a broad valley northeast of the lake, comprised one tent ring with a hearth and cache. A musk ox skull had been incorporated into the low wall at the base of the tent. The Gilman East Site (T1-At-3), on the delta near the end of the lake, showed evidence for regular occupation. Features 2 and 3, both tent rings, produced rare musk ox bones. Feature 5a, possibly an early house, yielded a three-pronged fish harpoon with Dorset affinities, and musk ox bones were quite common. The nearby Gilman West Site (T1-At-1) might have been a winter camp and yielded bones of hare and musk ox.

The Ruggles Outlet Site (Tk-Au-1) was the only definite winter camp near Lake Hazen. Feature 1 was a tent ring and produced cut tines of caribou antler, a drilled antler pot hook, and a few pieces of worked antler and ivory. Hare dominated the fauna, followed by musk ox, caribou, fox, goose, and char. Feature 2, a house, contained three artefacts of musk ox bone, including several meat sticks carved from musk ox ribs. The fauna resembled that of Feature 1. Maxwell believed that the artefacts had affinities with the Thule culture. The second stage had been seriously disturbed by later activities, and no traces of musk oxen were found. Finds from the third, probably recent, stage included two scrapers made from musk ox tibiae, accompanied by a fauna of musk ox, caribou, hare, goose, ptarmigan, fox, and char. The last occupants had apparently died of starvation.

The observed ratio of summer to winter sites was 100:4. The most likely pattern of seasonal movements would have been to winter on the coast and to move to the interior in summer, but coastal winter sites are rare. Winter sites in western Ellesmere Island, southeast of Lake Hazen on the Bache Peninsula, or even in Northwest Greenland may have been complementary to the summer sites studied. Alternatively, winter activities may have been concentrated on the sea-ice; in either case, the evidence suggests that the population of northern Ellesmere Island was small.

Musk ox hunting on Axel-Heiberg Island dates back at least 4000 years. Knuth (1967) reported three sites near Kettle Lake which seemed from their location to be specialised musk ox hunting sites. He assigned them typologically to the Pre-Dorset. [14]C dates were obtained from each: Kettle Lake South: 3930 $\pm$ 130 B.P. (K-1260); Kettle Lake: 3810 $\pm$ 130 B.P. (K-1261); and Kettle Lake North: 3760 $\pm$ 130 B.P. (K-1262). The nearby site of Air Force Valley, dated typologically and geologically to 4000–3000 B.P. (Andrews, McGhee, & McKenzie-Pollock, 1971) showed similar economic emphasis.

The preceding data suggest that musk oxen were more important in the archipelago than on the mainland, but that they were still a critical resource, particularly on Ellesmere Island, where caribou may have been periodically rare. On some more southerly islands, musk oxen were the only resident large herbivores, and reliance in winter was concentrated on fishing and hunting sea mammals. If either of these failed at traditionally exploited locations, opportunities to move in search of alternative supplies were more limited than on the mainland, and musk ox hunting became the principal alternative activity. In spring and summer the same applied if anticipated numbers or locations of caribou proved wrong. Finally, musk oxen tend to be more accessible on islands than on the mainland, because the islands are much smaller, or because glaciers or mountains limit grazing areas.

The frequent association of musk oxen with hare and fox bones, especially on Ellesmere Island, is striking. In defining critical resources, I suggested that one of their functions was to permit survival or travel in areas lacking alternative resources. Fox trapping, a winter activity, frequently necessitated journeys to areas away from the coast and without dependable large game other than musk oxen. The association of musk ox and fox bones is probably a good indication of the use of musk oxen as a critical resource. Taylor suggested that the large numbers of musk oxen at the Umingmak Site indicated a stress situation and the final inhabitants at Ruggles Outlet, who may have been relying on musk oxen, died of starvation.

Greenland (Map 9)

Studies of prehistoric man–musk ox relationships in Greenland are complicated by incomplete knowledge of the former distribution of musk oxen there. Vibe (1967) discussed the available evidence. Reports from early visitors suggest that musk oxen were rare or absent on the east coast south of 70°N in the early nineteenth century, although they were present before this time in some areas. An important southerly extension of musk oxen occurred in the second half of the nineteenth century.

Systematic archaeological research in East Greenland was initiated by Mylius-Erichsen and, after his death, by Thostrup on the Danmark Expedition (Thostrup, 1917). Thostrup subdivided the area surveyed into six geographical regions. The first two districts, Hagens Fjord and Danmarks Fjord, contained no sites with musk oxen. The third, Ingolf's Fjord, contained three sites but only one, at Eskimonaesset, with musk ox bones. The site was located close to the shore near a favoured landing place of walrus. It comprised one winter house, seven tent rings, and eight meat caches, containing bones of walrus, fjord seal, musk ox, and narwhal. The musk ox bones were probably associated with the winter house. Four sites were recorded in the next district, Skaerfjorden, but all lacked faunal remains.

The fifth district, Cape Bismarck, was explored intensively. A site at Syttenkilometernaesset comprised sixteen winter houses and fifteen tent rings. Faunal remains were abundant and included bean-goose, grey gull, polar bear, dog, walrus, bearded seal, fjord seal, caribou, musk ox, whale, and narwhal. The marine orientation of the economy is confirmed by the location of the site at a spot where the prevailing winds tend to keep the ice offshore, facilitating hunting in kayaks. Musk ox remains were rare and were associated only with two of the winter houses.

A site at Renskaeret included winter houses and tent rings. One musk ox skull was associated with a winter house. The presence of umiak-rests suggests that the site was visited at times of open water as well as in winter. No winter houses were discovered at Danmarkshavn, which contained forty-nine tent rings, six shelters, and fifteen fox traps. The fox traps suggest that the site was occupied at least early in winter. Musk ox, hare, polar bear, bearded seal, fjord seal, and caribou comprised the fauna. A nearby site close to Wendel's Point, probably a summer camp, yielded remains of dog, polar bear, walrus, fjord seal, caribou (including cast antlers), and musk ox.

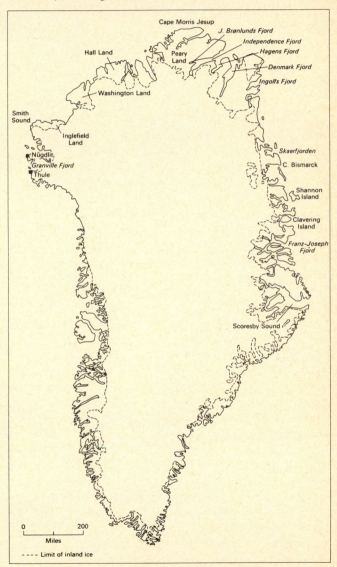

Map 9. Greenland: principal places mentioned in the text.

On the east coast of Stormbugt, Thostrup located a camp with six winter houses, twenty-four tent rings, two fox traps, many caches, and two graves. Musk ox bones occurred in only one winter house, where they were associated with hare, dog, walrus, bearded seal, fjord seal, caribou, and whale. A second site, near the head of Stormbugt, consisted of one tent ring, one shelter, one fox trap, and four caches, and was located close to a reef where walrus and large seals commonly rest; a few musk ox bones were found.

A camp at Stormnaes included tent rings, shelters, hearths, fox traps, and caches. The fauna was abundant and contained bean-goose, fjord seal, caribou, and musk ox. A nearby tent ring also yielded musk ox bones. A site at Snenaes was located on a section of beach normally free of snow and with access to a good water supply in summer. Remains of thirteen winter houses, eight tent rings, two shelters, thirteen fox traps, many caches, and three graves were located. The fauna from winter house 406 consisted of ptarmigan, hare, dog, bearded seal, fjord seal, caribou, and musk ox, including one musk ox skull.

Two tent rings and one shelter were located at Lakseelven, which is noted today for the early arrival of walrus and birds in spring and for its excellent salmon fishing. Polar bear and musk ox bones were recovered from one tent ring. A site at Saelsøen, close to a lake, included traces of twelve tent rings, one shelter, three traps, twenty-five permanent caches, and four temporary caches. Unusually, Thostrup noted (1917, pp. 292–3) that 'it was not reindeer hunting, as at other places, but mainly the musk-ox hunting, as is shown by the many bones we obtained'. Other faunal remains included dog, fjord seal, and caribou. One meat cache contained evidence suggesting a special relationship with musk oxen. The skeleton and flesh of a calf were preserved in anatomical order, but with a stone carefully placed between each bone; overlying this was a layer of hare flesh. Another important site, Rypefjeldet, had ten winter houses, forty-eight tent rings, thirteen shelters, and thirteen traps. Walrus, bearded seal, fjord seal, caribou, and musk ox remains were recovered from winter house 522. Winter houses 523 and 524 produced hare, dog, polar bear, walrus, bearded and fjord seal, caribou, and musk ox bones. Winter house 525 yielded hare, polar bear, fjord seal, and musk ox bones, and a meat cache contained musk ox underwool. Musk ox bones were associated with two of the tent rings.

At a distance of 1200 m east of Rypefjeldet, the site of Foraarsboplads, comprising thirty-six tent rings and one shelter, produced bones of musk ox, dog, polar bear, bearded seal, fjord seal, and caribou. The musk ox remains included skull fragments. Musk ox and fjord seal remains occurred in several adjacent meat caches.

In the sixth district, the coast between Shannon Island and Clavering Island, traces of occupation occurred in eight areas, but musk ox remains were not reported.

Thostrup suggested three periods of occupation for the East Greenland sites, the oldest separated from the two younger by a considerable interval. He estimated relative population sizes from the number of winter houses, assigning thirty-two to the oldest period, twenty to the intermediate, and only four to the final period. This agrees broadly with historical data, which suggest that Eskimos disappeared from East Greenland by the mid-nineteenth century. Knuth (1966–7) observed a similar trend in Northeast Greenland, assigning 43 sites with 157 traces of dwellings to his Independence 1 culture, but only 8 sites and 31 dwellings to the later Independence 2.

The first Thule Expedition conducted limited excavations in East Greenland. Freuchen (1915) reported that musk oxen and fjord seals were the principal faunal components at sites on both sides of the mouth of Jørgen Brønlunds Fjord, and he and Steensby (1910) believed that musk oxen had been a staple resource in East Greenland. The 1926 Cambridge University Expedition collected material from fourteen sites in East Greenland (Mathiassen, 1929), but no finds of musk oxen were reported. Rasmussen (1915) described a possible summer camp at Cape Knud Rasmussen, with numerous bones of seal and musk ox. Glob's (1946) review of archaeological sites in East Greenland mentioned only one site with musk ox bones.

Thule culture remains are known from East Greenland at Dødemandsbugten, on Clavering Island (Larsen, 1934; Degerbøl, 1935; Bandi & Meldgaard, 1952), where they may date to the sixteenth century. One of the earliest houses contained a pelvis, tibia, metatarsal, and phalanges of musk ox. Other musk ox finds from Dødemandsbugten may date to the eighteenth century. Hare bones were common in the latest house, but ringed seal, harp seal, bearded seal, walrus, narwhal, and polar bear dominated the fauna.

The earliest inhabitants of Northeast Greenland have been termed the Independence 1 people (Knuth, 1966–7). A coastal site of this group in Wyckoff Land was dated 3970 ± 120 B.P., but lacked a fauna. Nine ^{14}C dates from five Independence sites range between 4069 ± 120 B.P. (K-938) and 3730 ± 120 B.P. (K-1196) (Knuth, 1967). Independence 1 artefacts (Figure 7) include burins, bifacial points, micro-blades, and end-scrapers, which may have vague typological affinities with the Epigravettian tradition in North America. Knuth's proposed subdivisions of the Independence 1 are typological, and the economic basis remained constant. A single ^{14}C date of 2585 ± 110 B.P. (K-1059) may date an early stage of the Independence 2 (Knuth, 1967), which Larsen (1960), but not Knuth, believed to represent a new group of immigrants rather than a development of the earlier stage.

Independence 1 material is represented at Nedre Midsommer Sø, in Peary Land, and by a winter camp at Cape Holbaek (Knuth, 1966–7). The fauna from the latter included a few hares and foxes, and three adult and two musk ox calves, possibly a single family unit. Most authors share Knuth's (1952) belief that the economy of the Independence people was based on musk oxen, with seal, hare, brent goose, ptarmigan, and trout as subsidiaries. Caribou were rare or absent from most Independence sites. In my opinion this claim requires confirmation, especially by means of the location and excavation of coastal (particularly winter) sites.

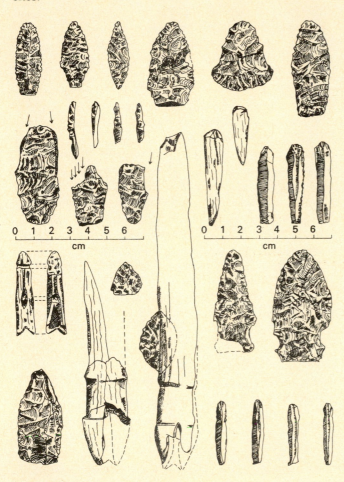

Figure 7. Artefacts of the Independence culture in Greenland (redrawn after Bandi, 1969).

The later stages of the Independence culture show Dorset influences. Several Dorset sites from Brønlunds Fjord have faunas comprising principally musk oxen (Johnsen, 1953). Surprisingly, of the thirty-one Dorset sites recorded in Peary Land, only one resembled a winter camp (Knuth, 1952). Organic remains were rare but indicated that musk oxen were taken, as well as river trout, hares, geese, and ptarmigan.

Thule elements have also been found in Northeast Greenland. North of Brønlunds Fjord, Knuth (1952) found several camp sites, including the nearly complete remains of an umiak at one. Other artefacts included whaling harpoons, sledge shoes, ground slate blades, trace buckles for a dog-sledge, and baleen tools. Faunal remains included Greenland whale, narwhal, bearded seal, ringed seal, musk ox, caribou, and arctic fox.

Mathiassen (1928) discussed finds made by L. Koch near Cape Webster, Washington Land, Northwest Greenland, in 1922. The artefacts suggested a relatively recent (Thule) date. Faunal remains, which were abundant, consisted principally of seal and polar bear, with smaller quantities of caribou and musk ox. A group of stones near Cape Tyson, Hall Land, was interpreted as the remains of a structure by Koch. An Eskimo informant told him that a musk ox skin had probably formed the superstructure. Bearded seal and musk ox bones were numerous in an adjacent midden, as well as fox, hare, and caribou. The artefacts resembled those from Naujan (Mathiassen, 1928; Bandi, 1969). Older finds are known from West Greenland, but these lie south of the known distribution of musk oxen on the west coast.

Musk ox bones occurred in middens near Thule, Etah, and along the south coast of Washington Land (Jensen, 1928, 1929). Holtved's (1944, 1954) studies of Inglefield Land revealed only limited utilisation of musk oxen, despite Rasmussen's (1921) belief that they had been staples, and Kane's (1856) statement that the Eskimos had exterminated them there. The earliest of these finds belonged to the Dorset culture, and the evidence suggested that musk oxen were an unimportant element of Dorset economies. Thule sites were more abundant than Dorset sites, but musk ox bones remained rare. House 7 at Inuarfigssuak produced a curved snow knife of musk ox horn, and a single skull was recovered from the passage of this house. The economy at Inuarfigssuak was predominantly marine, but hare, fox, and caribou were also exploited.

Several sites from near Cape Kent have been classified as transitional between the Thule and the later Inugsuk cultures (Holtved, 1954), and several of them contained both winter and summer dwellings. The faunal remains were chiefly seal and caribou, but musk ox, polar bear, whale, hare, and bird bones were also recovered. The musk ox bones included one skull, and one winter house produced a ladle of musk ox horn. An Inugsuk site was located on Ruin Island, three kilometers offshore from Inuarfigssuak. One house produced whale bones and pieces of musk ox skin and hair, and horn ladles were recovered from two houses. At the site of modern Thule, a house yielded a two-handed scraper made from a musk ox tibia. Another house, at Nûgdlît, near the mouth of Granville Fjord, which was probably contemporaneous with the Inugsuk occupation of Ruin Island, produced a ladle of musk ox horn.

With the possible exception of some Independence and

some Dorset occupants of Northeast Greenland, the evidence indicates that musk oxen were not an important element of traditional economies in Greenland. Musk ox exploitation may have been a subordinate element in a round of seasonal subsistence activities not yet fully appreciated. The data from Northeast Greenland suggest strongly that musk oxen were exploited as a critical resource because caribou were rare or absent. There is a similar correlation between fox and hare trapping and the presence of musk ox bones to that observed in the Canadian archipelago.

In view of my earlier statements that musk oxen cannot alone form the basis of viable economies, it is significant that the Independence people who depended more heavily than most others upon musk oxen declined markedly in numbers (Knuth, 1967). The disappearance of man from East Greenland in the nineteenth century also coincided broadly with the decline of caribou there, and the survival of musk oxen did not permit man's continued occupation.

Unfortunately, few detailed faunal analyses have been undertaken, and the skeletal elements and age and sex composition of musk ox samples have rarely been reported. At Dødemandsbugten, however, the bones represented suggested that the animals were killed away from the site and that only a few bones were brought back. The finds from Cape Holbaek may indicate the slaughter of an entire social unit, possibly in late summer, since only one bull was present, although the site was believed to be a winter camp. Negative evidence suggests that skulls, the most difficult skeletal element to transport, may have been rare: Thostrup's extensive survey, for example, mentioned their presence only four times.

The frequent association of musk ox bones with winter houses may imply that they were exploited as a critical resource when other food resources were rare, or during fox trapping journeys, which are a winter activity. Unlike Axel-Heiberg Island, few sites in Greenland were located in spots uniquely favourable for hunting musk oxen. Freuchen (1915), for instance, said that the area between Cape Rigsdagen and Hagens Fjord, in Independence Fjord, was poor territory for musk oxen, and that the southern shore of Independence Fjord was too narrow and too poor in food to support musk oxen.

Finally, evidence of seasonal patterns of movement in East Greenland makes it improbable that men and musk oxen often met, since human populations were often restricted to the immediate coastal littoral. Many sites in East Greenland contain both winter houses and summer tent rings, which indicates that they were visited at all seasons, if not occupied permanently. If musk oxen were hunted near the camps, local populations would quickly have been exterminated. Musk oxen tend to avoid heavily populated areas, and it is unlikely that they would have been near enough to most settlements to be easily hunted. The apparent abundance of marine resources renders it improbable that there was a significant need to hunt musk oxen, except perhaps occasionally in winter. On the other hand, the area between the inland ice and the coast in Greenland is often very narrow, and musk oxen must have been more accessible than on the Canadian mainland. In this respect Greenland should be compared with the Canadian islands rather than the mainland. Sites with a relatively large number of musk oxen often lie in areas where the coastal littoral is particularly narrow, and this may be significant.

Steensby (1910) and Knuth (1966–7) developed the theory of the musk ox way, according to which the spread of Eskimos from Alaska through the Canadian mainland and archipelago into Greenland was possible only by heavy reliance on musk oxen. Their publications suggest a purposive migration, in which case travel through some areas would have been impossible without musk oxen. If, however, as I believe, the Arctic was colonised principally by a process of natural population growth and expansion, to speak of a musk ox way probably exaggerates the importance of musk oxen, although undoubtedly they did contribute towards the colonisation of the Arctic in their rôle as a critical resource.

Finally, although musk oxen occur in varied technological contexts, there is a common association between the presence of musk ox bones and of large, frequently bifacial, points.

MAN–MUSK OX RELATIONSHIPS IN THE EURASIAN PLEISTOCENE

Russia

Musk oxen are known from only five Palaeolithic sites in Russia: Kostenki 1, level 1 (Klein, 1969); Mezin (Frenzel, 1960); Diuktai Cave (R. Powers, *pers. comm.*); Medvezh'ia Cave (Rogachev, 1964; Bader, 1965); and Dobranichivka, near Kiev (Pidoplichko, 1969).

Traces of a large structure, 35 m × 15–16 m, were recovered at Kostenki 1/1. A habitation pit (Figure 8) formed a part of this structure, to which it was connected by a low step. Mammoth bones, particularly scapulae and long bones, probably formed the supports of the structure, from which a single musk ox skull was recovered. The excavators suggested that the skull had rested on top of the covering of the structure. The absence of other musk ox bones, the pollen spectrum of the site, and the associated fauna suggest that the skull was probably a chance find and that musk

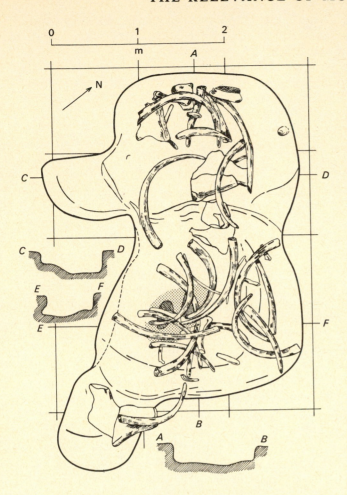

Figure 8. Habitation pit A at Kostenki 11, from which musk ox remains were recovered (redrawn after Klein, 1969).

and the shape of the horns render this claim implausible (Figure 9).

In contrast, evidence that musk oxen were exploited at Mezin, in the Desna Valley, is firm. Table 8 lists the fauna from Mezin, which is strikingly arctic. A single ^{14}C date of 21 600 $\pm$ 2200 B.P. (Chard & Workman, 1965) applies broadly to the musk ox remains and probably indicates that the site was occupied near the maximum of the Final Glacial. Traces of a substantial structure, probably a winter habitation, were recovered. No detailed information on the musk ox bones was published, but they may represent the slaughter of a single social unit in winter. Clearly, musk oxen were relatively unimportant economically. The numerous fox bones at Mezin are interesting in view of the connection between fox trapping and musk ox hunting observed in Greenland and elsewhere.

Table 8.   Mezin fauna

Species	Bones	Individuals	Per cent
Elephas primigenius	3979	116	20.2
Rhinoceros antiquitatis	17	3	0.5
Equus equus	659	61	10.6
Ovibos moschatus	188	17	3.0
Bison priscus	19	5	0.9
Megaceros giganteus	1	1	0.2
Rangifer tarandus	444	83	14.4
Ursus arctos	35	7	1.2
Gulo gulo	28	5	0.9
Canis lupus	1004	59	10.3
Alopex lagopus	1842	112	19.6
Vulpes vulpes	1	1	0.2
Lepus sp.	37	11	1.9
Marmota bobak	5	4	0.7
Lagopus lagopus	14	7	1.3

oxen did not occupy this area when Kostenki 1/1 was occupied or that they were not exploited. The fauna included some cold-adapted species, such as mammoth, woolly rhinoceros, wolverine, steppe fox, and caribou, but the presence of red deer and otter suggested more temperate conditions than those to which modern musk oxen are accustomed. The rodent fauna lacked lemmings and other exclusively arctic or peri-glacial species, and the pollen spectrum contained high proportions of pine, spruce, hazel, and alder. The single ^{14}C date, 14 020 $\pm$ 60 (GIN-86) (Klein, 1967), post-dates the glacial maximum, and the climate may have been continental rather than arctic. Musk oxen were also absent from broadly contemporaneous sites such as Anosovka 2/2 and 2/1, Markina Gora, and Kostenki 2 (Klein, 1969). Klein believed that an engraving from Kostenki 1/1 depicted a musk ox, but the lack of a hump

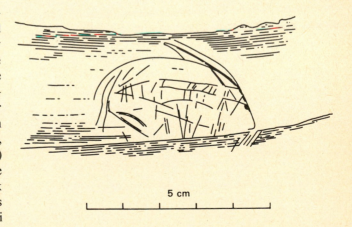

5 cm

Figure 9. Engraving on a bone from Kostenki 11 believed by some to represent a musk ox (redrawn after Klein, 1969).

A single musk ox bone was recovered from the Late Würm settlement at Dobranichivka, associated with mammoth, bison, caribou, wolf, arctic and common fox, wolverine, marmot, and arctic hare.

Each of these sites had Gravettoid industries with a high proportion of backed blades and bladelets, and large, leaf-shaped points occurred at Kostenki 1/1.

At Diuktai Cave in the Aldan District of Yakutia one unspecified musk ox bone was recovered from Level 6. Associated artefacts included 1 broken leaf-shaped point, 1 dihedral burin, 1 unifacial ivory point, and 224 fragments of mammoth ivory. The faunal remains were sparse. Two ^{14}C dates from unspecified levels probably apply broadly to the musk ox bone: 13 070 ± 90 B.P. (LE-784), and 12 090 ± 120 B.P. (LE-860).

Medvezh'ia Cave (Bear Cave) lies in the foothills of the northern Ural Mountains, on the upper reaches of the Pechora River. The extensive fauna included mammoth, woolly rhinoceros, bison or aurochs, musk ox, horse, reindeer, elk, cave bear, brown bear, cave lion, wolf, arctic fox, ermine, wolverine, sable, arctic hare, squirrel, water vole, field mouse, birds, and the most northerly occurrence in an archaeological context of saiga antelope. Bader (1965) described the artefacts as pre-Magdalenian, by which he meant Late Gravettian in the western European sense. Faunal collections from nearby Late Palaeolithic sites such as Byzovaia, Talitskii, and Kammenoe Kol'tso (*ibid.*) lacked musk oxen.

The Russian evidence is difficult to interpret. Late glacial finds of musk oxen in palaeontological contexts are rare, although musk oxen do appear in postglacial situations (Wilkinson, 1972c, Appendix A), and estimates of their late pleistocene distribution in Russia are difficult. The data from Mezin suggest that musk oxen inhabited parts of the Russian Plain at the height of the Final Glaciation, but they were absent from broadly contemporaneous sites in the Don Valley. I suggested earlier that musk oxen tended to be exploited in the modern Arctic largely because there was no alternative large herbivore if caribou or marine resources failed. The faunal remains from Upper Palaeolithic sites in Russia indicate that large herbivores were diverse and probably abundant, and there may have been little incentive to hunt musk oxen even if they existed. Many sites were located strategically near river valleys to exploit mammoth, caribou, and horse, for example, and it is unlikely that man encountered musk oxen frequently, since they probably spent much time on the windswept plains. The exploitation of musk oxen at Mezin may have been related to fox trapping or to a general shortage of alternative resources. Mezin dates from a period when many elements of the Pleistocene megafauna were probably declining numerically (Wilkinson, 1972d). The sparse data

from Diuktai and Medvezh'ia do not permit assessments of man-musk ox relationships there, except that musk oxen were insignificant economically.

Artistic data are equivocal. Abramova (1967) listed eight species frequently represented artistically, but quoted only one example of a musk ox. Vereschagin (1967), on the other hand, recorded thirteen species, including musk oxen, as common, but did not support his claim.

Central Europe

In Yugoslavia, musk oxen were associated with cultural remains at Potočka (Brodar, 1938; Zotz, 1951; I. Radovic, *pers. comm.*) and in the Schaflochhöhle (Vaňura, 1944), both in mountainous areas.

At Potočka, Layer C, a brown loam containing a so-called Aurignacian industry (Figure 10) with numerous bone points, blades, and also with leaf-shaped points, produced nine upper teeth, probably from a single musk ox: the molars from both sides, the left P^3 and P^4, and the right P^4. Potočka is located at 1700 m o.d., and Radovic believed that the teeth had been imported from Czechoslovakia. In East Greenland and Ellesmere Island, however, musk oxen occupy mountainous areas, and they may have lived near Potočka. A hoard of 55 bone points suggests that this may have been a task-specific site, which is supported by the fact that the fauna comprised 99 per cent cave bear.

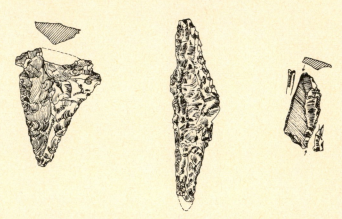

Figure 10. Artefacts from Potočka (¼ actual size) (redrawn after Zotz, 1951).

Several skull fragments from a single musk ox were found in a late pleistocene loam at the Schaflochhöhle, associated with cave bear, horse, and woolly rhinoceros. Although artefacts were recovered from the loam, they were not described, and their relationship to the musk ox remains was uncertain; it seems unlikely, however, that a non-human agency introduced such a large skull into the cave.

Musk ox remains occurred at several caves in the Moravian karst, but details of their antiquity and associations were rarely recorded. Skutil and Stehlík (1931) listed the following: Stierfelshöhle, Pekarna, Balearhöhle, Schoschuwkahöhle, and Teufelsloch. Stehlík (1941) later added Sipka Cave but omitted Pekarna, Balearhöhle, and Schoschuwkahöhle. Musil and Jelinek (1965) confirmed the presence of musk oxen in Layer 4 at Sipka Cave. They described the industry as Mousterian on the basis of its large points and dated it to Early Würm. It may, however, have had affinities with the Szeletian and large points occur as a minor element in some Upper Palaeolithic assemblages, so that a later date cannot safely be excluded. Křiž (1899) reported a few musk ox bones from Pekarna, associated with caribou and abundant hare and fox bones and with an industry containing flakes and blades.

The open site of Predmost (Zotz, 1951; Freund, 1952) yielded a rich fauna, including mammoth, woolly rhinoceros, musk ox, reindeer, arctic fox, arctic hare, banded lemming, and glutton. The associated industry (Figure 11) included backed blades, shouldered points, and end-scrapers, but leaf-shaped points also occurred. The site

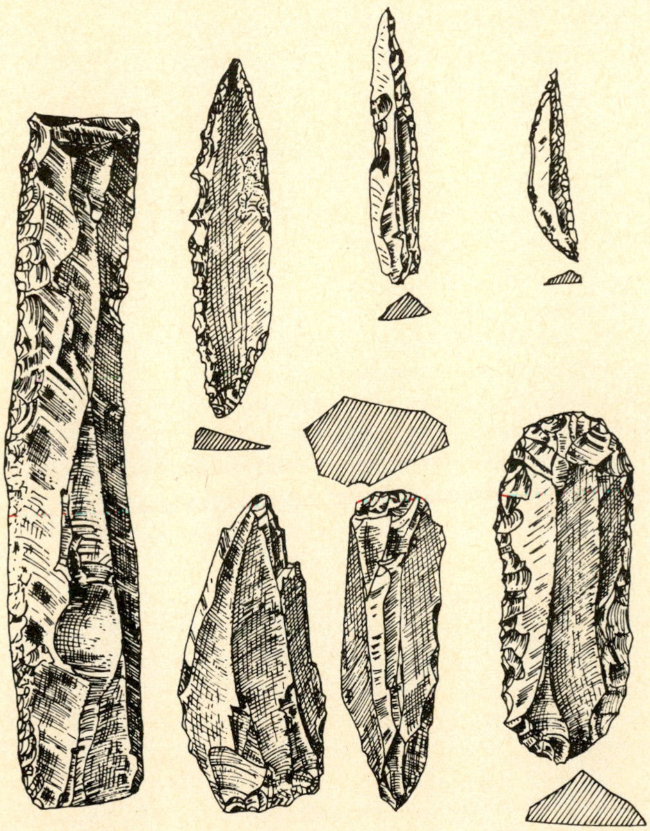

Figure 11. Artefacts from Predmost ($\frac{1}{4}$ actual size) (redrawn after Zotz, 1951).

probably dates to c. 20 000 B.P., and the fauna indicates a severe climate.

In Hungary, Vértes (1959) published faunal lists from the principal Mousterian sites. Musk oxen occurred in only one: at Pörgörlhegyer Cave, at 350 m o.d. in the Bakony Hills. Vértes dated the finds to Early Würm, but the presence of musk oxen makes this improbable. Although musk oxen are well documented in Europe up to the Middle Pleistocene (Wilkinson, 1972c), they do not reappear in central and western Europe until late in the Final Glacial. If the dating of Pörgörlhegyer and the identification of the musk ox bones are confirmed, this will be the first firm evidence for the presence of musk oxen in central and western Europe at this period and the first undisputed association of musk oxen with a Middle Palaeolithic industry.

Musk oxen were also reported from Czechoslovakia in a much earlier context at Stranská skalá, five kilometers northeast of Brno. Claims of early artefacts from Stranská skalá are unverified, but the site is broadly contemporaneous with the presence of man in the early Mindel at Vértesszöllös. Kahlke (1964) referred a single tooth to the large Middle Pleistocene genus, *Praeovibos priscus*, whereas Musil (1968) mentioned only *Ovibos*, and the matter remains unresolved. There is no evidence for human exploitation of musk oxen in Czechoslovakia at this early date. Late Pleistocene finds of musk oxen near Brno were mentioned by Skutil and Stehlík (1931) and by Stehlík (1941), but not apparently in archaeological contexts.

Western Europe

Finds of musk oxen are comparatively numerous in Switzerland, dating from the later Würm Glacial. In 1874 a lifelike carving of a musk ox was recovered from an unspecified level of Kesslerloch, near Thayngen (Hescheler, 1939), which is not unlike the carved head of a musk ox depicted by Boas (1901) (Figure 12). Musk ox bones themselves were first recovered only in the third series of excavations, when a phalange was found in a Magdalenian level (Koby, 1955). Another phalange was recovered from Schnurrenloch, in the Simmental (*ibid.*; Dehm, 1966). Its cultural context is uncertain, but it apparently dates from the Late Würm. Osborn (1923) reported the presence of musk oxen at Niedernau.

In Austria rare musk ox remains were reported from the Upper Palaeolithic site at Krems-Hundssteig, near Vienna, associated with arctic fox, wolverine, mammoth, woolly rhinoceros, caribou, horse, bison, red deer, arctic hare, ptarmigan, and hare (Osborn, 1923; Zotz, 1951). The artefacts from Krems included Aurignacian forms, but some scrapers and points on flakes were described as having a

Mousterian appearance (H. Obermaier, quoted by Zotz, 1951, p. 205).

In Germany, Hülle (in Andree, 1939) reported musk ox horn cores from Ilsenhöhle, associated with abundant caribou and horse. Sedimentological analyses suggested a cold climate. Hülle believed that the cave was a habitation site in earlier times, but the sparsity of finds suggested that at this time it was used only as a transient stop, which accords well with the exploitation of musk oxen as a critical resource. Artefacts were rare, but included blades.

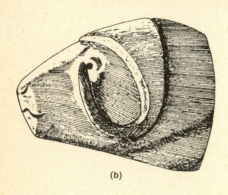

(b)

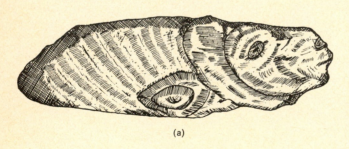

(a)

Figure 12. A sculpted musk ox from Kesslerloch (a) compared with a recent Eskimo carving (b) (redrawn after Kurtén, 1968, and Boas, 1901, respectively).

At least one fragment of a musk ox skull was recovered from the Balver Höhle, Westphalia (Andree, 1933), but its exact provenance and cultural context are unclear (Andree, 1939). Also in Westphalia, a skull fragment of musk ox from Herne was associated with an industry with large points and a fauna including mammoth, rhinoceros, horse, cattle, bison, pig, and caribou. Andree (*ibid.*) dated these finds geologically to the Würm Glacial. Musk ox skull fragments were associated with a large bifacial point and a similar fauna at Wettin (*ibid.*), but claims that these finds date from the Early Saale are improbable. At Treis 2, in Hesse, a crude flake industry with large points was accompanied by mammoth, woolly rhinoceros, pig, bison, elk, caribou, musk ox, cave lion, brown bear, wolf, and banded lemming, probably dating from late in the Final Glaciation.

Occasional palaeontological finds of musk oxen have been reported from Poland (Ryziewicz, 1933, 1955). Andree (1933) claimed the association of man and musk ox at Murek Cave, near Krakow, but the precise age and cultural associations of these finds are unknown.

In Belgium, Grevé (1900) mentioned musk ox bones from Dinorst and the Trou de Chaleux, but no details of these finds are known.

Evidence of associations of men and musk oxen in France dates from the Middle Pleistocene. Finds of musk oxen from river gravels at Précy (Oise) and Viry-Noureuil (Aisne) occurred in levels with hand-axes. Despite Gottsche's (1879) claim, there is no evidence that they were associated (Lartet & Christy, 1875). The only firm associations date from late in the Final Glacial. H. Movius (*pers. comm.*) found two musk ox teeth at the Abri Pataud, Dordogne. The first occurred in talus deposits, apparently associated with Perigordian IV material. The second, found ten years later, occurred within a Perigordian IV stratum. Movius (*pers. comm.*) shared the view of Dawkins (1872) that the presence of musk oxen did not necessarily indicate a cold climate: 'I should state that the presence of musk oxen in our Perigordian IV horizon is of very little climatic significance ... the analysis of the sediments from this stratum demonstrates beyond all cavil that temperate conditions prevailed.' Although experimental evidence (Wilkinson, 1972c) has demonstrated that musk oxen can survive in temperate climates, they cannot compete successfully with better-adapted animals and it is difficult to visualise why they should have colonised western Europe during a period of mild climate when they were absent in colder periods. Harlé (1901) reported a complete musk ox skull from the Aurignacian level of the Abri du Poisson, Gorge d'Enfer, Les Eyzies. Lartet and Christy (1875) found seven foot and leg bones of musk ox in an unspecified locality at Les Eyzies, which might have been the Abri du Poisson.

Artistic depictions of musk oxen in French Upper Palaeolithic art are more numerous and widespread than the remains of the animals themselves, but not all claims of musk oxen can be supported. Koby (1960) reported a musk ox from Gargas, in the Pyrenees. Giedion (1962, Fig. 188) claimed that an engraving overlain by meanderings from Altamira was a musk ox bull, but I am unconvinced. Both these finds occurred several hundred miles south of the known limit of musk oxen. Lemozi (1929) suggested that a large painting at Pech-Merle depicted a musk ox, but it might equally be a bison. At the Roc de Sers there is an indisputable bas-relief of an adult bull pursuing a man carrying a long stick over his shoulder. The provenance of this find is uncertain: Breuil (1952) stated that the frieze, which had fallen from the wall, overlay the lowest of three Solutrean levels, whereas Graziosi (1960) assigned it to the middle of the Upper Solutrean level. The realistic posture of the animal suggests that the artist was personally acquainted with musk oxen. A claimed musk ox from Chancelade (Lemozi, 1929) is probably a bison, but a very convincing bas-relief of a musk ox head was found in the Magdalenian levels at Le Fourneau du Diable, Dordogne (Graziosi, 1960). A sculpted head from the shelter at Laugerie-Basse (Breuil, 1952) probably came from a Magdalenian level. Breuil (*ibid.*) believed that the Magdalenian levels of La Mouthe had produced an engraved profile of a musk ox. The claim of Zervos (1959) for a musk ox head from the Magdalenian IV level at Bruniquel was not supported by Graziosi (1960). Mayet and Pissot (1915) found an engraving of a musk ox on a pebble from La Colombière, but later excavations by the Harvard University Expedition found only reindeer and woolly rhinoceros.

The preceding evidence is consistent with the hypothesis that musk oxen were exploited efficiently in the Eurasian Palaeolithic, since they were not exploited intensively or consistently anywhere. In fact, there is little reliable evidence that musk oxen were exploited at all before a late stage of the Final Glacial. In Russia, their exploitation was associated with technologies of a late Gravettian type, often associated with large points. In central Europe, there were several associations of musk oxen and industries with leaf points perhaps related to the Szeletian, but most musk ox remains were associated with late Upper Palaeolithic industries. In western Europe, musk oxen occurred predominantly with late Upper Palaeolithic industries.

Three questions emerge: whether musk oxen were present earlier in Eurasia but were not exploited; the nature of the stimulus to their exploitation in the Late Würm; and the precise nature of man–musk ox relationships.

Although there is good evidence for the presence of musk oxen in Eurasia up to the Middle Pleistocene (Wilkinson, 1972c, Appendix A), there are no reliable indications that they were present again until the later stages of the Last Glacial. Andree (1933) dated several finds to the Riss and Early Würm Glacials on geological grounds, but these lack a firm basis, and a survey of archaeological literature on Middle Palaeolithic sites revealed no indisputable occurrences of musk oxen. Ethnographic and archaeological data suggest that the technologies of these periods were adequate for hunting musk oxen, and larger animals were killed regularly. Two main possibilities exist: that musk oxen were absent; or that they were present but not exploited. The lack of evidence precludes a firm decision, but other cold-loving forms were present during Riss and Early Würm, and conditions are believed to have been suitable for musk oxen. Nonetheless, musk oxen were probably rare, and the possibility of their absence cannot be excluded.

Nor is the stimulus to the onset of musk ox exploitation clear. Evidence discussed below does not preclude the possibility that musk oxen were herded, although this seems improbable. I have suggested elsewhere (Wilkinson, 1972d) that the decline of the Pleistocene megafauna in North America began by *c.* 25 000 B.P. and probably accelerated after *c.* 16 000 B.P. This has not yet been demonstrated clearly for Eurasia, but I believe that the decline in North America is attributable to climatic changes which probably operated on a world-wide scale (Heusser, 1961).

Archaeological data support the hypothesis that demographic increases occurred in Eurasia during the Final Glaciation. If, as I believe, staple game resources began to decline by 25 000 B.P., the pressure of populations upon available resources must have increased, and crisis situations must have become more frequent. In such situations, the pressure to exploit musk oxen must have been intensified. Thus, musk ox exploitation in the late Upper Palaeolithic may have been stimulated by the pressure of populations on decreasing staple resources, and musk oxen probably played the rôle of a critical resource in permitting human populations to overcome periodic food shortages.

Detailed analyses of musk ox remains from archaeological sites are too sparse to permit firm conclusions regarding the exact nature of the exploitive relationship between men and musk oxen. Where they have been reported in detail, faunal collections frequently contain metapodials and phalanges. Skull fragments may also be relatively common, but the fact that skulls are easily identified may mean that they have been reported when other bones were not recognised. There are, however, few indications that entire skeletons occurred in archaeological sites. In most cases the musk oxen were probably killed and butchered at some distance from the sites and only the robes (with phalanges and metapodials) and chosen portions of the carcase were brought back to the sites. This suggests strongly that musk oxen were hunted rather than herded.

On the other hand, the age and sex composition of faunal samples from archaeological sites often suggests that very few (sometimes only one) animals occurred, which is inconsistent with earlier descriptions of musk ox behaviour and with ethnographic accounts of musk ox hunts. There is, however, little supporting evidence that musk oxen were husbanded for meat or wool. If they had been, many surplus males would have been available for slaughter, as well as older bulls and cows, and entire skeletons would have probably occurred. It is possible, of course, that the defensive behaviour of musk oxen has changed through time and that the static phalanx is a relatively recent development, but I consider this improbable. Alternatively, musk oxen may have been exploited selectively despite their defensive formation, but this too seems improbable in the light of the ethnographic record.

At the present time, it is not possible to exclude completely the hypothesis that musk oxen were herded in the Upper Palaeolithic (Wilkinson, 1972b). On the other hand, there is no evidence which supports this belief more than the hypothesis that they were hunted as a critical resource. The evidence does demonstrate that musk oxen were exploited efficiently, and there is nothing to suggest that man was an important agent of their extinction in Eurasia.

GENERAL CONSIDERATIONS

The archaeological evidence is consistent with the hypothesis that musk oxen in Eurasia and North America were hunted as what I have called a critical resource. In this respect there appears to have been a direct continuity between ethnographic and archaeological patterns of exploiting musk oxen.

The results of this inquiry justify the use of the predictive approach developed in the first section. Not only does this method permit a deepened understanding of man—musk ox relationships in the past, but it is practicable despite the fragmentary nature of the archaeological record. Indeed, the approach employed can be used to overcome some of the limitations of the archaeological evidence by suggesting the location of undiscovered sites and possibly by indicating previously undiscovered subsistence activities. It is axiomatic that the objective of human economies in all areas and periods and at every level of technological and social development is the provision of sufficient resources distributed as evenly as possible throughout the total subsistence cycle to support existing populations and to accommodate, wherever possible, their natural tendency towards expansion. The concept of integrated economies implies that the totality of economic activities observed archaeologically must attain this objective. If they do not, a knowledge of the available resources combined with the constraints implied by the concept of integrated economies permits accurate forecasts of the manner in which the subsistence cycle might have been completed.

The belief that animals *must* have been exploited in what I have called an efficient manner in the past if they were not to have been decimated or destroyed is shown by the effects of commercial exploitation of musk oxen during the late nineteenth and early twentieth centuries. On a time scale relevant to archaeological interests, this inefficient exploitation led instantaneously to the severe depletion of the resource in question. The decimation of musk oxen was so great that their continued exploitation even as a critical resource, became impossible. It was not the introduction to the Arctic of rifles or of European technology which permitted or stimulated the depletion of musk oxen, for I have shown that musk oxen were very susceptible to hunting with traditional weapons. The important factor was that musk oxen were elevated from the status of a critical resource to that of a staple resource, in the sense that they could be traded for food, rifles, and other items and thus made an important contribution to the seasonal subsistence cycle.

The relevance to prehistorians of these brief comments is that the only patterns of exploiting musk oxen which have survived for long periods or which show signs of succeeding on an economically important scale in the future are those which are efficient in the sense of my definition. I consider it inconceivable that inefficient exploitive practices could have been widely practised in any period or area of prehistory. This is not to say that they will never have occurred or that they cannot be seen occasionally in the historical and ethnographic records. Nonetheless, they are unlikely to have attained widespread importance. Where inefficient exploitive practices can be observed in the archaeological record, they will obviously have some significance for prehistorians, but it must be remembered that they are the exception rather than the rule.

Finally, the question remains whether the approach which I have outlined can be applied profitably to species other than the musk ox. In some respects musk oxen may be easier to study than many other species. Musk oxen have occupied comparable (although not identical) habitats at least since the later part of the Final Glacial. Whereas many other species became extinct at the close of the Final Glacial or adapted to the changed environmental conditions of the Postglacial, musk oxen in North America followed the retreating ice sheets northwards. Although musk oxen have been exploited intensively during the past two centuries, they have been much less affected by the direct and indirect effects of human exploitation than animals in more intensively occupied areas. Particularly in Europe and the Near East, for example, human alteration of habitats on a large scale must have had a profound effect on the behaviour and seasonal activities of many animals even when they themselves were not intensively exploited. It is reasonable to assume that the selective pressures affecting musk oxen have been relatively constant through time and space, and the behavioural and biological adaptations to these pressures observed in modern musk oxen can safely be extrapolated into the past. Where it can be shown that these adaptations have important consequences for human exploitation today, or where this can be demonstrated ethnographically, it is reasonable to assume that similar constraints operated in prehistory. Since one important effect of these constraints is often to influence the numbers of animals which can be cropped or the age and sex composition of the cropped segment of animal populations, this approach is often susceptible to direct, archaeological testing.

Whereas the biology and behaviour of musk ox populations in different parts of their range are identical in all important respects, many other species show marked variations. These are reflected in the large numbers of subspecies and geographical races recognised for many species by taxonomists, and in marked inter-regional differences in behaviour by different populations of the same species. Many of these adaptations may be of relatively recent origin and may plausibly be seen as adaptations to changing conditions since the Postglacial and to the direct and indirect effects of human exploitation. In such situations it is obviously much more difficult to apply the type of predictive approach developed in this paper.

Nonetheless, I believe that it is often possible to make allowances for relatively recent or localised influences and to evaluate retrospectively their likely importance in the past from knowledge of the environmental conditions which pertained then. The question of the general validity of the predictive approach to the study of man–animal relationships in the past can indeed be answered only by undertaking detailed studies of other species. Where similar studies have been conducted (by Clark, 1972, with special reference to the exploitation of red deer at the Mesolithic site of Star Carr, and by Sturdy, 1972, for reindeer-based economies in the Late Palaeolithic in northern Europe, for example) profitable insights have resulted. These findings, as well as theoretical considerations, encourage confidence that this method of study may be extended beyond the limited sphere of man–musk ox relationships to the problems of animal exploitation in the broader context of world prehistory.

ACKNOWLEDGEMENTS

My research was financed by the W. K. Kellogg Foundation, the Institute of Northern Agricultural Research (p. 73/3), and the office of the Vice-President for Research at the University of Alaska. I am indebted to John J. Teal, Jr and to E. S. Higgs for their advice and to H. N. Jarman for her criticism of the manuscript.

REFERENCES

Abramova, Z. A. (1967) Palaeolithic art in the U.S.S.R. *Arct. Anthrop.* **4**, 1–180.

Allen, J. A. (1913) Ontogenetic and other variations in musk oxen, with a systematic review of the musk ox group, recent and extinct. *Mem. Am. Mus. nat. Hist.* **1**, 103–226.

Anderson, D. (1970) Akmak: an early archaeological assemblage from Onion Portage, northwest Alaska. *Acta Arct.* **16**.

Anderson, J. (1856) Letter from the Chief Factor Anderson to Sir George Simpson, *J. R. geogr. Soc.* **26**, 18–25.

Anderson, R. M. (1930) Notes on the musk-ox and the caribou. In *Conserving Canada's Muskoxen*, ed. W. H. B. Hoare, pp. 49–53. Ottawa: F. C. Acland.

Anderson, S., & Poulsen, H. (1958) Two muskoxen (*Ovibos moschatus* Zimm.) in captivity. *Zool. Gart., Lpz.* **24**, 12–23.

Andree, J. (1933) Über diluviale Moschusochsen. *Abh. westf. Prov.-Mus. Naturk.* **4**, 5–34.

(1939) *Der eiszeitliche Mensch in Deutschland und seine Kulturen.* Stuttgart: F. Enke.

Andrews, J. T., McGhee, R., & McKenzie-Pollock, L. (1971) Comparison of elevations of archaeological sites in arctic Canada. *Arctic* **24**, 210–28.

Bader, O. N. (1965) The Palaeolithic of the Urals and the peopling of the north. *Arct. Anthrop.* **3**, 77–90.

Balikci, A. (1964) Development of basic socio-economic units in two Eskimo communities. *Bull. natn. Mus. Canad.* **202**.

Bandi, H.-G. (1969) *Eskimo Prehistory.* College, Alaska: University of Alaska Press.

Bandi, H.-G., & Meldgaard, J. (1952) Archaeological investigations on Clavering Island, Northeast Greenland. *Meddr. Grønland* **126**, 1–85.

Banfield, A. W. F. (1951) Notes on the mammals of the Mackenzie District, Northwest Territories. *Arctic* **4**, 112–21.

Barrow, J. (1818) *A Chronological History of Voyages into the Arctic Regions.* London: J. Murray.

Beechey, F. W. (1831) *Narrative of a Voyage to the Pacific and Beering's Strait.* London: H. Colburn & R. Bentley.

Bell, R. H. V. (1971) A grazing ecosystem in the Serengeti. *Scient. Am.* **225**, 86–93.

Bernier, J. E. (1910) *Report on the Dominion of Canada Government Expedition to the Arctic Islands and the Hudson Strait on Board the D.G.S. 'Arctic' (1908–9).* Ottawa: Government Printing Bureau.

Binford, L. R. (1968) Archaeological perspectives. In *New Perspectives in Archaeology*, ed. S. R. Binford & L. R. Binford, pp. 5–32. Chicago: Aldine.

Birket-Smith, K. (1929) *The Caribou Eskimos.* Copenhagen: Gyldendalske.

(1959) *The Eskimos.* New York: E. P. Dutton.

Bliss, L. C. (1971) Devon Island, Canada, high arctic ecosystem. *Biol. Conserv.* **3**, 229–31.

Boas, F. (1888) The Central Eskimo. *A. Rep. Bur. Ethnol.* **6**, 390–669.

(1901) The Eskimo of Baffin Land and Hudson Bay. *Bull. Am. Mus. nat. Hist.* **15**, 1–370.

(1907) Second report on the Eskimo of Baffin Land and Hudson Bay. *Bull. Am. Mus. nat. Hist.* **15**, 371–570.

Bos, G. N. (1967) Range types and their utilisation by muskox on Nunivak Island, Alaska. Unpublished M.S. thesis, University of Alaska, College, Alaska.

Breuil, H. (1952) *Four Hundred Centuries of Cave Art.* Montignac, Dordogne: Centre d'Études et de Documentation préhistoriques.

Brodar, S. (1938) Das Paläolithikum in Jugoslawien. *Quartär* **1**, 140–72.

Bruce, M. W. (1895) *Alaska.* Seattle: Lowman and Hanford.

Buckley, J., Spencer, D. L., & Adams, P. (1954) Muskox (*Ovibos moschatus*) longevity. *J. Mammal.* **35**, 456.

Campbell, J. M. (1959) The Kayuk complex of arctic Alaska. *Am. Antiq.* **25,** 94–105.

(1961a) The Tuktu complex of Anaktuvuk Pass. *Anthrop. Pap. Univ. Alaska* **9,** 61–80.

(1961b) The Kogruk complex of Anaktuvuk Pass, Alaska. *Anthropologica* **3,** 1–18.

Chard, C. S., & Workman, W. B. (1965) Soviet archaeological radiocarbon dates: 2. *Arct. Anthrop.* **3,** 146–50.

Chévigny, H. (1965) *Russian America.* New York: Viking Press.

Clark, J. G. D. (1972) Star Carr: a case study in bioarchaeology. *Addison Wesley Modular Publs.* **10,** 1–42.

Clarke, C. H. D. (1940) A biological investigation of the Thelon Game Sanctuary. *Bull. natn. Mus. Can.* **96.**

Collins, H. B. (1950) Excavations at Thule culture sites near Resolute Bay, Cornwallis Island, N. W. T. *A. Rep. natn. Mus. Can. 1949–50,* 49–63.

(1951) Excavations at Thule culture sites near Resolute Bay, Cornwallis Island, N. W. T. *Bull. natn. Mus. Can.* **123,** 49–63.

Critchell-Bullock, J. C. (1930) An expedition to sub-arctic Canada, 1924–5. *Can. Fld. Nat.* **44,** 53–9, 81–7, 111–17, 140–5, 156–62, 187–96, 207–13; **45,** 11–18, 31–5.

Damas, D. A. (1969) Characteristics of Central Eskimo band structure. In Contributions to anthropology: band societies, ed. D. A. Damas, pp. 116–38. *Bull. natn. Mus. Can.* **228.**

Dawkins, W. B. (1872) *The British Pleistocene Mammalia, vol. 3, part 5.* London: Palaeontographical Society.

Degerbøl, M. (1935) Animal bones from the Eskimo settlement in Dødemandsbugten, Clavering Island. *Meddr. Grønland* **102,** 173–86.

Dehm, R. (1966) Über den Weinheimer Ovibos-Fund und die Niederterrassen-Sande. *Mitt. bayer. Statsamml. Paläont. hist. Geol.* **6,** 143–53.

Dietrich, W. O. (1942) Ein neuer Moschusochs-Fund in der Mark Brandenburg. *Zentbl. Miner., Geol., Paläont.* Abt. B, 1942, 129–41.

Ehik, J. (1932) Eine interessante Angabe zum Vorkommen des Moschusochsen in Asia. *Z. Säugetierk.* **7,** 258–9.

Eidlitz, K. (1969) Food and emergency food in the circumpolar area. *Studia ethnogr. Ups.* **32.**

Ellis, H. (1748) *A Voyage to Hudson's Bay, by the 'Dobb's Galley' and 'California' in the Years 1746 and 1747.* London: H. Whitridge.

Ewer, R. F. (1968) *Ethology of Mammals.* London: Logos Press.

Foote, D. C. (1965) Exploration and resource utilization in northwestern arctic Alaska before 1855. Unpublished Ph.D. dissertation, McGill University, Montreal.

Ford, J. A. (1959) Eskimo prehistory in the vicinity of Point Barrow, Alaska. *Anthrop. Pap. Am. Mus. nat. Hist.* **47,** 1–272.

Franklin, J. (1823) *Narrative of a Journey to the Shores of the Polar Sea in the Years 1819, 20, 21, and 22.* London: J. Murray.

Freeman, M. R. (1970) Productivity studies of high arctic musk oxen. *Arct. Circ.* **20,** 58–65.

(1971) Population characteristics of musk-oxen in the Jones Sound region of the Northwest Territories. *J. Wldl. Mgmt.* **35,** 103–8.

Frenzel, F. (1960) Die Vegetations- und Landschafts-Zonen Nord-Eurasiens während der letzten Eiszeit und während der postglazialen Warmezeit. *Abh. math. naturwiss. Kl. Wiesbaden* **6.**

Freuchen, P. (1915) General observations as to the natural conditions in the country visited by the First Thule Expedition. *Meddr. Grønland* **51,** 341–70.

Freund, G. (1952) *Die Blattspitzen des Paläolithikums in Europa.* Bonn: Quartär-Bibliothek.

Giddings, J. L. (1960) The archaeology of Bering Strait. *Curr. Anthrop.* **1,** 121–38.

Giedion, S. (1962) *The Eternal Present.* London: Oxford University Press.

Glob, P. V. (1946) Eskimo settlements in Northeast Greenland. *Meddr. Grønland* **144,** 1–40.

Gottsche, C. (1879) Notiz über einen neuen Fund von Ovibos. *Verh. Ver. naturw. Heimatforsch.* **4,** 235–8.

Graziosi, P. (1960) *Palaeolithic Art.* London: Faber & Faber.

Greely, A. W. (1886) *Three Years of Arctic Service.* New York: Charles Scribner's Sons.

(1888) *Report on the Proceedings of the United States Expedition to Lady Franklin Bay, Grinnell Land.* Washington, D. C.: Government Printing Office.

Grevé, C. (1900) Die Verbreitung von *Ovibos moschatus* Blainv. einst und jetzt. *Loodusuur. Seltsi. Aastar.* **12,** 371–4.

Gubser, N. J. (1965) *The Nunamiut Eskimos. Hunters of Caribou.* New Haven and London: Yale University Press.

Hall, A. B. (1964) Musk-oxen in Jameson Land and Scoresby Land, Greenland. *J. Mammal.* **45,** 1–11.

Hanbury, D. T. (1904) *Sport and Travel in the Northland of Canada.* New York: Macmillan.

Harington, C. R. (1961) History, distribution, and ecology of the muskoxen. Unpublished M. Sc. thesis, McGill University, Montreal.

(1964) Remarks on Devon Island muskoxen. *Can. J. Zool.* **42,** 79–86.

Harlé, E. (1901) Un crâne de boeuf musqué des Eyzies (Dordogne). *Bull. Soc. géol. Fr. 1901,* 455.

Harp, E., Jr (1958) Prehistory in the Dismal Lake area. *Arctic* **11,** 217–49.

(1959) Ecological continuity on the Barren Grounds. *Polar Notes* **1,** 48–56.

(1961) The archaeology of the lower and middle Thelon, Northwest Territories. *Tech. Pap. Arct. Inst. N. Am.* **8.**

(1969–70) Late Dorset Eskimo art from Newfoundland. *Folk* **11–12,** 109–24.

Hartz, N., & Kruuse, Chr. (1911) The vegetation of Northeast Greenland. *Meddr. Grønland* **30,** 333–431.

Hearne, S. (1795) *A Journey from Prince of Wales Fort in Hudson Bay to the Northern Ocean in the Years 1769, 1770, 1771, and 1772.* London: A. Strahan & T. Cadell.

Henoch, W. E. S. (1964) Preliminary geomorphological study of a newly discovered Dorset culture site on Melville Island, N. W. T. *Arctic* **17,** 119–25.

Hescheler, K. (1939) Ein neuer Schädelfund von Moschusochsen aus dem Gebiete des diluvialen Reussgletschers. *Verh. schweiz. naturf. Ges. 1939:* 55–6.

Heusser, C. J. (1961) Some comparisons between climatic changes in northwestern North America and Patagonia. *Ann. N. Y. Acad. Sci.* **95,** 642–57.

Higgs, E. S., Vita-Finzi, C., Harris, D. R., & Fagg, A. E. (1967) The climate, environment and industries of Stone Age Greece, part III. *Proc. prehist. Soc.* **33,** 1–29.

Hoare, W. H. B. (1930) *Conserving Canada's Musk Oxen.* Ottawa: Department of the Interior.

Hoel, A. (1933) The Musk Ox. Number, Hunting, Capture, Introduction. Translation of a typewritten report. Quoted by E. Hone (1934), in The present status of the musk ox in arctic North America and Greenland. *Spec. Publ. Am. Comm. intl. Wldl. Prot.* **5.**

Holtved, E. (1944) Archaeological investigations in the Thule district. Part 1. Descriptive part. *Meddr. Grønland* **141,** 1–308.

(1954) Archaeological investigations in the Thule District. Part 3.

Nûgdlît and Comer's Midden. *Meddr. Grønland* **146**, 1–135.

Hone, E. (1934) The present status of the musk ox in arctic North America and Greenland. *Spec. Publ. Am. Comm. intl. Wldl. Prot.* **5.**

Hooper, C. L. (1881) *Report of the Cruise of the U.S. Revenue-Steamer 'Corwin'.* Washington, D.C.: Government Printing Office.

Hornaday, W. T. (1911) The musk-ox in Alaska. *Bull. N.Y. Zool. Soc.* **28**, 130.

Humphrey, R. L. (1966) The prehistory of the Utukok River region, arctic Alaska: early fluted point tradition with Old World relationships. *Curr. Anthrop.* **7**, 586–9.

Indrenius, A. A. (1756) Specimen academicum de Esquimeaux, gente americana. *Anthrop. Pap. Univ. Alaska* **5**, 83–90.

Ingstad, H. (1951) *Nunamiut.* Lonon: Allen & Unwin.

Irving, W. N. (1962) Fieldwork in the western Brooks Range, Alaska. *Arct. Anthrop.* **1**, 76–83.

Jarman, M. R., & Wilkinson, P. F. (1972) Criteria of animal domestication. In *Papers in Economic Prehistory,* ed. E. S. Higgs, pp. 83–96. Cambridge: Cambridge University Press.

Jenness, D. (1922) *The Life of the Copper Eskimos.* Ottawa: F. C. Acland.

(1946) *Material culture of the Copper Eskimo.* Ottawa: King's Printer.

Jennings, L. B., & Burris, O. E. (1971) *Muskox Report.* Juneau, Alaska: Alaska Department of Fish & Game.

Jennov, J. G. (1933) Der Moschusochse in Ost-Grönland. *Z. Säugetierk.* **8**, 40–6.

Jensen, A. S. (1928) The fauna of Greenland. In *Greenland,* ed. M. Vahl, G. C. Amdrup, L. Bobé, & A. S. Jensen, vol. 1, pp. 319–55. London: Oxford University Press.

(1929) Moskusoksen paa Grønland og dens fremtid. *Skand. naturf. Moede og Dansk Jagtidende* **46**, 274–8.

Jeremie, N. (1926) *Twenty Years of York Factory, 1694–1714* (translated from the French edition of 1720). Ottawa: Thorburn & Abbott.

Johnsen, P. (1953) Birds and mammals of Peary Land in North Greenland. *Meddr. Grønland* **128**, 1–135.

Kahlke, H. D. (1964) Early Middle Pleistocene (Mindel/Elster) *Praeovibos* and *Ovibos. Comment. biol. Soc. Sci. fenn.* **26**, 1–17.

Kane, E. K. (1856) *Arctic Explorations: the Second Grinnell Expedition in Search of Sir John Franklin.* Philadelphia: Childs and Peterson.

Kelsall, J. P. (1968) *The Migratory Barren-Ground Caribou of Canada.* Ottawa: Queen's Printer.

Kelsall, J. P., Hawley, V. D., & Thomas, D. C. (1971) Distribution and abundance of musk oxen north of Great Bear Lake. *Arctic* **24**, 157–61.

Klein, D. R. (1970) Tundra ranges north of the boreal forest. *J. Range Mgmt.* **23**, 8–14.

Klein, R. G. (1967) Radiocarbon dates on occupation sites of Pleistocene age in the U.S.S.R. *Arct. Anthrop.* **4**, 223–6.

(1969) *Man and Culture in the Late Pleistocene.* San Francisco: Chandler Publishing Company.

Knuth, E. (1952) An outline of the archaeology of Peary Land. *Arctic* **5**, 17–33.

(1966–7) The ruins of the musk-ox way. *Folk* **8–9**, 191–219.

(1967) *Archaeology of the Musk Ox Way.* Paris: École Pratique des Hautes Études.

(n.d.) *Report on Arctic Archaeological Research, Summer 1965.* Manuscript in the files of the National Museum of Canada, Ottawa. Quoted by J. T. Andrews *et al.* (1971) Comparison of

elevations of archaeological sites in arctic Canada. *Arctic* **24**, 210–28.

Koby, F.-E. (1955) Découverte d'un ossement d'ovibos dans la couche à ours du Schnurrenloch (Simmental). *Act. Soc. jurass. Emulation* **58**, 117–31.

(1960) Sur l'extension maxima vers le sud-ouest de quelques représentants de la faune froide Würmienne. *Anthropos* n.s. **2**, 101–7.

Koch, L. (1930) The Danish expedition to East Greenland in 1929. *Meddr. Grønland* **74**, 186–205.

Koldewey, K. (1874) *The German Arctic Expedition of 1869–70.* London: Sampson, Low, Marston, Low, & Searle.

Křiž, M. (1899) L'époque quaternaire en Moravie. *Anthropologie, Paris* **10**, 257–80.

Kurtén, B. (1968) *Pleistocene Mammals of Europe.* London: Weidenfeld and Nicolson.

Larsen, H. (1934) Dødemandsbugten: an Eskimo settlement on Clavering Island. *Meddr. Grønland* **102**, 1–185.

(1960) Eskimo-archaeological problems in Greenland. *Acta. arct.* **12**, 10–16.

(1968) Trail Creek: final report on the excavation of two caves on Seward Peninsula, Alaska. *Acta. arct.* **15.**

Larsen, H., & Rainey, F. G. (1948) Ipiutak and the arctic whale hunting culture. *Anthrop. Pap. Am. Mus. nat. Hist.* **42.**

Lartet, E., & Christy, H. (1875) *Reliquiae Aquitanicae.* London: Williams and Norgate.

Laughlin, W. S. (1967) Human migrations and permanent occupation in the Bering Sea area. In *The Bering Land Bridge,* ed. D. M. Hopkins, pp. 409–50. Stanford, California: Stanford University Press.

Laverdière, C. (1954) Les pâturages à boeufs musqués du nord de l'île d'Ellesmere. *Rev. Géogr. alp.* **13**, 735–43.

Lemozi, A. (1929) La grotte-temple du Pech-Merle. Quoted by H. Müller-Karpe (1966) *Handbuch der Vorgeschichte.* Munich: C. H. Beck'sche Verlagsbuchhandlung.

Lent, P. C. (1971) A study of behaviour and dispersal in introduced muskox populations. *Final. Rep. Arct. Inst. N. Am., Grant ONR-419.*

Leslie, P. H. (1965) Theoretical consideration of the intrinsic rate of natural increase. In *Muskoxen in Canada,* by J. S. Tener, pp. 152–5. Ottawa: Queen's Printer.

Lowther, G. R. (1962) An account of an archaeological site on Cape Sparbo, Devon Island. *Bull. natn. Mus. Can.* **180**, 1–19.

Lynge, B. (1930) Le boeuf musqué dans le Groenland est. *Norsk. Geogr. Tidskr.* **3**, 16–33.

McClintock, F. L. (1859) *The Voyage of the 'Fox' in the Arctic Seas.* London: J. Murray.

McClure, R. J. (1856) *The Discovery of the Northwest Passage by H.M.S. 'Investigator'.* London: Longman, Brown, Green, Longmans, & Roberts.

McDougall, G. F. (1857) *The Eventful Voyage of H.M. Discovery Ship 'Resolute' to the Arctic Regions.* London: Longman, Brown, Green. Longmans & Roberts.

MacFarlane, R. (1905) Notes on mammals collected and observed in the northern Mackenzie River district, Northwest Territories of Canada. *Proc. U.S. natn. Mus.* **28**, 673–764.

McKennan, R. A. (1965) The Chandalar Kutchin. *Tech. Pap. Arct. Inst. N. Am.* **17.**

MacKenzie, A. (1801) *Voyages from Montreal through the Continent of North America.* London: R. Noble.

MacMillan, D. B. (1928) *Etah and Beyond.* London: Chapman and Hall.

MacNeish, R. S. (1951) An archaeological reconnaissance in the

Northwest Territories. *Bull. natn. Mus. Can.* **123**, 24–41.

MacNeish, R. S. (1956) The Engigstciak site on the Yukon arctic coast. *Anthrop. Pap. Univ. Alaska* **4**, 91–111.

—— (1964) Investigations in southwest Yukon. Archaeological excavations, comparisons, and speculations. *Pap. Robert S. Peabody Fdn. Archaeol.* **6**, 201–488.

Madsen, J. (1901) Polarjagt af moskusoxer og bjørne. *Zool. Gart., Lpz.* **42**, 129–39, 159–69.

Manniche, A. L. V. (1912) The terrestrial mammals and birds of northeast Greenland. *Meddr. Grønland* **45**, 1–200.

Manning, T. H. (1956) Narrative of a second Defence Research Board expedition to Banks Island, with notes on the country and its history. *Arctic* **9**, 3–77.

Manning, T. H. & Macpherson, A. H. (1958) The mammals of Banks Island. *Tech. Pap. Arct. Inst. N. Am.* **2**.

—— (1961) A biological investigation of Prince of Wales Island, Northwest Territories. *Trans. R. Can. Inst.* **33**, 116–239.

Markham, C. R. (1875) *A Selection of Papers on Arctic Geography and Ethnology.* London: J. Murray.

Mathiassen, T. (1927) *Archaeology of the Central Eskimo.* Copenhagen: Gyldendalske.

—— (1928) Eskimos relics from Washington Land and Hall Land. *Meddr. Grønland* **71**, 183–216.

—— (1929) The archaeological collection of the Cambridge East Greenland expedition, 1926. *Meddr. Grønland* **74**, 139–66.

—— (1931) Contributions to the physiography of Southampton Island. In *Report of the Fifth Thule Expedition, vol. 1, pt. 2.* Copenhagen: Gyldendalske.

Maxwell, M. S. (1960) An archaeological analysis of eastern Grant Land, Ellesmere Island, Northwest Territories. *Bull. natn. Mus. Can.* **170**.

Mayet, L., & Pissot, J. (1915) Abri sous-roche préhistorique de la Colombière, près Poncin (Ain). *Annls. Univ. Lyon* **39**.

Musil, R. (1968) Stranská skalá: its meaning for Pleistocene studies. *Curr. Anthrop.* **9**, 534–9.

Musil, R., & Jelinek, J. (1965) Die Höhlen Sipka und Cértova dira bei Stramberk. *Anthropos, Brno* **9**.

Nares, G. S. (1878) *Narrative of a Voyage to the Polar Sea.* London: Sampson Low, Marston, Searle, & Rivington.

Nathorst, A. G. (1901) Le loup polaire et le boeuf musqué dans le Groenland oriental. *Géographie* **3**, 1–16.

Nelson, N. C. (1937) Notes on cultural relations between Asia and America. *Am. Antiq.* **2**, 267–72.

Nourse, J. E. (1879) *Narrative of the Second Arctic Expedition made by Charles F. Hall.* Washington, D.C.: Government Printing Office.

Ogilvie, W. (1893) Report on the Peace River and tributaries in 1891. *A Rep. Can. Dept. Interior Sess. Pap.* **13**, pt 7.

Osborn, H. F. (1923) *Men of the Old Stone Age.* New York: Charles Scribner's Sons.

Parry, W. E. (1821) *Journal of a Voyage (1st) for the Discovery of a Northwest Passage from the Atlantic to the Pacific.* London: J. Murray.

—— (1824) *Journal of a Second Voyage for the Discovery of a Northwest Passage from the Atlantic to the Pacific.* New York: E. Duyckinck, G. Long, & Collins.

—— (1828) *Journals of the First, Second and Third Voyages for the Discovery of a Northwest Passage.* London: J. Murray.

Pedersen, A. (1926–7) Der Moschusochsen ein Naturdenkmal. *Naturforscher, Berlin* 1926–7, 540–2.

—— (1936) Der Grönlandische Moschusochse. *Ovibos moschatus wardi* Lydekker. *Meddr. Grønland* **93**, 1–82.

—— (1942) Dansk Nordøst-Grønlands Expedition 1938–39. Säugetiere und Vögel. *Meddr. Grønland* **128**, 1–119.

Perry, R. (1883) *The 'Jeanette': a Complete and Authentic Narrative Encyclopedia of all Voyages and Expeditions to the North Polar Regions.* Chicago: Coburn and Newman.

Petrof, I. (1900) *The Population and Resources of Alaska, 1880.* Washington, D.C.: Government Printing Office.

Pidoplichko, I. G. (1969) *Pozdnepaleoliticheskie Zhilishtcha iz Kostei Mamonta na Ukraine (Late Palaeolithic Dwellings of Mammoth Bones in the Ukraine).* Kiev: Akademii Nauk Ukrainskoi S. S. R. Institut Zoologii.

Pike, W. M. (1892) *The Barren Ground of Northern Canada.* London & New York: Macmillan.

Rae, J. (1850) *Narrative of an Expedition to the Shores of the Arctic Sea, in 1846 and 1847.* London: T. & W. Boone.

Rasmussen, K. (1915) Report of the First Thule expedition. *Meddr. Grønland* **51**, 283–340.

—— (1921) *Greenland by the Polar Sea.* London: William Heinemann.

—— (1931) *The Netsilik Eskimos.* Copenhagen: Gyldendalske.

—— (1932) *Den store Slaederrejse.* Quoted E. Knuth (1966–7) The ruins of the musk-ox way. *Folk* **8–9**, 191–219.

Ray, P. H. (1900) *An International Polar Expedition to Point Barrow, 1881–1884.* Washington, D.C.: Government Printing Office.

Richardson, J. (1829) *Fauna boreali-americana.* Vol. 1. *Quadrupeds.* London: J. Murray.

—— (1836) Zoological remarks. In *Narrative of the Arctic Land Expedition of the Mouth to the Great Fish River and along the Shores of the Arctic Ocean in the Years 1833, 1834, and 1835,* by G. Back, pp. 475–522. London: J. Murray.

—— (1851) *Arctic Searching Expedition: a Journal of a Boat-Voyage through Rupert's Land and the Arctic Sea.* London: Longman, Brown, Green & Longmans.

Rogachev, A. N. (1964) Principal results and problems in the study of the Palaeolithic of the Russian Plain. *Arct. Anthrop.* **2**, 135–42.

Ross, J. (1819) *A Voyage of Discovery for the Purpose of Exploring Baffin's Bay and Inquiring into the Probability of a Northwest Passage.* London: J. Murray.

—— (1835) *Narrative of a Second Voyage in Search of a Northwest Passage, and of a Residence in the Arctic Regions during the Years, 1829, 1830, 1831, 1832, and 1833.* London: A. W. Webster.

Ross, J. C. (1835) Zoology. In *Appendix to the Narrative of a Second Voyage in Search of a Northwest Passage,* by J. Ross, pp. vii–xxiv. London: A. W. Webster.

Rousselière, G.-M. (1964) Palaeo-Eskimo remains in the Pelly Bay region. *Bull. natn. Mus. Can.* **193**, 162–83.

Russell, F. (1898) *Exploration in the Far North.* Iowa City: University of Iowa Press.

Rutherford, J. G., McClean, J. S., & Harkin, J. D. (1922) *Report of the Royal Commission to Investigate the Possibilities of Reindeer and Musk-ox Industries in the Arctic and Sub-Arctic Regions of Canada.* Ottawa: Department of the Interior.

Ryziewicz, Z. (1933) *Ovibos recticornis* n. sp. Ein Beitrag zur Systematik der Unterfamilie Ovibovinae. *Acad. Polon. Sci., Cracow* **2**, 71–87.

—— (1955) Systematic place of the fossil musk-ox from the Eurasian Diluvium. *Pr. wrocl. Tow. nauk.* **49**.

Sabine, J. (1823) Zoological appendix. In *Narrative of a Journey to the Shores of the Polar Sea in the Years 1819, 20, 21 and 22,* by J. Franklin, p. 647–68. London: J. Murray.

Schell, L. S. (1972) The musk ox underwool, qiviut; historical uses and present utilization in an Eskimo knitting industry. Unpublished M.A. thesis, University of Alaska.

Schwatka, F. (1885) *Nimrod in the North.* New York: Cassell.

Seton, E. T. (1929) *Lives of Game Animals,* vol. 3, pt 2. New York: Doubleday, Doran & Company.

Simpson, T. (1843) *Narrative of the Discoveries on the North Coast of America.* London: R. Bentley.

Skarland, I., & Giddings, J. L. (1948) Flint stations in central Alaska. *Am. Antiq.* **14,** 116–20.

Skutil, J., & Stehlík, A. (1931) Moraviae fauna diluvialis. *Přírodov. palaeolith. odděl. moravského. Zemsk. musea v Brně c. 19 Sborník Klubu brně* **14.**

Solecki, R. S. (1950) A preliminary report of an archaeological reconnaissance of the Kukpowruk and Kokolik rivers in N. W. Alaska. *Amer. Antiq.* **16,** 66–9.

Solecki, R. S., & Hackman, R. (1951) Additional data on the Denbigh flint complex in northern Alaska. *J. Wash. Acad. Sci.* **41,** 85–8.

Spencer, D. L., & Lensink, C. J. (1970) The muskox of Nunivak Island, Alaska. *J. Wildl. Mgmt.* **34,** 1–15.

Steensby, H. P. (1910) Contributions to the ethnology and anthropogeography of the Polar Eskimos. *Meddr. Grønland* **34,** 255–407.

(1917) An anthropogeographical study of the origin of Eskimo culture. *Meddr. Grønland* **53,** 141–228.

Stefansson, V. (1914a) The Stefansson-Anderson expedition of the American Museum; preliminary ethnological report. *Anthrop. Pap. Am. Mus. nat. Hist.* **14.**

(1914b) Prehistoric and present commerce among the arctic coast Eskimos. *Bull. geol. Surv. Can. anthrop. ser.* 3, **6.**

(1921) *The Friendly Arctic.* New York: Macmillan.

(1924) *The Northward Course of Empire.* New York: Macmillan.

(1946) *Not by Bread Alone.* New York: Macmillan.

Stehlík, A. (1941) *Ovibos moschatus cf. wardi* Lydekker z jeskyně 'Jezevčí dira' u Vilémovic. *Příroda. Brno,* **34.**

Sturdy, D. A. (1972) Reindeer economies in late Ice Age Europe. Unpublished Ph.D. dissertation, University of Cambridge.

Sverdrup, O. (1904) *New Land.* London & New York: Longmans, Green & Company.

Taylor, W. E., Jr (1964) Archaeology of the McCormick Inlet site, Melville Island, N. W. T. *Arctic* **17,** 125–9.

(1967) Summary of archaeological fieldwork on Banks and Victoria Islands, arctic Canada. *Arct. Anthrop.* **4,** 221–43.

Teal, J. J., Jr (1958) Golden fleece of the Arctic. *The Atlant.* **201,** 76–81.

Tener, J. S. (1963) Queen Elizabeth Islands game survey. *Occ. Pap. Can. Wldl. Serv.* **4.**

(1965) *Muskoxen in Canada.* Ottawa: Queen's Printer.

Thostrup, Chr. B. (1917) Ethnographic description of the Eskimo settlements and stone remains in Northeast Greenland. *Meddr. Grønland* **44,** 179–356.

Turner, L. M. (1886) *Contributions to the Natural History of Alaska.* Washington, D.C.: Government Printing Office.

Tyrell, J. W. (1902) Exploratory survey between Great Slave Lake and Hudson Bay, Districts of Mackenzie and Keewatin. *A. Rept. Dept. Interior* Pap. **25,** Appendix 26.

Vaňura, J. (1944) Über den Fund von *Ovibos moschatus wardi* Lydekker im mahrishen Karst. *Bull. int. Acad. cheque Sci.,* **44,** 159–89.

Vereschagin, N. K. (1967) Primitive hunters in the Soviet Union. In *Pleistocene Extinctions,* ed. P. S. Martin & H. E. Wright, Jr, pp. 365–98. New Haven & London: Yale University Press.

Vértes, L. (1959) Das Mousterien in Ungarn. *Eiszeitalter Gegenw.* **10,** 21–40.

Vibe, Chr. (1958) The musk ox in East Greenland. *Mammalia* **22,** 168–74.

(1967) *Arctic Animals in Relation to Climatic Fluctuations.* Copenhagen: C. A. Reitzel.

Vita-Finzi, C., & Higgs, E. S. (1970) Prehistoric economy in the Mount Carmel area: site catchment analysis. *Proc. prehist. Soc.* **36,** 1–37.

Wells, R. (1890) Arctic Eskimos in Alaska and Siberia. *Bull. Alaskan. Soc. nat. Hist. Ethnol.* **3.**

Whitney, C. W. (1896) *On Snow-Shoes to the Barren Grounds.* New York: Harper & Brothers.

Wilkinson, P. F. (1971a) Polle, archaeology, and man. *Arch. phys. Anthrop. Oceania* **6,** 1–20.

(1971b) The first verified occurrence of twinning in musk oxen. *J. Mammal.* **52,** 238.

(1972a) Current experimental domestication and its relevance to prehistory. In *Papers in Economic Prehistory,* ed. E. S. Higgs, pp. 107–18. Cambridge: Cambridge University Press.

(1972b) Oomingmak: a model for man-animal relationships in prehistory. *Curr. Anthrop.* **13,** 23–44.

(1972c) The relevance of musk ox exploitation to the study of prehistoric animal economies. Unpublished Ph.D. dissertation, University of Cambridge.

(1972d) Ecosystem models and demographic hypotheses: predation and prehistory in North America. In *Models in Archaeology,* ed. D. L. Clarke, pp. 543–76. London: Methuen.

(1973a) The musk oxen of Alaska. *Oryx* (in press).

(1973b) Behaviour and the domestication of the musk ox. In *Ethology and the Management of Large Ungulates,* ed. V. Geist. (in press).

Willey, G. R., & Phillips, P. (1958) *Method and Theory in American Archaeology.* Chicago: University of Chicago Press.

Zervos, C. (1959) *L'Art de L'Époque du Renne en France.* Paris: Cahiers d'Art.

Zotz, L. (1951) *Altsteinzeitkunde Mitteleuropas.* Stuttgart: Ferdinand Enke.

3. SOME REINDEER ECONOMIES IN PREHISTORIC EUROPE

D. A. STURDY

INTRODUCTION

In 1875 Lartet and Christy reported the predominance of reindeer bones in the Dordogne caves, and since that time an association of man and reindeer has been repeatedly observed in the archaeological record. Interpretations of this association have followed Nilsson's hypothesis that there was a hunter-gatherer age and in consequence all palaeolithic peoples have been dubbed 'hunters'. Little attempt has been made to define what this label may mean, or what variety of economies may be included within this broad categorisation. The rich data from the German late glacial sites lend themselves to an investigation of these problems. Further, the growing realisation that many prehistoric economies were based on deer, renders a study of reindeer-based economies particularly useful, since the principles arising from it may be expected to have a wider application to prehistoric studies.

Two lines of approach are pursued. First the study of the remains of the reindeer, particularly of antlers, which can give valuable information on the season in which animals were killed. Secondly fieldwork, particularly studies of topography and seasonal availability of grazing on both a regional and local scale, can indicate how particular economic objectives might have been achieved.

Many terms used in this paper were explained in Higgs (1972). The concept of the 'extended territory' was proposed by Sturdy (1972a). All chronological limits in this paper are intentionally approximate. The term 'Magdalenian' is used to designate late glacial industries with typological affinities to the French Magdalenian, but no equation between industries and cultures is implied.

The evidence from the antlers is considered first and is followed by a section tracing the migration routes of late glacial reindeer herds. The reactions to migratory movements of human groups dependent on these reindeer are assessed, and a final section discusses the detailed operation of some late glacial reindeer herds.

THE EVIDENCE FROM ANTLERS

This section presents the results of a study of faunal collections from German and Swiss Magdalenian sites. A close examination of the bones failed to produce any worthwhile insights into former economic practices, and an analysis of dental wear in 80 reindeer mandibles of which the season of death was known (Sturdy, 1972b) suggested that this technique was too inaccurate for investigating slaughtering patterns. Emphasis was therefore given to studying antlers, using the techniques developed by Bouchud (1966).

Antlers occur on both sexes of reindeer from the first year of life onwards. Some pregnant females carry only very small and poorly developed antlers, and others never develop antlers or cease to grow them late in life. Modern female reindeer and caribou seldom carry the two brow tines characteristic of adult males. Palaeolithic reindeer cows in France (Bouchud, 1966) and at Stellmoor, for example, often carried two brow tines, and the antlers were generally well developed, which has led to the conclusion that the late glacial reindeer of Europe occupied excellent habitats. Old males undergo a process known as 'going back', when the complicated tine structure and palmations characteristic of prime bulls are replaced by simpler but equally robust forms. The shape and thickness of the antler above the brow tines is highly variable in females. Some females develop bulbous antlers above the brow tines, composed principally of very spongy tissue with a thin layer of compact antler. Male antlers increase in size and complexity of tine structure and palmation up to the age of six or seven years. Female antlers are greatly affected by pregnancy and other factors, and no developmental age grades can be distinguished by inspection.

Ageing and sexing antlers

Figure 1 illustrates the terms employed to describe the different parts of reindeer antlers. Antlers still attached to the skull are described as 'massacred' antlers, which corresponds with Bouchud's 'bois de massacre'. Sexing such antlers is often very easy. Bouchud noted that the shape and form of the sutures on the skull near the base of the antlers was highly characteristic of old and young animals of both sexes. If this suture pattern is preserved, slaughtered reindeer can be aged and sexed by inspection. I have divided reindeer into three age groups: young and yearling, animals up to the beginning of their second year, in which fawns may be isolated; subadult, which among males means animals in their second to fourth years, and among females probably only those in their second and third years; and adult, when the sutures reach the complicated patterns which they retain for the rest of their lives.

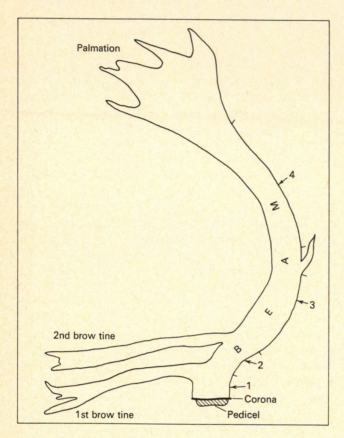

Figure 1. Sketch of a cast male reindeer antler to illustrate the terms used in the text. The numerals show the 'measurement positions'. Two measurements are taken at each position: the thickness, taken across the antler beam in the same plane as the length of the brow tines at the thinnest available point within the range shown on the beam; and the breadth, taken at right angles to this at the same point.

With cast antlers, or when the sutures surrounding the pedicel are not preserved on massacred antlers, sex and age can be established by inspection or measurement. Adult male antlers are distinctive and even small beam fragments can be recognised. Fawns have poorly developed corona and no tines, except a possible branching of the tip of the antler, and can be distinguished by inspection. Separating subadult from adult males and distinguishing age classes among females and young males is, however, more difficult. I have used Bouchud's (1966) measurement of the beam between the brow tines (or the equivalent position where

only one brow tine occurs) to distinguish adult from subadult males (Figures 2–3). Less than 3 per cent of subadult antlers fell within the range of adult males. Dubious cases that lie within the range of the known adult males have been included with the adults. While a few antlers thus assigned to the adults are probably subadult, these will be from older subadults and will be closer in development to the adult males. Interpretations of the seasonal slaughter pattern of animals represented are unlikely to be seriously distorted by such minor inaccuracies. Doubtful cases falling outside the range of adult males have been assigned to the subadult class. Unfortunately, it was not possible to distinguish young males from females. Figure 4 shows that the dubious cases cannot be assigned to any class at all. A few cases can be assigned tentatively to the subadult male class from the data in Figures 5 and 6, where antlers were measured rather higher up the beam. Figure 5 suggests that a beam width greater than 20.0 mm at this point represents subadult males. Admittedly measurements higher up the beam (position 3, Figure 6) include three females, but this reflects the curious shape of some female antlers. I have therefore included the thirteen dubious cases with beam widths above 20.0 mm in Figure 5 in the subadult male class.

Variations in the shape and size of female antlers do not correlate with age, and in the absence of sutures no ageing of the females can be performed. In the sample from Stellmoor 112 female antlers could not be assigned to any age class, and the seasons of their death could not be estimated. They are included in Figure 13, but not in Tables 1 and 2.

Antler development and seasonal dating

Antlers can also give information on the season at which animals were slaughtered (Bouchud, 1966). Before presenting my analyses, one point should be emphasised. All modern populations of reindeer make migratory movements; and even very small herds move about 30–50 km. The hypothesis adopted in this paper is that archaeological sites will tend to have been occupied in only one season, or in a group of seasons such as spring and autumn, but not continuously. This is based on the assumption that human groups usually exploit a restricted territory from any particular site, and the seasonal movements of the reindeer would have taken them beyond the practicable range of exploitation of any single site. Most of the graphs and diagrams illustrating seasonal occupation at the sites discussed might be taken to indicate year-round occupation from the antler remains. The purpose of the diagrams is, however, to establish likely hypotheses, and they are interpreted as showing which sites show an emphasis on particular seasons. The seasons thus isolated indicate the period of occupation which was economically most important and, unless other evidence conflicts with the presence of humans only during those important seasons, sites are assumed to have been occupied only in the main season. It is, of course, possible that some sites were occupied by small groups of old people, for example, outside their major period of occupation, but the economic importance of such sites nonetheless centres on their major season of occupation.

Although Bouchud (1966) concluded that sites on the Vézère were occupied in all seasons, he conceded that the reindeer would have been near them only in spring and autumn, and it was therefore necessary to invoke long marches by hunters into reindeer pastures in summer and winter to explain the data. Sturdy (1972b) showed that this would have meant starvation of the human groups, since the calories won would have been less than those expended. [Further objections to Bouchud's view are in Higgs (1972). *Editor.*] Bouchud's data can, however, be explained

in several ways and his published data are not inconsistent with the hypothesis that the reindeer at these sites were killed only in spring and autumn. Briefly, the statistical failure in his monograph is the assumption that, for example, six antlers which Bouchud states could represent any month from October to March should be assigned one to each of the six possible months. Statistically, if the basic hypotheses that the statisticians have to work on are not spelled out, this is the obvious course. But there is in fact no reason at all why all the antlers could not represent animals killed in any single one of the months, such as, for example, all in October. Where the raw data are published, and the occupation of sites all the year round is claimed, significant clumping of antlers in spring and autumn does occur, and the antlers which do not so clump are not inconsistent with an interpretation of spring and autumn killing. In other words, a second hypothesis of equal or greater probability can be constructed on the data. It does not, therefore, seem reasonable to conclude that the French Palaeolithic

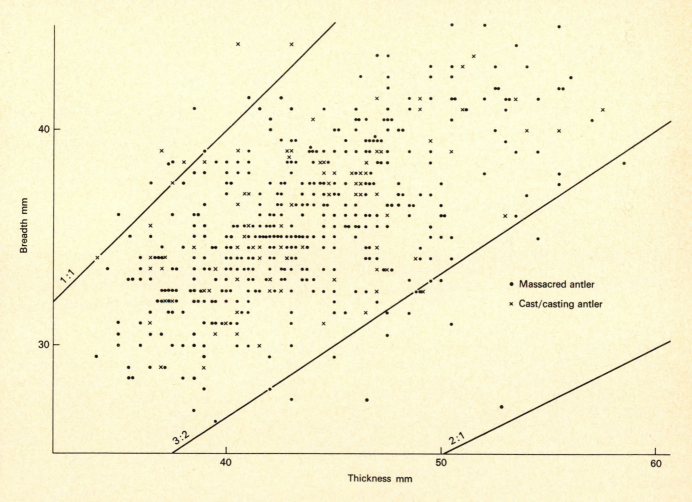

Figure 2. Adult male antlers: Stellmoor, Ahrensburgian. Beam measurements at position 2.

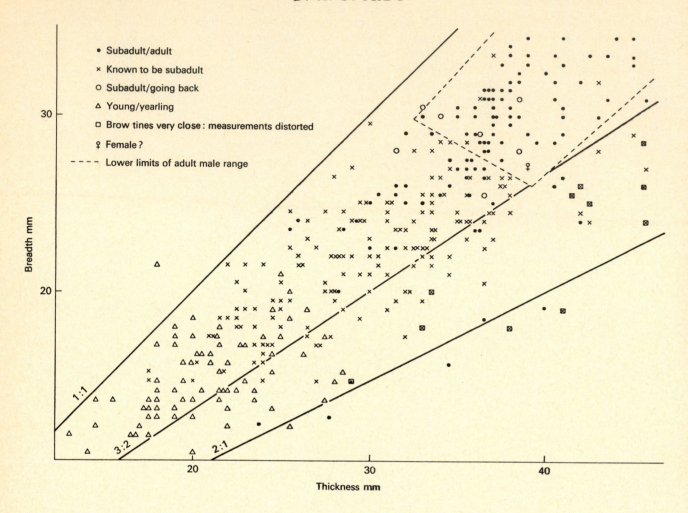

Figure 3. Subadult and young male antlers: Stellmoor, Ahrensburgian. Beam measurements at position 2.

economies were vastly different from any other economy in the distances which men were prepared to travel for their food. It should be stressed that the fault does not lie with Bouchud's analyses but with the statistical methods applied to them.

In the interpretation of tooth wear patterns, I must again differ from Bouchud, and the reasons for my differences will be presented in due course. But it must be emphasised once again that none of the results discussed in this paper would have been obtained without Bouchud's groundwork and the stimulus offered by his monograph.

Antler growth begins with the development of velvet, a protective covering of skin with thick, short fur. After three or four months the antlers reach their full development, and the outside of the antler begins to harden from the base upwards by a process resembling osteosclerosis. The amount of compact antler surrounding the spongy tissue of the core

varies with the distance from the base of the antler, and in adults the tips often have less than one millimetre of compact antler. The term 'fully compact' signifies a stage of compactness beyond which no further compacting occurs. On fully compact antlers the ratio of compact to spongy antler is at least 1:1 at the base, about 1:3 half way up, and less still higher up and towards the end of the brow tines. This ratio is expressed by the minimum width of the beam where the measurement is taken against twice the width of compact antler on one side of the piece measured in the same plane. Thus graphs of compact antler (Figures 5–10) show ratio lines of, for example, 2:1 when the measurements show 4:1.

The earliest sign of casting is a thin crack at the base of the antler. The crack is invisible at first, but soon becomes visible from the outside of the antler. Within a few days the pedicel and base of the antler become spongy, and a few days later the antler is cast. The fracture occurs in a characteristic fashion for males, females, and castrates. In the male a projection is always present below the corona on a cast antler, and the pedicel on the skull is concave at the top. Cast female antlers possess a hollow extending higher than the corona and forming a cup, and the pedicel is correspondingly convex. Among castrates both the pedicel and the antler have a characteristically rough surface. Castrates have only a very small amount of compact antler, since the antlers remain in velvet until they are shed, so that cast castrate antlers are easily recognised. The whole casting process from the appearance of the cast line (Bouchud's *sillon*) to the loss of the antler requires only between ten and fourteen days, and antlers showing incipient casting can be ascribed to a season with the greatest confidence.

The timing of the growth of modern reindeer antlers varies widely in different populations. Growth is influenced by seasonal changes, since reindeer introduced to South Georgia in the southern hemisphere (Bonner, 1958) adapted their pattern of antler growth to the new seasonal cycle there. The timings suggested by Bouchud (1966) are adopted in this paper, although it is recognised that they are only approximations, and I have always given the widest spread of dates within the period applicable to any one antler. Even if the months named are slightly inaccurate, there is no doubt about the season. The seasonal classification adopted is that of the modern Arctic: spring – May and June; summer – from the last week of June to the end of September; autumn – from October to mid-November; and winter – from mid-November to the end of April. These

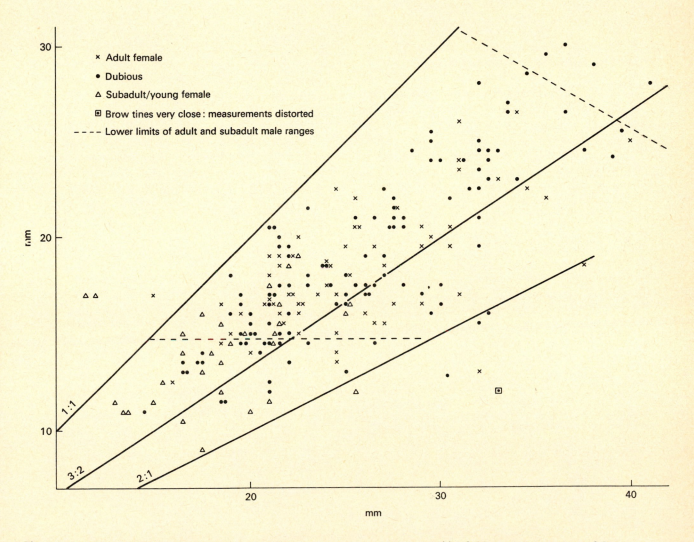

Figure 4. Female and dubious antlers: Stellmoor, Ahrensburgian. Beam measurements at position 2. Measurements to nearest 0.5 mm.

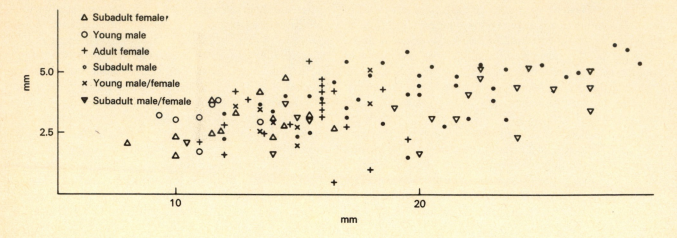

Figure 5. Compactness of some antlers at position 2: Stellmoor, Ahrensburgian. Measurements to nearest 0.5 mm.

seasons are slightly out of phase with those of temperate areas, because summer does not start until almost all the snow has melted, and winter begins with the first heavy snowfalls. The greater amounts of yearly sunshine, especially in the winter months, in late glacial Europe, might have brought the seasons nearer to modern temperature seasons, but this would not materially alter the conclusions presented below. It is also clear that the precise timing of the seasons varies in different years. It is uncertain whether this influences the development and casting of antlers, but modern accounts suggest that these small fluctuations are not reflected consistently in the antler phases. Therefore a site occupied only in autumn must be expected to show antlers from mid-September to mid-November, and sites occupied only in spring will show a comparable range.

The first growth on adult male antlers occurs in March, on subadult males in April, and on yearlings in May. Fawns may begin to show antlers very early in the summer following their birth or may not develop antlers at all until they are one year old. Adult males reach full antler develop-

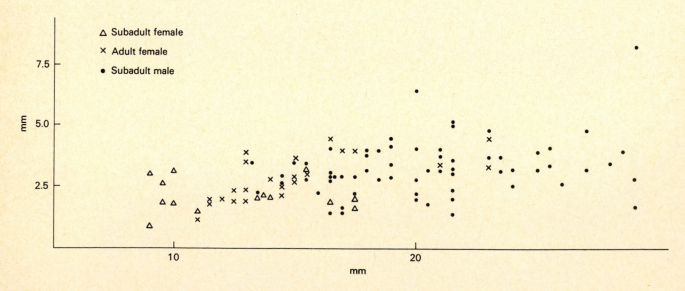

Figure 6. Compactness of some antlers at position 3: Stellmoor, Ahrensburgian. Measurements to nearest 0.5 mm.

ment by the end of June, when compacting begins, but in July the whole antler is still very tender and quite uncompact, except perhaps at the base. Compacting is nearly complete by late August, and the velvet starts to be shed. During September and the first half of October the antlers are polished, compact, and without velvet. The first signs of casting occur in mid-October, and the antler is shed at the beginning of November, immediately after the October rut. Subadult male antlers are not compact until September, the velvet being shed a little later than in the case of the adults. Three-year-olds shed their antlers in December, younger animals in January and February, and fawns lose their spikes in April and May.

The female pattern is slightly out of phase with that of adult males but corresponds quite closely to that of yearlings and fawns of both sexes. The first female growth on adults may occur in May, and in June on subadults, but there is little difference in the timing of antler growth between different classes of females. The antler may be considered fully compact in females by the middle of October. Females retain their antlers through the winter. Adults shed in April and younger animals in early May. Like the male fawns, female fawns, if they carry spikes, may shed them as late as early June, though this is rare. Growth on the pedicels starts very soon after the antlers have been shed, in contrast to adult males in which no growth occurs in winter although they are not carrying antlers.

It is clear from this that it is impossible to date certain classes of antlers except within broad limits. For example, a compact female antler may represent an animal killed during any month from October to April inclusive, and an antler classed as 'female or subadult male' could be representative of any time between September and May. Such antlers are not necessarily winter antlers, however, since the span involved also includes autumn and spring. Further, since antlers increase in compactness while still growing, it is clearly desirable to try to devise some means of assessing whether a massacred antler was fully compact or not. On all antlers where measurements can be taken, therefore, the amount of compact antler has been measured, and the results have been plotted in Figures 5 to 10 for various classes of animals. The Stellmoor graphs show considerable variation in the ratio of compact to total antler width, and I have assumed that antlers which were massacred but which lie within the size range of cast antlers can be considered fully compact. With the exception of five antlers (Figure 7) all the adult male antlers from the Ahrensburgian level of Stellmoor fall within the range for cast antlers and can be referred to the period after the shedding of the velvet. The presence of the five examples which fall outside the range corroborates Degerbøl's observations that the Stellmoor antlers were probably fully compact (Degerbøl & Krøg, 1959).

Using the techniques described, the seasonal diagrams of

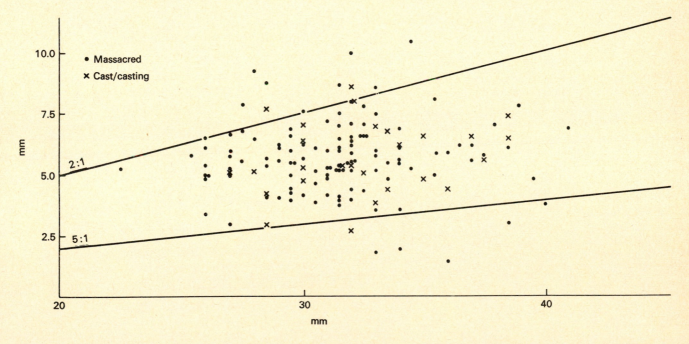

Figure 7. Compactness of adult male antlers at position 2: Stellmoor, Ahrensburgian. Measurements taken to nearest 0.5 mm. Ratio lines express total width of antler against total width of compact antler at the same point.

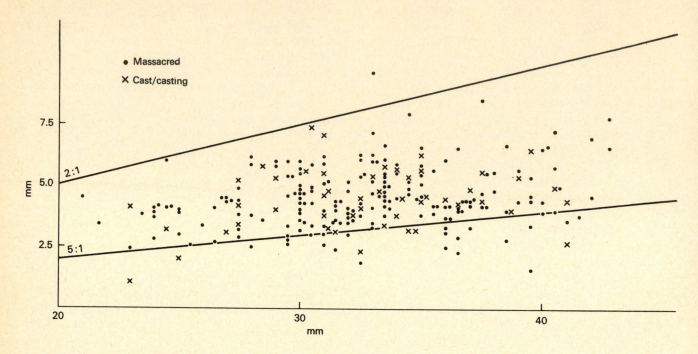

Figure 8. Compactness of adult male antlers at position 3: Stellmoor Ahrensburgian. Measurements to nearest 0.5 mm. Ratio lines express width of antler against total width of compact antler at the same point.

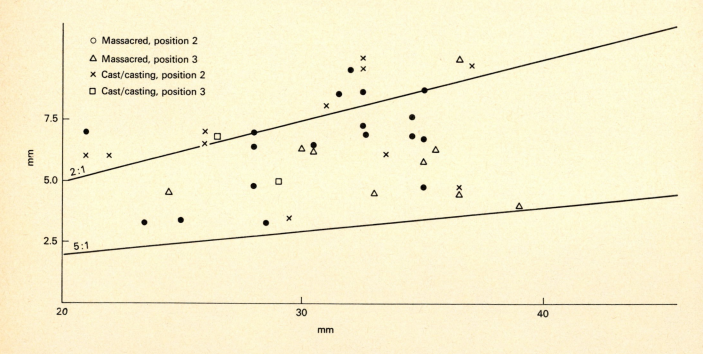

Figure 9. Compactness of adult male antlers at positions 2 and 3: various Magdalenian stations in South Germany and Switzerland. Measurements to nearest 0.5 mm. Ratio lines express width of antler against total width of compact antler at the same point.

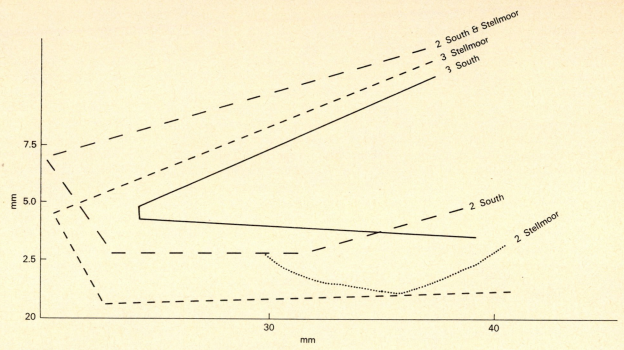

Figure 10. Comparison of the ranges of measurement of compact antlers from Stellmoor, Ahrensburgian, and the various Magdalenian stations of South Germany and Switzerland. Data from Figures 7–9. The numbers indicate positions–'2 South' shows the measurements at position 2 on antlers from South Germany and Switzerland.

Figures 11 to 14 have been built up. Where precise dating is impossible, as is often the case, the maximum range has been assigned to each antler. Two factors require further comment. First, antler dates are weighted towards those periods when the dates are certain, especially spring and autumn when the casting process gives exact dates. Thus it would theoretically be easy to find many sites with an ap-parent preponderance of spring and autumn antlers. On summer sites only the durable spring and autumn antlers, resulting from occasional 'late' or 'early' seasons, may be

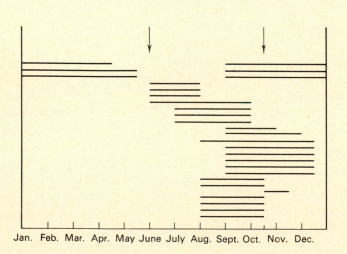

Figure 11. Antlers from Schussenquelle. The lines indicate the possible months in which the animals died. The arrows indicate the minimum period which will account for all the antlers, corresponding to a typical summer.

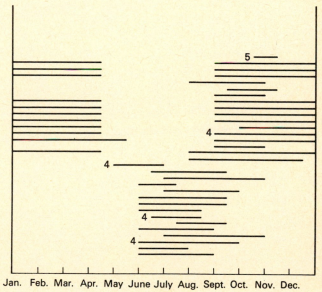

Figure 12. Antlers from Schweizersbild. The lines indicate the possible months in which the animals died. The numbers refer to those specimens which can be assigned to a layer: 4 = layer 4 (gelbe Kulturschicht) and 5 = layer 5.

preserved, and the soft summer antlers may have disappeared. Animals which were killed in summer probably had very spongy antlers, which would crumble easily, be eaten by rodents, or otherwise be destroyed more easily than the hard antlers from animals killed after the velvet has been shed, and this factor must be taken into account. However, if fragments of growing antler are preserved in a site, as in the Ahrensburgian level of Stellmoor, and no summer antlers occur, it is justifiable to preclude summer occupation of the site. Human groups may have brought cast antlers to summer sites from some distance away, in order to make tools. Therefore, if a site contains predominantly summer antlers but also a few cast male antlers this need not be taken to indicate autumn occupation. Equally, where a site shows a good deal of compact antler from massacred specimens, the cast antlers can be assumed to be reliable indicators of seasons. Despite the limitations outlined, the techniques described are adequate to provide a broadly accurate picture of the seasonal cycle of occupation of archaeological sites.

Results

Tables 1 and 2 present an analysis of the antlers from the Ahrensburgian level at Stellmoor. It is clear from the casting adult male antlers that the site was occupied in October. The absence of uncompact adult males, but the presence of uncompact subadult males (in very small numbers), suggests very strongly that on occasions occupation there began in September, but no earlier. The vast amount of compact antler recovered precludes the possibility that an appreciable quantity of cast antler was brought to the site. Therefore occupation from late October and early November until December is indicated. The growing male antlers show presence at the site in March or April, and the growing female antlers indicate May and the early part of June. The two uncompact female antlers could also be dated to the early autumn, or slightly earlier. Cast and casting females indicate spring occupation. The seasonal breakdown of all antlers is given in Figure 13. Turning to the males, the compactness figures show that at the most five males were killed before the antler was fully compact. September and October killing would account for this. The five apparently summer antlers require some further comment. The Stellmoor collection includes five or six definitely castrate antlers. Out of c. 1020 male antlers, it would be remarkable if there were not a few animals which had been accidentally castrated or had a natural hormone deficiency. It is not unreasonable that the five very lightly compact antlers in Figure 7 also represent castrates, perhaps im-

Table 1.   Stages of antler development at Stellmoor, Ahrensburgian

	Adult		Subadult		Yearling		Total	
	No.	Per cent	No.	Per cent	No.	Per cent	No.	Per cent
Total male:	708	69.7	232	22.8	77	7.6	1017	100.1
Massacred	584	82.4	209	90.0	70	91.0		
Uncompact	0	0.0	5	2.2	3	3.9		
Casting	99	14.0	1	0.4	1	1.3		
Cast	20	2.8	6	2.6	0	0.0		
Growing	5	0.7	11	4.7	3	3.9		
		99.9		99.9		100.1		
Total female:	68	60.1	42	37.2	3	2.7	113	100.0
Massacred	61	89.8	35	84.4	2	(66)		
Uncompact	0	0.0	2	4.8	1	(33)		
Casting	1	1.5	0	0.0	0			
Cast	3	4.4	0	0.0	0			
Growing	3	4.4	5	11.9	0			
		100.1		100.1				

Note. This is a breakdown of all the antlers which could be sexed and aged (1129 in total). Other antlers to which a season could be ascribed without accurate ageing or sexing are included in Figure 13.

Table 2. Stellmoor antler ages and sexes

	Slaughter patterns (per cent)		
Age and sex	Stellmoor	Skuncke 1	Skuncke 2
Adult male	63	39	6
Adult female	6	34	26
Subadult male	20	17	43
Subadult female	4	6	11
Young male	7	2	10
Young female	0.3	2	3
Adults	69	73	32
Subadults	24	23	54
Young	7	4	13

Note. The Stellmoor antler ages and sexes are set against the same figures for two slaughter patterns offered by Skuncke (1969) for modern Scandinavian reindeer ranching. The Stellmoor data fit quite closely to Skuncke's Plan 1 except that in Stellmoor the adult male figure is much higher and the adult female much lower than in Skuncke's Plan. The correspondence, however, in the general age groups (both sexes combined) is remarkably close. Skuncke's Plan 2 is clearly not compatible with the Stellmoor data.

perfect castrates, killed before the casting period for this class of animal in spring. Alternatively they may be genuine summer antlers belonging to male entires. Once again, 5 out of 1017 males is a totally insignificant number, and there is no reason to deduce from these antlers that full summer occupation at Stellmoor occurred. Castration of males may have occurred, but it cannot have been an important practice of the Stellmoor occupants; nor is it widely recorded in France (Bouchud, 1966).

An additional 38 out of 1241 antlers might represent animals killed in summer. Figure 13 shows how many antlers, by contrast, represent the winter months. Among the adult males at least 99 are definitely autumn, and many others definitely assigned to a period other than summer. Every one of the 38 antlers could represent reindeer killed in May or in the first fortnight of September. Taking these considerations into account, it is unlikely that summer occupation played a significant part in the economy of the occupants of Stellmoor. A big kill occurred in autumn, some killing occurred in spring, and at least sporadic deaths of animals occurred in winter.

Kollau (in Rust, 1943) believed that the Ahrensburgian and probably Hamburgian levels of Stellmoor represented summer occupation because of the presence of birds which

were certainly migratory summer visitors to the area, such as mallards. His case is, however, unverified. Mallards are the most adaptable of ducks and are resident today in West Greenland, for example, which probably has a similar winter climate to that of north Germany in the Younger Dryas. Moreover, summer immigrants could have been

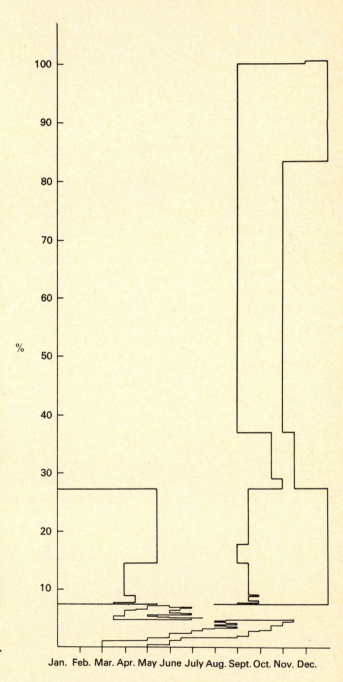

Figure 13. Antlers from Stellmoor, Ahrensburgian. The blocks indicate the possible range of months in which the animals died. The figure is arranged by per cent of 1241 antlers.

killed shortly before the site was abandoned in spring.

Kollau also classified Stellmoor as a summer occupation site because the adult male antlers were massacred, and he was able to isolate only six cast antlers. Degerbøl (in Degerbøl & Krøg, 1959) first suspected Kollau's interpretation. He observed that the Danish late glacial reindeer, when they could be assigned to a season, had died in winter, and he pointed out that it was improbable that Denmark and the Hamburg region would have been so different climatically and vegetationally that the reindeer visited them at different seasons. Further, he noted that the Stellmoor antlers were compact, and hence that killing probably did not occur until September. Since Kollau's analyses, the Stellmoor antlers were moved in large wooden crates without packing, and the jolting caused many of the apparently massacred antlers to become cast antlers. Thus they must have been very near to casting, since the antler is very solid until this time. This may account for the discrepancies between Kollau's counts of cast antlers and my own. Secondly, the publication of Bouchud's work has allowed the antler material to be assigned to the various seasons with much greater accuracy.

Figure 2 also disposes of any suspicion that two populations of reindeer may be present at Stellmoor. In France Bouchud (1966) was able to isolate 'woodland' from 'tundra' reindeer on the basis of the antler shape. Woodland forms have a more flattened beam than the tundra forms. This criterion is somewhat suspect, but it is clear that the adult male antlers fall into the tundra reindeer category from their shapes, as the ratio lines of widths against thickness in Figure 2 suggest. The subadult antlers (Figure 3), however, range more towards the flattened beam form, but this is a function of their youth rather than their subspecific status, since two populations of subadult reindeer but only one of adults is unlikely.

In summary, the Stellmoor antler collection suggests that the Hamburg region was very sparsely, if at all, used by the reindeer in summer. The most likely hypothesis is that this area was winter range, and that the humans who exploited the reindeer killed animals predominantly in autumn.

The number of antlers from the southern stations, in Switzerland and Germany, is much lower. The number of antler fragments from sites in High Germany (the region of the Swabian Alps and its environs) is so small compared with the number of bones that it is reasonable to suppose that differential preservation may have occurred, which possibly suggests summer occupation by reindeer of this region. Such antlers as are preserved from High Germany are assigned to months in Figure 14d. The single antler assigned to mid-October or early November is a cast adult male, which might have been taken to the site as raw material for artefacts. One of the few examples of a possibly

castrate antler comes from the Hohler Fels, but it is uncertain. Four definitely summer antlers are preserved from the Magdalenian layers at Vogelherd, the Bocksteinschmiede, and the Hohler Fels near Hutten. The other specimens are consistent with the hypothesis that occupation of the High German sites sometimes began in May, although this is not the only possible hypothesis. Certainly, at some sites the human group was present in spring, and at some in summer.

The results from the Swiss stations show that some sites, notably those in the Konstanz and Schaffhausen regions, which form the bottom half of Figure 14b, were occupied in

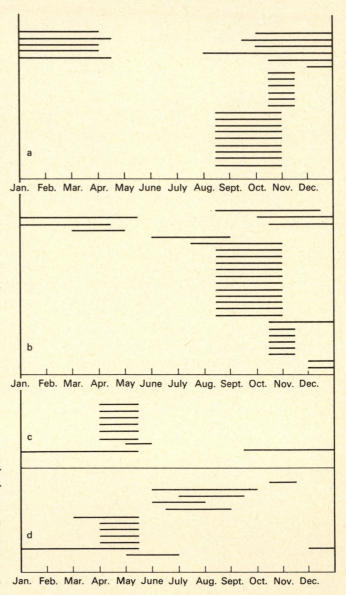

Figure 14. Antlers from various stations: a, Petersfels; b, miscellaneous Swiss stations; c, Wildscheuer; d, High Germany. The lines indicate the possible months in which the animals died.

autumn and winter. One definitely summer antler occurs at Kastelhöhle, where the tiny number of antler fragments (less than twenty fragments) relative to the large bone collection (over 1000 reindeer bones) suggests differential preservation of hard bones and soft summer antler. It is possible that here and elsewhere the rarity of antler indicates the slaughter of males in winter, when they do not carry antler, but in this case some sign of compact subadult male antler, not cast until December, would be expected. In the case of the one summer example from Kastelhöhle it seems likely that this site was, at one time at any rate, occupied in summer. Therefore it appears that Switzerland has served as both winter and summer territory for reindeer, possibly at different times.

This suggestion is borne out by the evidence from Schweizersbild, where there is ample evidence for winter and summer antler (Figure 12). Unfortunately, most of the layer labels have been lost from the specimens, but one autumn antler occurs in layer 5, three summer antlers in layer 4, and one equivocal piece (late summer to winter) also in layer 4. Discounting the last antler there is a hint that Schweizersbild was occupied in summer in layer 4 and in winter during layer 5. These two layers may represent the Allerød and the Younger Dryas respectively (Sturdy, 1972b), although the layers and the phases may not be coterminous. If such was the case, winter occupation of the site probably occurred during Allerød, and summer occupation during the Dryas phase. This would be consistent with the elevation of the site (472 m), which is intermediate between the Swabian Alps and the Rhine valley below Basel.

Because of its proximity the same might reasonably be expected of Petersfels, but here there are complicating factors. Most of the Petersfels bones were destroyed by bombing. Those that survive are the 'belles pièces', the artefacts such as bâtons and other drilled and shaped pieces. Summer antler does not make a good museum display, and if there was ever a summer component in the antlers it was probably destroyed with the bones in storage. The surviving evidence indicates occupation in autumn and winter, but summer occupation cannot be excluded. The Schweizersbild results represent the best picture of the three great sites between Engen and Schaffhausen, the Kesslerloch, Schweizersbild, and Petersfels. Peters' recovery of foetal bones from Petersfels shows that the site was also occasionally occupied in May or early June.

The Schussenquelle diagram (Figure 11) is also very incomplete. Most of the Schussenquelle material is preserved, but was inaccessible to me, and the evidence I have amassed may be biased since it was collected from small museums where a few pieces had been sent for display. The probable minimum period of occupation is indicated by arrows on the diagram, but it has been extended into autumn on the basis of a single cast male antler. Since there are several definitely summer antlers, this antler may have been brought to the site as raw material for artefacts, and Schussenquelle was probably occupied from June to mid-September. The female antlers with their wide range of monthly dates would not conflict with this view, although on the basis of the antlers alone year-round occupation of the site might be inferred. It is notable that there are no compact adult females, datable to after October, but the sample is small.

The antlers from the southern sites therefore fall into two groups. High Germany was probably occupied by reindeer only in summer. In Switzerland, particularly in the region between Engen and Schaffhausen and including the Central Swiss lowlands down to Geneva, summer and winter occupation is recorded, probably varying with the climatic phases of the Late Glacial. This view is based principally on the antlers, but is supported by other lines of evidence.

Finally, it is instructive to consider the antlers from one site in central Germany. Wildscheuer (Figure 14c) is near Steeden, on the Lahn between Frankfurt and Cologne. No single antler from this site displayed the characteristic palmations or beam size of male antler. There is a *prima facie* case, therefore, for supposing that the site was occupied at a time when males were not carrying antler. Since subadult males also have palmations, it is possible that the site was not occupied until after December, but this is less certain, since some fragments could conceivably represent two-year-old males. The summer and autumn months are unlikely seasons for the occupation of the site, since only one fragment could be assigned to autumn or winter. All the other fragments suggest spring occupation. The alternative hypothesis, that the human group at the site exploited only females does not appear particularly probable. Some distance further down the Rhine is the site of Teufelskuchen, in Olberg (Zotz, 1928), where remains of three reindeer foetuses occurred, although very few new milk teeth were present. The excavator therefore suggested that this site was occupied in May and the earliest part of June, corresponding to late spring. I have not been able to trace the bones from this site.

MIGRATION AND TRANSHUMANCE

Studies of modern caribou and reindeer migration (Kelsall, 1960; Banfield, 1954; Pruitt, 1959; summarised in Sturdy, 1972b, Chapter 4) suggest three major conclusions. Migration is desirable to maintain herds in a healthy state: only migration will prevent the overgrazing of arctic lichen pastures, which may take thirty years to recover from serious over-use and trampling. Migration may also prevent the diseases endemic in reindeer herds from reaching epidemic proportions. A second important factor determining the annual cycle of movement is probably regional differences in snow cover. Areas with soft, thin snow are preferred in winter. Although most modern large herds move north in summer and south in winter, the direction of migration is less important than snow cover conditions. Thirdly, reindeer tend to move in winter towards areas rich in lichen cover and away from such areas in summer. It is because of the softer, thinner snow and abundant arboreal lichens, therefore, that caribou herds in Canada seek the trees in winter. Because all modern populations of reindeer make some form of annual migration, and because of these three factors, this paper assumes that Würmian reindeer herds are likely to have made similar migrations. Some evidence supports this assumption: for example, the celebrated 'gaps' in Krause's bone measurements from Stellmoor, and the antler data already discussed. The alternative hypothesis that reindeer have changed their behaviour since the last glaciation seems implausible.

The migration of reindeer herds does not mean that all the reindeer in any one herd move in one mass between different areas. The majority will do this, but occasional animals will stay in the winter lands all the year round, and others will be found in the summer lands in winter, especially in completely wild herds – that is, herds where no human herd-following economy influences the movements of the animals (Banfield, 1954; Kelsall, 1960). This matter must be considered in assessing the resources available in, for example, summer grazing grounds during the winter, for human groups not practising a herd-following economy.

The basic hypothesis of this section is, therefore, that Würmian reindeer in Europe practised some form of seasonal movement. This poses two problems: whether the migrations were short-range (50 km or less) or long-range, and what were their directions. Modern migration patterns suggest that short-range migrations only occur where two conditions are met. First, there must be a considerable environmental change within a small area, particularly in snow cover and vegetation, and possibly also in temperature. Secondly, only very small herds or those living in restricted areas such as islands (Banfield, 1954) will practise short-range migrations in the absence of the first condition, for example in South Georgia (Bonner, 1958), the Pribilov Islands (Scheffer, 1951) and among greatly reduced caribou herds in Canada. The condition of substantial environmental differences within a small area is met in Switzerland, where the Rhine valley from Basel to Strasbourg and the lowlands between the Vosges and the Black Forest contrast sharply with the Jura, and here short-range migration is a plausible hypothesis. It is a less useful hypothesis in the *Flachland*, where the reindeer herds represented at

Stellmoor would have had to travel over 200 km in order to change their environment.

The human groups exploiting the reindeer herds at, for example, Petersfels, Schweizersbild, and Kesslerloch, were killing substantial numbers of animals. Even allowing for the depredations of various scavengers from the sites, at least 1500 reindeer are represented at these sites, and the true number was probably several times greater. It has been suggested that these sites represent sustained killing over a long period rather than a few large-scale slaughters. This is because the sites appear to span virtually the whole of the Late Glacial, certainly corresponding at least to the Younger Dryas. Several lines of evidence suggest that these sites were occupied for a few weeks annually rather than for occasional short periods. If this was not the case, it is difficult to explain the sustained existence of the human groups. If one assumes that the products of such sustained killing went to feed a minimum human group of at least five people (Clark, 1952), the exploited reindeer herds must have been large enough to support such groups while maintaining a stable herd size. The data in Skuncke (1969) show that the herds must have exceeded 300 animals. Larger human groups would require about 1000 animals, and such examples are indeed indicated by the archaeological evidence. Although this evidence is only circumstantial, it seems plausible that the reindeer herds were larger than those able to undertake short-range movements. Unless there is overwhelming evidence that short-range migrations were practised the data will be examined for evidence of long-range migrations.

The general migration pattern

The North European Plain today carries less snow cover, both in terms of snow depth and of number of days with snow cover, than the highland regions of High Germany, the Swiss Jura, and most of Czechoslovakia. Winter and summer temperatures are also slightly higher in the *Flachland* than in the highland areas to the south. Degerbøl and Krøg (1959) emphasised that the nature of the vegetation of late glacial Denmark indicates thin, non-persistent winter snow cover there. The prevailing winds in the Dryas phase were from the northwest (de Jong, 1967) and must have swept the plains relatively clear of snow, and total precipitation was probably lower than today (Galloway, 1965). Following Pruitt's observations that one important objective of reindeer migrations today is to move away from deep snow cover in winter, and away from the thinly covered winter areas in summer, the Würmian reindeer migrations probably moved from the highlands in summer to the *Flachland* in winter. In Germany this would have involved a southwards movement in summer and a northwards movement in winter. Other areas around the highlands with lighter snow cover and earlier above-freezing temperatures each year might also have been suitable for winter use. Discounting the small intra-montane depressions, because of cold-air sinkage, and noting that reindeer movements south from Germany and north Switzerland are blocked by the Alps, lowland areas of Hungary, which today lie in a rain-shadow, might have been suitable winter territory for reindeer. The lower parts of Moldavia, between the Siret and the Prut and between the Prut and the Dniester, and possibly also the Dobrogea region near the Black Sea, might also have been suitable winter grounds. Other areas such as the central Swiss lowlands, between Engen and Geneva and the Transylvanian tableland, are fairly high (*c.* 500 m) but are surrounded by mountains and possess some of the characteristics both of lowland and highland. They were probably marginal reindeer winter territory. The movements of reindeer, therefore, were probably from the highland areas of the Jura, the limestone plateaux of Germany, and the erosion platforms of the Carpathians in summer, to low-lying districts in winter. This hypothesis can be tested in several ways.

The temperature tolerance of reindeer was discussed by Banfield (1954). Combining his data with the Würmian summer and winter temperatures (Šegota, 1967; Degerbøl & Krøg, 1959), no parts of Europe were too cold for reindeer in winter except the highest mountain regions, which are characteristically so steep that gelifraction and solifluction would have made them unsuitable habitat for reindeer. Unless Würmian reindeer had different temperature tolerances from modern reindeer, winter temperature is not likely to have influenced seasonal migration patterns. Even if the temperature tolerance of the Pleistocene reindeer was different, modern data suggest that *Flachland* areas were slightly warmer in winter than highland areas. Summer temperatures are a different case, since it seems quite probable that during the Allerød period summer temperatures in the *Flachland* and elsewhere in Europe were probably uncomfortably close to the upper limit of temperature tolerance of reindeer.

Vegetational differences probably characterised highland and *Flachland* as well. The more acid, salty soils of the *Flachland* (Frenzel, 1968) recently exposed by retreating ice-sheets would have been even less nourishing than they are today. In contrast, the limestone plateaux of High Germany would have provided comparatively lush grazing. The first vegetation to colonise the *Flachland* was probably lichen mats, which now tend to grow on patches rejected by other plant communities. It is, of course, these lichen mats on which reindeer in winter are today so dependent. This suggestion must be used with caution, because the marshy

nature of much of the *Flachland* would have rendered large areas unsuitable for summer grazing. Summer use of the *Flachland* by animals would therefore have tended to concentrate on the better drained sandier soils. On the other hand, the widespread occurrence of permafrost might have offset the better drainage of the sandy regions, and the greater concentration of lichens is the more probable explanation of any relationship between sandy soils and late glacial economies. The high density of archaeological sites on sandy areas is demonstrated by the clusters of Ahrensburgian sites in Belgium, west and northwest of Aachen, and on the Lüneburger Heide southwest of Hamburg (Figure 15). Similar factors may have operated in

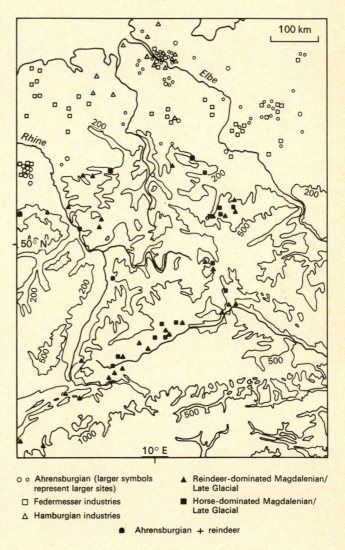

Figure 15. Distribution of major late glacial sites and site groups: general map, Switzerland and Germany.

eastern Hungary where, until recently, the acidity of the soils of the Hortobagy area impeded the growing of other than pasture plants, and where the glacial vegetation may have shown a greater percentage of lichen than the richer limestone and loess soils of other regions.

To summarise the discussion at this point; the modern tendencies of arctic reindeer herds to move towards taiga in winter and north on to tundra in summer cannot be strictly paralleled in late glacial Europe because there was, in the Dryas periods at least, no taiga to move towards. The principles which underlie modern movements can be paralleled in the Late Glacial. The soft snow of the modern taiga is replaced by the thinner snow cover of the late glacial *Flachland*, and the increased lichen growth of the modern taiga by the greater proportion of lichen in the sandy *Flachland*. Any trees in the Late Glacial may have been in the valleys of the highland areas, but these valleys are characteristically so steep that this has little bearing on the discussion, and they were in any case probably inaccessible in winter

Even today much of the *Flachland* area of Germany and Poland is covered by marsh. During the Late Glacial, as the result of permafrost conditions, it is reasonable to suppose that water-logged conditions were at least as common as today. While vegetation on tussocks, and the tops of plants growing with their roots in water, would have been available when the water was frozen in winter, such vegetation is much less accessible in summer. The marsh areas of the highlands are much less frequent and smaller in area, which reinforces the desirability of using the *Flachland* primarily in winter. The concentrations of insects, notably mosquitoes, were probably greater in the *Flachland*, because of much more extensive marsh; but this factor seems of little account, since insect plagues do not greatly influence migration patterns of modern reindeer (Banfield, 1954; Kelsall, 1960; Sturdy, 1972b). Nonetheless, it is one additional factor which might have increased the desirability of the highlands as summer pasture.

The seasonal evidence from antlers showed strong indications that the Stellmoor site was occupied between autumn and spring, and that the High German localities represented summer occupation. The sites in the Swiss lowlands indicated occupation in summer and winter, but probably not year-round occupation.

Migration patterns in Germany

The circumstantial evidence presented suggests that the highland regions were summer grazing and that the *Flachland*, and probably other lowland areas, were winter pastures. It remains to demonstrate that the reindeer in High Germany and in north Germany belonged to a single migratory population. The evidence for such a migration derives largely from consideration of the alternatives.

The evidence from the Stellmoor antlers suggests that these reindeer herds were in the area in winter. They might have spent the winter in four regions: eastwards towards Poland; westwards, northwestwards, or north in the areas now occupied by the North Sea, Sweden, and Jutland; southwards in the central German highlands; or southwards in the limestone plateaus of south Germany. The eastwards movement was postulated by Degerbøl (Degerbøl & Krøg, 1959), who believed that the Stellmoor region and Denmark were winter pastures for reindeer, at least in the Dryas phases. He therefore suggested that the summer might have been spent in Poland and that the annual migration cycle was along the Baltic. The disadvantage of this hypothesis is the lack of any determinable reason why the reindeer should have made such movements. Even if Poland in the Late Glacial, as today, had colder winters than northwest Germany, winter temperatures probably had little effect on migration patterns. More important, following the evidence given by de Jong (1967) for prevailing northwesterly winds over northern Europe in the Dryas phases, it seems probable that the present pattern, of decreased precipitation towards the east in Europe, obtained in the Late Glacial also. Hence, a westwards movement in winter would have involved a movement towards deeper snow, and therefore seems unlikely. Movements might, however, have been along the Baltic to the east in winter and west in summer, since these would have led away from deeper snow in winter and also away from the more frequent *Foehn* conditions in the west. Such a movement is belied by the Stellmoor antlers, and the presence of marshes in northwest Germany in summer.

A movement north into Scandinavia seems perfectly likely, and the presence of late glacial sites with tanged points in south Sweden (Taute, 1968) might support such a hypothesis. In fact such movements probably occurred, but the available pastures would have been too small to support the total reindeer population which is believed to have wintered in the *Flachland*.

Although migrations into central Germany would have been short, much of this area provides poor winter grazing. The soft rocks and broken relief of much of this area would have limited the available grazing range because of solifluction. The area around Gera where a concentration of late glacial sites occurs (Figures 15 and 19) is only a small part of the total available area. Figure 15 shows that the late glacial sites in highland Germany form a rough circle, down the Rhine, along the Swabian and Franconian Alps from Basel to Regensburg, and northwards east of Nuremburg, continuing with the Gera and associated groups at the edge of the *Flachland*, and following the edge of the highlands through the Harz foreland and the Hanover–Hameln areas back to the Rhine. Areas inside this circle show remarkably little late glacial occupation. Figure 16 takes the central section of the Rhine and adjacent lands. The sites marked fall into two groups: those actually lying on the Rhine (sites 4, 8, 9 and 12); and those in or adjacent to relatively flat areas (sites 1, 2, 3, 5, 6, 10, 11). The only

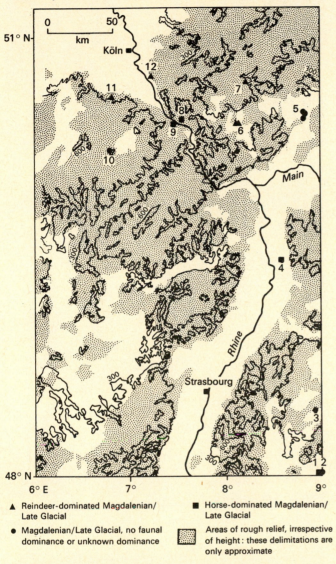

exception is site 7, Wildweiberhaus, which occupies gently rolling terrain close to more broken relief. The correlation of sites with the Rhine valley or with flatter areas within 30 km of the valley must be more than coincidence. Figure 17 shows that sites in northwest Germany follow the ap-

proximate edge of the highland or occupy flatter regions near the edge of the highland. Between Osterode (Steinkirche, 16) and Hameln and Hanover, the small find-spots of late glacial material follow the valleys. Numbers 13, 14, and 15 occur on the ecotone between broken country and *Flachland* at an altitude of 300 m. Figure 18 reiterates the distribution of sites around the edge of the highland. In Figure 19, the Gera group is on the ecotone (32 and 33); the Kniegrotte group (35) is adjacent to the flatter country; the other groups in the area (34, 36, and 37) lie on the edge of a long valley entering the highland, and are

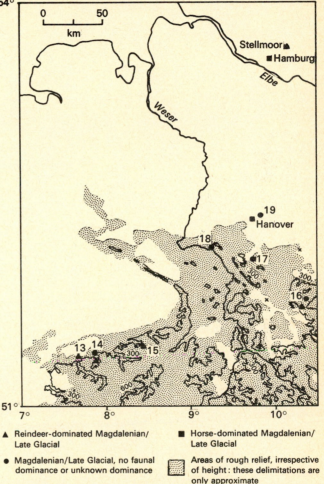

Fig 17. Distribution of late glacial sites and site groups in northwest Germany. 13—Martinshöhle; 14—Balverhöhle and Klusensteinhöhle; 15—Bilsteinhöhle, Schnopers Hol, H. Stein bei Callenhardt; 16—Steinkirche; 17—Banteln; 18—Oldendorf; 19 Hanover-Misburg. The small unnumbered crosses represent small find-spots in the area Hanover Hameln Harz.

broadly contiguous with the 300 m contour. The other major sites follow the limestone plateau country, and only Arnshausen an der Saale (38) provides any indication whatsoever that the vast intervening area of largely shaley rocks was occupied during the Late Glacial.

Figure 16. Distribution of late glacial sites and site groups in southwest Germany. 1—Probstfels; 2—Buttentalhöhle; 3—Niedernau; 4—Ilvesheim; 5—Lich Lolnhauserhof, Lich Albachertal and Bellersheim; 6—Wildhaus and Wildscheuer; 7—Wildweiberhaus; 8—Gonnersdorf; 9—Andernach; 10—Buchenloch; 11—Kartsteinhöhle; 12—Oberkassel.

Discussions of the late glacial distribution of archaeological sites are valueless unless there is good reason to believe that the discovered sites represent, in reasonable measure, the original distribution of sites. Until recently, prehistorians tended to confine their search for artefacts to areas with caves, and the distribution of

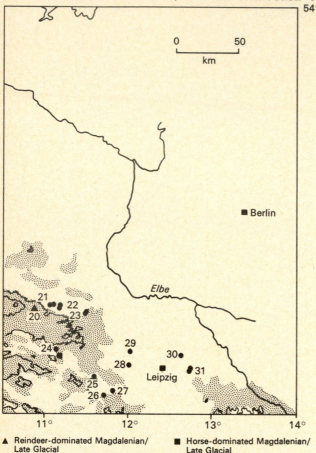

Figure 18. Distribution of late glacial sites and site groups in northeast Germany. 20–Zwergenloch; 21–Hessenberg, Königstein; 22–Konigsaue, Quedlinburg sites; 23–Aschersleben and Gatersleben; 24–Kyffhauser and Bennungen; 25–Altenburg; 26–Lengefeld; 27–Saaleck; 28–Kriegsdorf; 29–Galgenberg; 30–Groitzsch; 31–Wurzen, Wusten and Wusten Kirche.

Magdalenian sites in Germany may reflect only areas with a limestone substratum. On the other hand, open sites have been found in the Rhine valley, around the edge of the highlands, and within the highland belt itself; Munsingen, Gönnersdolf, Ilvesheim, the Hameln-Hanover-Harz group, the Lich group near Giessen, Arnshausen, the Regensburg sites, Lauterach, and several small find-spots illustrate this. Other considerations suggest that the distributional picture recorded is broadly accurate. In areas with soft underlying rock and broken relief, solifluction

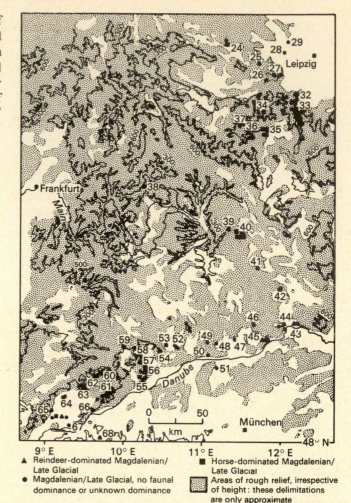

▲ Reindeer-dominated Magdalenian/ Late Glacial
■ Horse-dominated Magdalenian/ Late Glacial
● Magdalenian/Late Glacial, no faunal dominance or unknown dominance
▨ Areas of rough relief, irrespective of height: these delimitations are only approximate

Figure 19. Distribution of late glacial sites and site groups in southern Germany. 24–Kyffhauser, Bennungen; 25–Altenburg; 26–Lengefeld; 27–Saaleck; 28–Kriegsdorf; 29–Galgenberg; 32–Breitenbach; 33–Gera group, comprising Ahlendorf, Etzdorf, Gleina, Langenberg, Pohlitz, Pfortner Berg, Zwotzen, Liebschwitz, Zoitzberg, Binsenacker, Lindentaler Hyänenhöhle; 34–Hummelskain, Kahla-Lobschutz, Olknitz, Rothenstein; 35–Kniegrotte, Urdhöhle, Wuste Scheuer; 36–Herdloch, Ilsenhöhle, Lausnitz Abri Theure; 37–Rudolstadt group, Bärenkeller, Allendord, Wildpferdhöhle; 38–Arnshausen; 39–Draisendorf; 40–Fuchsenloch, die Breit, Gaiskirche, Zwergloch, Rennerfels; 41–Hohler Fels, Happurg; 42–Steinbergwand; 43–Keilstein, Keilberg Korche; 44–Burghöhle Loch, Obernederhöhle, Räuberhöhle; 45–Heidensteinhöhle, Klausen, Kastlhanghöhle; 46–Muhlbach; 47–Hohler Stein, Schambachtal; 48–Breitenfurterhöhle; 49–Altendorf; 50–Mauern; 51–Donaumoos; 52–Hahnenberg, Kaufertsberg; 53–Ofnet; 54–Hohlen Stein, Ederheim; 55–Bocksteinschmiede, Stadel (Hohlen Stein), Vogerherd; 56–Bärenfelsgrotte & Spitalhöhle, Maierhöhle, Irpfelhöhle; 57–Heidenheim; 58–Herwartstein; 59–Klein Scheuer; 60–Ursring; 61–Hohler Fels, Hutten, Gänserfelsen, Schmiechenfels, Sirgenstein, Hohler Fels bei Schelklingen, Brillenhöhle, Borgerhau; 62–Randecker Maar, Burkhardtshöhle, Papierfels; 63–Klopfjorgleshütte, Rappenfels; 64–Guppenlochfels, Karlshöhle; 65–Bitz & Heidensteinhöhle, Strassberg, Winterlingen, Nikolaushöhle, Annakapellenhöhle; 66–Lauterach; 67–Kohtalhöhle; 68–Schussenquelle.

phenomena would have been so great that suitable pasture for herbivores would have been widely dispersed among areas supporting only the tougher woody plants with extensive root systems. Much of highland central Germany, then, would have been marginal for reindeer grazing. Although these phenomena would also tend to destroy Palaeolithic open sites, the apparent lack of sites in highland central Germany probably does reflect sparse human occupation during the Late Glacial.

The areas of highland Germany most suitable for grazing, the flatter regions, are also those in which sites are most likely to be found, and this coincidence helps to diminish the effect of differential exploration in assessing the late glacial distribution of human occupation. In Hungary, on the other hand, few sites are known from regions presumed to have offered good grazing. When the enormous number of open sites in the *Flachland* from Brussels to Warsaw is considered – over five hundred examples are known of late glacial date – it seems odd that so few discoveries have been made in Central Germany, but the distribution of the better grazing grounds outside this region suggests that the known sites reflect at least the relative density of past human occupation of these areas.

Accepting this supposition, the distribution of the central German sites can be considered in greater detail. Figure 15 suggests a tendency for sites to cluster in three locations: in and around the Rhine valley; in the Osterode region southeast of Hannover; and in the reentrant of low ground running into the highlands around Gera. Assuming that the reindeer were moving from the *Flachland* near Hamburg to south Germany, two obvious routes present themselves to avoid the traversing of much difficult country: travelling down the Rhine valley, or taking the shortest route across the highlands by using the reentrant at Gera, and it is likely that human habitations would occupy one of these areas. At this point it is irrelevant whether they are pursuing casual hunting, migration hunting, herd-following, or any other form of exploitation. The distribution of known sites supports this hypothesis. Alternatively, one might assume that reindeer herds wintered on the *Flachland* and summered in highland central Germany and south Germany, or only in central Germany. Then there are three obvious migration routes: the two already mentioned, and the Weser valley with its long reentrant which ends in some of the highest country contained in the arc between the Alps, the Bohemian and Thuringian forest, and the Harz. Steinkirche, the nearest site to this route, is still some 60 km from it. Thus the distribution of archaeological sites and of grazing areas suggests that, if any reindeer herds wintered in the *Flachland* and summered in highland Germany, most of them moved all the way to the limestone plateau of High

Germany. This area is, however, considerably smaller than the part of the *Flachland* lying between the same lines of longitude. Even if the greater marsh areas of the *Flachland*, and the greater area of land required for one reindeer's winter grazing is considered, it is improbable that High Germany alone provided adequate summer food for all the herds which wintered between the modern Rhine and Elbe. Since eastwards movements were unlikely, some of the herds which wintered in north Germany may have moved north into what is today southern Sweden. Of the herds that moved south, some probably summered in such areas as the Eifel mountains, a few in central Germany, and most in south Germany.

This hypothesis is supported by several lines of evidence. The rarity of antler from Wildscheuer (Figure 16:6) pointed strongly to spring killing of reindeer. None of the pieces represented a summer occupation, although one piece could be assigned to autumn, winter, or spring. Foetal reindeer bones from Olberg suggested that some killing took place in late spring. Olberg lies on the Rhine valley, and killing in late spring in this area would be expected if the Rhine valley was a migration route for the reindeer. Oberkassel near Bonn is situated between the river and the hills east of the Rhine in this area, and it lies on the hypothetical route. Yet it is not in the Rhine gorge, where only sites showing predominance of horse killing have been found; this matter is of some significance to later discussions. The preference for reindeer cows to drop their calves in country with plenty of natural shelter would be met if parturition occurred during the spring migration through the areas suggested.

Antler evidence from sites between Petersfels and Draisendorf, near Nuremburg, suggests that some reindeer herds pastured in High Germany. If these herds moved away from the highland in winter, they might have gone to Hungary, northern France, or northern Germany. Northern France is the nearest area, and Stellmoor and Sagvar on Lake Balaton in Hungary are almost exactly equidistant from Petersfels and Draisendorf. The difference in accessibility of these areas is, however, considerable. As already observed, the Rhine valley provides a good route, except in the gorge, which is easily by-passed by continuing northwards where the Rhine bends west at Mainz and, passing through easy country near Wildscheuer, rejoins the river southeast of Bonn. The *Flachland* is then reached after about 300 km of travel. Moving to Hungary, no obvious by-pass of the Danube gorge between Passau and Linz exists. Although this country is far from impassable, flatter country is not reached until over 500 km have been traversed. The obvious route for such a migration is along or near the Danube, but the area from Regensburg to Krems near Vienna lacks Late Upper Palaeolithic material. Although neither the greater difficulties of the route nor the absence of human groups exploiting reindeer on this route is conclusive, the available evidence suggests that northwards movements from High Germany are the most likely. The same applies to northwesterly movements towards northern France. The obvious route lies through the Belfort gap between the Vosges and the Jura and past Chaumont towards Troyes. While the southern Rhine area is rich in Late Upper Palaeolithic discoveries, there are no known sites along this route. A more serious objection exists to such a movement: after 25 000 B.C. France apparently supported large reindeer herds, which migrated from lowland Aquitaine towards the Massif Central (Bouchud, 1966). Recent discoveries in northern France, notably at Pincevent (Leroi-Gourhan & Brezillon, 1966) suggest that another migration occurred between the Massif north and the Paris basin. It is, therefore, improbable that there was sufficient pasture in France to support reindeer from southern Germany as well as indigenous herds. Finally, the Rhine valley between Mainz and Basel, although probably good winter pasture, was too small to support the whole population of reindeer grazing in High Germany in summer, although a few herds may have wintered there.

No single piece of the evidence put forward here is worth more than passing consideration on its own. Argument can slowly dismantle each point separately. But the intention is not to attempt to indicate what must have happened. The purpose is to use each piece of circumstantial evidence to construct the most likely hypothesis, and to reveal greater shortcomings in the alternative hypotheses than are present in the preferred one. The sum of all the points raised in this section is the postulation of seasonal movement by reindeer herds in the Late Glacial between the *Flachland* in winter, and south Scandinavia and central and High Germany in summer. The majority of animals which passed into highland Germany continued south to summer on the limestone plateaux. It is considered that patterns of migration from north Germany into north Poland, from High Germany into France or the Rhine valley, and from High Germany into Hungary, are less likely hypotheses. The migrations which are considered more likely possibilities are mapped in Figure 20.

HUMAN TRANSHUMANCE

Human groups dependent at least seasonally on migratory reindeer herds can pursue one of three possible economies. They may follow the reindeer all the year round; they may live permanently in the range occupied by the reindeer only in one season; or they may place themselves on migration routes and hope to kill sufficient animals during the two migrations to provide enough food for the whole year. The first possibility is described as herd following. In most

modern herd-following economies the reindeer are effectively 'ranched' – using that term in the sense of Strickon (1965). Hunting economies – economies where the quarry is approached by stealth – based on herd following occur in one ill-documented case, and this may represent a transient

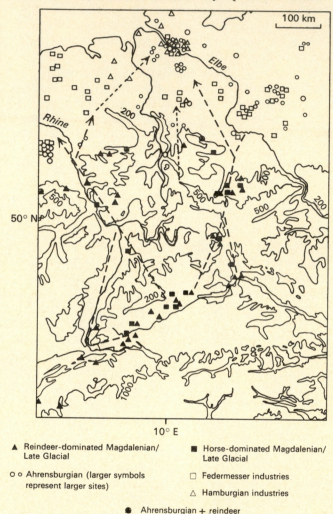

Figure. 20. Hypothetical reconstruction of reindeer migration and human transhumance in late glacial Germany. The arrows indicate the autumn migration.

▲ Reindeer-dominated Magdalenian/ Late Glacial

■ Horse-dominated Magdalenian/ Late Glacial

O o Ahrensburgian (larger symbols represent larger sites)

□ Federmesser industries

△ Hamburgian industries

⊕ Ahrensburgian + reindeer

phenomenon resulting from a highly fluid economic structure at a time of great economic change. Using the herds for only half the year – termed a one-season economy – can happen only where there are adequate resources other than reindeer to provide for the season in which the herds are absent. A full discussion of the impracticability of attempting to provide year-round subsistence from one-season hunting is offered by Sturdy (1972b). Migration hunting will have long-term viability only when the movements of the herds during migration are very strictly limited by natural features and are totally predictable. The case of the Kazan Eskimo, who starved in a season of great caribou abundance because the caribou changed their migration route, was discussed by Harper (1955). The weaknesses of these economies (Sturdy, 1972b) means that migration hunting can be entertained as a serious hypothesis only where there are very strict environmental limitations on migration routes.

The site of Petersfels, with its rich fauna, will be taken as the basis for discussing the resources available to the human groups in the Dryas. This site is located in a postulated summer range, and reindeer must have been rare or absent from October to May. The probable alternative resources are fish, birds, and small game, and any large herbivores wintering in the region, predominantly horse; although even horses probably abandoned this area in winter and they were exploited intensively only in the relatively mild Allerød (Sturdy, 1972b). Although birds are a possible alternative, forty ptarmigan per day are required to provide the fifteen kilocalories required daily by a family of five at an average ambient temperature of 0°C, and in the absence of extensive fishing or some other large herbivore, they could hardly have provided a staple food. The same consideration applies to hares. The daily requirements of a family of five demands at least seven hares. These two animals, the most common representatives of small game at Petersfels, must be trapped. While trapping is probably easier in winter, a daily average trapping success of four hares and fifteen to twenty ptarmigan seems highly improbable for any length of time. Sturdy (1972b) observed that winter resources of one-season hunting economies are based either on seals or reindeer. Neither were available at Petersfels in winter, nor were there any obviously abundant alternative resources. If a human group wintered at Petersfels it must have relied largely on reindeer killed in summer, supplemented by small game.

In the *Flachland*, the case of Stellmoor can be considered. This site was probably occupied in winter, when reindeer living locally were exploited. The summer resources of the *Flachland* are fish, birds and small game, and occasional large herbivores. The possibility of extensive salmon runs, such as were exploited by the Canadian Indians, cannot be discounted, although there is no positive evidence for them. Except near Hamburg and Hanover late glacial sites do not tend to cluster around river valleys. Near Hamburg the river was probably so wide that this area is not an obvious location for intensive fishing. Occasional fishing is indicated at Stellmoor by the presence of pike bones, but at the moment the possibility of summer dependence on fishing is not a particularly probable hypothesis. The remarks about dependence on small game already offered apply equally to the *Flachland*. A more likely hypothesis is that the groups which wintered at

Stellmoor moved north in summer to exploit seal off the coast. Finds of late glacial seal bones in Jutland show that some exploitation of seal occurred, but it is impossible to ascertain whether they represent the winter activities of groups largely dependent on reindeer similar to those at Stellmoor, or summer seal hunting, because the likely movements of the ringed seal in the late glacial seas are largely a matter of speculation. The finds of seal bones and walrus bones in Jutland (Møhl, 1970) are mapped in Figure 21.

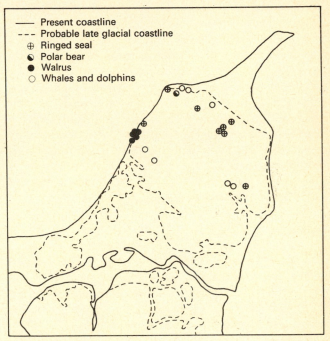

Figure 21. Late glacial bones of sea mammals in Jutland (simplified from Møhl, 1970, Fig. 1).

The possible reactions of human groups dependent on reindeer can be summarised in two probabilities. First, herd-following economies may have been practised. Sites such as Draisendorf in Bavaria and Stellmoor near Hamburg would be the product of the activities of the same human groups. Other groups which wintered in the *Flachland*, however, would have followed some herds north in summer, along the postulated migration routes into south Scandinavia. Stellmoor might therefore represent an agglomeration of groups wintering in the *Flachland* but summering in two or more areas. The group that moved north might also have hunted seal and walrus in summer, or seal and walrus hunting might have been a winter activity. Secondly, human groups might have remained more or less settled in the south German sites, living in winter on stored products. Other groups might have wintered in the *Flachland* by exploiting reindeer and lived off stored food in summer or have gone north to hunt seals. Two considerations may assist in selecting the more probable of these hypotheses.

The first consideration is theoretical. If two groups depend for their year-round subsistence on a given group of reindeer, the possibility of over-killing is considerable for obvious reasons.

Secondly, if this hypothesis were true, sites in central Germany would have to be explained as representative either of human groups exploiting reindeer in summer or of migration hunting. The case of Wildscheuer may be taken as an example. The antlers from this site can all be assigned to spring and, less certainly, to summer. The data are scanty: possibly summer occupation may have occurred, but there is no evidence for it. Killing only in spring is the most likely hypothesis on the data available. According to the hypothesis being tested, Wilscheuer should be a migration hunting site. The success of such sites depends on their being located in areas where there is a very high probability that the reindeer herds will pass. While Wildscheuer lies on a postulated migration route, the animals could easily pass up to 40 km east of the site, and their tendency to do so would have been increased if regular migration hunting took place at Wildscheuer. The site is not on a defile or even a particularly suitable crossing point of the Lahn; indeed, it occupies one of the least strategic positions on the whole postulated migration route. The location of Oberkassel is the same. The horse-dominated sites of Andernach and Feldkirchen–Gonnersdorf are on the most strategic points of the Rhine valley, where the gorge begins. Although Oberkassel lies on the suggested 'by-pass' of the gorge, it is not ideally situated for either of these routes. Therefore, while Wildscheuer and Oberkassel are probably transit sites they are unlikely to be migration hunting sites. The same applies to the Gera and related groups southeast of Leipzig which are located near the migration route but are not particularly well situated for migration hunting since they can be easily by-passed.

In summary, there were probably two major areas of reindeer winter pasture, the North European *Flachland* and the Hungarian basin. From these areas the reindeer migrated in spring towards summer ranges on the level, high plateaux of the Swabian and Franconian Alps and the Carpathians, with minor movement from the northwest *Flachland* into south Scandinavia. The human response to these movements is most likely to have been some form of herd following, since no practicable alternatives can be envisaged. It might be argued that the distances involved are too great for human groups. The distance from Stellmoor to Bavaria is over 500 km, and the other postulated routes are of similar length. Similar movements are, however, documented among modern Siberian groups.

A more serious difficulty is that the postulated transhumance pattern cuts across the classic industrial boundaries of the *Flachland* and highland industrial sequences. To suppose that industrial groupings represent social groups depends on the assumption that methods of tool-making reflect more than the functional requirements of the manufacturer, and also that there exist more than superficial differences between the highland and *Flachland* industries.

The first supposition may have some truth in it. There are several ways of making a tool which will serve a similar function, and it may be that such differences will characterise discrete social units. Such differences are perhaps observable in the clines of industrial types which can be observed between the Magdalenian of France and the Late Gravettian industries of Russia. Certain types are more frequent in France, for example, than in Slovakia. Similary, in the *Flachland*, the type artefacts of the Hamburgian and Swiderian I industries are different, and the Federmesser industries of the western *Flachland* differ slightly from those east of the Elbe and from the Tarnovian industries. These differences show that within each of the major areas, the *Flachland* and the highland, slight regional variations occur, which can (most economically) be explained as representative of social differences (Taute, 1968). This is, however, very different from asserting that the makers of the Moravian Magdalenian industries could not also make Swiderian artefacts. If the postulated transhumance did occur, the same social groups must have occupied two quite different environments in two different seasons. In summer they were relatively stationary, living in caves, and the nature of the relief would have enabled them to keep track of the reindeer without making more than small local movements. On the *Flachland*, the situation is quite different. Greater reliance must have been placed on tents, because there are no caves. The relief is flat, and if the reindeer herds were mobile there were no natural barriers to check their wanderings. In order to keep track of their principal food source, human groups would have had to be mobile. In summer small game would have had to have been shot whereas in winter with the snow cover it could have been more easily trapped. These and other differences would have led to considerably different tool requirements in summer and winter, particularly with certain specialised artefacts perhaps specific to the seasons. We do know that there is a similarity of industrial substratum, 'Epigravettian' in principle, which accounts for some 95 per cent or more of all the tools in all the industries. Superimposed on these are the type artefacts, which have been used in order to make classification possible. Thus the industries recognised may be valid typological units, but it is unjustified to equate them with social units without considering other possible explanations. As Vértes showed on Upper Palaeolithic industries in Hungary, the metrical and statistical attributes of the tools align with the raw material and not with typology or inferred social groups (Vértes, 1964–5), and this approach is therefore likely to yield unequivocal results. Further, Thomson (1939) has given a modern ethnographic instance of one family making, in the course of four seasons, four discrete artefactual industries. To conclude, there seems to be no reason why the hypothesis of transhumance should not assist attempts to interpret the lithic industries, and equally no reason why the existence of industries cutting across social groupings should surprise us.

THE DYNAMICS OF THE REINDEER ECONOMIES

This section advances hypotheses on the working of Late Palaeolithic reindeer economies. The case studies are based on fieldwork and on the study of detailed maps. Except in special circumstances, it is unjustified to assume that the sites known in any area represent more than a few of the sites which probably existed in the periods under consideration. It is an axiom of site catchment analysis that if the subsistence systems which are studied are likely to have involved more than a single site, there must be good reason to assume that the known distribution of sites reflects the actual distribution. Thus, it is quite feasible to study the site exploitation territory of a single site, but to study a system of extended territories where there is reason to believe that a single economic unit of humans occupied or used more than one site, presupposes very intensive exploration. Detailed data are therefore presented for only three intensively explored highland regions. Elsewhere, less detailed analyses are provided, and the conclusions drawn are more tentative. The three detailed analyses in the highland regions were made in the Laufen and Delemont basins of the Swiss Jura, the region between the Altmühl and the Danube of High Germany, and the area of the Moravian karst in Czechoslovakia. As a contrast, an analysis of the horse-based economy of Steinbergwand in Bavaria is included. Less detailed analyses are presented for the Engen–Schaffhausen region, the Swabian Alps, sites near Olten in the Swiss lowlands, some Bavarian sites, and a group of sites in the Ceahlua region of the eastern Carpathians. All these sites come under the heading of highland summer sites discussed above. Comparative data from the winter *Flachland* site of Stellmoor are offered.

The following discussion incorporates several important assumptions and limitations. Most of the economies studied were probably herd-following economies. Unless bone samples are very large or unless large numbers of antlers are preserved, attempts to discover the age and sex ratios of the animals killed are unlikely to yield reliable information. I have calculated (Sturdy, 1972b) that if reindeer forms 80 per cent of the diet, and if the minimum killing plan offered is taken, the annual productivity of 100 reindeer (i.e. the excess of calving rate over natural mortality factors, excluding predation) can support one person at 0°C. This estimate is an absolute minimum because the killing rate assumed (11 per cent per year) is very low, but it does allow for the effects of other predators. The 100 reindeer required for the yearly maintenance of one person will graze in summer at least 1400 hectares. Thus the theoretical density of deer on summer pasture is 7.15 deer per square kilometre, assuming no serious competition for food. An arbitrary figure of two-thirds of the theoretical deer density, based on the mean between summer and winter grazing requirements and several studies of deer densities, was adopted to calculate carrying capacities for ranges shared with other large herbivores. This figure, 4.75 deer per square kilometre for summer grazing, is used in all cases except where it is reasonable to assume that reindeer had almost exclusive use of a given area of grazing.

These figures imply extremely low human population densities. A herd of 100 reindeer requires at least 60 square kilometres for its annual grazing requirements, and the annual territory of a nuclear family of between four and five people must have been at least 300 square kilometres.

The economies described are truly predatory and some recapitulation of points about predation is useful. Banfield (1954), Kelsall (1957), and Mowat (1952) have shown that caribou are usually 'warily tolerant' of predation, and that predation tends to weed out the sickly animals. As a general rule a herd of animals is at a selective advantage if it tolerates predation which acts to its long-term advantage and at a selective disadvantage if it fails to tolerate such predation. Conversely, a herd of animals which tolerates predation which is not to its long-term advantage will tend to become extinct. Thus one can assume that reindeer economies which persisted for prolonged periods were not disadvantageous to the animals exploited.

Secondly, there is no *a priori* reason to believe that the reindeer need have been intolerant of human exploitive practices. The Canadian caribou are usually tolerant to the 'starting' method of predation discussed by Mowat (1952). The other method of predation practised by wolves occurs when caribou are scarce and consists of running down fit animals. During this process the animals become frightened. Sturdy (1972a) showed that frightened reindeer will rush past humans making a great deal of commotion, and that they will take routes not used in the normal course of events. I noted also that reindeer tend to move away from what is apparently a disturbance. A further principle can be formulated: that the killing of animals by stealth is to be distinguished from the killing of animals after an open approach. If the approach by stealth is not immediately successful – and a primitive hunter, as well as a wolf, must get very close to a reindeer to make sure of his kill – the animal will flee from the disturbance. This contrasts with the tolerance of open wolf predation. If one animal flees, it is likely to disturb other animals nearby. Hence a third principle is that hunting by stealth or by running animals down will tend to be successful only when the human group is highly mobile and can move away from areas where the deer have been disturbed. In a herd-following economy, the likely long-term selective advantage will go to human groups which establish a reaction by the reindeer to their predation similar to that towards wolves hunting by the 'starting' principle. Situations will obviously occur where it may be desirable to exploit a herd other than that customarily followed. It may not be important if, after killing a few animals, the herd then moves off. Indeed, in some circumstances it may be desirable that a given area of grazing should not be used by other animals than the followed herd.

THE CASE STUDIES

The remainder of this section is devoted to attempts to show what I consider may have actually happened in the Late Würm reindeer economies.

The Delemont and Laufen basins (for the sites see Rütimeyer, 1893; Sarasin, 1918; Bandi, 1947, 1969; Bay, 1952; Schweizer *et al.*, 1959)

Figure 22 plots the sites in relation to topography and other features. The map shows two major grazing areas for reindeer, the large Delemont basin to the west and the smaller Laufen basin in the east, linked by a steep little gorge passing close to Liesberg and by an area of comparatively easy country northwest of the Laufen basin. The Delemont basin can be divided into two regions: the higher northern region above 600 m and the lower southern region between 400 m and 600 m. The potential paths for leaving

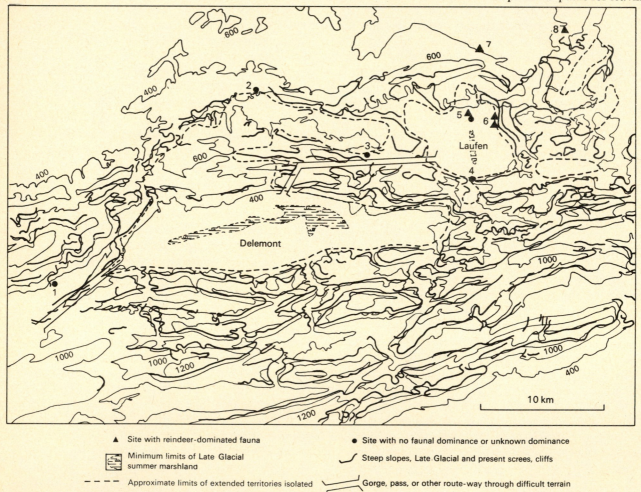

▲ Site with reindeer-dominated fauna

● Site with no faunal dominance or unknown dominance

▨ Minimum limits of Late Glacial summer marshland

〜 Steep slopes, Late Glacial and present screes, cliffs

– – – Approximate limits of extended territories isolated

〜 Gorge, pass, or other route-way through difficult terrain

Figure 22. The Laufen and Delemont Basins. 1–St Brais; 2–Neumühle; 3–Liesberg; 4–Thierstein; 5–Brugglihöhle, Kohlerhöhle; 6–Heidenküche, Kastelhöhle; 7–Buttenloch (Ettingen); 8–Birseck Ermitage, Hollenberg.

the Delemont basin run past the sites of St Brais, Neumühle, and Liesberg, and those for leaving the Laufen basin past Thierstein or past the sites in the Birs valley. The Delemont basin contains *c.* 175 km² of grazing, the Laufen basin 38.5 km², and subsidiary areas raise the total grazing area in and around the Laufen basin to *c.* 45 km². Taking the basins as summer grazing during the Dryas phases, and discounting their marshy areas as unsuitable for use in summer, the carrying capacity of the grazing land can be estimated. The faunal lists from the sites (Sturdy, 1972b) show that the only other important large herbivore was the ibex. Accepting the proposition of Higgs (1961) that all available important food sources tend to be exploited, it is reasonable to assume that no other large herbivore was present in sufficient numbers to influence the reindeer's use of grazing except the ibex. Although the present habits of ibex are not necessarily a very good indication of their habits in the past, it seems probable that most of them would have inhabited the steeper ground and higher small grazing patches in the Jura. It therefore seems justifiable in this instance to use the higher figures of theoretical deer density of 7.15 deer to the square kilometre during the summer months. The herds would then number some 1175 animals in the Delemont basin and 325 in the Laufen basin, corresponding to a total area of grazing of slightly less than 200 km². The total number of animals in both basins could have provided year-round food for about fourteen people or three nuclear families, assuming that a herd-following economy was practised.

The sites marked on the map represent only known sites. Not only have most of these sites been known for many years, but intensive exploration for Palaeolithic sites has taken place in this area since Rütimeyer and the Sarasin brothers found the majority of the sites marked, and I have also examined the area in great detail. From the point of view of an idealised hunting territory it might be supposed that at least one more site might be found with an exploitation territory approximating to the base situation of the ten-kilometre (two-hour) circle. Despite intensive exploration of the centre of the Delemont basin and the adjacent uplands, not a single worked flint was recovered. This evidence is inconclusive, but the long history of palaeolithic exploration in this area and the fact that Neumühle and Liesberg show that even very small artefact assemblages have been recovered suggest to me that little more of importance remains to be discovered about Magdalenian settlement in this area. If there are more sites they must be masked by thick slope deposits.

One striking feature of the situation observed is that all the major sites, and particularly those which can be considered as home bases, occur in the smaller of the two basins, the Laufen basin. The larger Delemont basin has

revealed sites only at its periphery close to routes of exit and entry, all of which have produced few artefacts. Further, the home bases in the Laufen basin – Thierstein and the Kaltbrunnental sites – have very restricted exploitation territories, especially the Thierstein. While the obvious exit points from the Laufen basin are 'covered' by either a home base or a smaller site, it is possible that the suitability of the caves for occupation influenced the distribution of sites more strongly than the exploitation territories available around them. Given the situation described, what economic practices could have provided long-term stability for both humans and reindeer in this area?

The first possiblity is that the animals were approached by stealth and were slaughtered by typical hunting methods – using bows and arrows, harpoons, or spears. If this were the case it is hard to see why the Delemont basin was largely unexploited while large sites occurred in the small Laufen basin. Further, the activities of a hunting band in an area as small as the Laufen basin would soon have alarmed the animals, which would have abandoned the region by going towards Delemont or crossing the Jura. If a hunting economy existed, it must have blocked all the exit points. The most likely exits from the Laufen basin are few, but frightened animals could have found routes across the Jura to the east. Thus, even if sites were located on the most feasible exit points from the basin, they would not have prevented the disappearance of frightened animals, and the number that could have been killed in flight would have been limited. Hunting by stealth does not therefore appear to be a likely hypothesis.

If a close-herding economy operated, the absence of sites in the Delemont basin is even harder to explain, and this possibility can be discounted because close-herding has not been successfully applied to any modern population of reindeer. The first conclusion, therefore, is that we are dealing in this area with an 'intermediate' economy. To understand the way in which such an economy might have operated, a hypothetical reconstruction of events in the spring of a late glacial year is offered.

According to the hypotheses already offered, the reindeer would arrive in the region in late spring after moving down the Rhine valley. To reach the basins, they would pass up the valley of the Birs from Basel, passing the sites along this route. A few reindeer might stay in the Laufen basin, but most would continue into the Delemont basin, perhaps via the gorge in order to arrive first in the lower part of the basin which would provide excellent late spring and early summer grazing, while the higher ground would have been grazed in high summer. The human groups might react in two ways. If a herd-following economy was practised, the humans would have been with the reindeer when they entered the Laufen basin. The objective of their economy at this season would have been to secure their food supply for the following four months of summer. As the deer split into two unequal groups when they reached the Laufen basin, it would have been advantageous for man to influence the splitting process, encouraging those animals which they intended to kill to remain in the Laufen basin, the exits from which were controlled by sites near Birs and Thierstein. Since the main herd in the Delemont basin represented the future capital of the groups in the Laufen basin, efforts would have had to be made to ensure that it did not leave the Delemont basin unobserved. This could have been achieved if a few people, probably young men, blocked the exits at St Brais and Neumühle. Some localities such as Neumühle need have been occupied only immediately before the autumn migration. Throughout the rest of the summer there was little reason for the reindeer to move, because there was adequate grazing and they were not being disturbed by human activity. This hypothesis explains the rarity of finds at St Brais and Neumühle, since their occupants would not have been taking part in any preparation of hides or slaughtering. Even if they did not rely for food on dried meat brought from the bases in the Laufen basin, or if they supplemented this food by occasionally killing ibex and small game, their situation would not have been comparable to that of home bases since they would have been concerned only to supply the short-term needs of a small group. Carcases would have been butchered where they were, and only artefacts used for hunting would have been brought to the site. At home bases, in contrast, tools for hide preparation and countless other purposes are constantly in demand through wear and breakage, and maximum use of carcases must be made, not only because one food-collector is supporting perhaps three or four persons, but also for manufacturing artefacts from bones and antler. Thus the concentration of debris from a one-day stay at a home base will surely be greater than at a site occasionally used by one or two active people.

In the Laufen basin there must have been a behavioural accommodation between men and reindeer such that the reindeer tolerated occasional hunting. Hunting by stealth is improbable, and there is no evidence that the reindeer were tame. Studies of wolf predation on caribou in Canada have, however, shown that caribou are tolerant of wolf predation, and there is no reason why they should not have established a similar relationship with human predators.

One logical extension of the economic methods outlined is to kill all the animals required for the summer at one time in the spring and to live on the stored meat, but the relatively warm late glacial summer may have discouraged this practice. The hypothesis outlined above explains well the unequal distribution and size differences of the sites in the Laufen and the Delemont basins and also illustrates two general principles. First, the late glacial exploitation of this area was probably based on the principle that the main herd is left alone by the humans as much as is compatible with retaining contact, thereby promoting its maximum summer growth. Secondly, the area offers an ideal illustration of the principle of the extended as opposed to the exploitation territories (Sturdy, 1972b). The exploitation territory was the Laufen basin, and those parts of the surrounding hills where ibex were killed. The extended territory was the total grazing area of the herd upon which the humans depended, including those regions not directly exploited by man – in the present case the Delemont basin. This system does not demand that the reindeer are tame, although it would be advantageous if they were amenable to being driven and to some form of 'cutting-out' designed to separate certain animals from the main herd in spring.

The Altmühl group (Schmidt, 1912; Birtner, 1933; Zotz, 1941; Gumpert, 1955; Freund, 1963; Taute, 1970)

Sites: Kastlhanghöhle, Klausen, Heidensteinhöhle near Neuessing; Hohler Stein im Schambachtal near Arnsberg. Between the Altmühl and the Danube lies a region of rolling plateau, into which the steep-sided Altmühl valley is incised (Figure 23).

Naturally defined grazing areas

The steepness of the Altmühl valley and tributaries, such as the Schambachtal, was probably accentuated by gelifraction and the sparse vegetation in the Late Glacial. This area was probably summer grazing for reindeer, its archaeological sites probably occupied by human groups practising some form of herd following. The Kastlhanghöhle is the major late glacial site and reindeer dominate its fauna. The precise time of occupation has an important bearing on the natural boundaries to grazing areas in this region. In early summer the Altmühl must have been in spate, and crossing it would have been extremely hazardous. The river and the steep cliffs must have formed an almost impassable barrier to reindeer until almost the end of July, and even in summer reindeer would probably not have attempted to cross the river except under duress. The Danube in this area is largely surrounded by marsh. Since at that time it drained the Black Forest, where snow probably persisted until late summer, the Danube would have formed a natural barrier to reindeer movement throughout summer, even though it did not run in a gorge. Further, by the time the Danube reaches this region it has been supplemented by several rivers running north from the Alpine ice-sheet, and summer melt-water from the glaciers would probably have inundated considerable areas as well as

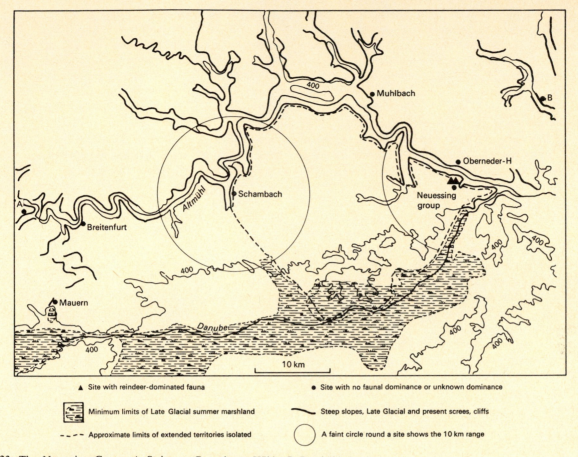

Figure 23. The Neuessing Group. A–Steinerner-Rosenkranz-Höhle; B–Burghöhle Loch.

swelling the flow of the river itself. Hence the group of sites at Neuessing would have been confined to exploiting reindeer on the plateau between the two rivers. The grazing areas can be divided conveniently into two sections. First, the plateau region, stretching from the confluence of the Altmühl and Danube to the steep little valley between Eichstätt and Mauern and covering an area of 855 km². The Schambachtal, however, cuts southwards into this plateau, and southeast of the Schambachtal there is an area where the Danube marshy areas stretch northwest. Although passage is free between these two extensions of the natural boundaries into the grazing area, it is convenient to define the region between the Schambach and the marsh extension and the confluence of the Danube as a sub-area within the main region, 275 km² in extent. Allowing for cliffs and the river which formed barriers, the exploitation territory of the Neuessing group (measured as two hours' walk from the sites) is 88 km², and that of the Schambachtal site is 153 km². Thus the Neuessing exploitation territory is only slightly larger than half the size (56.5 per cent) of the Schambachtal territory.

The economy

Horse, woolly rhinoceros, and other large herbivores existed in the region (Sturdy, 1972b), and it is not reasonable to ascribe the maximum density of deer to this summer grazing, even though the other large herbivores may not have competed seriously with the reindeer for food. Since the reindeer is the dominant food source at the site, it is reasonable to employ the lower density figure of 4.75 deer per square kilometre discussed above. The numbers of deer in the grazing areas and exploitation territories would have been c. 4000 over the whole plateau between the Altmühl–Danube confluence and the Mauern valley, c. 1300 in the smaller unit described, c. 725 within range of the Schambach site, and c. 420 within range of the Neuessing sites. Other relevant figures are the distance between the Schambach and Neuessing, which is 30 km, and between Schambach and the marsh extension to the southwest, which is slightly less than 10 km.

Clearly there were more than enough reindeer within range of the Neuessing sites to supply the needs of a large group over summer. However, the numbers of animals within the exploitation territory were inadequate to supply the yearly requirements of a nuclear family without destroying the herd. Even if the maximum grazing density is assumed for this area, the 625 deer which could have been supported would have supplied the needs of no more than a large nuclear family. It is likely, therefore, that the animals that summered within the exploitation territory of the Neuessing sites were only part of the whole herd on which the human group relied for its yearly subsistence. By definition, therefore, there existed an area outside the exploitation territory which supported resources on which the human group depended, i.e. the site had an extended territory.

The Neuessing sites are not, at first sight, particularly attractive for occupation. Other sites such as the Schambachtal have larger and more accessible exploitation territories. The Neuessing sites face north and receive very little sun, which argues against their winter occupation. In contrast, the Schambachtal receives sun until mid-afternoon. Nor are the Neuessing sites located advantageously for fishing since the fast, wide Altmühl must have been less suitable than the smaller, gentler stream of the Schambach. Nonetheless, the large number of Magdalenian flints at Neuessing (considerably over 5000) implies strongly that the Neuessing sites were the home base. The Magdalenian collection from the Schambach site is tiny and corresponds to a temporary camp similar to those discussed at Neumühle or Liesberg in Switzerland. There must, therefore, be some economic factor which explains the apparent attraction of Neuessing.

Figure 22 suggested the existence of a large basin without home bases and of a small basin which represented the exploitation territory of one or more home bases. In this instance the matter was particularly clear, because the exploitation territories and the inferred extended territories were geographically distinct. At Neuessing the exploitation territory must form part of any hypothetical extended territory. However, the principles suggested for the Delemont-Laufen basin sites might explain the anomaly at Neuessing. The extended territory would be the area in which the herds of reindeer that provided year-round subsistence grazed in summer, and the location of the sites would represent a compromise between the requirements of ensuring an immediate food supply without unnecessarily disturbing the reindeer and of retaining knowledge of any tendency of the deer to move out of a defined grazing area. The Schambachtal site, from which the country between the valley and the marshy lobe northwest of the Danube can be surveyed, was probably equivalent to the 'stop-gap' sites in the Delemont and Laufen basins. This hypothesis explains the paucity of finds at the Schambachtal site despite its apparently favoured location. The main sites occupy the edge

of the grazing area and minimise disturbances to the deer whilst providing easy access to food supplies. The extended territory of the Neuessing sites must have been the area between the Danube–Altmühl confluence and the line drawn down the Schambachtal and across to the lobe of marsh, and the exploitation territory lay at its eastern end. This area could have supported c. 1300 deer, enough to provide a year-round food supply for thirteen people especially if supplemented by other food resources known to have been available. The sparse Magdalenian remains from the Obernederhöhle across the Altmühl valley may represent a temporary camp used for hunting in the area across the river and contributing to the diet of the Neuessing families.

The Moravian karst (Zotz, 1941; Klíma, 1951, 1959; Skutil, 1953; Klíma et al., 1962; Valoch, 1965, 1967)

Archaeological exploration of this area has been intensive, and it is assumed that the distribution of known Magdalenian sites reflects broadly the actual distribution of late glacial occupations.

Naturally defined grazing areas

Figure 24 shows that the Moravian karst lies between the Svitava and Morava rivers, with a wide and rather low basin to the east, and rising ground separating the Moravian basin from the basin of Prague to the west. Much of the Moravian basin to the east is marshy today, and marshes were probably more extensive in the Late Glacial and would have rendered much of the basin unsuitable for reindeer grazing. In contrast, the karst areas are well-drained, and the Moravian karst probably provided summer pasture for reindeer.

The karst area itself consists of a limestone plateau, between 400 m and 600 m o.d. Around the periphery of this plateau the country is usually rough, and probably did not provide good grazing for reindeer although it might have been traversed during migrations. The southern karst is dissected by steep valleys, in which most of the known archaeological sites are located. I have divided the region into five ranges: the plateau; the region which lies between a line drawn from site group 9 on Figure 24 to the rough country to the east, and the southern and western extension of the plateau south of that line; the portion of the preceding region which is defined by the southern and western edges of the plateau and a line drawn north from site 4 to site 6 and thence east to the rough country; the enclave between the steep valleys in which site groups 7, 8, and 9 are situated; and the area on the plateau south of a line drawn northwest from site group 9 towards the rough country.

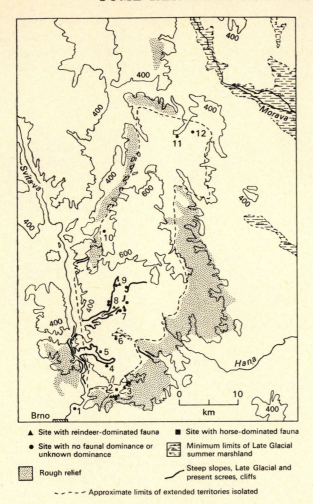

Figure 24. The Moravian karst. 1–Brno Malomerice; 2–Adlerova, Hadi, Krizova, Ochozska, Pekarna, Sveduv stul; 3–Nova Dratenicka, Vinckova, Zitneho; 4–Jachymka; 5–Byci skala; 6–Kolibky; 7–Balcarova skala, Ostrov, Veruncina, Vintok; 8–Katerinska, Konsky spad, Rytirska, Suchdol 9 and 10; 9–Michalowa skala, Kulna, Poustevna, Sosuvska; 10–Sklep; 11–Pruchodice, Sanova dira; 12–Jezevci dira.

Table 3. Possible grazing areas in the Moravian karst and their reindeer population in summer

Range	Area (km²)	Potential deer population
1: total	558	2650
2: southeast	162	780
3: southernmost	67	320
4: central enclave	12.5	59
5: western	35	167

The location of the sites

The major reindeer sites fall into two concentrations, each of which includes at least one home base, and there are also two sites dominated by horse. One of these is located with a group of reindeer sites, the other (Byci skala) is more isolated. These horse-dominated sites may belong to the Allerød phase or they may have been contemporaneous with the reindeer sites.

The Moravian karst plateau possesses numerous obvious exit points, as did the Delemont basin. Virtually the whole northeast edge of the plateau offers easy access to the Morava basin, and there is a further wide gap in the northwest. On the western side, a small gap is filled neatly by the site of Sklep. Further down on the west, the major sites of the northern concentration command the easier descent towards the Svitava. A gap in the southwest corner of the area is stopped by the site of Brno–Malomerice. Turning to the largest gap, in the northeast, it is interesting to find two small Magdalenian sites spaced over this gap. They do not 'stop' the gap as remarkably as Brno-Malomerice or Sklep, but they may have been supplemented by other undiscovered sites. The position of these two sites (actually three, but two occupying identical positions), and of Sklep and Brno-Malomerice precisely in natural entrances and exits, parallels the situation in the Delemont and Laufen basins and must be more than coincidence.

The northern concentration of sites

The sites which form group 9 on the map command a position from which one could observe movements of deer north or south of a line drawn east–west through the Moravian karst. A further curiosity is that the central enclave, over which considerable supervision could have been exercised by the occupants of the site groups 7, 8, and 9, would have supported 59 reindeer in summer. This would provide sufficient food for some fifteen people for the summer

These ranges are referred to hereafter as 1: total area, 2: southeast area, 3: southernmost area, 4: central enclave, and 5: western area. Because remains of large herbivores other than reindeer are frequent in the sites, a density of 4.75 deer per square kilometre has been used. The area and potential deer density of each region are tabulated in Table 3.

The entire Moravian karst would have supported in summer a herd of reindeer sufficient to provide the yearly requirements of about 30 individuals, approximately twice the number estimated for the Delemont–Laufen basins and the Altmühl area. It is, therefore, intriguing that the major reindeer sites in the area form two concentrations separated by 15–20 km.

months, with a small margin of surplus. Since the whole area of the karst provided grazing for enough reindeer to supply the year-round needs of six nuclear families, and since there are two major site concentrations in the region, the fact that the summer food requirements of three nuclear families were contained in the central enclave becomes significant. Those grazing areas which the author has been able to isolate with confidence would have supported food resources for people in multiples of 4.3 to 4.7 persons, roughly equivalent to a nuclear family (see summary). Because the figures discussed concentrate around three nuclear families the analyses may be revealing a consistent tendency which supports the hypotheses advanced earlier. The significant facts are that one of the major concentrations of sites commands a position from which movements of deer from the northern half of the karst area to the southern can be observed and is adjacent to an easily managed area capable of supporting three nuclear families in summer. The northern half of the karst would have supported enough reindeer to provide long-term annual subsistence for those three nuclear families. Finally, the distribution of sites suggests that movements of reindeer northwards out of this area could be observed and perhaps influenced by 'stop-gap' sites. One anomaly is, however, that although the exploitation territories of sites 11 and 12, which occupy possible 'stop-gap' positions, are extremely large and those of the sites in groups 7, 8, and 9 are relatively restricted, evidence for the most intensive occupation comes from the latter sites. One important corollary of considering the central enclave as the potential total exploitation territory of the northern concentration is the small margin of surplus which such an arrangement would provide. In the Jura basins and the Altmühl–Danube sites, the number of animals in the exploitation territories was probably much greater than the immediate summer requirements of the men exploiting them, but this was not the case with the central enclave. If the men were to live off the animals grazing in the central enclave, there would have been little margin for error in the selection of age and sex classes for killing. Indiscriminate killing is rare in the ethnographic records, and the faunal remains from Stellmoor suggested that some selection was practised in the Late Upper Palaeolithic of Europe. If, however, the central enclave was used as a natural corral for animals to be killed in summer, the selection would have had to take place before the animals entered the area, as was probably the case in the Jura basins but not in the larger Laufen basin. The central enclave was demonstrably used on a sustained basis, and some form of selection or conservation must therefore have been practised. In this case the economy can have differed in no essentials from that practised in parts of West Greenland today (Sturdy, 1972b).

In summary, the Moravian karst provided an ideal situation for exploiting reindeer. The year-round subsistence requirements of three families would have been provided by a herd of reindeer pasturing in the northern half of the karst. The animals required in summer could have been kept under close supervision by the three families if they occupied precisely the sites which they did occupy, and movements of the major herd could have been observed from the outlying 'stop-gap' sites. Such a strategy would have had long-term viability, would have minimised disturbances to the herds, and would have required little effort on the part of the human groups other than selecting which animals were allowed to enter the central enclave in spring.

The possible alternatives to this hypothesis are analogous to those discussed for the Jura basins and the Altmühl–Danube sites. Evidence from the southern concentration of sites may suggest which hypothesis is to be preferred.

The southern concentration

Site groups 2 and 3 on the map are economically identical since they relate to the same exploitation territories. A glance at the map will reveal that site groups 2 and 3 are so located that their exploitation territory is virtually the smallest that any possible location of an occupation site in the area could provide. Situated up against the rough country, and limited to the northwest by the Krtinsky stream and to the west by the Svitava valley, the exploitation territory corresponds exactly to range 3 and has an area equal to one-fifth of the maximum of a two-hour exploitation territory. The small site of Kolibky (site 6) is precisely 10 km over easy country from the home bases, and from this site movements of deer west or north out of range 3 could have been observed. Jachymka is 5 km from the home base and from this site one could have observed any deer attempting to move westwards down the Krtinsky valley. It may be assumed once again that the animals in the exploitation territory represented only part of the total herd supplying the yearly requirements of the groups. The number of deer in the exploitation territory of site groups 2 and 3 would have been insufficient to supply the annual requirements of one nuclear family, so that the site groups must have had extended territories, as did site groups 7, 8, and 9. Indeed the extended territories of the two site groups were probably the same: the whole area of the Moravian karst excluding the central enclave and at least part of the southernmost area where the animals which supplied the summer requirements of six nuclear families would have grazed. This hypothesis accounts for the position of the home bases and the smaller sites in relation to the topography and the natural grazing ranges of the animals.

If the pattern of exploitation hypothesised for the two halves of the Moravian karst is correct, the sites in the two major concentrations would not all have been occupied simultaneously. The six reindeer sites of groups 2 and 3 and some of those in the north might provide an example of an annually mobile home base, where the precise siting of a home base inside a general area is not critical and might be changed from year to year, for example to avoid exhausting firewood supplies. Nonetheless, sites such as Kulna in the north and Pekarna in the south, were particularly favoured as bases.

The hypothesis offered can be tested by considering some of the alternatives: for example, that the sites were hunters' villages; that they represent occasional visits of human groups to the area; or that they reflect a full herding economy.

The first hypothesis might be supported by the frequent remains of small game recovered from Balcarova skala, where bird bones were abundant, and Pekarna, where hare formed 37 per cent of the bones recovered. On the other hand, small game is unlikely to have provided a staple item of diet to any Late Upper Palaeolithic group. The 12 000 bird bones from Balcarova probably represented a maximum of 1200 birds, mostly ptarmigan, the meat from which would have been equivalent only to that from six male reindeer, or sufficient to feed a nuclear family for six days. The belief that a hunting economy based on large herbivores, particularly reindeer, was practised is belied by the positions of the southern sites in the least advantageous places for hunting. Where large concentrations of artefacts occur in disadvantageous positions for hunting, it is intrinsically improbable that hunting formed the basis of the economy.

The objections to the second hypothesis revolve around the fact that the exploitive strategies which it suggests would have been relatively unproductive. Even if occasional short visits were made, this does not explain why the sites were located in such unfavourable places for hunting. It could be argued that a single group visited each of the major sites in turn, and that the distribution of the small 'stop-gap' sites resulted simply from the function of those gaps as route-ways, but this leaves too many factors unexplained, and such an explanation would not fit the Altmühl or Jura basin situations. If the mobile hunting group hypothesis is correct, the area would have supported only one-third of the population capable of being supported if the main hypothesis advanced is correct, and in the long term this must render the mobile hunting group hypothesis less likely.

The hypothesis of a ranching economy as practised by the Lapps can be dealt with summarily. Fieldwork in Greenland (Sturdy, 1972a) showed that such an economy might give precisely the distribution of sites noted in this area. On the other hand, it seems superfluous to suggest that any form of semi-domestication occurred, because it is impossible to state exactly what this would have involved.

Steinbergwand (Gumpert, 1932)

In contrast to the reindeer-based economies, the horse-based economy of the Bavarian site of Steinbergwand shows how a site of similar date and material culture but in a different position can illuminate other economic practices. Figure 25 illustrates the situation. The site lies in a gentle valley away from the steep cliffs. To the east lie presumed marshes in what is now the valley of the Naab, which would have been most inhospitable to large herbivores in summer, especially to horses which prefer a firm footing. The marsh continues towards the south where it meets the main valley in which the site lies, at a point where the valley sides are very steep. To the south a steep side-valley offers a restriction on animal movement, and to the west the rough country would probably have carried only sparse vegetation. Only to the northwest is there uninterrupted country for any distance. The location of the site is interesting because in direct contrast to the previous three cases the limits to the practical area of exploitation correspond closely to a circle with a 10 km radius round the site (Figure 25). In this situation, there is no reason to assume that subsistence activities were conducted outside the exploitation territory.

The Schaffhausen–Engen group (Nuesch, 1896, 1904; Peters, 1930; Peters & Toepfer, 1932; Andree, 1939; Bandi, 1947; 1969; Mauser, 1970)

The general situation of this group is mapped in Figure 26, and the details of the smaller sites near Schweizersbild and Kesslerloch are mapped in Figure 27. The second map shows that the smaller sites are concentrated around the two major sites, to which they might have served as occasional alternatives. The fauna from Kesslerloch suggested that this site might have been occupied in the Oldest and Older Dryas phases and in Allerød, while Schweizersbild might be ascribed to the Allerød and Younger Dryas phases. For the present, it seems best to concentrate on the colder periods. I have also suggested (Sturdy, 1972b) that there might have been a period of reindeer importance at Petersfels corresponding to the Older Dryas/Oldest Dryas phase, followed by a period of horse dominance tentatively ascribed to the Allerød. This suggestion is based on the presence at these sites of two apparently incompatible faunal assemblages, one cold and the other relatively warm. Whether Bildstockfels played the same part to Petersfels as did Schweizersbild to Kesslerloch cannot be ascertained without radiocarbon dating. These

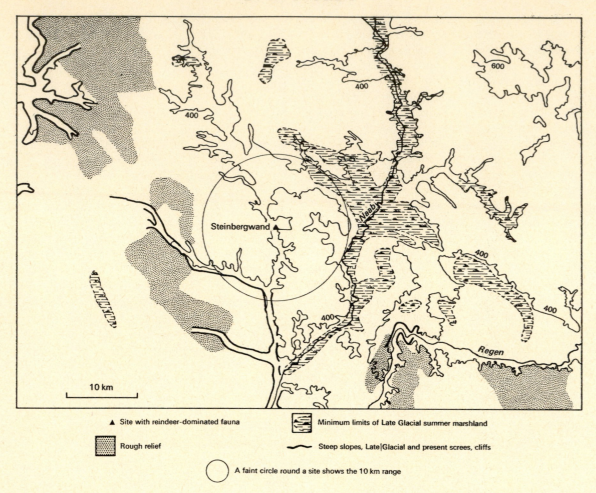

Figure 25. Steinbergwand.

sites were not analysed in detail because the areas in which they lie have been incompletely explored. There appear, for example, to be unexcavated shelters both towards the Bodensee and the Thur river.

Schweizersbild lies at the point where the distance between the Rhine and the hills above Schaffhausen narrows to its minimum. This is an anomalous position because the hills and river severely limit the size of the exploitation territory. Similarly, to the east a tongue of the marshes at the head of the Bodensee reaches northwest towards Kesslerloch, which lies in the gap of firm ground between this tongue of marsh and a line of bluffs separated from the hills behind by a narrow corridor. The marshes continue north and end in an area of undulating plateau country broken by a line of steep little valleys and reentrants. The sites of Petersfels and Bildstockfels lie close to this line of reentrants. To the west, the line of the hills above Schaffhausen follows northwest to a gap between the steep valley of the Wutachtal, where it turns southwest, and scarps to the northeast. Between these scarps and the

marshes of the higher course of the Danube there exists a narrow corridor. The small site of Leipferdingen is placed where movements of animals towards these gaps might be easily detectable. The disposition of these sites would have permitted their occupants to detect attempts by the reindeer to leave the area.

It is not necessary that the two pairs of major sites, Petersfels and Bildstockfels, Schweizersbild and Kesslerloch, should have been occupied simultaneously, since they all served similar functions. Variations in local conditions in the Oldest and Younger Dryas phases might explain why Kesslerloch was inhabited in the earlier phase and Schweizersbild in the later. The grazing area defined by the natural boundaries described is 375 km². The faunal collections from the sites suggest that reindeer was the only important large herbivore, and I have assumed a summer carrying capacity of 7.15 deer per km², giving c. 2700 deer for the whole area. Such a herd could have provided year-round food for 27 people. The lower figure of 4.75 deer per km² would give 1800 deer, providing year-round subsistence for four nuclear families. If the two pairs of major sites are taken to be home bases, each pair might have been occupied by two or three families. Leipferdingen might have been used in the same way as the St Brais and Neumühle sites, the Schambachtal site, or the lesser sites of the Moravian karst. According to the hypothesis proposed, the groups of sites near Schweizersbild and Kesslerloch would not represent villages but the 'annually mobile home base' discussed above.

Supporting evidence for this hypothesis comes from the Schweizersbild which occupies a somewhat peculiar position, since its exploitation territory and that of the smaller sites near it is reduced to an absolute minimum. Other south-facing shelters similar to Schweizersbild are available in the rising ground southwest of the site, and these shelters offer a more advantageous exploitation territory with commanding views. Kesslerloch also has an exploitation territory greatly restricted by marsh and by the bluffs

behind the site. Petersfels has a reasonably large exploitation territory, but that of Bildstockfels is severely reduced by its position in virtually the steepest part of the Wasserburgtal gorge, with easy access only to the northwest. In contrast, Leipferdingen, the site with the least evidence of occupation, has the best exploitation territory after Petersfels. An excellent cave 5 km northeast of Bildstockfels with an advantageous exploitation territory was also apparently ignored. These considerations imply that the location of the four home bases was not determined by the amount of resources in their exploitation territories. Their location near the gaps in the boundaries of a natural grazing area suggests that their principal function was to control access to this area.

A second hypothesis can be suggested. Figure 26 might indicate three extended territories related to the sites of Kesslerloch, Schweizersbild, and Petersfels/Bildstockfels respectively. The Schweizersbild extended territory would

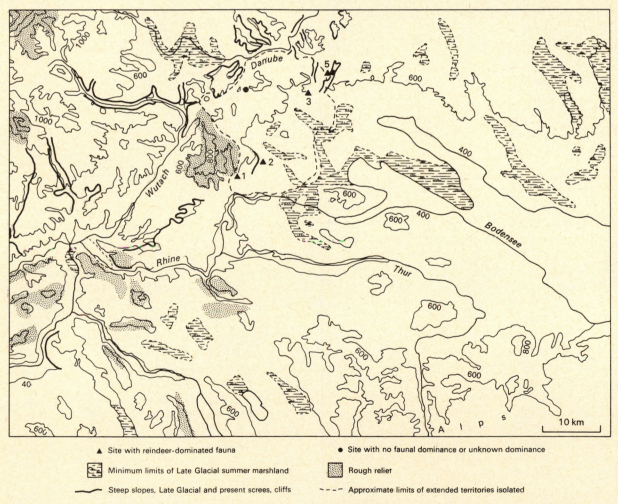

▲ Site with reindeer-dominated fauna   ● Site with no faunal dominance or unknown dominance

Minimum limits of Late Glacial summer marshland   Rough relief

——— Steep slopes, Late Glacial and present screes, cliffs   - - - - Approximate limits of extended territories isolated

Figure 26. The general situation of the Schaffhausen-Engen sites. 1—Schweizersbild; 2—Kesslerloch; 3—Petersfels; 4—Leipferdingen; 5—Bildstockfels.

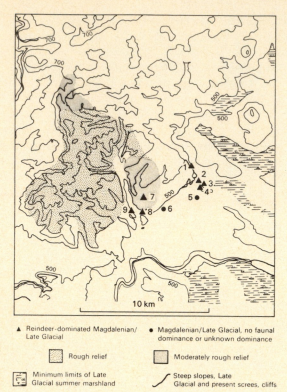

Figure 27. Schaffhausen Group, detail. 1–Kerzenstubli; 2–Kesslerloch; 3–Neue Höhle; 4–Vorder Eichen; 5–Untere Bsetzi; 6–Gsang; 7–Freudenthal; 8–Schweizersbild; 9–Langeberg.

▲ Reindeer-dominated Magdalenian/Late Glacial   ● Magdalenian/Late Glacial, no faunal dominance or unknown dominance

▢ Rough relief   ▢ Moderately rough relief

Minimum limits of Late Glacial summer marshland   Steep slopes, Late Glacial and present screes, cliffs

would contribute little to our understanding of how the economy might have worked, and the arguments adduced against such an hypothesis for the Moravian sites apply equally here.

The man–animal relationship implied by the first hypothesis is unlikely to have been a hunter–prey relationship for reasons already outlined. The sites may have been located to provide surveillance of the grazing area or their location for other reasons may have opened up the possibility of such surveillance. In either case, the man–animal relationship must have resembled that described for the Laufen basin, the Altmühl–Danube, and the Moravian karst sites.

Sites and site groups in the Swabian Alps

Exploration in this area is still too inadequate to attempt to construct a picture of prehistoric economic development in the area as a whole.

Veringenstadt and Strassberg groups (Schmidt, 1912; Peters, 1936; Paret, 1961)

The sites in this group are the two sites of Veringenstadt, Annakapellenhöhle, Nikolaushöhle, and two sites 8 km to the west at Strassberg and Kuhsthallhöhle near Winterlingen. The last site contained a preponderance of horse, but it is unknown whether it was contemporaneous with the other sites. Faunal remains and artefacts from Strassberg are rare, and it was probably not a home base. The Veringenstadt sites may have been a home base, although artefacts were much rarer than at other home bases such as Petersfels. Only Annakapellenhöhle contained a predominance of reindeer, and the lower deer density figure of 4.75 deer per km² was therefore adopted.

Figure 28 illustrates the area of the Swabian Alps under consideration. The Veringenstadt sites lie on the eastern edge of a block of grazing land of 202 km² surrounded by steep slopes, marshland, and strips of boggy ground, close to where a valley breaks the natural features described and provides access to the east. It does not appear particularly likely that this position was selected solely because of the presence of the two caves, since caves are abundant in this part of the valley. Hence the 'stop-gap' location of the Veringenstadt sites is probably significant. The site of Strassberg occupies a similar location.

If the position of the Veringenstadt sites and of Strassberg on easy crossing points is more than coincidence, some hypothesis can be postulated about the working of the economy. Deer grazing in the block of land to the west of the Veringenstadt sites would not normally be able to leave this area by the obvious routes without passing

be the area west of the site, north of the Rhine, east of the steep valleys at the edge of the Black Forest, and north to the deeply incised part of the Wutachtal. The Kesslerloch territory would lie south of the site between the Rhine and the Thur. The Petersfels extended territory would correspond with the natural grazing area described above or might include territory east of the site. This hypothesis is partially supported by the presence at Schweizersbild of stone from the Wutachtal. On the other hand, that part of the extended territory of Kesslerloch beyond the Rhine would have been poor pasture in the Older Dryas because it would probably just have become free of ice, and some parts of it might still have been glaciated. If this hypothesis is correct, small outlying sites should occur, particularly in the neck of land between the hills above Schaffhausen and the deep valley of the Wutach at its bend. Exploration of this area did reveal some indeterminate flints but they were insufficient to support this hypothesis.

A third possiblity, that exploitation occurred solely within the exploitation territories of the sites, would restrict exploitation to the natural grazing area defined above, perhaps with supplementary food-gathering activities occurring outside the site exploitation territories. This theory close to the humans living at the sites. Unless the animals were frightened or stampeded, groups occupying the Strassberg and Veringenstadt sites could be reasonably confident that their food supply would remain in a limited area. The area in question could have supported 950 animals, capable of providing year-round subsistence for 9 or 10 people or two nuclear families. Thus Annakapellenhöhle and Nikolaushöhle might have housed one family each. The Veringenstadt sites are also related to an extended territory to the west. Although this hypothesis cannot be proved, the evidence is consistent with it, and similar economic strategies could be more clearly documented in the other areas described above.

The evidence does not justify further interpretation of the Strassberg site, but it may have been analogous to the St Brais–Neumühle sites near the Delemont basin.

Finally, the two Magdalenian hearths at the Heidensteinhöhle near Bitz deserve comment. This site has yielded few tools and provides a good example of a temporary camp as a migration stop-over camp or, more probably, as a checking point used occasionally to see whether the herds were still within the extended territory of

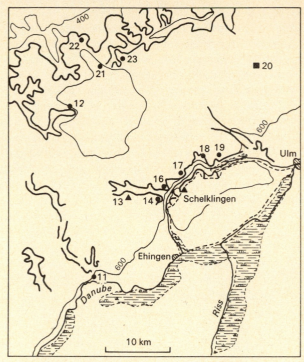

▲ Reindeer-dominated Magdalenian/ Late Glacial   ■ Horse-dominated Magdalenian/ Late Glacial

● Magdalenian/Late Glacial, no faunal dominance or unknown dominance   Minimum limits of Late Glacial summer marshland

◡ Steep slopes, Late Glacial and present screes, cliffs

Figure 29. The Hohler Fels, Schelklingen. 11–Lauterach; 12–Rappenfels; 13–H. Fels, Hutten; 14–Schmiechenfels; 16–Gänserfels; 17–Sirgenstein; 18–Brillenhöhle; 19–Borgerhau; 20–Ursprung; 21–Burkhardtshöhle; 22–Randecker Maar; 23–Papierfels. The Late Würm course of the Danube is shown, rather than its present course.

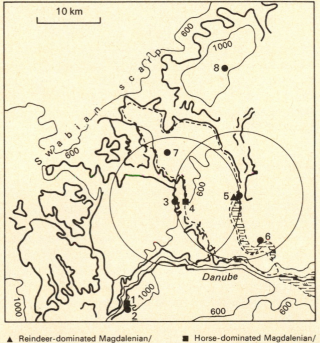

▲ Reindeer-dominated Magdalenian/ Late Glacial   ■ Horse-dominated Magdalenian/ Late Glacial

● Magdalenian/Late Glacial, no faunal dominance or unknown dominance   ◯ A faint circle round a site shows the 10 km range

◡ Steep slopes, Late Glacial and present screes, cliffs   Minimum limits of Late Glacial summer marshland

Figure 28. The Veringenstadt sites. 1–Probstfels; 2–Buttentalhöhle; 3–Strassberg; 4–Winterlingen; 5–Nikolaushöhle and Annakapellenhöhle; 6–Kuhstallhöhle; 7–Heidensteinhöhle; 8–Guppenlochfels. No. 5 is the supposed home base.

the Veringenstadt sites. Occupation of the site was extremely sporadic, which suggests that the exploitation of this area was not by the use of adjacent exploitation territories of ten kilometre radius, but on the extended territory principle.

Schelklingen, Hohler Fels (Schmidt, 1910, 1912)

This site lies just across the valley from the Sirgenstein (Figure 29) and shows a great preponderance of reindeer (Schmidt, 1912), although horse was not uncommon.

During the Late Glacial and main Würm periods, the Danube flowed along the course mapped in Figure 29. The Riss, which now joins the Danube south of Ulm, probably followed the present course of the Danube above Ulm. The low ground between the Pleistocene Danube and the Riss was almost certainly marshy, since the Danube has done little downcutting in this region during the Holocene. The

Danube flowed in front of Hohler Fels and must have hindered and sometimes prevented movements to Sirgenstein. As far as the reindeer were concerned, the most attractive grazing land near the site was the area enclosed between the modern course of the Danube and its Pleistocene course, amounting to 185 km². Because of an area of inundatable land in the first part of the course of the ancient Danube the most probable river crossing for deer wishing to leave this area would have been close to the small site of Schmiechenfels, where reindeer bones are slightly more numerous than horse but where no clear dominance of either species is apparent. The 185 km² of the area isolated would have supported 880 deer in summer, a herd capable of providing year-round food for two nuclear families averaging 4.4 people each. Whatever the precise economy practised in this area, the main site is located in a position which restricts the size of its exploitation territory. Proximity to the river might have been desirable, and several local Magdalenian sites have produced fish bones, but it is improbable that fish were a staple food. It is likely that this situation forms another variant on the pattern which has emerged elsewhere, in which the main sites lie on the edge of a block of grazing land and smaller sites block the exit points from that area. The Schelklingen site may provide an instance where the extended territory is only slightly larger than the exploitation territory, but where the general principles elucidated above still apply.

Other sites in the Swabian Alps

Figure 30 shows the positions of the other sites in this region. Detailed analysis is not possible because the data are insufficient to provide any means of evaluating alternative hypotheses. It is notable, however, that many sites, including those in which reindeer did not predominate, were situated on the edge of blocks of grazing territory. Three sites which did not lie on the edge of steep valleys which reduced the size of their exploitation territories, Guppenlochfels, Klopfjorgleshütte, and Heidensteinhöhle near Bitz, all yielded only very small collections of artefacts. The other site so located, Urspring, yielded a slightly larger collection of artefacts, and its fauna was dominated by horse. In contrast, this region contains twenty sites on the edge of steep valleys or scarp slopes, even though there was no lack of caves in other positions apparently offering larger exploitation territories. At present, although the exact nature of the economies practised can only be guessed at, there is a strong possibility that other sites may have been part of economies involving similar patterns of site location and probably similar methods of exploitation. The most obvious sites have now been found, but new discoveries show that the area is far from exhausted, and with better excava-

tion techniques and a less restricted approach to the search for sites much may yet be learnt.

Sites in Bavaria: Räuberhöhle (Lindner, 1961)

The exact extent of the Magdalenian occupation here cannot be determined because of inadequacies in the early excavations, but it is clear that reindeer was the dominant food animal throughout the Upper Palaeolithic occupation. Curiously, the site lies on a peninsula of land surrounded on three sides by steep cliffs or by the Danube, which must have impeded the movements of men and animals in summer. The site exploitation territory of Räuberhöhle was only slightly over 50 km², under one-sixth of the optimum exploitation territory defined by a radius of 10 km, and any hunting from the site would have rapidly exterminated local game resources. If the site was not a route or transit site (and it lies on no obvious route), it must have been somehow related to subsistence extraction. Its location is reminiscent of the situation of the northern concentration of sites in the Moravian karst, where sites clustered around a similar enclave. A smaller site, the Burghöhle Loch, occurs on the western valley which defines the peninsula, near a point where the cliffs become less steep and passage across the western valley is possible. Hunting or close-herding is inadequate to explain the location of the Räuberhöhle, but its position fits within the range of variation already observed for limited exploitation territories related to extended territories. The economy at Räuberhöhle probably resembled that suggested for the northern concentration of sites in the Moravian karst.

Draisendorf (Mollison, 1934)

Figure 31 illustrates the locations of Draisendorf, where reindeer dominated the fauna, and Rennerfels, a horse-dominated site. Draisendorf is interesting because it occupies the head of a peninsula of land surrounded by steep valleys and slopes and has a small exploitation territory of 37 km². Thus Draisendorf may illustrate another instance of a natural corral similar to Räuberhöhle and the northern part of the Moravian karst.

Stellmoor

Although the economy practised at Stellmoor may have been atypical of the economies of the north European plain it merits analysis, and other similar sites may be assumed to have existed.

Stellmoor is unusual firstly because it is located in a tunnel valley, which provides the only opportunity for concentrating animals by means of natural topography in a

Flachland. Secondly, the different skeletal elements are present in unusual proportions. Antlers are most numerous (1400), followed by phalanges and 200 distal ends of tibiae. Astragali, one of the most indestructible and easily recovered bones, however, number only *c.* 170.

The main periods of reindeer killing at Stellmoor were autumn and spring. A little killing may have occurred all winter but there is no evidence for summer killing. According to my analyses of their movements, reindeer wintered on the *Flachland* and must have been available for hun-

ting. Thus the marked autumn peak of killing and the absence of intensive winter killing require further explanation.

The location of Stellmoor may help to explain these apparent anomalies. The *Flachland* was unlikely to have had deep snow cover in winter except in the valleys, and deep snow drifts probably accumulated only in tunnel valleys, so that Stellmoor may have been quite unsuitable for occupation in mid-winter. If it was occupied its inhabitants would have had to rely on stored meat, but the relative rarity of

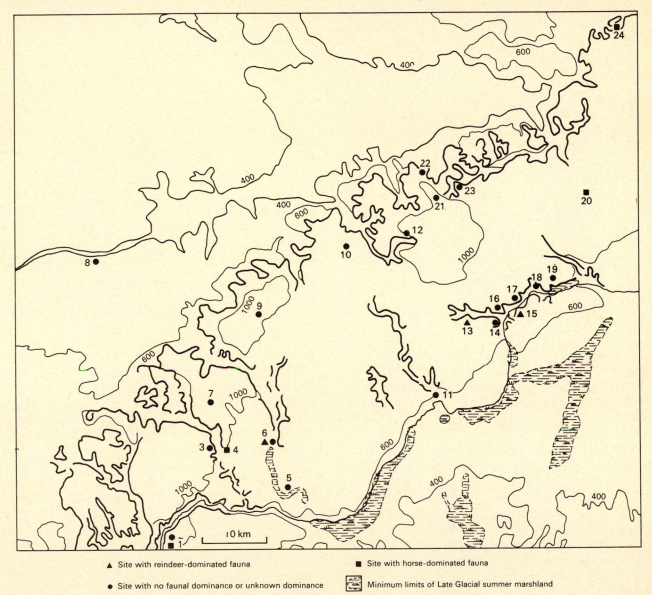

▲ Site with reindeer-dominated fauna   ■ Site with horse-dominated fauna

● Site with no faunal dominance or unknown dominance   ⬚ Minimum limits of Late Glacial summer marshland

Steep slopes, Late Glacial and present screes, cliffs

Figure 30. Sites in the Swabian Alps: general map. 1–Probstfels; 2–Buttentalhöhle; 3–Strassberg; 4–Winterlingen; 5–Kohtalhöhle; 6–Nikolaushöhle and Annakapellenhöhle; 7–Heidenstein (Bitz); 8–Niedernau; 9–Guppenlochfels; 10–Klopfjorgleshütte; 11–Lauterach; 12–Rappenfels; 13–H. Fels, Hutten; 14–Schmiechenfels; 15–Schelklingen; 16–Gänserfels; 17–Sirgenstein; 18–Brillenhöhle; 19–Borgerhau; 20–Urspring; 21–Burkhardtshöhle; 22–Randecker Maar; 23–Papierfels; 24–Klein Scheuer.

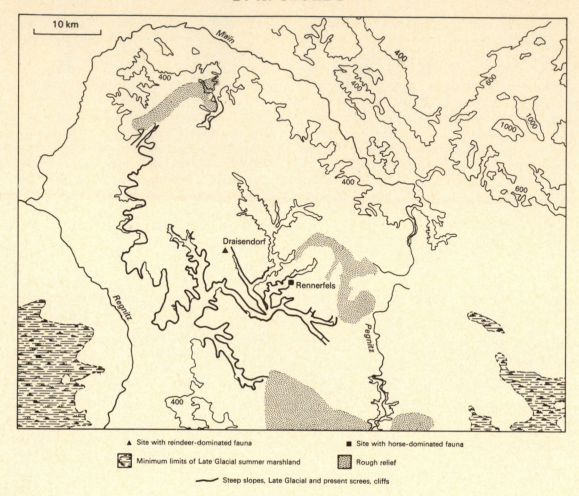

▲ Site with reindeer-dominated fauna　　　　■ Site with horse-dominated fauna

▨ Minimum limits of Late Glacial summer marshland　　▨ Rough relief

── Steep slopes, Late Glacial and present screes, cliffs

Figure 31. Draisendorf.

bone compared with antler renders this explanation unlikely.

The abundance of Hamburgian and Ahrensburgian sites on the *Flachland* may explain the rôle of Stellmoor. Because of the corralling facilities offered by the tunnel valley, Stellmoor may have been used in autumn and spring for slaughtering reindeer. The autumn slaughter would have provided food supplies for winter, the spring slaughter food for the journey south. The site would have been abandoned in autumn before snow-drifts made it inhospitable. But if the groups using Stellmoor in autumn moved elsewhere, why did they do so? If they had adequate meat they could have survived at Stellmoor, yet the bone evidence suggests they did not live on stored food at Stellmoor. One likely explanation is that they occupied one of the sites known on the neighbouring *Flachland*. One reason for doing this would have been to keep watch on the reindeer herds, which would also have permitted occasional killing of fresh meat.

Two further facts are relevant. First, there is the association between reindeer and Lyngby axes. Rust argued that a shouldered or tanged point fitted into the hollowed-out tine of a 'Lyngby axe' was used to kill the reindeer at Stellmoor, and this is corroborated by the perforations in the animals' shoulder blades. Killing was therefore probably done at close quarters. Secondly, the proportion of males to females in the kill is almost 10:1, indicating selective slaughter. Such slaughter might have occurred in two ways. In Canada today males and females often migrate in largely segregated bands. The Ahrensburgian level at Stellmoor might therefore represent successive kills of male bands. Alternatively, the occupants at Stellmoor may have avoided slaughtering females even though they were present. The extreme rarity of females renders this the more likely hypothesis. The tunnel valley is not such a good natural corral that any animals enclosed in it were at the mercy of man. For men to have been able to go amongst the reindeer and kill both selectively and at close quarters shows the difference between the economy practised at Stellmoor and the indiscriminate wounding of caribou at river crossings practised by the recent Caribou Eskimos. The Stellmoor finds indicate an economy in which the reindeer must have been either under human control or at least habituated to man.

It is possible that the autumn slaughters at Stellmoor were rare, but its occupation from the Hamburgian to the Ahrensburgian periods belies this hypothesis. In considering the Stellmoor finds, it is important to distinguish between year-round occupation of a site, living seasonally off stored food, and the seasonal occupation of an area, when the food required for that season is killed at the start of the season and stored. The former idea was rejected because it involved the exploitation of one resource by two human groups, whereas the alternative does not and is more consistent with the archaeological evidence.

The slaughter pattern hypothesised for Stellmoor is virtually identical to the autumn killing practised by the modern Lapps. One of its advantages is that the vital winter grazing is not consumed by animals which are not destined to survive the winter.

CONCLUSIONS

The arguments advanced suggest two generalisations for the reindeer economies studied. Herd following was probably universal among groups mainly dependent on reindeer. Both deer and men would have had to undertake migrations between winter ranges, such as the *Flachland*, the Hungarian plain and the Black Sea littoral, and summer ranges in the Jura, south German highlands, and the Carpathians.

Secondly, the reindeer in the highlands were exploited in a manner which permitted man to observe their movements with a minimum of disturbance to the animals. Thus sites are repeatedly located either on natural routes to blocks of naturally defined grazing or on the edge of such blocks, where their exploitation territories were characteristically much reduced from the theoretical optimum of 314 km². This pattern of distribution precludes the possibility that reindeer were hunted at random. Instead, the economies observed combined the use of a site exploitation territory within two hours' walk of the site and an extended territory supporting the resources on which the humans were dependent but which were not directly exploited by the humans. The two territories may be quite discrete, as in the Laufen–Delemont basins. The exploitation territory may be a geographical part of the extended territory, as in the Altmühl group, or two human groups may combine both types of territorial relationship, as in the Moravian karst. The Schaffhausen–Engen group illustrated a situation where the sum of the exploitation territories of four sites corresponded roughly to the extended territory of any one or all of them, but where the concept of the extended territory was required to understand the workings of the economy. Other variants occur but do not destroy the underlying principle that the animals required for one season are separated and kept near at hand, and that the movements of the main herd from which those animals are drawn are kept under observation.

The populations represented by the economies studied must have been small. Table 4 illustrates the close relationship between the size of the extended territories postulated and the size of the estimated populations of deer and men.

The correspondence between the number of people supported by any of these territories and a multiple of between 4.3 and 4.8 people (except at Keilstein) is interesting since

Table 4.   The sizes of the extended territories

	Area km²	No. deer/ km² (summer)	No. of deer	No. of people	In groups
Laufen–Delemont	200	7.15	1400	14	3 × 4.7
Altmühl–Danube	275	4.75	1300	13	3 × 4.3
Moravian Karst	558	4.75	2650	26–7	6 × 4.4
Schaffhausen–Engen	375	7.15	2700	27	6 × 4.5
		4.75	1800	18	4 × 4.5
Veringenstadt	202	4.75	950	9–10	2 × 4.75
Strassberg	190	4.75	900	9	2 × 4.5
Sirgenstein	660	4.75	3100	31	7 × 4.4
Schelklingen	185	4.75	880	8–9	2 × 4.4
Rheinfelden	200	4.75	950	9–10	2 × 4.75
Keilstein	212	4.75	1010	10	2 × 5.0

this is the average number of people expected in a nuclear family. The consistent ratio of the areas of the extended territories, always in multiples of from 90 to 110 km², is also unlikely to be a coincidence.

In the highland regions humans tended to occupy sites from which movements of deer out of a particular area could be observed. This is practicable in areas of high plateau dissected by obvious natural boundaries, but the situation was quite different in the *Flachland* areas occupied in winter. The anomalies of the Stellmoor finds can best be explained by postulating movement out on the plain to keep track of the movements of the deer. Although the evidence cannot reveal whether herd control was practised, it does indicate selective killing. Nonetheless the frequency of 'stop-gap' sites in the highlands might imply some human control over the movements of the reindeer they exploited. The 'stop-gap' and peripheral site location pattern suggests at least a pre-adaptation to herd control.

REFERENCES

Andree, J. (1939) *Der eiszeitliche Mensch in Deutschland und seine Kulturen.* Stuttgart: F. Enke.

Bandi, H.-G. (1947) *Die Schweiz zur Rentierzeit.* Frauenfeld: Huber & Company.

(1969) Le Paléolithique supérieur en Suisse. *Préhist. Spéléol. ariège* **24**, 55–71.

Banfield, A. W. F. (1954) Preliminary investigation of the barren-ground caribou, parts 1 and 2. *Wildl. Mgmt. Bull., Ottawa* ser. 1, **10A** and **10B**.

Bay, R. (1952) Die Magdalenienstation am Hollenberg bei Arlesheim. *Tätigkeitber. naturf. Ges. Basselland.* **19**, 164–78.

Birtner, F. (1933) Madeleinewerkstätte bei Neuessing, B-U Kelheim. *Bayer. VorgeschBl.* **11**, 55–7.

Bonner, W. H. (1958) The introduced reindeer of South Georgia. *Surv. Rep. Falkld Isl.* **22**, 1–8.

Bouchud, J. (1966) *Essai sur le Renne et la Climatologie du Paléolithique moyen et supérieur.* Perigueux: Imprimerie Magne.

Clark, J. G. D. (1952) *Prehistoric Europe: The Economic Basis.* Cambridge: Cambridge University Press.

Degerbøl, M. & Krøg, H. (1959) The reindeer in Denmark. *Biol. Skr.* **10**(4).

Edwards, R. Y. (1954) Fire and the decline of a mountain caribou herd. *J. Wildl. Mgmt.* **18**, 521–6.

Frenzel, B. (1968) The Pleistocene vegetation of northern Eurasia. *Science, N.Y.* **161**, 637–49.

Freund, G. (1963) Die ältere und mittlere Steinzeit in Bayern. *Jber. bayer. Bodendenkmalpflege* **4**, 9–67.

Galloway, R. W. (1965) A note on world precipitation during the last glaciation. *Eiszeitalter Gegenw.* **16**, 76–7.

Gumpert, K. (1932) Eine neue paläolithische und mesolithische Abrisiedlung an der Steinbergwand bei Ensdorf, Amberg. *Bayer. VorgeschBl.* **10**, 66–7.

(1955) Der altsteinzeitliche "Hohle Stein" bei Schambach, Ldkr. Eichstätt. *Bayer. VorgeschBl.* **21**, 13–21.

Harper, F. (1955) Barren-ground caribou of Keewatin. *Misc. Publs. Univ. Kansas* **6**, 1–163.

Higgs, E. S. (1961) Some Pleistocene faunas of the Mediterranean coastal areas. *Proc. prehist. Soc.* **27**, 144–54.

Higgs, E. S. (ed.) (1972) *Papers in Economic Prehistory.* Cambridge: Cambridge University Press.

Higgs, E. S. & Jarman, M. R. (1969) The origins of agriculture: a reconsideration. *Antiquity.* **43**, 31–41.

Higgs, E. S., Vita-Finzi, C., Harris, D. R., & Fagg, A. E. (1967) The climate, environment and industries of Stone Age Greece, part III. *Proc. prehist. Soc.* **33**, 1–29.

Jong, J. D. de (1967) *The Quaternary of the Netherlands.* In *The Quaternary, Volume 2,* ed. K. Rankama, pp. 301–426. London: Interscience.

Kelsall, J. P. (1957) Continued barren-ground caribou studies. *Wildl. Mgmt. Bull., Ottawa* ser. 1, **12.**

(1960) Co-operative studies of the barren-ground caribou. *Wildl. Mgmt. Bull., Ottawa* ser. 1, **15.**

Klíma, B. (1951) Křížova jeskyně v Moravském Krasu. *Archeol. Rozhl.* **3**, 109–30.

(1959) Archeologický výzkum jeskyně Hadí (Mokrá u Brna). *Antropozoikum* **9**, 277–89.

Klíma, B., Musil, R., Jelinek, J. & Pelisek, J. (1962) Die Erforschung der Höhle Sveduv Stul, 1953–1955. *Anthropos* **13**, 1–297.

Leroi-Gourhan, A. & Brezillon, M. (1966) L'habitation magdalénienne no. 1 de Pincevent, près Montereau. *Gallia Préhist.* **9**, 263–385.

Lindner, H. (1961) *Die altsteinzeitlichen Kulturen der Räuberhöhle am Schelmengraben bei Sinzing.* Kallmünz: Michael Lassleben.

Mauser, P. F. (1970) Die jungpaläolithische Höhlenstation Petersfels in Hegau. *Bad. Fundber.* **13.**

Møhl, U. (1970) Fangstdyrene ved de Danske strande. *Kuml,* 1970, 297–329.

Mollison, Th. (1934) Ein paläolithisches menschenähnliches Idol aus Oberfranken. *Bayer. VorgeschBl.* **12.**

Mowat, F. (1952) *People of the Deer.* London: Michael Joseph.

Nuesch, J. (1896) Die praehistorische Niederlassung am Schweizersbild bei Schaffhausen. *Neue Denkschr. schweiz. naturf. Ges.* **35**, 219–327.

(1904) *Das Kesslerloch, eine Höhle aus paläolithischer Zeit.* Zürich: Zurcher & Furrer.

Paret, O. (1961) *Württemberg in vor- und frühgeschichtlicher Zeit.* Stuttgart.

Peters, E. (1930) *Die altsteinzeitliche Kulturstätte Petersfels.* Augsburg: Dr. Benno Filser Verlag.

(1936) Die altsteinzeitlichen Kulturen von Veringenstadt. *Prähist. Z.* **27**, 173–95.

Peters, E. & Toepfer, V. (1932) Der Abschluss der Grabungen am Petersfels bei Engen. *Prähist. Z.* **23**, 155–99.

Pruitt, W. O. (1959) Snow as a factor in the winter ecology of the barren-ground caribou. *Arctic* **12**, 158–79.

Rust, A. (1943) *Die alt- und mittelsteinzeitlichen Funde von Stellmoor.* Neumünster in Holstein: Karl Wachholtz Verlag.

Rütimeyer, L. (1893) Neuere Funde von fossilen Säugetiere in der Umgebung von Basel. *Verh. naturf. Ges. Basel* **9**, 420.

Sarasin, F. (1918) In Die steinzeitlichen Stationen des Birstales Zwischen Basel und Delsberg, by H. G. Stehlin. *Neue Denkschr. schweiz. naturf. Ges.* **54**(2), 72–291.

Scheffer, V. B. (1951) The rise and fall of a reindeer herd. *Scient. Mon.* **73**, 356–61.

Schmidt, R. R. (1910) *Der Sirgenstein und die diluvialen Kulturstätten Württembergs.* Stuttgart.

(1912) *Die diluviale Vorzeit Deutschlands.* Stuttgart: E. Schweizerbartsche Verlagsbuchhandlung.

Schweizer, Th., Schmid, E., Bay, R., Stampfli, H. R., Forcart, L., & Fey,

L. (1959) Die Kastelhöhle im Kaltbrunnental, Gem. Himmelried. *Jb. solothurn. Gesch.* **32,** 3–88.

Šegota, T. (1967) Paleotemperature changes in the Upper and Middle Pleistocene. *Eiszeitalter Gegenw.* **18,** 127–41.

Skuncke, F. (1969) Reindeer ecology and management in Sweden. *Biol. Pap. Univ. Alaska* **8,** 1–82.

Skutil, J. (1953) Výzkum aurignackého sídliště v Řevnicich u Prahy. *Archeol. Rozhl.* **5,** 721–5.

Strickon, A. (1965) The Euro-American ranching complex. In *Man, Culture, and Animals,* ed. A. Leeds and A. P. Vayda, pp. 229–58. Washington, D.C.: American Association Advancement Science.

Sturdy, D. A. (1972a) The exploitation patterns of a modern reindeer economy in West Greenland. In *Papers in Economic Prehistory,* ed. E. S. Higgs, pp. 161–8. Cambridge: Cambridge University Press.

(1972b) Reindeer economies in late Ice Age Europe. Unpublished Ph.D. dissertation, University of Cambridge.

Taute, W. (1968) *Die Stielspitzen-gruppen im nordlichen Mitteleuropa.* Köln: Böhlau Verlag.

(1970) Die mittel- bis jungpaläolithische Stratigraphie im Hohlen Stein bei Böhmfeld (Bayern) und die Frage einer Höhlenbären-schädeldeposition. In *Actes VII Cong. Int. Sci. préhist. protohist.,* ed. J. Filip, pp. 308–11. Prague: Inst. Archéol. Acad. Echèch. Sci.

Thomson, D. F. (1939) The seasonal factor in human culture. *Proc. prehist. Soc.* **10,** 209–21.

Valoch, K. (1965) Magdalenien na Morave. *Anthropos* **12,** 1–105.

(1967) Paleolitické osidlení jeskyně Kolny u sloupu v Moravském Krasu. *Archeol. Rozhl.* **19,** 566–75.

Vértes, L. (1964–5) Das jungpaläolithikum von Arka in Nord-Ungarn. *Quartär* **15–16,** 79–132.

Zotz, L. (1928) Die paläolithische Besiedlung der Teufelskuchen am Ölberg bei Kuckucksbad. *Prähist. Z.* **19,** 1–53.

(1941) Eine Karte der urgeschichtlichen Höhlenrastplätze Gross-Deutschlands. *Quartär.* **3,** 132–55.

4. PREHISTORIC SETTLEMENT AND LAND USE IN SOUTHERN BULGARIA

R. W. DENNELL AND D. WEBLEY

This paper attempts some preliminary assessments of the economic basis and development of Neolithic and Bronze Age settlements in southern Bulgaria. In recent years, the density and continuity of prehistoric settlement in this region have elicited much investigation and comment. Most of this attention has been directed towards the chronological and cultural aspects of these settlements, or particular features of their development, such as their metallurgy. Despite this degree of interest, little is known of the basic economy, of the animal and crop husbandry, and almost nothing of the underlying primary factors which influenced and perhaps directed the frequency, location, continuity of occupation, and development of these sites.

In order to investigate these problems, two areas were selected for investigation, one c. 35 km square, centred around the modern town of Nova Zagora 300 km east of Sofia, and the other in the region of Čelopeč 200 km west of Nova Zagora.

The Nova Zagora area is especially suitable for study. It affords a well-defined cross-section of a wide valley system which, by reason of the density of archaeological sites, must have been highly suitable for prehistoric settlement. Secondly, a wide variety of soils is found within this area, which provided an opportunity of examining whether or not soil types influenced the location of prehistoric sites. Thirdly, more archaeological exploration has occurred in this area than elsewhere in Bulgaria; most of the settlements have already been surveyed, and some excavated. Moreover, excavations at some of these sites, especially at Karanovo (Georgiev, 1961) and Ezero (Georgiev & Merpert, 1965), attest not only the high degree of cultural development within this area in prehistory, but also provide a convenient chronological framework within which prehistoric settlement can be considered.

In contrast, the Čelopeč region contains only a few Neolithic and later sites which are generally smaller and occupied for shorter periods than those of the Nova Zagora region.

Data for this study have been collected by means of site location analysis (Higgs & Vita-Finzi, 1972). By this means an endeavour has been made to assess the factors underlying the location of sites and the prehistoric economic development of the area. Excavations have indicated that some form of mixed farming economy was practised from the sites. Therefore, emphasis was placed on the collection of information about soils, which it was suspected would have been an important factor controlling the location of sites and agricultural practices.

THE NOVA ZAGORA REGION

Figures 1 and 2 show the prehistoric settlements within the Nova Zagora region. The northern boundary of this area is marked by the hills of the Sredna Gora, which rise to c. 500 m o.d. Most of these hills are covered with a thin stony soil, in places barely able to support rough grazing. However, there are some widely scattered pockets of alluvial soil on which some cultivation is feasible.

South of these hills, there extends a wide plain, about 150 m o.d., broken by occasional outcrops of the Sredna Gora, such as the hills of Svetli Iljija. Today this area is one of Bulgaria's most fertile regions, where wheat, maize, fruit, cotton, and tobacco are grown. Although the plain at first sight appears uniform, it can be divided into two sharply contrasting zones. The northern part contains more settlements, modern as well as prehistoric, and also a greater, and generally lighter, range of soils than the southern part. The latter area consists almost entirely of smolnitzas (see below), which have only recently been drained and opened for cultivation. Thus as one traverses this region from north to south, there is a progression from the thin, stony, and infertile soils of the Sredna Gora to the deep, clayey, and immensely fertile smolnitzas.

The climate of the whole area is less extreme than it is in much of Bulgaria, and is more Mediterranean than Continental. In summer mean temperatures are rarely above 25°C and rarely below freezing in winter. The mean rainfall is about 500 mm per annum, most of which is concentrated in the winter season. The region is well-provided with water, both from springs and rivers. The availability of water would probably not have been a critical factor affecting human settlement.

Soils

Within Bulgaria, over sixty distinct soils have been

recognised (Koniev, 1966). For our purposes it is sufficient to discern four groups.

(1) Cinnomonic Forest Soils. This is one of the main soil groups in southern Bulgaria. It was originally formed during Pliocene and early Pleistocene times under more extreme bio-climatic conditions than today. In its unaltered form it is found only in isolated pockets at the edges of valleys. On slopes of greater than 2 per cent, and especially those of more than 6 per cent, these Forest Soils are found in varying states of erosion and are characterised by a much smaller proportion of clay and silt particles. They are found most commonly in a leached form, marked by high acidity and low phosphate levels. Where pseudo-podsolisation has occurred, they are low in nitrogen, phosphates, and organic matter.

(2) Chernozem-smolnitzas. This important group of soils has accumulated in basins overlying Pliocene and lower Pleistocene deposits. In general they originated on the lowest elevations and gentlest gradients of a valley system, where drainage was impeded, and thus the deposition of

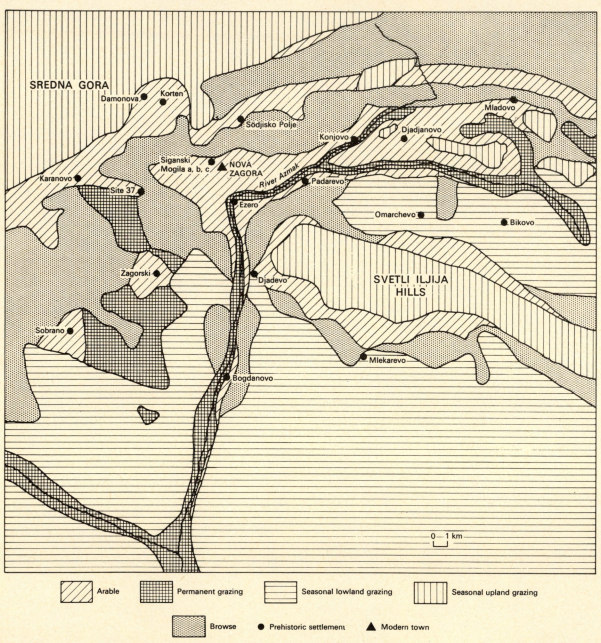

Figure 1. Neolithic and Eneolithic settlement and land use in the Nova Zagora region.

clay particles was facilitated. As they were also formed under conditions where humidity exceeded evaporation, the decomposition of organic matter was arrested, and in consequence drainage was impeded still further. They are associated in their early stages of formation with a meadow-bog type of vegetation. As organic matter accumulates, this is succeeded by a grass steppe, or on the better drained parts, by tree and scrub cover.

(3) Diluvial sandy soils. These soils, found at the foot of hills as fans and shelves, are derived from hill deposits

which have been resorted by erosion. These soils are stony and well-drained, but their grain size depends to a large extent upon local factors, such as the gradient of the parent slope and the rate of erosion. Fed by silt-laden waters, they are intermittently recharged with plant nutrients. Today, vines, lavender, or oats are grown on these soils, which are regarded as greatly inferior to more fertile but heavier soils, such as the smolnitzas.

(4) Riverine soils. Two types of riverine soils can be distinguished, one formed mainly of sand, the other of clay.

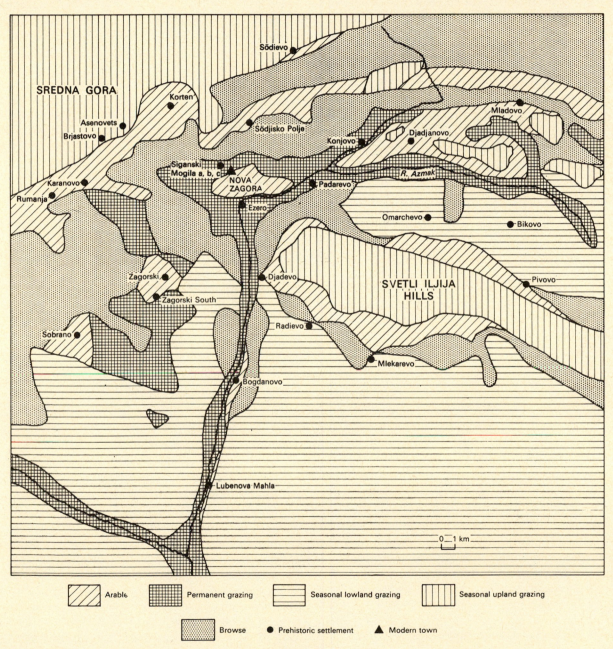

Figure 2. Early Bronze Age settlement and land use in the Nova Zagora region.

The sandy type of riverine soil (a) is found along the upper reaches of a river, where the gradient is steep, and thus the carrying capacity of the river is greater. More commonly in the Nova Zagora region, however, riverine soils are characterised by a high clay content. (b) These are found further downstream, where the gradient decreases, and the slower flowing waters allow the deposition of clay and silt particles. As the Nova Zagora plain is virtually level right up to the Sredna Gora hills, riverine clays are common along all the rivers in this area. Moreover, the formation of smolnitzas in the lower part of the plain (see below) would have reduced the river gradient further; as a result, clay and silt particles would have been deposited progressively further upstream.

Many of the above soil types grade into each other and result in a variety of 'soil ecotones'. These can be particularly advantageous to a primitive technology. Fertile soils too heavy to till are mechanically more amenable where there is an admixture of the less fertile sandy soils, and the sandy soils are made more water retentive and more productive by the inclusion of a heavier component.

The tillage potential

With a Neolithic or Bronze Age technology, only the lighter, better drained soils of the Nova Zagora region would have been accessible for cultivation. Thus arable agriculture would have been limited to the diluvial sandy soils, the sandy riverine soils, the eroded form of the Forest Soils, and the leached form where it was adjacent to one of the lighter soils. Wheat would have been best suited to the heavier of the soil ecotones and barley to the lighter sands, so that the ratio of these two cereals would have varied from site to site according to the soil distribution pattern. Neither the heavy, poorly drained chernozems and smolnitzas nor the riverine clays would have been workable at that time. Only by means of large-scale drainage and the advent of heavy ploughs and tractors has the high fertility of these soils been released for crop cultivation and even today the heavier riverine clays are usually associated with wet meadows or marsh.

The grazing potential

There is a wide variety of soils which are unsuitable for arable agriculture but which are of varying potential for animal grazing. We have classified them as follows.

(1) Year-round grazing. Animals could have been pastured throughout the year only in areas with soils which retained enough moisture to provide good grazing throughout the dry summer months. The most important source of such grazing would have been some of the smolnit-zas on the lowest parts of the plain, where drainage is most impeded, and the riverine clays along the River Azmak and its tributaries. Although these soils would have supported year-round grazing, they would have been of critical importance in the late summer when the other soils became too dry to provide good grazing.

(2) Seasonal grazing. Within this category we have recognised two types. (a) Lowland grazing. This could have occurred on those smolnitza soils which are too dry in summer to provide grazing throughout the year, and too heavy to be tilled. (b) Upland grazing. Upland grazing could have taken place on the Sredna Gora and its associated outcrops such as the Svetli Iljija hills. Because the hill soils in this region are thin and stony, and rainfall is low, hill grazing in summer is parched and sparse.

(3) Browse. It is difficult to estimate how extensive the prehistoric tree cover might have been, but some soils would have supported forest vegetation. It is certain to have been more widespread than today, and forest would probably have covered some of the Cinnomonic Forest Soil. Such tree cover would have provided a useful source of browse, winter fodder, and shelter for livestock.

Geomorphological change

We have discussed the landscape as though it had remained largely unchanged through time. However, the possibility of different conditions during the period under consideration must be taken into account.

There is no reason to suppose that the main formations of the Cinnomonic Forest Soils and the diluvial sandy soils were not already in existence when the area was occupied in the sixth millennium B.C. At Karanovo, and also at Kazanluk 100 km to the west, the initial Neolithic settlements were founded on diluvial fans which graded into Cinnomonic Forest Soils. The site of Djadevo (Figure 1:19), believed to contain a Neolithic horizon, also overlay a Cinnomonic Forest Soil. We found no evidence that either of these soil types had changed substantially since that time.

Greater hazards are involved in dating the smolnitza formations in this area, for their age varies according to their location and source. In Czechoslovakia, chernozems overlying marls have been dated to c. 5000 B.P., and those on clays to c. 9000 B.P. (Nemecek, 1971). The ages of chernozem-smolnitza formations from various locations in Europe generally support the hypothesis that they were formed in early postglacial times. Near Goljama Detelina, 35 km south of Nova Zagora, a deep gully exposed smolnitzas which directly and conformably overlie gravels believed to be of Pleistocene age. This would suggest that some at least of the smolnitzas in the Nova Zagora region were already in existence when agricultural communities were founded. Figure 1 illustrates the probable geomorphology of the region prior to and during the Neolithic.

There is, however, some evidence that smolnitzas continued to form after this date. At Brezevo, 30 km northeast of Plovdiv, a chernozem formation was observed overlying an occupation horizon which can be dated to the Early Bronze Age (Detev, 1954). This evidence could indicate a secondary phase of smolnitza formation, although it does not preclude the possibility that such soils were formed continuously until the Bronze Age. Whichever viewpoint is taken, it is possible that some minor Neolithic sites may have been buried by subsequent smolnitza formations. At the same time, we do not feel that this need seriously affect our observations. As smolnitzas are formed where drainage is impeded, it seems unlikely that such areas would have been favourable for prehistoric settlement of the kind studied in this paper.

The formation of smolnitzas in the Early Bronze Age appears to have been accompanied by other geomorphological changes, some of which could have had profound effects upon the agricultural economies of the area studied. These changes involved erosion in the Sredna Gora, and deposition in the plain.

At Brjastovo (Figure 2), an Early Bronze Age settlement on the edge of the Sredna Gora had been severely eroded; however, a nearby Late Bronze Age and Iron Age site had not been so affected. A similar situation was found at Omarchevo (Figure 2), to the north of the Svetli Iljija hills: this Early Bronze Age tell had been severely eroded, although an overlying tumulus of Iron Age, or possibly later date, had not suffered erosion. At Djadevo, pottery-laden gravels adjacent to the site indicated that erosion had been severe during or after the Early Bronze Age. This site rises to 18 m in height, but it appears that only the top 3 m represent archaeological deposits, the lower 15 m resulting from erosion of the surrounding plain rather than the accumulation of occupational debris. Much of the material eroded from the hills must at this time have been deposited on the plain. Prior to this erosional episode, while the drainage pattern must have been similar, soil depth on the hills would have been greater and would have supported a denser vegetation than is found on them today.

It seems likely that the deposition of the large sheet of riverine clay along the upper reaches of the River Azmak is connected with the above erosional phase and was of Early Bronze Age date or slightly later. In the vicinity of Ezero and further downstream near Lubenova Mahla (Figure 2), Early Bronze Age pottery was found overlying a leached form of the Cinnomonic Forest Soil, and was sealed by riverine clay. A similar situation is found at Brezevo, where an Early Bronze Age horizon was covered by a smolnitza formation. At Ezero there is a sharp difference between the

Late Neolithic and Early Bronze Age layers. Whereas the former are light-coloured and similar to the eroded form of the Cinnomonic Forest Soil, the Early Bronze Age levels are like the darker and heavier riverine clays. Although tells are largely a result of the accumulation of occupational debris, their deposits are also derived from the soils contemporaneous with and adjacent to the settlement and would be expected to be representative of them. Another indication of the increasingly impeded drainage around Ezero is the appearance in Early Bronze Age levels of *Lycopus europaeus*, a plant suited to damp and marshy conditions, as well as an increase in the quantity of shell-fish and fish remains (Dennell, in Merpert, Georgiev, & Katincherov, in press).

The deposition of these riverine clays would have considerably reduced the area available for cereal cultivation, for even today, much of this soil is unsuitable for crop cultivation and is used instead as pasture for cattle. It appears that these soils have never attracted settlement: in spite of the numerous tumuli found in this area dating to Iron Age and medieval times, virtually none are found on the riverine clays. It is possible that the abandonment of many of the tells in this area was due in part to the deposition of such clay formations. The effects of these changes upon the land utilisation is shown by the contrast between Figures 1 and 2.

Sites and economies

The general features of the sites have been described elsewhere (Georgiev, 1961; C. Renfrew, 1969; Tringham, 1972). Unexcavated sites have been dated by surface pottery collections (Table 1). All of them are tells and represent the greatest known concentrations of prehistoric settlements within the area. It is possible that there were other living sites, relating to summer grazing on the Sredna Gora and on the smolnitzas, which were of too ephemeral a nature to leave evidence in the archaeological record.

Evidence from excavations is at the present time minimal, for little of the data has been both adequately collected and studied. Einkorn, emmer, and pulses have been recovered from Karanovo 1 contexts at Karanovo (J. M. Renfrew, 1969), Chevdar, and Kazanluk, and barley is also present at the latter two sites (Dennell, 1972, 1973). A little more is known of the Early Bronze Age crop husbandry. At Ezero, emmer, six-rowed naked barley, and legumes appear to have continued as the main crops. The main elements of a rotational system were therefore present, and in order to maintain fertility and reduce the area under fallow, such a system may have been practised. At the nearby and slightly later site of Siganski Mogila, emmer and lentils have been recorded.

Table 1. Height and estimated dating of sites in the Nova Zagora region

Site	Height	Neo-lithic	Eneo-lithic	Bronze Age	Iron Age
Rumanja	6 m			×	
Karanovo	12 m	×	×	×	
Brjastovo	2 m			×	
Asenovets	3 m				×
Damonova	3 m	×			
Korten	12 m	×	×	×	
Södjisko Polje	6 m	?	×	×	
Södievo	2 m			×	
Site 37	3 m	×			
Siganski Mogila: a	4 m			×	
b	3 m	×			
c	3 m		×		
Ezero	12 m	×	×	×	
Padarevo	10 m	×	×	×	
Konjovo	6 m		×	×	
Djadjanovo	10 m	×	×	×	
Mladovo	10 m	×	×	×	
Sobrano	10 m	×	×	×	
Zagorski	12 m	×	×	×	
Zagorski South	3 m		×		
Djadevo	3 m	?	×	×	
Omarchevo	4 m		×	×	
Bikovo	6 m	×	×	×	
Pitovo	3 m		?	×	
Bogdanovo	3 m		×	×	
Radievo	4 m		×	×	
Mlekarevo	6 m	?	×	×	
Lubenova Mahla	3 m		×	×	

As no faunal material from Neolithic sites in the Nova Zagora region has yet been studied, it is necessary to refer to other Neolithic sites in southern Bulgaria. At Chevdar and Kazanluk the commonest animals were caprines, which still form the mobile element in the traditional economies of the Balkans. Cattle, deer, and pig were also exploited. Our territorial analysis shows some poorer land which is probably suitable mainly for sheep or goat husbandry and richer, wetter clay land suitable for exploitation by cattle. At Bikovo and Ezero in the Eneolithic and Early Bronze Age levels the same association of species is recorded, but cattle were reported as the commonest animals (Ivanov, 1965). However, subsequent data collection by sieving at Ezero suggests that better recovery techniques might reverse this conclusion, and that caprines

were in fact in the majority. It must be remembered that cattle produce so much more meat per individual than the caprines, that if the latter are in the minority, they are likely to have played only a very minor rôle in the production of animal protein. The territorial analysis suggests that there was in fact a considerable opportunity for caprine exploitation.

Area exploitation and site territories

The territories of Neolithic and Eneolithic sites are shown in Figure 3, and those of Early Bronze Age sites in Figure 4. Territorial overlaps have been omitted and it is evident not only that the individual sites were located so that they could exploit the resources within their territories to good and even the best advantage, but also that the sites were so distributed that, given even a measure of site contemporaneity, they fully exploited the entire region.

The average distance between sites is about 5.2 km. Several pairs of sites, however, such as Karanovo and Rumanja (Figure 2), Brjastovo and Asenovets (Figure 2), Korten and Damonova (Figure 1), and Zagorski and Zagorski South (Figure 2), are much less than 5 km apart and appear to have been competing for the same resources. This may have been true for the Korten–Damonova and Zagorsky–Zagorsky South pairs. Damonova is a small tell, which was occupied only during the Karanovo IV period, whereas the nearby site of Korten is a large tell with Neolithic through Bronze Age levels. Either they represent a situation where, for a short period of time, the resources of an area were more effectively exploited from two different points within that area, or Damonova may be an instance of a short-term unsuccessful attempt to over-exploit an area. A similar situation is seen in the case of Zagorski, a large tell occupied from the Neolithic to the Bronze Age, and Zagorski South, a small tell occupied only during the Eneolithic period. With the other paired sites, however, there would have been little competition, as they were either not occupied contemporaneously or the period of overlap was very short. As Table 1 shows, Asenovets was occupied later than Brjastovo; Rumanja, believed to be of Early Bronze Age date, was occupied later than the major occupation at Karanovo, where there is only one thin Early Bronze Age horizon.

The economic orientation toward arable agriculture is evident from the high density of sites in the northern part of the region, where the good arable soils are most extensive (Figures 1 and 2), and from the location of sites on or near these soils. Chisholm (1968) has pointed out that net agricultural output drops at least 15–20 per cent with each kilometre that a parcel of land is removed from a farmstead. Thus it can be seen that the sites in the Nova Zagora region are situated so as to take the best advantage of the available arable land. This is particularly noticeable in the case of the Neolithic settlement pattern, in which almost every site is located on potentially arable soil. By Eneolithic and Bronze Age times the amount of good arable land had decreased and the number of sites increased, thus forcing settlement of the more marginal areas with poor drainage and less workable soils.

It seems likely that the economies of these sites included a mobile pastoral, as well as a primary arable, element: the mobile-cum-sedentary economy. During the Neolithic period the quantity of year-round grazing would have been very limited, and it seems unlikely that the available seasonal grazing cycle would have remained undiscovered. In fact, it would have required strict control to prevent the animals from following it themselves. One can visualise this simple seasonal cycle as the wintering of flocks on the better drained lowland areas and movement to the hills for spring and early summer. Later in the summer parching of the upland grazing would have reduced its carrying capacity, and

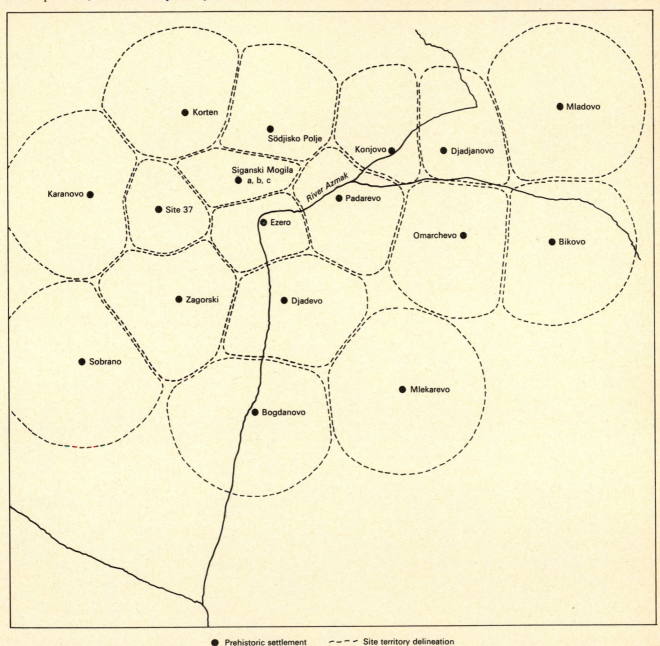

● Prehistoric settlement   - - - - Site territory delineation

Figure 3. Neolithic and Eneolithic site territories (omitting overlap) in the Nova Zagora region.

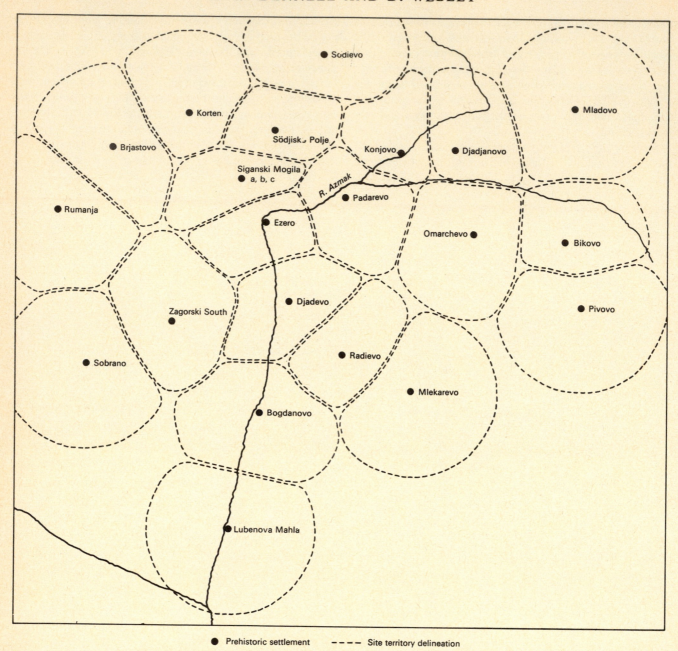

● Prehistoric settlement　　- - - - Site territory delineation

Figure 4. Early Bronze Age site territories (omitting overlap) in the Nova Zagora region.

while most of the stock could have remained on the hills, the immediately productive animals would probably have returned to the lowlands to make use of the stubble fields and the richer grazing provided by areas of heavy, water-retentive soils. By this means there could have been a greater animal population than could have otherwise been maintained. By the Early Bronze Age the area of year-round grazing had increased, but a continuation of the seasonal pattern described for the Neolithic period would

have allowed higher stocking levels through the utilisation of all the newly available grazing resources.

The site territories can be divided into three classes based on the amount of potentially arable land within a 2 km radius of the site (Tables 2–4): (1) greater than 50 per cent arable (with a Neolithic or Bronze Age technology), (2) 25–50 per cent arable, and (3) less than 25 per cent arable. It is well known that land used for cereal production will support a higher population than a similar area of land used for meat production. It is therefore of great interest to note the correlation between tell height, length of occupation, and the category into which its territory falls. The largest tells, such as Karanovo with a height of 12 m, are associated with territories composed of large amounts of potentially arable land, and the smallest, such as Södievo with a height of only 2 m, have territories consisting mainly of potentially grazing land. There are a number of factors which may have influenced tell size, such as the type of building material used and the rate of reconstruction. However, it seems reasonable to suppose that the larger tells, which were associated with the potentially most productive site territories, were actually the larger settlements.

Table 2. Percentage representation of land use categories within 2 km radius of site: sites with greater than 50 per cent arable

| Site | Arable | Permanent | Grazing seasonal | | Browse |
			Lowland	Upland	
Ezero (Neolithic)	81.3	16.4	–	–	2.3
Korten	79.8	–	–	15.4	4.8
Siganski Mogila (Neolithic)	74.5	–	–	–	25.5
Damonova	64.4	–	–	35.6	–
Djadjanovo	59.8	31.8	–	8.4	–
Konjovo (Eneolithic)	59.6	16.5	–	2.3	21.6
Rumanja	59.0	–	–	21.1	19.9
Mladovo	58.1	8.5	–	7.2	26.2
Karanovo	55.2	13.1	–	11.3	20.4

Table 3. Percentage representation of land use categories within 2 km radius of site: sites with 25–50 per cent arable

| Site | Arable | Permanent | Grazing seasonal | | Browse |
			Lowland	Upland	
Zagorski	47.4	27.9	12.2	–	12.5
Sobrano	46.5	19.2	7.0	–	27.3
Djadevo (Eneolithic)	39.4	14.8	20.5	5.3	20.0
Asenovets	38.5	–	–	56.3	5.2
Padarevo (Neolithic)	37.1	16.5	–	–	46.4
Zagorski South	35.1	48.5	14.1	–	2.3
Siganski Mogila (Bronze Age)	35.0	39.5	–	–	25.5
Brjastovo	31.5	–	–	65.7	2.8
Konjovo (Bronze Age)	30.5	45.6	–	2.3	21.6
Södjisko Polje	28.7	–	–	0.6	70.7
Ezero	27.3	70.4	–	–	2.3

Table 4. Percentage representation of land use categories within 2 km radius of site: sites with less than 25 per cent arable

Site	Arable	Permanent	Grazing seasonal Lowland	Grazing seasonal Upland	Browse
Djadevo (Bronze Age)	23.7	30.5	20.5	5.3	20.0
Mlekarevo	22.0	–	54.0	–	24.0
Radievo	20.7	–	48.7	4.2	26.4
Pitovo	18.8	–	46.3	27.2	7.7
Södievo	17.2	–	–	50.0	32.8
Bogdanovo	14.6	18.3	24.6	–	42.5
Site 37	13.6	30.2	–	–	56.2
Omarchevo	10.5	–	80.1	–	9.4
Lubenova Mahla	8.8	12.5	78.7	–	–
Padarevo (Bronze Age)	5.7	47.9	–	–	46.4
Bikovo	–	2.3	97.7	–	–

The estimated prehistoric population of the Nova Zagora region

A good yardstick for measuring the success of an economy is the level of population which it can maintain. To date there has been little coherent study of prehistoric demography, but we can obtain some rough estimate of the level of population likely to have been supported on these settlements.

One method is to consider the productivity of the largest component of the economy. In the case of settlements with territories composed of a large proportion of potentially arable land, this is likely to have been cereals. We have suggested that in this region most cereal cultivation would have occurred within a radius of about 2 km from the settlement, or within an area of about 12.6 km². At the largest sites about 60 per cent of the land within this area, c. 760 ha, could have been tilled. It is scarcely conceivable that all of this could have been planted in cereals each year, for such a practice would soon have led to exhaustion of the soil, and the abandonment of the settlements. As these sites were occupied for several centuries, some form of agricultural directive must have operated. Some alternation between cereals and fallow would have been a minimum requirement, and we have applied here the system used in Greece prior to the Second World War, when in any one year half the arable land was under grain and the rest fallow (see Naval Intelligence Division Geographical Handbook Series, 1944, *Greece*, volume II, p. 49). As was suggested above, legumes may have played some part in the rotation system. In this case the area under cereals in any one year would have been smaller but the yield per hectare would have been considerably higher, and total yield would certainly not have been less than in a simple fallow system.

Prehistoric crop yields are unlikely to have been higher than they were in medieval, classical, or recent times. A figure of c. 400 kg/ha would not seem excessively high (Slicher van Bath, 1963). In Greece in 1922, using unimproved wheat varieties and traditional farming techniques, 500–600 kg/ha was the average yield. Of the 400 kg, at least one-quarter, and possibly one-third, would have been required as seed for the following year. The total minimum amount of grain left for consumption would have been about 100 000 kg. Clark and Haswell (1967) have calculated that 210 kg of grain per person is the minimum annual cereal consumption which would provide adequate calories and protein for a population subsisting entirely on cereals. At this rate of consumption the territory associated with one of the large sites could have supported about 480 people. Given the other food resources available, however, this must be considered a minimum estimate.

Estimates of population can also be obtained by considering the size of the settlement. At various Near Eastern sites the density of settlement averaged 125 persons per hectare (Russell, 1958). In southern Bulgaria, the largest tells cover an area of c. 3 ha. If we assume densities similar to those of the Near East, the population of such tells would have been c. 375 people.

Taking into account the two figures we have arrived at, an estimate of between 400 and 500 inhabitants for the population of the largest tells may bear some resemblance to the actual prehistoric situation. If so, the nine largest sites in this region would have had a total population of 3600–4500, and the area as a whole, probably about 10 000 inhabitants by the Early Bronze Age. This is a density of c. 10 persons/km². As a measure of economic success this figure compares favourably with population densities of less than 25 persons/km² for eastern Thrace in 1928 (Naval Intelligence Division Geographical Handbook Series, 1944, *Greece*, volume II). At that time some cash crops were grown, but wheat, barley, cattle, caprines, and pigs formed the basis of the economy. About 20 per cent of the land was under cultivation, which is comparable to the amount of potentially arable land in the Nova Zagora region in Neolithic times.

THE ČELOPEČ REGION

The Čelopeč area (Figure 5) consists of a highly dissected intermontane valley about 500 m o.d., in which the settlements are found, surrounded by the Sredna Gora and the Stara Planina mountains which rise to over 1500 m o.d. The precipitation of this region is over twice that of the Nova Zagora region; in winter, most of this falls as snow, which persists for over three months. As most of the soils in this area are thin and stony, they are unsuitable for continuous crop cultivation. This is possible only on isolated pockets of diluvial sandy soils along the flatter parts of river valleys. A further restriction on human settlement is the difficulty of access to the alpine pastures of the Sredna Gora and Stara Planina mountains. Although such seasonal grazings are close at hand and of good quality, the mountain slopes are precipitous and difficult to ascend except via side valleys. These, however, are few and far between. The most advantageous situation for a settlement, and the only one where prolonged occupation would have been possible, would thus be a location from which the inhabitants could exploit both the small amount of soil which could be repeatedly cultivated, and the summer grazing in the mountains via a side valley. As can be seen (Figure 5), it is precisely in such locations that tell settlements are situated. The date of each site is shown in Table 5. We have not made allowance for those communities which may have utilised the grazing potential of the remaining soils which were unsuitable for continuous cultivation. Evidence of their settlements has so far escaped detection, and it seems

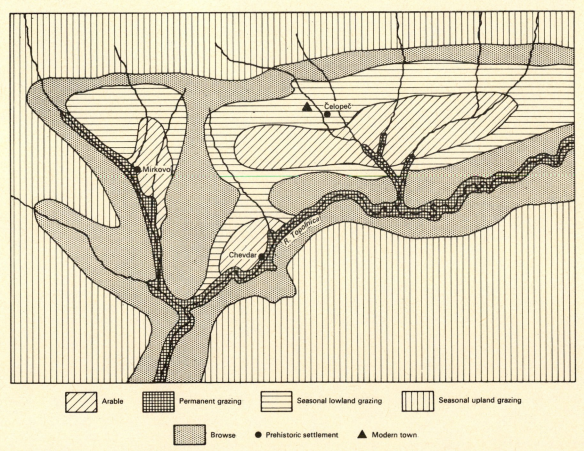

Figure 5. Prehistoric settlement and land use in the Čelopeč region.

probable that the tells, by reason of their repeated occupation, were in the most advantageous site locations in this area.

Table 5.   Height and estimated dating of sites in the Čelopeč region

Site	Height	Neolithic	Bronze Age
Čelopeč	5 m	×	×
Chevdar	2 m	×	
Mirkovo	2 m	×	

In contrast to the Nova Zagora region, the Čelopeč area, with only a few locations suitable for continuous settlement, is of low economic potential. As a result, the sites in this area are widely separated from their neighbours, and can thus be regarded, to a much larger extent than those in the Nova Zagora region, as relatively isolated, independent communities (Figure 6).

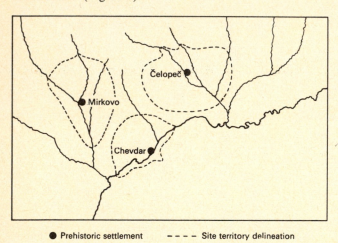

● Prehistoric settlement   - - - - Site territory delineation

Figure 6. Prehistoric site territories in the Čelopeč region.

INTERPRETATION

In the Nova Zagora region in Neolithic and Bronze Age times the settlements were so close together that communication and exchange between them would have been easily accomplished and each site may be regarded as a part of an inter-dependent and integrated unit of considerable economic strength. The intervention of a Bronze Age technology made little difference.

The observed deposition of the riverine clays changed this apparently stable situation. As has been supposed by Vita-Finzi for similar events in medieval times in brittle environments in the Mediterranean region (Vita-Finzi, 1969) such geomorphological changes may have been due to

climatic changes but in Bulgaria there is no evidence for this. On the other hand the development of territorial analysis enables us to bring some redress to the traditional explanation of prehistoric economic changes by reference to climatic change. By the Bronze Age the agricultural potential of the region was fully exploited. The area of potentially arable land was, however, with the available technology of the time, severely restricted. Even if a primitive plough had been developed, it is unlikely that it could have significantly increased the area under cultivation by tackling areas of heavier land, and sustained population pressure would have been brought to bear on the existing pastoral resource. In consequence the removal of vegetational cover on the unstable uplands could have resulted in unforeseen erosion and consequent deposition in the valleys and lowland areas to an extent which would have impelled drastic economic and social change. How this change was brought about, by invasion or by an indigenous response is, from the point of view of the development of agriculture, a secondary consideration.

REFERENCES

Chisholm, M. (1968) *Rural Settlement and Land Use,* 2nd ed. London: Hutchinson.

Clark, C. & Haswell, M. R. (1967) *The Economics of Subsistence Agriculture,* 3rd ed. London: Macmillan.

Dennell, R. W. (1972) The interpretation of plant remains: Bulgaria. In *Papers in Economic Prehistory,* ed. E. S. Higgs, pp. 149–60. Cambridge: Cambridge University Press.

— (1973) The economic development of Bulgaria during the Neolithic and Bronze Age. In *Proceedings of the 1st International Congress of Thracology, Sofia.*

Detev, P. (1954) Tell près du village de Bikovo. *Godisnik na Muzeite v Plovdivski Okrug* **1,** 151.

Georgiev, G. I. (1961) Kulturgruppen der Jungsteinzeit und Kupferzeit in der Ebene von Thrazien. In *L'Europe à la Fin de l'Age de la Pierre,* ed. B. Soudsky & E. Plesova, pp. 45–81. Prague.

Georgiev, G. I. & Merpert, N. I. (1965) Raskopki mnogosloinovo poseleniya u sela Ezero. *Izvestia Archeologicheskaya Institut* **27,** 129–59.

Higgs, E. S. & Vita-Finzi, C. (1972) Prehistoric economies: a territorial approach. In *Papers in Economic Prehistory,* ed. E. S. Higgs, pp. 27–36. Cambridge: Cambridge University Press.

Ivanov, S. (1965) Kosti zhivotnih iz mnogosloinovo poseleniya u sela Ezero. *Izvestia Archeologicheskaya Institut* **27,** 160–2.

Koniev, B. (1966) *Pochvena Karta na Bulgaria.* Sofia.

Merpert, N. I., Georgiev, G. I., & Katincherov, R. (In press) Ezero site monograph. Moscow.

Naval Intelligence Division Geographical Handbook Series. (1944) *Greece.*

Nemecek, J. (1971) Determinations of the age of organic material by C14. *Rostlina Vyruba* **17** (7), 745–51.

Renfrew, C. (1969) The autonomy of the south-east European Copper Age. *Proc. prehist. Soc.* **35,** 12–47.

Renfrew, J. M. (1969) The archaeological evidence for the domestication of plants: methods and problems. In *The Domestication of Plants and Animals,* ed. P. J. Ucko & G. W. Dimbleby, pp. 149–72. London: Duckworth.

Russell, J. C. (1958) Late ancient and medieval populations. *Trans. Am. phil. Soc.* **48** (3), 1–152.

Slicher van Bath, B. H. (1963) *The Agrarian History of Western Europe A.D. 500–1850.* London: Edward Arnold.

Tringham, R. (1972) *Hunters, Fishers and Farmers of Eastern Europe.* London: Hutchinson.

Vita-Finzi, C. (1969) *The Mediterranean Valleys.* Cambridge: Cambridge University Press.

5. PREHISTORIC TERRITORIES AND ECONOMIES IN CENTRAL ITALY

G. W. W. BARKER

The purpose of this paper is to summarise the evidence for an economic prehistory in central Italy. The available evidence consists of: the material culture of the prehistoric sites; faunal and plant samples from excavations, both published and unpublished; and the location of the sites. Among the topics discussed first are the climatic and environmental constraints at work in central Italy; the basic pattern of agricultural exploitation since the classical period; and the relevance of the exploitation territory of the individual site to the study of prehistoric economies in central Italy. An attempt is then made to construct an economic prehistory of central Italy, from the Middle Palaeolithic until the Bronze Age.

THE PHYSICAL LANDSCAPE

The area discussed stretches from the northernmost Apennines south of the Po valley down the peninsula to the Sangro and Liri rivers (Figure 1). It can be divided into four regions.

(a) The Anti-Apennines consist of plains and uplands which extend from the Tyrrhenian coast east to the Val di Chiana, the middle Tiber, and the Sacco-Liri basin. By the Tyrrhenian Sea is a wide plain edged by low hills, which in northern Lazio and Toscana is called the Maremma. Around Rome is the Campagna, a similar area, and to the south is the Pontine plain, formerly marshland. Much of the western plain was malarial in historical times but has since been drained and as reclaimed land is termed *bonifica*. Volcanic hills extend from the Monti Volsinii in the north to the Alban Hills south of the Tiber. Fertile soils overlie the soft *tufo* rock (cemented volcanic ash). To the north, the Tuscan uplands consist of gentle hills and undulating plateaux, mostly less than 800 m in height apart from the southernmost mass of Monte Amiata (1734 m). The hills are still recognisable as the landscape of the Florentine and Sienese Renaissance artists: small farms screened by cypresses, cereal fields, fruit trees, olives, and vines. Nevertheless, there are extensive chestnut, oak, and beech forests (38 per cent of the total vegetational cover in Toscana) and wide areas of pasture. To the south of the Alban Hills the rivers flow down from the central Apennines into the Sacco–Liri basin; between the basin and the

Pontine plain is the bare limestone massif of the Monti Lepini, Ausoni, and Aurunci.

(b) The Pre-Apennines are an ill-defined chain of hills west of the main ridge, from Pratomagno (1592 m) in the north to the Monti Simbruini (2156 m) in the south. Between these two masses there is a series of low hills running through Umbria and Lazio. The rivers flow westwards from the main ridge, often through wooded gorges, into several intermontane basins, thence west again to the Tiber and Arno systems. The valley floors are farmed like the basins, but there is extensive forest cover on the slopes of the hills, particularly above the Nera and Salto systems.

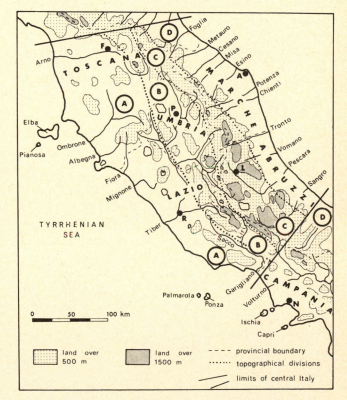

Figure 1. Central Italy: general topography. (A) Anti-Apennines, (B) Pre-Apennines, (C) high Apennines, (D) eastern lowlands. Solid circles indicate the capitals of the provinces: F–Florence (Toscana), A–Ancona (Marche), P–Perugia (Umbria), R–Rome (Lazio), L–L'Aquila (Abruzzi). N–Naples (Campania).

111

(c) The high Apennine chain begins in the Alpi Apuane north of the Arno and curves south down the peninsula. Many of the peaks are above 2000 m and the highest peak, the Corno Grande of the Gran Sasso in Abruzzi, is 2921 m above sea level. Here in Abruzzi the single ridge separates into a number of limestone masses with intermontane basins, forming a broad dissected plateau region. The basins are farmed, the lower slopes heavily wooded, whilst above them are high plateaux or karstic basins between 1300 and 1700 m above sea level, the summer pastures for the transhumant flocks.

(d) The eastern lowland strip is a low plateau of clays, sands, and chalks rather than a plain, which has been dissected by the rivers into parallel ridges and valleys. There is a succession of long flat-topped spurs, often badly gullied, separated by alluvial valleys. Many of the latter were malarial until recently and all the medieval villages occupy the higher ground.

Three major vegetational zones can be distinguished in central Italy, defined on the basis of altitude associated with plant types (Houston, 1964). The evergreen zone of the Anti-Apennines, the western side of the Pre-Apennines, and the eastern lowlands is characterised by coniferous forests and macchia, and reaches up to about 750 m. Above this, deciduous species such as oak and chestnut dominate to heights of 1000 to 1300 m, whence the beech woods reach up to about 2000 m. These broad divisions are correlated with certain climatic conditions, but local variations in vegetation are of course related to local climatic, edaphic, and biotic factors.

Although the climate of central Italy is 'Mediterranean', with hot summers and humid winters, relief and altitude bring wide variations (Figure 2). The winters are extremely cold in the high Apennines (Figure 2a), where snow can cover the ridges and *altipiani* for several months (Figure 2d); elsewhere the temperature is cool, except on the Tyrrhenian coastlands. In summer both western and eastern lowlands are extremely arid (Figure 2b). Rainfall varies from 500 to 3000 mm according to elevation (Figure 2c), with spring and autumn maxima. The intermontane basins of the Apennines have less rainfall than the surrounding hills and tend to have extremes of heat in the summer and cold in winter.

THE RURAL LANDSCAPE

The main components of the rural economy in central Italy have traditionally been *coltura promiscua* (interculture) and *pastorizia* (pastoralism). *Coltura promiscua,* a system dating at least from the Roman period, dominates the rural landscape of our area today, and trees grow intermingled with cereals and other crops on almost half the cultivated

area (Houston, 1964, p. 435, Fig. 177). The system is admirably adapted on a number of counts to the limiting factors of climate and environment. The vine is naturally suited to interculture with trees as a creeper and, as the roots of the vines, trees, and leguminous crops occupy different soil levels, they do not compete with one another. The system helps to resist erosion, as Columella realised (*De Re Rustica.* II.2.24); furthermore, it raises the ground temperature by several degrees in winter and provides a longer growing season and shelter against excessive heat in summer. The use of the elm also provides fodder for local stock.

The effect of the summer drought is extreme on the lowlands, and the pastures are desiccated by June. Lack of summer rainfall is a major limiting factor to a pastoral

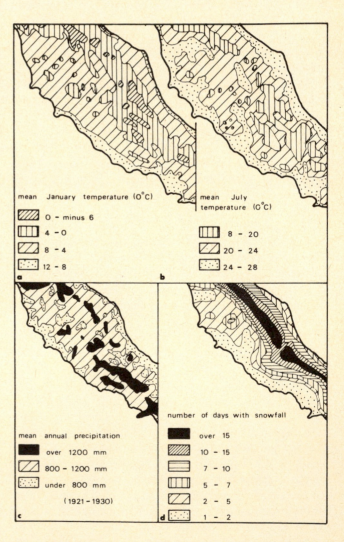

mean January temperature (0°C)

/////	0 – minus 6
|||||	4 – 0
	8 – 4
.....	12 – 8

mean July temperature (0°C)

|||||	8 – 20
/////	20 – 24
.....	24 – 28

mean annual precipitation

███	over 1200 mm
/////	800 – 1200 mm
.....	under 800 mm

(1921 – 1930)

number of days with snowfall

███	over 15
/////	10 – 15
	7 – 10
|||||	5 – 7
/////	2 – 5
.....	1 – 2

Figure 2. Central Italy: (a) winter and (b) summer temperatures, (c) mean annual precipitation (1921–30), and (d) snowfall (adapted from *Italy*, 1944, vol. 1).

economy. On the other hand, the pasture of the high Apennines is available from late May, after the last snows have melted, until the first snows on the highest *altipiani* in early October. Thus the most efficient system of stock and pasture management is the utilisation by transhumance of both lowland and upland grazings. This system also avoids the danger of vitamin A deficiency in sheep, which can result from prolonged grazing on withered pasture (Fraser & Stamp, 1961, p. 284), and reduces parasite infestation. Transhumance is well-documented in the area from Roman times (White, 1970) onwards. It was at its most organised when Abruzzi was part of the Kingdom of Naples, when enormous flocks were taken from the Abruzzi *altipiani* down to the Tavoliere or Foggia plain in Apulia (Braudel, 1972, pp. 85–91). Transhumance continued as an important part of the rural economy until the postwar years of this century. Though reduced, transhumant flocks survive in central Italy today (Barbieri, 1955; Müller, 1938; Ortolani, 1941. Figure 3 is a reconstruction of the traditional routes used to walk the flocks between the lowland and upland pastures until the last war. The heavier dots show the three classic *tratturi* or drove roads which cut artificial routes across the valleys parallel to the coast from the Tavoliere to the Abruzzi *altipiani*: Campo Imperatore on Gran Sasso (9), the Maiella and Piano delle Cinquemiglia (10), Monte Velino (8), and Monte Matese (11). The natural routes from the Abruzzi pastures are directly west or east to the lowlands. The western valley routes, which I also describe as *tratturi*, are shown by the lighter dots in Figure 3.

The transhumance patterns recorded from the Roman period until today are adapted to the major natural constraints of seasonal grazing and water supply in central Italy and as such are an invaluable ethnographic record when we turn to man-animal relationships in prehistory. Mobility of one kind or another has been the solution in historical times to the major limiting factors of livestock economy, and it is a reasonable hypothesis that prehistoric livestock economies would also have adapted wholly or partially to these factors.

THE EXPLOITATION TERRITORY

Prehistoric economies in central Italy have not been intensively studied in the past, but the main cultural phases have been equated with a series of economic 'stances' assumed to be valid for the entire area. An unspecialised hunting and gathering economy is assumed for the pre-Neolithic groups, a sedentary economy of cereal cultivation and stock keeping in the Neolithic, a fully transhumant economy in the 'Apennine' phase of the Bronze Age, and finally a return to a sedentary mixed economy in the 'Subapennine'

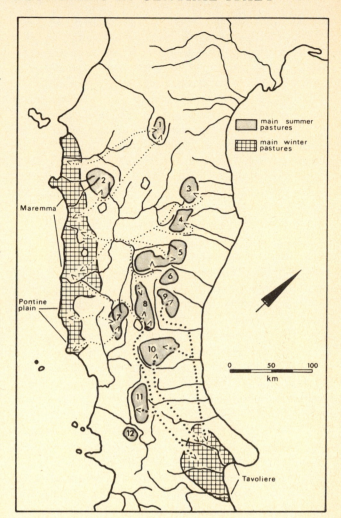

Figure 3. Central Italy: *tratturi* and pastures. Heavy dots mark the classic *tratturi* to Apulia, lighter dots show the valley routes to the western plains. 1–Pratomagno, 2–Monte Amiata, 3–Monte Catria, 4–Monte Pennino and Monte Penna, 5–Monti Sibillini, 6–Monti della Laga, 7–Monti Simbruini, 8–Monte Velino, 9–Gran Sasso, 10–Maiella and Piano delle Cinquemiglia, 11–Monte Matese, 12–Camposauro.

phase of the Bronze Age. The prehistoric sites have been regarded as transitory, seasonal, or permanent according to these *a priori* assumptions taken from the cultural framework. Thus all Palaeolithic and Apennine Bronze Age sites are assumed to have been transitory or seasonal, all Neolithic and Late Bronze Age sites to have been permanent. On the other hand, the ethnographic record reveals hunting and gathering groups which store food and which are sedentary, transhumant groups which build houses and grow and store grain. It is difficult to demonstrate from the archaeological evidence of most sites whether the occupation was unequivocally permanent, seasonal, or transitory. In central Italy, moreover, economic data are often minimal; thus we have no more than half a dozen cereal samples from over seventy Neolithic sites and perhaps a dozen from nearly a hundred Bronze Age sites. Therefore we must surely take into account not only the assemblage of a site, but also the possibilities inherent in its location.

We can assume that the conditions in the immediate vicinity of most prehistoric sites were usually the principal concern of the inhabitants in the extraction of their subsistence. The area around the prehistoric site ought to tell us at least as much about the economy of the group as general environmental considerations. Clearly, however, in order to relate the location of a given site to the archaeological evidence of the site, and then to compare site with site, we need to establish criteria whereby we can circumscribe an area and quantify the resources within it. I have used the technique of territorial analysis proposed by Higgs and Vita-Finzi (1972): a one-hour distance on foot from a Neolithic or post-Neolithic site and a two-hour distance on foot from a pre-Neolithic site being taken as the territorial boundaries. There must have been instances when the exploitation of the territory of a given site entailed journeys beyond our artificial limits, but the calculation of the one- or two-hour territory is likely to encompass the area habitually exploited. Our territories are hypothetical reconstructions under modern conditions, but at least they serve as a guide to the resources for which the prehistoric site was occupied, and, according to Lee's discussion of Bushman groups (Lee, 1968, 1969) and Chisholm's of modern peasant economies (Chisholm, 1968), if anything show a larger rather than a smaller area than was probably utilised by the prehistoric group. The main categories of land use employed in all of the maps are shown in Figure 4, any variants to this key being shown in the key to the individual map. Caves and shelters are represented by triangles, open sites by circles; all scales are in kilometres, and north is at the top of all the maps.

PALAEOLITHIC ECONOMIES

In spite of its limitations the Alpine glacial sequence provides the best available climatic framework for our area. It seems justifiable to think in terms of two primary cold phases in the last glaciation, separated by a warmer interstadial. Pollen diagrams (Dubois & Zangheri, 1957; Lona, 1957–62a, b; Bonatti, 1961, 1963, 1966, 1970; Menendez Amor & Florschütz, 1963, 1964; Van der Hammen, Wijmstra, & Van der Molen, 1965; Bottema, in Higgs *et al.*, 1967; Frank, 1969) demonstrate that the cooler phases of the Würm in the northern Mediterranean were characterised by increasing aridity rather than precipitation: they are dominated during glacial periods by pollen of a steppe or open vegetation, such as *Artemisia*,

Ephedra, Helianthemum, and *Thalictrum,* which must have developed in cold and arid conditions.

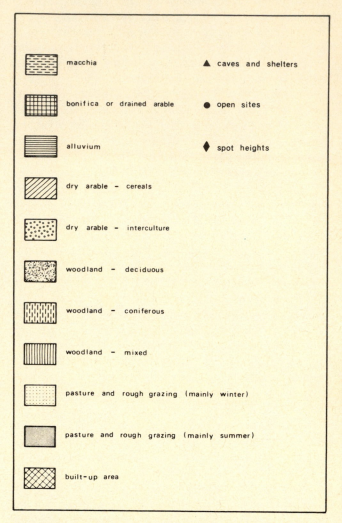

Figure 4. Land utilisation in central Italy: key to the maps.

Southern Campania

An important succession of Palaeolithic industries has been established in southern Campania from excavations in a number of caves at Marina di Camerota (Figure 5:1). The Middle and Upper Palaeolithic faunal samples allowed more complete analysis than was possible elsewhere, and hence the sites are discussed below, although they lie outside central Italy proper.

At the Grotta del Poggio the lower layers contained a denticulated Mousterian industry, the proportions of which decreased with time (Palma di Cesnola, 1969a), overlain in the topmost layer by a small evolved Mousterian assemblage. An evolved Mousterian in the adjacent Grotta della Cala was dated by ^{14}C to 40 000 B.P. (Palma di

Cesnola, 1969b). Above was an evolved Gravettian assemblage, which was dated to 27 000 ± 1700 B.P. and continued in the three overlying layers. The levels above this appear to be Epigravettian (Palma di Cesnola, 1971). Both caves also provide evidence of climatic change. A 'warm' interglacial fauna was present in the lower levels at the Grotta del Poggio, but was absent in the upper levels. In the Grotta della Cala microfaunal evidence suggests a succession from a damp woodland to a colder and drier environment (G. Bartolomei, *pers. comm.*). The change to a colder and drier climate after an interstadial *c.* 40 000 B.P. corroborates the pollen diagrams in the northern Mediterranean referred to above.

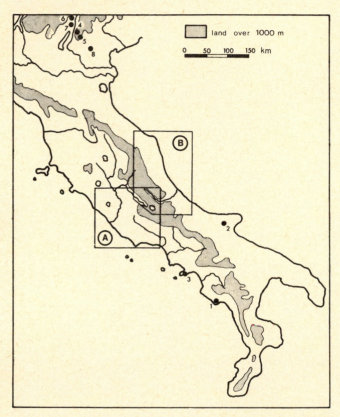

Figure 5. Location of areas in central Italy covered by maps in Figures 9, 10 and 20: (A) see Figures 9 and 10, (B) see Figure 20. Sites discussed in text outside central Italy: 1–Camerota caves, 2–Grotta Paglicci, 3–Grotta la Porta di Positano, Grotta Erica, 4–Ponte di Veia, 5–Riparo Tagliente, 6–Riparo Vatte di Zambana, 7–Romagnano Loc, 8–Molino Casarotto.

A single species, the red deer, was the dominant meat source at both Middle and Upper Palaeolithic sites at Camerota. Climatic change, as we saw above, was inferred from faunal and microfaunal evidence, and the period almost certainly encompassed some marine regression which would have altered the territories available to the

caves; nevertheless, the percentage of red deer was remarkably unaffected and varied from over 70 per cent to over 90 per cent.

Middle Palaeolithic faunal samples are available from the Grotta del Poggio and the Grotta Taddeo (Vigliardi, 1968a) and Upper Palaeolithic samples from the Grotta della Cala and the Grotta Calanca (Vigliardi, 1968b). The age at death of the deer at three of the caves was reconstructed from stages of tooth eruption and wear in mandibles (Figure 6), using the data from deer of known age from Rhum (Lowe, 1967). The shortcomings of this method are acknowledged, but they do not invalidate the general killing patterns which emerge. The total number of mandibles from the Camerota caves is fairly small, but at least the Upper Palaeolithic samples reveal a similar pattern to the very large sample from the Grotta Polesini near Rome (Figure 6:4), discussed

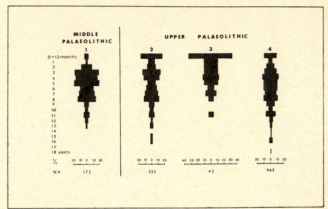

Figure 6. Mortality ages of red deer (*Cervus elaphus*), constructed from mandibular tooth eruption and wear, using the stages given by Lowe (1967). 1–Grotta del Poggio, 2–Grotta della Cala, 3–Grotta Calanca, 4–Grotta Polesini.

in the following section. At the Grotta del Poggio (Figure 6:1) the Middle Palaeolithic group killed mature animals: 80 per cent of the deaths fell between the third and eighth years. At the Grotta della Cala (Figure 6:2), however, and at the contemporaneous shelter the Grotta Calanca (Figure 6:3), the Upper Palaeolithic groups (*c.* 27 000–25 000 B.P.) still killed the deer between these ages, but also selected young deer in their first year. Calving probably took place in June and July, and on tooth eruption data the first-year deaths at the Upper Palaeolithic caves occurred in the second six months of life. Therefore, one feature of the Upper Palaeolithic economies at the Camerota caves and the Grotta Polesini seems to have been the systematic killing of young deer during the winter months.

The two-hour exploitation territory associated with the Camerota caves is roughly semi-circular, and covers an area of 86 km² (Figure 7). From sea level at the caves the land rises to M. Bulgheria at 1224 m (Figure 8:3); precipitous slopes fall away on the north side of the mountain. To the west is the gorge of the Mingardo river; to the east is the gorge of the Vallone di Marcellino and the hill of Penniniello (Figure 8:5), separated from the cliffs of M. Bulgheria by a wide saddle (Figure 8:4). The prehistoric caves at Camerota lie on either side of a third, central gorge some 3 km long: on the west are the Grotta Calanca (Figure 7a:2) and the Grotta Taddeo (Figure 7a:3), and on the east, the Grotta della Cala (Figure 7a:4) and the Grotta del Poggio (Figure 7a:5). This gorge runs due north and opens out into a wide bowl surrounded by hills. The nearby site of Cala delle Ossa (Blanc & Segre, 1953b; Figure 7a:1) at the mouth of the Mingardo river also contained rich Middle and Upper Palaeolithic industries.

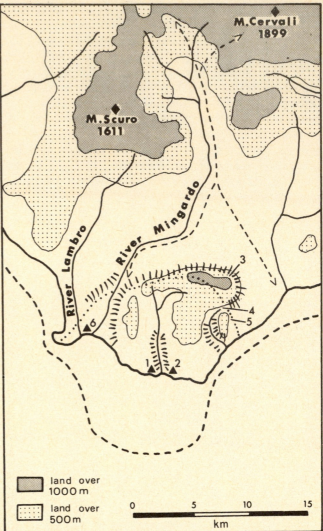

Figure 8. Suggested annual territory at Camerota; light broken lines indicate modern sheep transhumant routes; heavy broken line indicates sea regression of 100 m; dotted line shows the two-hour territory from the caves (see Figure 7). 1—Grotta Calanca and Grotta Taddeo, 2—Grotta della Cala and Grotta del Poggio, 3—Monte Bulgheria (1224 m), 4—saddle, 5—Penniniello (660 m), 6—Cala delle Ossa.

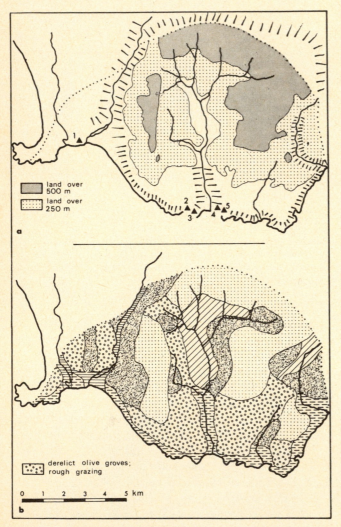

Figure 7. The two-hour territory at Camerota. a, topography: 1—Cala delle Ossa, 2—Grotta Calanca, 3—Grotta Taddeo, 4—Grotta della Cala, 5—Grotta del Poggio; b, land use.

A drop in sea level of 100 m would have effectively doubled the territory by exposing a plain several kilometres long in front of the caves, but to the west and east the bedrock shelves steeply and a change in sea level would not have added significantly to the territory in these areas. The heavy broken line in Figure 8 shows the seaward extension of the territory in the extreme situation of a 100 m drop in sea level; according to Milliman and Emery (1968), the marine regression at *c.* 30 000–25 000 B.P. was probably only in the order of 30 m below present sea level.

In the present situation (Figure 7b) pasture and rough grazing cover some 70–80 per cent of the total territory.

Most of the pasture is at its best in the winter months. Apart from the ridge top of M. Bulgheria, the pastures of the middle and lower slopes are withered and brown in summer. Transhumant flocks, which still use the area, winter on the lowlands and are driven up on foot to the extensive summer pastures at the head of the Mingardo river; their routes are shown by the lighter broken lines in Figure 8. The uplands would have been even more inhospitable during Würmian winters, when the snow line at Camerota would have reached at least down to 1000 m.

Red deer movements in a situation like that at Camerota would probably have been strongly seasonal, as they are wherever seasonal constraints make this necessary or profitable. The deer remain on the lowlands during the winter months, apart from occasional forays to higher ground if weather permits. In the spring the stags move up to the hills and are joined by the hinds, their yearlings, and calves, after calving in June and July. In southern Campania the changes in topography are drastic; distances are short and in some cases winter and summer territories would have overlapped. At Camerota limited summer pastures were probably available on top of the ridge of M. Bulgheria; on the other hand, very extensive summer pastures lay at the head of the Mingardo, 30–40 km to the north (Figure 8). Inland Middle and Upper Palaeolithic flint scatters have been found at high altitudes on these summer pastures (Lazzari, 1959; Pericoli, 1959; Stradi & Andreolotti, 1964), which we saw above are still used by transhumant flocks. The evidence for a winter mortality peak in the Upper Palaeolithic cave samples, the presence of inland flint scatters, the modern transhumance in the area, and the seasonal movements of red deer today make it a reasonable hypothesis that both Middle and Upper Palaeolithic bands occupied the Camerota caves during the winter months, but moved inland to the upper Mingardo during the summer.

The mortality patterns for the deer at Camerota (Figure 6) are unlikely to represent an unsystematic catch-as-catch-can kill. A number of reasons can be suggested for the selective slaughter of red deer: Darling (1937, p. 48) has noted that maintaining a young hind stock keeps the herd vigorous and productive; the winter coat of both stags and hinds is at its best early in the season, in November; rutting stags may not have been killed, for their meat has an unpleasantly strong taste and odour; are 'yeld' or barren hinds are thought to provide the best venison. Modern culling policy (that is, a policy not simply designed to produce the best 'heads' for a shoot) in some areas selects the yeld hinds together with late calves and their dams (Guinness, Lincoln, & Short, 1971).

It is difficult to interpret the first-year deaths at the Upper Palaeolithic sites. By the end of the first year, English park deer have reached the size of mature animals, whereas, probably because of the poor quality of the feed, Scottish yearlings are still only half this size. This suggests that at Camerota the calves and yearlings would have provided a reasonable meat source only under certain grazing conditions. The yearling hide is preferable for its suppleness to the hide of an older deer, but it was probably only worth killing the yearling if it had almost reached the size of the mature animal, after which the increase in area of the hide would have been negligible. The maintenance of two deer for one year would have required the same amount of pasture as one deer for two years, but the first system would only have supplied much more meat than the second under good grazing conditions. There could therefore be several possible explanations of the first-year deaths, but a modern situation adds a cautionary note. In a reindeer economy in West Greenland, the nature of the cull varies from year to year (Sturdy, 1972): more does are killed in a good calving year, while in a bad year the Lapp herders (introduced to manage the reindeer) select barren does, older animals, and young males. Despite these annual fluctuations, however, Sturdy comments that, were the main autumn camp to be excavated in a few thousand years, 'the only major trend to emerge from the bones about killing proportions might be a tendency to select young males' (Sturdy, 1972, p. 166).

Whatever the composition of the kill, however, the selection of the Camerota caves by the Palaeolithic bands is probably significant, in that the territory is effectively walled in on three sides by precipitous slopes. In the spring, regardless of marine regression, the only exits to the inland pastures for the deer were either through the Bulgheria-Penniniello saddle (Figure 8:4) or the gorge between the caves (between 1 and 2 in Figure 8). In the Lapp systems of loose herding in West Greenland, strategic positions like this saddle are occupied by small parties for a few days (Sturdy, 1972); the fact of human presence drives the deer away and thus the seasonal movements of the deer are manipulated by the herders to suit their own needs. If the Bulgheria–Penniniello saddle were occupied in spring by such a party, the only other route to the summer grazings would have been down the gorge between the caves and westwards to the Mingardo estuary. Occupation of the Cala delle Ossa would have been a control on the deer spilling into the lower Lambro valley (Figure 8:6).

There is considerable variation reported in the carrying capacities of different types of grazing for red deer. Darling gives estimates ranging from 1 deer: 100 acres to 1 deer: 40 acres on Scottish moorland and up to 1 deer: 5 acres in modern deer parks (Darling, 1937, pp. 36–40). The lowest ratio of 1 deer: 100 acres (40.5 hectares) would give a minimum figure of 209 deer in the present territory of the Camerota caves (if it were all free from snow), or 400 deer with maximum marine regression. If we assume that each family unit consisted of two adults and three children, and that the nutritional requirements per day were 3000 calories per man, 2400 per woman and 2000 per child, then the total requirements for a microband of two, three, or four family units would have been 22 800, 34 200 and 45 600 calories per day respectively. These would have been met by 10.9, 16.3, and 21.7 kg of meat daily, using the figures given by Clark (1972, p. 27). On the island of Rhum in Scotland a herd of some 1200 deer is maintained at a stable population level by shooting one-sixth of the mature stags and hinds each year (Lowe, 1969). In Table 1 I have calculated the meat yields of a one-fifth and one-sixth kill of the hypothetical Camerota herd, adopting Fraser and King's figure of 109.5 kg dead weight for a stag and assuming that approximately 60 per cent of the dead weight provided usable meat (Fraser & King, in Clark, 1954).

Table 1. Yields of meat from minimum and maximum two-hour territories at Camerota

Territory (km²)	Population (numbers of deer)	Kill : Yield (numbers of deer)	Dead-weight (kg)	Meat (kg)	Daily supply (kg)
86	209	1/5 : 41.8	7963	4779	13.1
86	209	1/6 : 34.8	6629	3977	10.9
162	400	1/5 : 80	15240	9144	25.1
162	400	1/6 : 66.6	12687	7612	20.8

According to these calculations, a one-sixth kill would have supported exactly two family units in the present two-hour territory. With a marine regression of 20 or 30 m below the present-day sea level, the area could probably have supported a total of three family units, but even with the maximum marine regression it is unlikely that a microband of more than four units could have extracted its livelihood from the Camerota territory. If the hypothesis of a mobile economy between the caves and the upper Mingardo is accepted, the annual territory of the microband would have been in the order of 450 km².

The Camerota faunal samples have given us an insight into the Palaeolithic economies of one area in peninsular Italy. In the first place, red deer was the dominant meat source for both Middle and Upper Palaeolithic bands; secondly, the deer probably moved between winter and summer grazing areas, in turn followed by the Palaeolithic bands; thirdly, the system of exploitation changed in the Upper Palaeolithic and, although the details may elude us, became in some way more intensive; finally, the territory of

the caves can be correlated with Sturdy's example of herd following practised in the modern reindeer economies in West Greenland, a system which involves a degree of manipulation at certain times of the year, particularly in the spring and autumn. This remains an hypothesis, but one which is testable in the future. The Greenland analogy fits the evidence of the kill and the location of the sites at least as well as those of other systems of animal predation employed by modern hunter–gatherers.

Southern Etruria and the central Apennines

Stratified evidence in Lazio which is comparable to that of the Camerota caves is extremely sparse. The Middle Palaeolithic industries manufactured on beach pebbles and found in dunes and caves on the western coast are defined loosely as Pontinian (Blanc, 1957; Tozzi, 1970), but it is apparent that the term embraces more than one type of Mousterian industry. At the Grotta del Fossellone, for example (Figure 9:5), the early Mousterian industry on top of a 6–8 m beach evolved into a micro-Mousterian form in the higher levels, with greatly increased percentages of denticulated tools (as in the Grotta del Poggio). Our knowledge of inland Middle Palaeolithic sites in Lazio is even more meagre, but there is some evidence for Mousterian exploitation of the inland valleys in the last glaciation, at the Grotta di Cassino (Figure 9:24), Pofi (Figure 9:21), Pontecorvo (Figure 9:23), and Valle Radice near Sora (Figure 9:22). The industries are characterised by tools made by the Levallois technique from large cores. In the past they have sometimes been regarded as distinct from the Pontinian assemblages, but the dichotomy seems basically to be the result of the very different raw materials available in the in-

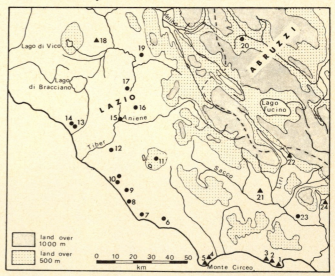

Figure 9. Lazio: Middle Palaeolithic sites (listed with references in Appendix I: 1).

land valleys as opposed to on the coastal beaches (Biddittu, Cassoli, & Malpieri, 1967).

In central Italy, only the Grotta del Fossellone provides direct evidence for the end of the Middle and beginning of the Upper Palaeolithic. Above the sterile Terra Rossa overlying the topmost Mousterian layer was a rich industry designated 'Circeian' (Blanc, 1939b) and a huge faunal sample; whereas the Mousterian fauna had included *Equus caballus, Sus scrofa,* and *Dama dama* and had been dominated by *Bos primigenius*, the fauna now consisted almost entirely of *Cervus elaphus* and *Equus hydruntinus*. Most of the upper deposit had been washed away by sea action, but enough remained to show that backed blade industries succeeded the 'Circeian', associated with the same 'cold' fauna.

The later development of Upper Palaeolithic industries in central Italy is also poorly understood. Although Upper Palaeolithic and Epipalaeolithic sites are numerous, none contains deeply stratified deposits. All the later Upper Palaeolithic sites dated by ^{14}C in central Italy belong to the latter part of the last glaciation c. 15 000 B.P. and later, and the period between c. 25 000 and 15 000 B.P. remains a blank. The Epigravettian typology proposed by Laplace (1964, 1966) has been widely accepted in Italy, and the assemblages between c. 15 000 B.P. and the Neolithic have been classified as *Epigravettiano antico, evoluto,* or *finale*. The first phase, Laplace suggested, lasted until c. 14 000 B.P., the second to perhaps 9000 B.P., and the third until the Neolithic. This system is not without its faults: first, the chronology is largely speculative; secondly, a number of basic criticisms can be made about the typology; thirdly, such a system may interpret in chronological terms variations between assemblages which may only reflect functional differences resulting from the activities of a single group in different parts of its annual territory. Therefore the validity of well-defined Early, Middle, and Late Epigravettian phases in the industries is questionable. Nevertheless, the basic hypothesis of an evolving backed blade tradition in Italy is in accord with the stratigraphical and chronological data, particularly those of northern and southern Italy, which suggest that backed blade industries were used up to the end of the last glaciation and, in evolved and sometimes specialised form, continued into the Postglacial; indeed, in some areas they were the basis of the Neolithic industries which followed. The central Italian sequence, however, is particularly difficult to establish, but it seems likely that Radmilli's (1954–5) 'Bertonian facies' of the Upper Palaeolithic may result largely from differences in raw material between the lowlands and the high Apennines. Of the sites shown in Figure 10, early Epigravettian deposits are known from sites 7, 12, 18, 21, and 22, and later Epigravettian deposits from 4, 6, 17, 19, and 20.

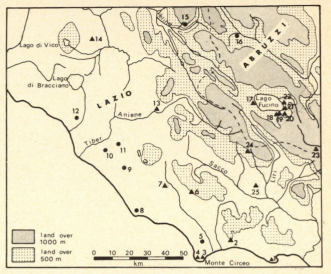

Figure 10. Lazio: Upper Palaeolithic and Epipalaeolithic sites (listed with references in Appendix I: 2).

Middle Palaeolithic economies

The scattered sites of Figure 9 are probably a palimpsest of many thousands of years. The distribution could result from a trend over time, so that individual stages are blurred, or it could show a successful and long-term exploitation pattern. As at Camerota, the Middle Palaeolithic industries probably span the early cold phase of Würm and the interstadial c. 40 000 B.P. Clearly the Middle Palaeolithic data of Lazio are very limited; nevertheless, there appears to be a basic disparity between the distribution of Middle and Upper Palaeolithic sites in Figures 9 and 10: the Middle Palaeolithic sites are confined to the coastal lowlands and lower valleys, whereas the distribution of the Upper Palaeolithic sites reaches inland to the central Apennines. [For evidence in Greece, see Higgs & Webley (1971). *Editor.*] The argument will be put forward below that the disparity reflects changes in exploitation which can be detected in changing faunal samples and changing site territories.

The annual movements of herbivores such as red deer and horse in central Italy will probably have taken place over far greater distances than at Camerota, where the winter and summer grazing areas for the deer probably lay within a short distance of each other. Annual migrations are largely controlled by the distance between winter and summer pastures and in extreme cases (the caribou of North America, for example) annual deer territories are dumb-bell shaped, involving treks of hundreds of miles each spring and autumn (Darling, 1937, p. 96). In southern Etruria, although a certain amount of summer pasture for herbivores would have been available on the ridge between the Sacco and Pontinian plain, the major upland pastures would probably have been at the head of the Velino, Aniene, and Liri rivers and around the Fucine Lake. Würmian snow lines in the central Apennines, thought to have lain between 1700 and 2000 m (Butzer, 1972, p. 293), would not have had a considerable effect on the summer upland pastures, which are mostly between 1200 and 1700 m. In winter, however, snow cover may have reached as low as 500 m (Higgs *et al.*, 1967) and would have obliterated these grazing areas. During the Würm, both horse and deer herds would probably have sought the higher pastures in the summer, particularly in the cold phases before and after the interstadial, when under glacial conditions the aridity of the lowlands may have been even more pronounced than under modern conditions.

Upper Palaeolithic sites are known from the central Apennines and the western lowlands, and the faunal samples from most of the Upper Palaeolithic sites of Figure 10 show a consistent bias towards the large herbivores, particularly *Cervus elaphus* and either *Equus caballus* or later *E. hydruntinus* (Appendix III: 2). In contrast, no Middle Palaeolithic sites are found above the lower valleys on the western side of the Apennines, and the food debris from the sites known to us demonstrates the exploitation of a broad spectrum of game: *Palaeoloxodon antiquus*, *Dicerorhinus merckii*, *Cervus elaphus*, *Bos primigenius*, *Equus caballus*, *Sus scrofa*, *Capra ibex*, and occasionally *Hippopotamus amphibius* (Appendix III: 1). However, the full range of species does not occur at every Middle Palaeolithic site, and it is evident from the three examples given below that site location will have affected the portion of the spectrum which could have been exploited.

Red deer was by far the most abundant animal in the faunal sample at the Grotta di S. Agostino (Figure 9:1), but was associated with roe and fallow deer, cattle, horse, pig, ibex, and occasional fragments of the woodland rhinoceros *Dicerorhinus merckii*. The exploitation territory of the site extends from a small coastal plain in front of the cave (Figure 11a:1), over a succession of low hills to the foot of the limestone massif of the Monti Aurunci on the northeastern edge of the territory. The coastal plain would have been increased in times of marine regression. Today the hills are covered for the most part with rough grazing and extensive olive groves (Figure 11b) and in the past would probably have provided grazing for the cattle, deer, and horse, killed in the territory. The topography is very similar to that of the Camerota territory and, as at Camerota, the rolling hills probably carried grazing for the herbivores which was at its best during the winter. Ibex probably summered on the heights of the Monti Aurunci, but winter conditions would have forced it down to the lower slopes at the edge of the territory north and east of the Itri river. Thus for the exploitation of both the larger her-

bivores and ibex the site was probably occupied during the winter months.

Thirty kilometres to the west of these sites, another group of caves offered a different range of resources to a Middle Palaeolithic band. Some of these caves, such as the Grotta del Fossellone (Figure 12a:3) and the Grotta delle Capre (Figure 12a:4), are large and sheltered, have complex assemblages and large faunal samples, and can reasonably be interpreted as base camps. The territory exploited from these caves reaches from Monte Circeo north over the Pontine plain, which would also have extended south of the caves in a period of marine regression (Figure 12a): a drop in sea level of 50 m would have increased the two-hour territory by more than a third, while a drop of 100 m would have almost doubled the territory, leaving the mountain isolated in the middle of a wide plain. The ibex which

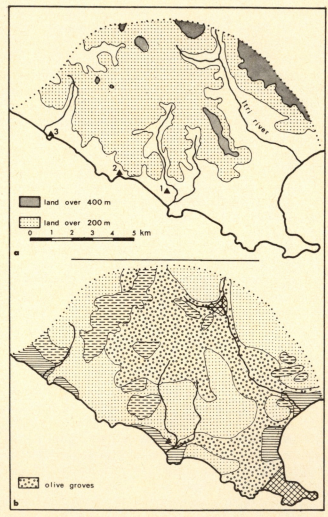

Figure 11. Grotta di S. Agostino: two-hour territory. a, topography: 1—Grotta di S. Agostino, 2—Grotta dei Moscerini, 3—Grotta di Tiberio; b, land use.

appears in the faunal lists would have been hunted on the slopes of the mountain, but the major food sources — cattle, horse, elephant, rhinoceros, and hippopotamus — were all presumably killed nearby on the Pontine plain. The Pontinian surface sites found to the north over the plain (Figure 9:8—10) could well be related to the Monte Circeo caves as transitory and/or butchering camps.

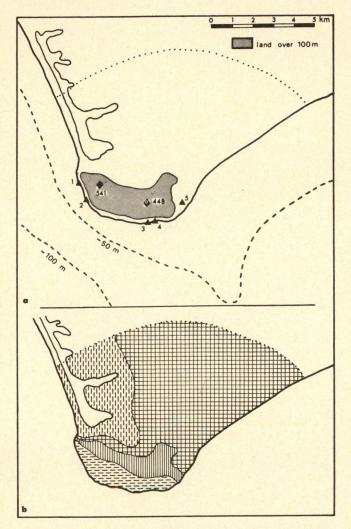

Figure 12. Monte Circeo: two-hour territory (dotted line). a, topography: 1—Grotta Breuil, 2—Riparo Blanc, 3—Grotta del Fossellone, 4—Grotta delle Capre, 5—Grotta Guattari; b, land use.

Inland, the cave at Valle Radice near Sora (Figure 9:22) is situated at the southern end of the narrow Liri valley on the edge of the Apennines (Figure 13). The territory extends over a drained river basin to the south and includes some of the steep hills above the Liri valley to the north. Deer, cattle, and rhinoceros were reported as the main animals killed. The rhinoceros and perhaps cattle were probably killed on the Sora plain south of the site, and ibex was hunted oc-

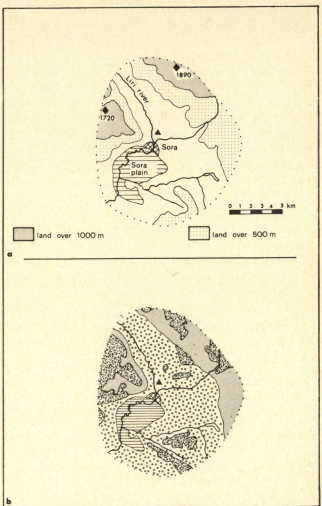

Figure 13. Valle Radice, Sora: two-hour territory. a, topography; b, land use.

casionally, probably on the steep flanks of the Liri valley. If, as I suggested at the beginning of the section, the red deer sought inland grazing areas in the summer, then an obvious route to the high Apennines would have been the Liri valley. Thus the deer would have traversed the Valle Radice territory in the spring and autumn. The Grotta di Cassino (Figure 9:24) occupied an identical situation at the entrance to an Apennine valley and was used to exploit a similar range of animals.

The annual territories of the red deer and horse probably encompassed lowland winter pastures such as the Pontine plain and Sacco basin, and highland summer pastures around the upper valleys of the Aniene and Liri rivers. The territories of the known Middle Palaeolithic sites, however, do not include the upland grazing areas. At the same time, a heavy bias towards one or two animals is not recorded in

121

the faunal samples. Elephant, rhinoceros, and hippopotamus are common in lowland deposits dating to the last interglacial in central Italy. It is unlikely that they were migratory and they probably found sufficient grazing on the lowland plain and in the inland valleys to remain there throughout the year. They persist in the first cold phase of the Würm but seem to have disappeared by the interstadial.

Until these animals became rare before their extinction in central Italy, it was probably more economic for Middle Palaeolithic exploitation to remain on the lowlands, than to follow the deer and horse into the hills during the summer. Thus the known Middle Palaeolithic sites in Lazio probably bear witness to systematic but generalised economies, embracing the coastal plain and inland valleys and utilising a series of seasonal base camps and related transitory sites, whose territories provided differing portions of the total spectrum of the available game. The Neanderthal population apparently maintained this kind of economy during the early part of the Würm, although the gradual extinction of the big game during this period must have made the generalised economy confined to the lowlands less and less profitable.

Late Upper Palaeolithic economies

The macrobotanical evidence of the Canale Mussolini (Blanc, 1957) section shows the development of a fir forest on the coastal plain of Lazio in the cold and dry conditions of the early part of the Würm. At the same time the section of a pollen diagram from Lago Vico in lowland Lazio dating to the same period is dominated by *Artemisia* and other components of steppe vegetation, again reflecting cold and arid conditions (Frank, 1969). After the interstadial *c.* 40 000 B.P. the same steppe vegetation reappears in the Vico diagram and also dominates the diagram from the nearby Lake Monterosi, which dates to the later part of the Würm and has a ^{14}C date of *c.* 25 000 B.P. from a basal level (Bonatti, 1961, 1970). However, the *Artemisia* and related steppe types may not necessarily have been the main vegetation around the lake basins. The diagrams also show small percentages of oak and other deciduous tree pollen and, if the situation of the Ioannina basin in Epirus is applicable to lowland Lazio (Higgs & Webley, 1971), such forest cover may have been fairly widespread in the area: much of the steppe pollen may have reached the Monterosi and Vico basins from the Pre-Apennines and Apennines to the east. On the other hand, faunal assemblages from the late Upper Palaeolithic sites of this period imply the existence of a certain amount of open vegetation both in lowland Lazio and the high Apennines: red deer and *Equus hydruntinus*, the steppe horse, dominate the majority of the samples from the late Würmian sites of Figure 10 (Appendix III: 2). It is unlikely that these samples simply show human bias out of all proportion to the available game resources and one must assume that the conditions in both lowland and upland areas were favourable to deer and horse. In the preceding section I suggested that, although the deer and horse herds probably summered in the uplands in the early part of the Würm, Middle Palaeolithic economies were limited to the western lowlands: the Middle Palaeolithic bands used some sites which probably lay on the migration routes, such as Valle Radice and the Grotta di Cassino, but do not seem to have followed the herds inland. The distribution of the late Upper Palaeolithic sites shown in Figure 10 suggests that the human bands now followed the game inland during the summer months and returned with it in the autumn. If this was the case, their annual territories would have broadly resembled those of the transhumant shepherds in historical times, which encompassed the same kind of seasonal pastures in Lazio and the central Apennines (Figure 3).

The possible 'Early Epigravettian' sites on the lowlands of Lazio are very few, and it is more profitable to turn to the several 'Evolved Epigravettian' sites in Figure 10. The large faunal sample from the Grotta Polesini (Figure 10:13) is an invaluable yardstick against which to measure these sites. The cave is situated on the right bank of the Aniene, some 2 km from the foot of the first hills of the Apennines (Figure 14). A huge flint assemblage, a quantity of decorated bonework (Marshack, 1969), and an enormous faunal sample suggest that the site was probably a preferred site. The faunal sample was dominated by red deer, which occurred with consistent frequencies of *c.* 70 to 80 per cent, and steppe horse. Most of the deer (over 60 per cent) were killed between three and eight years (Figure 6:4), but over 10 per cent of the total kill consisted of year-old animals — again, as at Camerota, probably killed in the winter months, if calving took place in June and July. The mortality data correlate closely with those of the Upper Palaeolithic deer at Camerota and a similar interpretation can be applied to the Grotta Polesini sample.

The long-term preference for the cave is all the more significant in the light of the evidence for a consistent killing pattern of the deer. In the winter, the cave could have been used to exploit the deer and horse on the low rolling hills north and south of the Aniene (Figure 14a). In the spring, the game would have been moving inland up the Aniene, from the plains into the central hills. A few kilometres into the hills, the Aniene river flows down a wide valley, but for the last kilometre before the point of egress onto the Roman plains the river winds through a narrow defile between the heights of Tivoli. The Grotta Polesini is situated some fifteen minutes downstream from the gorge. From the cave, an Upper Palaeolithic band could easily exploit the deer and horse during the spring and autumn, when the restricted route into the hills would have greatly facilitated the kind of selection seen in the deer mortalities at the site.

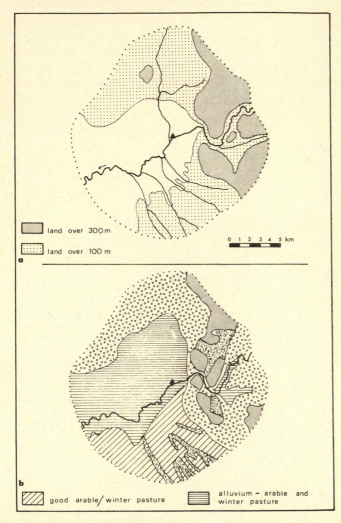

Figure 14. Grotta Polesini: two-hour territory. a, topography; b, land use.

Two other Epigravettian sites are known on the edge of the Pontine plain, both used for the exploitation of deer and horse. Half of the Grotta Jolanda (Figure 10:6) territory extends northeast over the hills to the foot of the main ridge of the Monti Lepini (Figure 15), the other half over the Pontine plain. A winter snowline at *c.* 500 m would not have had much effect on the low hills edging the plain, but the grazing available to the red deer and horse in the summer would probably have been limited to the Lepini ridge, on the very edge of the territory. At the same time, the cave lies near the main pass through the Monti Lepini which connects the Pontine plain with the Sacco and Liri valleys. The Amaseno valley (Figure 15a) provides the main entrance to or exit

from the plain. In the same fashion, the Cisterna shelter (Figure 10:7) is situated at the southern end of the valley which separates the Monti Albani and Lepini (Figure 16); transhumant flocks winter in the territory today and in spring are still driven through the gap in the hills north of the site, round the head of the Sacco valley and up onto the Monti Simbruini. Two sites with similar Epigravettian tool-kits are also known out on the plains: Palidoro (Figure 10:12) and Riparo Blanc (Figure 10:4; Figure 12:2).

Two kinds of sites seem to have been selected by the Epigravettian bands: some were preferred out on the coastal plains for their access to the winter grazing areas of the game; others were occupied because, in addition to the first factor, they also controlled obvious entrance and egress points on the edge of the plains, probably used by the deer and horse in spring and autumn. The red deer sample

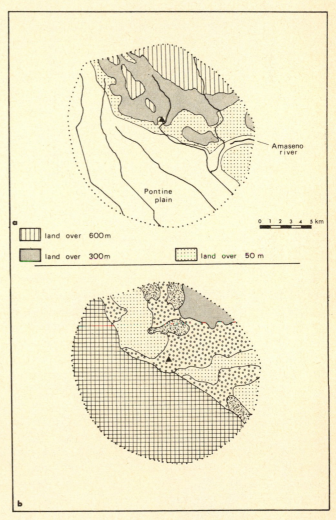

Figure 15. Grotta Jolanda: two-hour territory. a, topography; b, land use.

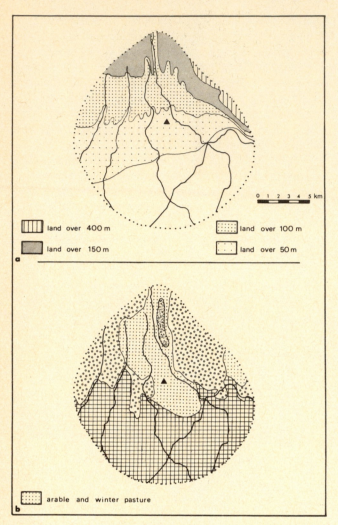

Figure 16. Cisterna: two-hour territory. a, topography; b, land use.

resemblance. In the Pleistocene the lake filled the basin and lake deposits are reported at the base of two of the caves. Considerable annual fluctuations in the extent of the lake have been recorded in the recent past: in wet years in the last century the lake increased by perhaps a kilometre in the southeastern corner near Ortucchio village (Craven, 1838). (The lake was first drained by the Romans and again in the last century.) All of the caves would have been near the lake shore, but fish bones, numerous in the Mesolithic deposits, have only been found in insignificant numbers in the Pleistocene occupation layers. The late glacial deposits roughly contemporary with the lowland sites discussed above consist of the upper levels of the Riparo Maurizio (Figure 17a:2) and of the Grotta Maritza (Figure 17a:5), the lower levels of the Grotta di Ortucchio (Figure 17a:3) and of the Grotta la Punta (Figure 17a:4), and the small deposit in the Grotta di Ciccio Felice (Figure 17a:6).

Radmilli (1959, 1968a) has suggested that some of the caves around the lake were occupied in the winter months,

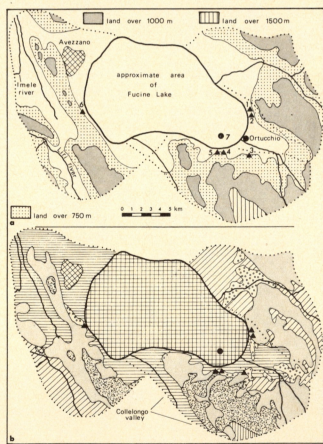

Figure 17. The Fucine basin: two-hour territories. a, topography: 1—Grotta Clemente Tronci, 2—Riparo Maurizio, 3—Grotta di Ortucchio, 4—Grotta la Punta, 5—Grotta Maritza, 6—Grotta di Ciccio Felice, 7—Ortucchio open site; b, land use.

at the Grotta Polesini demonstrates the systematic killing pattern practised towards the end of the last glaciation at one such site in lowland Lazio, which is situated on a probable migration route of the deer herds. If the hypothesis of seasonal migration is correct, then most of the red deer and horse would have summered inland, where several 'Evolved Epigravettian' sites are known in the hills east of the Roman plains (Figure 10).

Six major Epigravettian sites have been excavated on the edge of the Fucine basin in these central Apennines (Figure 10:17–22). Sites 1 and 2 in Figure 17 are within a few yards of each other, as are sites 4 and 5. Three territories are marked in Figure 17, showing the area available today in summer conditions. The northeastern territory is from sites 1 and 2, the southeastern is from sites 4 and 5, the western is from site 6. The territory of site 3 extends further east than that of sites 4 and 5, but in shape and size bears a close others in the summer; in other words, that the annual territory of an Epigravettian band would have encompassed the lake basin where, he suggested, the deer and horse would have been hunted. On the other hand, in the summer the natural grazing areas would probably have been not the small enclosed plains at the level of the lake but the rolling hills which edge the basin to the west, south, and east, where extensive sheep pastures now lie (Figure 17b). These areas cannot support the flocks from late October to spring under modern conditions. It is true that the basin itself has a milder climate than the surrounding hills and today snow rarely lies for more than a few days at a time on the basin floor. On the other hand, the carrying capacity of deer and horse in the basin, which was almost filled by the lake in the last glaciation, must have been extremely small. The enclosing hills would have been at least as important to an Epigravettian band hunting the large herbivores as the floor of the basin, and a winter snowline at even 750 m would clearly have obliterated the greater part of the three territories in Figure 17. It is therefore unlikely that the large herbivores could have remained in any numbers in the winter territories available to the Fucine caves, and I would argue that the onset of the Würm winter would have forced the game away from the central Apennines down the Aniene and Liri valleys to the winter grazing of the western lowlands.

The richest site in the Fucine basin, in terms of numbers of artefacts, was the Riparo Maurizio on the eastern shore of the lake. There were some 1500 artefacts and 5000 waste flakes in the shelter (Radmilli, 1963a). On the other side of the Ortucchio plain, however, the assemblages in the caves of Maritza, la Punta, and Ortucchio were all extremely small, with very few waste flakes. The richest faunal sample was also in the Riparo Maurizio, consisting primarily of red deer and steppe horse (Appendix III: 2). Furthermore, the Riparo Maurizio was a sheltered cave, facing southwest, whereas the southern caves are at the foot of north- and east-facing cliffs. The size and content of the flint assemblage, the large faunal sample, and the situation of the cave all suggest that the Riparo Maurizio was the preferred site or home base. Furthermore, the faunal samples of the caves are explicable in terms of the topography and resources of the modern territories. From the Riparo Maurizio the territory extends eastwards over rolling hills and over half of the territory consists of summer pasture for the Fucine flocks. From the southern caves, however, the territory is more rugged and reaches in places almost to 2000 m; even in late spring snow lingers on the north-facing slopes. Thus ibex and chamois are absent from the Grotta Clemente Tronci and Riparo Maurizio faunal samples (both dominated by deer and horse), but were killed from the southern caves and occasionally from the Grotta di Cic-

cio Felice (Figure 17a:6). The smaller and less favoured (and less favourable) sites can be plausibly interpreted as part of an economic system which pivoted on the Riparo Maurizio as a home base during the summer and involved movement between several sites round the lake, in order to exploit the different range of game available in the different territories.

Many of the large herbivores could well have moved beyond the territories shown in Figure 17 in the summer months, particularly southeast into what is now the Abruzzi National Park. Evidence from this area, however, is very rare, consisting of a few surface scatters and a single late glacial site at the head of the Sangro river, the Grotta Achille Graziani (Figure 10:23). The concept of the 'extended territory' proposed by Sturdy (1972, p. 164) might be relevant to our situation: 'The area that supports resources used by the inhabitants, but that lies outside the exploitation territory and is rarely visited by man. As such, the resources in a site extended territory must be mobile.' The territories shown in Figure 17 probably encompass the area habitually used by the Epigravettian bands in the summer months for the extraction of their subsistence; beyond the territories, however, the highland south and east of the Fucine basin may well have been an 'extended territory' into which some of the game moved as the snows melted.

The onset of the Würm autumn and winter would have gradually forced the red deer and steppe horse down from the Abruzzi highlands to lower ground; many would have moved down towards the western lowlands. The two major routes down to Lazio, the valleys of the Aniene and Liri rivers, originate from the country northwest of the Fucine basin, to the west of Avezzano (Figure 17a). Some of the game would have come down to the basin from the highlands via the Ortucchio plain (Figure 17a) and Collelongo valley (Figure 17b). They would then have had to move round the southern or eastern shore of the lake; in spring, the movement would have been reversed. In either case the Epigravettian caves used to exploit deer and horse (Riparo Maurizio, Grotta Maritza, and Grotta di Ciccio Felice) lay along their routes at the neck of the extended territory like Itivnera, the killing station in Sturdy's example of Lapp herding in Greenland; all three caves are situated where only a narrow strip of land exists between the hills and the former shoreline of the lake.

The tool-kits of the lowland sites on the edge of the Roman plains, which were used primarily for the exploitation of deer and horse, were dominated by backed blades and points (Laplace, 1964). In the Fucine caves (except the Grotta Maritza), however, the repertoire of flint types was very different and, in particular, backed blades and points were relatively unimportant (*ibid.*). The faunal evidence

(Appendix III) demonstrates that other game was regularly exploited from the Fucine sites. The Grotta Maritza, however, has high percentages of backed tools in the same levels in which deer percentages are highest (Grifoni & Radmilli, 1964); the lack of waste flakes also distinguishes this assemblage from those of the other Fucine caves. I suggested above that the cave was not a preferred living site like the Riparo Maurizio and one interpretation of the assemblage difference might be that the cave was selected as a killing station, was occupied at either end of the summer, and that the tool-kit was taken across from the home base for the purpose. In West Greenland the reindeer are driven 'by allowing the deer to see or smell a man in a given position, so that they will move away from the scent or sight in a desired direction' (Sturdy, 1972, p. 167). The Riparo Maurizio lies at the foot of the hills on the floor of the basin; on the Greenland analogy, occupation of this site in the autumn would probably have driven the large herbivores across the Ortucchio plain along the southern edge of the lake past the Grotta Maritza, which is 50 m above the basin floor, on a precipitous slope and invisible in the rocks from below. Furthermore, like Itivnera, the cave is situated by a natural corral or killing ground: immediately west of the cave is a small basin a kilometre square, enclosed on three sides by precipitous slopes and on the fourth by the shoreline of the lake (Figure 17a). This interpretation reconciles the various data in a plausible system of exploitation, on the assumption that the differences observed in the archaeological record of the Fucine caves are meaningful and not simply the result of sampling bias.

Epipalaeolithic economies

The pollen diagrams from the volcanic hills north of Rome document marked changes in vegetation at the end of the Würm. The *Artemisia* and other steppe pollen in the Monterosi diagram lasted until *c.* 15 000 B.P., and then was replaced between 15 000 and 12 000 B.P. by that of a less arid grassland; by 10 000 B.P. the diagram was registering considerable percentages of arboreal pollen of the broad leaved trees. In the Postglacial, oak pollen was absolutely dominant, but at first it was the pollen of *Quercus petraea*, a species more favoured by a cool climate than other Italian oaks (Bonatti, 1970). The Baccano (Bonatti, 1966) and Vico (Frank, 1969) diagrams corroborate this sequence; the minor oscillations known from the intensive pollen studies in northen Europe are not recorded in the available pollen evidence from Italy.

Campania, Lazio, and the Fucine Lake

Although the onset of postglacial conditions produced con-

siderable changes in the pollen diagrams, it is not clear to what extent these reflect changes in the lowlands. The local pollen rain from the deciduous trees around the basins in the Postglacial is probably a major element in the diagrams, but the disappearance of *Artemisia* and other steppe vegetation could also indicate postglacial changes in the vegetation of the Apennines. As in other parts of Europe (Jarman, 1972), red deer continues to be a dominant or an important element in many Epipalaeolithic and early Neolithic faunal samples. This may indicate that it was able to adapt to environmental change (increased tree cover), or that the change was not sufficient to require adaptation on the part of the deer. *Equus hydruntinus*, on the other hand, quickly disappeared from the faunal record in central Italy. Other changes in the faunal samples correlate with the onset of the Postglacial in central Italy and suggest changes in the man–animal relationships which had developed in the late Würm. The changes in the flint industries at some sites in this period seem to corroborate the hypothesis of significant postglacial adaptations in prehistoric economies.

In the Fucine basin, postglacial archaeological deposits are known in the caves of la Punta, Ortucchio, and perhaps in the topmost levels of Maritza, as well as at the open camp near Ortucchio (Cremonesi, 1962; Figure 17a:7). The cave assemblages are poor but are associated with large microfaunal samples. The excavation of specialised postglacial fishing and shell-gathering sites and of these caves prompted Radmilli's hypothesis of an 'economic crisis'; according to this, the postglacial environment reduced the numbers of larger game to such an extent that the human population of central Italy was reduced to fishing, shell-gathering, and hunting small game – even rodents (Radmilli & Tongiorgi, 1958; Radmilli, 1960a; Radmilli & Cremonesi, 1963). The samples of postglacial Epigravettian industries in the Fucine caves are extremely small, consisting of scattered hearths in deposits which are otherwise sterile archaeologically but rich in microfauna; in these same levels, however, the numbers of larger mammals, such as deer, ibex, and pig are not insignificant (Cremonesi, 1968a, table 3). Furthermore, there is now direct evidence to suggest that the microfauna in the caves was not related to human activities. In the basal layers of the Grotta di Ortucchio the microfauna was contained in pellets of unspecified predatory birds (Cremonesi, 1968a). Since the publication of the excavations, bird pellets have also been recognised in the upper levels (G. Bartolomei, *pers. comm.*).

The acidity of the soil has destroyed all faunal remains at the open site near Ortucchio, but the location of the site suggests that, as at the Eneolithic and Bronze Age camps in the same locality, the exploitation of lake resources (both fish and fowl) was the primary activity. The caves on the edge of the basin were no longer the preferred sites, but were still used occasionally to hunt deer, pig, and ibex.

Specialised tool-kits, associated with midden deposits, are known from several sites on the western or Tyrrhenian coast; the Postglacial clearly brought changes in the economy practised at these sites, but the phenomenon is open to more than one interpretation. The earlier levels at the Grotta la Porta di Positano (Figure 5:3), the Grotta Erica nearby (Bonuccelli, 1971), and Riparo Blanc (Figure 10:4) contained 'Evolved Epigravettian' assemblages associated with ibex (especially at Grotta la Porta), red deer, roe deer, and pig. The upper layers contained a specialised 'Final Epigravettian' assemblage, and at the Grotta la Porta and Riparo Blanc these levels have been dated to *c.* 8500 B.P. (Appendix II), with Neolithic pottery occurring in small quantities at the top of the Riparo Blanc stratigraphy. At all three sites fish bones increased in numbers sharply in the postglacial levels and shell middens accumulated in the caves. The rapid dwindling of deer and ibex at this time in the coastal caves might in part confirm the hypothesis of significant climatic change in the Postglacial; however, the changes detected at these sites could be the result of alterations in exploitation patterns by the inhabitants of the caves; it is also possible that, as sea levels rose at the end of the Würm, activities formerly carried out at sites of different altitudes were telescoped into the territories of the coastal sites known to us above the present sea level. Shells are known in small quantities, for example, from both Middle and Upper Palaeolithic deposits in the Monte Circeo caves.

Several 'Final Epigravettian' sites inland demonstrate other facets of the postglacial economy west of the Apennines. The Grotta di Peschio Romaro near Collepardo lies at *c.* 600 m above sea level on the edge of the Monti Simbruini Pre-Apennines (Figure 10:24). The flint assemblage is unpublished but included backed blades and microliths, and lacked the denticulated tools of the coastal sites. To the north are the precipitous slopes of the Monti Ernici, which rise to almost 2000 m directly behind the cave (Figure 18). Even today, ibex is found in these mountains and the faunal sample of the cave consisted almost entirely of ibex. Other sites, such as the several small caves (the 'Cavernette Falische') on the western tributary streams of the Tiber (Figure 10:14), were utilised to exploit larger game (deer and cattle). At Petescia in the Valle Ottara, above the valley of the middle Velino (Figure 10:15), excavation revealed an assemblage of backed blades and points associated with a small faunal sample composed almost entirely of red deer. The territory reaches north up the Valle Ottara just onto the summer pastures of the Monte Terminillo, but also extends across the Velino valley (Figure 19). Both of these valleys serve as routes to summer pastures today, and the camp

would have been ideally placed as a spring or autumn site to exploit seasonal movements of the deer.

The Epigravettian sites in Lazio dating to the Postglacial are very few and their faunal evidence meagre, but cumulatively the data imply significant adaptations in exploitation patterns. I have argued previously that the lowland sites of Lazio were related to upland sites in the Fucine basin in the latter part of the last glaciation, within a single economic system exploiting primarily red deer and

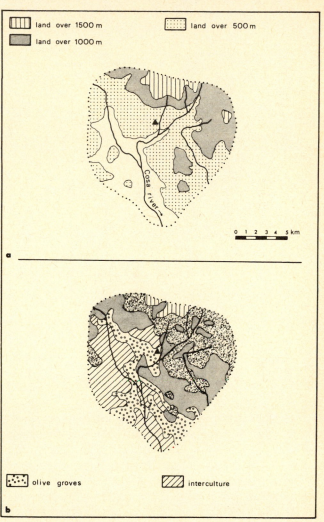

Figure 18. Grotta di Peschio Romaro: two-hour territory. a, topography; b, land use.

horse. The postglacial sites, however, no longer document a heavy concentration on these animals. The seasonal movements of red deer were exploited at Valle Ottara, ibex was hunted from the Grotta di Peschio Romaro, cattle and deer from the Faliscan shelters; the lake resources were utilised in the Fucine basin and coastal sites in Lazio were selected for fishing and shell-gathering. The disappearance

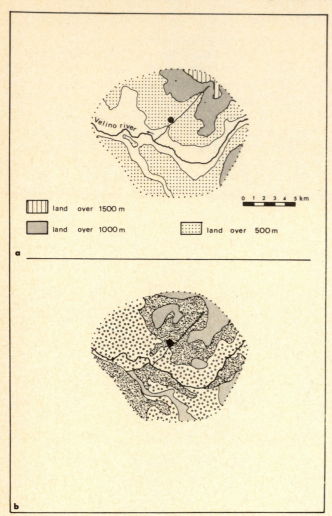

Figure 19. Valle Ottara: two-hour territory. a, topography; b, land use.

site is the earliest of the three; it was situated in the valley of the Misa river, on the ecotone between the dissected plateau of the eastern lowlands and a low ridge of hills which is the easternmost outcrop of the Apennines (Figure 21). The ridge widens and gets higher to the south, where it is cut by the two connected gorges of the Sentino and Esino rivers. The Grotta della Ferrovia is a few hundred metres into the Esino gorge, the Gola della Rossa, with access up a tributary stream onto the heights of Monte Pietroso to the south (Figure 22). The late glacial assemblage was associated with red deer and ibex, the early postglacial assemblage with ibex. The third site, the Grotta del Prete, containing a postglacial industry of truncates, small backed blades, backed points, and a few geometrics, yielded a date of 9990 ± 190 B.P. The faunal sample consisted of red deer and ibex, together with small percentages of pig. The cave situated at the western end of the Gola del Sentino (Figure 23), and the territory reaches east down the gorge, south up the Esino, and west into the Sassoferrato basin, a basin

of the steppe horse from the faunal assemblages in the Postglacial correlates with the increase of tree cover suggested by the pollen diagrams in Lazio. During this period the late Epigravettian sites in the area demonstrate the development of economic diversification: particular sites seem to have been selected for the exploitation of specific resources, only one of which now was red deer.

Marche

Until the last few years, all the Upper Palaeolithic and Epipalaeolithic assemblages known in Marche were surface scatters recovered from river terraces. We now know of three sites, however, which are the first documentation of the Epigravettian sequence in Marche: Ponte di Pietra (Figure 20:2), the Grotta della Ferrovia (Figure 20:4) and the Grotta del Prete (Figure 20:3). The Ponte di Pietra open

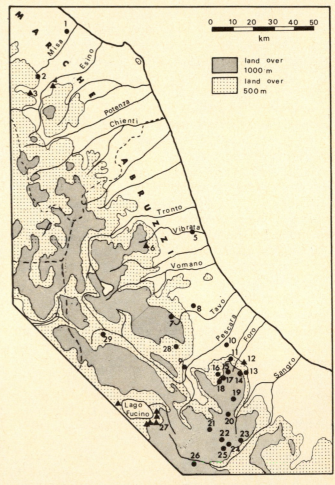

Figure 20. Marche and Abruzzi; Upper Palaeolithic and Epipalaeolithic sites (listed with references in Appendix I: 2).

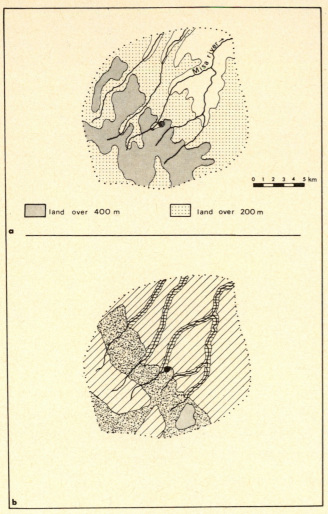

Figure 21. Ponte di Pietra: two-hour territory. a, topography; b, land use.

to the east were probably much less favourable in the summer months (Figure 2b and c); almost certainly, however, the annual territories encompassed areas on either side of the ridge (about 5–10 km wide), and all three sites were located by the routes probably used by the deer in spring and autumn. The sites could also have been used to hunt ibex on the ridge; in Marche, as in Lazio, ibex seems to have become more important in the Postglacial and was probably the main meat resource for the inhabitants of the Grotta del Prete.

Abruzzi

In southern Abruzzi, Upper Palaeolithic and Epipalaeolithic sites are known from the central Apennines to the coast. Inland, 'late Bertonian' surface scatters have

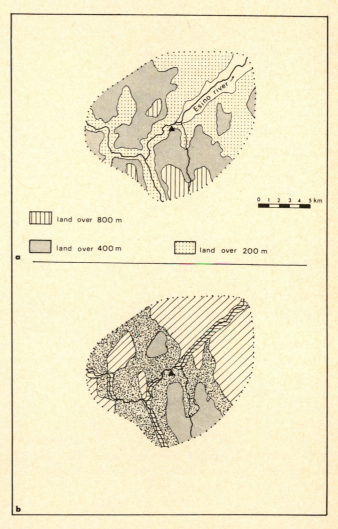

Figure 22. Grotta della Ferrovia: two-hour territory. a, topography; b, land use.

between the ridge and the main Apennines. All three Epigravettian sites lie at the end of narrow valleys which cut through the ridge.

There are marked local climatic differences today between the country east of the ridge, the heights above the gorges (summer pastures for local flocks), and the Sassoferrato basin to the west. The main summer pastures today for transhumant flocks are west of the Sassoferrato basin in the central Apennines (Figure 5:3 & 4). Surveys have not been carried out on the heights of these northern Apennines as they have to the south in Abruzzi, but Middle and probably Upper Palaeolithic surface scatters are known at c. 1000 m above sea level, above Norcia in the Monti Sibillini (Calzoni, 1928a). The summer territories of the prehistoric deer may have lain west of the Sassoferrato basin, or simply west of the ridge, for as today the lowlands

129

caves on the edge of the basin were still used occasionally in the Postglacial for their access to the game on the hills above the lake. Similar assemblages with very small backed blades, backed points, geometric microliths, and microburins, are known on the coastal lowlands (Ripoli; Figure 20:5) and in the intermontane basins (Capo d'Acqua; Figure 20:28). The small faunal sample at Capo d'Acqua was dominated by red deer, but cattle, pig, and roe deer were also present. The camp was located at the head of the Tirino river in the Capestrano basin (Figure 24), and the territory reaches north to the edge of the Gran Sasso pastures. Like the Marche sites, therefore, the camp was probably selected both for the local resources of the lake basin (cattle, pig, roe deer), and the mobile resource (red deer), for the deer would probably have traversed the basin in spring and autumn during their movements to and from

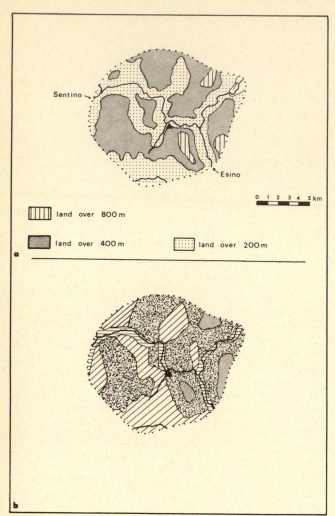

Figure 23. Grotta del Prete: two-hour territory. a, topography; b, land use.

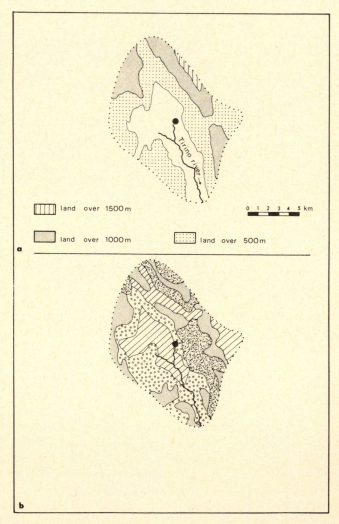

Figure 24. Capo d'Acqua: two-hour territory. a, topography; b, land use.

been found mostly between 1000–1500 m, but some are as high as 2000 m; all are in areas still used each summer by the transhumant flocks from Apulia (Figure 3:9 and 10). Although difficult to place in a chronological sequence, their economic rôle as summer camps is fairly secure. On the lowlands an open site was excavated at Campo delle Piane (Figure 20:8); other lowland surface sites are known below the Maiella (Figure 20:10); and a small Epigravettian assemblage with red deer and ibex was found at the foot of the Maiella in the Grotta del Colle (Figure 20:12), situated, like the Marche sites, on the ecotone between lowlands and Apennines.

The number of unequivocally postglacial Epigravettian sites in Abruzzi is small. The Fucine caves and the Ortucchio open site were discussed earlier: the Ortucchio camp was probably a fishing and fowling site, whilst the

the Gran Sasso slopes. Despite the lack of stratigraphic control, therefore, the distribution and location of both the 'Bertonian' and late Epigravettian sites known in Abruzzi suggest that the economic systems of the Postglacial were similar to those postulated for Marche, both in the range of resources exploited and in the short-distance movements necessary for such exploitation.

PALAEOECONOMIES EAST OF THE APENNINES: NEOLITHIC TO BRONZE AGE

The cultural framework

Postwar excavations by Lollini at several sites have pieced together the basic Neolithic succession in Marche. Four of them in particular are the backbone of the sequence (Lollini, 1965). At Maddalena di Muccia (Figure 25:53), ^{14}C dated to 4630 $\pm$75 B.C., practically all the pottery consisted of coarse bowls and jars, either plain, incised, or impressed. One carinated sherd was of *figulina* ware. There was in addition a handful of dark brown/black burnished sherds. This pottery was associated with heavy- and light-duty polished axes, obsidian – mostly tiny unretouched blades – and a geometric industry. A similar ceramic but quite different lithic assemblage was found in the excavations at Ripabianca di Monterado (Figure 25:39), a site on the coastal plain dated to 4310 $\pm$ 85 B.C., 4260 $\pm$ 75 B.C., and 4190 $\pm$ 70 B.C. Pottery shapes and decoration were much as at Maddalena di Muccia, but there was a larger repertoire of finer wares. Unlike the Maddalena tool-kit, geometrics were absent from the lithic industry save for one trapeze; the assemblage included the Ripabianca burin (Broglio & Lollini, 1963), which is found at other Neolithic sites in northern Italy. The third major site of S. Maria in Selva (Figure 25:50) probably dates to the late fourth millennium or later. The lithic industry can still be related to that of Ripabianca, but new elements are pressure-flaked points, both foliate and barbed and tanged; such points are very common on the later Neolithic sites of the Marche. *Figulina* is an important component of the pottery, often with incised or studded decoration, a feature of several other assemblages of this phase in Marche. The other main group of fine wares varies from dark brown to dark grey, carefully smoothed but rarely burnished. A few sherds of 'Lagozza' ware stand out by their rarity and quality. The coarse ware has a particular mica fill which is found in the coarse wares of several late and final Neolithic sites in the Marche. The last main Neolithic site in the sequence is Attiggio (Figure 25:48). Its stratigraphy overlaps with the late Neolithic sites above and also links up with the Conelle Eneolithic. In level 6, *figulina* disappears

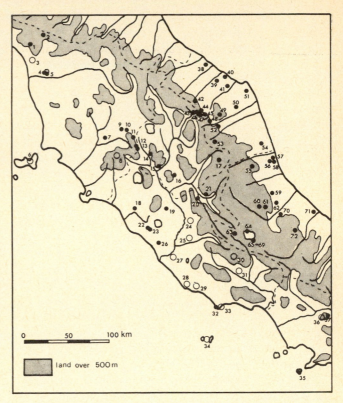

Figure 25. Central Italy: Neolithic sites (listed with references in Appendix I: 3). Solid circle—domestic site; blank circle—possible surface site.

but the dark smoothed and burnished wares continue; and the lithic industry is dominated by pressure-flaked arrowheads. A radiocarbon determination dates level 6 to 2720 B.C. The assemblage has many similarities with the 'Subneolithic' levels at la Romita di Asciano on the other side of the Apennines; in turn, level 4 at Attiggio can be compared with the 'Eneolithic' levels at la Romita ^{14}C dated to 2298 $\pm$ 115 B.C.

In Abruzzi, the situation is similar to that in the north; almost a score of Neolithic sites is known, but there is only a handful of key sites, the most important being Grotta dei Piccioni (Figure 25:70). Level 6 here has impressed and red-painted pottery, and a date of 4297 $\pm$ 130 B.C. An impressed ware open site, Villaggio Leopardi (Figure 25:59), was dated to 4228 $\pm$ 135 B.C. Level 6 at Grotta dei Piccioni included dark brown to black smoothed and burnished wares as in Marche; the other fine ware was *figulina*, occasionally red-painted. The Villaggio Leopardi coarse ware was similar to that at Grotta dei Piccioni and was accompanied by both dark-faced wares and plain *figulina*. The same repertoire was also found at Capo d'Acqua (Figure 25:61), together with one red-painted sherd. At all three sites the early Neolithic flint industry consisted of blades and flakes both retouched and unworked, scrapers, a few truncated and denticulated tools, occasional blades with 'sickle gloss', and, equally rare, backed blades. The succeeding layer 5 at the Grotta dei Piccioni was dated to 2820 ± 105 B.C. Layer 5 is roughly contemporaneous with S. Maria in Selva and Attiggio layer 6, the 'Eneolithic' layer 3 contemporaneous with Attiggio layer 4. As in the north, pressure-flaked arrowheads play an important part in the tool-kits. Obsidian is present but always rare. The dark burnished wares are popular, often decorated with scratched geometric motifs as at S. Maria in Selva and other Marche sites; impressed decoration on coarse wares has disappeared; the same fashions of *figulina* decoration also appear in these levels as in the later Marche sites, including stud decoration, bands of thin incised lines and more sophisticated painting styles, including rectilinear and curvilinear patterns in dark brown paint and bands of red paint: 'classic Ripoli' traits. The same gradual pottery and flint developments are also found in the smaller stratigraphies of the Fucine caves, particularly the Grotta Maritza (Figure 25:66) and the Grotta la Punta (Figure 25:67). All the wares are present from the very first, but particular fabrics become much more popular in the later Neolithic. At Ripoli itself (Figure 25:57), the 'type site' of Abruzzi most traits place the main occupation in the later Neolithic and there are now three ^{14}C dates supporting this hypothesis: 3680 ± 80 B.C., 3610 ± 150 B.C., and 3150 ± 120 B.C. (unpublished).

The assemblages of Marche and Abruzzi discussed above can be related to each other to provide the first framework for the Neolithic. Grotta dei Piccioni has provided an invaluable stratigraphical sequence. At the same time, it is absurd to persist in calling levels 6 and 5 (and their counterparts at other sites) respectively 'Middle' and 'Late' Neolithic, in deference to the illusory 'Early Neolithic' defined as an Impressed Ware phase: as in southern Italy, both impressed and painted wares are amongst the earliest kinds of pottery used on the eastern seaboard of central Italy. All the major wares of the later Neolithic were present from the outset, parts of developing traditions which lasted some two thousand years or more.

The assemblage of level 6 at Attiggio in the early third millennium is an obvious development of the assemblages of sites like S. Maria in Selva; by the second half of the millennium, however, the content of level 4 shows that an early version of the Conelle 'Eneolithic' culture was just beginning to develop. In layer 4 sherds were recovered of *vasi a fiasco*, the funerary ware of the Eneolithic Rinaldone burials, which are particularly common west of the Apennines but are also known sporadically in Marche. In Abruzzi there is the same kind of local continuity between level 5 at the Grotta dei Piccioni and the Eneolithic layer 3, dated to 2356 ± 105 B.C.; this is particularly evident in the coarse

wares, but the same dark-faced wares continue, with the scratched decoration which grows ever more popular. The same developments are found in the stratigraphies of the Fucine caves, with, however, the new element of sherds with *punteggio* or dotting. This decorative style has been found in abundance at Ortucchio, an open site a kilometre out onto the floor of the lake basin from the caves, known as the type site of the Abruzzi Eneolithic (Puglisi, 1959b, 1965).

Later developments are poorly documented stratigraphically. The lack of a good stratified settlement is particularly unfortunate in Marche, for it is virtually impossible to place in order the classic Apennine Bronze Age sites (Rellini, 1931) or to relate their development chronologically to the situation west of the Apennines. In Abruzzi, Apennine decoration is virtually absent from all sites except two. Largely because of this, levels overlying Ortucchio 'Eneolithic' levels at several sites have been defined as 'Subapennine' – Late Bronze Age – by the excavators. Yet the same sites demonstrate the basic continuity between the local wares of the Eneolithic and post-Eneolithic levels. It is impossible to bring conclusive arguments to bear on the hypothesis that there must be a settlement hiatus in Abruzzi between the Eneolithic and Late Bronze Age. However, the persistence of Ortucchio sherds into 'atypical' and 'late' Bronze Age levels which lack Apennine sherds could as well argue that the local 'Eneolithic' was very long lasting and developed into a *local* Bronze Age, with a different ceramic repertoire from that of the Apennine Bronze Age in Marche or west of the Apennines. Only in the latter part of the second millennium does the Bronze Age of Abruzzi lose its isolation. Only two sites in Abruzzi, north and west of the Fucine lake, share in the classic Apennine Bronze Age tradition: the Grotta a Male in the north (Figure 26:79) and, to the west, a cave in the Val di Varri (Figure 26:46). Their pottery closely resembles that of the western lowland sites.

The prehistoric economies

Marche, 4500–3000 B.C.

It was suggested above that the Epipalaeolithic exploitation of the Marche probably ranged from the inland valleys (perhaps even the central mountains) to the coastal lowlands. The earliest Neolithic site of Maddalena di Muccia (Figure 25:53) lies on the edge of the central Apennines; the other early Neolithic sites are situated on the lowlands. A basic part of the Maddalena di Muccia tool-kit is rooted in the Epipalaeolithic assemblages of the Marche, although the geometric microliths recovered in profusion at Maddalena di Muccia were an unimportant component of the Epipalaeolithic industries known to us. Obvious new

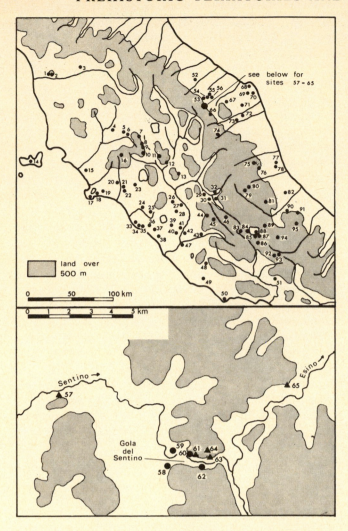

The faunal sample implies that much of the lower ground was wooded, and that caprines made a much smaller contribution to the diet than either pig or deer. A similar situation has been found at the Early Neolithic site of Molino Casarotto in northern Italy (Jarman, 1971; Figure 5:8). The site was ill-placed either for large-scale caprine exploitation or cereal cultivation: the main summer grazing for the caprines lies to the west on the hills and the arable hills to the north have much higher cereal yields today than the lower ground by the rivers, which is much heavier and stonier. Furthermore, like the Epipalaeolithic camps before, the Early Neolithic site was located at the end of exit valleys from the hills: like those sites, Maddalena di Muccia may have been selected at least partially to exploit the spring and autumn movements of the deer. Whether or not we are dealing with an intrusive group is for the moment unimportant: the pottery-using group at Maddalena di Muccia

Figure 26. Central Italy: Bronze Age sites (listed with references in Appendix I: 4). Detail of Sentino gorge (Gola del Sentino) has the same contour as the main map.

elements in the assemblage are the polished axes, occasional obsidian blades, and pottery. The faunal assemblage consisted of 50 per cent pig, almost 25 per cent red deer, 15 per cent caprines, and 8 per cent cattle.

The site lay on the right bank of the Chienti river at the junction with a western tributary stream, just over 400 m above sea level (Figure 27). Rolling hills are to the north and east, while to the south and west the country rises to about 1000 m – the edge of the main Apennine hills. These slopes are heavily forested today, while the arable north, east, and south of the site covers over half of the available area (Figure 27b). The farm at the site has an 18-metre well, but there is a spring about 1 km to the southeast. The farm cattle are taken up onto the lower mountain slopes in summer, but are stalled in the winter.

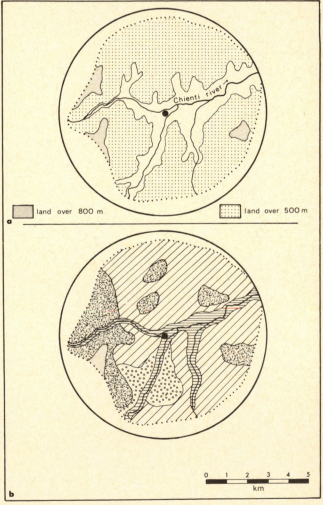

Figure 27. Maddalena di Muccia: one-hour territory. a, topography; b, land use.

133

selected a site in the same kind of position as the sites used by the Epigravettian bands and manufactured much the same kind of tool-kit; equally, save for the replacement of the ibex by sheep or goat, the animal resources exploited were identical.

Ripabianca di Monterado (Figure 25:39) is located on the left bank of the Cesano river, about 40 m above sea level in a wide alluvial plain (Figure 28a). The heavy soil of the plain has been drained for intensive interculture, the plateau region above is used for extensive cereal cultivation. Cattle levels were as at Maddalena di Muccia (6 per cent), pig was less important (19 per cent), and deer quite insignificant, but caprine frequencies jumped from 15 per cent at Maddalena to 64 per cent at Ripabianca. The group clearly concentrated on caprines, yet under modern conditions the site would be extremely unfavourable to them in summer. The successful exploitation of caprines would have necessitated

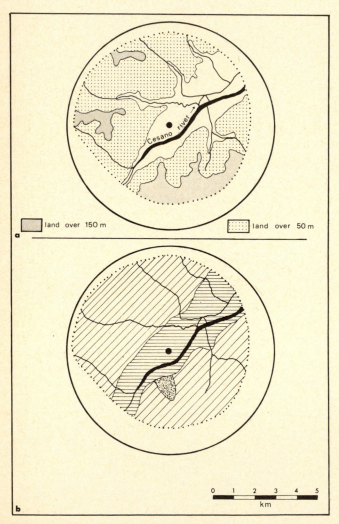

Figure 28. Ripabianca di Monterado: one-hour territory. a, topography; b, land use.

seasonal movements between the central mountains and the lowlands. The nearest summer pastures lie 30–40 km away at the head of the Cesano river, where a Neolithic site has recently been found (Figure 25:42). The location of Ripabianca di Monterado was not suitable for cereal cultivation without a plough, for the lighter soils are those of the plateau, not the plain; the heavy soils of the plain would, however, have supplied winter grazing for the caprines. From the evidence of Maddalena di Muccia and Ripabianca di Monterado, caprines seem to have thrived after their introduction, and the differences between the Ripabianca and Maddalena tool-kits may be related to this fact.

S. Maria in Selva (Figure 25:50) probably dates to the end of the fourth millennium. The faunal sample comprised 33 per cent caprines, 31 per cent cattle, 20 per cent pig, and 16 per cent deer. Although the caprines and cattle were almost certainly herded, it is possible that the deer and some of the pigs were hunted. The several sites loosely referable to the later Neolithic (including S. Maria) have large numbers of pressure-flaked projectile points in a wide variety of shapes. At Molino Casarotto such a point was found attached by twine to a wooden shaft (Barfield, 1971, plate 11), and the points found at these later Neolithic sites can reasonably be interpreted as arrowheads. The composition of the faunal assemblages from many of these sites in Marche indicates that hunting probably provided an important contribution to the diet. Furthermore, measurements taken from pig tibiae from central Italian Neolithic and Eneolithic sites clustered in two discrete groups: the group of larger animals was as large as the Pleistocene pig, whereas the smaller group was as small as Bronze Age specimens. The two clusters, in the light of the increase of deer killed and the proliferation of projectile points at this time, can reasonably be interpreted one as the controlled herd and the other as a wild stock. At S. Maria, five specimens fell in the smaller and seven in the larger group.

S. Maria is the first site in Marche from which cereal remains have been recovered: daub contained grains of bread wheat and barley (Evett & Renfrew, 1971). Both earlier sites were ill-placed for early cereal cultivation, being on heavy soils in river valleys. S. Maria, however, was on a low ridge above the flood plain of the Potenza river, on the light soils of the dissected plateau (Figure 29). Barley is the commonest cereal found on the Neolithic sites of the eastern lowlands (Evett & Renfrew, 1971), and the sites from which it has been recovered are, like S. Maria, on the plateau. Barley is well suited to the lighter soils, it ripens earlier than wheat, and is generally the hardier crop. Today the S. Maria farm sows in October and November and harvests at the beginning of July. If the grain in the daub can be related directly to grain cultivation at the site, it would

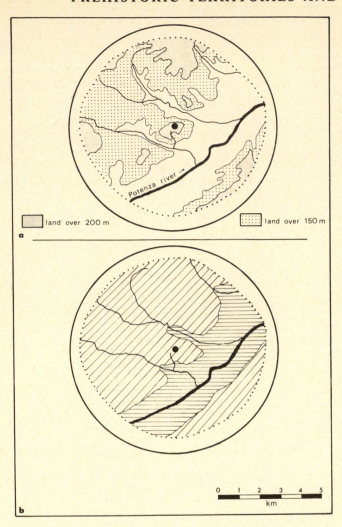

land over 200 m   land over 150 m

Figure 29. S. Maria in Selva: one-hour territory. a, topography; b, land use.

dei Baffoni (Figure 25:45), and the Grotta del Mezzogiorno (Figure 25:44), in the Gola del Sentino and Sassoferrato basin, can be linked with the lowland sites on the basis of the identical mica filler found in the pottery of the two areas. The pottery assemblages at the three upland sites are simplified versions of those of the lowland settlements; no evidence of cereals has been recovered; the faunal samples consist mostly of pig, red deer, and some caprines. All the specimens of pig tibiae from Donatelli cluster in the larger group. The territories, particularly of the two caves, are extremely restricted by the topography of the gorge. What arable there is is very poor, and all the sites seem best interpreted as short-term camps, utilised by shepherds from the eastern settlements such as S. Maria in Selva. Certainly they are situated on the first summer pastures to be reached by groups coming up-river from the lowlands.

At Berbentina (Figure 25:43), however, to the west of these sites, caprines were clearly the most important part of the stock economy, but swine were also significant and most of the tibiae, unlike at Donatelli, fell into the smaller group. Percentages of swine, cattle, and caprines were respectively 9 per cent, 31 per cent, and 60 per cent. There is no cereal evidence, and it is probably significant that the settlement was located on some of the poorest land for cereals today; the yields both north and south of the site are poor in the extreme. Both inland settlements like Berbentina and lowland settlements like S. Maria would have needed alternative pastures for their sheep and cattle; sites such as Donatelli and the Sentino caves in the hinterland and Coppitella di Iesi on a lowland flood plain may indicate the kind of seasonal camps utilised by the large settlements. Maddalena di Muccia and Ripabianca di Monterado were probably used by mobile or transhumant groups; the evidence of the later Neolithic sites in Marche suggests that the integration of cereal cultivation into these economies on the lowlands was accompanied by the development of more intensive patterns of exploitation of both lowland and upland resources.

Marche, 3000–1000 B.C.

The final Neolithic and Eneolithic domestic sites of the third millennium B.C. known in Marche document the same pattern of exploitation as that of the later Neolithic. Attiggio (Figure 25:48), on the one hand, was situated south of the Sassoferrato basin and, like Berbentina, on the edge of the main Apennines. Faunal percentages were relatively stable between levels 6 and 4.

	pig (per cent)	cattle (per cent)	caprines (per cent)	red deer (per cent)
level 6	47	17	30	6
level 4	46	23	22	9

follow that some of the group must have remained at the site from October until July; after the harvest the ground would have benefited from being broken up to prevent evaporation; thus the indications are that we are dealing with a more or less permanent settlement. On the other hand, it is unlikely that sheep and cattle could have been maintained at the site during the summer months, when conditions would have been as unfavourable as at Ripabianca. The most accessible summer pastures would have been 40–50 km away at the head of the Potenza river. Other later Neolithic sites occupy very similar positions to that of S. Maria, overlooking the coastal plain: Saline di Senigallia (Figure 25:40) and San Biagio (Figure 25:38); Coppitella di Iesi (Figure 25:41), however, is situated at the widest point of the Esino river in a very similar position to that of Ripabianca.

Three upland sites, Donatelli (Figure 25:46), the Grotta

The ditched settlement of Conelle (Figure 26:55), on the other hand, was located on the eastern lowlands, east of the ridge separating the Sassoferrato basin from the coastal plateau. The faunal sample comprised 60 per cent pig, 23 per cent cattle, 11 per cent caprines and 6 per cent red deer. Pigs were thus very important to both settlements, but their distal tibia measurements divide the sample equally between the large and small forms. As in the later Neolithic, the Eneolithic groups maintained their own swine, but hunting deer and pig may have supplied almost a third of the meat protein. The few Eneolithic burials in Marche are, like the later Neolithic domestic sites, both on the ridges of the plateau like Conelle (Contrada San Rocco, Osimo, Recanati) and in the river valleys (Fonte Noce).

Despite the richness of the Apennine Bronze Age sites in Marche, we noted above that far less is known about the processes of their development than in other areas of central Italy. The Bronze Age levels in the Grotta dei Baffoni (Figure 26:63) contained a small faunal sample dominated by pig, divided into two distinct groups according to size; there were also cattle, caprines, and red and roe deer. Fuller information comes from the Grotta del Mezzogiorno (Figure 26:64). The Bronze Age deposit was divided into two levels, IIb (the lower level) and IIa. The faunal percentages published by Tongiorgi (1956) were as follows:

	pig (per cent)	cattle (per cent)	caprines (per cent)
level IIa	24	10	66
level IIb	28	23	49

Red deer was also present in both levels. The high percentages of caprines at the cave were an important component of Puglisi's thesis of Bronze Age pastoralism (Puglisi, 1959a).

The Grotta dei Baffoni is a large cavern some 50 m deep, with an entrance some 9 m wide and 4 m high, facing due south. It lies at the eastern end of the Gola del Sentino, 70 m above the river. The Grotta del Mezzogiorno, on the other hand, is situated high up in the cliffs at the end of the gorge, c. 600 m above sea level, reached only by a circuitous and arduous route. The territories of both caves are severely restricted by the topography of the gorge and both are heavily forested (Figures 30 and 31). Grazing areas are limited to the Pierosara valley and the flood plain of the Esino-Sentino confluence. The pottery of the Grotta del Mezzogiorno has clearer associations with that of the lowland sites east of the gorge, such as Bachero (Figure 26:67) or Filottrano (Figure 26:71), than with that of a settlement west of the gorge (between Donatelli and Berbentina) called Monte San Croce (Figure 26:57). The Grotta dei Baffoni, however, can more easily be related to

this and other sites west of the gorge. The rich assemblage at Monte San Croce was found by quarry work, which broke into a cave 150 m above the right bank of the Sentino (Figure 32). Cereal yields today near the site are even poorer than at either Berbentina or Donatelli, both on the terraces below the site and on the arable to the east (Figure 32b). Cattle were reported as the main animal killed at the site, whilst pig, caprines, and red deer were also present in the faunal sample.

About a dozen Bronze Age sites are known on the Marche lowlands, but we have faunal data only from two and cereal evidence from none. The type site of Santa Paolina di Filottrano (Figure 26:71) is on the right bank of the Musone river on an isolated spur (Figure 33). The position is very similar to that of S. Maria in Selva and cereal yields are again very high, averaging 35–40 quintals/hectare

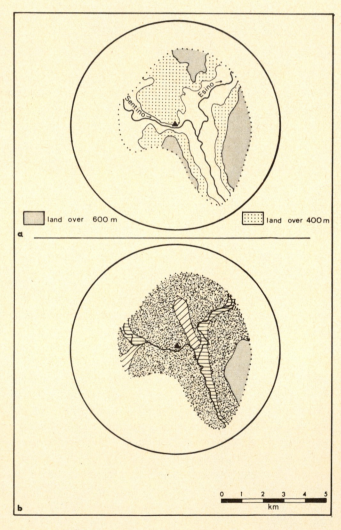

Figure 30. Grotta dei Baffoni: one-hour territory. a, topography; b, land use.

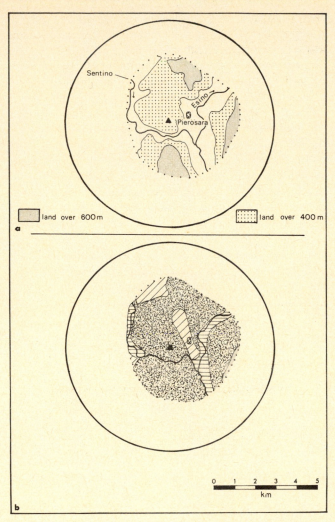

Figure 31. Grotta del Mezzogiorno: one-hour territory. a, topography; b, land use.

poor water supply were probably as severe limiting factors on the lowlands in the Bronze Age as today.

At S. Maria in Selva, the percentages of the three kinds of stock were roughly equal; so too in the Bronze Age the stock economy of the lowland sites seems to have been based equally on cattle, swine, and caprines. Caprines almost certainly could not have been kept in the territories of the lowland settlements in the summer, and most cattle too were probably driven inland. It would have been difficult enough to keep plough oxen on the sites during the summer months: the lack of fodder was probably as insoluble a problem as in classical times, when most Roman peasants could scarcely afford to keep the oxen team, let alone meat or dairy cattle, throughout the year (White, 1970, pp. 276–84). The caprines and most of the cattle were probably taken inland in the spring; if such a system did operate, the Grotta del Mezzogiorno is explicable as the

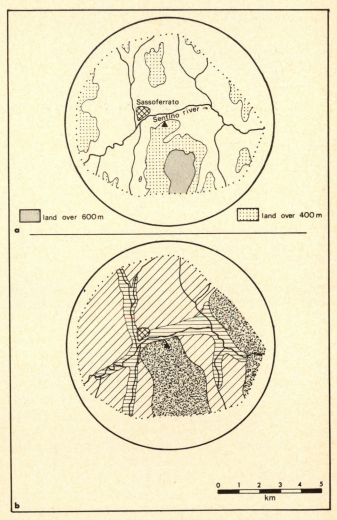

Figure 32. Monte San Croce: one-hour territory. a, topography; b, land use.

(compared with no more than 20 q/ha in the Sassoferrato basin). [A quintal is 100 kg; 1 quintal/hectare is equivalent to about 4/5 cwt/acre.] Percentages of cattle, caprines, and swine were roughly equal and red deer were killed occasionally. Bachero (Figure 26:67), about 15 km up-river, was also on an isolated hill, almost an acropolis, connected by a neck of land to the main spur. Barley on the alluvium below the site (Figure 34) gives yields of 25–30 q/ha today, while yields of 35–40 q/ha are obtained from wheat on the higher ground. Relative percentages of stock were again fairly equal: 31 per cent pig, 37 per cent cattle, and 32 per cent caprines, whilst red deer constituted about 10 per cent of the total sample. Montefrancola di Pollenza (Figure 26:72) was also an acropolis site surrounded by good arable land. All the farms in the area today have wells 10–20 m deep to secure a perennial water supply. The absence of summer pasture and

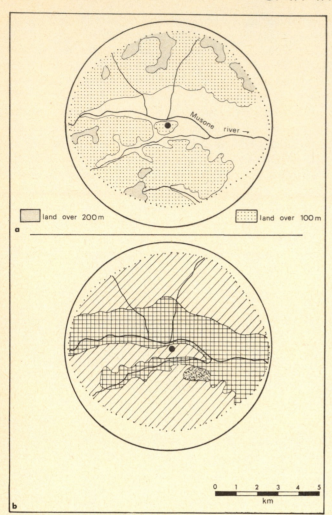

Figure 33. Santa Paolina di Filottrano: one-hour territory. a, topography; b, land use.

century B.C., when Pompey boasted that he had only to stamp his foot in Picenum, and vast numbers of men would answer his summons to arms (White, 1970, p. 70). By this time the Ager Gallicus (the Marche lowlands) was exploited by small intensive farms for cereal, olive, and vine cultivation, with very little emphasis on stock keeping (White, 1970, p. 78), despite the proximity of the summer pastures. This pattern endures today, changed only by the draining of the malarial river valleys and the establishment of small farms there in recent times. The Bronze Age lowland settlements, however, still had limited flocks and herds, yet the latter had gone by the Roman period. Without plant remains, we can only speculate on the development of cereal agriculture, and olive and vine cultivation, between the Late Neolithic and the classical period. The change in the faunal samples of the inland sites, particularly the dwindling percentages of caprines, correlates broadly with the growth of settlement evidence on the lowlands; both

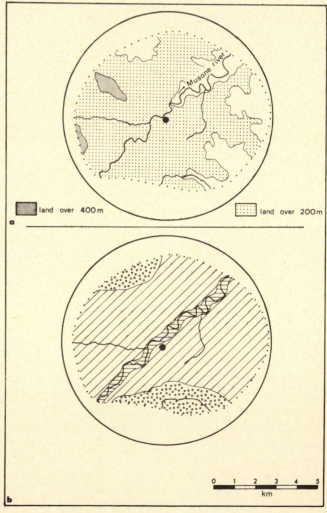

Figure 34. Bachero: one-hour territory. a, topography; b, land use.

kind of site with limited pastures which would have been used in spring and autumn. Summer camps were probably also used, such as Pievetorina (Figure 26:74), on the edge of the main summer pastures. At the same time, however, inland settlements were clearly fairly numerous, particularly in the Sassoferrato basin (Figure 26:57–61), but changes developed in the stock keeping of the area. Caprines in particular grew less and less important: caprines made up 60 per cent of the fauna at Berbentina, 30 per cent in Attiggio level 6, 22 per cent in Attiggio level 4, and were insignificant at Monte San Croce. One hypothesis to explain this would be that the lowland pastures needed for a caprine economy were no longer accessible to the inland groups.

By the Roman period the rural population of Marche seems to have been considerable: 'quondam uberrima multitudine' (Pliny, *Nat. Hist.* III.13.18). The area was the recruiting ground for the armies of the civil wars in the first trends could be an indication of the increasing rural population at the end of the second millennium which we have documented in the classical sources at the end of the first millennium B.C. If this hypothesis is correct, developments in the later Bronze Age on the lowlands would have excluded the Sassoferrato groups from the winter pastures, which must have been so important to the Berbentina settlement in the later Neolithic.

Abruzzi, 4500–2500 B.C.

The earliest Neolithic ^{14}C date in Abruzzi of 4297 ± 130 B.C. comes from level 6 in the Grotta dei Piccioni (Figure 25:70), the level with impressed and incised coarse ware, red-painted and plain *figulina*, and dark faced wares. Variations of this early pottery have been found at sites on the eastern lowlands of both northern and southern Abruzzi and in the Apennine basins. These sites seem to fall into two broad categories.

The first group consists of sites located on the best light soils of the dissected plateau. Villaggio Leopardi (Figure 25:59), for example, was a lowland open site on a spur which juts out from the ridge north of the Tavo river (Figure 35a): the site has been dated to 4228 ± 135 B.C. The lower slopes carry cereal arable with interculture on the ridge round the town of Penne (Figure 35b). Cereal yields today are high, on average 30–5 q/ha; daub examined from the site contained seeds of emmer and barley (Evett & Renfrew, 1971). Catignano (Figure 25:62), just over 10 km to the southeast, exploits an almost identical territory. In northern Abruzzi Pianaccio (Figure 25:58), 4 km south of Ripoli, occupied a ridge position very like that of S. Maria in Selva (Figure 36). The faunal samples at Villaggio Leopardi and Catignano consisted mainly of caprines and swine; cattle were relatively unimportant. The caprine economies probably encompassed summer pastures outside the territories and such pastures today are within a few hours of all these 'arable' settlements.

The second group of early sites was located on the upper limit of the arable, immediately below the Apennine summer pastures (Figure 25:55, 61, 70). The Grotta Sant' Angelo (Figure 25:55) in northern Abruzzi is a large and sheltered cave facing due south, situated 600 m above sea level on the Salinello river, at its point of egress from the Monti della Laga (Figure 37a). There are some summer pastures within the territory (Figure 37b), but the main summer pastures are on the hills immediately above and west of the territory. The arable east of the site is very poor, giving some 10–15 q/ha of wheat today compared with 30–40 q/ha further down the Salinello by Pianaccio. The faunal sample is still being studied but the bias of the stock seems to be towards caprines. The Grotta dei Piccioni

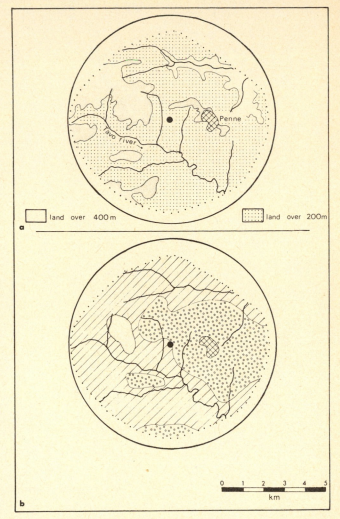

Figure 35. Villaggio Leopardi: one-hour territory. a, topography; b, land use.

(Figure 25:70) is also a spacious cave, at *c*. 300 m above sea level; the cave, which faces southeast, is 100 m above the Orta river, high on the wall of an impressive gorge (Figure 38b). The faunal sample contained 40 per cent caprines, 25 per cent swine, 13 per cent cattle, and 20 per cent red deer. At Capo d'Acqua (Figure 25:61) the Early Neolithic one-hour territory just reaches to the edge of these (Figure 38b). The faunal sample consisted of 40 per cent caprines, 25 per cent swine, 13 per cent cattle, and 20 per cent red deer. At Capo d'Acqua (Figure 25:61) the early Neolithic site was, like the Epipalaeolithic camp, located at the head of the Tirino river. The small faunal sample was dominated by red deer, while cattle, swine, and caprines were also present. The site would probably have been too wet in winter for caprines, but the lowland pastures are immediately beyond the two-hour territory shown in Figure 24. In summer,

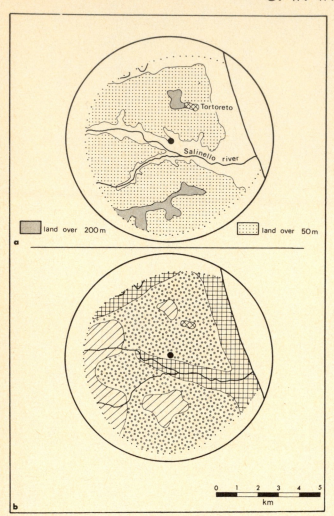

Figure 36. Pianaccio: one-hour territory. a, topography; b, land use.

In the later Neolithic of Abruzzi, the second group of lowland sites, together with the inland camps, was still utilised by shepherd groups. On the lowlands, however, significant developments seem to have taken place by the latter part of the fourth millennium B.C. In the Vibrata and Salinello region of northern Abruzzi, a century of research has revealed an enormous concentration of sites belonging to the later Neolithic (Rellini, 1934), which are on average 2–3 km apart, both on the ridges and in the valley bottoms. The Pianaccio ridge settlement (Figure 36) was also occupied by a Late Neolithic group with plain and trichrome painted *figulina*. Ripoli itself (Figure 25:57) was situated to the north, on a terrace of the Vibrata river 4 km from the sea (Figure 39); the central part of its territory embraces the *bonifica* of the valley floor. Red and roe deer constituted almost one-fifth of the total faunal sample, with cattle forming 25 per cent and caprines and swine 28 per cent each.

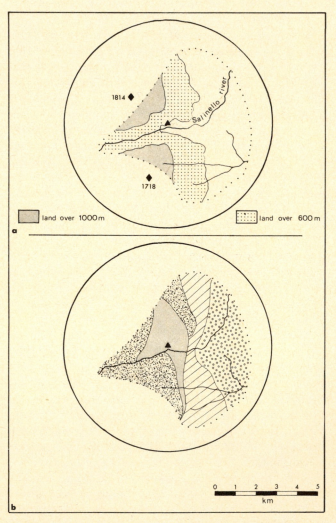

Figure 37. Grotta Sant' Angelo: one-hour territory. a, topography; b, land use.

likewise, the main pastures are not within the territory, but to the northwest and west on the Gran Sasso.

The Early Neolithic groups of this second cluster seem to have selected sites at the limit of the arable, like the Grotta Sant' Angelo and Grotta dei Piccioni, as base camps; such sites have limited pastures within the territories, extensive pastures within easy reach, but were, as a result, away from the prime agricultural land for early cereal cultivation. Similar sites had been utilised at the foot of the Apennines by Epigravettian bands in both Marche and Abruzzi. The Epigravettian bands in Abruzzi probably followed game inland in the summer and the economies of the second Neolithic group involved the same kind of seasonal mobility. Thus we find Neolithic groups with caprine economies in the Fucine basin (for caprines made up 80 per cent of the faunal sample at the Grotta la Punta) with pottery identical to that of the Grotta dei Piccioni; these groups would have wintered in lowland areas.

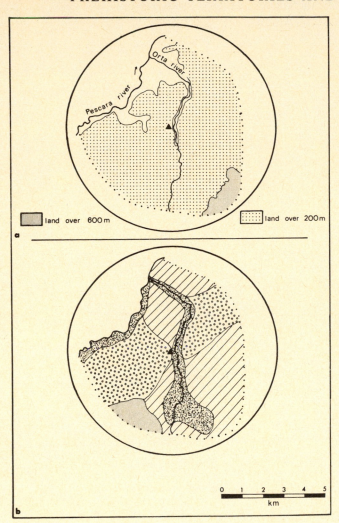

Figure 38. Grotta dei Piccioni: one-hour territory. a, topography; b, land use.

dominated the small faunal samples of the Grotta delle Marmitte (Figure 25:60), in the Capestrano basin a few kilometres north of Capo d'Acqua, and Paterno (Figure 25:64), on the northern side of the Fucine basin. Furthermore, their pottery is closest to that of the lowland arable sites of the Late Neolithic, whereas the scratched decoration, 'Diana' forms, and dark burnished wares in the Fucine caves demonstrate closest associations with the Grotta dei Piccioni assemblage (layer 5). There is as curious a dichotomy between the assemblages of the southern Fucine caves and that of Paterno on the other side of the lake, as there is between the Grotta dei Piccioni and Fossacesia on the lowlands. Thus the two clusters of sites detected in the earlier Neolithic of Abruzzi, of mainly agricultural and mainly pastoral settlements, may have persisted into the later Neolithic.

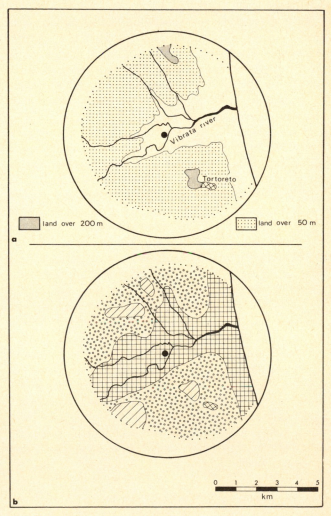

Figure 39. Ripoli: one-hour territory. a, topography; b, land use.

Daub from the site contained grains of emmer and barley, as well as bread wheat, which would have been better suited to the heavier soils of the river valleys (Evett & Renfrew, 1971). In southern Abruzzi, a new Ripoli site with an enormous *figulina* assemblage has been found near Fossacesia (Figure 25:71) on a terrace of the Sangro, in an identical situation to that of Ripoli and with a very similar faunal sample. All the sites have pressure flaked arrowheads and hunting was still important. Thus the expansion of settlement at this time (to include the valley floors) was probably accompanied by more developed agricultural systems.

Livestock was still a significant part of the lowland economies and presumably would still have been taken inland to summer pastures. Inland, two small later Neolithic sites have been excavated in recent years which might be shielings related to the lowland settlements. Caprines

Abruzzi, 2500–1000 B.C.

The heavy bias towards caprines in the Neolithic layers at the Grotta la Punta in the Fucine basin continued throughout the Bronze Age (although the sample is poorer in the upper layers). The lake itself was also exploited in the second millennium B.C., when Ortucchio 'Eneolithic' and then Bronze Age fishing settlements ringed the lake. Bronze Age economies in lowland Lazio also involved the use of summer pastures, but the contemporaneous material culture of the Fucine sites shows almost no influence from the Lazio sites. The upland Apennine Bronze Age sites are all to the west of the Fucine lake, even though large areas of pasture lie north and east of the lake, and it is therefore possible that the shepherds from the western lowlands were excluded from the Fucine pastures. It is unlikely, however, that these resources were not exploited in the Bronze Age. Near Collarmele to the east of the lake (Figure 26:89), for example, a small Bronze Age site was discovered at over 1000 m above sea level (Figure 40a). The territory consists almost entirely of pasture, exploited today by flocks from the Fucine villages (Figure 40b), which are brought up in the spring. From the faunal sample, it is apparent that the Bronze Age site, too, was a shepherds' camp, but we cannot tell whether the flocks wintered on the eastern lowlands or, as today, were stalled in the Fucine villages.

Other Bronze Age settlements on the eastern lowlands follow the pattern established in the later Neolithic. Bronze Age settlements are known on the plateau ridges and in the valleys in the Vibrata area of northern Abruzzi (Figure 26:77 and 78); west of these sites, the Grotta Sant' Angelo was still utilised in the Bronze Age and another camp has been found, also at the foot of the Monti della Laga, a few kilometres to the south at Campovalano (Figure 26:76). Further south, Bronze Age sites are known on the lowland plateau (Figure 26:82), at the foot of the Maiella like the Grotta dei Piccioni (Figure 26:90 and 91), and on the highest pastures of the Maiella, where a Bronze Age camp was excavated at Blokhaus (Figure 26:95) over 2000 m above sea level, immediately by the stalls of modern transhumant flocks (Figure 41). As in Marche, we have no cereal evidence and little faunal evidence for the period in Abruzzi. We know of fishing villages round the Fucine lake, transhumant shepherds in the Fucine caves, at Blokhaus, Collarmele and the Grotta dei Piccioni; at the same time, presumably, small agricultural settlements such as Campo delle Piane (Figure 26:82) proliferated on the good arable of the coastal plateau.

Neolithic beginnings east of the Apennines

The major associations of the earliest pottery on the Adriatic side of the Apennines in central Italy are with the

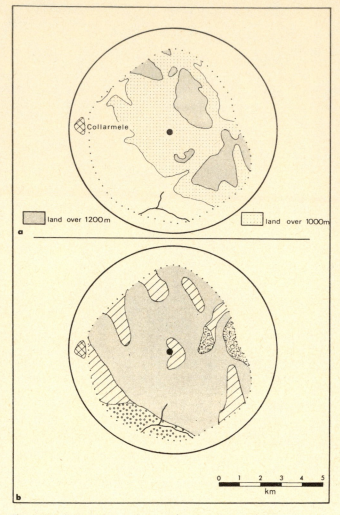

Figure 40. Collarmele: one-hour territory. a, topography; b, land use.

impressed and red-painted wares of the first Neolithic in Apulia. Here there is considerable evidence of related Epipalaeolithic and Neolithic flint industries and economies in many coastal areas, apart from the Tavoliere or plain of Foggia, where no Epipalaeolithic sites but scores of Early Neolithic sites are known (see also Jarman and Webley, below). The latter, found from the aerial photography of Bradford in the postwar years, have been the strongest element in the 'colonist hypothesis'. Thus Ruth Whitehouse has argued that Neolithic farmers arrived on the shores of southern Italy from the eastern Mediterranean c. 5000 B.C.; an existing Mesolithic population on the periphery of the colonised areas adopted some Neolithic skills, principally the ability to make pottery (impressed ware), but occasionally stock keeping too (Whitehouse, 1968a, 1968b, 1971).

The Epipalaeolithic assemblages in southern Italy have

mostly been recovered from coastal caves. In central Italy, however, Epipalaeolithic sites are known across the peninsula, and I suggested earlier that the exploitation of coastal resources was but one element in the economic systems which developed in the Postglacial. East of the Apennines, I have argued, Epipalaeolithic economies in both Marche and Abruzzi involved short-distance mobility between the coast and the hinterland. We cannot hazard any guesses on the size of the Epipalaeolithic population on the Adriatic side of the Apennines, but the economic systems of the human groups probably ranged from the lowland plain to the central Apennines. This population must be integrated into models of Neolithic beginnings.

On the present radiocarbon dates, pottery (impressed and *figulina*) had appeared in Marche, together with domesticated caprines, by *c.* 4500 B.C., in Abruzzi perhaps a little later. Some five millennia thus separate the groups at

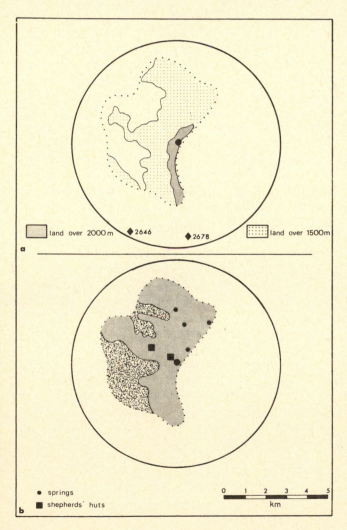

land over 2000m ◆2646 ◆2678 land over 1500m

a

● springs
■ shepherds' huts

0 1 2 3 4 5
km

b

Figure 41. Blokhaus: one-hour territory. a, topography; b, land use.

the Grotta del Prete and Maddalena di Muccia, but the origins of the Maddalena tool-kit can reasonably be found in the Grotta del Prete industry. In Abruzzi, the Epipalaeolithic assemblage at Capo d'Acqua is probably later than that of the Grotta del Prete; likewise, it is more obviously the parent of the early Neolithic assemblage at the same site. At both Maddalena di Muccia and Capo d'Acqua, the economy of the early Neolithic group was much the same as that of the Epipalaeolithic, augmented now by the herding of a few caprines. Furthermore, like the Epipalaeolithic sites, many early Neolithic camps (Capo d'Acqua, Grotta dei Piccioni, Grotta Sant' Angelo, Maddalena di Muccia) were situated at the foot of the central Apennines, on the highland/lowland junction. In Marche, Ripabianca di Monterado shows the rapid increase in sheep and goat herding in the second half of the fifth millennium B.C., but cereal cultivation is not documented until the fourth millennium. A millennium before this in Abruzzi we have evidence of two groups of sites, one with a heavy bias towards sheep and goat herding, the other with a mixed economy of cereal cultivation and mixed stock keeping. The location of both groups is related to the resources necessary for the two kinds of economy.

Three simple hypotheses can be constructed from the data. The first is that all our sites are of Epipalaeolithic groups which integrated caprines and cereals gradually into their mobile economies between roughly 4500 and 4000 B.C. This hypothesis is supported by the essentially Epipalaeolithic nature of the earliest Neolithic flint industries and economies, the gradual change in the Marche faunal samples (and particularly the increase in caprine percentages), and the close correlation in the selection of Epipalaeolithic and many early Neolithic camps.

Obsidian blades, probably from Lipari and Palmarola, are a feature of the earliest Neolithic sites of Marche and Abruzzi; they bear witness to the kind of exchange systems which existed across Italy at this time; none has so far been found in an Epipalaeolithic assemblage. The mass of pottery is probably locally made, but the half dozen or so sherds of fine red-painted ware contrast so obviously with the soft chalky *figulina* that we can reasonably interpret the red-painted ware as an import and the likeliest source is Apulia. In this first hypothesis, therefore, the likeliest source of the cereals and caprines which appear in the area at the same time as the obsidian and red-painted ware would also be Apulia, where the first Neolithic sites date to the early fifth millennium B.C. On the other hand, the Villaggio Leopardi group of sites might argue against this simple hypothesis, for the mixed economy of wheat and barley cultivation and stock breeding (probably involving inland shielings) appears fully fledged at these sites on the soils best suited to early agriculture.

The second hypothesis would be that all or most of our sites are the villages of Neolithic colonists, either from southern Italy or the eastern Mediterranean: 'the new race which entered Italy at the end of the palaeolithic period' (Peet, 1909, p. 165). It is difficult to reconcile most of the evidence of the Marche and Abruzzi sites with such an hypothesis, unless we argue that colonists arriving on the shores of central Italy would have had to adapt so drastically to the limiting factors imposed on a stock economy and to the abundant existing resources of game and so on, that they manufactured tool-kits inevitably very similar to those of the Epipalaeolithic groups. Thus the Epipalaeolithic and most of the Neolithic groups practised mobile economies over the same areas, selecting the same kind of sites, sometimes even the same sites.

A third hypothesis would be a version of the preceding two. The greater part of the evidence supports the first hypothesis, of negligible population change, but rather of a series of adaptations at different rates by the indigenous human groups to new resources. At the same time, the Abruzzi arable sites could perhaps be the settlements of new groups, whose origins lay ultimately to the south. Yet they, too, would have had to adapt their economies to the seasonal pastures and the annual territories would have resembled those of the Epipalaeolithic hunting groups in the same area.

PALAEOECONOMIES WEST OF THE APENNINES: NEOLITHIC TO BRONZE AGE

The cultural framework

The site usually regarded as the type site in the west, the Grotta Patrizi near Sasso (Figure 25:22), contained a Neolithic burial and a large number of funerary goods: pottery, flintwork, polished axes, and a number of shell and bone ornaments. The dark brown pottery was decorated with broad incised lines and small pits or impressions. The flint tools were usually made from parallel sided blades and consisted mostly of trapezes, truncated blades, and scrapers. From the obvious similarities with the pottery and flintwork of the Emilian Fiorano sites, Radmilli (1953b) suggested that the Grotta Patrizi was an extension of the Fiorano culture to the western side of central Italy. He therefore proposed the Grotta Patrizi as the type site and the term Fiorano-Sasso has since been accepted to suggest linked cultures.

Stratigraphic evidence for the chronological position of the Sasso sites is sparse and ambiguous. The one reliable stratigraphy, at la Romita di Asciano near Pisa (Figure 25:4), is far to the north and seems to show mostly local conditions which bear little relation to developments further south. A basal 'Middle Neolithic' deposit included sherds of a typical Fiorano-Sasso *boccale* and a sherd of black burnished ware with comb-impressed decoration, or *ceramica dentellata* (Peroni, 1962–3). The 'Late 'Neolithic' levels contained 'Lagozza' sherds in dark burnished fabrics. Our only date for a Sasso site, 4130 ± 200 B.C., comes from the Grotta dell'Orso in Tuscany.

Recently excavations at Pienza in Tuscany (Figure 25:9) and Palidoro in Lazio (Figure 25:26) have produced evidence that *ceramica dentellata* is at least as early as Sasso ware and may be earlier. The lowest levels at Pienza contained *ceramica dentellata* and other impressed and incised sherds; in the levels above, Ripoli trichrome ware was found with unpainted *figulina*, two sherds of red-painted *figulina*, and a few Sasso sherds; in the topmost levels of the Neolithic deposit the Ripoli trichrome ware was associated with other 'late' types, such as a 'Diana' *ansa a rocchetto*. At Palidoro, the *ceramica dentellata* in the lower part of the stratigraphy was found with sherds of painted *figulina*. Higher up were sherds of Ripoli trichrome ware, Sasso ware, and an *ansa a rocchetto*. The two stratigraphies conflict in some ways, but the comb-impressed ware seems to be earlier than Sasso ware at both sites and the Sasso ware is associated at both sites with Ripoli trichrome ware. Apart from the three sites discussed above, *ceramica dentellata* from early excavations in the Grotta Lattaia (Figure 25:12) and Grotta dell'Orso (Figure 25:11) has now been found.

On the eastern side of the Apennines, the shapes and decoration of the impressed and incised wares in Marche and Abruzzi are closely comparable to those of the early pottery in southeast Italy (Whitehouse, 1969), Yugoslav Dalmatia (Batovič, 1966), and Albania (Korkubi & Andrea, 1972): an 'eastern province' of early impressed pottery. On the other side of the Apennines, the Sasso and comb-impressed wares can best be regarded as the primary wares of the Tyrrhenian Neolithic, although the relationship to each other on the present data is problematical. Thus Sasso is a pottery style almost identical to the Fiorano style of northern Italy, while the *ceramica dentellata* lies within a western and central Mediterranean province of impressed wares. In a sense, therefore, the Apennine watershed divides not only the regional pottery groups of central Italy but also two larger provinces of early pottery in the Mediterranean.

Later Neolithic developments are little clearer. In the upper levels at Palidoro and middle levels at Pienza, Sasso sherds are found with Ripoli trichrome *figulina*, but later they are not found in Neolithic sites where Ripoli trichrome *figulina* still appears. The assemblages of the later sites, such as Cola ïI di Petrella (Figure 25:63), Norcia (Figure

25:17), la Romita di Asciano 'Late Neolithic', Tre Erici (Figure 25:18), and Valle Ottara (Figure 25:21), share general similarities in pottery, fabrics and shapes, and occasionally isolated 'imports', with other parts of Italy. Nevertheless, underneath these general associations, there remains the very local component of most of the later Neolithic assemblages. It seems fruitless at the present time to tag any of the pottery in these Tyrrhenian sites with a label from a three stage system of Early, Middle, and Late Neolithic phases. We have no idea about the timespan of Sasso pottery before and after c. 4000–3500 B.C. (in ^{14}C years), nor that of the different painted styles of *figulina* before and after c. 3500–3000 B.C. In central Italy as a whole, and especially west of the Apennines, any rigid classification beyond 'earlier' and 'later' Neolithic must beg fundamental questions which are unanswered by the available stratigraphic evidence.

The Rinaldone burials west of the Apennines can now be related to a few settlement sites. In la Romita di Asciano the 'Late Neolithic' assemblage evolved into a 'Subneolithic' and thence an 'Eneolithic' assemblage. Sherds of the Rinaldone *bottiglia* or *vaso a fiasco*, the most common vessel of the Rinaldone burials, were recovered from the middle and upper layers of the 'Eneolithic' deposit; the middle layer was dated to 2298 ± 115 B.C. Incised decoration appeared in the topmost 'Eneolithic' level, a forerunner of the Polada incised wares of the following 'Early Bronze Age' levels (Peroni, 1962–3, pp. 406–8). Apart from these isolated sherds, however, there was a ceramic continuity between the Late Neolithic, Subneolithic, and Eneolithic layers at the site. Rather different Eneolithic domestic wares have been found to the south in the Grotta dell'Orso, decorated by smearing or incising before firing (Cremonesi, 1968b, p. 253). Other coarse pottery was decorated with applied cordons, often thumb-impressed. Similar decoration was used in the Eneolithic deposit at Tre Erici (Östenberg, 1967, p. 56), where the domestic assemblage was also associated with sherds of Rinaldone *bottiglia*. Three radiocarbon dates place the Eneolithic settlement at the end of the third millennium: 2075 ± 100 B.C., 2005 ± 200 B.C., and 1850 ± 80 B.C.

The radiocarbon dates from Attiggio, Grotta dei Piccioni, la Romita di Asciano, and Tre Erici have destroyed the hypothesis of an 'Eneolithic horizon' (Puglisi, 1959a, 1959b and 1965): the duration of the Eneolithic assemblages was at least in the order of half a millennium. Secondly, where Late or Final Neolithic layers are stratified below an Eneolithic deposit there is demonstrable continuity between the main ceramic and lithic types of the two groups.

Our best means of dating the Rinaldone graves is the appearance of the *vaso a fiasco* sherds in the domestic sites

^{14}C dated to between c. 2300 and 1800 B.C.: Attiggio, la Romita di Asciano, and Tre Erici. On the calibrated chronology, the period of the graves would fall in the first half of the third millennium and could have begun before 3000 B.C.

Puglisi (1959a) defined the Apennine Bronze Age as a culture which practised an economy of transhumant pastoralism and his arguments have met with wide acceptance, although mostly drawing on cultural rather than direct economic evidence. Recently, however, the 'pastoralist hypothesis' has been questioned by Östenberg (1967), whose excavations at Luni recovered rock-cut house foundations and evidence for a mixed economy of stock keeping and cereal cultivation.

Peroni (1959) suggested that his first phase, the 'Apennine', was probably full Bronze Age. However, a series of graves excavated in the south has produced pottery with sufficient links both with the Eneolithic and the Apennine tradition to cause the introduction in recent years of the term 'Protoapennine'. The local development of the Apennine axe handle from the earlier elbow handle in the south has been convincingly demonstrated by Lo Porto (1964, p. 134, Figure 9) at the settlement of Porta Perone near Taranto. In central Italy, elbow handles occur in late Neolithic contexts at Ripoli (Cremonesi, 1965, p. 113, Figure 10:8) and axe handles are known from a few Rinaldone graves, such as Punta degli Stretti (Minto, 1913, p. 133, Figure A). The settlement evidence also gives little support to the hypothesis of a cultural dichotomy between the Eneolithic and Bronze Age assemblages. 'Protoapennine' deposits *sensu strictu* may exist in Lazio at Tre Erici (Luni) and Palidoro (Peroni, 1965); intermediate deposits between the local Eneolithic and full Bronze Age have been excavated at several sites on the eastern side of the Apennines, but the settlement evidence shows almost as much regional variation in the Bronze Age material culture as in the Eneolithic. In this situation, terms such as Protoapennine, Apennine, and Subapennine, applied throughout central Italy as a rigid chronological sequence, can only serve to obscure processes of cultural change.

Östenberg distinguished three levels of Bronze Age occupation at Luni (Figure 26:24), which he called Apennine I, II, and III. The dating pivots on Apennine II, which has ^{14}C dates of 1245 ± 75 B.C. and 1170 ± 75 B.C., together with two sherds of Mycenaean IIIB pottery (1300–1230 B.C.). The excavator chose a short chronology and dated Apennine I to 1350–1250 B.C., II to 1250–1150 B.C., and III to 1150–1000 B.C. On the other hand, calibration would push the Apennine II ^{14}C dates back to c. 1500 B.C., and Apennine I would then fall in the first half of the second millennium. Certainly the short chronology leaves an uncomfortably long gap between the Eneolithic deposit at Tre

Erici below Luni *c.* 2000/1800 B.C. (in ^{14}C years) and Luni Apennine I; yet a clear linear relationship was seen between the pottery of the two groups and Eneolithic decoration still appeared in Apennine I. There are therefore reservations about the wider implications of the sequence.

Apennine I decoration developed trends seen in the local Eneolithic and included *punteggio* as well as 'classic' Apennine motifs. Axe or tongue handles had appeared in the Eneolithic. They continued in Apennine I and II, but were rare in III; instead, handles gradually developed the exotic forms known in the Late Bronze Age, with horns and animal heads. The typical Apennine motifs flourished in the early stages but grew less common in time. The stratified phases at Luni (as at the Grotta a Male) thus largely corroborate the main typological system of Peroni (1959), but emphasise how gradually different elements appear and disappear. Classic 'Subapennine' forms in fact occur sporadically very early in the sequence, but only become more common much later; typical 'early' handle forms still appear occasionally in Apennine III.

Apennine Bronze Age sites are known on the coastal plain and lowland hills of Etruria; in the hills north and east of Monte Amiata in central Toscana and western Umbria clustered around Belverde, which may have been an important religious or social centre (Trump, 1966, pp. 118–19); and in the Pre-Apennines and central Apennines. The similarities between the Apennine pottery used on the lowland sites of southern Etruria (Luni, Malpasso, Marangone, Narce, Palidoro, Pian Sultano, Torre Chiaruccia) and the inland sites to the east (Grotta a Male, Ponzano, Toffia, Val di Varri, Valle Ottara) are very close indeed and the hypothesis will be put forward in the following section that economic, as well as cultural, relationships are represented by the archaeological record of these sites.

The prehistoric economies

The Tyrrhenian Neolithic, 4500–2500 B.C.

I suggested above that postglacial economies on the Tyrrhenian side of the Apennines involved the exploitation

of a more diverse range of resources than before: the Epipalaeolithic bands probably moved from area to area, utilising the seasonal resources of the coast (Riparo Blanc), the inland valleys (Valle Ottara), and the high peaks (Grotta di Peschio Romaro). Our only ^{14}C dates come from the two midden sites, the Grotta la Porta di Positano and Riparo Blanc, both of the mid-seventh millennium B.C. After this there is an hiatus in the record; if the stratigraphies of Palidoro and Pienza are accepted, the first Neolithic pottery on this side of central Italy should date to some time in the fifth millennium and perhaps is as early as the impressed pottery of southern France or Praia a Mare in Calabria. However, because of the ambiguity of the evidence, the Early Neolithic sites with *ceramica dentellata* and Sasso pottery will be discussed together in this section.

Our most complete picture of an Early Neolithic economy west of the Apennines comes from the faunal and plant samples recovered at Pienza. In the earlier Neolithic levels (*ceramica dentellata* and Sasso), caprine percentages were very high; in the later phases, caprine and cattle percentages were roughly equal. Table 2 shows the percentages of the identifiable fragments. The estimation of the minimum number of individuals from different anatomical elements confirmed the bias towards the caprines in the earlier Neolithic levels. According to modern mortality data of tooth eruption and bone fusion (Silver, 1969), most of the caprine deaths occurred in the third year or even later; nearly all of the cattle were over 2–4 years old at death; most swine died in the second, third, or later years.

A sample of carbonised plant remains was also recovered by the flotation method from the quarry section at Pienza; the preliminary analysis is given in Table 3 (H. N. Jarman, *pers. comm.*).

Pienza lies in the eroded *crete senesi* of inland Toscana: the town is situated on the edge of a flat spur 400 m above sea level, north of the Orcia river (Figure 42a). Most of the territory (65 per cent) consists of cereal fields and pasture; the former today yield some 30 q/ha, compared with up to 50 q/ha on the land exploited by Late Neolithic groups in Marche. Most of the remaining land in the territory is reserved as pasture and rough grazing (Figure 42b). Water

Table 2.   Percentages of identifiable bone fragments from Pienza

Context	Cattle Per cent	Caprines Per cent	Pig Per cent	Dog Per cent	Red deer Per cent	Roe deer Per cent
Bronze Age levels	33	36	17	7	7	–
Later Neolithic levels	36	35	18	5.5	5.5	–
Earlier Neolithic levels	16	62	12	8.5	1	0.5

scarcity is a major limiting factor today to settlement in this part of Toscana. Water has to be pumped to the town in the summer months; a single spring flows throughout these months and its outlet is less than fifty metres from the prehistoric settlement.

Table 3.   Plant remains from Pienza

Context	Identification	Comment
Later Neolithic levels	*Hordeum* sp.	present
Sasso levels (above the hearth)	*Gramineae*	present
Sasso/*ceramica dentellata* levels (at and below the hearth)	*T. aestivum* var. *compactum*	very common
	T. dicoccum	fairly common
	Hordeum distichum var. *nudum*	common

The principal limiting factor, however, for cattle or caprines is the shortage of winter pasture. Pienza, like other upland villages of Toscana, kept flocks in the past; necessarily they were mobile, summering on the pastures of the Val d'Orcia, wintering on the Maremma. Nowadays the Maremma has been reclaimed for arable land and transhumance is much reduced. Nevertheless, remnants of the old practices remain: the *Fiera del Cacio*, a shepherds' festival dominated by a market for *pecorino* or sheep's cheese, still takes place in the town in September, the month when the local shepherds would have been preparing to move down to the Maremma. Obviously the stock economy of the earlier Neolithic group consisted primarily of sheep and goat herding, integrated with the cultivation of barley, emmer, and club wheat. Whether or not optimum use had to be made of the available resources in the territory, the prehistoric stock economy must have been adapted in some way to the absence of pasture in the winter for the flocks. Sheep kept in the territory today have to be stalled and fed on fodder in winter. This might have been Neolithic practice, but the preferred solution in the past has been the utilisation of winter pasture outside the Pienza territory on lower ground. Part or most of the group probably remained at Pienza during the year, to sow the grain in late autumn (on the modern analogy) and harvest in mid-July; but in winter, shepherds probably took the flocks down to the lowlands some four to five days' march away.

Several Neolithic sites are known in the same part of Toscana, but economic information about them is very limited. At Grotta dell'Orso (Figure 25:11), a cave about twenty kilometres southeast of Pienza, the faunal sample included 23 per cent cattle, 33 per cent caprines, 30 per cent swine, 2 per cent red deer, and 3 per cent roe deer (Grifoni, 1967). The cave is situated on the northern edge of the ridge of Monte Cetona, about 500 m above sea level

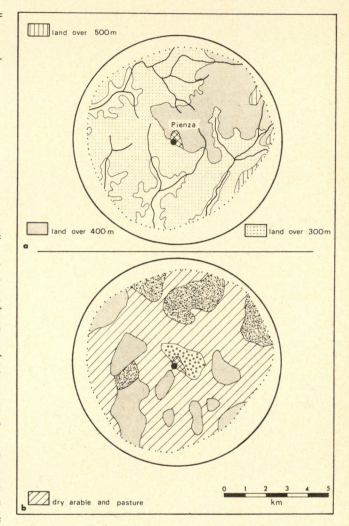

Figure 42. Pienza: one-hour territory. a, topography; b, land use.

(Figure 43a). To the east, poor arable (with wheat yields of 20–5 q/ha) and extensive oak copses drop down to the Val di Chiana; to the west, pastures lie above the forested slopes of Monte Cetona (Figure 43b). The territory today, with its lack of pasture compared to the Pienza territory and extensive woodland on Monte Cetona, appears to be a reasonable guide to the prehistoric situation, for the caprines decrease and cattle and swine increase in importance, compared with the Pienza faunal sample.

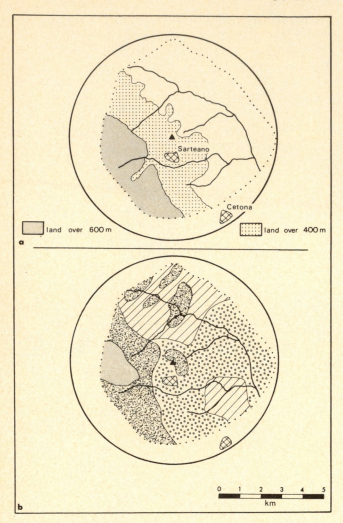

Figure 43. Grotta dell'Orso: one-hour territory. a, topography; b, land use.

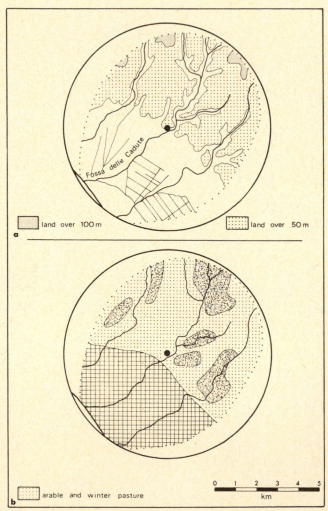

Figure 44. Palidoro: one-hour territory. a, topography; b, land use.

stock economy, at another more detailed evidence of cereal cultivation combined primarily with sheep and goat herding.

Three early Neolithic sites are known on the western lowlands on the other side of Monte Amiata: Grotta Patrizi, Palidoro, and Tre Erici. The Grotta Patrizi, a burial cave, is situated on the edge of the Roman Maremma (Figure 25:22); until the postwar land reforms, the whole plain from the cave to the sea was used for winter sheep pasture. Palidoro (Figure 25:26) lies on the edge of drained *bonifica*; behind the shelter are rolling pastures and cereal fields (Figure 44), the winter pasture of the Maremma. Tre Erici is to the north on the edge of the Tuscan Maremma and about half of the territory (illustrated below in the discussion of the Bronze Age settlement of Luni) consists of winter pasture and rough grazing (Figure 50b). The Neolithic assemblage, which included sherds with Sasso grooved decoration, was

Neolithic deposits have also been found in other caves a few kilometres to the south, in similar positions on the edge of the Cetona ridge: the Grotta Lattaia (Figure 25:12) and the Grotta di Gosto (Figure 25:13). The Grotta Lattaia in particular is a large and sheltered cave and had rich prehistoric deposits, but no stratigraphic details were recorded from the excavations, which were given only a cursory report (Calzoni, 1940). Neolithic artefacts have been found in similar circumstances in the Tane del Diavolo on the other side of the Val di Chiana (Figure 25:14) and in the Grotta di San Francesco in Umbria (Figure 25:15), whilst a large Sasso assemblage has been found in the network of caves called the Pozzi della Piana nearby (Figure 25:15). The indications are therefore of a group of settlements in central Toscana and Umbria north and east of Monte Amiata; at one site we have evidence of a mixed dated to 3445 ± 80 B.C. Obviously we cannot link these sites directly with the inland settlements, for the total distribution is probably a palimpsest of many hundreds of years, but they might be an indication of the kind of stock movement practised by the inland Neolithic settlements, whereby a few shepherds and herdsmen took the mobile stock down to lowland grazing in winter.

A ^{14}C date of 3440 ± 145 B.C. suggests that the Neolithic level F at Valle Ottara (Figure 25:21) is roughly contemporaneous with Neolithic Tre Erici. The small faunal sample was dominated by red deer (65 per cent), caprines were by far the most significant of the stock animals (23 per cent), and cattle were unimportant. The flint industry was fundamentally similar to the Epipalaeolithic industry at the same site. The pottery consisted of coarse ware with a few sherds of *figulina*. The one-hour territory at Valle Ottara (Figure 45) is heavily forested, the area being made up of 45 per cent deciduous woodland, 37 per cent

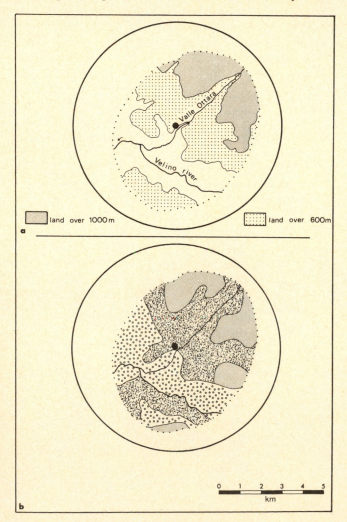

Figure 45. Valle Ottara: one-hour territory. a, topography; b, land use.

poor arable, and 18 per cent summer pasture. As at Maddalena di Muccia, the economy of the group was essentially like that of the Epipalaeolithic group in the area, with the addition of a few caprines. Like Maddalena di Muccia, too, the site was placed in the same way as the local Epipalaeolithic camp, at the foot of the main summer pastures, on an obvious route up to Monte Terminillo (the Valle Ottara).

Thus, despite the changes to the landscape caused by millennia of agricultural exploitation, the faunal samples of both Pienza and Valle Ottara are closely related to the natural resources of the territories defined today and demonstrate different economic stances in response to different local conditions. The location, assemblage, and faunal sample of Valle Ottara seem to show the gradual integration of Neolithic stock keeping into the economy of the Apennines *c.* 3500 B.C. Yet, perhaps at a much earlier date, the settlement at Pienza in the Tuscan uplands relied almost totally on stock keeping (especially caprines) and cereal cultivation. If the hypothesis of a mobile stock economy is correct, however, then from the first, the Early Neolithic economy at Pienza would have been fully adapted to the limiting factors of climate and pasture in Toscana.

Östenberg (1967, pp. 162–3) argued for two lithic traditions in the Neolithic of the west: a Sasso-Fiorano and a 'native' tradition. In the north, the Fiorano flint assemblages contain long parallel-sided blades, small scrapers, numbers of trapezes, rhomboids, and transverse arrowheads, occasional backed blades and microburins, together with a variety of burin types (Barfield & Broglio, 1965; Bagolini, 1971a; Perini, 1971). In central Italy the same kind of flint industry has been found in the Grotta Patrizi, the Grotta dell'Orso, Pozzi della Piana, and la Romita di Asciano, in each case associated primarily with Sasso pottery. The assemblages of Valle Ottara and the Faliscan caves (Figure 25:19) also have burins and scrapers, microburins and trapezes, but lack the long blades so distinctive of the Sasso and Fiorano sites and also have many more backed blades, some microlithic. Recent excavations in the Grotta Bella in Umbria (Figure 25:16) have also found Neolithic levels with *figulina* pottery, a fauna dominated by red deer, and a blade industry. The two different kinds of economy which we have suggested were in existence by the mid-fourth millennium B.C. in Etruria, exemplified by Pienza and Valle Ottara, correlate broadly with the two pottery and lithic traditions.

As in Marche and Abruzzi, three simple theories about Neolithic beginnings in Etruria can be constructed. The first and second would be that we are dealing with single populations west of the Apennines, wholly intrusive or wholly indigenous. To accept the first theory of Neolithic intrusive groups, we would have to argue as in Marche and Abruzzi that local resources were such as to induce some colonist groups, for example at Valle Ottara, to turn to the large-scale exploitation of red deer, with concomitant changes in the flint industry. Furthermore, we would have to explain the absence of Sasso ware from inland sites and the use instead of *figulina*. According to the second theory, caprines and cereals would have percolated gradually into Etruria (like the obsidian blades found at many early Neolithic sites), to be gradually integrated into local Epipalaeolithic economies. The differences in the flint assemblages would then have to be explained by differing activities, but the problem remains of the contemporaneous Sasso and *figulina* wares at Tre Erici and Valle Ottara.

The third theory would be that the archaeological record represents two economic groups. The group at Valle Ottara was essentially Epipalaeolithic in its tool-kit and economy, but also herded a few caprines. At about the same time, Sasso groups were in Toscana and Lazio, with identical pottery and flint assemblages to those of the Fiorano sites in northern Italy. The Pienza data suggest that the Sasso groups probably practised stock keeping (particularly of sheep) and cereal cultivation. A secondary hypothesis could be constructed, that the two economic groups were also two cultural or social groups (the one an intrusive group related to the Fiorano culture of the north); however, the Fiorano assemblage has been shown to be rooted firmly in the Epipalaeolithic of the north (Bagolini, 1971a, 1971b), and this hypothesis would have to rely principally on the negative evidence that we do not know of any Epipalaeolithic sites in Toscana and Umbria.

Evidence for the later Neolithic economies on this side of the Apennines is even more fragmentary than for the earlier Neolithic. At Pienza, cereal evidence is limited to the presence of barley in the later Neolithic levels; in the stock economy, caprine levels dropped to 35 per cent and cattle levels rose from 16 per cent to 36 per cent. The lessening in importance of caprines at Pienza could have been from pressure on, or changes affecting, pastures within the territory or on the lowlands. We cannot tell, for we have little contemporaneous economic data from sites in central Toscana and none from the lowlands. The basic equilibrium between cattle and caprines was maintained in the Bronze Age levels at the site; this was the case too in the Bronze Age levels at the Grotta dell'Orso (Cremonesi, 1968b, p. 317).

Inland at this time we know of two Late Neolithic sites. One is at Norcia (Figure 25:17), 600 m above sea level and at the limit of the arable, immediately below the *altipiano* of Castelluccio. The other, the Grotta Cola II di Petrella, lies at the head of the Liri river (Figure 25:63), 1000 m above sea level: the assemblage was extremely poor and associated with caprines and red deer, while half of the

territory consists of summer grazing today. Thus in the latter part of the Neolithic west of the Apennines, as on the eastern side, two groups may be represented in the archaeological record: on the one hand, the groups of central Toscana and western Umbria practising cereal cultivation and mixed stock economies; and on the other, inland groups at the limit of the arable, with economies probably heavily biased towards mobile stock. The origins of these two groups, if confirmed by more reliable data, might reasonably be derived from the two groups detected in the earlier Neolithic west of the Apennines.

Northern Etruria, 2500–1000 B.C.

The Eneolithic domestic assemblages are so poor that we have practically no economic evidence of any value from them and we can only make a few general observations on the distribution of the graves and settlements. In the Neolithic, it has been argued that the inland sites were probably settlements, which sent most of their stock down the Ombrone and Fiora valleys for the winter months. The Rinaldone graves and settlements of northern Etruria encompass the same area, from the central hills to the Maremma. The distribution of Eneolithic graves and domestic sites might therefore be an indication that the Neolithic pattern of exploitation continued into the Enolithic. The beginnings of copper metallurgy in central Italy are beyond the scope of this paper; but, by whatever process knowledge of metallurgy was introduced, the copper ores of Toscana would have been within the annual territories of the Rinaldone groups.

As in the Neolithic and Eneolithic, the Bronze Age settlements extended from the Maremma to the hinterland (Figure 26); by and large, however, they cluster into three groups: one in the uplands, one on the middle Fiora, and one on the northern Maremma. The first group clusters round Belverde (Figure 26:9), the richest Apennine Bronze Age site in central Italy.

Belverde is situated on the eastern flank of Monte Cetona (Figure 46). Wheat yields immediately round the site and below the Grotta Lattaia (Figure 46a:2) are good for this part of Toscana: some 30 q/ha. The Late Bronze Age camp of Casa Carletti, however, lies at the upper limit of the arable where yields are poor and the land is used primarily for pasture (Figure 26:10). The Bronze Age deposit at Tane del Diavolo (Figure 26:11), a cave 20 km southeast of Belverde, seems to contain most of the Belverde phases, whereas the assemblage of the Grotta di San Francesco (Figure 26:12), further east on the middle Tiber, is much poorer and belongs to the latter part of the Bronze Age like Casa Carletti. The territories of both sites are dominated by oak and chestnut forests – 60 per cent of the Tana del

Diavolo territory, 80 per cent of the Grotta di San Francesco territory. The cultivated land, however, is very different: the cereal yields near the Tana are high, whereas the arable below the higher site, the Grotta di San Francesco, is extremely poor.

Apart from Pienza, the upland sites around Belverde (the Grotta dell'Orso, Grotta di San Francesco, Tane del Diavolo) have faunal samples dominated by caprines, with swine being the second most numerous species. Equally, apart from at Pienza, extensive woodland areas are within easy reach of the sites today, whilst a certain amount of summer pasture is also available. From Belverde we know that wheat, barley, millet, beans, peas, and perhaps vines were cultivated in the area during the Bronze Age, as today. Wheat and horse beans were also found at the Tane del Diavolo. Apart from the absence of the olive, the evidence from Belverde implies that the classical pattern of inter-culture in the Tuscan and Umbrian hills was already developing in the Bronze Age. At the same time, unlike today, caprines were clearly an important part of the stock economy, but all the territories lack winter pasture. Stalling may have been one solution, but we have evidence neither for nor against this hypothesis. The archaeological evidence of several lowland sites suggests that the stock economies were probably much as in the Neolithic, entailing the use of winter camps on the Maremma.

Here the second group of sites is known, on the Maremma proper and on its edge. The Grotta dello Scoglietto (Figure 26:15), for example, is situated on the edge of the Ombrone estuary (Figure 47); the site contained a poor assemblage of coarse wares. Abundant wild pig was reported from the site (still hunted today in the Ombrone pine forests); caprines and cattle were the principal stock of the group. The territory in front of the cave, now *bonifica*, was probably much better drained in the Bronze Age, for alluviation in historical times has appreciably extended the estuary (Vita-Finzi, 1969). Other sites on or near the Maremma with territories consisting entirely of winter pasture or rough grazing are the Grotta delle Sette Finestre (Figure 26:19) and Cala dei Santi (Figure 26:17). These sites are all on or on the edge of the Maremma, have faunal assemblages of caprines and cattle, have poor assemblages of coarse ware which is identical to the coarse wares of the inland sites, and can reasonably be interpreted as the kind of winter camps utilised by the inland settlements north and east of Monte Amiata.

The third group of sites lies between the Maremma and the uplands, up-river from the Maremma on the middle Fiora. Of these sites the Grotta Misa (Figure 26:22) has provided the fullest economic evidence. Carbonised plant remains – wheat, millet, and beans – were found near a clay oven in the cave. The fauna consisted of the main stock animals, particularly caprines and cattle, while pig and deer were also reported. The pottery is mostly undecorated and coarse, but several large storage pots were recovered. The cave is situated on the left bank of the Fiora river; a perennial tributary stream of the Fiora in fact flows through the cave. Half of the territory (Figure 48) carries deciduous oak forests, and half good arable and winter pasture. The Grotta Nuova (Figure 26:21) was a Late Bronze Age site 4 km to the north, with a similar faunal sample and territory. A

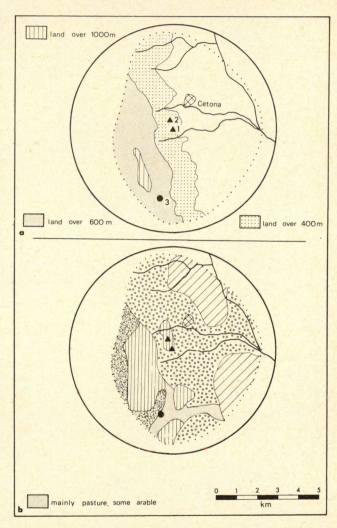

Figure 46. Belverde: one-hour territory. a, topography: 1–Belverde, 2–Grotta Lattaia, 3–Casa Carletti; b, land use.

Bronze Age settlement has also been excavated recently near Scarceta on the other side of the Fiora (Figure 26:20), with a similar range of material to that of the Grotta Misa, including oven fragments, 'milk boilers', strainers, and so on. Emmer and barley were found at the site, but we have only a list of fauna without percentages: caprines, cattle, swine, dog, red and roe deer. The territory is again

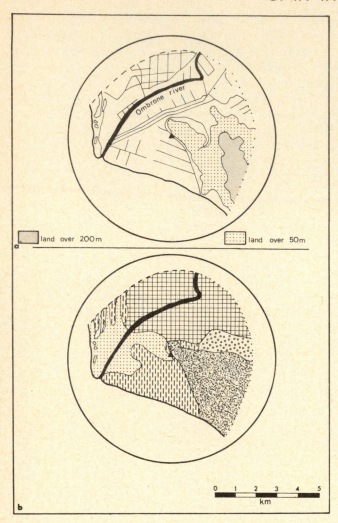

Figure 47. Grotta dello Scoglietto: one-hour territory. a, topography; b, land use.

model: a first stage of Neolithic inland settlements with lowland shielings; a second stage of lowland and upland Apennine Bronze Age settlements, using alternative seasonal pastures; and perhaps a third stage at the end of the Bronze Age when the upland settlements were augmented by peripheral sites like Casa Carletti and the Grotta di San Francesco – sites with caprines and swine, right on the edge of the arable.

If this model is accepted and the prehistoric sites document the extension of arable farming and the use of alternative sheep pasture during the Bronze Age in northern Etruria, then a secondary hypothesis might be that these changes were gradual responses to increasing population pressure in the area. The following stage would be the development of the complete dichotomy between transhumant shepherds using the Maremma and the high Apennine pastures on the one hand, and on the other, the hill villages

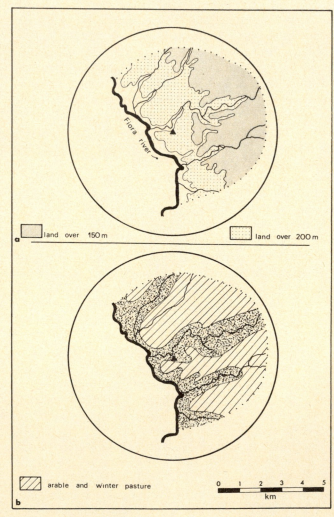

Figure 48. Grotta Misa: one-hour territory. a, topography; b, land use.

dominated by woodland, with a small area of good arable and winter pasture.

I have argued that the lowlands of Etruria during the Neolithic were probably exploited only by shepherd groups from the inland settlements. By the Bronze Age, however, two groups of settlements are known: one, as before, north and east of Monte Amiata, the other now on the middle reaches of the Fiora. Caprines, however, were still by and large the most important stock animal in both groups and in each case were probably transhumant. From the middle Fiora settlements like the Grotta Misa, the nearest summer pastures were directly above on Monte Amiata, two or three days' journey away, while I suggested above that the Maremma sites were probably the winter camps used by the Belverde settlements. From the available evidence from the Neolithic to the Late Bronze Age, we can construct a simple of Toscana and Umbria growing cereals, olives, and vines, with a few swine and plough oxen. This has been the situation in historical times and had probably developed by the Roman period; the economic systems postulated in the Late Bronze Age might bear witness to the first development of separate social and economic groups.

Southern Etruria and the central Apennines, 2500–1000 B.C.

As in the north, we can only speculate about Eneolithic economies from the distribution of the graves. These are known on the western lowlands, the Roman plains, in the Sacco valley, and in the central Apennines. The inland graves have been interpreted as the evidence of the incursions of Rinaldone warrior bands into the hinterland (Radmilli, 1957), but, from the material continuity at Tre Erici between the Neolithic and Eneolithic levels, the two groups of graves (lowland and highland) could as reasonably be correlated with the Neolithic patterns of exploitation discussed at the beginning of this section. There are far more data, however, about Bronze Age settlement (Figure 49); an outline discussion has already been published elsewhere (Barker, 1972), but selected sites and their territories will be examined below so that the system which emerges can be integrated into the total picture of Bronze Age economies in central Italy. The three most important sites in the area excavated in recent years are Luni and Narce on the lowlands and the Grotta a Male in the central Apennines.

Luni (Figure 49:1) is an acropolis site in northern Lazio, north of the Tolfa mountains. The territory south of the Mignone river is covered almost entirely by deciduous woodland (Figure 50b); arable lies on the edge of the territory, but half of the territory carries winter pastures or rough grazing. Cattle constituted 45–53 per cent of the Apennine Bronze Age faunal sample, caprines 22–6 per cent, and swine 20–5 per cent (Gejvall, in Östenberg, 1967), but there is some evidence that cattle may be over represented. Cattle were usually raised to full growth, most swine died in the second and third years, most caprines died in the first three years (especially in the first year). Carbonised club wheat, barley, horse beans, grass pea, and acorns were recovered in Luni Apennine II (Östenberg, 1967, p. 279).

Narce (Figure 49:5) was also an acropolis site and, like Luni, was utilised from the Bronze Age into the Etruscan period. The topography today (Figure 51a) consists of a plateau cut by a series of stream ravines. The prehistoric site was located at a point where the ravine opens out into a

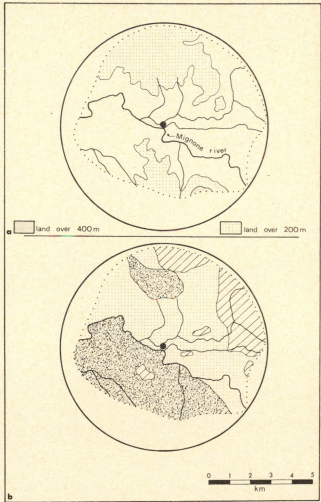

Figure 50. Luni: one-hour territory. a, topography; b, land use.

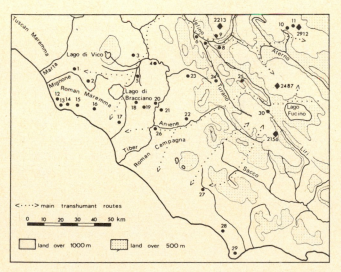

Figure 49. Southern Etruria and the central Apennines: Bronze Age sites (listed in Appendix I: 5).

valley several hundred metres wide; the Treia, like the Mignone, is a perennial river. The modern land use is shown in Figure 51b: the valley floor is used for vine and nut cultivation and pasture, the hill slopes and ravine walls carry deciduous woodland and above them are the main arable and pasture lands. Caprine percentages were consistently high in the seven main levels of the settlement (from the Apennine Bronze Age to the Iron Age), varying from 45 per cent to almost 60 per cent (the latter in the earliest layer). Both cattle and swine frequencies were usually between 20 per cent and 30 per cent, apart from the low figure of 10 per cent for swine in the first level. The mortality data were similar to those of Luni: most cattle and swine were slaughtered in their second or third year, and most caprines during their first three years (nearly half by the end of the first year). Also as at Luni the carbonised plant remains (recovered by flotation) consisted mostly of wheat (emmer in this case), with some barley and legumes (H. N. Jarman, *pers. comm.*). Swine and cattle policy at Luni and Narce were much as at Neolithic Pienza, but caprine policy had changed remarkably, for most caprines at Pienza died in their third year or even later.

Between a third and a half of the Narce territory carries good winter pasture, grazed by considerable transhumant flocks in the winter months up to the last war. At Luni, the farms on the peripheral arable (Figure 50b) find it worthwhile to keep a few small flocks, but numbers have to be kept low because of the lack of pasture in the summer: winter under-grazing is the result. Mobility has been the preferred solution to the limiting factors of lowland stock economies in both territories. The faunal samples from the two sites demonstrate that the flocks were a substantial part of the Bronze Age stock economies and transhumance to upland shielings would have been the simplest solution then as in the recent past. This hypothesis is supported by the faunal sample from the Grotta a Male in the central Apennines (Figure 49:10).

The Grotta a Male is a large cavern 950 m above sea level. To the north, the territory (Figure 52) rises gently for about a kilometre, then stops at the southern wall of the Gran Sasso; to the south, the land also rises to 1500 m. About 10 per cent of the territory carries woodland, over 30 per cent consists of the poor arable of the modern village of Assergi, and almost 60 per cent still carries summer pasture. In the winter, however, conditions are extremely harsh and the Assergi flocks have to be stalled in the village. Level 4 at the site contained Apennine decorated pottery, level 3 dates to the latter part of the Bronze Age, and level 2b to the end of the Bronze Age. There is a remarkable change in the fauna of these levels (Pannuti, 1969). In level 4, red and roe deer made up almost a quarter of the animals killed, caprines dominated the sample (60 per cent), cattle were unimportant (6 per cent), and swine absent. In the later levels, however, deer percentages were insignificant; cattle and caprine percentages were approximately equal, constituting about two-thirds of the total faunal sample; swine appeared as 8 per cent of the sample in level 3 and rose to 18 per cent in level 2b. In the earlier levels, therefore, the site was apparently used by shepherd groups, like the Grotta Cola II in the later Neolithic. The percentages of cattle and swine in levels 3 and 2b and the material richness of level 3 suggest that, though the flocks were probably still taken down to the lowlands in winter, a permanent settlement was established in the cave. It was from level 3 that a stone mould for a flanged axe was recovered (Pannuti, 1969, p. 220, Fig. 41), an indication of bronze working in the cave at this time.

These developments in the Grotta a Male would appear to correlate very generally with the appearance of cereals in

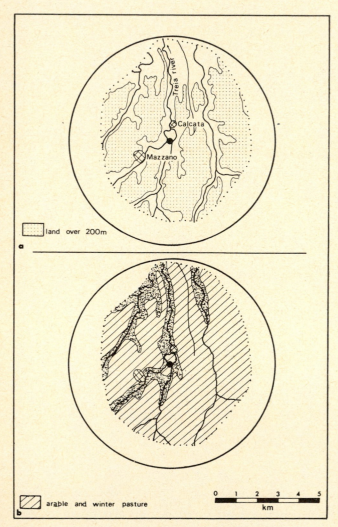

land over 200m

arable and winter pasture

0 1 2 3 4 5
km

Figure 51. Narce: one-hour territory. a, topography; b, land use.

the upper levels at Luni and Narce, the increase in cereal pollen in nearby deposits (Bonatti, 1970), and the increase in settlement evidence on the Etrurian lowlands towards the end of the second millennium B.C. (Ward-Perkins, Kahane, & Murray Threipland, 1968, pp. 14–17). The evidence of the earlier levels at the three sites, however, together with that of other sites in Etruria and the highlands, suggests that most sites with early Apennine incised ware were used by primarily stock keeping groups. In the historical past, the transhumant flocks wintered on the Maremma and Campagna and summered on the Abruzzi *altipiani* (Figure 3:5–7, 9). From the record of the earlier Apennine Bronze Age sites, the shepherds and herdsmen probably travelled over much the same distance from the Maremma to the central Apennines, by similar routes (Figure 49).

There is a series of sites with classic Apennine incised ware at roughly ten-kilometre intervals down the Maremma: the Civitavecchia open sites (Figure 49: 12–14), Pian Sultano (Figure 49:15), the Grotta 'le Croce' at Sasso Furbara (Figure 49:16), and Palidoro (Figure 49:17). We have little economic data, but the fauna at Pian Sultano consisted of cattle and caprines, the pottery assemblage included 'milk boilers', and clearly stock keeping was an important part of the economy of the group. Areas of pasture dominate all the territories of these sites; desiccated in summer, the pasture still provides winter grazing for modern transhumant flocks. The territories of Cisterna (Figure 49:27) and the Grotta Polesini (Figure 49:22) on the Roman Campagna are also situated in areas of winter pasture.

From the coastal lowlands, the *tratturi* first followed the Tiber north to the Velino confluence or cut across the Tiber and Sabine hills northeast to the Rieti basin. Bronze Age sites are known on both routes (Figure 49:6–9, 23). Two small sites were found in the Rieti basin, for example, at Campo Avello (Figure 49:6) and Valviano (Figure 49:7). The basin was marshy and too wet for sheep in Roman times (Varro, *De Re Rustica*, II.2.17). The camps are situated on the edge of the basin and might represent the kind of transitory camps used during transhumance. Further up-river are two more sites, at Ponzano (Figure 49:8) and Valle Ottara (Figure 49:9). Both their territories are heavily wooded with limited areas of arable and pasture (Figure 45b), both sites are well situated for use as temporary camps with enough pasture for a few days in spring or autumn. Beyond these sites, the transhumant route left the Velino and went southeast to the L'Aquila basin, thence either south to Monte Velino or north to Gran Sasso. The Gorotta a Male, situated on the second route, was clearly first utilised by a shepherd group and has very extensive summer pastures available within the territory (Figure 52b); there are both general and specific links between the Valle Ottara and

Grotta a Male assemblages. Thus the early Apennine Bronze Age sites in Figure 49 can be related to each other in an economic system of mobile stock keeping from the Maremma to Gran Sasso; the annual territories would have been dumb-bell shaped between these areas, hinging on spring and autumn camps such as Toffia (Figure 49:23) and the Velino camps.

It is apparent that the exploitation of the Grotta a Male had changed drastically by the latter part of the Bronze Age, when a permanent settlement was probably established in the cave. Summer pastures for the caprines were available round the site, but it is possible that the flocks were taken onto Gran Sasso when the snows melted. A Late Bronze Age shepherds' camp was excavated on Campo Pericoli here (Figure 49:11), 2000 m above sea level west of the Corno Grande, the highest peak of Gran Sasso (Figure 53). The pottery was coarse and poorly made, but was

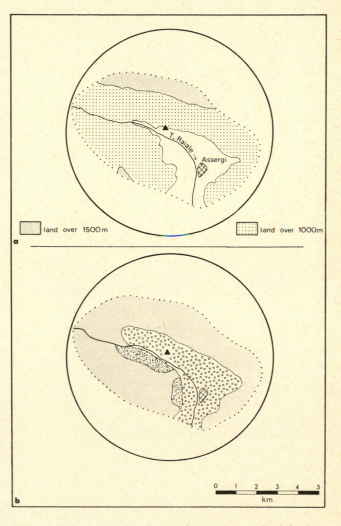

Figure 52. Grotta a Male: one-hour territory. a, topography; b, land use.

155

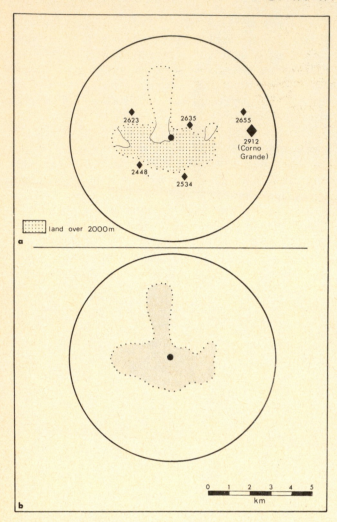

Figure 53. Campo Pericoli: one-hour territory. a, topography; b, land use.

likened to the later wares of Valle Ottara and Ponzano (Leopardi, Radmilli, & Rozzi, 1954–5). Occupation of the camp is only conceivable in the summer months.

The shepherd villages of the last century in Abruzzi were usually situated, like the Grotta a Male, at the foot of the *altipiani*; the shepherds went up to the high pastures in summer and down to the lowlands of Etruria in winter, staying in the villages only for a few weeks at either end of the summer. Socially they were a discrete group when they came down to the lowlands, where their winter huts can still be seen occasionally (Close-Brooks & Gibson, 1966). 'The most frequent landmarks are the conical shepherds' huts, usually on the higher grounds, inhabited during about half the year by a race of men so cut off from all social and civilizing influences that one might expect to find the lowest brutality, and all the fiercest passions, in a moral soil thus neglected' (Heman's *Story of Monuments in Rome,* after

Hare, 1875, p. 21). Perhaps the beginnings of this social dichotomy can be found in the later Bronze Age, as lowland and upland settlements developed in the latter part of the second millennium B.C.: there is a striking difference between the assemblages of poor coarse wares in the Faliscan caves and shelters (Figure 49:3) on the transhumant route to the Maremma and those of the contemporaneous levels at the Narce settlement, less than 20 km to the south.

The hypothesis of more developed exploitation systems suggested by the Grotta a Male is supported by another cave deposit of the central Apennines in the secluded Val di Varri (Figure 49:25). From the cave at 800 m above sea level (Figure 54a) the topography rises to 1374 m 3 km away on Monte Val di Varri. About 60 per cent of the territory is forested (Figure 54b): oak and beech on the heavier and chestnut on the lighter soils. Charcoal found in the excavations consisted almost entirely of chestnut. Poor

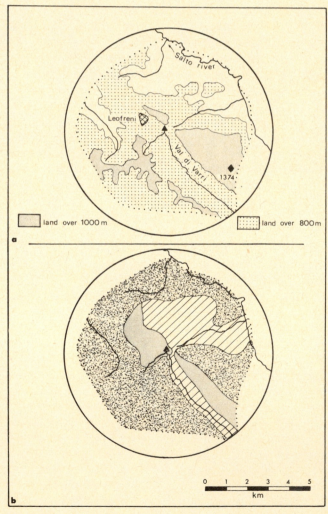

Figure 54. Val di Varri: one-hour territory. a, topography; b, land use.

arable, mostly around the modern village of Leofreni, constitutes about 25–30 per cent of the territory. Occasional wheat seeds were found in the deposit and a fairly large sample of horse beans, so often found on the Apennine Bronze Age sites and one of the commonest fodder crops of the classical period (White, 1970). The fauna was dominated by pig, whilst caprines and cattle were also present in significant quantities. Bauxite was used as filler for the pottery and the excavators reported that the nearest deposit known is 20 km to the east, on Monte Velino, the nearest *altipiano* (Güller & Segre, 1948). The summer pastures round the site are limited and the archaeological evidence implies that the cattle and caprines were taken up to Monte Velino in the summer. In the winter, as at the Grotta a Male, the stock would either have had to be stalled or taken down to the Roman plains. At the same time there appears to have been some cereal cultivation in the Val di Varri and at least one other crop was grown. Perhaps, on the analogy of pre-war villages in the Apennines, chestnut flour was as important as wheat flour to the Bronze Age settlement. There must have been some contact between the villages of the Fucine lake and the shepherds from the lowlands, or later from inland sites such as Val di Varri. Nevertheless, the archaeological record of the Fucine sites shows remarkably little influence from the neighbouring sites of the Apennine Bronze Age.

In the preceding discussion I have put forward a model of social and economic change, arguing that the exploitation of southern Etruria and the central Apennines intensified during the Bronze Age. In the latter part of the second millennium B.C., shepherd groups from villages in the middle and higher Apennines utilised the westernmost pastures of the Maremma in the winter, whilst the intervening lowland settlements practised more limited stock keeping and grew a variety of crops (Figure 55). The faunal evidence at Pienza and Narce demonstrates the increasing intensification of stock management between the Neolithic and the Bronze Age in Etruria; Bronze Age economy also seems to have involved the cultivation of a wider spectrum of crops than before. One hypothesis to account for the changes in Bronze Age economies documented both on the Etrurian lowlands and in the high Apennines would be that the phenomenon was a response to population pressure, seen in the archaeological record as a growth of settlement evidence in the Apennines and on a larger scale, on the western lowlands, towards the end of the second millennium B.C.

If the hypotheses put forward above for the Bronze Age are subsequently borne out, it might be possible in time to reconcile the prehistoric with the historical situation. By the second half of the first millennium B.C. the indigenous tribes of central Italy were in existence and were

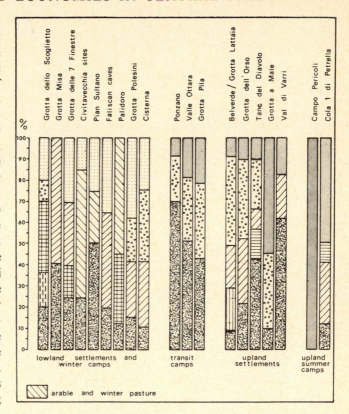

Figure 55. Summary of modern land use in the one-hour territories of twenty Apennine Bronze Age sites in southern Etruria and the central Apennines, with their suggested exploitation (adapted from Barker, 1972a, p. 198, fig. 10).

documented by the classical writers. In Abruzzi, for example, the main tribal groups were the Vestini, the Marrucini, the Paeligni, and the Marsi. Their territorial boundaries are not clear, but the main areas of occupation are known. The territory of the Vestini was north of the Pescara river and reached from the Adriatic to the Gran Sasso. South of the Pescara, the territory of the Marrucini likewise extended over the lowlands from the sea to the Maiella. The other two tribes, however, occupied inland territories which did not have access to the eastern lowlands: the Paeligni in the Sulmona basin, the Marsi in the Fucine basin and hills to the south. In the Bronze Age in Abruzzi, I argued that, although fishing settlements were probably situated in the Fucine basin, the caprine economies of the Fucine caves and Collarmele would have utilised winter pasture on the eastern lowlands. Half a millennium later, the Marsi and Paeligni occupying the Apennine intermontane basins seem to have been landlocked tribes.

There are two main hypotheses to explain the development of the separate inland and coastal territories of the historical tribes. One is that the tribal areas were not rigid economic areas: thus shepherds from the inland tribes could have been a socially discrete group (like the Abruzzi shepherds of more recent times), still able to go down to the Adriatic coast in winter unhampered by the tribal boundaries. On the other hand, it is possible that the Abruzzi tribal territories do in fact reflect basic patterns of exploitation, thus having economic as well as social and political significance. In Marche, for example, I suggested earlier that there is evidence for heavy population densities on the eastern lowlands by the classical period, probably accompanied by the disappearance of mobile stock keeping and the development of intensive agriculture. Equally in Abruzzi the tribal territories may bear witness in part to the new economic configurations of an increasing rural population. Population pressure in the lakeside settlements of the Fucine basin at the end of the second and during the first millennium B.C. might have induced the intensive exploitation of the lake and land resources in the area. Any flocks would have had to be stalled in winter in the Fucine villages, as today. At the same time, the lowland groups excluded from the central mountains (the Marrucini and the Vestini) would have been able to use only the summer pastures nearest to the coastal lowlands: the eastern slopes of the Gran Sasso and Maiella, on the very edge of the Apennines.

West of the Apennine watershed, too, the tribal territories suggest complex developments between the end of the Bronze Age and republican Rome. The archaeological record shows that the Apennine Bronze Age culture reached from Etruria to the hills north and west of the Fucine basin; yet the Marsi territory extended from the lake west to the Monti Simbruini, the Aequi occupied the area between Gran Sasso, Monte Velino, and the Pre-Apennine valleys, whilst the Latin and Etruscan tribes controlled the western lowlands. Thus as in Abruzzi the prehistoric pattern is replaced by separate hill and lowland tribal territories. On the one hand, there is the prehistoric record of southern Etruria discussed above, of lowland settlements side by side with the winter camps of shepherds from the central Apennines; on the other, the mythology of the *Aeneid*. The period ought to be one of the most fertile areas of research, for testing within the historical framework the archaeological models constructed for the end of the prehistoric period; yet in reality remarkably little is known about the subsistence economies of the Iron Age, including both Etruscan and early Roman, and the cultural developments of the first part of the first millennium B.C. are almost totally divorced from domestic economic data.

SUMMARY

In establishing the archaeological framework of this paper,

I argued first that the existing data often support new hypotheses about the culture history of the area at least as well as other theories proposed in the past, while new excavations tend to support the former rather than the latter. These have shown, for example, the polythetic nature of the change in the material culture from the Neolithic to the end of the Bronze Age, seen both in the stratigraphies of particular sites and through series of new sites in each province, which argues against older theories that major phases and sub-phases can be equated with major cultural changes and often population upheaval throughout central Italy. Equally, it is impossible to divorce much of the Neolithic settlement evidence completely from the late Epigravettian assemblages of central Italy. There is at every stage a remarkable regionalism in the Neolithic and post-Neolithic material culture; at its most extreme, this is represented by extraordinary disparity between assemblages close in time and space. At the same time, the new excavations reveal the same kind of complexity in the prehistoric economies, demonstrating that the existing data can no longer be ordered in simple stages applicable to the whole of central Italy and equated with major cultural phases. Even though the recovery of economic data has been a subsidiary concern in the past, we are now at a stage when we can construct tentative hypotheses about changing economies in the different areas of central Italy. These suggest that we are not dealing with a series of simple economic stages, of pre-Neolithic hunting and gathering, Neolithic settled agriculture, Apennine Bronze Age pastoralism, and Subapennine and later settled agriculture.

During the last glaciation, for example, it is unlikely that static systems of predation were maintained by the Palaeolithic population of central Italy. West of the Apennines, Middle Palaeolithic economies were based on a broad spectrum of game such as elephant, rhinoceros, red and roe deer, horse, cattle, and ibex. The annual territories of the Middle Palaeolithic bands did not extend inland beyond the lower valleys, for although animals such as red deer and horse probably moved into the high Apennines during the summer, it was more economic to remain in the lowlands and exploit the range of resources available, than to concentrate on one or two species and follow their seasonal movements. After the interstadial *c.* 40 000 B.P., the cold and arid conditions of the Würm again favoured red deer and horse, which could move between the seasonal upland and lowland grazing. The big game such as elephant and rhinoceros had disappeared by the interstadial and in this situation it would now have been more economic to follow the seasonal migrations of the deer and horse; and the distribution of late Upper Palaeolithic sites on the western side of central Italy suggests that the human annual territories did in fact embrace both the western plains and the central Apennines. In both areas sites were selected at the ends of the valleys which were probably the migration routes of the deer and horse, each thus controlling the neck of an 'extended territory' in which the game summered or wintered, while a few sites were also used in the 'extended territories' themselves: on the coastal plains of Lazio or high in the Apennines above the Fucine basin.

The development of mobile economies for the exploitation of one or two animals in the latter part of the last glaciation in this area contrasts with the situation in southern Campania. There the rugged topography favoured red deer throughout the last glaciation and both Middle and Upper Palaeolithic bands appear to have concentrated on its exploitation, following the deer up-river for the summer months and wintering on the coast at Camerota. In both southern Campania and Lazio, however, the Upper Palaeolithic bands regularly killed immature red deer as well as mature deer, whereas the Middle Palaeolithic band at Camerota killed only mature deer, between their third and eighth years. We lack this kind of data on the eastern side of central Italy, but a study of the territories of the late Upper Palaeolithic sites reveals another and rather different economic system at the end of the Würm. The annual territories of the Epipalaeolithic bands west of the Apennines were dumb-bell shaped, spanning the lowland plains of Lazio, the connecting Pre-Apennine valleys, and the Fucine basin. Distances are shorter on the other side of the Apennines between the Adriatic coast and the mountains, and I suggested that short-distance mobile economies developed in Marche and Abruzzi hinging on base camps at the junction between the lowlands and the Apennines. This pattern of movement is documented as at the end of the last glaciation and continued in the Postglacial, based primarily on the exploitation of red deer and ibex. On the western side of the Apennines, however, the Postglacial brought significant changes in Palaeolithic economies. The extinction of the steppe horse *Equus hydruntinus* in the Postglacial coincides with considerable afforestation in three pollen diagrams in Lazio, and the late Epigravettian economy was adapted to the changes in the available resources: particular sites were used in different seasons to exploit specific resources such as red deer, ibex, or shell-fish, but the economic system as a whole no longer concentrated on any one resource to the exclusion of the others.

The problem of the first 'Neolithic economy' has dominated the study of economic changes in the prehistory of Italy, as in most areas of Europe, but I have argued against the utility of defining one economic system as 'typically Neolithic' and comparing it with a 'typical' Epipalaeolithic or Mesolithic economy. Instead, I have tried to demonstrate that we are dealing with dynamic rather than static economic systems, all adapted in some way to the major constraints of the environment of central Italy. Thus developments within the Neolithic and Bronze Age in central Italy are no less significant than the first appearance in an area of the modern plant and/or animal domesticates at a prehistoric site. At the same time we cannot assume identical economic developments and an equal rate of change over a wide area and the evidence of central Italy indeed argues against such an hypothesis.

Tables 4 to 6 summarise the evidence of the territories constructed for the major Neolithic and post-Neolithic sites, showing the basic location of each site, the major resources available, and the suggested exploitation. In accordance with Chisholm's (1968) assertion that it is the area within one kilometre that is most important to a farming settlement, it is for this area that the percentages of major resources are shown.

The percentage of tree cover found today (and shown in the maps) has been translated into a percentage of potentially arable or potentially grazing land.

Table 4 illustrates the diversity of economic systems which emerge from the archaeological record of the fifth and first half of the fourth millennia B.C. in central Italy. Some groups followed seasonal patterns of movement essentially identical to those of the Epipalaeolithic bands: the economic basis was sometimes twofold (as at Maddalena di Muccia), consisting of hunting game and raising some stock, whilst other groups seem to have been primarily transhumant shepherds (Ripabianca di Monterado). Large-scale hunting was still apparently the principal means of subsistence *c.* 3500 B.C. at Valle Ottara. On the Abruzzi lowlands, however, other groups practised creal agriculture as well as stock keeping and, probably lacking the ard, occupied the lighter soils best suited to their crops; a few kilometres inland on the edge of the Apennines were other, primarily stock keeping, communities (Table 4, a and b). On the western side of the Apennines the period saw the development of subsistence economies very different from that of Valle Ottara: inland settlements raised both crops and stock, and probably sent their flocks and herds down to the Maremma in the winter to sites such as Palidoro and Tre Erici (Table 4, c).

By the second half of the fourth millennium B.C. on the Adriatic side of central Italy, cereal agriculture had apparently extended to include not only the light soils of the coastal plateau but also the heavier soils of the valley floors (Table 5, a and b). Inland settlements had probably appeared by this time in Marche. Sites like Berbentina were probably all-year-round settlements and it is likely that both inland and lowland communities sent their stock to complementary grazing areas for part of the year, a system represented in the archaeological record by seasonal camps

Table 4. Resources and suggested exploitation of prehistoric territories: fifth to mid-fourth millennium B.C.
(1: arable/potentially arable, heavy soils; 2: arable/potentially arable, light soils; 3: pasture/rough grazing, probably summer; 4: pasture/rough grazing, probably winter)

Site	Location	Resources (Per cent, 1 km)				Suggested exploitation
		1	2	3	4	
(a) Marche						
Maddalena di Muccia	Lowland/highland junction	35	65			Spring/autumn camp: hunting, some herding
Ripabianca di Monterado	Lowland: valley floor	96	4			Winter camp: caprine herding
(b) Abruzzi						
Catignano	Lowland: ridge		100			All-year-round settlement: stock + cereals
Villaggio Leopardi	Lowland: ridge		100			All-year-round settlement: stock + cereals
Fonti Rossi	Lowland/highland junction		79	21		Settlement or camp: mainly stock (caprines)
Grotta dei Piccioni	Lowland/highland junction		76		24	Settlement or camp: mainly stock (caprines)
Grotta Sant' Angelo	Lowland/highland junction			100		Settlement or camp: mainly stock (caprines)
Capo d'Acqua	Inland	83	17			Summer or autumn/spring camp: stock + hunting
Grotte Maritza/la Punta	Inland	40	15	45		Summer camp: stock, especially caprines
(c) Etruria						
Grotta Patrizi	Lowland		17		83	Winter camp: stock keeping
Palidoro	Lowland	17	33		50	Winter camp: stock keeping
Tre Erici	Lowland		10		90	Winter camp: stock keeping
Grotta Lattaia	Inland		79	21		All-year-round settlement: stock + cereals
Grotta dell'Orso	Inland		100			All-year-round settlement: stock + cereals
Pienza	Inland		77	23		All-year-round settlement: stock + cereals
Valle Ottara	Inland		76	24		Spring/autumn camp (and perhaps summer): hunting and stock keeping

160

Table 5. Resources and suggested exploitation of prehistoric territories: late fourth and third millennia B.C.
(1: arable/potentially arable, heavy soils; 2: arable/potentially arable, light soils; 3: pasture/rough grazing, probably summer; 4: pasture/rough grazing, probably winter)

Site	Location	Resources (Per cent, 1 km)				Suggested exploitation
		1	2	3	4	
(a) Marche						
Conelle	Lowland: ridge	34	66			All-year-round settlement: stock, cereals, hunting
Saline di Senigallia	Lowland: ridge	43	57			All-year-round settlement: stock + cereals
San Biagio	Lowland: ridge	6	94			All-year-round settlement: stock + cereals
S. Maria in Selva	Lowland: ridge	22	78			All-year-round settlement: stock + cereals
Coppitella di Iesi	Lowland: valley floor	100				Winter camp: caprine herding?
Attiggio	Lowland/highland junction		90	10		?All-year-round settlement: stock + cereals
Berbentina	Inland	31	69			All-year-round (or summer?) settlement: esp. caprines
Donatelli	Inland	47	53			Summer camp: stock, esp. caprines, + hunting
Grotta dei Baffoni	Inland	2	13	85		Spring/autumn camp: stock keeping + hunting
Grotta del Mezzogiorno	Inland		11	89		Spring/autumn camp: stock keeping + hunting
(b) Abruzzi						
Fossacesia	Lowland: valley edge	60	40			All-year-round settlement: stock, cereals, hunting
Pianaccio	Lowland: ridge	37	63			All-year-round settlement: stock + cereals
Ripoli	Lowland: valley floor	94	6			All-year-round settlement: stock + cereals
Grotta dei Piccioni	Lowland/highland junction		76		24	Settlement or camp: mainly stock (caprines)
Grotta Sant' Angelo	Lowland/highland junction			100		Settlement or camp: mainly stock (caprines)
Grotte Maritza/la Punta	Inland	40	15	45		Summer camp: stock keeping?
Grotta delle Marmitte	Inland	12	43	45		Summer camp: stock keeping (caprines)
Paterno	Inland	52	34	14		Summer camp: stock keeping
(c) Etruria and Apennines to the east						
Grotta Lattaia	Inland		79	21		All-year-round settlement: stock + cereals
Norcia	Inland	63	37			?Settlement or perhaps spring/autumn camp: esp. stock
Cole di Petrella	Inland		30	70		Summer camp: stock keeping

Table 6. Resources and suggested exploitation of prehistoric territories: second millennium B.C.

(1: arable/potentially arable, heavy soils; 2: arable/potentially arable, light soils; 3: pasture/rough grazing, probably summer; 4: pasture/rough grazing, probably winter)

Site	Location	Resources (Per cent, 1 km)				Suggested exploitation
		1	2	3	4	
(a) Marche						
Bachero	Lowland: ridge	21	79			All-year-round settlement: stock + cereals
Montefrancola di Pollenza	Lowland: ridge	24	76			All-year-round settlement: stock + cereals
San Paolina di Filottrano	Lowland: ridge	52	48			All-year-round settlement: stock + cereals
Grotta dei Baffoni	Inland	2	13	85		Spring/autumn camp: stock, esp. caprines
Grotta del Mezzogiorno	Inland		11	89		Spring/autumn camp: stock, esp. caprines
Monte San Croce	Inland	25	75			All-year-round settlement: stock, cereals, hunting
Pievetorina	Inland	17	10	73		Summer or spring/autumn camp: stock keeping
(b) Abruzzi						
Campo delle Piane	Lowland: ridge		100			All-year-round settlement: stock + cereals
Tortoreto, Costa del Monte	Lowland: ridge		100			All-year-round settlement: stock + cereals
Tortoreto, Fortelezza	Lowland: valley floor	35	65			All-year-round settlement: stock + cereals
Grotta dei Corvi	Lowland/highland junction		28	72		Spring/autumn camp: stock keeping
Grotta dei Piccioni	Lowland/highland junction		76		24	Settlement or camp: mainly stock
Grotta Sant' Angelo	Lowland/highland junction			100		Settlement or camp: mainly stock
Blokhaus	Inland			100		Summer camp: caprine herding
Collarmele	Inland		24	76		Summer camp: caprine herding
Grotte Maritza/la Punta	Inland	40	15	45		Summer camp: mainly caprines
(c) Northern Etruria						
Grotta Misa	Lowland	10	39		61	All-year-round settlement: stock + cereals
Grotta dello Scoglietto	Lowland				90	All-year-round settlement: stock + cereals
Cala dei Santi	Lowland		25		75	Winter camp: stock keeping
Grotta 7 Finestre	Lowland	31	43		26	Winter camp: stock keeping
Belverde	Inland		86	14		All-year-round settlement: stock + cereals
Casa Carletti	Inland		20	80		All-year-round settlement: stock + cereals
Grotta Lattaia	Inland		79	21		All-year-round settlement: stock + cereals
Grotta dell' Orso	Inland		100			All-year-round settlement: stock + cereals
Tane del Diavolo	Inland	9	24	67		All-year-round settlement: stock + cereals
Grotta di S. Francesco	Inland		100			Spring/autumn transit camp: stock (later perhaps a permanent settlement)

162

(d) Southern Etruria and the high Apennines

Site	Location	Resources (Per cent, 1 km)				Suggested exploitation
		1	2	3	4	
Luni sul Mignone	Lowland		10		90	All-year-round settlement: stock + cereals
Narce	Lowland	14	30		56	All-year-round settlement: stock + cereals
Cisterna	Lowland	50			50	Winter camp: stock keeping
Faliscan caves	Lowland		55		45	Winter camp: stock keeping
Grotta 'le Croce'	Lowland		17		83	Winter camp: stock keeping
Grotta Polesini	Lowland	46	40		14	Winter camp: stock keeping
Malpasso	Lowland		60		40	Winter camp: stock keeping
Marangone	Lowland		54		46	Winter camp: stock keeping
Palidoro	Lowland	17	33		50	Winter camp: stock keeping
Pian Sultano	Lowland		17		83	Winter camp: stock keeping
Torre Chiaruccia	Lowland		70		30	Winter camp: stock keeping
Grotta a Male	Inland		67	33		All-year-round settlement: stock + cereals
Val di Varri	Inland		33	67		All-year-round settlement: stock + cereals
Campo Pericoli	Inland			100		Summer camp: caprine herding
Cole di Petrella	Inland		30	70		Summer camp: caprine herding
Grotta a Male	Inland		67	33		Summer camp: caprine herding
Grotta Pila	Inland		10	90		Spring/autumn transit camp: stock keeping
Ponzano	Inland		47	53		Spring/autumn transit camp: stock keeping
Valle Ottara	Inland		76	24		Spring/autumn transit camp: stock keeping

like Coppitella and Donatelli (Table 5, a). Further south in Abruzzi the same kind of parallel systems had probably developed, whereby shepherds from lowland settlements (Fossacesia) went inland in the summer (Paterno), whilst the inland Fucine caves were related to sites on the edge of the lowlands like the Grotta dei Piccioni (Table 5, b). On the western side of the Apennines the Grotta Lattaia seems to be the same kind of site as the earlier Tuscan settlements grouped around Pienza; the Cole di Petrella cave can only be a summer camp; Norcia is perhaps the same kind of inland settlement situated on poor quality arable as Berbentina in Marche and might imply similar trends in settlement expansion (Table 5, c). Thus although the details are not clear, more intensive (though varying) systems of exploitation were probably developing in this period consistent with an increased population in central Italy. In northern Abruzzi, for example, in the ten-kilometre stretch of the lower Vibrata valley, the one area investigated regularly during he past hundred years, almost twenty sites, loosely dated to the latter part of the Neolithic, are known around Ripoli and are situated in some cases little more than one kilometre apart.

In the second millennium B.C. on the Adriatic side of the Apennines there seem to be both lowland and inland settlements (Table 6, a and b): the lowland settlements were probably still related to summer camps inland, but the absence of winter camps on the lowlands could indicate changes in the stock economies of the inland groups. On the other side of the Apennines developments are more complex. In northern Etruria, for example, we saw that the Neolithic economy involved all-year-round settlements in the Tuscan hill country and winter camps on the lowlands. By the middle of the second millennium B.C. there were inland settlements and lowland camps as before, as well as new lowland all-year-round settlements such as Grotta Misa and Grotta dello Scoglietto (Table 6, c); finally, towards the end of the millennium, we find peripheral sites like Casa Carletti at the limit of the arable above the main settlements like Belverde – further evidence of the increasingly intensive exploitation of Etruria and the expansion of prehistoric settlement. In the middle of the second millennium B.C. in southern Etruria lowland communities such as Luni raising stock and cereals probably used shielings in the Apennines such as the Grotta a Male, reached via transit camps in the intervening valleys (Ponzano, Valle Ottara). At the same time, however, there is a number of winter camps on the Maremma which must also have been occupied by transhumant shepherds (Table 6, d). In the second half of the millennium permanent settlements developed in the uplands where the shepherds were probably both socially and economically separate from the lowland communities.

The one-hour territory used in the main discussion and the one-kilometre circle in Tables 4–6 are of course hypothetical areas thought on several counts to provide significant information about the factors governing prehistoric site location. It is impossible to estimate the real size of the exploited territories on the basis of the distribution maps of known prehistoric sites; nevertheless, it appears from the tables that the one-kilometre circle is at least as significant a factor of site location as the one-hour territory for groups practising cereal agriculture in central Italy. For example, the cereals found at S. Maria in Selva are those we would expect in a Neolithic community cultivating the lighter soils of the ridge rather than the heavier soils of the valley floor; the one-kilometre circle covers much of the spur of light soils on which the settlement was located (Table 5, a), whereas the one-hour territory reaches right across the floor of the Potenza valley (Figure 29). The situation recurs in Marche at Bronze Age sites such as Santa Paolina di Filottrano, Bachero and Montefrancola di Pollenza (Table 6, a and Figures 33–4). In the case of seasonal camps used for stock keeping, however, the one-kilometre area seems much less significant: at some sites the resources of the immediate locality differ considerably from those of the one-hour territory, but at others they are identical. As today, it seems, a prehistoric stock keeping group was little affected by the resources within a few minutes' walk of the habitation, but probably ranged up to an hour from the home base in search of grazing. The correlation in central Italy between cereal-based economies and the one-kilometre area on the one hand, and between stock-based economies and the one-hour territory on the other, may be relevant to the study of palaeoeconomies in other areas of prehistoric settlement, in the construction of predictive locational models.

I have argued in this paper that the economic prehistory of this region—so far from being (as currently viewed) a series of major economic phases correlating with cultural phases—was in fact a complex story of differential rates of change in different parts of the peninsula. On the other hand, although short-term changes were not uniform and contemporary from area to area, the overall view is one of increasingly intensive exploitation systems, probably intimately related to the pressures of increasing population. Of course the ideas put forward in the paper cannot be more than preliminary hypotheses: although the data are now too complex to fit the simplistic models used in the past, their inadequacy prevents us from testing new hypotheses against the old as rigorously as we would wish. Each stage of the inquiry has emphasised the dangers of shoring up the obsolete models of rigid cultural and economic stages, and of building grandiose models anew on little better foundations. Nevertheless, by integrating the excavated evidence with a study of the prehistoric territories, we can construct at least the first framework of an economic prehistory in central Italy.

The intensification of economic systems during the prehistoric period down to the end of the second millennium B.C. can be compared with the settlement archaeology of the first millennium B.C. in one area, southern Etruria. For over twenty years the British School at Rome has carried out an intensive survey north of Rome in the *Ager Veientanus*, the territory of the city of Veii, which was conquered by Rome in 396 B.C. (Ward-Perkins, Kahane, & Murray Threipland, 1968). The sites discovered by the survey (in an area of some 170 km^2) date to the centuries which embrace the growth and political dominance of Rome. Therefore a number of factors apart from subsistence economics—the Roman conquest of 396 B.C., the construction of trunk roads through the area, the establishment of the *Pax Romana* and the growth of Rome as the principal market for local produce, for example—has affected the distribution of the sites. Nevertheless, the single trend which emerges from the survey is the steady growth of the rural population in the *Ager Veientanus*:

Pottery type	Date	Number of sites
Bronze Age	down to *c.* 900 B.C.	5
Archaic Iron Age	8th, 7th centuries B.C.	24
Bucchero	6th, 5th centuries B.C.	153
Black-glazed	last 3 centuries B.C.	237
Terra sigillata	30 B.C.–A.D. 150	316
Red polished	2nd century A.D.	312

Despite evidence for abandonment of some sites, for example, after the Roman conquest in 396 B.C., 'for every farm that was given up, two more can be seen to have continued in occupation under the same or under new masters' (Ward-Perkins, Kahane & Murray Threipland, 1968, pp. 145–6). The trend continued in the late Republic and early Empire: in the last two centuries B.C. 'there was no less steady growth of settlement in the open countryside' (*ibid.* p. 148) ... and 'for every two sites already occupied under the Republic a third came into being during the 150 odd years following the accession of Augustus' (*ibid.* p. 149). In this one area at least, population pressure appears to have been a significant factor affecting rural settlement during the first millennium B.C. and the first centuries A.D., until the pattern altered drastically under the impact of the political and military crisis of the third century A.D. (*ibid.* p. 152). The extraordinary growth of settlement in the *Ager Veientanus* during the climactic centuries of the Roman Republic and early Empire was intimately related to the urban development of Rome; but the processes of settlement intensification should be regarded not only as a response to the political events of classical history, but also as the culmination of a long-term trend which can be traced through the economic prehistory of central Italy from the beginning of the last glaciation until the first millennium B.C.

APPENDIX I: CENTRAL ITALY – THE PREHISTORIC SITES

1. Middle Palaeolithic sites

Figure 9

1 – Grotta di S. Agostino; 2 – Grotta dei Moscerini; 3 – Grotta di Tiberio; 4 – Grotta Guattari; 5 – Grotta del Fossellone, Grotta delle Capre, Grotta Breuil; 6 – Canale Mussolini, Agro Pontino; 7 – Anzio, Nettuno; 8 – Lido di Lavinio; 9 – Ardea; 10 – Pratica di Mare, Pomezia; 11 – Alban Hills; 12 – Acilia; 13 – Torrimpietra; 14 – Palidoro; 15 Monte delle Gioie, Saccopastore, Sedia del Diavolo; 16 – Invioletta, Montecelio; 17 – Borghetto; 18 – Cavernette Falische; 19 – Poggio Mirteto; 20 – Ponte Peschio; 21 – Cava Giovanni Pompi, Pofi; 22 – Valle Radice, Sora; 23 – Pontecorvo; 24 – Grotta di Cassino.

Site no	Site	Reference
12	Acilia	Malatesta & Pannuti, 1957.
11	Alban Hills	Radmilli, 1962.
7	Anzio, Nettuno	Zei, 1953a.
9	Ardea	Blanc, 1937.
17	Borghetto	*Ibid.*
6	Canale Mussolini	Blanc, 1936, 1957.
21	Cava Pompi, Pofi	Fedele, 1962; Fedele, *et al.*, 1962.
18	Cavernette Falische	Rellini, 1920.
5	Grotta Breuil	Taschini, 1970.
5	Grotta delle Capre	Blanc & Segre, 1953a.
24	Grotta di Cassino	Vaufrey, 1928.
5	Grotta del Fossellone	Blanc, 1939b; Blanc & Segre, 1953a.
4	Grotta Guattari	Blanc, 1938–9b, 1939a.
2	Grotta dei Moscerini	Tozzi, 1970.
1	Grotta di S. Agostino	*Ibid.*
3	Grotta di Tiberio	*Ibid.*
16	Invioletta, Montecelio	Radmilli, 1962.
8	Lido di Lavinio	Zei, 1953a.
15	Monte delle Gioie	Blanc, 1933–4, 1938–9a, 1957; Taschini, 1967.
14	Palidoro	Blanc, 1955a; Chiappella, 1956.
19	Poggio Mirteto	Radmilli, 1951–2a.
23	Pontecorvo	Biddittu & Cassoli, 1968.
20	Ponte Peschio	Leopardi *et al.*, 1957.
10	Pratica di Mare	Zei, 1953a.
15	Saccopastore	Blanc, 1933–4, 1938–9a, 1957.
15	Sedia del Diavolo	*Ibid.*
13	Torrimpietra	Blanc, 1958a, 1958b.
22	Valle Radice	Biddittu *et al.*, 1967; Chiappella, 1962.

2. Upper Palaeolithic and Epipalaeolithic sites

Figure 10

1 – Grotta di S. Agostino; 2 – Riparo Salvini, Terracina; 3 – Grotta del Fossellone; 4 – Riparo Blanc; 5 – Agro Pontino; 6 – Grotta

Jolanda, Sezze Romano; 7 – Cisterna; 8 – Anzio, Nettuno; 9 – Pomezia; 10 – Acilia; 11 – Osteria Malpasso; 12 – Palidoro; 13 – Grotta Polesini; 14 – Cavernette Falische; 15 – Valle Ottara; 16 – Ponte Peschio; 17 – Grotta di Ciccio Felice; 18 – Grotta Maritza; 19 – Grotta la Punta; 20 – Grotta di Ortucchio; 21 – Riparo Maurizio; 22 – Grotta Clemente Tronci; 23 – Grotta Achille Graziani; 24 – Grotta Peschio Romaro, Collepardo; 25 – Pofi.

Figure 20

1 – Misa terraces; 2 – Ponte di Pietra; 3 – Grotta del Prete; 4 – Grotta della Ferrovia; 5 – Vibrata terraces & Ripoli; 6 – Grotta Sant' Angelo & Grotta Salomone; 7 – Rigopiano, 1200 m; 8 – Campo delle Piane; 9 – Popoli, 'le Svolte'; 10 – S. Maria delle Piane, Manopello; 11 – Montepiano, 650 m; 12 – Grotta del Colle, Rapino; 13 – Le Piane di Rapino; 14 – Madonna della Mazza di Pretoro, 1000 m; 15 – Colle Tondo di Pretoro, 1000 m; 16 – Valle Giumentina, 700 m; 17 Fornelli di Caramanico, 1000 m; 18 – Colle Vento di Caramanico, 1000 m; 19 – Rifugio della Maiella, 2050 m; 20 – Campo di Giove, 1200 m; 21 – Piano delle Cinquemiglia, 1200 m; 22 – Piano di Roccaraso, 1250 m; 23 – Pescopennatoro, 1000 m; 24 – Piano dell' Aremogna, 1450 m; 25 – Serra Veticosa, 1650 m; 26 – Grotta Achille Graziani, 1020 m; 27 – Fucine caves – see Figure 4, sites 17–22; 28 – Capo d'Acqua; 29 – Ponte Peschio.

Fig.	no	Site	Reference
10	10	Acilia	Malatesta & Pannuti, 1957.
10	5	Agro Pontino	Bietti, 1969; Blanc, 1937.
10	8	Anzio, Nettuno	Zei, 1953a.
20	20	Campo di Giove	Pigorini, 1875.
20	8	Campo delle Piane	Leopardi & Radmilli, 1951–2; Radmilli, 1954–5.
20	28	Capo d'Acqua	Tozzi, 1966.
10	14	Cavernette Falische	Barra Incardona, 1969; Rellini, 1920.
10	7	Cisterna	Segre, 1956, 1957.
20	15	Colle Tondo	Radmilli, 1959.
20	18	Colle Vento	*Ibid.*
20	17	Fornelli	*Ibid.*
20	27	Fucine caves	listed under Fig. 10, sites 17–22.
10	23	Grotta Achille Graziani	Radmilli, 1955.
20	26	Grotta Achille Graziani	*Ibid.*
10	17	Grotta di Ciccio Felice	Radmilli, 1951–2a.
10	22	Grotta Clemente Tronci	Radmilli, 1956a.
20	12	Grotta del Colle	Leopardi *et al.*, 1954–5.
20	4	Grotta della Ferrovia	Lollini, 1966.
10	3	Grotta del Fossellone	Blanc, 1939b; Blanc & Segre, 1953a.
10	6	Grotta Jolanda	Zei, 1953b.
10	18	Grotta Maritza	Grifoni & Radmilli, 1964.
10	20	Grotta di Ortucchio	Cremonesi, 1968a.
10	24	Grotta Peschio Romaro	unpublished.
10	13	Grotta Polesini	Radmilli, 1953a.
20	3	Grotta del Prete	Lollini, 1966.
10	19	Grotta la Punta	Cremonesi, 1968a.

Fig.	no	Site	Reference
10	1	Grotta S. Agostino	Tozzi, 1970.
20	6	Grotta Sant' Angelo	Radmilli, 1963b.
20	14	Madonna della Mazza	Radmilli, 1959.
20	1	Misa terraces	Leonardi, 1960.
20	11	Montepiano	Leopardi *et al.*, 1954–5.
10	11	Osteria Malpasso	Malatesta & Pannuti, 1957.
10	12	Palidoro	Blanc, 1955a.
20	23	Pescopennatoro	Radmilli, 1959.
20	13	Piane di Rapino	*Ibid.*
20	24	Piano dell' Aremogna	*Ibid.*
20	21	Piano delle Cinquemiglia	*Ibid.*
20	22	Piano di Roccaraso	*Ibid.*
10	25	Pofi	Fedele, 1962.
10	9	Pomezia	Zei, 1953a.
10	16	Ponte Peschio	Leopardi *et al.*, 1957.
20	29	Ponte Peschio	*Ibid.*
20	2	Ponte di Pietra	unpublished.
20	9	Popoli, 'le Svolte'	Radmilli, 1959.
20	19	Rifugio di Maiella	Leopardi *et al.*, 1954–5.
20	7	Rigopiano	Radmilli, 1959.
10	4	Riparo Blanc	Taschini, 1964, 1958.
10	21	Riparo Maurizio	Radmilli, 1963a.
10	2	Riparo Salvini	Taschini, 1964, 1968.
20	10	S. Maria delle Piane	Arias, 1964; Leopardi, *et al.*, 1954–5.
20	25	Serra Veticosa	Radmilli, 1959.
20	16	Valle Giumentina	*Ibid.*
10	15	Valle Ottara	Acanfora, 1962–3.
20	5	Vibrata terraces & Ripoli	Bravi, 1951–2; Radmilli & Cremonesi, 1963.

3. Neolithic sites in Figure 25

1 – Grotta all'Onda; 2 – Grotta delle Campane; 3 – Padule di Massaciuccoli; 4 – Riparo la Romita di Asciano; 5 – Grotta del Leone; 6 – Isola d'Elba; 7 – Montalcino; 8 – Monte Amiata; 9 – Pienza; 10 – Grotta del Beato; 11 – Grotta dell'Orso; 12 – Grotta Lattaia; 13 – Grotta di Gosto; 14 – Tane del Diavolo; 15 – Grotta di San Francesco & Pozzi della Piana; 16 – Grotta Bella, Montecastrilli; 17 – Norcia; 18 – Tre Erici; 19 – Cavernette Falische; 20 – Campo Avello (?); 21 – Valle Ottara; 22 – Grotta Patrizi; 23 – Grotta 'le Croce', Sasso; 24 – Poggio Mirteto (?); 25 – Contrada le Caprine (?); 26 – Palidoro; 27 – Acilia (?); 28 – Anzio & Nettuno; 29 – Canale Mussolini; 30 – Trisulti; 31 – Pofi; 32 – Riparo Blanc; 33 – Monte Circeo; 34 – Isole Pontine; 35 – Grotta delle Felce; 36 – Camposauro (?); 37 – Vitulano – la Palmenta (?); 38 – San Biagio; 39 – Ripabianca di Monterado; 40 – Saline di Senigallia; 41 – Coppitella di Iesi; 42 – Serra San Abbondio & Arcevia; 43 – Berbentina; 44 – Grotta del Mezzogiorno; 45 – Grotta dei Baffoni; 46 – Donatelli & Pianello di Genga; 47 – Caverna di Frasassi; 48 – Attiggio; 49 – Collemorico, Serrone; 50 – S. Maria in Selva; 51 – Monte Colombo; 52 – Serrapetrona; 53 – Maddalena di Muccia; 54 – Offida; 55 – Grotta Sant' Angelo; 56 – San Donato; 57 – Ripoli; 58 – Pianaccio; 59 – Villaggio Leopardi, Penne; 60 – Grotta 'le Marmitte', Capranica; 61 – Capo d'Acqua; 62 – Catignano; 63 – Grotta

Cola II di Petrella; 64 – Paterno; 65 – Grotta San Nicola; 66 – Grotta Maritza; 67 – Grotta la Punta; 68 – Grotta la Cava; 69 – Grotta di Ortucchio; 70 – Grotta dei Piccioni; 71 – Fossacesia; 72 – Fonti Rossi.

Site no	Site	Reference
27	Acilia	Malatesta & Pannuti, 1957.
28	Anzio & Nettuno	Zei, 1953a.
42	Arcevia	Alessio, *et al.*, 1967.
48	Attiggio	Lollini, 1959a, 1965.
43	Berbentina	Lollini, 1965.
20	Campo Avello	Peroni, 1951–2.
36	Camposauro	Buchner, 1950.
29	Canale Mussolini	Blanc, 1957.
61	Capo d'Acqua	Bonuccelli & Faedo, 1968.
62	Catignano	Radmilli, 1971.
47	Caverna di Frasassi	Rellini, 1931.
19	Cavernette Falische	Rellini, 1920.
49	Collemorico, Serrone	Rellini, 1934.
25	Contrada le Caprine	Radmilli, 1951–2a.
41	Coppitella di Iesi	unpublished.
46	Donatelli	Lollini, 1965; Puglisi, 1959b.
72	Fonti Rossi	Rellini, 1914.
71	Fossacesia	Radmilli, 1970, 1971.
45	Grotta dei Baffoni	Radmilli, 1953c.
10	Grotta del Beato	Radmilli, 1968b.
16	Grotta Bella, Montecastrilli	Guerreschi, 1971.
2	Grotta delle Campane	Malatesta, 1951.
68	Grotta la Cava	Tozzi, 1962.
63	Grotta Cola II	Radmilli, 1957.
23	Grotta 'le Croce', Sasso	Rellini, 1933.
35	Grotta delle Felce	Rellini, 1923–4.
13	Grotta di Gosto	Grifoni Cremonesi, 1969a.
12	Grotta Lattaia	Calzoni, 1940; Grifoni Cremonesi, 1969a.
5	Grotta del Leone	Tongiorgi, 1950.
66	Grotta Maritza	Grifoni & Radmilli, 1964.
60	Grotta delle Marmitte	Grifoni Cremonesi, 1969b.
44	Grotta del Mezzogiorno	Puglisi, 1956a.
1	Grotta all'Onda	Graziosi, 1944.
11	Grotta dell'Orso	Grifoni, 1967.
69	Grotta di Ortucchio	Cremonesi, 1968a.
22	Grotta Patrizi	Radmilli, 1951–2b, 1953b.
70	Grotta dei Piccioni	Radmilli, 1959, 1962.
67	Grotta la Punta	Cremonesi, 1968a.
55	Grotta Sant' Angelo	Radmilli, 1965a, 1965b, 1967b, 1968b.
15	Grotta di San Francesco	Mochi, 1914.
65	Grotta San Nicola	Borzatti von Löwenstern, 1962b; Radmilli, 1960b.
6	Isola d'Elba	Zecchini, 1969a.
34	Isole Pontine	Buchner, 1949.
53	Maddalena di Muccia	Lollini, 1965.
7	Montalcino	unpublished.
8	Monte Amiata	Blanc, 1937, Sestini, 1934.
33	Monte Circeo	unpublished (Bietti-Sestieri, *pers. comm.*).

Site no	Site	Reference
51	Monte Colombo	Dall'Osso, 1915.
17	Norcia	Calzoni, 1939.
54	Offida	Rellini, 1934.
3	Padule di Massaciuccoli	Blanc, 1937.
26	Palidoro	Peroni, 1965.
64	Paterno	Fraia, 1970.
58	Pianaccio	Leopardi, *et al.*, 1954–5.
46	Pianello di Genga	Colini, 1914; Rellini, 1931.
9	Pienza	Calvi Rezia, 1968, 1969, 1972.
31	Pofi	Fedele, 1962.
24	Poggio Mirteto	Radmilli, 1951–2a.
15	Pozzi della Piana	Passeri, 1970.
39	Ripabianca di Monterado	Broglio & Lollini, 1963; Lollini, 1965.
32	Riparo Blanc	Taschini, 1964, 1968.
4	Riparo la Romita di Asciano	Peroni, 1962–3.
57	Ripoli	Cremonesi, 1965; Radmilli, 1967a; Rellini, 1934.
40	Saline di Senigallia	unpublished.
38	San Biagio	Rellini, 1934.
56	San Donato	Leopardi, *et al.*, 1954–5.
50	S. Maria in Selva	Lollini, 1965.
52	Serrapetrona	Rellini, 1934.
42	Serra San Abbondio	Lollini, 1971.
14	Tane del Diavolo	Calzoni, 1933.
18	Tre Erici	Östenberg, 1967.
30	Trisulti	Alonzi, 1965.
21	Valle Ottara	Acanfora, 1962–3.
59	Villaggio Leopardi	Cremonesi, 1966.
37	Vitulano – la Palmenta	Buchner, 1950.

4. Bronze Age sites in Figure 26

1 – Romita di Asciano; 2 – Grotta del Leone; 3 – Stabbia; 4 – Montalcino; 5 – Romitorio di Pienza; 6 – Grotta del Beato; 7 – Grotta dell'Orso; 8 – Grotta Lattaia; 9 – Belverde; 10 – Casa Carletti & Monte Cetona summit; 11 – Tane del Diavolo & Tane del Faggio; 12 – Grotta di San Francesco; 13 – Grotta Bella; 14 – Monte Giove, Elba; 15 – Grotta dello Scoglietto; 16 – Monte Amiata; 17 – Cala dei Santi; 18 – Cosa; 19 – Grotta delle Sette Finestre; 20 – Scarceta; 21 – Grotta Nuova; 22 – Grotta Misa; 23 – Selva; 24 – Luni sul Mignone; 25 – San Giovenale; 26 – Cavernette Falische; 27 – Monte Ramiano; 28 – Narce; 29 – Campo Avello; 30 – Valviano; 31 – Ponzano; 32 – Valle Ottara; 33 – Malpasso; 34 – Marangone; 35 – Torre Chiaruccia; 36 – Pian Sultano; 37 – Grotta 'le Croce', Sasso; 38 – Palidoro; 39 – Fosso di Formello; 40 – Veii, Piazza d'Armi; 41 – Vallelunga; 42 – Riserva della Torretta; 43 – Grotta Polesini; 44 – Toffia; 45 – Grotta Pila; 46 – Val di Varri; 47 – Roma – San Omobono; 48 – Cisterna; 49 – Canale Mussolini; 50 – Grotta Cona, Monte Circeo; 51 – Cassino; 52 – Grotta del Grano; 53 – Giacometti quarry & Ponte del Goro, Arcevia; 54 – Pieve, Arcevia; 55 – Conelle; 56 – Crocifisso; 57 – Monte San Croce; 58 – Spineto; 59 – Pianello; 60 – Gola di Frasassi; 61 – Caverna di Frasassi; 62 – Grotta delle Moniche; 63 – Grotta dei Baffoni; 64 – Grotta del Mezzogiorno; 65 – Monte la Rossa, Serrasanquirico; 66 – Attiggio; 67 – Bachero; 68 – Ancona; 69 – Fontevecchia, Camerano; 70 – Massignano;

71 – Santa Paolina di Filottrano; 72 – Montefrancola di Pollenza; 73 – Tolentino; 74 – Pievetorina; 75 – Grotta Sant' Angelo & Grotta Salomone; 76 – Campovalano, Campli; 77 – Costa del Monte, Tortoreto; 78 – Fortelezza, Tortoreto; 79 – Grotta a Male; 80 – Campo Pericoli; 81 – Grotta delle Marmitte, Capranica; 82 – Campo delle Piane; 83 – Cola I di Petrella; 84 – Grotta di Ciccio Felice; 85 – Grotta Maritza; 86 – Collelongo; 87 – Grotta la Punta; 88 – Ortucchio; 89 – Collarmele; 90 – Grotta dei Piccioni; 91 – Grotta dei Corvi, Serramonesca; 92 – Grotta del Fauno, Camosciara; 93 – Grotta Achille Graziani; 94 – Lago del Scanno; 95 – Blokhaus.

Site no	Site	Reference
68	Ancona	Lollini, 1956, 1959b.
66	Attiggio	Lollini, 1959a.
67	Bachero	Lollini, 1959b.
9	Belverde	Calzoni, 1954, 1962.
95	Blokhaus	Radmilli, 1959.
17	Cala dei Santi	Segre, 1959.
29	Campo Avello	Peroni, 1951–2; Radmilli, 1953d.
80	Campo Pericoli	Leopardi, *et al.*, 1954–5.
82	Campo delle Piane	*Ibid.*
76	Campovalano	Radmilli, 1971.
49	Canale Mussolini	Blanc, 1937.
10	Casa Carletti	Calzoni, 1936.
51	Cassino	Pantoni, 1949.
61	Caverna di Frasassi	Rellini, 1931.
26	Cavernette Falische	Rellini, 1920.
48	Cisterna	Segre, 1956.
83	Cola I di Petrella	Radmill, 1957.
89	Collarmele	Radmilli, 1965b.
86	Collelongo	*Ibid.*
55	Conelle	Brizio, 1899.
18	Cosa	Bronson & Uggeri, 1968.
77	Costa del Monte	Radmilli, 1965b.
56	Crocifisso	Brizio, 1899.
69	Fontevecchia, Camerano	Lollini, 1968.
78	Fortelezza, Tortoreto	Radmilli, 1965b.
39	Fosso di Formello	Ward-Perkins, *et al.*, 1968.
53	Giacometti quarry, Arcevia	Alessio, *et al.*, 1967.
60	Gola di Frasassi	Lollini, 1968.
93	Grotta Achille Graziani	Radmilli, 1965b.
63	Grotta dei Baffoni	Radmilli, 1953c, 1956b.
6	Grotta del Beato	Radmilli, 1968b.
13	Grotta Bella	Guerreschi, 1971.
84	Grotta di Ciccio Felice	Radmilli, 1965b.
50	Grotta Cona, Monte Circeo	Radmilli, 1965a.
91	Grotta dei Corvi	Radmilli, 1965b.
37	Grotta 'le Croce'	Rellini, 1933.
92	Grotta del Fauno	Radmilli, 1965b.
52	Grotta del Grano	Graziosi, 1943.
8	Grotta Lattaia	Calzoni, 1940; Grifoni Cremonesi, 1969a.
2	Grotta del Leone	Tongiorgi, 1950.
79	Grotta a Male	Pannuti, 1969; Peroni, 1969; Rellini, 1938.

Site no	Site	Reference
85	Grotta Maritza	Grifoni & Radmilli, 1964.
81	Grotta delle Marmitte	Grifoni Cremonesi, 1969b.
64	Grotta del Mezzogiorno	Puglisi, 1956a.
22	Grotta Misa	Rittatore, 1951.
62	Grotta delle Moniche	Rellini, 1931.
21	Grotta Nuova	Rittatore, 1951.
7	Grotta dell'Orso	Cremonesi, 1968b.
90	Grotta dei Piccioni	Radmilli, 1962, 1965b.
45	Grotta Pila	Radmilli, 1951–2a.
43	Grotta Polesini	Radmilli, 1953a.
87	Grotta la Punta	Cremonesi, 1968a.
75	Grotta Sant' Angelo	Radmilli, 1965b.
12	Grotta di San Francesco	Mochi, 1914.
75	Grotta Salomone	Radmilli, 1965b.
15	Grotta dello Scoglietto	Rittatore, 1951.
19	Grotta delle Sette Finestre	Blanc, 1955b.
94	Lago del Scanno	Radmilli, 1965b.
24	Luni sul Mignone	Östenberg, 1967.
33	Malpasso	Barbaranelli, 1954–5; Peroni, 1953.
34	Marangone	Barbaranelli, 1957.
70	Massignano	Lollini, 1959b.
4	Montalcino	unpublished.
16	Monte Amiata	Sestini, 1934.
10	Monte Cetona summit	Cipolloni, 1971.
72	Montefrancola di Pollenza	Lollini, 1959b.
14	Monte Giove, Elba	Zecchini, 1969b.
27	Monte Ramiano	Jones, 1963.
65	Monte la Rossa	Lollini, 1959b.
57	Monte San Croce	Lollini, 1957.
28	Narce	Peroni & Fugazzola, 1969; Ward-Perkins, 1969, 1970.
88	Ortucchio	Radmilli, 1965b.
38	Palidoro	Blanc, 1955a; Peroni, 1965.
59	Pianello	Rellini, 1931.
36	Pian Sultano	Puglisi, 1954, 1956b.
54	Pieve, Arcevia	Brizio, 1899.
74	Pievetorina	Rellini, 1931.
53	Ponte del Goro	Brizio, 1899.
31	Ponzano	Acanfora, 1960–1.
42	Riserva della Torretta	Ward-Perkins, *et al.*, 1968.
47	Roma – San Omobono	Gjerstad, 1966.
1	Romita di Asciano	Peroni, 1962–3.
5	Romitorio di Pienza	*Ibid.*
25	San Giovenale	Östenberg, 1967.
71	Santa Paolina di Filottrano	Rellini, 1931.
20	Scarceta	Soffredi, 1972.
23	Selva	Rittatore, 1951.
58	Spineto	Rellini, 1931.
3	Stabbia	Dani, 1966.
11	Tane del Diavolo	Calzoni, 1938.
11	Tane del Faggio	Borzatti von Löwenstern, 1968.
44	Toffia	Barich, 1969.

Site no	Site	Reference
73	Tolentino	Radmilli, 1962.
35	Torre Chiaruccia	Barbaranelli, 1954–5.
46	Val di Varri	Güller & Segre, 1948.
41	Vallelunga	Ward-Perkins *et al.*, 1968.
32	Valle Ottara	Acanfora, 1962–3.
30	Valviano	Calzoni, 1949; Radmilli, 1953d.
40	Veii, Piazza d'Armi	Stefani, 1922.

5. Southern Etruria and the central Apennines: Bronze Age sites in Figure 49

1 – Luni sul Mignone; 2 – San Giovenale; 3 – Cavernette Falische; 4 – Monte Ramiano; 5 – Narce; 6 – Campo Avello; 7 – Valviano; 8 – Ponzano; 9 – Valle Ottara; 10 – Grotta a Male; 11 – Campo Pericoli; 12 – Malpasso; 13 – Marangone; 14 – Torre Chiaruccia; 15 – Pian Sultano; 16 – Grotta 'le Croce', Sasso; 17 – Palidoro; 18 – Fosso di Formello; 19 – Veii, Piazza d'Armi; 20 – Vallelunga; 21 – Riserva della Torretta; 22 – Grotta Polesini; 23 – Toffia; 24 – Grotta Pila; 25 – Val di Varri; 26 – Roma – San Omobono; 27 – Cisterna; 28 – Canale Mussolini; 29 – Grotta Cona, Monte Circeo; 30 – Grotta Cola I di Petrella.

APPENDIX II: RADIOCARBON DATES IN CENTRAL ITALY (UNCALIBRATED AND QUOTED AS PUBLISHED)

Site	Lab. no.	Date B.P.	S.D. (±)		Publication in *Radiocarbon*
1. Middle Palaeolithic					
Canale Mussolini	GrN 1353	55 000			9.1967: 103
	GrN 1798	50 000			9.1967: 103
	GrN 2501	48 600	2300		9.1967: 103
	GrN 2572	58 000	500		9.1967: 103
Grotta della Cala (Camerota)	F ?	>40 000			unpublished, see Palma di Cesnola, 1969a
2. Upper Palaeolithic and Epipalaeolithic					
Grotta di Ortucchio	Pi 23	12 619	410		1.1959: 106
Grotta la Porta di Positano	Pi 10	8 619	200		1.1959: 106
Grotta del Prete	R 645	9 990	190		12.1970: 602
Grotta la Punta	Pi 153	10 581	100		3.1961: 100
	Pi 152	14 488	800		3.1961: 100
Palidoro 8–6	R 83	13 000	700		6.1964: 79
Riparo Blanc	R 341	8 565	80		10.1968: 358
Grotta della Cala (Camerota)	F 9,10,11	27 000	1700		see Palma di Cesnola, 1971
	F 8	25 800	2500		see Palma di Cesnola, 1971
	F 5,6,7	25 300	2400		see Palma di Cesnola, 1971
3. Neolithic					
Attiggio layer 6	?	4 670	314	2720	see Lollini, 1965
Grotta dell'Orso	R 676	6 080	200	4130	unpublished
Grotta dei Piccioni layer 6	Pi 46	6 247	130	4297	3.1961: 100
layer 5	Pi 49	4 770	110	2820	3.1961: 100–1
Maddalena di Muccia	R 643a	6 580	75	4630	12.1970: 603–4
Ripabianca di Monterado	R 598	6 210	75	4260	12.1970: 602–3
	R 598a	6 140	70	4190	12.1970: 602–3
	R 599a	6 260	85	4310	12.1970: 602–3
Ripoli Hut 6	R 665	5 560	150	3610	13,1971: 397
Hut 12	R 664	5 630	80	3680	13.1971: 397
Hut 3	Pi ?	5 100	120	3150	unpublished
Tre Erici layer 10	St 1344	5 395	80	3445	7.1965: 285–6
Valle Ottara layer F	Pi 28	5 398	145	3448	1.1959: 106
Villaggio Leopardi	Pi 101	6 578	135	4228	3.1961: 100

Site	Lab. no.	Date B.P.	S.D. (±)	Date B.C.	Publication in *Radiocarbon*
4. Eneolithic					
Grotta dei Piccioni layer 3	Pi 50	4 306	105	2356	3.1961: 101
Romita di Asciano layer 10	Pi 100	4 248	115	2298	3.1961: 102
Tre Erici layer 8	St 1343	3 800	80	1850	7.1965: 285–6
	St 2043	4 025	100	2075	9.1967: 436
	St 2042	3 955	200	2005	9.1967: 436
5. Bronze Age					
Ancarano di Sirolo	R 608	3 140	60	1190	13.1971: 396–7
	R 608a	3 100	60	1150	13.1971: 396–7
	R 608a/1	3 190	50	1240	13.1971: 396–7
Arcevia, Giacometti quarry, layer 5	R 275	3 265	55	1315	9.1967: 352
Colle dei Cappuccini, Ancona	Pi 94	2 780	95	830	3.1961: 103
Grotta Misa	Pi 54	3 030	75	1080	3.1961: 103
	R 9	2 870	60	920	7.1965: 217
	R 24	2 700	60	750	7.1965: 217
Luni sul Mignone	St 1340	2 865	80	915	7.1965: 285–6
	St 1345	3 195	75	1245	7.1965: 285–6
	St 1346	2 785	70	835	7.1965: 285–6
	St 2045	3 120	75	1170	9.1967: 437
Narce layer 2	St 2397	3 005	100	1055	unpublished
layer 3	St 2395	2 990	100	1040	unpublished
layer 3	St 2396	2 910	105	960	unpublished
Ortucchio	Pi 80	3 366	130	1416	3.1961: 102–3
Tre Erici layer 6	St 1341	2 775	100	825	7.1965: 285–6
layer 6	St 1147	3 075	70	1125	7.1965: 285–6
layer 3	St 1340	2 865	80	915	7.1965: 285–6

APPENDIX III: PRINCIPAL MAMMALIAN FAUNA REPORTED AT MIDDLE AND LATE UPPER PALAEOLITHIC SITES WEST OF THE APENNINES

1. Middle Palaeolithic sites (Figure 9)

× present
×× common

Site no.	Site	Hippopotamus amphibius	Palaeoloxodon antiquus	Dicerorhinus merckii	Dama dama	Capreolus capreolus	Cervus elaphus	Bos primigenius	Equus caballus	Sus scrofa	Capra ibex	Marmota marmota
6	Canale Mussolini		×	×		×	×	×	×	×		
21	Cava Pompi, Pofi		×	×			×	×	×	×		
5	Grotta delle Capre	×	×	×	×						×	×
24	Grotta di Cassino		×	×			×	×	×	×		
5	Grotta del Fossellone				×		×	×	×	×		
4	Grotta Guattari		×	×			×	×	×		×	
1	Grotta di S. Agostino			×	××	××	××	×	×	××	××	×
3	Grotta di Tiberio					×	×	×				
15	Monte delle Gioie	×	×	×	×			×				
23	Pontecorvo		×	×			×	×	×	×		
20	Ponte Peschio	×		×				×				
15	Saccopastore	×			×		×	×				
15	Sedia del Diavolo	×	×	×	×			×				
13	Torrimpietra		×					×				
22	Valle Radice			××			×	××	××		×	×

2. Late Upper Palaeolithic sites (Figure 10)

× present
× × common

Site no.	Site	Dama dama	Capreolus capreolus	Cervus elaphus	Bos primigenius	Equus caballus	Equus hydruntinus	Sus scrofa	Capra ibex	Rupicapra rupicapra	Marmota marmota
5	Canale Mussolini			× ×			× ×		×		
14	Cavernette Falische			×	×	×	×				
7	Cisterna	×		×	×	× ×	× ×				
23	Grotta Achille Graziani		×	×	×	×			×	× ×	× ×
17	Grotta di Ciccio Felice			× ×	×	×	×	×	×	×	× ×
22	Grotta Clemente Tronci			× ×	×	× ×	×	×	×		×
3	Grotta del Fossellone	×	×	× ×	×		× ×	×	×		
6	Grotta Jolanda			× ×	×			×	×		
18	Grotta Maritza upper			× ×	×	×	×	×	×	×	×
18	Grotta Maritza lower			×	×	×	×	×	×	×	×
20	Grotta di Ortucchio			× ×	×			×	×	×	×
13	Grotta Polesini		×	× ×	×		× ×	×	×	×	×
19	Grotta la Punta			×	×				×		
12	Palidoro			× ×	×	×	×				
4	Riparo Blanc		×	× ×			× ?	×	×		
21	Riparo Maurizio upper		×	× ×	×	×	× ×				×
21	Riparo Maurizio lower		×	× ×	×	× ×	×				×
15	Valle Ottara			× ×	×				×		

REFERENCES

Acanfora, M. O. (1960–1) Saggio di scavo a Ponzano (Cittaducale). *Bull. Paletnol. ital.* **69–70**, n.s. **13**, 233–41.

(1962–3) Gli scavi di Valle Ottara presso Cittaducale. *Bull. Paletnol, ital.* **71–2**, n.s. **14**, 73–154.

Alessio, M., Bella, F., Bachechi, F., & Cortesi, C. (1967) University of Rome Carbon-14 dates V. *Radiocarbon* **9**, 346–67.

Alonzi, A. (1965) Notizie sul Quaternario della Valle del Liri (Sora-Cassino). *Quaternaria* **7**, 271–7.

Arias, C. (1964) La stazione di superficie a Piano di S. Maria di Arabona. *Atti Soc. tosc. Sci. nat.* Ser. A, **71**, 40–50.

Bagolini, B. (1971a) Considerazioni preliminari sull'industria litica dei livelli neolitici di Romagnano (Trento) (scavi 1969–1970). *Preistoria Alpina* **7**, 107–33.

(1971b) Ricerche sulla tipometria litica dei complessi epipaleolitici della Valle dell'Adige. *Preistoria Alpina* **7**, 243–76.

Barbaranelli, F. (1954–5) Ricerche paletnologiche nel territorio di Civitavecchia. *Bull. Paletnol. ital.* **64**, n.s. **9**, 381–400.

(1957) Facies appenniniche e industria litica alla stazione del Marangone (Civitavecchia). *Bull. Paletnol. ital.* **66**, n.s. **11**, 277–87.

Barbieri, G. (1955) Osservazioni geografico-statistiche sulla transumanza in Italia. *Riv. geogr. ital.* **62**, 15–30.

Barfield, L. H. (1971) *Northern Italy before Rome.* London: Thames and Hudson.

Barfield, L. H. & Broglio, A. (1965) Nuove osservazioni sull'industria de Le Basse di Valcaloana (Colli Euganei). *Riv. Sci. preist.* **20**, 307–44.

Barich, B. (1969) Nuove testimonianze appenniniche in Sabina. *Bull. Paletnol. ital.* **78**, n.s. **20**, 41–77.

Barker, G. W. W. (1972) The conditions of cultural and economic growth in the Bronze Age of central Italy. *Proc. prehist. Soc.* **38**, 170–208.

(1973) Cultural and economic change in the prehistory of central Italy. In *Explanations of Culture Change: Models in Prehistory*, ed. A. C. Renfrew, pp. 359–70. London: Duckworth.

Barra Incardona, A. (1969) La nuove ricerche nelle cavernette e nei ripari dell'Agro Falisco. *Atti Soc. tosc. Sci. nat.* Ser. A, **76**, 101–24.

Batovič, S. (1966) *Stariji Neolit u Dalmaciji.* Zadar: Arheološki Muzej Zadar.

Biddittu, I., Cassoli, P., & Malpieri, L. (1967) Stazione musteriana in Valle Radice nel Comune di Sora (Frosinone), *Quaternaria* **9**, 321–48.

Biddittu, I., & Cassoli, P. (1968) Una stazione del paleolitico inferiore a Pontecorvo in provincia di Frosinone. *Quaternaria* **10**, 167–97.

Bietti, A. (1969) Due stazioni di superficie del paleolitico superiore nella pianura Pontina. *Bull. Paletnol. ital.* **78**, n.s. **20**, 7–39.

Blanc, A. C. (1933–4) Saccopastore II. *Riv. Antrop.* **30**, 479–81.

(1936) Sulla stratigrafia quaternaria dell'Agro Pontino e della bassa versilia. *Boll. Soc. geol. ital.* **15**(2), 375–96.

(1937) Nuovi giacimenti paleolitici del Lazio e della Toscana. *Studi etruschi* **11**, 273–304.

(1938–9a) Il giacimento musteriano di Saccopastore nel quadro del Pleistocene laziale. *Riv. Antrop.* **32**, 223–4.

(1938–9b) 'L'uomo fossile del Monte Circeo'. Un cranio neandertaliano nella Grotta Guattari a San Felice Circeo. *Riv. Antrop.* **32**, 1–16.

(1939a) L'uomo del Monte Circeo e la sua età geologica. *Boll. Soc. geol. ital.* **63**(1), 201–14.

(1939b) Un giacimento aurignaziano medio nella Grotta del Fossellone al Monte Circeo. *Atti Soc. ital. Prog. Sci.* **27**(6), 215–21.

(1955a) Giacimento del paleolitico superiore ad *Equus hydruntinus* e sovrapposti livelli con ceramica neolitica? e dell'età del bronzo, nella cava di travertino di Palidoro (Roma). *Quaternaria* **2**, 308–9.

(1955b) Giacimento con fauna pleistocenica a marmotta e livelli a ceramiche ed inumazione dell'età del bronzo, nella Grotta delle Sette Finestre ad Ansedonia. *Quaternaria* **2**, 309–10.

(1957) On the Pleistocene sequence of Rome. Paleoecologic and archaeologic correlations. *Quaternaria* **4**, 95–109.

(1958a) Torre in Pietra, Saccopastore e Monte Circeo. La cronologia dei giacimenti e la paleogeografia quaternaria del Lazio. *Boll. Soc. geol. ital* **8**(4–5), 196–214.

(1958b) Torre in Pietra, Saccopastore, Monte Circeo. On the position of the Mousterian culture in the Pleistocene sequence of the Rome area. In *Hundert Jahre Neanderthaler*, ed. G. H. R. Von Koenigswald, pp. 167–74. Utrecht: Kemink en Zu.

Blanc, A. C. & Segre, A. G. (1953a) Excursion au Mont Circé. *Livrets-guide des Excursions du IV Congrès International du Quaternaire, Rome-Pise.*

(1953b) Excursion dans les Abruzzes, les Pouilles et sur la côte de Salerne. *Livrets-guide des Excursions du IV Congrès International du Quaternaire, Rome-Pise.*

Bonatti, E. (1961) I sedimenti del Lago di Monterosi. *Experientia* **17**, 1–4.

(1963) Stratigrafia pollinica dei sedimenti postglaciali di Baccano, lago craterico del Lazio. *Atti Soc. tosc. Sci. nat.* Ser. A, **70**, 40–8.

(1966) North Mediterranean climate during the last Würm glaciation. *Nature, Lond.* **209**, 5027, 984–5.

(1970) Pollen sequence in the lake sediments. In *Ianula – an Account of the History and Development of the Lago di Monterosi, Latium, Italy.* ed. G. E. Hutchinson, pp. 26–31. (*Trans. Am. phil. Soc.* **60**, part 4.)

Bonuccelli, G. (1971) L'industria mesolitica della Grotta Erica di Positano. *Riv. Sci. preist.* **26**, 347–72.

Bonuccelli, G. & Faedo, L. (1968) Il villaggio a ceramica impressa di Capo d'Acqua. *Atti Soc. tosc. Sci. nat.* Ser. A, **75**, 87–101.

Borzatti von Löwenstern, E. (1962a) Industria litica rinvenuta nella zona di Prata (Grosseto). *Riv. Sci. preist.* **17**, 225–60.

(1962b) Scavi nella Grotta S. Nicola nel Bacino del Fucino. *Riv. Sci. preist.* **17**, 205–22.

(1968) Notizario. *Riv. Sci. preist.* **23**, 414–15.

Braudel, F. (1972) *The Mediterranean and the Mediterranean World in the Age of Philip II*, Vol. 1. London: Collins.

Bravi, M. (1951–2) Il paleolitico superiore nella Valle di Vibrata. *Bull. Paletnol. ital.* n.s. **8**, parte 4, 92–9.

Brizio, E. (1899) Il sepolcreto gallico di Montefortino presso Arcevia. *Monumenti antichi* **9**, 617–808.

Broglio, A. & Lollini, D. G. (1963) Nuova varietà di bulino su ritocco a stacco laterale nella industria del neolitico medio di Ripabianca di Monterado (Ancona). *Annali Univ. Ferrara* Sez. 15, **1**, 143–55.

Bronson, R. C. & Uggeri, G. (1968) Notizario. *Riv. Sci. preist.* **23**, 412–13.

Buchner, G. (1949) Ricerche sui giacimenti e sulle industrie di ossidiana in Italia. *Riv. Sci. preist.* **4**, 162–86.

(1950) Appunti sulle collezioni preistoriche e protostoriche del Museo Nazionale di Napoli, in occasione del loro riordinamento. *Riv. Sci. preist.* **5**, 97–107.

Butzer, K. W. (1972) *Environment and Archaeology.* London: Methuen.

Calvi Rezia, G. (1968) Notizario. *Riv. Sci. preist.* **23**, 410–11.

(1969) L'età neolitica nell'abitato preistorico di Pienza (Siena). *Studi etruschi* **37**, 355–9.

(1972) Resti dell'insediamento neolitico di Pienza. *Atti 14 Riunione Istituto Italiano per la Preistoria e Protostoria*, 285–99.

Calzoni, U. (1928a) L'industria di Abeto di Norcia. *Archo. Antrop. Etnol.* **58**, 97–8.

(1928b) I tipi di industria aurignaziana nell'Umbria. *Archo. Antrop. Etnol.* **58**, 153–4.

(1933) Scoperte preistoriche nelle Tane del Diavolo presso Parrano (Orvieto). *Archo. Antrop. Etnol.* **63**, 267–74.

(1936) Resti di un abitato preistorico a 'Casa Carletti' sulla Montagna di Cetona. *Studi etruschi* **10**, 329–39.

(1938) Lo strato superiore delle 'Tane del Diavolo' presso Parrano (Orvieto). *Studi etruschi* **12**, 225–35.

(1939) Un fondo di capanna scoperto presso Norcia (Umbria). *Bull. Paletnol. ital.* n.s. **3**, 37–50.

(1940) Recenti scoperte a Grotta Lattaia sulla Montagna di Cetona. *Studi etruschi* **14**, 301–4.

(1949) Notizario. *Riv. Sci. preist.* **4**, 220.

(1954) *Le Stazioni Preistoriche della Montagna di Cetona. Belverde I.* Florence: Olschki, Quaderni di *Studi etruschi* 1.

(1962) *Le Stazioni Preistoriche della Montagna di Cetona. Belverde II.* Florence: Olschki, Quaderni di *Studi etruschi* 2.

Chiappella, G. V. (1956) Scavo nel giacimento superiore di Palidoro, Roma. *Quaternaria* **3**, 263–4.

(1962) Saggi di scavo in Val Radice (Sora) e rinvenimenti di abbondante fauna pleistocenica con pachidermi. *Quaternaria* **5**, 301–2.

Chisholm, M. (1968) *Rural Settlement and Land Use.* London: Hutchinson University Library.

Cipolloni, M. (1971) Insediamento 'Protovillanoviano' sulla vetta del Monte Cetona. *Origini* **5**, 149–91.

Clark, J. G. D. (1954) *Excavations at Star Carr, an Early Mesolithic Site at Seamer, near Scarborough, Yorkshire.* Cambridge: Cambridge University Press.

(1972) Star Carr: a case study in bioarchaeology. *McCaleb Module in Anthropology* **10**, 1–42.

Close-Brooks, J. & Gibson, S. (1966) A round hut near Rome. *Proc. prehist. Soc.* **32**, 349–52.

Colini, G. A. (1914) Necropoli di Pianello presso Genga (Ancona) e l'origine della civiltà del ferro in Italia. *Bull. Paletnol. ital.* **39**, 19–68.

Craven, K. (1838) *Excursions in the Abruzzo,* Vol. 1. London: Bentley.

Cremonesi, G. (1962) I resti degli ultimi mesolitici del Fucino. *Atti Soc. tosc. Sci. nat.* Ser. A, **69**, 447–56.

(1965) Il villaggio di Ripoli alla luce dei recenti scavi. *Riv. Sci. preist.* **20**, 85–155.

(1966) Il villaggio Leopardi presso Penne in Abruzzo. *Bull. Paletnol. ital.* **75**, n.s. **17**, 27–49.

(1968a) Contributo alla conoscenza della preistoria del Fucino: la Grotta di Ortucchio e la Grotta la Punta. *Riv. Sci. preist.* **23**, 145–204.

(1968b) La Grotta dell'Orso di Sarteano – i livelli dell'età dei metalli. *Origini,* **2**, 247–331.

Dall'Osso, I. (1915) *Guida Illustrata del Museo Nazionale di Ancona.* Ancona: Museo Nazionale.

Dani, A. (1966) Resti di capanne della tarda età del bronzo presso Stabbia (Firenze). *Archo. Antrop. Etnol.* **96**, 65–71.

Darling, F. F. (1937) *A Herd of Red Deer: a Study in Animal Behaviour.* Oxford: Oxford University Press.

Dubois, C. & Zangheri, P. (1957) Palynologie de quelques sédiments tourbeux de la basse plaine du Po. *Bull. Serv. Carte géol. Als. Lorr.* **10,** 145–50.

Evett, D. & Renfrew, J. M. (1971) D'agricoltura neolitica italiana: una nota sui cereali. *Riv. Sci. preist.* **26,** 403–9.

Fedele, P. (1962) Prospezioni nel territorio di Pofi. *Quaternaria* **5,** 321–2.

Fedele, P., Blanc, A. C., Cardini, L., & Cassoli, P. (1962) Segnalazione e prospezione di un nuovo giacimento con industria musteriana e un'ulna umana fossile della cava di pozzolana 'Giovanni Pompi' in contrada S. Lucia nel territorio di Pofi (Frosinone). *Quaternaria* **5,** 339–40.

Fraia, T. de (1970) Tracce di uno stanziamento neolitico all'aperto presso Paterno (L'Aquila). *Atti Soc. tosc. Sci. nat.* Ser. A, **77,** 289–307.

Frank, A. H. E. (1969) Pollen stratigraphy of the Lake of Vico (Central Italy). *Palaeogeogr. Palaeoclimatol. Palaeoecol.* **6,** 67–85.

Fraser, F. C. & Stamp, J. T. (1961) *Sheep Husbandry and Disease.* London: Crosby, Lockwood and Sons, Ltd.

Gjerstad, E. (1966) *Early Rome IV. Synthesis of Archaeological Evidence.* Lund: Skrifter utgivna av Svenska Institutet i Rom, 4°, **17.**

Graziosi, P. (1943) Stazione preistorica delle Gole del Furlo presso Fossombrone. *Archo. Antrop. Etnol.* **73,** 115–22.

(1944) La Grotta all'Onda. *Archo. Antrop. Etnol.* **72,** 73–100.

Grifoni, R. (1967) La Grotta dell'Orso di Sarteano – il neolitico. *Origini* **1,** 53–115.

Grifoni, R. & Radmilli, A. M. (1964) La Grotta Maritza e il Fucino primo dell'età romana. *Riv. Sci. preist.* **19,** 53–127.

Grifoni Cremonesi, R. (1969a) I materiali preistorici della Toscana esistenti al museo archeologico di Perugia. *Atti Soc. tosc. Sci. nat.* Ser. A, **76,** 151–94.

(1969b) La grotta cultuale delle 'Marmitte' presso Ofena (L'Aquila). *Atti Soc. tosc. Sci. nat.* Ser. A, **76,** 151–94.

Guerreschi, G. (1971) Notizario. *Riv. Sci. preist.* **26,** 479–80.

Guerri, M. (1963) L'industria litica delle stazioni di superficie sulla Maielletta. *Atti. Soc. tosc. Sci. nat.* Ser. A, **70,** 244–61.

Guinness, F., Lincoln, G. A., & Short, R. V. (1971) The reproductive cycle of the red deer hind (*Cervus elaphus*). *J. Reprod. Fert.* **27,** 427–38.

Güller, A. & Segre, A. G. (1948) La stazione enea del grottone di Val di Varri nell'Appennino abruzzese. *Riv. Antrop.* **36,** 269–81.

Hare, A. J. C. (1875) *Days near Rome.* London: Daldy, Isbister and Co.

Higgs, E. S. & Vita-Finzi, C. (1972) Prehistoric economies: a territorial approach. In *Papers in Economic Prehistory,* ed. E. S. Higgs, pp. 27–36. Cambridge: Cambridge University Press.

Higgs, E. S., Vita-Finzi, C., Harris, D. R., & Fagg, A. E. (1967) The climate, environment and industries of stone age Greece: part III. *Proc. prehist. Soc.* **33,** 1–29.

Higgs, E. S. & Webley, D. (1971) Further information concerning the environment of Palaeolithic man in Epirus. *Proc. prehist. Soc.* **37,** part II, 367–80.

Houston, J. M. (1964) *The Western Mediterranean World.* London: Longmans.

Italy. (1944) Geographical Handbook Series of the Naval Intelligence Division, 5 volumes.

Jarman, M. R. (1971) Culture and economy in the north Italian Neolithic. *World Archaeology* **2**(3), 255–65.

(1972) European deer economies and the advent of the Neolithic. In *Papers in Economic Prehistory,* ed. E. S. Higgs, pp. 125–47. Cambridge: Cambridge University Press.

Jones, G. D. B. (1963) Capena and the Ager Capenas. Part II. *Papers of the British School at Rome* **31,** 100–58.

Korkubi, M. & Andrea, Z. (1972) L'agglomération néolithique de Cakran (Fieri). *Studia Albanica* **9,** 15–31.

Laplace, G. (1964) Les subdivisions du leptolithique italien. *Bull. Paletnol. ital.* **73,** n.s. **15,** 25–63.

(1966) *Recherches sur l'Origine et l'Évolution des Complexes Leptolithiques.* Paris: Boccard.

Lazzari, A. (1959) Insediamento del paleolitico superiore all'ingresso della Grotta di Castelcività (Salerno). Supplement to *Boll. Soc. Nat. Napoli* **25.**

Lee, R. B. (1968) What hunters do for a living, or how to make out on scarce resources. In *Man the Hunter,* ed. R. B. Lee & I. DeVore, pp. 30–48. Chicago: Aldine.

(1969)! Kung bushman subsistence: an input-output analysis. In *Environment and Cultural Behaviour,* ed. A. P. Vayda, pp. 47–79. New York: Natural History press.

Leonardi, P. (1960). Nota preliminari sul paleolitico inferiore e medio e sulle alluvione quaternarie delle Marche. *Riv. Sci. preist.* **15,** 1–25.

Leopardi, G., Pannuti, S., & Radmilli, A. M. (1957) Esplorazione paletnologiche in Abruzzo – anno 1956. *Bull. Paletnol. ital.* **66,** n.s. **11,** 239–68.

Leopardi, G. & Radmilli, A. M. (1951–2) Giacimento preistorico all'aperto di Campo delle Piane (Pescara). *Bull. Paletnol. ital.* n.s. **8,** parte 4, 89–92.

Leopardi, G., Radmilli, A. M., & Rozzi, R. (1954–5) Esplorazioni paletnologiche in Abruzzo. *Bull. Paletnol. ital.* **64,** n.s. **9,** 343–78.

Lollini, D. G. (1954–5) Saggi di scavo a Massignano di Ancona. *Bull. Paletnol. ital.* **64,** n.s. **9,** 379.

(1956) L'abitato preistorico e protostorico di Ancona. *Bull. Paletnol. ital.* **65,** n.s. **10,** 237–62.

(1957) Stanziamento appenninico di Monte di S. Croce (Sassoferrato). *Bull. Paletnol. ital.* **66,** n.s. **11,** 289–301.

(1959a) Notizario. *Riv. Sci. preist.* **14,** 320.

(1959b) Appenninici, Protovillanoviani e Piceni nella realtà culturale delle Marche. *Atti 2 Convegno di Studi etruschi,* 45–60.

(1965) Il Neolitico nelle Marche alla luce delle recenti scoperte. *Atti 6 Congresso Istituto Italiano per la Preistoria e Protostoria,* Vol. 2, 309–15.

(1966) Notizario. *Riv. Sci. preist.* **21,** 418.

(1968) Notizario. *Riv. Sci. preist.* **23,** 413.

(1971) Notizario. *Riv. Sci. preist.* **26,** 371–2.

Lona, I. (1957–62a) I depositi lacustri Euganei: archivio paleontologico del tardo glaciale e del periodo postglaciale. *Memorie Biogeogr. adriat.* **5,** 3–11.

(1957–62b) Studio pollinologico del deposito lacustre di Fimon (Vicenza). *Memorie Biogeogr. adriat.* **5,** 13–7.

Lo Porto, F. G. (1964) La tomba di S. Vito dei Normanni e il 'Proto-Appenninico B' in Puglia. *Bull. Paletnol. ital.* **73,** n.s. **15,** 109–42.

Lowe, V. P. W. (1967) Teeth as indicators of age with special reference to red deer (*Cervus elaphus*) of known age from Rhum. *J. Zool.* **152,** 137–53.

(1969) Population dynamics of the red deer (*Cervus elaphus*) on Rhum. *J. Anim. Ecol.* **38,** 425–7.

Malatesta, A. (1951) Ricerche preistoriche nella valle della Lima (Lucca). *Riv. Sci. preist.* **7,** 79–83.

Malatesta, A. & Pannuti, S. (1957) Giacimento preistorico di superficie presso Acilia. *Bull. Paletnol. ital.* **66,** n.s. **11,** 269–75.

Marshack, A. (1969) Polesini. A reexamination of the engraved Upper Palaeolithic mobiliary materials of Italy by a new methodology. *Riv. Sci. preist.* **24,** 219–81.

Menendez Amor, J. & Florschütz, F. (1963) Sur les éléments steppiques dans la vegetation quaternaire de l'Espagne. *Boln. R. Soc. esp. Hist. nat.* **61**, 121–33.

(1964) Results of the preliminary palynological investigation of samples from a 50-metre boring in southern Spain. *Boln. R. Soc. esp. Hist. nat.* **62**, 251–5.

Milliman, J. D. & Emery, K. O. (1968) Sea levels during the past 35 000 years. *Science* **162**, 1121–3.

Minto, A. (1913) Avanzi di suppellettili funebri eneolitiche di Punta degli Stretti nel Monte Argentario. *Bull. Paletnol. ital.* **38**, 132–5.

Mochi, A. (1914) La Grotta di San Francesco presso Titignano (Umbria). *Archo Antrop. Etnol.* **44**, 64–85.

Müller, E. (1938) Die Herdenwanderungen im Mittelmeergebiet. *Petermanns geogr. Mitt.* **84**, 364–70.

Ortolani, M. (1941) Pastorizia transumante e bonifica integrale. *Geopolitica* **3**, 276–80.

Östenberg, C. E. (1967) *Luni sul Mignone e Problemi della Preistoria d'Italia.* Lund: Acta Instituti Romani Regni Sueciae 4°, **25**.

Palma di Cesnola, A. (1969a) Il musteriano della Grotta del Poggio a Marina di Camerota (Salerno). *Scritti sul Quaternario in Onore di Angelo Pasa,* pp. 95–135. Verona: Museo Civico di Storia Naturale.

(1969b) Le ricerche e gli scavi a Marina di Camerota (Salerno) durante il biennio 1968–1969. *Riv. Sci. preist.* **24**, 195–217.

(1971) Il Gravettiano evoluto della Grotta della Cala a Marina di Camerota (Salerno). *Riv. Sci. preist.* **26**, 259–324.

Pannuti, S. (1969) Gli scavi di Grotta a Male presso L'Aquila. *Bull. Paletnol. ital.* **78**, n.s. **20**, 147–67.

Pantoni, A. (1949) Montecassino. *Atti Accad. naz. Lincei: Notizie degli Scavi* Ser. 8, **3**, 143–67.

Passeri, L. (1970) Ritrovamenti preistorici nei Pozzi della Piana (Umbria). *Riv. Sci. preist.* **25**, 225–51.

Peet, T. E. (1909) *The Stone and Bronze Ages in Italy.* Oxford: Oxford University Press.

Pericoli, S. (1959) Industria di tipo musteriano nella Grotta di Castelcività. Supplement to *Boll. Soc. Nat. Napoli* **25.**

Perini, R. (1971) I depositi preistorici di Romagnano-Loc (Trento). *Preistoria Alpina* **7**, 7–106.

Peroni, R. (1951–2) Stazione preistorica di Campo Avello (Cittaducale). *Bull. Paletnol. ital.* n.s. **8**, parte 4, 126–9.

(1953) La stazione preistorica di Malpasso presso Civitavecchia. *Bull. Paletnol. ital.* n.s. **8**, parte 5, 131–45.

(1959) Per una definizione dell'aspetto culturale 'subappenninico' come fase cronologica a sè stante. *Atti Accad. naz. Lincei* Ser. 8, **9**, 3–253.

(1962–3) La Romita di Asciano (Pisa) – riparo sotto roccia utilizzato dall'età neolitica alla barbarica. *Bull. Paletnol. ital.* **71–72**, n.s. **14**, 251–372.

(1965) Significato degli scavi nel deposito a ceramiche di Palidoro. *Quaternaria* **7**, 309–11.

(1969) Osservazioni sul significato della serie stratigrafica di Grotta a Male. *Bull. Paletnol. ital.* **78**, n.s. **20**, 249–58.

Peroni, R. & Fugazzola, M. A. (1969) Ricerche preistoriche a Narce. *Bull. Paletnol. ital.* **78**, n.s. **20**, 79–145.

Pigorini, L. (1875) Stazioni litiche della provincia di Sulmona. *Bull. Paletnol. ital.* **1**, 135–6.

Puglisi, S. M. (1954) Civiltà appenninica e sepolcri di tipo dolmenico a Pian Sultano. *Riv. Antrop.* **41**, 3–32.

(1956a) Gli scavi nella Grotta del Mezzogiorno. *Bull. Paletnol. ital.* **65**, n.s. **10**, 499–521.

(1956b) I 'dolmen' con muri a secco a Pian Sultano (S. Severa). Nuovi scavi e precisazioni. *Bull. Paletnol. ital.* **65**, n.s. **10**, 157–74.

(1959a) *La Civiltà Appenninica. Origine delle Communità Pastorali in Italia.* Florence: Sansoni.

(1959b) Le civiltà del Piceno dalla preistoria alla protostoria alla luce delle più recenti scoperte. *Atti 2 Convegno di Studi etruschi,* 29–44.

(1965) Sulla facies protoappenninica in Italia. *Atti 6 Congresso Istituto Italiano per la Preistoria e Protostoria,* Vol. 2, 403–7.

Radmilli, A. M. (1951–2a) Attività del Museo Nazionale Preistorico ed Etnografia 'L. Pigorini' – Anni 1946–51. *Bull. Paletnol. ital.* n.s. **8**, parte 4, 63–80.

(1951–2b) Notizie preliminari sulla Grotta sepolcrale 'Patrizi' di Sasso Furbara. *Bull. Paletnol. ital.* n.s. **8**, parte 4, 100–4.

(1953a) Gli scavi della Grotta Polesini. *Bull. Paletnol. ital.* n.s. **8**, parte 5, 23–31.

(1953b) Attività del Museo Nazionale Preistorico 'L. Pigorini' – Anno 1952. *Bull. Paletnol. ital.* n.s. **8**, parte 5, 37–48.

(1953c) Scavi nella Grotta dei Baffoni presso San Vittore di Frasassi. *Bull. Paletnol. ital.* n.s. **8**, parte 5, 117–30.

(1953d) Esplorazioni paletnologiche nel territorio di Rieti. *Bull. Paletnol. ital.* n.s. **8**, parte 6, 17–24.

(1954–5) Un nuovo facies del paleolitico superiore italiano presente in Abruzzo. *Bull. Paletnol. ital.* **64**, n.s. **9**, 73–105.

(1955) Il paleolitico superiore nella Grotta Achille Graziani (Parco Nazionale d'Abruzzo). *Atti Soc. tosc. Sci. nat.* Ser. A, **62**, 479–95.

(1956a) Il paleolitico superiore nella Grotta Clemente Tronci a Venere dei Marsi, territorio del Fucino. *Boll. Soc. geol. ital.* **85**, 94–116.

(1956b) Gli scavi nella Grotta dei Baffoni. *Bull. Paletnol. ital.* **65**, n.s. **10**, 523–33.

(1957) Insediamento neolitico nella Grotta Cola II a Petrella di Cappadocia. *Atti Soc. tosc. Sci. nat.* Ser. A, **64**, 40–8.

(1959) Gli insediamenti preistorici in Abruzzo. *L'Universo* **39**, 861–98.

(1960a) Considerazioni sul Mesolitico italiano. *Annali Univ. Ferrara,* Sez. 15, **1**, 29–48.

(1960b) Notizario. *Riv. Sci. preist.* **15**, 234.

(1962) *Piccola Guida della Preistoria Italiana.* Florence: Sansoni.

(1963a) Il paleolitico superiore nel Riparo Maurizio. *Atti Soc. tosc. Sci. nat.* Ser. A, 70, 220–43.

(1963b) *La Preistoria d'Italia alla Luce delle Ultime Scoperte.* Florence: Istituto Geografico Militare.

(1965a) Notizario. *Riv. Sci. preist.* **20**, 375.

(1965b) Considerazioni sull'età del bronzo in Abruzzo. *Abruzzo* (Rivista dell'Istituto di Studi abruzzesi) **3**, 135–49.

(1967a) I villaggi a capanne del neolitico italiano. *Archo. Antrop. Etnol.* **97**, 53–62.

(1967b) Notizario. *Riv. Sci. preist.* **22**, 444–6.

(1968a) La situazione degli studi paletnologici in Abruzzo. *Atti 2 Convegno Nazionale della Cultura Abruzzese, Abruzzo* **6**, 45–58.

(1968b) Notizario. *Riv. Sci. preist.* **23**, 410 & 416.

(1970) Notizario. *Riv. Sci. preist.* **25**, 424.

(1971) Notizario. *Riv. Sci. preist.* **26**, 483–4.

Radmilli, A. M. & Cremonesi, G. (1963) Note di preistoria abruzzese. *Atti 7 Riunione Istituto Italiano per la Preistoria e Protostoria,* 127–53.

Radmilli, A. M. & Tongiorgi, E. (1958) Gli scavi nella Grotta la Porta di Positano. Contributo alla conoscenza del mesolitico italiano. *Riv. Sci. preist.* **13**, 91–109.

Rellini, U. (1914) L'età della pietra sulla Maiella. *Bull. Paletnol. ital.* **40**, 30–42, 95–100.

(1920) Cavernette e ripari preistorici nell'Agro Falisco. *Monumenti antichi* **26**, 8–181.

(1923–4) La Grotta delle Felci a Capri. *Monumenti antichi* **29**, 305.

(1931) Le stazioni enee delle Marche di fase seriore e la civiltà italiana. *Monumenti antichi* **34**, 129–280.

(1933) Caverna preistorica a Sasso di Furbara. *Atti Accad. naz. Lincei: Notizie degli Scavi* Ser. 6, **9**, 395–7.

(1934) *La Più Antica Ceramica Dipinta in Italia*. Rome: Collezione Meridionale Editrice.

(1938) Caverna preistorica del periodo di transizione ad Assergi (Aquila). *Bull. Paletnol. ital.* n.s. **2**, 65–7.

Rittatore, F. (1951) Scoperte di età eneolitica e del bronzo nella Maremma Tosco-Laziale. *Riv. Sci. preist.* **6**, 3–33.

Segre, A. G. (1956) Scoperte di paleolitico e del bronzo nei travertini di Cisterna (Latina). *Riv. Antrop.* **43**, 367–82.

(1957) Contributo allo studio del Quaternario dell'Agro Pontino: il travertino di Cisterna Latina. Giacimenti del paleolitico superiore e del bronzo. *Quaternaria* **4**, 191–4.

(1959) Giacimenti pleistocenici con fauna e industria litica a Monte Argentario (Grosseto). *Riv. Sci. preist.* **14**, 1–18.

Sestini, A. (1934) Indizi di stazioni preistoriche nei giacimenti di farina fossile del Monte Amiata. *Studi etruschi* **8**, 315–17.

Silver, I. A. (1969) The ageing of domestic animals. In *Science in Archaeology*, ed. D. Brothwell & E. S. Higgs, pp. 283–302. London: Thames and Hudson.

Soffredi, A. (1972) L'abitato preistorico di Scarceta (Manciano). *Atti 14 Riunione Istituto Italiano per la Preistoria e Protostoria*, 45–59.

Stefani, E. (1922) Veii – esplorazione dentro l'area dell'antica città. *Atti Accad. naz. Lincei: Notizie degli Scavi* **19**, 379–404.

Stradi, F. & Andreolotti, S. (1964) Secondo rinvenimento in superficie di industrie del paleolitico superiore e medio sul Monte Alburno (Salerno). *Atti 8 e 9 Riunione Istituto Italiano per la Preistoria e Protostoria*, 291–301.

Sturdy, D. A. (1972) The exploitation patterns of a modern reindeer economy in west Greenland. In *Papers in Economic Prehistory*, ed. E. S. Higgs, pp. 161–8. Cambridge: Cambridge University Press.

Taschini, M. (1964) Il livello mesolitico del Riparo Blanc al Monte Circeo. *Bull. Paletnol. ital.* **73**, n.s. **15**, 65–88.

(1967) Il 'Protopontiniano' rissiano di Sedia del Diavolo e di Monte delle Gioie (Roma). *Quaternaria* **9**, 301–19.

(1968) La datation au C14 de l'abri Blanc (Mont Circé). Quelques observations sur le mésolithique en Italie. *Quaternaria* **10**, 137–65.

(1970) La Grotta Breuil al Monte Circeo. *Origini* **4**, 45–78.

Tongiorgi, E. (1950) Notizario. *Riv. Sci. preist.* **5**, 121.

(1956) Osservazioni paleontologiche nella Grotta del Mezzogiorno. *Bull. Paletnol. ital.* **65**, n.s. **10**, 535–40.

Tozzi, C. (1962) Resti neolitici e sepolture nella Grotta la Cava (Bacino del Fucino). *Atti Soc. tosc. Sci. nat.* Ser. A, **69**, 1–8.

(1966) Il giacimento mesolitico di Capo d'Acqua (L'Aquila). *Bull. Paletnol. ital.* **75**, n.s. **17**, 13–25.

(1967) Giacimenti paleolitici in superficie sulle montagne abruzzesi. *Atti Soc. tosc. Sci. nat.* Ser. A, **74**, 107–19.

(1970) La Grotta di Sant' Agostino (Gaeta). *Riv. Sci. preist*, **25**, 3–87.

Trump, D. H. (1966) *Central and Southern Italy before Rome*. London: Thames and Hudson.

Van der Hammen, T., Wijmstra, T. A., & Van der Molen, W. H. (1965) Palynological study of a very thick peat section in Greece and the Würm glacial vegetation in the Mediterranean region. *Geol. Mijnb.* **44**, 37–9.

Vaufrey, R. (1928) Le paléolithique italien. *Arch. Inst. Paléont. hum.*, Mémoire 3.

Vigliardi, A. (1968a) Il musteriano della Grotta Taddeo (Marina di Camerota, Salerno). *Riv. Sci. preist.* **23**, 245–59.

(1968b) Prima campagna di scavi nel deposito paleolitico superiore di Grotta Calanca (Marina di Camerota, Salerno). *Riv. Sci. preist.* **23**, 271–314.

Vita-Finzi, C. (1969) *The Mediterranean Valleys*. Cambridge: Cambridge University Press.

Ward-Perkins, J. B. (1969) In: British archaeology abroad. *Antiquity* **43**, 99–100.

(1970) In: British archaeology abroad. *Antiquity* **44**, 187–8.

Ward-Perkins, J. B., Kahane, A., & Murray Threipland, L. (1968) The Ager Veientanus, north and east of Rome. *Papers of the British School at Rome* **36**, 1–218.

White, K. D. (1970) *Roman Farming*. London: Thames and Hudson.

Whitehouse, R. (1968a) Settlement and economy in southern Italy in the Neothermal period. *Proc. prehist. Soc.* **34**, 332–67.

(1968b) The early Neolithic of southern Italy. *Antiquity* **42**, 188–93.

(1969) The neolithic pottery sequence of southern Italy. *Proc. prehist. Soc.* **35**, 267–31.

(1971) The last hunter-gatherers in southern Italy. *World Archaeology* **2**, 239–54.

Zecchini, M. (1969a) Rinvenimento di industrie litiche in alcuni località dell'Isola d'Elba. *Atti Soc. tosc. Sci. nat.* Ser. A, **76**, 1–13.

(1969b) Ceramiche di tradizione subappenninica rinvenute a Monte Giove (Isola d'Elba). *Atti Soc. tosc. Sci. nat.* Ser. A, **76**, 88–100.

Zei, M. (1953a) Stazione preistoriche del Lido di Lavinio (Lazio). *Bull. Paletnol. ital.* n.s. **8**, parte 5, 83–102.

(1953b) Esplorazione di grotta nei pressi di Sezze-Romano. *Bull. Paletnol. ital.* n.s. **8**, parte 5, 102–7.

ACKNOWLEDGEMENTS

I am grateful to Dr J. B. Ward-Perkins, Director of the British School at Rome, for his constant support during my tenure of the Rome Scholarships in Classical Studies, 1969–70 and 1970–1. I received enormous help from many Italian and foreign archaeologists in universities, museums, institutes and *Soprintendenze* throughout Italy. I am particularly grateful, however, to Dott. G. Calvi Rezia (Milan University), Professor C. E. Ostenberg (Swedish Institute in Rome). Professor A. Palma di Cesnola (Siena University), Dr T. W. Potter (Lancaster University), Professor A. M. Radmilli (Pisa University), and Dott. A. Vigliardi (Florence University).

6. SETTLEMENT AND LAND USE IN CAPITANATA, ITALY

M. R. JARMAN AND D. WEBLEY

One of the difficulties besetting many attempts to relate archaeological sites and their populations to their environments has been the reliance upon zonal framework provided by (and stemming from the requirements of) a variety of other disciplines. Archaeologists lacked a set of hypotheses and methods specifically appropriate to their own data and needs. A particular inadequacy of the zonal framework stemming from the concerns of other disciplines has been its inability to allow particular sites to be studied in terms of their precise location and the environmental resources which this offers. A site located in a zone (be this climatic, geographic, botanical, or ecological) may not necessarily be best described in these terms, for sites are frequently located in exceptional, rather than typical, positions within zones. The techniques of 'catchment analysis' and 'territorial analysis' (Higgs & Vita-Finzi, 1972; Jarman, 1972) allow a measure of improvement, permitting the area of prime archaeological significance (the site itself) to become the determining factor. The assumptions, hypotheses, and methods laid out in those papers were employed in our analysis of the sites discussed here.

This paper concerns the investigation by such means of the settlement of the region of Capitanata, the northern part of Apulia in southeast Italy. The results of the analyses can be conveniently divided into two groups: those on the Tavoliere, and those of the Gargano peninsula. Not only do these areas form recognisable geographical and economic units, but there are regularities visible in the features of archaeological settlement within each region. Figure 1 indicates the position of the sites concerned and of geographical features mentioned in the text.

THE TAVOLIERE

Topography

The Tavoliere as a whole can be viewed as a series of parallel ridges running roughly west to east, the altitude decreasing to the east. At the western edge of the Tavoliere the ridges run up into the foothills of the Apennines, attaining a maximum height of *c.* 400 m in the area concerning us. In the central area the ridges rise to no more than 50–100 m, dropping still further to the low-lying coastal area to the east. With the exception of the Fiume Fortore, which defines the northwestern limit of the Tavoliere and runs northward into the Adriatic to the west of the Gargano, the basic drainage pattern is west to east, from the Apennines into the Gulf of Manfredonia.

Soils

We have classified the soils of the area partly on the basis of their physical and chemical properties, but our primary consideration has been the economic potential and land use capability of the different formations. This provides us with a picture which is directly related to the exploitive potential of the site territories.

Two main soil categories are of particular importance for most of the Tavoliere sites, although others are occasionally present. The first class comprises a variety of heavy clays and alluvial deposits. They are, in the main, Pleistocene in age and have many parallels elsewhere in the Mediterranean area.

(1a) A deep brown alluvium, at least 3 m thick, covers the majority of the area between Foggia and Manfredonia. Mechanical analysis shows it to be a vertisol whose surface commonly cracks as it dries.

(1b) In some valley bottoms and at the foot of some hill slopes the drainage is impeded, creating water-logged soils and seasonal marsh conditions. In many places the marshes remained undrained until the recent historical past.

(1c) In the west of the Tavoliere most of the soils contain considerable quantities of rounded pebbles, probably indicating the existence of relict river beds. The soils vary in heaviness due to the varying proportions of clay and silt particles.

(2) On the ridges, and even on slight prominences, there often occurs a *crosta*, or calcium carbonate crust, which comes to within 10 cm of the surface in places but is on average *c.* 30–80 cm below the surface. It is often *c.* 1 m thick, and below it the silt continues. In the western area the *crosta* soils contain rounded pebbles similar to those in the alluvial deposits there. The *crosta* is hard and impervious to both root and water penetration. Ditches cut into the *crosta* at Passo di Corvo and other Neolithic sites show that its formation must be earlier than this period. Dates for the Scaramella sites indicate occupation during the first half of

the fifth millennium B.C. Since the basic alluvial deposit in which the *crosta* is found dates from the Late Pleistocene, the *crosta* must be later. It is possible that the lowering of the water-table during the Holocene (due to slope modification as well as aridity) led to its formation, but the reasons for such deposits are complex and not fully understood. Although their dates will have varied according to local conditions, it is instructive to consider some dated examples of comparable formations. Calcic layers have been ^{14}C-dated to 8380–11 580 B.P. in the central Sahara (Delibrius & Datil, 1966), and 7000–8000 B.P. in Russia (Vinogradov, Mamedov, & Stepanov, 1969). Core samples from the Black Sea (Deuser, 1972) showed that at about the

same date the fresh water had become salt. Further confirmation comes from soil calcium carbonate levels in the Tambov region of Russia, where that chemical has been accumulating for 7000 years in a chernozem and for 8500 years in a meadow soil (Kovda & Samilova, 1968).

(3) At the junction between the slopes of the Gargano and the plain there is a narrow band of rendsina soils, which is thin and contains much limestone near the hills and thickens and merges into the alluvial (Class 1) soils as the ground surface falls to the plain.

(4) The limestone hills have a very thin and incomplete cover of Terra Rossa, thicker only in the natural basins in which it collects from the steadily eroding slopes. At the

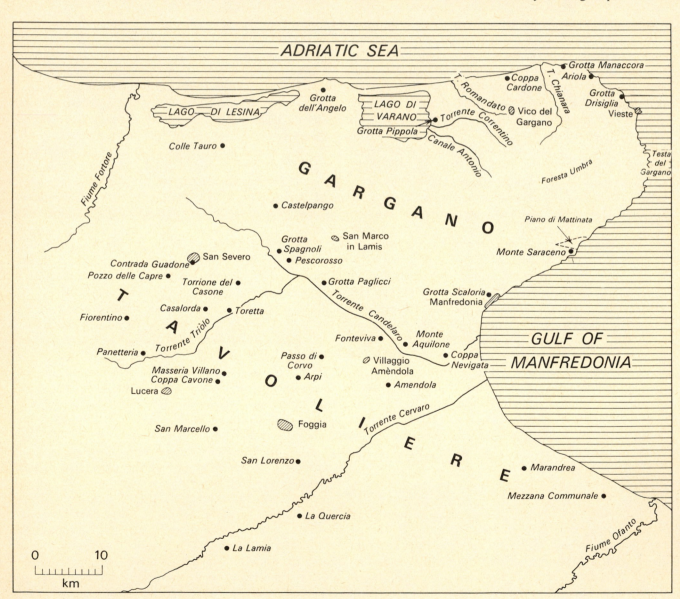

Figure 1. Map of Capitanata showing sites and geographical features mentioned in text.

edge of the hills the Terra Rossa forms mixtures with the rendsina and alluvium.

Climate and agricultural potential

The agricultural potential of the area, both today and in the past, is partly a function of the climate. Meteorological data, presented as ten-year averages (Appendix I), were obtained from the Villaggio Amèndola airport (39 m o.d.), which is situated centrally in the Tavoliere and can be taken as representing the plain as a whole. It was not possible to obtain figures for the Gargano, but the figures for Potenza (1367 m o.d.) give an indication of upland climate, although it would be expected that Gargano rainfall would be lower, and temperatures higher, than those for Potenza. The annual rainfall for Amèndola was 455 mm, as compared with 662 mm at Potenza. The maximum mean air temperatures were 21.3°C and 15.2°C at Amèndola and Potenza respectively, and the minimum mean air temperatures were 9.8°C and 7.8°C. Minor differences between these and official meteorological statistics are caused by the fact that the latter are calculated from January to December, whereas ours are related to the cereal growing season, and are calculated from August to July. The relative humidities of the two areas were comparable. In both areas the annual distribution of these meteorological factors was similar, with most rain falling between October and December, and least in July and August. The temperature range (the difference between maximum and minimum) was greater at Amèndola.

Correlation coefficients were calculated between the monthly meteorological means for each of ten years and the wheat production for the province of Foggia. A highly significant negative correlation was observed between wheat yield and maximum mean temperature in November, December, and February: the lower the maximum temperature in these months, the greater the subsequent yield. In addition, a positive correlation was observed between wheat yield and April rainfall: the more rain, the greater the yield. These figures relate to the physiological needs of the plant. The minimum rainfall usually needed to sustain cereal growth is about 300–400 mm per year, but the annual distribution is equally important, and 150 mm can suffice where soil water storage and rainfall run parallel to plant growth. For the Tavoliere, with a rainfall figure of 455 mm, wheat production is possible with few total crop failures; but the best yields are tied to the amount of April rain, which is needed to fill the ear. Absence of sufficient spring rainfall is a common cause of low yields today.

The other limiting factor, winter temperature, is related to the fact that winter wheat requires a cold period in order to flower and produce grain (vernalisation). The negative cor-

relation between maximum winter temperatures and yield is a manifestation of a degree of non-vernalisation and shows that winter temperatures are too high. Warm winters result in good vegetative growth to the benefit of pastures and stock. The climatic evidence supports the view that the Tavoliere is particularly suitable for winter grazing. While wheat can be satisfactorily grown, yields very considerably, and the high yearly variation in the rainfall means that economies based exclusively on cereals would be at a far greater risk than those based on animals. An economy combining both arable and pastoral elements would benefit from the high yield potential of the former and the lower risk of the latter.

Modern exploitation

The modern exploitation of the Tavoliere is based primarily upon cereals, especially wheat. Where there is sufficient water to support irrigation, sugar beet is a common rotation crop, others being *fava* (a leguminous fodder crop), lucerne, and vegetables. This form of land use, with the addition of intensive market gardening, occupies virtually all the most productive soils, including those in Class 1, and many of the Class 2 soils. Wide expanses of lighter soils (Class 2), however, carry vines and olives. The large area of light *crosta* soils around the modern town of San Severo primarily carries these crops, and they occur commonly throughout the Tavoliere where cereal agriculture is unprofitable for reasons of soil depth, water availability, or topography. Wheat yields average 30–5 quintals per hectare [A quintal is 100 kg; thus 1 quintal per hectare is roughly equivalent to 4/5 cwt per acre.] in good years, but the yield is very variable from year to year, depending on a variety of factors (see above). In poor years yields can fall to 10–15 quintals per hectare even on large and technically advanced farms with the advantages of machinery and fertilisers. These generally achieve better average yields than small family farms which cannot afford the capital expenditure necessary for the higher returns. This dichotomy is reinforced by the fact that small holdings are increasingly being forced onto the poorer soils by the economic competition of the large consortia. The small holdings thus frequently average only c. 20 quintals per hectare, with 25 quintals per hectare as a maximum in good years, and only 6–8 quintals per hectare in poor years; in very bad years virtually total crop failure can occur.

The Tavoliere is today an important area of winter grazing for sheep, one of the main areas for winter grazing being the region of limestone soils in the northeast of the Tavoliere (cf. commentary on Monte Aquilone and Coppa Nevigata, Appendix II). This is a low plateau extending at an altitude of c. 100 m from the southeastern edge of the

Gargano characterised by shallow Terra Rossa soils, thin scrub vegetation, and scarcity of water. Because of these limitations arable exploitation is impossible, and indeed the area becomes parched and deserted very early in the summer and is of ltttle use even as rough grazing until the autumn rains. Other areas are also primarily used as winter grazing; in particular where there is a good soil depth but steep slopes impede plough agriculture; or where the *crosta* is so near the surface that ploughing is difficult and expensive, and results in a poor stony tilth. These conditions occur, for instance, in parts of the western Tavoliere (cf. commentary on Fiorentino, Appendix II) where some stretches have only recently come under the plough. Cultivation produces a stony, nearly white tilth which is almost pure *crosta*, and which can support poor olives and vines, but not cereals.

Some animals are maintained on the Tavoliere throughout the year, but these are fed during the summer almost exclusively on artificial feed, or fodder bought for cash; some cattle find summer grazing in the artificial cuts in which the rivers now flow, for these obtain enough moisture from the rivers to allow plant growth nearly throughout the summer. The area involved is not large, however, providing strips only a few metres wide on either side of the river.

Some of this pattern, however, is a recent development; before the Second World War there was a greater emphasis on pastoralism than now, with a consequent lessening of the importance of arable crops. There is a number of reasons for this trend. Modern technology, in particular the use of the caterpillar tractor and the draining of marshes, has made available to arable exploitation areas which previously could only be grazed. Government subsidies encourage arable as opposed to pastoral exploitation. A further contributory factor is the difficulty in getting sufficient labour to do the arduous and lowly job of herding large numbers of animals.

We may thus expect that in the past a narrower selection of soils would have been given over to arable production, and more animals would have been carried on the Tavoliere. The arable crops would have been more restricted: the cultivation of crops requiring irrigation would have been impracticable, and longer fallow (again encouraging the pastoral aspect of the economy) would have been necessary in the absence of chemical fertilisers.

Site location

When we consider the relationship of sites to soils, one fact is immediately apparent. Sites are by no means randomly distributed on the Tavoliere, in spite of claims (Tiné, 1968) that they are relatively evenly scattered over the plain. With two exceptions (Coppa Nevigata and Monte Aquilone) all the sites whose territories were analysed are situated on the *crosta* (Class 2) soils, even though these only account for *c.* 20 per cent of the Tavoliere as a whole. Thus there seems to be a strong preference for Class 2 soils, and an avoidance of other soils, for the location of Neolithic sites. The two exceptions in our sample require further consideration.

The site of Monte Aquilone is in an unusual location, being situated upon Class 3 soils, which are not of great extent on the Tavoliere, accounting for only *c.* 2 per cent of the total area. The limestone bedrock which forms the prominence just to the east of the site is fairly close to the surface at the site itself. This, and the elements in the surface soil derived from hill-wash combine to produce a relatively light soil, resembling in texture the *crosta* soils more than the heavy alluvia. Coppa Nevigata, on the other hand, is on Class 1a soils, and during its occupation the site would have been on the edge of the Lago Salso, which with the Lago Verzentino would have truncated the terrestrial territory to the south and east (see Figure 14). The site is very different from the others considered in this paper, a fact which may be connected with its anomalous locational features. It is a small, low mound, with several superimposed occupation levels dating from the Early Neolithic to the Iron Age. No indication of structures was found at the site. It appears to have been occupied, during the Neolithic period at least, primarily for the exploitation of cockles (*Cardium edule*) from the adjacent Lago Salso. The small size of the site may indeed be taken as an indication of the ephemeral nature of the occupations. Most of the other sites in the sample are ditched settlements which measure anything up to 800 m in diameter. The size of the sites, and the labour involved in digging the ditches, demonstrate clearly the importance of the sites and significance of the occupations.

We must therefore ask what factors may have influenced Neolithic site distribution so strongly. Two linked features of the Class 2 soils seem likely to have been of importance. It has been mentioned already that many of the heavier clay soils have only recently been ploughed. This is partly due to the recent development of many poorly drained and marshy areas, but is also related to the difficulties inherent in ploughing heavy soils except with sophisticated agricultural machinery. Indeed, even today the effects of this restraint can be seen in the prevalence of 'caterpillar' or 'crawler' tractors on the Tavoliere farms. Before the advent of tractor ploughing some of the heavy soils could be ploughed with horses; but this was limited to very small areas, as weather conditions necessary to permit this were short-lived, and less than the 0.5 hectare usual for lighter soils could be ploughed in a day by a good pair of horses. If we assume that Neolithic agriculture on the Tavoliere would have relied on hand tools to break the soil, then the constraints introduced by heavy soils would have been yet more stringent.

The other factor to be considered is the reaction of the various soils to different weather conditions. Travel in the Tavoliere in wet conditions clearly illustrates the superior drainage of the Class 2 soils over the Class 1 soils. Even a relatively brief spell of rain renders the clays unworkable, difficult to walk over, and leaves water standing on the surface, whereas the lighter *crosta* soils stay drier for much longer, both by reason of their superior permeability and also because the soils are commonly found on eminences and slopes. It is thus easy to see why the Class 2 soils may have attracted settlement, particularly in cases where the site was to be occupied during the winter. Returning to the site of Monte Aquilone discussed above, it is of interest to note that the Class 3 soil on which it is situated drains more easily and can be more readily ploughed than can Class 1 soils, and the site location can be considered in these respects to be comparable with those on Class 2 soils.

There thus appears to be good reason for suggesting that the Neolithic sites of the Tavoliere are located with reference particularly to the requirements of arable agriculture and good drainage. Of these two factors the former seems likely to have been the more compelling; had drainage been the primary consideration, one would have expected more evidence of Neolithic settlement on the limestone hills which, while barren and infertile, provide the best-drained situations. Site location was concerned with the exploitation of the most fertile soils accessible to the available technology.

Site territories

The territories of twenty-one Neolithic sites were analysed in detail. Results of these individual analyses can be seen in Appendix II. The following is a synthesis of this data. The territories are all nearly circular, an indication that relief is not in general sufficiently severe greatly to distort the 'ideal' circular territory. A few individual sites, such as Fonteviva and Colle Tauro show a slight distortion due to topographic features. A few of the territories are truncated by lakes or the sea or by both. In some cases these lakes exist to the present day, but others have been drained during the last few centuries and would almost certainly have influenced the shape and nature of the territory at the time the site was occupied. The territories have been delimited assuming an arable agricultural economy, a one-hour limit being adopted (Higgs & Vita-Finzi, 1972; Jarman, 1972). The perimeters of the one-hour territories vary from a minimum of *c.* 4.3 km to a maximum of *c.* 5.3 km from the site, but most of the perimeters lie between 4.5 and 5.0 km from the site. This is again a strikingly close approximation to the 'ideal' 5.0 km one-hour limit proposed by the model. In view of the significance that the 1 km threshold has in many

modern farming economies (Chisholm, 1968) we have given special attention to the area within 1 km of the site. The 1 km ring contains the area which is optimally situated for arable exploitation in particular; beyond this distance the labour costs involved rise sharply, and the returns diminish accordingly. For pastoral exploitation the effects of distance are to some degree mitigated in that animals can frequently graze while on the move to and from distant pastures.

Reasons were given above for considering the sites of Monte Aquilone and Coppa Nevigata separately from the majority of Tavoliere Neolithic sites. If, however, the hypothesis is accepted that the hill-wash soils at the former site fulfil the same economic function as the *crosta* soils elsewhere, it is possible to consider Monte Aquilone with the other ditched settlements. Assuming that the light soils were exploited primarily as arable it can be seen from Table 1 that (excluding Coppa Nevigata for the reasons given above) 27–99 per cent of the land area within 1 km of the sites falls into the arable category, either *crosta* or hill-wash soils. Colle Tauro is also excluded from these figures, and is discussed separately below (p. 182). The average figure is *c.* 64.5 per cent. It should not be forgotten that some of the site territories are significantly curtailed by lakes, and Table 1 also indicates the approximate areal extent of soils in the territories. The other main soil type occurring within the 1 km ring is Class 1 alluvium, which could not have been cultivated and must presumably have been exploited primarily as pasture in prehistoric times; only at Monte Aquilone, Coppa Nevigata, and Colle Tauro do other soils occur in significant proportions within 1 km of the site.

Viewing the territories as a whole the same two soil types dominate, but whereas arable soils account on average for two-thirds of the area within 1 km of the site, they amount to less than two-fifths of the area of the whole territory (Table 2). There is thus a tendency for the sites to be so located that an unusually high proportion of the closely adjacent soils are of arable potential, a higher proportion than exists in the territory as a whole. On the other hand none of the sites is confined to a single soil type within the 1 km ring, although at Passo di Corvo the Class 1 soils come only just within 1 km of the site (see Appendix II). In general, soils suitable for pastoral exploitation predominate in the territories, comprising mainly Class 1 soils with the addition of thin limestone hill soils in some instances. The sites are most commonly located at or near the junction of the two main soil types, although virtually always actually on the *crosta* soils. The sites are customarily situated within a short distance (up to *c.* 1.5 km) of a water course. It is also noticeable that several of the sites are adjacent to small areas of impeded drainage with the formation of marsh soils. It was observed in the field that today the junctions of

Table 1. Soils within 1 km of Tavoliere sites

	Alluvium		Crosta		Thick limestone soils		Thin limestone soils		Marsh		Total area
	Area (km²)	Per cent	Area (km²)	Per cent	Area (km²)	Per cent	Area (km²)	Per cent	Area (km²)	Per cent	(km³)
La Lamia	0.39	12.3	2.75	87.7	–	–	–	–	–	–	3.14
La Quercia	1.34	42.8	1.80	57.2	–	–	–	–	–	–	3.14
Mezzana Comunale	0.75	34.5	1.42	65.5	–	–	–	–	–	–	2.17
Marandrea	0.39	13.7	2.46	86.3	–	–	–	–	–	–	2.85
San Lorenzo	1.47	47.1	1.66	52.7	–	–	–	–	0.01	0.2	3.14
San Marcello	0.82	26.0	2.32	74.0	–	–	–	–	–	–	3.14
Coppa Cavone	2.28	72.5	0.86	27.5	–	–	–	–	–	–	3.14
Villano	1.15	36.5	1.99	63.5	–	–	–	–	–	–	3.14
Amèndola	1.11	35.3	2.03	64.7	–	–	–	–	–	–	3.14
Passo di Corvo	0.03	0.8	3.11	99.2	–	–	–	–	–	–	3.14
Fonteviva	0.73	23.1	2.41	76.9	–	–	–	–	–	–	3.14
Monte Aquilone	0.40	12.8	–	–	1.84	58.7	0.90	28.5	–	–	3.14
Coppa Nevigata	0.85	47.5	–	–	0.72	40.1	0.22	12.4	–	–	1.79
Panetteria	1.02	32.5	2.12	67.5	–	–	–	–	–	–	3.14
Fiorentino	1.10	35.0	2.04	65.0	–	–	–	–	–	–	3.14
Casalorda	0.99	31.5	2.15	68.5	–	–	–	–	–	–	3.14
Torretta	1.76	56.0	1.38	44.0	–	–	–	–	–	–	3.14
Pozzo delle Capre	1.12	35.8	2.02	64.2	–	–	–	–	–	–	3.14
Torrione del Casone	1.95	62.1	1.15	36.3	–	–	–	–	0.05	1.6	3.14
Contrada Guadone	0.09	3.0	3.05	97.0	–	–	–	–	–	–	3.14
Colle Tauro	2.35	74.9	0.15	4.8	–	–	0.64	20.3	–	–	3.14

marsh and *crosta* soils are frequently chosen as the sites for wells, as the water-table is commonly most accessible here. It seems likely that this was also a factor influencing site location in Neolithic times.

The sites are frequently found on the top of eminences, either considerable hills (such as those in the west of the region) or barely perceptible rises (nearer the Adriatic coast). It has on occasion been suggested that altitude itself is of significance in the pattern of Neolithic settlement on the Tavoliere, but this is unlikely in view of the discrepancy of about 200 m between the heights of sites such as La Lamia and Fiorentino in the west, and Marandrea and Mezzana Comunale in the east. It seems more likely that the effective correlation is, as suggested above, with the soil conditions occurring commonly on the eminences, and not with altitude.

One further site on the Tavoliere, not included in the above discussion, calls for particular comment: the site of Colle Tauro. This is located in the northwestern corner of the Tavoliere, between the Gargano and the lower Fortore River, just to the south of the Lago di Lèsina. Certain features distinguish the location and territory of this site

from those discussed above. In particular the territory is characterised by the low proportion of Class 2 soils and the high proportion of thin limestone soils (Class 4). In this respect, of the sites considered hitherto, it is comparable only with Coppa Nevigata. Unlike Coppa Nevigata, however, the site itself is situated on light soil; but these only cover about 5 per cent of the area within 1 km of the site, and about 2 per cent of the territory as a whole. Compared with the ditched villages the territory is remarkable for the absence of any large areas of light soil, and must therefore have been without a considerable arable element in its exploitation. In view of the unusual features of its territory, it is of interest that the archaeological remains at Colle Tauro differ considerably from those of the other Tavoliere sites we have discussed. There were no signs of ditches or structures, and the major part of the finds were flints. The pottery is typologically distinct from the vast majority of the pottery from the sites considered above; whereas the latter are customarily identified as Early-Middle Neolithic, Russi (1969) categorises the pottery assemblage from Colle Tauro as Eneolithic–Bronze Age.

Table 2. Soils within the one-hour exploitation territory of Tavoliere sites

	Alluvium		Crosta		Thick limestone soils		Thin limestone soils		Marsh		Total area
	Area (km²)	Per cent	Area (km²)	Per cent	Area (km²)	Per cent	Area (km²)	Per cent	Area (km²)	Per cent	(km²)
La Lamia	42.0	53.5	36.5	46.5	–	–	–	–	–	–	78.5
La Quercia	46.2	60.4	30.2	39.6	–	–	–	–	–	–	76.4
Mezzana Comunale	19.2	47.3	21.3	52.7	–	–	–	–	–	–	40.5
Marandrea	14.7	37.1	23.5	59.1	–	–	–	–	1.5	3.8	39.7
San Lorenzo	53.3	71.4	21.4	28.6	–	–	–	–	–	–	74.7
San Marcello	48.4	62.3	29.3	37.7	–	–	–	–	–	–	77.7
Coppa Cavone	53.6	68.2	24.9	31.8	–	–	–	–	–	–	78.5
Villano	61.3	79.0	16.2	21.0	–	–	–	–	–	–	77.5
Amèndola	35.7	54.9	29.4	45.1	–	–	–	–	–	–	65.1
Passo di Corvo	43.7	64.5	24.0	35.5	–	–	–	–	–	–	67.7
Fonteviva	24.5	37.0	24.1	36.4	6.1	9.3	10.2	15.4	1.2	1.9	66.1
Monte Aquilone	21.4	27.1	16.4	20.7	17.8	22.6	23.3	29.6	–	–	78.9
Coppa Nevigata	6.7	21.6	–	–	5.1	16.2	19.4	62.2	–	–	31.2
Panetteria	48.6	67.8	23.1	32.2	–	–	–	–	–	–	71.7
Fiorentino	47.7	67.1	23.4	32.9	–	–	–	–	–	–	71.1
Casalorda	52.1	68.8	23.6	31.2	–	–	–	–	–	–	75.7
Torretta	59.5	75.8	19.0	24.2	–	–	–	–	–	–	78.5
Pozzo delle Capre	44.4	62.5	26.6	37.5	–	–	–	–	–	–	71.0
Torrione del Casone	37.1	57.7	27.4	42.3	–	–	–	–	–	–	64.5
Contrada Guadone	26.8	39.5	41.0	60.5	–	–	–	–	–	–	67.8
Colle Tauro	37.0	56.1	1.1	1.9	0.4	0.7	27.2	41.3	–	–	65.7

THE GARGANO

The Gargano presents a less coherent picture. Sites are much less common. Such as exist are frequently poorly-known cave deposits, or scatters of flint and pottery with little or no stratigraphy. Eleven sites from the Gargano were analysed in detail, some of which were occupied during a number of periods (e.g. Grotta Paglicci, Grotta Drisiglia). The results of individual analyses can be seen in Appendix II, the following section being a synthesis of this data.

Topography

The Gargano is a limestone massif which forms a promontory jutting into the Adriatic Sea north of the Tavoliere. The periphery of the massif is dissected by steep, deeply-cut valleys running radially. Two areas within the Gargano are characterised by different types of topography. The northeastern corner has a convoluted surface of steep-sided hills separated by sinuous valleys. The very broken terrain makes movements difficult except along the valleys. Elsewhere the Upper Cretaceous limestone gives a different land surface. The edge of the Gargano rises steeply from the plain to some 500–600 m. From here northward stretches a plateau area, which, while it contains further hills and steep gradients in places (rising to over 1000 m), is for the most part easy of access relative to the northeastern area, until the surface drops steeply down to the low-lying area around the Lago di Varano. Areas of lowland are very rare, being confined to the few considerable river flood plains such as the Piano di Mattinata and Canale Antonio valley.

Soils

The soils can be classified in the same way as those of the Tavoliere (see p. 177). However, crosta soils (Class 2) do not occur at all in the Gargano, and Class 1 soils are very rare and confined to the lower valleys of the few rivers. Most of the area carries only thin limestone soils (Class 4) varying slightly in character from the more broken topography of the Lower Cretaceous to the northeast to the flatter Upper Cretaceous elsewhere. Some Class 3 soils occur on the fringes of the rare alluvial deposits.

Modern exploitation

The modern exploitation of the Gargano can be considered under five headings.

Arable

The small areas of Class 1 soil are partly exploited as arable. In some areas, particularly in the lowland area around the Lago di Varano, the main crop is wheat, with yields of *c*. 25 quintals per hectare in good years. In the lower Chianara valley, and in the low-lying area around the site of Grotta Drisiglia, market gardening for vegetables is important. The other main exploitation of arable soil is viticulture, important in some areas around the Lago di Varano and in small patches elsewhere.

Marginal arable

Many small areas, although unsuitable, are under today's conditions of high population pressure exploited as low-grade arable. An example of this is the small area of cereals around the modern town of Vico del Gargano. Here steep slopes and shallow soils constitute obstacles to arable exploitation, as is shown by the generally poor yields (averaging less than 20 quintals per hectare, and sometimes as low as 6 quintals per hectare). Many such areas are capable of supporting only barley cultivation for animal fodder, and require long fallow periods. The characteristic form of exploitation for marginal arable soils on steep slopes is the intensive cultivation of olives in terraced fields. This occupies most of the Piano di Mattinata and many of the other minor valleys. Almonds, and around the site of Coppa Cardone, carobs occur in similar situations.

Pasture

Some flatter areas, particularly in the natural basins in the plateau area to the north of San Marco in Lamis, have small areas of improved pasture. Characteristically, valleys are terraced in a series of shallow steps running down the slope. Other areas have been improved simply by clearance of surface stone. These areas provide summer pasture, especially for cattle.

Rough grazing

Most of the Gargano is exploited as rough grazing. This varies in character from open areas dominated by herbaceous plants, usually with a great deal of limestone bedrock exposed on the surface, to a thick evergreen scrub, with few grasses. These areas are grazed by sheep, cattle, and particularly by goats. Cattle are largely confined to the flatter areas with richer grazing, less steep slopes, and less impenetrable scrub. The main summer grazing area for sheep is in the Abruzzi, not in the Gargano, and while many sheep do graze here the goat is the predominant animal, thriving on the scrub vegetation and untroubled by the rough topography. Some stock remains in the Gargano all the year round, but more commonly the area is used for summer grazing only, the stock moving to the Tavoliere, or (a few) to the lowland areas on the north and east coasts of the Gargano, during the winter. This is necessitated by the heavy snowfall (up to 2 m) which frequently occurs for short spells. The small numbers of animals maintained there throughout the year must be stalled and fed on hay and artificial feeds during the cold and snowy weather.

Many areas of rough grazing have in addition 'rough' olives and almonds. These, while clearly introduced and to some extent tended, receive little attention other than at the harvest and are not comparable to the intensively exploited olives and almonds of the alluvial valleys.

Forestry

Some areas are today exploited for soft woods which are planted and cropped on a planned basis. The Foresta Umbra retains in addition a certain amount of deciduous forest. These areas are largely confined to the northeastern area of the Gargano, and the forestry exploitation is usually run in combination with a limited level of pastoralism, sufficient to make use of the available rough grazing without endangering tree growth.

Even comparatively recently, however, the picture was perceptibly different. Several factors in the past operated to keep the amount of arable land at a lower level than at present. In particular, lower yields would have made it less profitable, while longer fallows and the difficulty of cultivating the heavier soils with ox or horse ploughs would have restricted the area it was possible to exploit in this way. Some areas now under arable, such as the low-lying area around Grotta Drisiglia, have only recently been drained from marshy or lagoon conditions. Similarly, many areas now used primarily for forestry were, until less than a century ago, exclusively used as rough grazing. Thus in the past a still higher percentage of the Gargano as a whole would have been used for pastoralism, and more animals would have been carried on the Gargano during the summer. Economic forces today, here as in many other areas in the Mediterranean region, are tending to restrict and break down the traditional system of transhumant pastoralism. Improvements in agricultural technology are steadily removing the winter grazing in the lowlands on the north and east coasts of the Gargano. Not only are areas of former winter grazing such as marsh and heavy clays now being drained and ploughed, but fertilisers and nitrifying crops are reducing the important areas of fallow land which were available for winter grazing. At the same time concentrate feeds permit modern farmers to maintain stock over the winter in areas where this would not have been possible before. Thus there is a tendency today for a greater variety in pastoral practice than was formerly possible, and while the majority of the stock are still managed according to the traditional transhumant pattern, there is an overall decline in the importance of livestock and a less rigidly seasonal exploitation of the upland grazing areas.

Site location

All the sites analysed are located at the periphery of the Gargano, rather than in the central area. This is to some extent determined by the choice of sites made for analysis. Sites are certainly known from the central area, such as those in the Foresta Umbra (Palma di Cesnola, 1960–1; Russi, 1969). To a large degree, however, the sites analysed in detail illustrate a real and significant feature of site location: that there are very few sites from the large central area, whereas the periphery has yielded many. In particular, along the southern edge overlooking the Tavoliere, and along the northern coast from the Lago di Lèsina to Vieste, large numbers of sites testify to an important prehistoric exploitation of the area.

Site territories

All the site territories are greatly distorted from the circular 'ideal' pattern, showing the impact of the rugged topography on movement and exploitation. Eight of the eleven site territories are seriously curtailed by the sea or lake shores, which occur in most cases c. 0.5–1.0 km from the site. The territories have been delimited assuming a mobile pastoral economy, a two-hour limit being adopted (Higgs & Vita-Finzi, 1972; Jarman, 1972). Sizes of territories vary from c. 55 km² to c. 191 km² with an average of c. 115.6 km². The perimeters of the territories, excluding those imposed by the Adriatic Sea or the Lago di Lèsina and Lago di Varano, vary from c. 4.4 km to c. 9.5 km from the site, with average minimum values of c. 5.7 km, and average maximum values of c. 8.7 km. They circumscribe the maximum area likely to have been consistently exploited from the sites in question, as exploitation at a greater distance would require too much expenditure of time and energy in travelling. As can be seen, large areas in the central Gargano, including a high percentage of the best grazing, are not exploitable from the sites whose territories have been mapped.

Most of the sites analysed are located close to areas of lowland, and all contain lowland within their territories (Tables 3 & 4). Today these areas are largely exploited as arable, with intensive olive and vine production also occurring. There remain small areas of marshland, such as the patch adjacent to the site of Ariòla, and these are exploited as summer grazing. In the past, as noted above, far more of this area would necessarily have been used for grazing. The only major arable areas would probably have been on the light soils occurring within the territories of sites along the southern edge of the Gargano.

Thus the Gargano sites are unlikely to have been concerned to an important degree with arable exploitation. The

Table 3. Soils within 1 km of Gargano sites

	Alluvium		Crosta		Thick limestone soils		Thin limestone soils		Marsh		Total area
	Area (km²)	Per cent	Area (km²)	Per cent	Area (km²)	Per cent	Area (km²)	Per cent	Area (km²)	Per cent	(km²)
Grotta Spagnoli	0.30	9.5	–	–	0.54	17.2	2.30	73.3	–	–	3.14
Pescorosso	0.04	1.3	–	–	0.36	11.3	2.74	87.4	–	–	3.14
Grotta Paglicci	–	–	–	–	–	–	3.14	100.0	–	–	3.14
Grotta Scaloria	–	–	–	–	0.32	10.2	2.82	89.8	–	–	3.14
Monte Saraceno	–	–	–	–	0.70	26.9	1.90	73.1	–	–	2.60
Grotta Drisiglia	–	–	–	–	–	–	1.35	69.2	0.60	30.8	1.95
Ariòla	–	–	–	–	–	–	1.59	72.6	0.60	27.4	2.19
Grotta Manaccora	–	–	–	–	–	–	1.60	100.0	–	–	1.60
Coppa Cardone	–	–	–	–	–	–	2.55	100.0	–	–	2.55
Grotta Pippola	–	–	–	–	1.06	34.2	2.04	65.8	–	–	3.10
Grotta dell' Angelo	–	–	–	–	–	–	3.14	100.0	–	–	3.14

Table 4. Soils within the two-hour exploitation territory of Gargano sites

	Alluvium		Crosta		Thick limestone soils		Thin limestone soils		Marsh		Total area
	Area (km²)	Per cent	Area (km²)	Per cent	Area (km²)	Per cent	Area (km²)	Per cent	Area (km²)	Per cent	(km²)
Grotta Spagnoli	122.3	64.1	16.0	8.4	6.7	3.5	46.0	24.0	–	–	191.0
Pescorosso	99.0	60.4	6.3	3.8	7.5	4.6	51.0	31.2	–	–	163.8
Grotta Paglicci	109.8	60.6	0.8	0.4	6.2	3.4	64.5	35.6	–	–	181.3
Grotta Scaloria	1.2	0.9	–	–	29.3	20.4	107.0	74.7	5.8	4.0	143.3
Monte Saraceno	–	–	–	–	8.3	14.9	47.0	85.1	–	–	55.3
Grotta Drisiglia	1.5	1.7	–	–	22.8	25.1	64.0	71.0	2.0	2.2	90.3
Ariòla	1.5	1.8	–	–	21.0	24.8	60.0	71.0	2.0	2.4	84.5
Grotta Manaccora	–	–	–	–	15.5	23.8	48.5	74.7	1.0	1.5	65.0
Coppa Cardone	–	–	–	–	9.0	10.3	78.5	89.7	–	–	87.5
Grotta Pippola	–	–	–	–	30.0	25.5	87.5	74.5	–	–	117.5
Grotta dell' Angelo	17.0	18.4	–	–	9.5	10.4	65.5	71.2	–	–	92.0

most important sites – those with large collections of material or multiple occupations – are correlated with areas of good soil cover around the periphery of the Gargano. Conspicuous here is the great concentration of sites, mainly flint scatters, around the Lago di Lèsina and Lago di Varano. An area with a noticeable lack of sites is the eastern extremity, the Testa del Gargano, which is devoid of lowland with good soil cover.

An advantage offered by the sites on the southern and western edges of the Gargano is that they are located so as to provide both upland and lowland resources within a short distance of the site. Snow depths of up to 2 m during the winter make the central Gargano unprofitable for winter exploitation, during which time the lowlands, which rarely get more than a transient snow cover, can be grazed. As the lowland grazings become desiccated in late spring increasing use can be made of the uplands which receive more rainfall and provide a certain amount of good forage throughout the summer. Sites at the periphery of the Gargano have accessible within their two-hour territories at least some upland grazing, and their proximity to the hills means that the whole central area can be exploited on the basis of small-scale movements of a few days' duration, whereas occupants of sites further away would be forced to resort to long-term seasonal movements. The lowlands around the lakes to the northwest are particularly favoured and provide unusually good grazing. Low altitude and the proximity of the Adriatic ensure freedom from winter snow, while the lakes provide conditions for sustained plant growth in the summer. As we have noted this area contains an unusually dense scatter of prehistoric sites. The scatter

of small, poorly known sites from the central Gargano presumably relate to dispersed summer pastoralism. Battaglia (1956) has noted the similarity between some 'Eneolithic' features on the Gargano plateau and modern pastoralists' enclosures.

PATTERNS OF SETTLEMENT

A number of general hypotheses can be advanced to interpret the distribution and location of archaeological sites. In the first instance it can be questioned whether the distribution is representative of the prehistoric situation, or whether the available evidence is seriously distorted by sampling error. Such an hypothesis, which is frequently proposed to account for differential or non-random site distributions, illustrates a basic shortcoming of all archaeological data. They are subject to a number of factors which may affect their deposition, preservation, and discovery, and consequently there is always a chance that the degree of distortion will exceed our capacity to accommodate it in our explanatory models. If we are to pursue the subject, however, we must make use of such data as we have and attempt to reduce as far as possible the impact of such uncontrollable factors.

It does not appear likely here that site distribution has been seriously affected by post-depositional factors. It is possible that erosion of hill slopes has destroyed evidence of some sites, particularly in the Gargano. Similarly, some low-lying sites on the Tavoliere may have been covered by accumulations of recent silt. The area has been subject to considerable and detailed archaeological research for more than half a century, however, and it is unlikely that considerable numbers of sites have been missed by chance, especially after aerial surveys. Civil engineering and hydrological projects have ensured that much is known about sub-surface features of the area and have presented frequent opportunities for the discovery of buried sites. While it is highly probable that individual sites remain to be discovered, it seems unlikely that the overall distribution patterns have been much affected by the vagaries of preservation and discovery. The Gargano has probably been more seriously influenced than the Tavoliere. Much of the country is topographically rough and difficult to cover on foot because of dense scrub vegetation. Steep slopes with little soil cover decrease the chances of the data being preserved. Here again, however, sites are known, and research such as that of Battaglia (1956) has shown the existence of artefacts in the valley soils of many streams. Even though these are probably for the most part derived from sites higher up on the slopes they indicate occupation of the area and demonstrate satisfactorily that evidence both exists and is being recovered.

The assumption made in this paper is that site distribution is related primarily to the distribution and availability of exploitable resources. The resources themselves change with time; those accessible also change with developing technology; and thus major shifts of site distribution occur, as well as changes consequent upon population fluctuations. This assumption can be shown to be justified in a variety of modern situations, and indeed it can be argued that this factor is a major constant in human behaviour, although of course individual or 'cultural' choice can have a minor short-term effect.

THE PALAEOLITHIC AND MESOLITHIC

The favoured location of pre-Neolithic sites is along the perimeter of the Gargano, in particular on the southern and southwestern edges, where are situated not only the well-known sites of Grotta Paglicci and Grotta Spagnoli, but also a number of caves and shelters with minor occupations. Upper Palaeolithic material is reported from the Grotta dell'Angelo on the northwestern edge of the Gargano. Grotta Drisiglia, on the northeast coast of the promontory has a Mesolithic, or at least non-pottery, level. Palaeolithic tools have been found in a number of valley deposits in the interior of the Gargano, notably in the Correntino and Romandato valleys and in the Foresta Umbra. Most, if not all, of these latter assemblages are redeposited, and so cannot be taken to represent precise settlement locations, but they do indicate occupation in their vicinity. A striking feature is the almost complete absence of signs of occupation on the Tavoliere, the only

exception being the report of a possible Palaeolithic occupation at Lucera in the west.

It is often supposed that Palaeolithic occupation is largely restricted to areas where caves and rock shelters provide ready-made dwellings, but much evidence to the contrary has accumulated. Palaeolithic open sites are not uncommon and they are often found in situations which indicate occupation under conditions of extreme climatic severity. It is clear that Palaeolithic man was quite capable of thriving without the existence of fortuitously sited caves where this was advantageous, and that therefore there are likely to have been other or additional factors involved in the near absence of Palaeolithic sites on the Tavoliere.

Most of the sites are so located as to be able to exploit the northern edge of the Tavoliere and the southern edge of the Gargano. There is some evidence for exploitation of the central Gargano areas, particularly to the east, and it seems likely that the whole of the Gargano was exploited at least on an occasional basis. Small surface flint scatters are indeed found widely throughout the Gargano, but they are difficult or impossible to date unless found in some datable deposit, as those of the Foresta Umbra (Palma di Cesnola, 1960–1). It is, of course, wrong to assume that Middle and Upper Palaeolithic and Mesolithic site locations and exploitation patterns will necessarily have been the same; there is considerable evidence from elsewhere in Europe that this is not the case. Unfortunately, the number of sites at present known from Capitanata does not allow a more refined analysis, although one might speculate that the basic pattern may have been one or two home bases on the landward edges of the Gargano, with a scatter of transit sites in its interior. One aspect of settlement does appear to link all the pre-Neolithic periods, however: the virtual absence of sites on the Tavoliere.

The territories of the major sites offer optimum exploitation potential at the junction of highland and lowland. This is a commonplace in many areas of Europe both for prehistoric and modern settlement, as this provides the opportunity for the most efficient integration of both upland and lowland resources. This is particularly pronounced for animal-based economies, whether they be hunters, herd-followers, or pastoralists, as there is frequently a seasonal pattern of movement of herbivorous animals from highland to lowland; sites located on the junction of these two major complementary economic zones can exploit both with a minimum of expenditure of time and effort. Both uplands and lowlands can frequently be exploited on a short-term basis, with a single home base sufficing for the whole year. Necessary movements can be accomplished in a short time, on a weekly or even daily basis. As well as its greater efficiency in resources exploitation, such a system has the advantage of a high degree of flexibility, an ability to take account of minor fluctuations in local conditions more fully than is possible when long-distance movement on a seasonal basis is necessary. Sites in the interior of the Gargano can reasonably be interpreted as short-term summer transit or kill sites. None so far known is substantial or has provided a massive collection, and they were probably for the most part never more than surface scatters which have since been redeposited in the river valleys.

The scarcity of evidence for occupation on the Tavoliere indicates (according to our basic assumption that settlement is related primarily to available resources) that this was an area of low economic potential during the pre-Neolithic period. This conclusion appears surprising at first, as it might be supposed that the Tavoliere would have supplied good winter grazing during the Pleistocene. Indeed, there is little doubt that the Tavoliere would have carried some herbivores during the winter, but its carrying capacity is likely to have been seriously affected by the extent of marshland at the time. Even as late as about A.D. 1900, there existed on the Tavoliere about 30 000 ha of permanent lagoon and marshland. Further areas of seasonal marshland followed the major watercourses.

There are, however, difficulties in interpreting the probable Pleistocene situation, as some factors have changed to an unknown degree. Sea level would have been lower than that at present and may to some extent have affected inland drainage patterns. More important, it is thought that the coastal lagoons and marsh owe their existence in some degree to the presence of dunes which impede drainage of the major rivers into the sea. This feature is not firmly dated, and while it might be a glacial marine regression feature, it could also be a post-Pleistocene phenomenon linked with the Holocene rise in sea level. Both these factors may have tended to reduce the amount of marshland relative to the recent situation. On the other hand there are some indications that the Upper Pleistocene climate may have been moister in the north Mediterranean than is today's, whether by reason of increased or more evenly distributed precipitation, or reduced insolation. This is not accepted by all workers, but it seems certain that snowfall was increased, and that surface run off was probably therefore at a higher level than today due to melt water. Both these factors could have increased the areas of surface water and marshland relative to the present situation. The presence of the *crosta* may lend some support to this suggestion. Calcification can occur when leaching of mineral salts is limited and seasonal aridity causes greater evaporation than precipitation; the salts crystallise at the boundary of wet and dry soil. This can occur in arid zones by water movement up profiles, but where impeded drainage does not permit the lowering of the water-table, seasonal aridity can also cause the calcium carbonate to be precipitated. The horizontal bedding of the Tavoliere *crosta* suggests that this kind of phenomenon may have played a part in its formation. Our suggested date for these salt-enriching processes, 10 000–8000 B.P. (see pp. 177–8), suggests that different conditions, possibly including a high seasonal water-table above the top of the present *crosta* may have existed prior to this.

The geological and palaeoclimatic information at present available therefore will not give us unequivocal answers on this point, and we are forced to return to our primary information, the site distribution pattern. This suggests that the Tavoliere was of low economic potential during the pre-Neolithic period, the most likely explanation for which appears to be that it was due to the amount of surface water, especially in winter and spring when the hills would have been inhospitable or indeed uninhabitable. From this point of view it is worth pointing out that the Tavoliere is thought to have been covered by the sea in the Pliocene, and that on the geological time scale one can view the area as having undergone an increasing desiccation since then. Another interpretation of the evidence is possible, however. Since the sea would have been considerably below modern levels, it is possible that lowland sites existed on or near the Upper Pleistocene coastline, now submerged. There is no evidence available which permits us to evaluate this hypothesis, but the absence of sites on the modern Tavoliere remains a strong argument against any hypothesis of an important exploitation of the lowland area at this time.

Viewing the situation as a whole it is not surprising that there are relatively few Palaeolithic sites in Capitanata. The Gargano is an isolated and relatively small area of high ground which even today is largely unsuited to winter occupation because of snowfall, and which during Pleistocene glacial periods would presumably have been even less appropriate for other than summer occupation. If, as suggested here, much of the Tavoliere was in fact of low grazing potential, much of the winter grazing must have been found in the relatively narrow band of land between the southern scarp of the Gargano and the Torrente Candelaro, with the possible addition of some of the lower slopes of the Gargano if snow conditions permitted it. While it is certain that some animals did indeed graze parts of the Tavoliere, the marshy conditions of river valleys would reduce the carrying capacity of the area and constitute barriers to north–south movement. Of the common food animals at Grotta Paglicci, only the pig is well adapted to marsh conditions, although cattle would have been able to exploit the fringes of marshland to some extent where necessary. There would thus have been a high degree of pressure on winter grazing, and animal populations as well as their dependent human populations would have been kept at a low level.

THE NEOLITHIC

The Neolithic site distribution exhibits a most striking change in pattern from the preceding situation. Air photography has indicated the presence of about 300 ditched enclosures on the Tavoliere attributed to the Neolithic period. Where excavation or surface collections have been undertaken this attribution has been confirmed, and it seems reasonable to suppose that the majority, at least, of these sites are indeed Neolithic. In a sense it can be said that the Tavoliere is covered with a scatter of Neolithic ditched villages, but this should not be taken as indicating either a random or a completely even distribution. As we have noted above (p. 180), Neolithic settlement location on the Tavoliere is strongly correlated with soil type, the light, freely draining *crosta* soils being chosen in almost every case. We have interpreted this as indicating the critical importance of arable agriculture in affecting site location, but it should be noted that although this does imply an important cereal component in the economy as a whole, the precise balance of animal to plant products is not clear; an important component in all the analysed territories is heavy alluvial soil which must have been exploited by pastoralism.

An important factor is the essential difference between animal resources, which are mobile and easy to transport over short distances, and plant resources which are more expensive of time and energy to exploit at long distances from the site. In the average Tavoliere territory about two-thirds of the area within 1 km of the site is soil suitable for arable cultivation. This means that *c*. 200 ha of arable land would have been available within the 1 km limit, which encloses the area of optimum potential as far as labour costs are concerned.

It is difficult to arrive at realistic estimates of wheat yields during the Neolithic. Certainly they would have been lower than those of today when agricultural technology has advanced and more productive varieties of crops have been developed. Columella's figure of about a four-fold average return for Roman wheat production is strikingly comparable with the figures given by Slicher van Bath (1963) for much of western Europe in the Middle Ages, quoting seed corn:yield ratios of *c*. 1:3 to 1:4. Today seed is sown at a rate of about 2.5 quintals per hectare on the poorer arable soils on the Tavoliere. If we assume that amounts of seed corn sown per hectare in the past were comparable to those of today (perhaps a less hazardous assumption than might at first appear: Slicher van Bath indicates that this figure has not changed greatly in western Europe between the Middle Ages and the present day), then we might expect average yields in the order of 8–10 quintals per hectare for the Roman period. Prior to this period any estimates must be

still further in the realms of speculation, but any lower seed: yield ratio than 1:2 would render cultivation uneconomic. Thus we may take *c*. 5 quintals per hectare as a probable minimum average yield for Neolithic cultivation, the actual figure in all likelihood falling somewhere between this value and *c*. 10 quintals per hectare.

Even assuming a very extensive rotation, with a given area of land being put under cereals only once every ten years, the area within 1 km of the site could have produced yields in the order of ten metric tons of grain for consumption annually, in addition to seed. Such a quantity would provide 500 g of cereals each per day throughout the year for about fifty-five people, a substantial community. This is not to suggest that these precise figures necessarily express accurately the average crop production and population sizes actually involved, but they indicate the important general conclusion that typical site situations offered a high potential for cereal production, and that in most cases the limiting factor upon the area cultivated was probably not the availability of suitable land, but some other factor such as summer water shortage or the high labour requirement of preparing the ground, especially with hoes or other manually operated tools. Areas not under arable cultivation would have provided important grazing for sheep, goats, and cattle, fallow land presumably also being grazed.

The Gargano presents a very different picture of Neolithic occupation. Most sites known are surface scatters of flint, pottery occurring relatively rarely. Some caves contain Neolithic levels; Grotta Pippola and Grotta Drisiglia in the north, and Grotta Scaloria in the southeast. Most occupations are classified on the basis of flint and pottery typology as Late Neolithic, Eneolithic, or 'Campignian'. It is usual to consider that these sites represent a separate, and more backward, population from that inhabiting the Tavoliere. Typical is Bradford's view (Bradford & Williams-Hunt, 1946) that the Gargano was then and now remote and isolated, with 'a primitive economy and outlook'. This is thought to explain both the relative scarcity of sites in the Gargano, and their apparent 'cultural' poverty. This hypothesis does provide one explanation of the available data, but despite the anecdote cited by Bradford (*ibid*. p. 193) to illustrate this point, a different hypothesis can also be advanced.

Today, and certainly throughout living memory, the Tavoliere and Gargano have been economically integrated, as is customary for adjacent areas possessing complementary seasonal resources. This is not to say that there are no groups or individuals who remain in either area permanently. The Tavoliere in particular has a large permanent population, and may have done so from Neolithic times onward. Nevertheless the majority of the Gargano is exploited seasonally, as summer grazing, and carries high summer populations of both humans and livestock, which winter on the Tavoliere when much of the Gargano is under snow. The Gargano is today an integral part of the economic system practised on the Tavoliere, and the two areas are exploited primarily by the same population.

There is little reason to suppose that in the past the Gargano was exploited in an essentially different fashion. Any permanent occupation would be restricted to very low levels by the absence of any high-productivity arable land and the climatic restraints upon winter exploitation. The availability of adjacent lowland grazing areas on the Tavoliere which would have been at their most productive in winter and spring, being too dry for extensive exploitation in summer and early autumn, would have urged a mobile seasonal exploitation of the two areas. The archaeological evidence, as usually interpreted, appears to contradict this conclusion, but it is capable of alternative interpretations. Even on the basis of conventional typological classification some of the Gargano sites are thought to be 'Middle Neolithic' and thus contemporaneous with some of the Tavoliere occupations. A more compelling reason for associating upland and lowland sites is found in the common occurrence in the Tavoliere sites of flint tools which are typologically 'Campignian'. The commonest example is the 'Campignian tranchet axe' which has been found at many of the classic ditched settlements such as Passo di Corvo, Marandrea, and Casone; other elements in the Tavoliere Neolithic industries are also described as being 'Campignian' in technique. A further indication of extensive contact between the Tavoliere and the Gargano is the fact that much of the flint on the Tavoliere sites proves to have come from Garganian raw material. Such occurrences are usually recorded without further comment or are quoted as evidence for an occupation subsequent to the main Neolithic occupation.

Thus we are faced with the situation of a lowland occupation characterised by large, substantial sites, and a pottery-dominated technology; and a highland occupation characterised by cave sites, and small surface scatters and redeposited valley collections, with a flint-dominated technology. 'Campignian' pottery does exist, but is uncommon, poor, fragmentary, and uncharacteristic. There are few ^{14}C dates for the lowland sites (such as there are indicate occupation commencing by c. 5000 B.C.) and none at all for the 'Campignian' sites, and the inference of a considerable dissynchronism of the upland and lowland occupations rests purely upon typological arguments. On the other hand, our economic hypothesis suggests that the two areas were likely to have been occupied at the same time and exploited as a single economic system. This is the only practicable way of exploiting the Gargano effectively and of realising the full potential of the Tavoliere. Exploitation of

either area in isolation limits both animal and human populations to those supportable in the lean season (the winter in the Gargano, the summer in the Tavoliere), whereas the mechanism of transhumance permits a more effective economy by taking advantage of complementary seasonal resources. In addition to these considerations there are, as we have noted, artefactual indications that there was extensive contact between the two areas.

We need not be overly swayed by the gross differences in the nature of the sites or their artefacts. It is clear that permanent or semi-permanent lowland sites whose primary concern was with cereal agriculture for much of the year cannot be expected to be similar or to have the same tool-kits as upland sites occupied on a mobile and transitory basis for the purposes of pastoralism. In particular it is a commonplace that such upland sites are characterised by a scanty and relatively crude assemblage; few tools are required for pastoralism, and pottery is likely to be absent or of a coarse and 'atypical' kind where present. In view of the fact that the 'Campignian axe' links the upland and lowland sites, it is interesting to note that today a small hatchet is frequently the only tool carried by shepherds in the Gargano.

It should be mentioned that the Apennines were probably also exploited from the Tavoliere as summer grazing. The Apennines are outside the primary study area from which we have field data, but it seems likely that during the Neolithic period, as is known to have been the case in Roman and medieval times, the Tavoliere carried more animals in winter than could be accommodated in the Gargano in summer, and that considerable numbers spent the summer to the west. Although there are no indications of the long distance movements or the *tratturi* which existed in subsequent periods, it seems more than likely that exploitation of the areas of the Apennines adjacent to the Tavoliere was an integral part of the economy of at least some communities.

As a speculation, then, we can suggest the following as a probable annual agronomic cycle for the area. From October until May virtually the whole of the population would have been concentrated on the Tavoliere, although it is possible that some of the low-lying areas on the seaward margins of the Gargano carried small populations of humans and livestock. The stock would have been on the areas of permanent grazing on the Tavoliere afforded by the soils unsuited to arable exploitation. These would have been in particular the heavy clay valley soils (our Class 1), but areas with limestone bedrock or very thick *crosta* close to the surface, or with steep slopes would also have been exploited primarily as winter grazing, as would fallow land. The areas of arable to be sown would need to have been prepared in time for the planting of cereals in November or early December.

The dry late springs and summers mean that cereals must be winter sown to do well, as spring planted cereals would not receive enough moisture to fill the ears. It is not possible to say precisely when the land would have been prepared for sowing, or how much would have been cultivated. Today ploughing starts as soon as the harvest is over, but if we assume some form of hoe or digging stick agriculture, it is unlikely that any except the lightest soil could have been broken during the summer when it was baked dry. Most of this work would necessarily have been confined to the period between the first rains – probably late September or early October – and the sowing. The Roman agronomists recommended that land should be ploughed up to four times before sowing, to keep the ground free of weeds, and to facilitate root penetration. Where, as on the Tavoliere, water was a severe limiting factor, the removal of weeds was of prime importance to prevent moisture loss through evapotranspiration, and the land might be rested for two years to husband the water. Repeated working of the ground before planting may also have been a feature of Neolithic agronomic practice.

In May or early June most of the livestock would have left the Tavoliere for the Gargano and adjacent highlands, enough of the human population moving with them to control them and protect them from predators on their way to the summer pastures. The Tavoliere would still have held the majority of the human population, however, as the cereal harvest would have been later in June or in early July. There are a number of ways in which the economy could have been managed during the remaining summer months. It is possible that after the harvest the grain would have been stored – pits which may have been for this purpose have been found on some Tavoliere sites – and the remaining population could then have followed the animal herds and herders to the summer pastures. There are reasons for thinking that this is unlikely to have been the general pattern, however. Apart from the more congenial summer climate offered by upland areas, there would have been little to be gained by such a movement, as the labour requirements of the pastoral activities would not have necessitated it. More important, considerable labour would have been needed to process the harvest (threshing and winnowing) and to start preparing the ground for the next year's cereal crop. The existence of pigs on Tavoliere sites would have meant that at least a small population probably remained there throughout the summer to tend them, unless they were left to their own devices for three to four months every year; pigs are not well adapted to substantial transhumantic movement, and although it is possible, it is not likely that they were taken to the summer pastures. It seems probable, then, that when the main animal population left a small 'killing-herd' remained on the plain to sustain the animal protein requirements of the human population during the summer, and that thus the Tavoliere carried a substantial permanent human population in Neolithic times, possibly more than half the winter population. Numbers of animals remaining on the Tavoliere in the summer would necessarily have been small, being limited by fodder shortage and especially by water shortage. Almost no rain falls on the Tavoliere today between May and October, and despite many claims that the 'Atlantic' period was one of increased summer rainfall there is little or no direct evidence of this as far as the Tavoliere is concerned. Fodder crops (the pulses *Vicia* and *Lathyrus* are reported from Passo di Corvo (Follieri, 1971)) may have been used to alleviate shortage of forage, while the areas of marsh and damp soil would have provided vegetation and possibly surface water for at least the late spring. Subsurface water may well have been relatively accessible throughout the summer.

A further aspect of the economy of the area is represented by the site of Coppa Nevigata, which seems to have functioned at this time primarily as a base for exploiting cockles. It does not appear that this was ever of great importance in the area, however. Coppa Nevigata is small, and there are no other comparable sites known. The shellfish seem only to have had the status of a minor, occasional resource for a group or groups, and they are unlikely to have represented a critical factor in the occupation of Capitanata as a whole.

It is clear that a number of human social organisations could accommodate this economic system. It is possible that two separate communities were involved, with a mobile, wholly pastoral group spending the summers in the hills and the winters on the Tavoliere, and a lowland sedentary population based almost entirely on arable agriculture. Some arrangement would have been made between the two communities in order to satisfy the winter grazing requirements of the pastoralists, although use could also be made of the areas (especially in the southeastern Tavoliere) where there were few ditched settlements due to the relative rarity of suitable arable land. The numbers of stock kept by the lowland community would have been severely limited by the dryness of the summer season. An alternative is that a single population was involved with all its members on the Tavoliere in the winter but with some individuals from the settlements taking the herds up to the hills for the summer. Possible variations of these two basic schemes are numerous, including commercial transactions for the acquisition of winter grazing, or for the summer pasturing by 'specialist herders' of stock owned by lowland settlements. These considerations must remain speculative, however; the archaeological evidence does not permit us to choose between the possible explanations, and indeed a combination of different organisations may well have operated in the past as it does today. It seems unlikely in this case that such factors were critical in the long-term evolution of human populations on the Tavoliere.

THE QUESTION OF ABANDONMENT

The Eneolithic, Bronze Age, and Iron Age periods are difficult to study in our area as there is an apparent lack of sites from the Tavoliere, a lack which is all the more striking in contrast to the unusually large number of Neolithic sites. This has been interpreted as showing the virtual abandonment of the Tavoliere. A number of reasons has been advanced to account for this, in particular a hypothetical change to a drier, more continental climate. Other factors are thought to have been improverishment of the soil due to 'generations of misuse', and a 'wind of change' stemming from elsewhere in Europe (Whitehouse, 1968). The disruptive features inherent in this 'wind' are thought to have been metallurgy and textile technology, wide trade relations, a livestock-based economy, and a propensity for mobility.

Even a relatively minor change to a drier climate could clearly have had a dramatic impact upon the Neolithic economy in the Tavoliere, particularly if this was strongly cereal-oriented, as suggested above. Today one year in four is considered by local farmers to be a failure due to lack of rain, and only about one year in two or three produces good yields. A tendency to less rain, particularly in spring, would turn the Tavoliere from a good marginal area into an uneconomic area for dry agriculture. Such a change would also shorten the period of availability of winter grazing. There is, however, no direct evidence that a drier period occurred on the Tavoliere, although it has been inferred that this was a general European feature at approximately this date. In view of the apparent widespread nature of this phenomenon – the Sahara appears to have started drying up after a moister 'subpluvial' phase at about the same period – it may be felt to be a reasonable hypothesis that southern Italy would also have been affected, but positive supporting evidence is lacking.

As far as the other proposed causes of change are concerned, it is difficult to see how they can have been directly responsible for the visible changes. There is no evidence whatever that the Tavoliere soils suffered impoverishment during the Neolithic or since, and most of even the poorer soils are still producing fair annual cereal yields, given sufficient moisture. None of the elements enumerated as forming the disruptive 'wind of change' seem likely in themselves to have been a threat to an established cereal-oriented economy. Copper, and eventually bronze and iron, metallurgy are indeed more easily and directly applicable to arable pursuits than to pastoralism. Textile technology and long distance trade seem unlikely to have affected the basic economic patterns, unless it is supposed that these were so important as to create a largely commercial economic system on the Tavoliere, based on a textile export industry, in place of the former subsistence economy. Mobility, as we have seen, was certainly an important feature built into the economy of the area, and would not necessarily be a disruptive force in any case. As for the livestock-oriented economy, even if we accept the hypothesis of an intrusive 'culture' and economy, as long as the arable exploitation of certain soils remained more profitable than pastoralism it would be unlikely in the long term to be superseded. Where suited to the local environment cereal agriculture almost always produces higher returns in calorific terms than a livestock economy, and will thus support a larger population. Even assuming the influx of a hostile pastoralist population it seems more probable that they would adapt in time to the local economic conditions and requirements than that they would ignore the most effective exploitation pattern available to them, thus maintaining their population at a vulnerable and unnecessarily low level.

Thus of the hypotheses so far advanced, that of the cataclysmic impact upon settlement of a relatively minor climatic change is the only convincing one. An additional factor which may have emphasised the effect of this change is the lowering of the water-table, a process which may have been going on throughout the Holocene. We must, however, take the consideration of these factors a stage further and try to estimate their actual effect upon the environment and human communities. There is certainly no indication that any climatic change involved was large in absolute terms. As far as Capitanata is concerned it seems probable that at worst winter rain would have continued dependable, and the Tavoliere can thus be expected to have continued to provide winter grazing at least from late November until March or April. In the Gargano, and especially in the Apennines, the growing season would come later in spring than on the plain due to the persistence of snow cover and more spring precipitation. Thus grazing would be available on the lower slopes of the hills in spring, and in the higher areas during the summer and early autumn.

Thus while a climatic change on the scale envisaged could have occasioned a drastic reorganisation of the economy, it seems unlikely that it would have forced complete abandonment of the lowlands. A critical change as far as dry cereal agriculture is concerned appears possible, but the same change would not have destroyed the value of the Tavoliere as a source of winter grazing. Indeed, as long as the adjacent highland areas were occupied, the economic pressures in favour of such an exploitation pattern would have been powerful and self-evident. As we indicate above, the only way in which to realise the economic potential of either the Gargano or the Tavoliere involves an element of mobile seasonal exploitation; with a decrease in or cessation of arable agriculture on the Tavoliere this aspect of the economy would have been of even greater importance. The existence of a relatively large number of Eneolithic–Iron Age sites in the Gargano thus implies that the Tavoliere must have been exploited to a considerable extent.

It is also probable that the economic strain was increased by the deleterious effect of the drier climate on the grazing of the Gargano and the lower, more accessible slopes of the Apennines. It is clear that a factor in the success of Roman and medieval pastoralism in the area was their exploitation of the high Abruzzi pastures a considerable distance from the Tavoliere. The long distance transhumant pattern may not have been established in prehistoric times (it would not have been necessary during the Neolithic when sufficient summer grazing could have been found close to the Tavoliere), and this may have exacerbated the post-Neolithic economic crisis.

The evidence of site distribution appears to be at odds with this hypothesis. The majority of the sites with characteristic Bronze Age and Iron Age pottery are found on the perimeter of the Gargano, particularly along the north coast and on the junction with the Tavoliere, leaving an apparent vacuum on the Tavoliere itself. The absence of accurate dates for the various typological entities remains an obstacle to an assessment of the accuracy of this picture, however. It has long been remarked that the evidence from air photographs shows that many of the ditched settlements had several phases of occupation with a number of different ditches. As Bradford (1949) pointed out this of itself argues a long period of occupation, especially when one considers the huge labour involved in digging such large ditches. Whitehouse (1969) has clearly shown the regional nature of many of the Neolithic wares that were at one time believed to represent stages of development over wide areas of southern Italy, and warned that 'there is no reason to believe that changes occurred rapidly or that they occurred at the same time in different places'. It seems possible that the ditched villages may have been occupied for a longer time than the conventional interpretation of the ceramic evidence suggests.

Furthermore, the recent work of Russi (1966, 1967) in the San Severo area has indicated the existence of pottery scatters which include wares not characteristic of typical Neolithic assemblages, and although these are not dated, it seems not unlikely that some of these may represent post-Neolithic occupations. By Late Iron Age times there are substantial sites on the plain, such as at Torre Fiorentina, Arpi, and Casalorda, which have been identified with the pre-Roman Daunian occupation. Here again the absolute dating of these sites is unknown, and their chronological relationship to typical 'Early Iron Age' sites such as Coppa Nevigata, Grotta Pippola, and Manaccora is uncertain. The usual hypothesis encountered in the literature is of an unsophisticated 'typical Iron Age' occupation of the Gargano, with the Tavoliere essentially deserted until the later, sophisticated Daunian occupation. The considerations outlined above in favour of the joint exploitation of the two areas together apply here, too, and it seems possible, in the absence of contrary evidence from ^{14}C dates, that the differences in the typology of the two groups of sites represent functionally related variations rather than a chronological succession.

On balance, the arguments that the Tavoliere and Gargano were exploited as a unit are substantial, but it cannot be contested that considerable changes in the pattern of occupation appear to be indicated. While it seems more than possible that the ditched settlements were longer-lived than is usually inferred from the pottery typology, there is nothing positively to suggest that they continued unchanged as the centres of occupation until the Iron Age. The vast majority of the known Early Neolithic sites are from the plain, and there certainly appears to be a subsequent increase in the number of sites in the Gargano. The number of settlements on the Tavoliere in these later periods is obscure, but they seem almost certain to have been fewer and/or less substantial than those of the Neolithic.

This leads us back to the plausible, but so far unsupported hypothesis that a climatic change provoked a drastic change in the economy and settlement pattern. If we assume that a decrease in rainfall essentially destroyed the Tavoliere cereal economy and that pastoralism became thereafter the prime basis of the economy of both uplands and lowlands, many of the observed facts can be accommodated. If the climatic change consisted partly in the contraction of the period during which the Tavoliere received rainfall, and thus the period during which it provided grazing, then we can envisage a situation in which the lowlands became the subsidiary element in the economy rather than the dominant. With arable agriculture impossible, and summer grazing virtually non-existent, the Tavoliere must have been without summer occupation and there would have been no permanent sites. If seven to eight months per year were spent in the upland areas one can indeed expect to find the major and more stable 'home base' sites in, or on the edge of the hills, and only insubstantial sites in the lowlands. The economy at this time would necessarily have been almost exclusively pastoral, and would for this reason have resulted in a considerably lower level of human population than in the preceding Neolithic period with its more productive mixed cereal and stock economy. Some minor cereal production may have been possible in those small areas of the uplands which permitted this through the conjunction of sufficient spring precipitation and soil depth; but not only are such places rare, especially in the Gargano, but they also tend to carry heavy red soils which present considerable obstacles to cultivation. Cereals are thus unlikely to have made a substantial contribution to the economy, and the resultant low population may be seen as a possible contributory factor to the scarcity of lowland sites of this period.

A second possible hypothesis, but one equally without positive supporting evidence, is that the development of settlement in Capitanata at this time was heavily influenced by events of far wider importance and greater power than those inherent in Capitanata itself. It is clear — and this is exemplified in the historical exploitation of the area (see below) — that once a small but originally self-sufficient unit becomes integrated into a much larger and more complex economic unit then events far outside the area can have an important determining influence upon the nature of the local economy. Subsistence requirements can become subservient to or even be totally eclipsed by production for export. Furthermore it is possible that internal processes, such as the steady build-up of population to a point beyond which it could be maintained given the available technology, may have caused a temporary disruption in the economic development of the area. For neither of these suggestions is there directly corroborative evidence, however, as far as Capitanata is concerned.

THE CLASSICAL AND MEDIEVAL PERIODS

Evidence for the occupation of the area in historic times is, of course, far more substantial than that for the prehistoric periods, but its interpretation is hampered because it is widely dispersed and much of it apparently mutually contradictory. The broad picture usually given is of an initial period in which occupation was based upon large and prosperous settlements such as at Arpi, followed by the decay of this system after the Hannibalic Wars and the appearance of one based upon regular, planned centuriated settlement. In the Imperial period the centuriation system seems to have broken down to be replaced by an increasing commitment to large-scale transhumant pastoralism. The Tavoliere became the winter grazing area for stock, especially sheep, which summered for the most part in the high Abruzzi, often as much as 200–300 km from the Tavoliere. After the break-up of the Roman Empire there is a period of which little is known, although it has been suggested that the economic system remained substantially unaltered. During the Norman and subsequent medieval occupations transhumance remained an important and apparently increasing feature of the economy.

The classical period

As far as the earlier historic period is concerned, it is clear that arable agriculture had again become a mainstay of the economy. From this we must infer that the dry oscillation had ended, and that once again dry-farming of cereals was possible. An additional factor may well have been the availability of a more effective agricultural technology, including ploughs, which would have extended both the range of soils and the area which could be cultivated. The large and prosperous Daunian cities must have required highly productive agricultural economies to support their populations. Site location on the Tavoliere again concentrates upon the light, well-drained *crosta* soils, and indeed many of the sites of this, as of the subsequent Roman and medieval periods, are adjacent to or precisely overlie earlier ditched settlements.

Bradford (1950) pointed out the close relationship between the centuriated field system and the low plateaux, the low-lying ground 'which they did not choose to centuriate' being blank. This shows that the Neolithic preoccupation with light and well-drained soils continued, in spite of technological advances. It has been suggested that the primary land usage of the centuriated system was the commercial production of vines and olives, but there are a number of factors which should make us wary of this conclusion. Varro refers to the wheat production of Apulia, which was, like Sicily, one of the major wheat producing areas for the urban populations elsewhere in Italy in the late Republican period. Another consideration is the likelihood that in some areas evidence of centuriation has not survived, and that these are more likely to have been grain growing areas than olive or vine areas, as these latter leave characteristic traces (pits and trenches dug through the *crosta* to assist root penetration) which are unlikely to have been widely destroyed. It has been noted that most of the surviving traces of centuriation are situated in the western part of the Tavoliere. This is no doubt in part due to the fact that a high proportion of the eastern Tavoliere, particularly to the south, is covered with heavy alluvial soils, and was thus in any case poorly suited to arable exploitation; but it seems unlikely that the areas of *crosta* soil to the northeast of Foggia, for instance, would not have been at least partially cultivated; they would have had considerable wheat producing potential, although it is true that they may not have been centuriated. One further factor may have operated to increase the apparent ratio of vine and olive cultivation to other forms of land use. The pits and trenches cut through the *crosta* by Roman, as by modern, farmers, leave an unmistakable and virtually indelible record in the air photographs. This means that any area which has been under olives or vines is likely to show these traces, even if, as is probable, its land use changed from time to time, and it carried cereals at other periods during the Roman occupation.

It is probable that the transhumant exploitation of the Tavoliere and its surrounding highlands was carried on in conjunction with intensive arable exploitation. This is contrary to the hypothesis put forward by Delano Smith (1967) that 'only such livestock were kept as could be contained within the farming unit and supplied from its own fallow and waste land grazing'. There is good evidence to suggest that a degree of mobile exploitation of seasonal pastures was widespread in peninsular Italy in Bronze Age times (cf., for example, Barker, 1972), and, as we have noted above, there are strong arguments in favour of viewing this as a feature of the Tavoliere economy from at least Neolithic times onwards. By the time Varro was writing, in the first century B.C., the large-scale movement of flocks of sheep from the Tavoliere along the *calles* to the high pastures in Samnium was already established. We do not know how early the practice was established in this highly organised form, but presumably it must have been at the very latest prior to 50 B.C., and in all likelihood considerably earlier. Much of the centuriation visible in the air photographs appears to be dated to the Gracchan period of land reforms, which presumably started in approximately 120 B.C. With an elaborate system of controlled and commercially organised transhumance thus presumptively in existence during the first half of the first century B.C., and with large areas of land on the Tavoliere only centuriated for the first time a generation or two prior to this, it seems most improbable that the two patterns of exploitation did not overlap in time, or that they were not in fact well integrated.

The commonsense arguments in favour of a mobile exploitation of upland and lowland resources in Neolithic and Bronze Age times are not less applicable for the Roman period. Much of the Tavoliere was still not economically cultivable in Roman times. To make anything like full use of the grazing offered by these and fallow areas in winter, and of the Gargano and Apennine uplands in the summer, some form of transhumance would have been necessary. There is nothing to make us believe that the Romans willingly ignored such opportunities, and it seems probable that such a pastoral system continued unchanged in its essentials from previous millennia. We do not know precisely when the large scale commercial transhumant routes, or the markets which they were supplying, came into being. Varro shows that the system was in operation by the mid-first century B.C., but this must be taken as a *terminus ante quem*.

With the Late Republican period and the advent of the Empire the importance of the pastoral aspect of the economy of the area is thought to have increased at the expense of arable agriculture. While there is considerable

evidence of the great importance of transhumant pastoralism at this time, there is little positive evidence that this occasioned an eclipse of arable agriculture. The growth of *latifundia* (large, extensively farmed estates) seems to have been interpreted by some authors as synonymous with the appearance of wasteful commercial enterpries devoted to livestock husbandry. This was far from the truth. As White (1970) points out, *latifundia* could equally be concerned primarily with cereal production, like those in the lowland plains of Sicily, where they appear to have been combined successfully with large-scale commercial sheep transhumance. It is important to realise here that sheep and cereal farming need not be competitive. As long as there exist sufficient areas of lowland grazing which cannot be profitably cultivated – and such soils covered much of the Tavoliere until technological change permitted the heavy alluvial soils to be ploughed – a joint pastoral and arable exploitation is bound to be more productive than any system exclusively based upon the one or the other. The *latifundia* did not in general form an all-exclusive system of land use, and even where there was a number of large estates they were commonly interspersed with subsistence small-holdings engaged in a mixed farming economy which was probably very little removed from that practised during the Neolithic.

We should remember, too, that most of the references of the classical writers to 'Apulia' can be seriously misinterpreted if it is not appreciated that 'Apulia' is a large and varied province, with gross differences in economic potential. Thus when Seneca talks of the 'deserts' of Apulia we need not suppose that he is referring to the Tavoliere, and when he condemns the *latifundia* in Apulia 'as large as kingdoms', he is likely to be indicating the barren limestone hills of central and southern Apulia. Much of the area to the south of the Tavoliere, in particular the Murge, is in fact illsuited to any exploitation other than extensive pastoralism.

There is thus little need to assume that the Tavoliere was given over wholly to the winter grazing requirements of sheep, and the probabilities are that cereals continued to be grown there, at least on a subsistence basis. As Stevens (1966) indicates, by the time of Marcus Aurelius (second century A.D.) Apulia was again producing wheat for export, due to the loss of the imports from Egypt and Africa; this was manifest in the consequent competition for the lowland between pastoralists and cultivators, a competition which had apparently intensified by the time of the Gothic kingdom. The growth of the *latifundia* may perhaps be more clearly seen in terms of the factors which brought them about – the plentiful slave labour force; the existence of commercial and communications systems sufficiently stable and sophisticated to make them a profitable business enterprise; and the existence of large urban markets for their products – than in an overall readjustment of basic economic strategies.

As far as the Gargano is concerned, there is little to suggest that settlement or land use changed greatly over this period. The limiting factors on exploitation remained unaltered, and while it seems probable that olives were first planted here at about this time there is no evidence to support the suggestion. The Gargano must thus have been used, as before, primarily for summer grazing. It is possible that the increased organisation of and emphasis on commercial pastoralism caused an increase in competition for winter grazing, in which case the lower slopes of the Gargano may be expected to have been exploited as an 'overflow' area from the Tavoliere. This would apply particularly to the northern coast whose climate was moderated by the influence of the sea, and offered relatively extensive lowlands around the Lago di Lèsina and Lago di Varano. The richness of the pasture apparently also acquired for this small area a reputation as good horse breeding country.

The medieval period

Much has been made in the literature of the medieval pastoral exploitation of the Tavoliere, which follows broadly the pattern of the Roman system, with permanent droveways linking lowlands to the summer pastures in the Abruzzi. From the Norman dynasty until the nineteenth century the economy is thought to have been dominated by the transhumant sheep flocks, which travelled in ever-increasing numbers from the summer pastures in the high Abruzzi to the Tavoliere along the established and legally protected *tratturi*. As time went on the system became increasingly controlled under the *Dogana della Mena delle Pecore*, and the resultant revenues became the established right of the sovereign or, when the crown was weak, of the local landlords. Large areas were set aside as permanent grazing, and the areas which it was permitted to cultivate were strictly limited. In the mid-seventeenth century, apparently, about eighty per cent of the Tavoliere was under grazing (Delano Smith, 1967). This situation continued little changed until the Napoleonic intervention in the early nineteenth century, when the laws enforcing the maintenance of land under pasture were briefly relaxed, to be finally removed in the 1860s. A dramatic increase in arable agriculture is witnessed at this point, the area of land in cultivation doubling within a decade.

The tendency in the literature has been to concentrate attention almost entirely on the transhumant pastoralism to the virtual exclusion of other aspects of the economy. Thus we find Lenormant (1883) writing 'La vaste plaine du Tavoliere . . . est animée seulement pendant les mois d'hiver par les immenses troupeaux qui descendent des montagnes; le reste de l'année elle demeure un désert où l'on n'aperçoit pas un seul être vivant.' Despite this affirmation he mentions in passing elsewhere that since 1865 'la production des céréals se développe sur la plus vaste échelle'. Repeatedly we find the existence of, and the litigation involving, the *Dogana della Mena delle Pecore* quoted as demonstrating the overwhelming importance of pastoralism, disregarding the fact that in order for there to be such numbers of legal disputes between arable farmers and pastoralists, there must have been a considerable and continuing population of the former.

Monarchs from the thirteenth-century Frederick II onwards enforced the payment of damages to landowners whose crops were damaged by the flocks, and although the areas where arable cultivation was permitted were controlled, and a rotation was enforced which included herbage for winter grazing, it seems probable that enough arable land was maintained under cereals to provide the needs of the local population throughout the period. In many ways the arable land and cereal yields would have benefited from the system, which guarded against too frequent cropping and ensured that the land would be well-manured. Presumably enough grain was produced to supply the population of Foggia, a substantial town from at least the twelfth century onwards, which had attained a population of over 30 000 by 1860.

The probability that local settlements were self-sufficient in this respect is suggested by the fact (Vitrani, 1968) that the largest area of authorised and protected arable land was adjacent to Foggia, the main population concentration. Bradford's (1949) analysis of air photographs gives us additional indications that there was more cultivation on the medieval Tavoliere than the conventional picture would imply. At the fortified farm of Torrione del Casone crop marks indicate intensively cultivated fields stretching 'for three-quarters of a mile in several directions' around the farm. Precisely similar traces were noted at San Lorenzo. The three-quarters of a mile referred to by Bradford is a remarkably close approximation to the 1 km threshold which we have taken as defining the area of maximum potential productivity for arable agriculture, and it is debatable whether more extensive territories could have been effectively exploited as arable land by the sites in question.

As far as the Early Medieval period is concerned there is good evidence that the rôle of wheat production was not confined to the satisfaction of local demands. Apulia has been estimated to have supplied as much as 86 000 quarters of wheat to the cities of northern Italy in the fourteenth century; and while as we have noted, 'Apulia' is not to be taken as synonymous with 'the Tavoliere', this area is the major one in Apulia with a wheat-producing potential, and any surplus from the province is almost certain to have come largely from here. As far as the later historical period is concerned, Vitrani (1968) indicates a steady, if slow, increase in the area of arable land on the Tavoliere from the seventeenth to mid-nineteenth century.

When considering the apparently low percentage of cultivated land on the Tavoliere, it is instructive to examine the available soils in the light of their suitability for pre-mechanical agriculture. The Tavoliere is variously recorded as covering c. 350 000–450 000 ha (depending on where its limits are defined). Of these some 30 000 ha remained as permanent marsh until c. 1900 A.D., and a further 40 000 ha were subject to regular autumn and winter flooding (Colaciccio, 1955). Only c. 20 per cent of the soils are easily worked *crosta* soils, the remaining soils being highly variable in particle size and structure. About 50 per cent of the area would have been totally unsuited to arable exploitation of the time. The remaining c. 30 per cent would have been cultivable but would have presented a variety of obstacles to such an exploitation pattern, from poor yields to difficult textures which could only be dealt with during short periods of the year under ideal weather conditions and when the draught beasts were in peak condition. It should not be forgotten that before the availability of tractors, the capacity of farms to plough extensive areas of the heavier soils was greatly limited by their capacity to maintain large numbers of horses or oxen. A good pair of horses, at the beginning of the season, would plough only about one hectare of heavy soil in three days, but by the end of the ploughing season this rate might have declined by 50 per cent. Before the Second World War farmers maintained approximately one horse for every ten to fifteen hectares they needed to cultivate, a major consideration as they needed not only winter pasturage but also expensive high quality feed at the end of the summer in order to put them in good condition for the autumn ploughing. Thus we should not be too surprised that the picture we get of the medieval Tavoliere does not correspond to the modern one in which nearly 80 per cent of the area is under arable exploitation.

The Gargano in this period was clearly occupied, but as usual far less is known of this area than of the Tavoliere. As in earlier periods sites are concentrated on the peripheries of the Gargano, including the open site on top of the small hill of Pescorosso, some 200 m above the plain, and 400 m below the edge of the plateau to the north; and the fortified site of Castelpango, situated on the edge of the plateau itself. Both these sites overlook the Tavoliere, but others, such as that on the Isola di San Clemente in Lago di Lèsina, and the Grotta dell'Angelo, exploit the northern edge of the hills. It seems certain that some of the many minor pottery scatters to be found on the surface throughout the Gargano are of medieval date, and others are Roman. However, such sites rarely provide sufficient material to encourage typological analysis, and they remain unstudied; there is thus no incontrovertible evidence as to their date.

It is difficult to explain any of the sites mentioned other than in terms of pastoral exploitation, although Castelpango may in addition have fulfilled a defensive rôle. However, in view of the fact that the majority of the local population must have lived on the plain, it is difficult to envisage precisely how this latter function would have been carried out. The exploitation territory of Pescorosso (Figure 24) would have permitted a mixed economy to have been practised, the hills to the north being used for mobile pastoralism, the hillwash soils below offering poor, but adequate arable. Further out on the plain the heavy soils of the Candelaro and Triòlo valleys would have provided good spring grazing. As was pointed out earlier, such a site location provides in many ways an ideal situation for a small holding. The uplands are close enough to be exploited in the most flexible way, with long distance movement being largely unnecessary. A single 'home base' can serve the annual needs, and even in the summer absence from it could be organised on a day-to-day or week-to-week basis. The present-day small-holding in the valley just below the site of Pescorosso is conducted on a precisely comparable basis. The small occupation in the Grotta dell'Angelo must have been exclusively concerned with pastoral exploitation. On the steep western side of Monte d'Elio, its territory (Figure 33) includes almost no land that could have been exploited as arable, and none at all occurs within 1 km of the site. The likelihood is that the Gargano played the same part in the economic system as it had in Roman times, being primarily exploited as summer grazing by those flocks which did not go to the Abruzzi, with olives and small patches of arable in favoured areas as possible but undemonstrated subsidiary elements.

It seems, then, that there has been too great a tendency to view the historical period on the Tavoliere as being wholly concerned with the rise of transhumant pastoralism. The prehistoric perspective indicates that this was almost certainly a development of the basic economic pattern which had been in existence for several millennia, and was only new in detail and degree. Certainly it seems to be established that pastoralism was an important commercial concern on the Tavoliere in the post-Roman period, and that this was of considerable but varying importance as far back as early Imperial Rome. It is possible that for a period in Roman times wheat exports from the Tavoliere ceased, at the time of maximum imports from North Africa, but this was probably only a brief hiatus; and even in medieval times the subsistence farming aspect of the Tavoliere economy appears to have continued with little change, with commercial wheat farming being of importance during at least the early part of the period.

If we consider why there should have been such variations in the commercial exploitation of the Tavoliere, we may speculate that this may have been connected with the scale and external conditions of the political and economic systems of which Apulia was a part. Under the Roman Empire and again after the *Risorgimento* the Tavoliere was a part of a unified Italian state. This facilitated communications and commercial transactions in general, and more importantly, Apulia was directly exposed to the market forces operating from the major urban centres elsewhere in Italy. As we have seen, the possession by the Roman Empire of alternative sources of grain may have occasioned a decline in cereal production on the Tavoliere for a short period. The commercial and industrial florescence of northern Italy in the medieval period created market forces which overcame the disunity and obstacles presented by poor communications. The apparent decline of wheat exports in the later historic period seems likely to have been caused by a more complex conjunction of phenomena than is often acknowledged. Certainly eagerness on the part of individual sovereigns and landlords to extract easy profits must have been a factor, but this seems unlikely to have been so long-lived a feature if it were operating in the face of clearly more profitable alternatives. A number of additional factors may have contributed to stimulate or confirm the trend to transhumant pastoralism in Apulia: the decline in the rate of growth of the north Italian cities, a more intensive and productive exploitation of the Po plain, and an increasing development of overseas trading relations by the northern maritime powers. With the unification of Italy, it is undoubtedly true that an initial stimulus to arable exploitation came from the removal of legal restrictions in 1865. However, the sustained growth in the importance of arable crops (the area under cultivation rose by about 100 000 ha in the first 50 years of the twentieth century) reflects the national and international markets now available, and the consequent provision of government aid and encouragement to cereal production.

GENERAL PERSPECTIVES

Looking at the prehistoric and historic settlement of the area in broad terms, two major episodes seem to have been of particular importance and to have caused significant change in what may otherwise be thought of as a continuum. These are the appearance of cereal-dependent economies with the Neolithic, and the apparent hiatus in the development of such economies which, we have argued, may have been caused by a critical climatic deterioration.

Pre-Neolithic occupation appears to have concentrated upon the hills, in particular on the southern margins of the Gargano. With Neolithic occupation the pattern was dramatically altered, with a vast preponderance of sites upon the plain. The Palaeolithic economy was based on herbivores which in their exploitation of the seasonally variable grazing resources must have imposed a pattern of seasonal movement upon the human population. While it is probable that vegetable foods contributed to the diet, it is difficult to see any of the plants which are likely to have been available as providing dietary staples. One can view the animal husbandry aspect of the subsequent exploitations as economic and ecological counterparts to the herbivores of the Palaeolithic economy. The obvious and important new element in the Neolithic economy is the exploitation of cereals, and this seems to have been the major determining factor both in the overall shift of the primary occupation sites to the plain and also in individual site location. If our estimated date for the formation of the *crosta* is correct, it follows that the Neolithic occupation of the Tavoliere began soon after the earliest time that cereal cultivation was made possible although it should be remembered that until the *crosta* was broken and mixed with the topsoil the light, easily-cultivated and well-drained soils would not be available. The period between the Neolithic and early historic times appears to be characterised again by a settlement pattern based largely on the Gargano, and for this and the other reasons already discussed it seems reasonable to suggest that the economy of this period depended upon herbivores, the economy and settlement pattern being thus broadly comparable with that of the Palaeolithic.

Our conclusion that there was a direct link between lowland settlement and cereal agriculture has a more general importance in addition to its specific explanatory value as far as the Tavoliere is concerned. A conspicuous feature of the Early Neolithic settlement of southern Italy is the concentration of settlement in a few relatively confined areas of lowland. As we have noted, this does not necessarily mean that there was no exploition of the uplands, and indeed it seems almost certain that some such areas were important sources of summer grazing. However, the major sites, and, as we have argued for the Tavoliere, the major economic emphasis, are centred on low-lying areas which have a high potential for arable agriculture. Apart from the Tavoliere, which we have studied in detail, concentrations of Neolithic sites are known from the Matera area of Basilicata and from the coastal lowlands of Sicily. Both these areas are characterised by the presence of light lowland soils of sufficient extent and depth to encourage the exploitation of cereals as a staple, and to permit the growth of substantial human populations. Areas of heavy alluvial lowland soil like that in the lower Bradano valley were avoided, as was seen to have been the case on the Tavoliere.

Table 5. Wheat yields (ten-year averages)
in some provinces of southern Italy

Province	Quintals per hectare
Caserta	20.4
Foggia	19.6
Chieta	16.3
Matera	14.5
Salerno	14.0
Bari	13.1
Taranto	13.0
Potenza	12.4
Benevento	12.3
Avellino	12.0
Lecce	9.9
Brindisi	9.6

Table 5 shows that wheat yields in southern Italy today are very variable, with the province of Foggia (which includes the Tavoliere) giving the second highest average yields. Caserta, the only province giving slightly higher yields, makes use of the highly fertile volcanic soils which are expensive of labour to cultivate, and are primarily exploited for viticulture, not for cereal agriculture. The modern cereal production of Foggia relative to the rest of Apulia, and of the Tavoliere in particular relative to the rest of the province of Foggia, can be seen in Tables 6 and 7. The Tavoliere is indeed the main cereal-producing area of southern Italy, and although we cannot take this directly as an index of its Neolithic importance because of the different soils and technology now in use, the coincidence of this and other modern centres of wheat production with the prime areas of Early Neolithic occupation is too striking to be ignored. It is also of interest that the Tavoliere, with the highest figures for grain production in southern Italy, also appears to have the greatest density of Neolithic sites, and thus presumably the highest Neolithic population.

Table 6. Wheat production (quintals) in Apulia (1967)

Province	Soft wheat	Hard wheat
Foggia	1 372 800	5 361 900
Bari	518 000	650 200
Taranto	153 600	291 200
Brindisi	144 600	52 700
Lecce	—	317 500

Apart from the two substantial breaks in the continuity of development, the basic features of settlement and economy in the study area appear to have been relatively stable. It has been the custom for archaeology to seek to document cultural change, and most archaeological activity is directed towards the definition of fine degrees of such development. This has sprung from the traditional archaeological need to provide itself with a reliable chronology, and while it remains an important objective in some situations, it should not be allowed to blind us to the fact that there are other approaches which may repay attention. It is possible to focus attention upon the features which unite different occupations, on the threads of continuity rather than the indications of change: an approach more appropriate to the analysis of factors controlling human behaviour than the traditional one, which concentrates upon the evidence for human inventiveness.

As far as Capitanata is concerned it has been usual to emphasise the apparent fluctuation of occupation between lowland and highland, and the oscillation between arable-dominated and pastoral-dominated economies. For the later periods it has been customary to point to the evidence for the effect of malaria, of wars, and of individuals. All of

Table 7. Hard wheat production in different areas
of the province of Foggia (1967)

Zone	Production	
	Quintals	Per cent
Tavoliere	4 249 769	76.0
Subapennine	1 064 599	19.0
Gargano	281 761	5.0

these have certainly had an impact upon the situation, but this may have been exaggerated in the literature. For example, while malaria is likely to present a considerable obstacle to an incoming human population, indigenous populations tend to become adapted to the disease in a number of ways and to be less seriously affected than might be supposed. A striking example of such a mechanism is the 'sickle cell' genetic anomaly which occurs in many malarial areas and is known to have been present in some areas of southern Italy in the recent past.

Change there has certainly been, but we should not ignore the contrary evidence for consistent factors and trends. Thus as Puglisi (1948) pointed out, the flint industries of the Gargano present an almost unchanging picture from the 'Eneolithic' to the Iron Age; and, as we have argued, some of these industries are likely to be earlier still.

A more striking constant in the occupation of the Tavoliere is the nature of locations chosen for sites. Bradford (Bradford & Williams-Hunt, 1946) pointed to the Neolithic preference for small rises, and our field evidence confirms this. In fact, our data suggest that the primary correlation is with the *crosta* soils, and a further observation of interest is that in the conducting of territorial analyses it was our repeated experience that minor patches of *crosta* soil carried traces of small Roman and medieval occupations. This can be added to the regular occurrence of Roman and/or medieval sites directly overlying Neolithic settlements, whether the former represent substantial occupations (as at Fiorentino and Torrione del Casone, for example) or pottery scatters (as at Il Casone). This continuity of settlement location can indeed be seen to continue to the present day. Many of the ditched settlements contain within them modern farms, and at San Lorenzo the medieval tower is within a few yards of an existing farm. Similarly it is noticeable that settlements being built today tend to avoid the alluvial soils, even when such soils form a major part of their exploitation territories.

Another aspect of continuity has been the primary economic importance of cereals, in particular wheat, from the Neolithic onwards. It does appear that this trend may have been broken for a time between the Neolithic and Daunian occupations, but this aside it has been a major constant. Arable agriculture may have suffered a minor decline in importance during the later historical period, but the significance of this appears to have been exaggerated in the literature, for it seems that wheat remained a staple as far as the subsistence economy was concerned throughout this period. Today, it has regained its position as the major export and cash crop, and wheat production is still increasing.

APPENDIX I: METEOROLOGICAL DATA (TEN-YEAR AVERAGES) FROM VILLAGGIO AMENDOLA (39 m o.d.) AND POTENZA (1367 m o.d.). Figures in brackets denote per cent variations over ten years.

	Rainfall (mm)		Maximum mean air temperature (°C)		Minimum mean air temperature (°C)		Relative humidity (per cent)	
VILLAGGIO AMÈNDOLA								
August	19.6	(30.6)	32.0	(5.0)	17.9	(1.8)	52.7	(2.5)
September	45.4	(27.3)	27.9	(3.9)	15.3	(1.4)	62.1	(3.0)
October	58.3	(32.9)	22.6	(5.7)	11.5	(0.2)	71.3	(1.2)
November	40.4	(14.6)	17.8	(7.8)	7.8	(3.9)	72.9	(1.5)
December	63.0	(18.1)	12.4	(8.9)	4.4	(7.1)	76.8	(1.6)
January	47.2	(15.2)	11.2	(8.9)	2.7	(19.6)	77.2	(1.5)
February	32.5	(13.5)	12.3	(17.8)	2.9	(15.5)	72.7	(0.6)
March	28.2	(26.9)	15.1	(9.3)	4.6	(7.2)	69.0	(2.8)
April	30.8	(28.6)	19.5	(8.7)	7.2	(4.6)	67.0	(2.4)
May	38.2	(15.4)	24.3	(4.9)	11.1	(3.1)	60.4	(1.4)
June	33.4	(38.3)	28.6	(3.8)	15.2	(2.6)	54.7	(2.9)
July	17.5	(24.2)	31.7	(3.5)	17.6	(2.2)	49.9	(2.4)
Mean	37.9	(23.8)	21.3	(7.4)	9.8	(5.8)	65.6	(2.0)
POTENZA								
August	31.5	(17.5)	25.1	(2.2)	15.6	(1.7)	50.9	(3.5)
September	49.2	(12.7)	21.3	(2.4)	12.9	(1.7)	61.8	(2.4)
October	64.4	(21.3)	16.6	(3.0)	9.2	(5.3)	69.8	(2.4)
November	112.0	(22.1)	12.3	(3.0)	6.2	(5.5)	71.1	(1.3)
December	83.7	(10.7)	7.3	(8.2)	2.5	(16.6)	77.6	(0.7)
January	67.4	(14.3)	5.7	(8.4)	0.6	(33.8)	77.1	(1.3)
February	46.5	(14.1)	6.7	(10.5)	1.0	(44.6)	72.2	(1.6)
March	48.5	(15.3)	9.0	(3.0)	2.7	(11.4)	69.3	(2.6)
April	48.9	(24.3)	13.6	(4.3)	5.9	(7.4)	62.4	(2.5)
May	41.1	(20.9)	17.9	(2.8)	9.6	(5.2)	58.4	(3.0)
June	42.6	(21.0)	21.8	(1.7)	12.8	(2.6)	57.8	(2.6)
July	26.5	(28.3)	24.8	(1.9)	15.1	(2.5)	51.4	(3.2)
Mean	55.2	(18.5)	15.2	(4.3)	7.8	(8.3)	65.0	(2.3)

APPENDIX II: SITE EXPLOITATION TERRITORIES

For the sites on the Tavoliere one-hour territories have been analysed, those from the Gargano being two-hour territories. The scale is indicated by the solid circles, of 1 km and 5 km radius in Figures 2–22, and of 1 km and 10 km radius in Figures 23–33.

La Lamia (Figure 2)

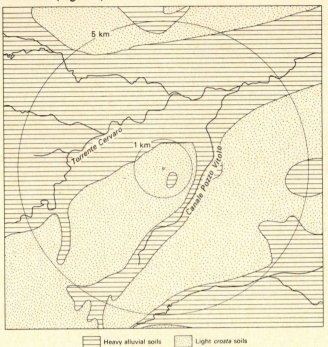

Figure 2. One-hour site exploitation territory of La Lamia.

Territory

Not walked, commentary based on hypothetical 5 km ring.

Topography and drainage

To the north the ground falls steeply from the site, at *c.* 240 m, to the Cervaro valley, *c.* 180 m at 2 km from the site. To the northwest the ground drops sharply to *c.* 200 m after 1 km, rising very slightly from there until the edge of the territory. To the west the ground falls to the Cervaro valley at *c.* 215 m, 3 km from the site, therafter rising to *c.* 240 m by the edge of the territory. To the southwest the ground rises to *c.* 330 m at the edge of the territory. To the south the ground rises to *c.* 280 m after crossing the valley of the Canale Pozzo Vitolo. To the east the ground falls to *c.* 195 m at 1.5 km from the site, rising again to *c.* 230 m by the edge of the territory. The general drainage pattern is from west to east.

Soils

The river valleys and some basins at higher altitudes are covered with heavy clay soils, which account for *c.* 54 per cent of the soils

within the territory. The rest of the territory (*c.* 46 per cent) has light *crosta* soils. The site is on *crosta* soils, which total *c.* 88 per cent of the area within 1 km of the site, clay soils covering the remaining *c.* 12 per cent.

Modern exploitation

The primary crop throughout the territory is wheat, with vegetables and sugar beet occurring as rotation crops. Vines occur in some areas of lighter soil, and some of the steepest slopes are exploited as rough grazing.

La Quercia (Figure 3)

Territory

Nearly circular, the perimeter varying from *c.* 4.6 km to *c.* 5.2 km from the site. Total area *c.* 75 km².

Topography and drainage

To the north the ground drops steeply from the site at *c.* 120 m to *c.* 105 m at 1 km from the site, falling thereafter to *c.* 90 m at the edge of the territory. To the west the ground rises slightly throughout the territory, reaching *c.* 140 m at the edge. Southward the ground rises gently to *c.* 155 m at 3 km from the site, drops to *c.* 140 m at the Valle del Forno at 4 km, and then rises steeply to *c.* 160 m at the edge of the territory. To the east the ground drops gently throughout the territory, reaching *c.* 80 m at the edge. The drainage pattern is basically from southwest to northeast. The site is on the northern edge of the ridge overlooking the Cervaro valley from the south.

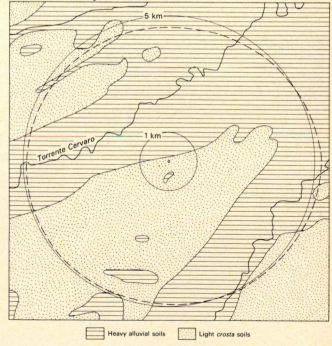

Figure 3. One-hour site exploitation territory of La Quercia.

Soils

The river valleys, and much of the low-lying ground to the northeast of the site are covered in heavy clay soils, which amount to *c*. 60 per cent of the territory as a whole. The higher ground is largely covered with light *crosta* soils, which account for the remaining *c*. 40 per cent of the territory. The site is on *crosta* soils, which cover *c*. 57 per cent of the area within 1 km of the site, clay soils covering the other *c*. 43 per cent.

Modern exploitation

Cereals are the primary crop throughout the territory, with sugar beet and fodder crops as rotation crops. Vines and olives occur only in small plots. In some areas, particularly to the east of the site, the richer soils are exploited as intensive market gardens. Most of the sheep in the area are in the Abruzzi during the summer, returning to the territory in the autumn. In the past, when there was more grazing area and there were more animals in the area, a proportion of them remained in the area throughout the summer. At the present time a number of cows are maintained in the area throughout the year, fed in summer primarily upon concentrate feed and fodder crops. Average wheat yields in good years are 30–40 q/ha, and 20–5 q/ha in poorer years.

Mezzana Comunale (Figure 4)

Territory

Not walked, commentary based on hypothetical 5 km ring. The territory would be nearly semi-circular, being truncated to the

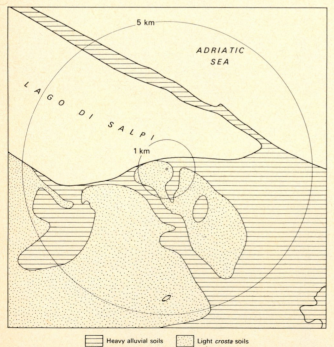

Figure 4. One-hour site exploitation territory of Mezzana Comunale.

northeast by the coast and the Lago di Salpi, drained in the nineteenth century. Total area *c*. 40 km².

Topography and drainage

To the north, west, and east the land surface is essentially flat, consisting of the bed of the old lake, or its margins. To the southwest, south, and southeast the land rises slowly and steadily from *c*. 4 m at the site to *c*. 20–5 m at the edge of the territory.

Soils

Most of the soils in the east of the territory, and those bordering the Lago di Salpi and streams draining into it, are heavy clays which account for *c*. 47 per cent of the area of the territory. Elsewhere, in particular in the central and southern area of the territory, are *crosta* soils totalling *c*. 53 per cent of the territory. The site itself is on *crosta* soils which cover *c*. 65 per cent of the area within 1 km of the site, clays accounting for the other *c*. 35 per cent.

Modern exploitation

Wheat and vines are the main crops grown within the territory, the former particularly on the clay soils, the latter usually on the more stony areas. Olives occur in some areas, and the marsh areas bordering the Lago di Salpi are used for grazing.

Marandrea (Figure 5)

Territory

Nearly semi-circular, being truncated to the north and east by the Lago di Salpi, which was drained and largely turned into salt-pans in the nineteenth century. The perimeter varies from *c*. 4.5 km to *c*. 5.0 km from the site. Total area *c*. 40 km².

Topography and drainage

To the north and east lies the area of the old lake, which is essentially flat. To the west and southeast there is likewise little relief, with the exception of a few small isolated humps to the west of the site which rise a few metres above the surrounding plain. To the south the ground rises steadily but very gradually to some 15 m above the altitude of the site (*c*. 6 m) at the edge of the territory. The main drainage is the Fosso della Pila, running into the Lago di Salpi from the south.

Soils

In the western portion of the territory, along the stream courses, and scattered elsewhere, the soil consists of a heavy stoneless clay, amounting to *c*. 37 per cent of the territory. The other main soil present is a light *crosta* soil which predominates in the southern part of the territory (*c*. 59 per cent). A small area of marsh, the Marana di Lupara, is also present (*c*. 4 per cent). The site is on

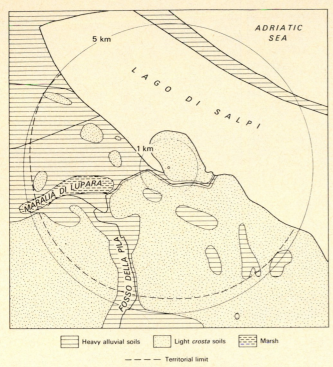

Figure 5. One-hour site exploitation territory of Marandrea.

crosta soils, *c.* 86 per cent of the area within 1 km of the site being of this type, *c.* 14 per cent being heavy clays.

Modern exploitation

Present-day exploitation is very variable, for while wheat is the commonest crop, several others are of significance. On the low-lying clay soils near the site market gardens occur, with some intensive vine production. Vines are also found on some of the more stony *crosta* soils. Sugar beet is in places grown in rotation with cereals, but this is a recent practice in the area. Adjacent to the site to the west, and in the Marana di Lupara are areas of marsh grazing, which provide the best areas of winter and spring grazing and are exploited in particular by cattle. Cereal yields are very variable, but average 30–40 q/ha in good years, 0–20 q/ha in bad years. Modern technology is necessary to achieve high yields, and until recently the yield was 10–20 q/ha in good years.

San Lorenzo (Figure 6)

Territory

Nearly circular, the perimeter varying from *c.* 4.8 km to *c.* 5.0 km from the site. Total area *c.* 75 km².

Topography and drainage

To the north the ground drops steadily but slowly throughout the territory, from the site at *c.* 75 m to *c.* 60 m at the edge. To the west and south the level rises steadily, reaching *c.* 110 m by the

west edge of the territory, *c.* 100 m by the south edge. To the east the ground descends very gently towards the Cervaro valley, reaching *c.* 65 m by the edge of the territory.

Soils

The river valleys and most of the eastern half of the territory carry heavy clay soils, which cover *c.* 71 per cent of the territory. On higher ground, particularly to the west and northwest of the site, light *crosta* soils occur, totalling *c.* 29 per cent of the territory. The site itself is on *crosta* soils, which cover *c.* 53 per cent of the area within 1 km of the site, clay soils accounting for *c.* 47 per cent. Immediately adjacent to the site to the west is a small patch of marsh soil which, however, covers only *c.* 0.2 per cent of the area within 1 km of the site.

Modern exploitation

The main crop in the territory is wheat, but vines occur as an important secondary crop. Sugar beet is grown as a rotation crop with wheat. The relatively high proportion of vines on clay soils and of small market gardens may be related to the proximity of the large modern town of Foggia (adjacent to the northern edge of the territory). Very few animals are now kept in the area all year round, as there is little summer grazing; before the *bonifica* (*c.* 1900) there was much more grazing as much of the low-lying area was seasonally water-logged, and was left as grazing. The majority of the sheep population (then as now) spent the summer in the Abruzzi.

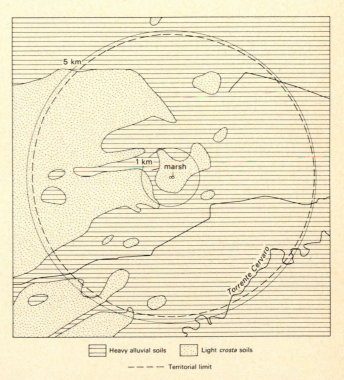

Figure 6. One-hour site exploitation territory of San Lorenzo.

San Marcello (Figure 7)

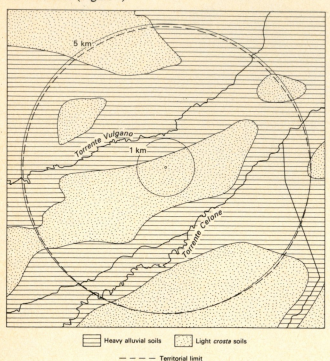

Figure 7. One-hour site exploitation territory of San Marcello.

Territory

Nearly circular, the perimeter varying from *c.* 4.9 km to *c.* 5.1 km from the site. Total area *c.* 80 km².

Topography and drainage

To the north the ground drops sharply from *c.* 140 m to *c.* 125 m within 200–300 m of the site, continuing to fall gently thereafter to the Vulgano valley and beyond, reaching a height of *c.* 100 m at the edge of the territory. Due west of the site the ground stays relatively level, skirting a ridge which lies to the south and meeting the Vulgano at *c.* 4 km from the site. Running southwest of the site is a ridge which rises steadily to *c.* 225 m at *c.* 4.5 km from the site. Southward the level remains fairly level to the Celone valley at *c.* 3.5 km from the site, then rising to *c.* 200 m at the edge of the territory. The territory as a whole can be considered as a series of parallel ridges and valleys, oriented southwest–northeast with height decreasing northeastward. The site occupies a position on the northern edge of a ridge.

Soils

The river valleys and many flatter areas are covered by heavy clay soils, which account for *c.* 62 per cent of the territory. The remaining *c.* 38 per cent of the area has light *crosta* soils. The site is on *crosta* soils, which total *c.* 74 per cent of the area within 1 km of the site, clays covering the other *c.* 26 per cent.

Modern exploitation

Wheat is the main crop throughout the territory, particularly on the heavy clay soils, where sugar beet occurs as a rotation crop. On poor soils with much *crosta*, and in small plots around farms, vines and olives are grown. Some cattle are maintained in the territory throughout the year, but only graze in the spring, being fed on hay and artificial feeds at other times of the year. In the past there was more pasture and there were more animals in the area. Good grain yields in the valley are 40–50 q/ha, *c.* 30 q/ha on the ridge. Poor years give *c.* 20–30 q/ha in the valley, *c.* 10 q/ha on the ridge.

Coppa Cavone (Figure 8)

Territory

Not walked, commentary based on hypothetical 5 km ring.

Topography and drainage

To the north the ground remains essentially flat for some 2.5 km, then falling lightly to the valley of the Sàlsola. To the west the ground rises slowly and steadily to a level of *c.* 60 m above the site (at *c.* 75 m); likewise the ground rises gently to the south, to *c.* 40 m above the site. To the east the level falls gently to the valley of the Vulgano. Immediately to the south of the site the Canale Bonifica drains eastward into the Vulgano.

Soils

The river valleys and the entire southeastern portion of the territory carry heavy clay soils, which cover *c.* 68 per cent of the

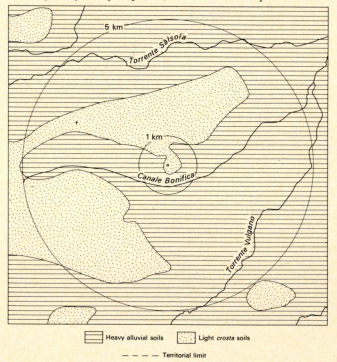

Figure 8. One-hour site exploitation territory of Coppa Cavone.

territory. Much of the area between the Sàlsola and the Canale Bonifica has light *crosta* soils, which also appear to the southwest of the site, amounting to *c.* 32 per cent of the territory. The site itself is on *crosta* soils, which cover *c.* 27 per cent of the area within 1 km of the site, the remaining *c.* 73 per cent being covered by heavy clays.

Modern exploitation

The primary crop throughout the territory is wheat. To the south small areas of irrigated vegetables occur, and patches of vines and olives occur widely throughout the territory adjacent to farms. Sugar beet and forage crops occur as rotation crops with cereals. Good average yields of wheat are *c.* 30–5 q/ha, with *c.* 20 q/ha in poor years. Cattle are maintained in the area throughout the year, subsisting largely on hay and artificial feeds in summer; sheep summer in the Abruzzi, only returning to the area in winter.

Masseria Villano (Figure 9)

Territory

Nearly circular, the perimeter varying from between *c.* 4.9 and *c.* 5.0 km from the site. Total area *c.* 75 km².

Topography and drainage

To the north the ground falls gently to the Sàlsola valley at *c.* 3 km from the site, and is flat thereafter. To the west and south the ground rises gently and steadily from the site (at *c.* 70 m) to *c.* 105

m in the west and *c.* 95 m in the south. To the east the level falls slowly to the Vulgano valley, at *c.* 55 m. To the south of the site runs a tributary of the Vulgano, the Canale Bonifica.

Soils

The area between the Sàlsola and the Canale Bonifica has a substantial proportion of light *crosta* soils, which amount to only *c.* 21 per cent of the territory as a whole. The remainder of the territory, including the river valleys, is covered with heavy clay soils (*c.* 79 per cent). The site itself is on light *crosta* soils which form *c.* 64 per cent of the soils within 1 km of the site, the other *c.* 36 per cent being heavy clay soils.

Modern exploitation

The main crop is wheat, which is grown in rotation with forage crops and sugar beet. Vegetable market gardening and vines, with some olives, occur in small patches. Average wheat yields are 30–5 q/ha in a good year on large farms, with 20–5 q/ha on small holdings. In bad years yields fall to 10–15 q/ha. A small number of sheep is maintained in the area throughout the year.

Amèndola (Figure 10)

Territory

Nearly circular, the perimeter varying from 4.5–4.9 km from the site. An area in the southeastern portion of the territory was until *c.* 1900 submerged under the Lago Contessa. Total area *c.* 65 km².

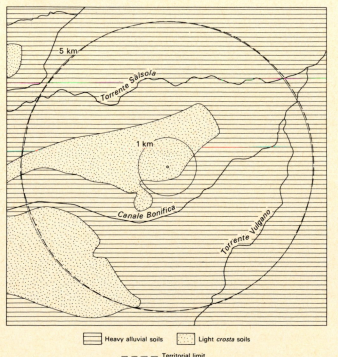

Figure 9. One-hour site exploitation territory of Masseria Villano.

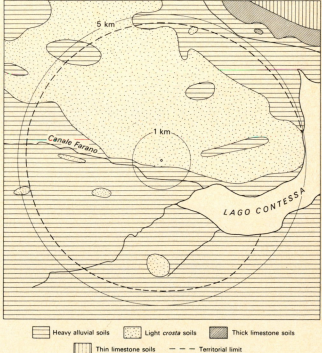

Figure 10. One-hour site exploitation territory of Amèndola.

Topography and drainage

To the north the land rises gently for about 2 km and then falls slowly to the perimeter of the territory. To the west the valley of the Canale Farano separates higher ground to the north and south. To the south the ground falls quickly from the site to the Canale Farano, rising gently thereafter. To the east the land slopes gently down to the edge of the territory.

Soils

Heavy alluvial deposits account for *c.* 55 per cent of the territory, *crosta* soils for the remaining *c.* 45 per cent. The site is situated on *crosta* soils, *c.* 65 per cent of the area within 1 km of the site falling into this class, the remaining *c.* 35 per cent being alluvial soils.

Modern exploitation

Arable exploitation, especially cereals with some sugar beet and arboriculture, predominates throughout the territory, with small areas of rough grazing confined to patches of marshy soil in the river valley to the south, and to very stony areas to the north. Average yields are *c.* 30 q/ha in a good year, *c.* 8–10 q/ha in a bad year.

Passo di Corvo (Figure 11)

Territory

Nearly circular, the perimeter varying from between 4.6 km and 4.9 km from the site. Total area *c.* 70 km².

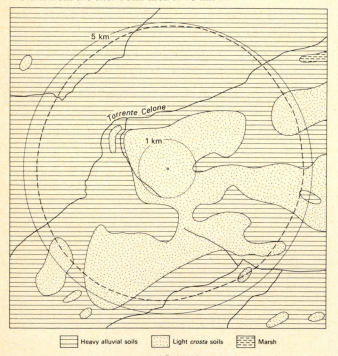

Figure 11. One-hour exploitation territory of Passo di Corvo.

Topography and drainage

The ground falls away fairly steeply to the valley of the Celone to the north, rising more gently on the further side of the valley. To the west the downward slope is more gradual, while to the south the ground rises gently after a minor valley at about 1 km from the site. Eastward the surface is practically level. The site is thus on the crest of a low ridge oriented basically east–west, overlooking the Celone valley.

Soils

Most of the valley soils, especially to the north of the site, are heavy alluvial deposits, which account for *c.* 65 per cent of the territory. The remaining *c.* 35 per cent are *crosta* soils. The site itself is on *crosta* soil which covers almost all the area within 1 km of the site (*c.* 99 per cent), *c.* 1 per cent being alluvium.

Modern exploitation

Wheat is the primary crop through most of the territory, with vines in small plots around farm houses, and more extensively to the south of the site. Sugar beet is uncommon. Small areas of grazing for animals are limited to river courses, especially the canal banks. Average wheat yields in good years are 30–40 q/ha, with *c.* 20 q/ha in bad years. In the recent past yields as low as 8–10 q/ha were recorded.

Fonteviva (Figure 12)

Territory

Nearly circular, the perimeter varying from *c.* 4.3 km to *c.* 4.8 km from the site. The distance to the northern perimeter of the site is influenced by the steep slopes encountered in this direction. Total area *c.* 65 km².

Topography and drainage

To the north the surface slopes gently down to the Candelaro valley at *c.* 1.5 km from the site and rises steeply to more than 100 m from about 2.5–3.5 km. The Candelaro runs approximately northwest–southeast. To the west and south of the site the land rises gently; to the east it falls slowly to the Candelaro at *c.* 1.5 km, thereafter rising to the limestone hills at *c.* 4 km from the site.

Soils

To the north and east the limestone hills carry a thin Terra Rossa soil, which accounts for *c.* 15 per cent of the site territory. Between this and the clays of the Candelaro and Celone valleys is a band of hill-wash soils, lighter than the clays, but much deeper than the hill soils. These deeper limestone soils amount to *c.* 9 per cent of the territory. The river valleys carry heavy clays (*c.* 37 per cent), and a small area (*c.* 2 per cent) to the northwest of the site contains grey marsh soils. Most of the area to the west and south of the site is covered by *crosta* soils, totalling *c.* 37 per cent of the territory. The site itself is situated on *crosta* soils, which account for *c*. 77 per cent of the area within 1 km of the site, heavy clays forming the other *c*. 23 per cent.

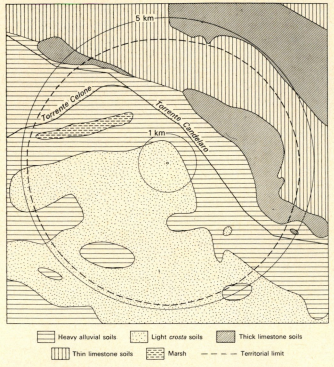

Figure 12. One-hour site exploitation territory of Fonteviva.

Modern exploitation

The limestone hills to the north carry rough grazing, exploited to some extent all the year round, but primarily in winter. The hill-wash soils carry a variety of crops, varying from low-yield cereals and fodder crops in the poorer, stony areas to irrigated sugar beet on the better soils. The *crosta*, clay, and marsh soils are predominantly under wheat, with some sugar beet, and patches of olives and vines around farmsteads. Good yields on these soils are 30–5 q/ha. Animals (in summer) are largely confined to stall-fed cattle.

Monte Aquilone (Figure 13)

Territory

Nearly circular, the perimeter varying between 4.9 and 5.3 km from the site. Total area *c*. 80 km².

Topography and drainage

To the north and east hills climb to about 100 m above the site at *c*. 25 m. To the northwest, west, south, and southeast runs the low-lying Candelaro valley, beyond which the land rises gently.

Soils

The hills to the north and east of the site bear thin limestone soils, with much bedrock exposed in most areas, although in the northeastern section of the territory there is an area of deeper Terra Rossa which lies on a plateau. The former soil accounts for *c*. 30 per cent of the site territory, the latter *c*. 12 per cent. At the base of the hills, and separating them from the heavy clays, is an area of mixed Terra Rossa and pieces of bedrock washed down from the hills, and including some *crosta*. This soil covers *c*. 10 per cent of the territory. Heavy clays (*c*. 27 per cent) follow the course of the Candelaro, and beyond is an area of light *crosta* soils (*c*. 21 per cent). To the extreme southeast the territory is impinged on by a small area of the Lago Salso and the Lago Verzentino. The site itself is situated on the light slope-wash soils at the foot of the hills. These soils constitute *c*. 59 per cent of the soils within 1 km of the site, while thin limestone soils constitute *c*. 28 per cent and heavy clays *c*. 13 per cent.

Modern exploitation

The thin limestone soils on the hilly areas and isolated patches of very stony *crosta* soil carry rough grazing, in particular winter pasture for sheep and goats which spend the summer in the hills. The area of thicker Terra Rossa on the plateau is under marginal arable exploitation, with cereals, especially barley, being the main crop. The hill-wash soils vary in potential from poor arable to good arable, those close to the site being deep and of high productivity. The clays and *crosta* soils are exploited as high productivity arable land, with wheat and sugar beet as the main crops. On the clay, *crosta*, and hill-wash soils, good yields are 30–5 q/ha, with 0–8 q/ha in poor years.

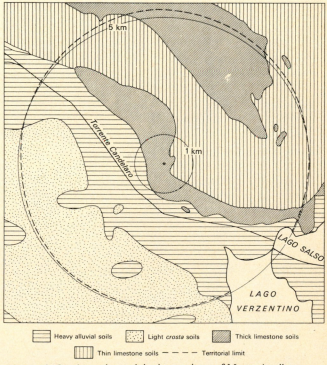

Figure 13. One-hour site exploitation territory of Monte Aquilone.

Coppa Nevigata (Figure 14)

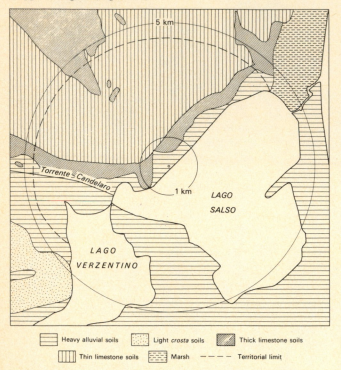

Figure 14. One-hour site exploitation territory of Coppa Nevigata.

Legend: Heavy alluvial soils | Light *crosta* soils | Thick limestone soils | Thin limestone soils | Marsh | --- Territorial limit

Territory

Roughly semi-circular, being truncated to the east and south by the former Lago Salso and Lago Verzentino, drained since 1900. A small segment of land lying between the two lakes may, however, have been accessible to exploitation. The perimeter of the territory varies from *c.* 4.5–4.7 km from the site. Total area *c.* 30 km².

Topography and drainage

To the north and northwest the land rises fairly steadily to a maximum of *c.* 100 m above the level of the site (*c.* 10 m). These hills are drained by small, but steep-sided, seasonal gullies. To the west the valley of the Candelaro, and to the south, the surface is flat, with almost no relief. Drainage was greatly impeded until the recent land reclamation projects.

Soils

Most of the area within the territory is covered by thin stony soils (Terra Rossa) with much limestone bedrock at or just below the surface. This accounts for *c.* 62 per cent of the territory. Deeper limestone soils around the edges of the hills cover *c.* 16 per cent, the remaining *c.* 22 per cent containing heavy alluvial clays. The site itself lies on heavy clay, and within a 1 km distance of the site *c.* 12 per cent of the area carries thin limestone soils, *c.* 40 per cent deeper limestone soils, and *c.* 48 per cent alluvial clays.

Modern exploitation

The thin limestone hill soils carry sparse vegetation which is utilised as winter rough grazing by sheep and goats which spend the summer in the Gargano and Abruzzi. The deeper limestone soils which are found between the hills and the heavy clays are of variable quality, depending largely on depth; they are exploited primarily as arable areas, with wheat and barley grown in rotation with hay in fallow years. On the clays wheat and irrigated sugar beet predominate. Wheat yields average 30–5 q/ha in good years, *c.* 16 q/ha in bad years.

La Panetteria (Figure 15)

Territory

Nearly circular, with the perimeter varying from *c.* 4.6 km to *c.* 5.0 km from the site. Total area *c.* 70 km².

Topography and drainage

To the north the ground rises quite steeply to *c.* 200 m (some 60 m above the site) at a distance of 2 km, dropping from there into the valley of the Canale Pontesano (*c.* 110 m), rising again to *c.* 150 m by the edge of the territory. To the west the relief is hummocky, rising to over 200 m at the edge of the territory. About 1 km to the south of the site, and flowing roughly west–east, is the Triòlo river, which falls from *c.* 170 m to *c.* 100 m from the western to the eastern extremities of the territory. South of the Triòlo the ground rises slightly, thereafter remaining relatively flat to the edge of the

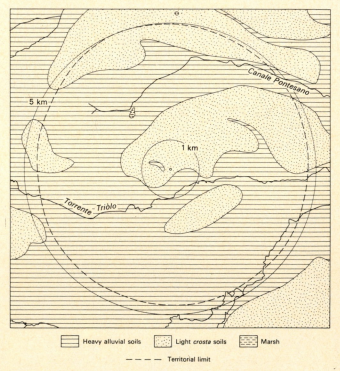

Legend: Heavy alluvial soils | Light *crosta* soils | Marsh | --- Territorial limit

Figure 15. One-hour site exploitation territory of Panetteria.

territory. The site is thus on the southern edge of a ridge running east–west between two river valleys.

Soils

Broadly speaking the high ground, and in particular the steeper slopes, are covered with light *crosta* soils, which comprise *c.* 32 per cent of the area within the territory. The river valleys and areas of unpronounced relief carry heavy clays, totalling *c.* 68 per cent. The site is on *crosta* soils, which account for *c.* 68 per cent of the soils within 1 km of the site, clays occurring over the other *c.* 32 per cent of the area.

Modern exploitation

The territory is almost exclusively exploited by arable agriculture, wheat being the dominant crop. Small amounts of sugar beet and maize occur to north and west of the site, and some olives and vines, particularly to the south. Good average wheat yields are 30 q/ha, with up to 40 q/ha at best, and as low as 20 q/ha in a poor year. With horse ploughing, average yields used to be 10–15 q/ha, with a 20 q/ha maximum. Some sheep remain in the area all year round, but their summer feed consists of hay and other fodder crops.

Località Fiorentino (Figure 16)

Territory

Nearly circular, the perimeter varying from *c.* 4.8 km to *c.* 5.0 km from the site. Total area *c.* 70 km².

Topography and drainage

To the north the ground drops steeply from *c.* 200 m to *c.* 110 m to the Canale S. Maria at *c.* 1.0 km from the site. A low ridge separates the Canale S. Maria from the Canale di Figurella, *c.* 3.5 km from the site, after which the ground level again rises gently. To the west the level falls steeply to the Canale S. Maria, thereafter rising slowly to the edge of the territory. To the south the ground falls steadily to *c.* 140 m at Il Canaletto, *c.* 3.5 km from the site, after which the level rises again. To the east the level falls slowly throughout the territory, being *c.* 130 m at the edge. The territory as a whole can be seen as a series of parallel valleys and ridges, oriented approximately west–east. The site occupies a position on the crest of one of the ridges.

Soils

The river valleys and much of the lower lying land are covered with heavy clays in which riverine gravels also appear in some areas. This soil accounts for *c.* 67 per cent of the territory. The ridges, and in particular areas with steep slopes, carry a light *crosta* soil, with the *crosta* in some cases very near the surface, giving a very thin stony soil; these soils total *c.* 33 per cent. The site is on *crosta* soil, which accounts for *c.* 65 per cent of the area within 1 km of the site; the other *c.* 35 per cent being heavy clay soils.

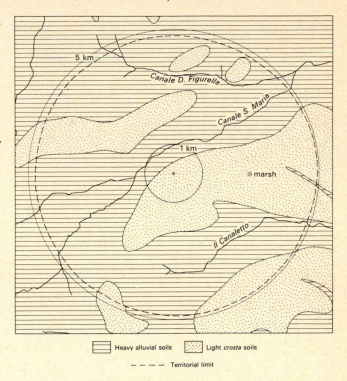

Figure 16. One-hour site exploitation territory of Fiorentino.

Modern exploitation

The valley and lower slope soils grow primarily wheat, with sugar beet and vegetables as rotation crops. Flatter areas on the ridges are exploited in the same way, but many of the slopes are too steep to permit this, and especially along the northern edge of the ridge to the east of the site soils are often too thin and poor to allow arable agriculture. On the better of these areas olives and vines are grown, but much of it is given over to rough grazing. To the south of the site the slope is less extreme, and there is a mixture of cereals with vines and olives, with little rough grazing. On the ridge the best arable soils yield up to 30 q/ha in a good year. The valley clays yield up to 45 q/ha in a good year, 25 q/ha in poor–average years. Some cows are maintained all year round, fed in summer on artificial feeds. Sheep come in winter from the Abruzzi. Until recently there was a higher percentage of rough grazing and far more animals were maintained.

Località Casalorda (Figure 17)

Territory

Nearly circular, the perimeter varying from *c.* 4.8 km to *c.* 5.2 km from the site. Total area *c.* 75 km².

Topography and drainage

To the north the surface remains relatively flat, though to northwest there is a slight but steady gain in altitude to the edge of the territory. To the west the ground is flat across the valleys of the Canale Ferrante and the Canale S. Maria (at *c.* 3.5 km from

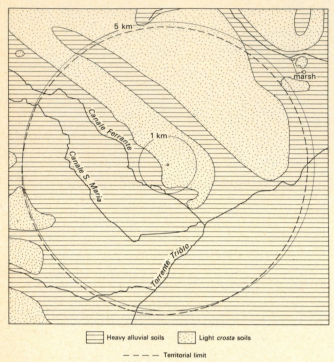

Heavy alluvial soils ▫ Light *crosta* soils

– – – – Territorial limit

Figure 17. One-hour site exploitation territory of Casalorda.

the site), thereafter rising slightly to the edge of the territory. Southward the level is essentially flat throughout across the Ferrante, S. Maria, and Triòlo valleys. To the east the ground falls steadily from the site (at *c.* 65 m) to the Triòlo valley (at *c.* 45 m) to the east. Drainage is basically from west to east.

Soils

The river valleys, and most of the southern and western sections of the territory, have heavy clay soils, which cover *c.* 69 per cent of the territory. Higher areas, particularly in the north and northeast sections, carry light *crosta* soils, which account for the remaining *c.* 31 per cent. The site itself is on *crosta* soils, which total *c.* 69 per cent of the area within 1 km of the site, the other *c.* 31 per cent being clay soils.

Modern exploitation

The main crop in most of the territory, particularly on the clay soils, is wheat, with sugar beet and fodder crops grown as rotation crops. However, considerable areas on the lightest soils are taken up with small vineyards, olives occurring less commonly. Some cows are pastured in the territory throughout the year, living on artificial feed and fodder crops during the summer. *C.* 30–40 q/ha are average wheat yields in good years.

Località Torretta (Figure 18)

Territory

Not walked, commentary based on hypothetical 5 km ring.

Topography and drainage

To the north the ground stays relatively level, sloping down very slightly into the Canale Vènole at the edge of the territory. To the northwest the ground rises gently throughout the territory from *c.* 50 m at the site to *c.* 80 m at the edge; while westward the ground rises to *c.* 65 m in the first 3 km from the site, remaining level thereafter. To the south the ground rises marginally, and to the east it falls marginally. The drainage pattern is broadly speaking from west and southwest to east and northeast.

Soils

Much of the area in the northwest segment of the territory, particularly higher ground, carries light *crosta* soils, which total *c.* 24 per cent of the territory as a whole. Heavy clay soils cover virtually the remainder of the territory (*c.* 76 per cent) with the exception of traces of marsh soil to the north. The site itself is on *crosta* soils which account for *c.* 44 per cent of the soils within 1 km of the site, the remaining *c.* 56 per cent being clay soils.

Modern exploitation

The primary crop throughout most of the territory is wheat, but in some areas, particularly on the lightest soils in the northwestern area, vines are the main crop. Some cattle are maintained in the area throughout the year, fed in summer on artificial feeds and fodder crops. The main animal exploited is, however, the sheep, which spends the summer in the Abruzzi, returning to the area in the autumn. Average wheat yields in a good year are 30–40 q/ha.

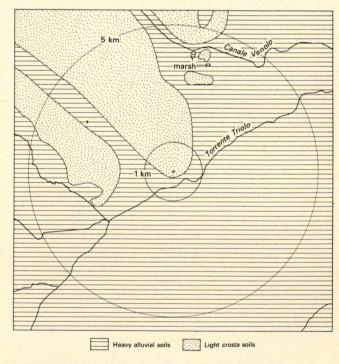

Heavy alluvial soils ▫ Light *crosta* soils

Figure 18. One-hour site exploitation territory of Torretta.

Pozzo Delle Capre (Figure 19)

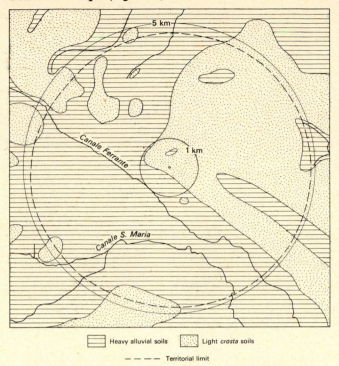

Figure 19. One-hour site exploitation territory of Pozzo delle Capre.

Territory

Nearly circular, with the perimeter varying from *c.* 4.5 km to *c.* 4.9 km from the site. Total area *c.* 70 km².

Topography and drainage

To the north the surface remains relatively flat for *c.* 2.5 km from the site, dropping gently thereafter towards the Radicosa valley. To the west the ground falls gently to the Canale Ferrante at *c.* 2 km from the site, after which the level steadily rises, reaching *c.* 130 m (*c.* 30 m above the site) at the edge of the territory. To the south the ground drops *c.* 25 m to the valleys of the Ferrante and S. Maria, rising again to *c.* 100 m at the edge of the territory. To the east the ground slopes down throughout the territory to *c.* 70 m at its perimeter.

Soils

The river valleys, and most of the area to the west and south of the site, are covered with heavy clays which account for *c.* 63 per cent of the area within the site territory. Many of the higher areas in the territory, in particular the eastern and northeastern section, are covered with light *crosta* soils, which total *c.* 37 per cent of the territory. The site is on *crosta* soils, which cover *c.* 64 per cent of the area within 1 km of the site, the remaining *c.* 36 per cent being under heavy clays.

Modern exploitation

Wheat is the main crop on the clay soils, with olives and vines occurring on the *crosta* soils, olives dominating. In good years wheat yields reach 40 q/ha, but 20–5 q/ha is common in poorer years.

Torrione del Casone (Figure 20)

Territory

Nearly circular, with the perimeter varying from *c.* 4.5 to *c.* 4.7 km from the site. Total area *c.* 65 km².

Topography and drainage

To the north the ground remains relatively flat to the edge of the territory, although to the northeast the level falls gently towards the Candelaro valley. To the west the surface rises steadily to *c.* 30 m above the site (at *c.* 45 m) at the edge of the territory. To the south the ground remains essentially level to the edge of the territory, while to the east the ground drops gently down the valley of the Canale Vènolo, falling by *c.* 10 m by the edge of the territory. The overall drainage pattern is from west to east.

Soils

The river valleys, and most of the eastern half of the territory, are covered with heavy clay soils which account for *c.* 58 per cent of the territory as a whole. The remaining *c.* 42 per cent are light

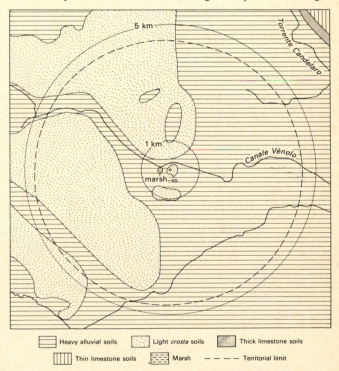

Figure 20. One-hour site exploitation territory of Torrione del Casone.

crosta soils, with the exception of traces of marsh soil. The site itself is on light *crosta* soils which account for *c.* 36 per cent of the area within 1 km of the site; clay soils account for *c.* 62 per cent, with a trace (*c.* 2 per cent) of marsh soil.

Modern exploitation

The primary crop throughout the territory is wheat, with vines occurring particularly in areas with very light, stony soils. Sugar beet, vegetables, and fodder crops are grown as rotation crops. Olives occur rarely, and grazing is confined to river banks and rare marshy areas. Sheep are grazed in the area during the winter, but spend the summer in the Abruzzi mountains. Wheat yields in good years average 30–40 q/ha, in poor years 20–5 q/ha.

Contrada Guadone (Figure 21)

Territory

Nearly circular, with the perimeter varying from *c.* 4.5 km to *c.* 4.9 km from the site. Total area *c.* 70 km².

Topography and drainage

To the north the ground falls gently from the site, at *c.* 85 m, to the Radicosa valley at *c.* 45 m. To the northwest the ground remains fairly level, while to the west it rises slowly to *c.* 100 m. To the south the ground falls slightly over the first 3 km, thereafter rising to the edge of the territory. To the east the level drops gently to *c.* 65 m at the edge of the territory.

Soils

Much of the north of the territory and the valley of the Canale Vènolo are covered with heavy clay deposits, which total *c.* 39 per cent of the territory. The remaining *c.* 61 per cent of the territory carries light *crosta* soils. The site itself is on *crosta* soils, which cover *c.* 97 per cent of the area within 1 km of the site, clay soils extending only to *c.* 3 per cent. These figures are to some degree hypothetical, however, as the modern town of San Severo covers a considerable proportion of the area within 1 km, obscuring the soil cover.

Modern exploitation

The main crop within the territory is olives, with vines as the second major element. This appears to be related to the preponderance of light soils in the San Severo area and to the cool and humid winds which particularly affect this area. Some wheat is grown, particularly on the heavier soils, which also support market garden plots near the city. In a good year wheat yields average 30 q/ha, in poorer years *c.* 20 q/ha.

Colle Tauro (Figure 22)

Territory

Nearly circular, with the perimeter varying from *c.* 4.5 km to *c.* 4.8 km from the site, except to the north, where the territory is truncated by the Lago di Lèsina, *c.* 3.5 km from the site. Total area *c.* 65 km².

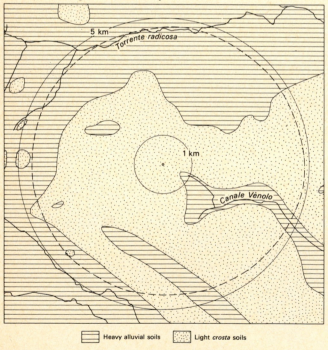

Figure 21. One-hour site exploitation territory of Contrada Guadone.

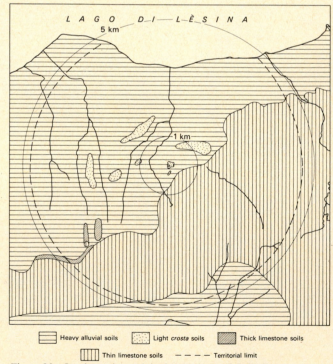

Figure 22. One-hour site exploitation territory of Colle Tauro.

Topography and drainage

To the north the surface slopes down from the site at *c.* 25 m, to the lake at sea level. To the west the ground is essentially level. To the south the ground rises steadily to *c.* 130 m at 3.5 km from the site, falling to *c.* 85 m by the edge of the territory. To the east the ground rises sharply to *c.* 160 m at 2 km from the site, rising only gently thereafter, reaching *c.* 180 m at the edge of the territory. The basic drainage pattern is to the north, from the ridge which occupies much of the southern portion of the territory into the Lago di Lèsina.

Soils

Most of the low-lying northern and western section of the territory is covered with heavy clay soils which total *c.* 56 per cent of the territory as a whole. The high ground to the south and east of the site has a scanty limestone soil, with much bedrock at or near the surface, which covers *c.* 41 per cent of the territory. Small patches of light *crosta* soil occur in the low-lying areas (*c.* 2 per cent), while at the foot of the limestone hills occur some areas of hill-wash soils (*c.* 1 per cent) which vary from light, stony soils to heavy clays in texture. The site itself is on light *crosta* soil, which covers *c.* 5 per cent of the area within 1 km of the site. Heavy clays account for *c.* 75 per cent and thin limestone soils for *c.* 20 per cent of this area.

Modern exploitation

Wheat is the primary crop on all the clay soils, and on much of the hill-wash and *crosta* soils. Sugar beet occurs as a rotation crop. Some of the lighter soils have vines, or (more rarely) olives. The thin limestone hill soils carry a scrub vegetation with *Quercus ilex* and other shrubs and grasses. These are used as permanent grazing for cattle and goats, as well as seasonal (winter) grazing for sheep which spend the summer in the Abruzzi.

Grotta Spagnoli (Figure 23)

Territory

Semi-circular to the southwest, but much curtailed to the north and east by the topographic influence of the Gargano. The perimeter varies from *c.* 4.4 km to *c.* 9.2 km from the site. Total area *c.* 190 km².

Topography and drainage

To the south and west of the site lies the Tavoliere plain, which rises westwards very gently from *c.* 25 m at the Candelaro, just over 1 km from the site, to *c.* 60 m at the perimeter of the territory. Due north of the site the altitude rises steeply to *c.* 400 m at *c.* 1 km from the site, then dropping into the Stignano valley; *c.* 5 km from the site the ground begins to rise again, reaching *c.* 400 m by the perimeter. Eastward the ground rises steeply to *c.* 600 m at 1.5 km from the site, broken plateau land stretching at that altitude to

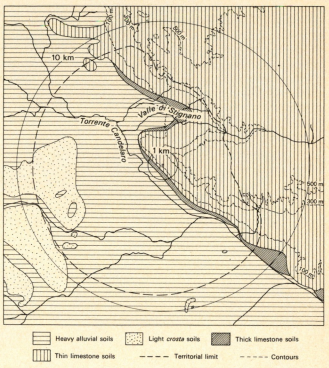

Figure 23. Two-hour site exploitation territory of Grotta Spagnoli.

the edge of the territory. The slopes of the Gargano are dissected by steep-sided gullies draining into the Candelaro valley which runs basically from the northwest to the southeast along the foot of the Gargano. The Stignano runs east–west into the Candelaro *c.* 3.5 km northwest of the site. The site, at an altitude of *c.* 150 m, is on the junction of the upland and lowland zones.

Soils

The Tavoliere to the south and west of the site is primarily covered with a heavy alluvial soil, which accounts for *c.* 64 per cent of the territory. A small area to the west of the site, towards the edge of the territory, carries light *crosta* soils, totalling *c.* 8 per cent. Between the Candelaro valley and the Gargano slopes lies a narrow band of light hill-wash soils (*c.* 4 per cent), the remaining *c.* 24 per cent being thin limestone soils on the Gargano hills. The site itself is on thin limestone soils, which account for *c.* 73 per cent of the area within 1 km of the site, the remaining area comprising hill-wash soils (*c.* 17 per cent) and heavy alluvium (*c.* 10 per cent).

Modern exploitation

The portion of the territory on the Tavoliere is exploited primarily as arable, with wheat as the main crop. Fodder crops and irrigated sugar beet occur as rotation crops, and a small area is used for intensive vegeculture. Towards the western extremity of the territory intensive olive and vine cultivation is the general mode of exploitation of light *crosta* soils. In a good year wheat yields average *c.* 30–40 q/ha, dropping to *c.* 20 q/ha in poorer years. The band of hill-wash soils separating the Tavoliere from the Gargano is utilised primarily for olive cultivation, but the less stony areas carry cereals. Cereals grown on this soil are, however, less productive than those on the plain. The Gargano hill slopes and plateau are virtually exclusively used as rough grazing, mainly for sheep and goats. While some flocks are based in this area all the year round, only coming down to the lower slopes and plain in periods of heavy snow cover, and subsisting in winter to some extent on artificial feeds, the Gargano is primarily used as a summer grazing area for animals which winter on the plain.

Pescorosso (Figure 24)

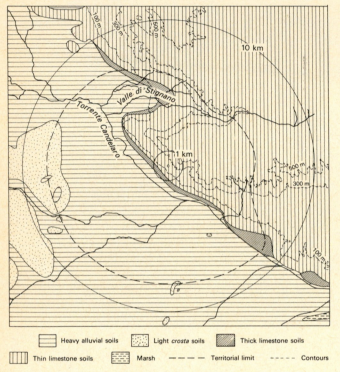

Figure 24. Two-hour site exploitation territory of Pescorosso.

Territory

Semi-circular to the southwest, but distorted to the north and east by the topographic influence of the Gargano. The perimeter varies from *c.* 4.9 km to *c.* 8.6 km from the site. Total area *c.* 165 km².

Topography and drainage

To the south and west lies the Tavoliere plain, essentially flat at an altitude of *c.* 30–40 m. The site is at *c.* 200 m, the land sloping down from it to the southwest, where the Candelaro valley lies at *c.* 1.5 km from the site. Due north of the site the altitude climbs steeply to over 600 m at *c.* 1.5 km from the site, then falling sharply into the Stignano valley. To the northwest the level rises to *c.* 600 m within 1 km of the site; broken plateau land stretches for a further 3 km, after which the ground falls steeply into the Stignano valley. To the east the ground reaches *c.* 600 m at *c.* 2 km from the site, thereafter remaining roughly level. The slopes of the Gargano are dissected by deep, steep-sided gulleys running

from the crest down to the Tavoliere where the Candelaro valley, following the edge of the hills southeast, is the major drainage feature of the territory. The Stignano flows east-west, running into the Candelaro towards the northwestern extremity of the territory. The site is situated at the junction of the upland and lowland zones.

Soils

Almost all the territory to the south and west of the Candelaro carries heavy alluvium, which accounts for *c.* 60 per cent of the territory. Small patches of *crosta* soil in this area total only *c.* 4 per cent of the territory. Immediately to the northeast of the Candelaro, between the river and the Gargano is a narrow band of light hill wash soils, amounting to *c.* 5 per cent of the territory; the remaining 31 per cent (the Gargano) carrying thin limestone soils with much limestone bedrock exposed. The site itself is on thin limestone soils, which cover *c.* 88 per cent of the area within 1 km of the site, the remaining area carrying hill wash soils (*c.* 11 per cent) and a trace (*c.* 1 per cent) of alluvium.

Modern exploitation

The portion of the territory on the Tavoliere is exploited almost exclusively by arable agriculture; wheat is the primary crop with fodder crops and irrigated sugar beet as common rotation elements. Wheat yields vary from 30–40 q/ha in good years, to about 20 q/ha in poorer years. The band of hill-wash soil separating the Tavoliere from the Gargano is primarily utilised for olive and almond production, but the least stony areas carry some cereals. The Gargano is virtually entirely used as rough grazing, especially as an area of summer grazing for sheep and goats which winter on the Tavoliere. However, some farms situated at the base of the hill slopes are able to graze the Gargano and slopes throughout most of the year, moving stock to the Tavoliere only during periods of considerable snow cover.

Grotta Paglicci (Figure 25)

Territory

Semi-circular to the southwest, but considerably distorted and restricted elsewhere by the topographic influence of the Gargano. The perimeter varies from *c.* 4.6 km to *c.* 9.5 km from the site. Total area *c.* 180 km².

Topography and drainage

The area to the south and west of the site is essentially flat, the land beyond the Candelaro being part of the Tavoliere plain, below 50 m in altitude. North of the Candelaro the lower slopes of the Gargano rise steeply to over 500 m within *c.* 2.5 km of the site, achieving a maximum altitude of nearly 700 m towards the northern extremity of the territory. The southwestern facing slope is dissected by deeply incised valleys, running roughly parallel to each other, a factor considerably restricting movement other than along the valleys. To the south of the site on the Tavoliere drainage is mainly through the Candelaro to the southeast, and the tributaries running into the Candelaro from the southwest. The site, at just over 100 m, is thus at the junction of the upland and lowland zones.

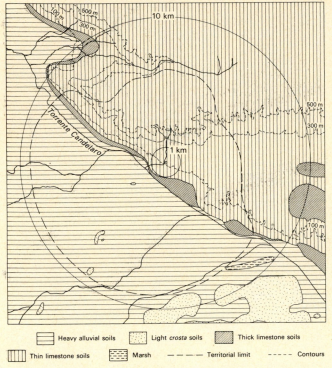

Figure 25. Two-hour site exploitation territory of Grotta Paglicci.

Soils

The Tavoliere to the south of the Candelaro is virtually entirely covered by heavy alluvium, which accounts for *c*. 61 per cent of the area within the territory, but a trace of light *crosta* soil (less than 1 per cent) also occurs in this sector. Immediately adjacent to the north bank of the Candelaro, between the river and the Gargano, a narrow, discontinuous band of light hill-wash soils occurs (*c*. 3 per cent), sloping up from the plain itself. The rest of the territory contains exclusively thin limestone soils (*c*. 36 per cent) with much limestone bedrock occurring at the surface, and only rare small pockets of slightly thicker Terra Rossa. The site itself is on thin limestone soils, which account for 100 per cent of the area within 1 km of the site.

Modern exploitation

The portion of the territory which extends on the Tavoliere is exclusively exploited by arable agriculture, with wheat as the main crop, fodder crops and irrigated sugar beet occurring as rotation crops. Wheat yields vary from 30–40 q/ha in good years, to about 20 q/ha in poorer years. The band of light rendsina soils separating the Tavoliere proper from the hills carries some cereals in the least stony areas, but is primarily exploited by olive and almond cultivation. The Gargano is almost entirely utilised as rough grazing, especially for sheep and goats, but with the local

hardy white Pugliese breed of cattle occurring in areas where there is sufficient water for their summer requirements, and sufficient capital to provide for supplementary summer fodder. The lower slopes of the Gargano are commonly grazed on a year-round basis (a day's journey easily sufficing to move stock either to the plain or to the higher slopes when necessary). The major part of the Gargano is, however, used primarily as an area of summer grazing for stock (particularly goats, which thrive on the thick scrub vegetation which covers much of the Gargano) which winter on the Tavoliere. Small pockets of deeper soil occur in the northern sector of the territory, the best of which can support poor arable exploitation, but this is usually confined to barley, and yields are so poor as to discount this as a significant economic practice.

Grotta Scaloria (Figure 26)

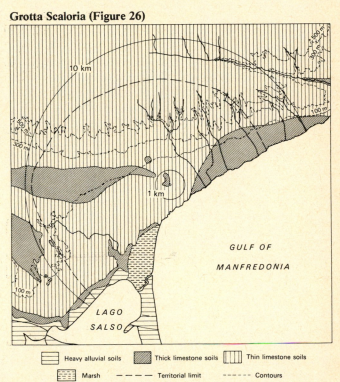

Figure 26. Two-hour site exploitation territory of Grotta Scaloria.

Territory

To the southeast of the site the territory is truncated by the Gulf of Manfredonia at *c*. 1.5 km from the site, while to the south–southwest the Lago Salso impinges at just over 7 km. The perimeter of the territory describes a relatively smooth arc varying in distance from the site from 7.0 km in the north and northwest, where the topographic impact of the Gargano is evident, to *c*. 9.5 km. Total area *c*. 145 km².

Topography and drainage

The site is at an altitude of *c*. 40 m, and a line running approximately southwest from it coincides roughly with the 50 m contour. To the south and east lies the Gulf of Manfredonia. Due west of the site the ground rises gently but steadily reaching an altitude of *c.* 120 m by the edge of the territory. To the north, the level rises slowly until the 150 m contour, *c.* 2.5 km from the site, after which the gradient increases, reaching the 500 m contour at *c.* 4.5 km from the site, and a maximum height of *c.* 750 m by the edge of the territory. Drainage is primarily from the high ground of the Gargano through steep, deeply incised gullies running south-southeast into the Gulf of Manfredonia.

Soils

Most of the territory carries thin limestone soils, which cover *c.* 75 per cent of the territory. Three main areas occur of thicker light limestone soils: northeast of the site, between the Gargano and the coast; west of the site, in a shallow basin on the low limestone plateau extending south from the Gargano; and along the southern edge of this plateau. These soils account for *c.* 20 per cent of the territory. The remaining area includes some coastal marsh deposits (*c.* 4 per cent) and a small area of heavy alluvium (*c.* 1 per cent) in the southwestern sector of the territory. The site is on thin limestone soils, which account for *c.* 90 per cent of the area within 1 km of the site, the remaining *c.* 10 per cent being a small pocket of thick Terra Rossa.

Modern exploitation

The thin limestone soils are used primarily for rough grazing, although in some areas olives and almonds are grown in addition. While those of the soils in this category below *c.* 300 m are especially used as winter grazing areas, the higher slopes in the north of the territory are in use primarily during the summer, although some stock remains in this area throughout the year. The thicker limestone soils are exploited primarily for wheat, with fodder crops grown as rotation crops. The small area of heavy alluvium in the territory is entirely used for arable agriculture, with wheat the main crop, irrigated sugar beet and lucerne occurring as rotation crops. On this heavy soil wheat yields rise as high as 40 q/ha in good years, averaging *c.* 30 q/ha, but on the lighter, stonier soils 25 q/ha is the maximum, with 20 q/ha a good average yield, dropping to 7–8 q/ha in poor years. Total failure of the crop is not unusual on the poorest soils now in use as arable.

Monte Saraceno (Figure 27)

Territory

The site is *c.* 0.5 km from the Gulf of Manfredonia, which considerably truncates the site territory to the southeast. The perimeter of the territory forms an irregular arc with a major distortion to the west of the site due to the effect of the Carbonara valley. The perimeter varies from *c.* 5.4 km to *c.* 7.4 km from the site. Total area *c.* 55 km².

Topography and drainage

The site at *c.* 250 m lies just to the south of the low-lying Piano di Mattinata in the lower Carbonara valley. West of the site the land

rises to *c.* 500 m at 4.5 km from the site, reaching *c.* 600 m by the edge of the territory. To the southwest lies the coastal plain, the Pianura di Macchia, sloping from the foot of the Gargano at *c.* 100 m down to the coast. The Pianura di Macchia is traversed by a series of deeply incised parallel gullies running down from the Gargano to the sea. To the north of the site the Piano di Mattinata stretches for *c.* 2 km, the land thereafter rising steeply, reaching *c.* 500 m by the edge of the territory. To the northeast, beyond the Piano di Mattinata, high ground again approaches the coast, with steep cliffs from 50–100 m high. The Carbonara runs roughly west–east in a deep, steep-sided valley until it reaches the Piano di Mattinata, *c.* 2 km from the coast. The only other considerable valley, the Tar di Lupo, runs north–south, entering the Gulf of Manfredonia *c.* 2 km north of the Carbonara.

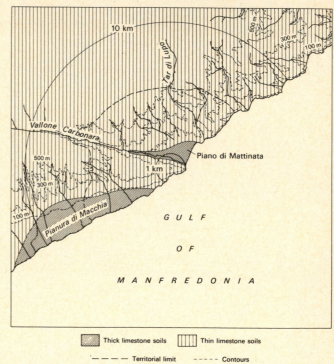

Figure 27. Two-hour site exploitation territory of Monte Saraceno.

Soils

Apart from the Piano di Mattinata and the Pianura di Macchia, the whole territory is covered by thin limestone soils, which total *c.* 85 per cent of the territory. The low-lying plains have thicker limestone soils, which account for the remaining *c.* 15 per cent of the territory. The site itself is on thin limestone soils, which account for *c.* 73 per cent of the area within 1 km of the site, the remaining 27 per cent being limestone valley soils.

Modern exploitation

The thin limestone soils are primarily used as rough grazing, but rough olives, and in particular almonds, commonly occur in conjunction with the rough grazing. The steep slopes of the lower valleys of the Carbonara and the Tar di Lupo have been extensively terraced, often producing plots of ground just wide enough to take a single row of trees. The plains are used almost exclusively for intensive olive and almond cultivation, the yield being up to double for olives grown here relative to the rough olives on the hillsides. Vines occur rarely on the Pianura di Macchia.

Grotta Drisiglia (Figure 28)

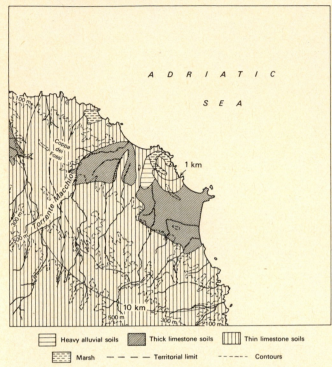

Figure 28. Two-hour site exploitation territory of Grotta Drisiglia.

Territory

To the north and east of the site the territory is truncated by the Adriatic Sea within a few hundred metres of the site. The perimeter of the territory forms an irregular arc varying from c. 7.2 km to c. 8.9 km from the site. Total area c. 90 km².

Topography and drainage

The site itself is at an altitude of c. 25 m, the level rising to over 100 m some 1.5 km to the south of the site, then falling again to c. 40 m before rising to c. 250 m at the edge of the territory. To the southwest the ground rises to a maximum altitude of c. 400 m at the edge of the territory, while to the west the Macchio valley separates these hills from the Coppa dei Fossi (c. 250 m) to the north. The basic drainage pattern of the territory is northeastwards, and while towards the outer edges of the territory the valleys form steep-sided gullies, the lower Macchio valley runs in a gently sloping floodplain some 1.5–2.0 km wide.

Soils

The majority (c. 71 per cent) of the territory is covered with thin limestone soils, which occupy almost all the land above 100 m. Two major lowland areas contain thicker hill-wash soils, which

total c. 25 per cent of the territory. Adjacent to the site is a substantial, horseshoe-shaped area of marsh soil, similar deposits occurring further along the coast to the northwest. Marsh soils account for c. 2 per cent of the territory, the remaining c. 2 per cent being heavy alluvial soil adjacent to the marsh deposits. The site is on thin limestone soils, which cover c. 69 per cent of the area within 1 km of the site. Marsh soils account for c. 31 per cent of this area.

Modern exploitation

The area of marsh soils adjacent to the site are at present used primarily for intensive market gardening, tomatoes being the main crop. This area of marsh has been recently drained however, and was previously exploited as an area of grazing, as is the other main area of marsh in the territory at this time (cf. commentary on Ariòla). The small area of heavy alluvial soil is partly used for market gardening, partly for cereals. The majority of the thick limestone soils are used for intensive olive cultivation, but the flattest, most productive of these soils carry wheat and vines, as well as olives. The thin limestone soils are used mainly as rough grazing, with olives and almonds occurring in some areas.

Ariòla (Figure 29)

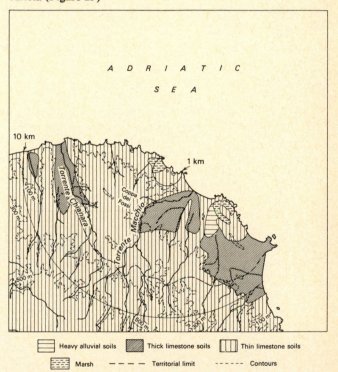

Figure 29. Two-hour site exploitation territory of Ariòla.

Territory

To the north and east the territory is truncated by the Adriatic Sea within a few hundred metres of the site. The perimeter forms an irregular arc varying from c. 6.2 km to c. 9.0 km from the site. Total area c. 85 km².

Topography and drainage

To the south of the site the ground rises to *c.* 150 m at 1.5 km from the site, then dropping into the Macchio valley, at *c.* 2 km, before rising again to *c.* 350 m by the edge of the territory. To the southwest and west of the site the ground rises to *c.* 300 m at *c.* 4 km from the site, thereafter falling towards the Chianara valley which approximates to the perimeter of the territory. Apart from the Macchio, flowing northeast into the sea to the southeast of the site, and the Chianara, flowing north into the sea to the west of the site, drainage in the territory is limited to narrow gullies running northeast and north from the Coppa dei Fossi.

Soils

c. 71 per cent of the territory carries thin limestone soils, which occupy almost all the high ground. The larger river valleys contain a thicker limestone soil, which accounts for *c.* 25 per cent of the territory. The site is adjacent to a considerable area of marsh, which with other similar areas amounts to *c.* 2 per cent of the territory as a whole, the remaining *c.* 2 per cent being an area of heavy alluvial soil in the southeastern sector of the territory. The site is on thin limestone soils, which account for *c.* 73 per cent of the area within 1 km of the site, marsh soils accounting for the remaining *c.* 27 per cent.

Modern exploitation

The area of marsh adjacent to the site today is used as grazing, particularly for cattle. This is a favoured area of summer grazing, as the relatively high water-table ensures a longer season of plant growth. In winter, however, it is flooded, and the stock must be moved elsewhere. Other areas of marsh deposit in the territory have been recently drained, and are used for intensive market gardening (cf. commentary on Grotta Drisiglia). The areas of limestone valley soils are used primarily for intensive olive production, but the best of these soils grow wheat. The thin limestone soils are used as rough grazing, especially for cattle and goats. Cattle grazing the marsh areas in summer spend about half of each day in the more wooded areas of inland grazing, which are in places under forestry management. Rough olives occur occasionally inland.

Grotta Manaccora (Figure 30)

Territory

The site is immediately on the coast, and to the north the territory is truncated by the Adriatic Sea. The perimeter of the territory forms an irregular arc to the south of the site, varying from *c.* 5.5 km to *c.* 7.9 km from the site. Total area *c.* 65 km².

Topography and drainage

To the west of the site land rises steeply from the coast forming an irregular cliff, broken only by the valley of the Chianara at *c.* 3 km from the site, and by a minor valley just before the edge of the territory. To the east the cliffs become lower, and are broken in the area of the Palude Sfinale, *c.* 4 km from the site, and by the Macchio valley at *c.* 6–8 km from the site. Due south of the site the ground rises fairly steeply and steadily, reaching *c.* 300 m at 3 km from the site, remaining at approximately this height from there to the edge of the territory. Apart from the Chianara and Macchio valleys which flow in considerable flood plains in their lower reaches, the drainage is primarily through steep, narrow gullies flowing down the northern slopes of the Coppa dei Fossi and Coppa del Fornaro.

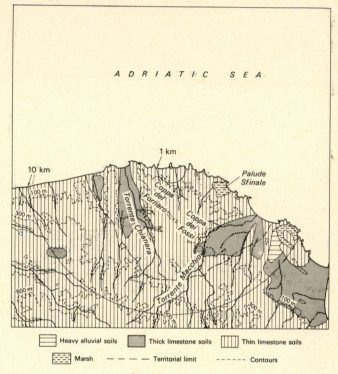

Figure 30. Two-hour site exploitation territory of Grotta Manaccora.

Soils

The majority of the territory (*c.* 75 per cent) carries thin limestone soils, which cover most of the land above 100 m. The lower reaches of the larger river valleys, in particular the Macchio and Chianara, contain substantial areas of thicker limestone soils, totalling *c.* 24 per cent of the territory. The remaining *c.* 1 per cent is marsh soil, the main area being the Palude Sfinale to the east of the site. The site is on thin limestone soils, which account for 100 per cent of the area within 1 km of the site.

Modern exploitation

The thin limestone hill soils are almost exclusively used for rough grazing, although some rough olives occur with the grazing in some areas; patches also occur of planned afforestation. The rough grazing is used primarily for cattle and goats; and while small numbers of animals are maintained on the coast throughout the year, the majority spend the summer months on the higher ground further inland, spending only the winter on the coast. The area of marsh to the east of the site is used as summer grazing for cattle in particular, being flooded in the winter. The limestone valley soils are used mainly for intensive olive production, but the most productive areas of these soils support wheat, with some small market gardens. Average yields for wheat are *c*. 10–20 q/ha, with up to 25 q/ha in especially good years and as low as 3 q/ha in poor years.

Coppa Cardone (Figure 31)

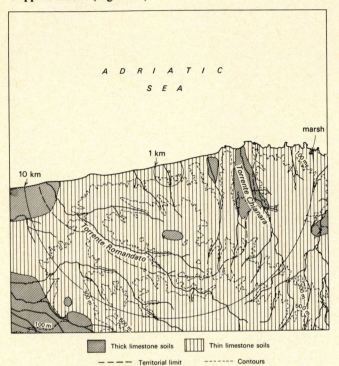

Figure 31. Two-hour site exploitation territory of Coppa Cardone.

Territory

To the north the territory is truncated at *c*. 0.5 km from the site by the Adriatic Sea. The perimeter of the territory thus forms an irregular semi-circle varying from *c*. 5.7 km to *c*. 9.0 km from the site. Relatively easy routes of access along the coast to the west are seen in the extent of the territory in this direction, whereas to the south, and particularly to the east the topographic impact on the size of the territory is evident. Total area *c*. 85 km².

Topography and drainage

Immediately to the north of the site, which is at *c*. 50 m, the ground drops steeply to the coast, *c*. 0.5 km away. This slope continues in the form of a low cliff *c*. 5.5 km along the coast to the west of the site. Beyond this point the coast topography is less pronounced, flatter ground sloping down towards the Lago di Varano. To the east the coastal line of hills is broken by a minor valley at *c*. 3.0 km from the site and by the more considerable Chianara valley at *c*. 5.0 km. To the south the ground rises steadily, reaching *c*. 500 m at the southern extremity of the territory. The basic drainage pattern is south–north, with the major excep-

tion of the Romandato valley, running from the south of the territory northwestwards.

Soils

The great majority of the territory (*c*. 90 per cent) is covered with thin limestone soils, which in some areas have been terraced to form small stony fields. The remaining 10 per cent consists of thicker limestone soils, almost all of which are concentrated in two valleys in the eastern sector of the territory and in the low-lying area between the lower Romandato valley and the Lago di Varano. The site itself is on thin limestone soils, which account for 100 per cent of the soils within 1 km of the site.

Modern exploitation

The thin limestone soils are terraced in places, particularly in the northern half of the territory, to produce small stony fields. The primary crop is olives, with carobs and less frequently almonds occurring among them. A large proportion of these soils however, especially inland, are used as rough grazing, combined with softwood forestry in some areas. The areas of deeper limestone soil are primarily used for cereals, especially wheat, with forage crops as rotation crops. However, these soils also support some intensively cultivated olives, and (near the mouth of the Romandato) vines. Wheat yields reach 20–30 q/ha in good years, but average only 10–20 q/ha, and drop as low as 3 q/ha in poor years. Small herds of Friesian or Brown Swiss cattle for milk production are maintained in the area near the coast throughout the year. Many sheep and goats, as well as the hardy Pugliese breed of beef cattle spend only the winter months on the coast, spending the rest of the year in the hills.

Grotta Pippola (Figure 32)

Territory

To the west the territory is truncated by the Lago di Varano, the shores of which approach to within *c*. 1 km of the site. To the north, the territory is also slightly curtailed by the Adriatic Sea. The perimeter of the territory forms an irregular ring varying from *c*. 5.9 km to *c*. 8.3 km from the site, the shape being considerably influenced by the topography of the hills and valleys. Total area *c*. 115 km².

Topography and drainage

Due west of the site, at *c*. 60 m, the ground falls quite steeply to the Lago di Varano, *c*. 1 km from the site; while to the north the level drops more gently, reaching the coast *c*. 5.5 km from the site. To the east of the site the Correntino and Antonino valleys reach up into hills which attain an altitude of 300–500 m by the edge of the territory. Southward the ground slopes down slightly into the Correntino and Antonino flood plains, rising again at *c*. 4 km from the site, reaching 300–500 m at the edge of the territory. These two rivers drain east–west into the Lago di Varano, the other major river being the Romandato, which drains northwestward into the Adriatic.

Soils

The majority of the territory is covered with thin limestone soils, which account for *c.* 75 per cent of the territory. The lower valleys of the Correntino and Antonino form a substantial block of thicker limestone soil to the south of the site, another occurring in the low-lying area in the north of the territory between the Lago di Varano and the lower Romandato valley. This soil accounts for the remaining *c.* 25 per cent of the territory. The site is on thin limestone soils, which account for *c.* 66 per cent of the area within 1 km of the site, thicker limestone soils covering the remaining *c.* 34 per cent.

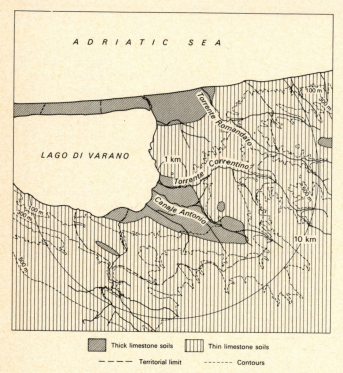

Figure 32. Two-hour site exploitation territory of Grotta Pippola.

Modern exploitation

On the thicker limestone soils, particularly in the lower-lying and less stony areas, wheat is the primary crop, with irrigated maize and vegetables occurring as a secondary element. To the north, between the Lago di Varano and the lower Romandato valley, vines are an important crop. In the poorer, more stony areas of this soil olives are the main crop, almonds occurring less frequently. The thin limestone soils are utilised primarily as rough grazing, especially for sheep, but rough olives are commonly associated with the grazing. Wheat crops on the thicker soils average *c.* 25 q/ha in good years. A number of the sheep and goats in the area are maintained on a semi-sedentary basis, being maintained on fodder crops, artificial feeds, and prunings from the olives during the lean period. However, an important seasonal element remains

the dominant feature of the animal economy, with the lowland grazing areas providing winter grazing for stock which spends the summers in the higher areas of the Gargano.

Grotta dell' Angelo (Figure 33)

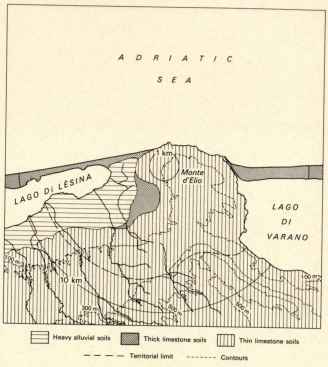

Figure 33. Two-hour site exploitation territory of Grotta dell' Angelo.

Territory

To the north of the site the territory is truncated at just over 1 km from the site by the Adriatic Sea. To the east, the Lago di Varano impinges at the edge of the territory, as does the Lago di Lèsina to a lesser extent to the west. The perimeter of the territory forms an arc from *c.* 6.4 km to *c.* 8.6 km from the site, distorted by the high ground lying to the south-southwest of the site. Total area *c.* 90 km².

Topography and drainage

To the north and west of the site, which is at just over 100 m, the ground falls steeply in the first 0.5 km, thereafter sloping more gently down, reaching the Adriatic *c.* 1.5 km from the site to the north, and reaching the Adriatic and the Lago di Lèsina at *c.* 4 km to the west. A low-lying plain some 2 km wide borders the southern edge of Lago di Lèsina, the land sloping up to the south of this reaching an altitude of 300–500 m at the edge of the territory. To the east of the site the ground rises to over 200 m in the first 2 km, falling to the Adriatic and Lago di Varano at *c.* 5 km from the site. The basic drainage pattern is northwestwards from the Gargano into the Lago di Lèsina.

Soils

The majority of the territory, including all the area above 50 m, carries thin limestone soils, which account for *c.* 71 per cent of the territory. Bordering the eastern and southern edges of the Lago di Lèsina is a low-lying plain which is covered with a heavy clay soil, primarily derived from Terra Rossa deposits washed down from above. This soil covers *c.* 19 per cent of the territory. In one small area between the hills and the clay deposit, admixture of a more stony hill-wash and the clays produces a light soil, while on some coastal stretches mixture of the clays with sandy deposits has produced a comparable soil. This light soil accounts for the remaining *c.* 10 per cent of the territory. The site is on thin limestone soils which account for 100 per cent of the soils within 1 km of the site.

Modern exploitation

The predominant thin limestone soils are used for rough grazing, which in some of the flatter areas contains sparse rough olives. In areas of steeper topography, however, such as in the vicinity of the site, the soil is very scanty, a high percentage of the surface (up to 50 per cent) being bare limestone rock, the vegetation being a thick woody scrub. This area, although it carries some animals throughout the year is primarily used for winter grazing of sheep and goats which spend the summer higher up in the Gargano. The light soils are used primarily for wheat, but in some areas support irrigated sugar beet and maize, vegetable crops, and intensively cultivated olives. The wheat yields on this soil are, however, lower than on the clay soils bordering on the Lago di Lèsina, on which are grown irrigated fruit and vegetables, sugar beet and fodder crops, as well as the main crop, wheat. Wheat yields in this latter area can equal 30–40 q/ha in a good year.

REFERENCES

Barker, G. (1972) The conditions of cultural and economic growth in the Bronze Age of central Italy. *Proc. prehist. Soc.* **38,** 170–208.

Battaglia, R. (1956) Ricerche e scoperte paletnologiche nel Gargano (1955–1956). *Riv. Sci. preist.* **11,** 1–30.

Bradford, J. S. P. (1949) 'Buried landscapes' in southern Italy. *Antiquity* **23,** 58–72.

(1950) The Apulia Expedition: an interim report. *Antiquity* **24,** 84–95.

Bradford, J. S. P. & Williams-Hunt, P. R. (1946) Siticulosa Apulia. *Antiquity* **20,** 191–200.

Chisholm, M. (1968) *Rural Settlement and Land Use,* 2nd ed. London: Hutchinson.

Colaciccio, G. (1955) *La Bonifica del Tavoliere.* Foggia: S. Pescatore.

Delano Smith, C. (1967) Ancient landscapes of the Tavoliere, Apulia. *Publ. Inst. Brit. Geogr.* **41,** 203–8.

Delibrius, G. & Datil, P. (1966) Calcareous formations of lacustrine origin in the upper Quaternary in the mountainous region of the central Sahara and their dating. *C. R. Acad. Sci. Paris* **262D,** 55–8.

Deuser, R. G. (1972) Core samples from the Black Sea. *J. geophys. Res.* **77,** 1071.

Follieri, M. (1971) Researches on prehistoric agriculture. Paper presented at the Third International Congress of the Museum of Agriculture, Budapest.

Higgs, E. S. & Vita-Finzi, C. (1972) Prehistoric economies: a territorial approach. In *Papers in Economic Prehistory,* ed. E. S. Higgs, pp. 27–36. Cambridge: Cambridge University Press.

Jarman, M. R. (1972) A territorial model for archaeology: a behavioural and geographical approach. In *Models in Archaeology,* ed. David L. Clarke, pp. 705–33. London: Methuen.

Kovda, V. A. & Samilova, E. M. (1968) Possibility of determining the age of hydromorphic soils from their $CaCO_3$ content. *C. R. Acad. Sci. U.R.S.S.* **182,** 1201–3.

Lenormant, F. (1883) *À Travers l'Apulie et la Lucanie.* Paris: Lévy.

Palma di Cesnola, A. (1960–1) Risultati paletnologici di una prima esplorazione della Foresta Umbra. *Bull. Paletn. ital.* **13,** 153–86.

Puglisi, S. M. (1948) Le culture dei capannicoli sul promontorio Gargano. *R. C. Accad. Lincei.* **8,** 3–57.

Russi, V. (1966) Notizario. Provincia di Foggia. *Riv. Sci. preist.* **21,** 430–1.

(1967) Notizario. Provincia di Foggia. *Riv. Sci. preist.* **22,** 449–51.

(1969) Notizario. Provincia di Foggia. *Riv. Sci. preist.* **24,** 375–7.

Slicher van Bath, B. H. (1963) *The Agrarian History of Western Europe A.D. 500–1850.* London: Edward Arnold.

Stevens, C. E. (1966) Agriculture and rural life in the later Roman Empire. In *The Cambridge Economic History,* Vol. 1, ed. M. M. Postan, pp. 92–124. Cambridge: Cambridge University Press.

Tiné, S. (1968) Alcuni dati circa il sistema di raccolta idrica nei villaggi neolitici del Foggiano. *Atti XI e XII Riun. scient. Ist. Ital. Preist. Protost.* 69–73.

Vinogradov, A. V., Mamedov, E. D. & Stepanov, I. N. (1969) Ancient soils in the Kyzylkun sands. *Pedology, Leningr.* **9,** 33–45.

Vitrani, G. (1968) Progressi e prospettive del'agricoltura della Capitanata. *La Bonifica* **22,** 27–46.

White, K. D. (1970) *Roman Farming.* London: Thames and Hudson.

Whitehouse, R. D. (1968) Settlement and economy in southern Italy in the Neothermal Period. *Proc. Prehist. Soc.* **34,** 332–67.

(1969) The Neolithic pottery sequence in southern Italy. *Proc. prehist. Soc.* **35,** 267–310.

APPENDIX A. SITE CATCHMENT ANALYSIS:
A concise guide to field methods

A brief statement of some of the relevant field techniques accompanied the discussion of site catchment analysis in the first volume of this series (Higgs & Vita-Finzi, 1972). The present outline attempts to treat the question of methods more systematically. The exercise can be justified on several counts. To begin with, any assessment of the findings hitherto obtained must take into account the nature of the data, and hence the procedures by which they were obtained. Secondly, site catchment analysis depends for its success on a large body of comparative information, and this in turn requires that field procedures be standardised as far as possible. Thirdly, those who accept the validity of a territorial approach to site interpretation, but are hesitant to discuss soils, landforms, vegetation, and other attributes of the territory, may be encouraged to do so once they are given some kind of guidance. And, finally, constructive criticism of the criteria adopted for demarcating the territories, and for subdividing them into terrain categories, cannot be discussed in the absence of a formalised set of provisional ground rules.

It is as well to remind oneself that the aim of the site catchment analysis *when applied to a prehistoric site* is to assess the resource potential of the area exploited from that site. The two essential preliminary steps are consequently to define the area and to ascertain how far its character and its soils today deviate from those prevailing at the time of occupation.

DELIMITING THE TERRITORY

The minimum number of 'radii' required to define the boundary of the exploitation territory is four. For simplicity the cardinal directions (N, S, E, W) have been adopted as the standard. A radius measured by one hour's walk is used for agricultural sites, and one equivalent to two hours for hunting and gathering sites. Where the nature of the site is in doubt it is advisable to adopt the longer radius and at the same time to record the position of the one-hour boundary. Additional radii can then be walked to areas where interpolation between the four measured points is hampered by rough terrain, the presence of marshy ground, cliffs, or other obstacles.

COMPOSITION OF THE TERRITORY

This heading subsumes two operations: an estimate of the changes undergone by the catchment since the period under review, and an evaluation of the terrain (in terms of potential productivity) duly corrected for such changes. The terrain classification recommended here is intended to make some correction possible in retrospect. Thus a marsh now present may be eliminated from the territorial map should it become obvious that it is a recent development; conversely marshy soils can be given full marsh status if their drainage is subsequently found to post-date occupation (cf. Vita-Finzi & Higgs, 1970).

Stage 1 (outward journey)

Since the primary aim of this stage is to define the boundary point, detours and halts must be avoided; if they are unavoidable, suitable correction must be made to the time–distance measurement. The observer should record in his log book:

(a) Gross changes in soil colour and texture. Where possible, draw boundaries between major soil types. Note that texture (i.e. grain-size) is the chief item of information required, and that a little practice will enable the observer to class a soil as silt-clay, sandy silt, and the like with considerable accuracy.

(b) Ground slope, to be measured at regular intervals with the help of a pocket alidade. A useful strategem is to sight back at objects which the observer has found to be at eye level, so as to obtain a reading in degrees directly. Pronounced breaks of slope will facilitate the drawing of soil boundaries. Prominent features likely (or known) to be marked on published topographic maps will of course facilitate the extrapolation of soil and topographic boundaries well beyond the transect line.

(c) The presence of pits, gully walls, and other sources of sections in the material underlying the ground being traversed.

(d) Sources of water: wells, springs, and the like.

Stage 2 (return journey)

During this stage the observer will:

(a) Inspect the sections observed on the outward journey for artefacts, charcoal, and other clues to the age of the host deposit. Thus the presence of sherds in the banks of a stream which has cut into a plain within the territory is taken to indicate that the plain is either contemporaneous with the sherds or younger. It is essential to determine the depth of the contact between the dated deposit and the underlying rock or sediment, and if possible to estimate how steeply the contact slopes, as this will give some impression of the older topography prior to its burial.

(b) Measure the depth of water in wells, estimate the flow of springs, and in other ways estimate water resources. The first requires a marked line and a weight which is manifestly clean.

(c) The crucial task of Stage 2 is to integrate the various observations into a map of potential productivity. The following categories have been found widely applicable:

Class I: land which is potentially or already suitable for arable cultivation. Possible qualifications are a slope of less than 15°, an absence of large stones and boulders (note evidence of *épierrage*), soil depth and texture guaranteeing good drainage.

223

Irrigated land must be distinguished as a percentage of the total, as should the proportion now devoted to arable as distinct from grazing. Existing tree cover should be noted but ignored in the assessment of the site potential.

Class II: rough grazing land where there is a major impediment to tillage, such as excessive slope, a large proportion of rock outcrops, etc. Localised cultivation, such as vines, olive trees, and the like, must be recorded and the area they occupy assessed as a percentage.

Class III: unproductive land – swamp, sand, bedrock, etc. subject to correction for drainage, irrigation, and other factors, or for natural changes.

Miscellaneous: land which is difficult to classify is better recorded under this head and subsequently allocated according to the needs of the investigation.

Once the four axes have been fully developed, the rest of the catchment map can be filled in by further ground inspection coupled with reference to air photographs, existing land use and soil maps, and other sources.

MODERN PARALLELS

It is essential to check the findings of site catchment analysis with a study of present-day land potential. The value of matching a nearby agricultural site with a modern subsistence farm is self-evident; yet there is much to be gained from making analogous comparisons even when all the modern farms in the area are engaged in cash-crop production, or when the site represents a hunting and gathering economy. The modern farm will still give some indication of the more productive soils, or of those areas most suited to pasture; again, seasonal changes in productivity are likely to be manifested however advanced the technology, and these must be understood before embarking on a reconstruction of patterns of animal migration.

Information should be obtained by the customary methods of sampling local opinion. A number of prepared questions should be used, bearing on yields, mechanical implements, sources of tractive power, fertilisers, and other items likely to yield a map of productivity and the extent to which it has been distorted by technology. Information on earlier periods is also valuable. Some of the points to be raised both at village and at farm level are listed below.

Plants

(1) Yield of barley, wheat, and fodder crops per unit of land per annum, and gross differences in yield within the territory or in terrains analogous to those represented within the catchment.
(2) What crop rotation is practised.
(3) Time of year when crops are sown and harvested.
(4) How far away from the village it is thought profitable to exploit the land.
(5) Extent of land exploited by the villages. This is not necessarily the same as the village boundary, and should be plotted on a map.
(6) What fertilisers, particularly artificial, are used.
(7) The reasons for some suitable land not being ploughed.
(8) Changes in the land, in the territory, and in techniques within the memory of living inhabitants.
(9) Changes in water supplies.
(10) Degree of self-sufficiency.
(11) Supplementary food sources (e.g. fishing, hunting, and gathering activities).

Animals

(1) Numbers of different species within the herds. The age at which they are discarded. Lambing or calving percentage. Predator loss. Value of main crops, wool, meat, milk, etc., and their order of priority.
(2) Distance and routes travelled to and from pastures. Time taken to do so.
(3) How long herdsmen stay away from their villages.
(4) Weight of two-year-old animal at death. Percentage of meat per carcase. Its value.
(5) Location of pastures for particular purposes – young rather than old animals, milk pastures, winter, summer, spring, and autumn pastures.

It is often helpful to make an inventory of tools currently in use, as this provides a guide to the magnitude of technological change. Particular attention should be paid to threshing floors, sledges, ploughs, and sources of power (e.g. water). Experience teaches that information obtained from local informants is likely to be more reliable than figures from official sources, which are commonly not related to the precise territories with which the investigation is concerned.

REFERENCES

Higgs, E. S. & Vita-Finzi, C. (1972) Prehistoric economies: a territorial approach. In *Papers in Economic Prehistory,* ed. E. S. Higgs, pp. 27–36. Cambridge: Cambridge University Press.

Vita-Finzi, C. & Higgs, E. S. (1970) Prehistoric economy in the Mount Carmel area of Palestine: site catchment analysis. *Proc. prehist. Soc.* **36,** 1–37.

APPENDIX B. RELATED TERRITORIES AND ALLUVIAL SEDIMENTS

C. VITA-FINZI

A site territory which has been defined in terms of its potential exploitation by man is unlikely to be coterminous with the territories of other site occupants or with the catchments from which have been derived water, sediment, game and other mobile components of the territory itself. For example, the Palaeolithic site territory of the Wadi el Mughara caves on Mount Carmel is far larger than the hunting territory of the barn owls that also occupied the caves; it includes windblown and waterlaid deposits derived from outside its boundaries; and it overlaps with the home range of former deer, gazelle, and cattle populations (Higgs & Vita-Finzi, 1972).

Which of these *related territories* are to be defined and analysed depends on the aims of the investigation. Thus a study of the faunal remains in the Wadi el Mughara caves has to consider the contribution made by owl predation, and will ultimately confront the issues of game movement and territoriality, but it is concerned with stream erosion and deposition only if these processes have changed the character of the site territory. Hence, whereas the owl and game territories have to be examined in their entirety, those portions of the relevant river basins that lie outside the site territory can largely be ignored. The emphasis would of course be reversed in a review of river sedimentation in which faunal remains were to serve primarily as local environmental indicators.

Nevertheless, even when the investigation sets off with clearly defined objectives, a full list of related territories requiring attention can rarely be drawn up prior to site catchment analysis, as it is this which will reveal, for example, how far a site territory is likely to have furnished the resources required for year-round occupation. Moreover some measure of re-survey will probably be needed whether the related territories in question are of the *overlapping* or the *nested* type (Figure 1), as greater detail is

usually required for evaluating the relationships between territories than for making a preliminary assessment of the economic potential of a site territory. This is not to deny that, as all related territories lie by definition within the site catchment (as distinct from the site territory), judicious planning of the initial survey could obviate a return visit to areas difficult of access for physical or political reasons.

This paper attempts to show how the concept of related territories can be of help in the interpretation of alluvial sequences and hence in the reconstruction of physical changes undergone by site territories during and since occupation. The need to take such changes into account when evaluating site location is stressed elsewhere in the present volume (p. 223–4).

FLUVIAL ACTION AND TERRITORIAL CONDITIONS

The alluvial record can be made to yield information on topographic, pedological, and hydrological conditions at different times. It is hardly necessary to add that this threefold classification is one of convenience and that it separates items which are closely interrelated, witness the marsh soils (*tirs*) that have developed within shallow surface depressions (*merjas*) in the Rharb Plain of Morocco (Pujos, 1958–9). The omission of climate from the list is intentional. Fluvial geology is a better guide to local ground conditions than it is to the regional atmosphere. Moreover, the archaeologist tends to gain more from information on the soil and water available to the occupants of a site than from an impression of the temperature or rainfall which he enjoyed. As it is, the continuing emphasis laid on palaeoclimate in environmental archaeology probably owes more to the needs of chronology than to cryptodeterminism (Vita-Finzi, 1973).

The requisite information is derived from the age, morphology, texture, structure, and composition of the deposits making up the alluvial sequence, and from the character of the intervening erosional or non-depositional episodes (Vita-Finzi, 1969a). The focus of interest will shift according to local circumstances and the requirements of each study. In a coastal location, for example, the age and history of a delta is of greater interest than its composition when the availability of land at different times is under discussion, and all aspects of the sequence can be interpreted with these two questions in mind.

The components of the alluvial record to be discussed here are grain-size distribution and the surface texture of individual sedimentary particles. Both illustrate the fact that sedimentary no less than human characteristics are the products of both *heritage* and *environment* (Pettijohn, 1957, p. 7), and that, by implication, the alluvial evidence obtained within a site territory may need to

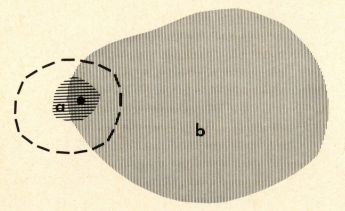

Figure 1. Related territories: a–nested and b–overlapping. The site is shown by the blob and the site territory by the broken line.

GRAIN-SIZE DISTRIBUTION

The mechanical composition of an alluvial fill is one clue to the volume and regime of stream flow during its accumulation, to the conditions prevailing in the zone of deposition, and, by extension, to the morphology of the valley at different stages in the past. Deposits characteristic of a flood-plain environment, for example, can often be differentiated from those laid down by alluvial fans at a mountain front, and connote contrasting topographies and discharge regimes. Correct interpretation – which of course demands corroborating evidence from other sources – brings the added benefit of enabling local observations to be extrapolated, or at any rate of indicating the range of variability to be expected. Thus the identification of a deposit as fluvioglacial in origin brings in its wake an awareness that it is likely to include a wide range of textures sometimes abruptly juxtaposed.

One can see how some or all of these items may enter into a site study. Perennial stream flow would favour year-round occupation where (in the absence of springs or wells) ephemeral flow might hamper it. High seasonal discharge coupled with overbank flooding would invite certain modes of cultivation, especially if the sediment laid down by the floods represented a net gain in nutrients. Irrigation by gravity flow may have been practicable prior to stream incision. Former soil patterns (Webley, 1972) can also be inferred from alluvial history at least as regards drainage capacity and the probable response to different methods of cultivation.

Many attempts have been made to identify grain-size distributions diagnostic of particular sedimentary environments (Kukal, 1971). Being intended primarily for the geologist engaged in palaeogeographical reconstruction on a regional scale, they rarely aim beyond distinguishing between fluvial, littoral, marine, lacustrine, and glacial settings, although, once combined with structural attributes (such as bedding), textural parameters may help to identify, say, between the deposits of braided and those of meandering streams.

The statistical techniques employed in these analyses generally match the observed grain-size population with a log-normal distibution or with some mixture of log-normal distributions. Quite apart from the assumptions inherent in all parametric statistics (Bradley, 1968), this approach has two serious drawbacks: it implies that there are no stream velocities of zero (Griffiths, 1967, p. 272), and it presupposes that the material being transported was capable of attaining a normal distribution. The former is of immediate concern once we turn our attention to semi-arid areas in which the cessation of flow is at least as important as fluctuations in flow to the evaluation of riverine territories. The problem of potential grain-size distributions becomes obvious once we consider the texture of an alluvial deposit derived from a loess-mantled source area, as only the addition of material which is not silt-sized can appreciably alter the characteristically well-sorted nature of the sediment whatever the agency responsible or its transport.

Both obstacles can to some extent be circumscribed by using the texture of the parent material, rather than a statistical model, as the standard with which the observed population is compared; in other words, by isolating heritage so as to reveal the effects of environment. The parent deposit is of course no longer present, but, provided its identity with an existing sedimentary unit can be established with conviction, the problem of sampling is no greater than under more usual circumstances. In any case, where – as in the examples cited below – 'grab' sampling is preferred to an elaborate (and prohibitively expensive) sampling programme, anxiety about the *statistical* validity of the results is somewhat misplaced.

The results obtained by applying the 'parent–daughter' method to four Mediterranean valleys are illustrated in Figure 2; further examples have been given elsewhere (Vita-Finzi, 1969b, 1971). In all four cases, the younger of the fills present in the reach sampled (broken line) consists largely of material derived from the older fill (solid line). Hence deviations between the two grain-size distributions reflect the conditions that accompanied redeposition, granted the limitations introduced by the field procedures.

It will be noted that the graphs refer almost exclusively to particles finer than 2 mm in diameter, that is to say to the sand, silt, and clay fractions. Other graphic methods of grain-size analysis take the entire population into consideration; that developed by Passega (1957) combines the mean with a measure of the coarsest material present. We are confronted with a choice between apparent objectivity and what van der Plas (1962, p. 152) has stigmatised as sampling procedures 'determined by a hypothesis of the investigator'. The reasoning behind the decision to exclude particles coarser than sand ran as follows. Maximum grain-size is a measure of competency, but this is primarily a reflection of peak discharge. If we are interested in distinguishing between perennial, seasonal, and ephemeral flow, that is in the relative importance of zero discharge, our attention must be focused on the finest grades and in particular those which are unlikely to be deposited unless flow ceases completely. Hence sampling should aim at obtaining the finest material present at the chosen location; and this 'arbitrary' procedure should be reaffirmed by excluding material coarser than the chosen limit from laboratory analysis.

The older fill includes a sufficiently wide range of grain-sizes for selective transport to be reflected in the mechanical composition of deposits derived from it. As it happens the younger fill in every case displays 'silt-clay depletion' (Vita-Finzi, 1971), which is attributable to deposition by streams whose discharges were sufficiently sustained (though not necessarily to the extent of being perennial) for the preferential export of suspended load from the basins and which attained peaks low enough for the retention of coarse silt and sand within the basins. The modern streams are characterised by shortlived high discharges and are undergoing erosion.

As the younger fill dates from about A.D. 300–1800, the above hydrological conclusions bear on site territories exploited during the Middle Ages, although they are also helpful in tracing changes undergone by the landscape since earlier periods of occupation. Once we shift our interest to the conditions that accompanied deposition of the older fill, which dates from about 40 000–10 000 years ago, the absence of an even older alluvial fill means that the 'parent' can no longer be sampled at the same

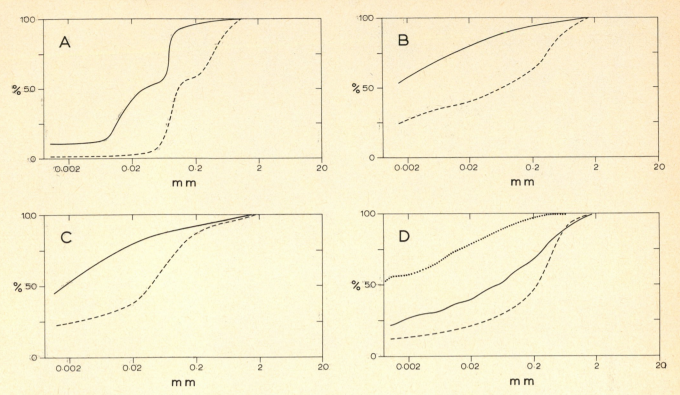

Figure 2. Cumulative grain-size distribution curves for 'parent-daughter' pairs of alluvial sediments: A–Wadi Megenin, Libya; B–Lower Aposelemis, Crete; C–Avgo, Greece; D–tributary of Louros shown in Plate I. Solid line = older fill; broken line = younger fill; dotted line = source deposit.

place as its 'daughter' deposit. In other words we are forced to define a related territory within which comparative material may legitimately be sought.

This is not to deny that the grain-size curve for the older fill as it stands tells us something of its origin. A low degree of sorting is characteristic, though not diagnostic, of deposition by mudflows and ephemeral streams, a finding which tallies with the evidence of morphology and of sedimentary structure. Even so there remains the question of how far the fill deviates in its texture from the source material.

Plate I shows part of the Louros valley in Epirus (Greece), about 1 km south of the site of Asprochaliko and well within its exploitation territory (Higgs & Webley, 1971, Figure 5). The road cuts through a lateral fan, b, composed of older fill (the Red Beds of previous accounts) and the Louros may be seen at the base of the photograph bordered by younger fill (or Valley-floor Alluvium – c). The area, a, from which the older fill was largely derived (Higgs & Vita-Finzi, 1966, p. 5) is a hollow in the limestone hills in which soil washed down from the surrounding slopes has accumulated; it thus represents a (nested) related territory which must be delimited when the origin of the older fill comes under discussion. Were the origin of the deposits in the hollow themselves the subject of genetic study, a further related territory could be drawn to encompass all the tributary slopes.

As Figure 2d shows, the deposits in a are richer than the older fill in the finer grades. One must therefore postulate either the ad-

dition of coarser material or the loss of fine particles during transit to the fan. In the absence of a suitable silt source the latter alternative seems the more probable. The possibility that wind action was responsible for some or all the clay depletion cannot be excluded, especially when evidence for seasonal aridity during deposition of the older fill (Higgs et al., 1967) is taken into account. Lustig (1965) has invoked reapportionment of the finer fractions by wind to explain variations in the clay-silt ratio of alluvial fan deposits in California. Nevertheless a more economical explanation is that the processes responsible for fan deposition also promoted some removal of clay in suspension. This is compatible with the presence of some bedding within the fill.

A corollary of clay export from the tributary valley is its accumulation or storage in transit within the trunk valley. In considering the exploitation patterns around Asprochaliko one must consequently bear in mind the possibility that the Louros valley proper was occupied by clay-rich sediments prone to waterlogging during the wet season, and to excessive desiccation in the dry months; the source area, a, was of course similar as regards sediment type but drew on a far smaller drainage catchment. A further corollary is that the texture and drainage characteristics of the fan deposits, which already benefited from steep slopes and the addition of gravel, would be improved by the removal of part of their clay fraction. Thus, in addition to the limestone slopes, one can recognise three land units whose dis-

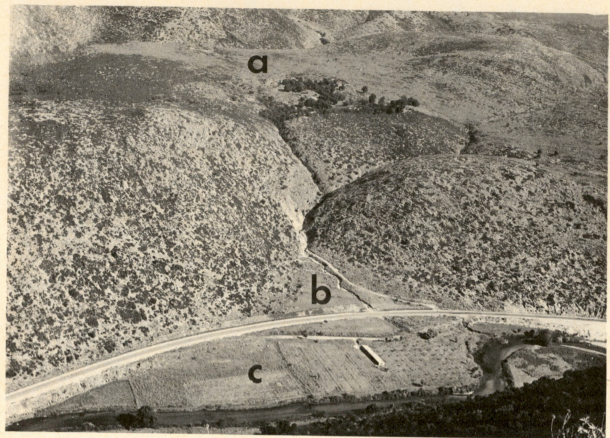

Plate I. Tributary of the middle Louros, Greece, and its catchment.

tinctiveness became increasingly evident as deposition of the older fill progressed: the source area, a, clay-rich, poorly drained, and subject to erosion; the fan, relatively well-drained and by the same token unlikely to retain soil moisture in the dry season; and the main valley, likely to exhibit marked seasonal contrasts in its moisture characteristics.

GRAIN SURFACE TEXTURE

The need to distinguish between inherited and acquired features also arises in the study of the surface textures exhibited by individual sedimentary particles. The advent of the scanning electron miscroscope has led to an active search for textures diagnostic of different depositional environments (Krinsley & Donahue, 1968). The usual procedure has been to collect samples from ancient sediments whose history was well known or from modern sediments whose environment was self-evident. Although redeposition is sometimes betrayed by the presence of two or more superimposed sets of textures, the risk remains that the latest of the textures is not the product of the environment from which the sample was collected and represents an earlier episode. Laboratory simulation (Margolis & Krinsley, 1971) is one means of circumventing the problem; another is the parent–daughter method discussed above.

In northern Tripolitania (Libya) the comparative approach has revealed consistent differences between the two valley fills both as regards the texture of the constitutent quartz grains and the debris adhering to their surfaces (Vita-Finzi & Krinsley, unpubl.). Once again the differences bear on conditions at the location sampled and during redeposition of material derived from the older fill (Jefara Alluvium) to form the younger (Lebda Alluvium). The loss of debris consisting of iron oxides and quartz fragments, and the chemical attack displayed by the grain surfaces thus exposed, all point to the prevalence of waterlogged conditions during medieval aggradation. In conjunction with evidence for sustained flow, they indicate high water-tables in the valley floors for at least several months of the year.

For a similar analysis of conditions during the earlier aggradational phase the entire river catchment needs to be considered, and the textural properties of its deposits compared with the Plateau Silts (Hey, 1962) of the interfluve areas which supplied the valley fills. To go one step further would be a formidable task, as the Plateau Silts appear to originate in the Sahara and were presumably transported to the Tripolitanian hills by wind.

In order to evaluate textural interpretation in an archaeological context, it was applied to samples taken from the two fills at the foot of the site of Rakefet in Israel (Vita-Finzi & Higgs, 1970, Fig. 7). The exploitation territory which has been demarcated for this Palaeolithic cave is dominated by rough grazing (45 per cent) and

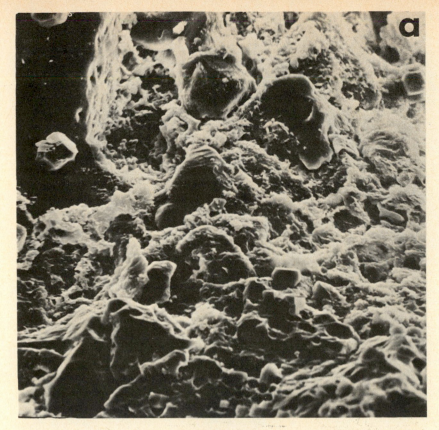

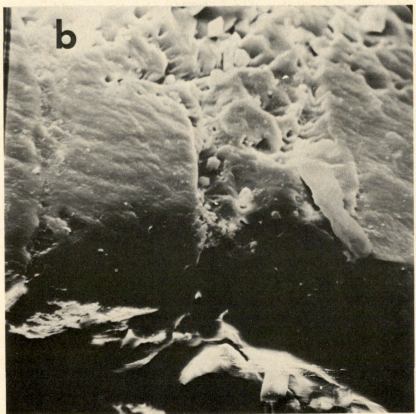

Plate II. (See caption on p. 230.)

229

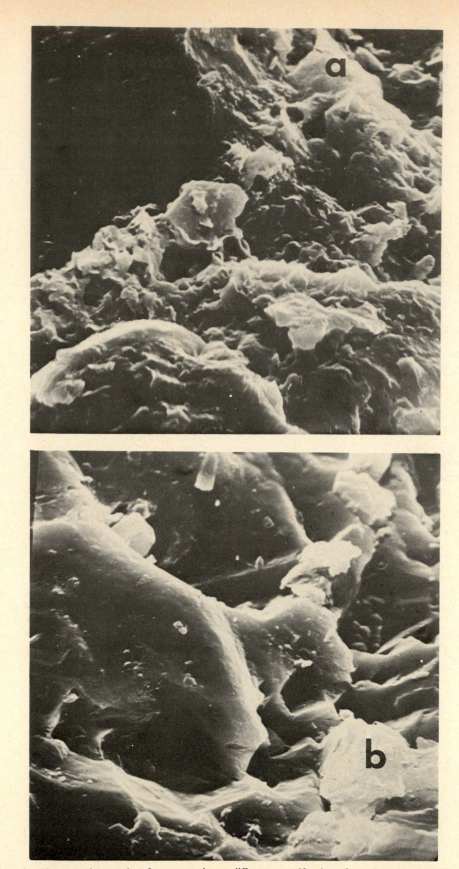

Plates II and III. Scanning electron micrographs of quartz grains at different magnifications from the younger (b) and older (a) fills near Rakefet, Israel.

potentially arable land (47 per cent) whose former productivity would clearly depend on the available moisture as well as on the lithological features on the basis of which it was mapped.

As in the Libyan examples, grains from the parent deposit are mantled by debris cemented to their surfaces by reprecipitated silica (Plates IIa and IIIa). The derived grains display relatively little surface debris, and their surfaces are more extensively pitted (Plates IIb and IIIb). Some of the debris consists of iron oxide, whose loss during redeposition is confirmed by Fe_2O_3 determinations. The bulk appears to be made up of quartz material. For it to be loosened, and for pits in the grain surface to be developed and enlarged, conditions favouring quartz solution are required. The simplest explanation – that the younger fill was exposed to circulating groundwater with a high pH (Wolfe, 1967) – is supported by the presence of carbonate overgrowths on particles from both fills. Waterlogged conditions would, of course, also favour the loss of iron oxides.

The older fill consists of redeposited Terra Rossa and limestone gravel, and is locally cemented by calcium carbonate. Its accumulation in the valley floor was at the expense of the slopes bordering the stream upstream of the site territory; we may thus envisage an overlapping related territory whose impoverishment during Palaeolithic occupation gradually tilted the balance in favour of sites such as Rakefet with ready access to zones of accumulation. After about 10 000 years ago, however, the older fill became prone to erosion, and it was not until about 2000 years ago that some of this eroded material began to be retained within the catchment (in the guise of the younger fill) and was favoured by plentiful soil water for several months in the year. To judge from sherds within the younger fill, its deposition dates at the earliest from Roman and Byzantine times. This period, and that immediately preceding the eighth millennium B.C., may be taken as the times when valley-floor exploitation near Rakefet was most favoured by local physical controls.

Despite the concentration on alluvial matters, the above examples may suffice to show that related territories can serve as a means of extending the area from which may be drawn information relating to a site without compromising the validity of the local picture. That the concept is applicable to botanical remains is demonstrated if only implicitly by studies which try to define the provenance of pollen grains subsequently incorporated into a single deposit, or which draw a distinction between the environmental implications of a pollen count and those of the stream by which they were transported (Vita-Finzi & Dimbleby, 1971; see also Brush & Brush, 1972). It may be that artefacts will also be found amenable to this approach and that the distinction between 'inherited' and 'acquired' tool types could provide a measure of environmental adaptation. The cumulative graphs employed by some archaeologists are derived from sedimentological practice (Bordes, 1955) and would lend themselves to graphical comparison, but for the comparison to have value it will have to be based on a classification that is more strictly functional.

ACKNOWLEDGEMENTS

I am indebted to Mr N. T. Moore and Prof. D. H. Krinsley for help with the electron microscopy, and to Dr D. A. MacLeod for Plate I.

REFERENCES

Bordes, F. (1955) Preface to Les industries moustériennes et pré-moustériennes du Périgord, by M. Bourgon. *Archs. Inst. Paléont. hum.* **27**, 5–6.

Bradley, J. V. (1968) *Distribution-free Statistical Tests.* Englewood Cliffs, N.J.: Prentice-Hall.

Brush, G. S. & Brush, L. M., Jr. (1972) Transport of pollen in a sediment-laden channel: a laboratory study. *Am. J. Sci.* **272**, 359–81.

Griffiths, J. C. (1967) *Scientific Method in the Analysis of Sediments.* New York: McGraw-Hill.

Hey, R. W. (1962) The Quaternary and Palaeolithic of northern Libya. *Quaternaria* **6**, 435–49.

Higgs, E. S. & Vita-Finzi, C. (1966) The climate, environment and industries of Stone Age Greece: Part II. *Proc. prehist. Soc.* **32**, 1–29.

(1972) Prehistoric economies: a territorial approach. In *Papers in Economic Prehistory,* ed. E. S. Higgs, pp. 27–36. Cambridge: Cambridge University Press.

Higgs, E. S. & Webley, D. (1971) Further information concerning the environment of Palaeolithic man in Epirus. *Proc. prehist. Soc.* **37**, 367–80.

Higgs, E. S., Vita-Finzi, C., Harris, D. R., & Fagg, A. E. (1967) The climate, environment and industries of Stone Age Greece: Part III. *Proc. prehist. Soc.* **33**, 1–29.

Krinsley, D. H. & Donahue, J. (1968) Environmental interpretation of sand grain surface textures by electron microscopy. *Bull. geol. Soc. Am.* **79**, 743–8.

Kukal, Z. (1971) *Geology of Recent Sediments.* London: Academic Press.

Lustig, L. K. (1965) Clastic sedimentation in Deep Springs Valley, California. *U.S. geol. Survey Prof. Pap.* **352-F.**

Margolis, S. V. & Krinsley, D. H. (1971) Submicroscopic frosting on eolian subaqueous quartz sand grains. *Bull. geol. Soc. Am.* **82**, 3395–406.

Passega, R. (1957) Texture as characteristic of clastic deposition. *Bull. Am. Ass. Petrol. Geol.* **41**, 1952–84.

Pettijohn. F. J. (1957) *Sedimentary Rocks,* 2nd ed. New York: Harper & Bros.

Pujos, A. (1958–9) Présentation de la carte des sols du Rharb à l'échelle de 1/100,000e par P. Divoux. *Soc. sci. nat. du Maroc, Section de pédologie.*

van der Plas, L. (1962) Preliminary note on the granulometric analysis of sedimentary rocks. *Sedimentology* **1**, 145–57.

Vita-Finzi, C. (1969a) Fluvial geology. In *Science in Archaeology,* ed. D. Brothwell & E. S. Higgs, 2nd ed., pp. 135–50. London: Thames & Hudson.

(1969b) Late Quaternary alluvial chronology of Iran. *Geol. Rdsch.* **58**, 951–73.

(1971) Heredity and environment in clastic sediments: silt/clay depletion. *Bull. geol. Soc. Am.* **82**, 187–90.

(1973) *Recent Earth History.* London: Macmillan.

Vita-Finzi, C. & Dimbleby, G. W. (1971) Medieval pollen from Jordan. *Pollen et Spores* **13**, 415–20.

Vita-Finzi, C. & Higgs, E. S. (1970) Prehistoric economy in the Mount Carmel area of Palestine: site catchment analysis. *Proc. prehist. Soc.* **36**, 1–37.

Webley, D. (1972) Soils and site location in prehistoric Palestine. In *Papers in Economic Prehistory,* ed. E. S. Higgs, pp. 169–80. Cambridge: Cambridge University Press.

Wolfe, M. J. (1967) An electron microscope study of the surface texture of sand grains from a basal conglomerate. *Sedimentology* **8**, 239–47.

APPENDIX C. LIST OF OTHER PUBLICATIONS BY THE EARLY HISTORY OF AGRICULTURE PROJECT
(in chronological order)

THEORY AND METHODS

Higgs, E. S. & Jarman, M. R. (1969) The origins of agriculture: a reconsideration. *Antiquity* **43**.

Higgs, E. S. & Vita-Finzi, C. (1970). Prehistoric economies in the Mount Carmel area of Palestine: site catchment analysis. *Proc. prehist. Soc.* **36.**

Jarman, M. R. (1971) Culture and economy in the North Italian Neolithic. *World Archaeology* **2**(3).

Jarman, M. R., Vita-Finzi, C., & Higgs, E. S. (1972) Site catchment analysis in archaeology. In *Man, Settlement and Urbanism,* ed. P. J. Ucko, R. Tringham, G. W. Dimbleby. London: Duckworth.

Jarman, M. R. (1972) A territorial model for archaeology. In *Models in Archaeology,* ed. D. L. Clark. London: Methuen.

Higgs, E. S. (1972) Archaeology and domestication. Burg Wartenstein Symposium No. 56: *Origin of African Plant Domesticates.*

ENVIRONMENT AND ECONOMY

Higgs, E. S., Vita-Finzi, C., Harris, D. R. & Fagg, A. E. (1967) The climate, environment and industries of Stone Age Greece, part III. *Proc. prehist. Soc.* **33.**

Harris, D. R. & Vita-Finzi, C. (1968) Kokkinopilos – a Greek badland. *Geog. Journ.* **134**(4).

Hutchinson, Sir Joseph (1969) Erosion and land use in the Epirus region of Greece. *Agric. Hist. Rev.* **17.**

Higgs, E. S. & Webley, D. (1971) Further information concerning the environment of Palaeolithic man in Epirus. *Proc. prehist. Soc.* **37**(2).

Dennell, R. W. (1973) The economic development of Bulgaria during the Neolithic and Bronze Age. In *Proceedings of the 1st International Congress of Thracology, Sofia.*

FAUNAL ASSEMBLAGES AND ANIMAL HUSBANDRY

Payne, S. (1968) The origins of domestic sheep and goats: a reconsideration in the light of fossil evidence. *Proc. prehist. Soc.* **34.**

(1969) A metrical distinction between sheep and goat metacarpals. In *The Domestication and Exploitation of Plants and Animals,* ed. P. J. Ucko & G. W. Dimbleby. London: Duckworth.

Jarman, M. R., Fagg, A. E. & Higgs, E. S. (1969) The animal remains from Grimthorpe. In An Iron Age hill fort at Grimthorpe, by I. M. Stead. *Proc. prehist. Soc.* **34.**

Jarman, M. R. & Jarman, H. N. (1969) The fauna and economy of Early Neolithic Knossos. *Ann. Brit. School Arch., Athens* **63.**

Jarman, M. R. (1970) The prehistory of Upper Pleistocene and Recent cattle: part I. *Proc. prehist. Soc.* **35.**

(1970) Isera (Trentino), Cava Nord: fauna report. *Studi Trentini di Scienze Naturali* 47.

(1972) The fauna; the obsidian. In Myrtos: an early Bronze Age settlement in Crete, by P. Warren. *Brit. School at Athens, Suppl. Vol.* No. 7.

Reports on the following sites were published (1972): Ellington, Huntingdonshire; Breedon-on-the-Hill, Leicestershire.

Reports on the following sites were completed and accepted for publication: Staines, Cheddar, and Photolivos.

FLORA AND PLANT DOMESTICATION

Field, B. (1969) Preliminary report on the botanical remains. In Choga Mami, 1967–8: a preliminary report, by J. Oates. *Iraq* 31.

Dennell, R. W. (1970) Seeds from a Medieval sewer. *Econ. Bot.*

(1972) Stone Age farming in Bulgaria. *Illustrated London News.*

(1973) Phylogenesis of *T. dicoccum*: a reconsideration. *Econ. Bot.*

(in press). The plant remains from Ezero. In *Ezero*, by Georgiev, Merpert, & Katancherov.

COLLECTED PAPERS

Papers in Economic Prehistory (1972) Edited by E. S. Higgs and published by the Cambridge University Press. Contents:

Higgs, E. S. & Jarman, M. R. – The origins of animal and plant husbandry.

Jarman, H. N. – The origins of wheat and barley cultivation.

Higgs, E. S. & Vita-Finzi, C. – Prehistoric economies: a territorial approach.

Jarman, H. N., Legge, A. J. & Charles, J. A. – Retrieval of plant remains from archaeological sites by froth flotation.

Payne, S. – Partial recovery and sample bias: the results of some sieving experiments.

Payne, S. – On the interpretation of bone samples from archaeological sites.

Jarman, M. R. & Wilkinson, P. F. – Criteria of animal domestication.

Legge, A. J. – Cave climates.

Wilkinson, P. F. – Current experimental domestication and its relevance to prehistory.

APPENDIX C

Legge, A. J. – Prehistoric exploitation of the gazelle in Palestine.

Jarman, M. R. – European deer economies and the advent of the Neolithic.

Dennell, R. W. – The interpretation of plant remains: Bulgaria.

Sturdy, D. A. – The exploitation patterns of a modern reindeer economy in west Greenland.

Webley, D. – Soils and site location in prehistoric Palestine.

French, D. H., Hillman, G. C., Payne, S. & Payne R. J. – Excavations at Can Hasan III 1969–1970.

Payne, S. – Can Hasan III, the Anatolian aceramic, and the Greek Neolithic.

Foreword by Grahame Clark and Conclusion by Sir Joseph Hutchinson.

NAME INDEX

SUBJECT INDEX

237